Postwar Years: Normalcy, 1918-1923

American Democracy and the World War

★ ★ ★

POSTWAR YEARS

NORMALCY, 1918-1923

FREDERIC L. PAXSON

COOPER SQUARE PUBLISHERS, INC.
NEW YORK
1966

Preface

BETWEEN *1913 and 1923 the people of the United States were tested by peace, by war, and by demobilization. They took a long stride in the readjustment of their federal government to the facts of a changing life, and an even longer stride as they adjusted themselves to those facts. Never did all the people agree with what was accomplished; never did the momentary majority like all that it was forced to do; never were minorities satisfied. The visible confusion of the period was the necessary consequence of the democratic process, in which minorities operate as brake and prod upon majorities. Yet when driven to it they massed their strength for a great military stroke.*

Two earlier volumes, of the three of which this is the last, were written before a second World War drove the United States to repeat the stroke: PRE-WAR YEARS 1913—1917 (1936), *and* AMERICA AT WAR 1917—1918 (1939)—*both published by the Houghton Mifflin Company. In all of the three it has been my attempt to prepare a fair picture of democracy as it functioned in the United States in an interval separating two distinct phases of American civilization. Its behavior as it lived from day to day was its real normalcy; what many of its people called normalcy, and craved, was a symptom of nostalgia in the presence of problems whose solutions were as yet unknown.*

FREDERIC L. PAXSON

Berkeley, California
February 23, 1948

Contents

Chapter I ★ Post-Armistice

At eleven o'clock (Paris time) on the morning of Monday, November 11, 1918, the people of the United States started back from the various fronts of war upon which their efforts had been concentrated for nineteen months. They were eager to resume the life which war had interrupted, or to begin the adult life which war had postponed for youth in the armies, or to reestablish careers where they had been dropped, or to take advantage of possibilities opened to them by war experience, or to dig in and hold the gains which war had brought them—and to enjoy the American way of life. Of all the reasons which have been advanced to account for the participation of the United States in the European war, the most convincing is the belief then prevailing that a German victory would leave America forever unsafe unless the United States should remain always ready for instant mobilization; the language of Germans both before the war and throughout its course spoke menacingly of the advantage and conquest to be attained by German arms.

The people of the United States had not wished to go to war. Only in terms of security and peace of mind had they expected profit from the defeat of Germany, but they had fought deliberately and angrily as the pattern of German hopes was displayed from day to day. Their reinforcement of the Allied effort in its thirty-third month was built upon an unusual power of imagination. Many nations have gone desperately to war to defend their frontiers against invasion; many have gone for trade, or conquest, or dynastic advantage; but never before 1917 had a people crossed an ocean in force to prevent the wrong belligerent from winning, when they themselves were not lured by hope of gain or impelled by fear of immediate destruction.

[1]

War was foreign to the American generation which fought it. The rush back to peace began when the news of the "false armistice" broke a few days too soon, and again when in the middle of the night the Department of State announced that the real Armistice had been signed at five o'clock, Paris time, effective at eleven. The war was not over; only combat had ceased. It still remained uncertain whether the defeated enemy would respect the terms of what was in effect an unconditional surrender. There might easily be hitches in the negotiation of the final peace. The Allies, who accepted avidly the American reinforcement in means and men while danger was at their frontiers, might be less than ready to implement the sort of peace which inspired the American mind. No Ally had bound itself even to the Fourteen Points until the last moment.

Yet no slogan had carried faster or farther in the United States than that of a "war to end wars." The concept of a postwar league to enforce the peace had been elaborated for Americans as though it were readily obtainable. Only a minority of the people appreciated the significance of the congressional election of November 5, 1918, in which the administration of Woodrow Wilson suffered sharp defeat. A Congress Republican in both houses was assured for March 4, 1919. With the war not over, and the peace yet to be shaped, the Americans who had delivered the reinforcement in arms deserted the making of the peace. They hurried from the war effort to resume their way of life.

That way of life was gone; and as the months ahead brought disillusion about peace, they brought also realization that many an old equilibrium had been jolted by the release of new hopes and fears. The domestic problem resumed its ascendancy over the American mind, and by its immediacy pushed into the background the new dream of an international world. The moment was lost at which the weight of the United States might, perhaps, have steadied the world. Realities of the local landscape quickly took American attention as the demobilized nation rebuilt itself. Nostalgia glorified the old way of life until it seemed more attractive than it ever really was. The new way, put together by trial and error, gave a positive pattern to the five years following the Armistice—a pattern which meant for many Americans a more open future than the past had ever held.

In the five years after 1918 the dominant fact in American public life was the return to power of the Republican party organization without a program which could command the support of its full membership. In the sixty years from the inauguration of Abraham Lincoln until 1921, except for three interludes comprising only sixteen years in all, this organization made the presidents; and for eight of the sixteen years, which Grover Cleveland and Woodrow Wilson divided, the Republican organization had control of part or all of Congress and was in a position to hobble Democratic presidents in their effort to administer the affairs of the United States. In the sessions when Democrats held that control at the Capitol their treatment of Republican presidents showed the slight difference between the two great parties in matters of politics. The leaders of the dominant Republican party nearly convinced themselves that they had a right to rule, and lack of votes kept the minority party from much share in parliamentary leadership. No general grievance was deep enough or lasting enough to enable any new party to crowd out of the picture either of the major parties. Republican leaders, before they threw away the presidency in 1912, almost convinced the outside world that their tenure in office was normally to be expected. Foreign powers, eager to know whether the United States meant what the Democrats in office said it meant, sometimes took counsel with Republicans.

In the five years after the Armistice the goal of full power was attained, and the Republican party—such as it was—was enabled to preside over a dozen mad years in a new era of national experience. In the drive for recovery of position it took its first trenches in the election which was held just before the Armistice was signed. It advanced from control of Congress to control of the presidency in two years more. It advanced as if it were solidly a party, regardless of the deep schisms splitting up its unities. The schisms were on sectional lines, East against West; on doctrinal lines, progressive against stalwart; on biological lines, age against youth. But encircling this internal fight for party control there was a temporary bond, sufficient for election purposes, in the common antipathy of Republicans to Democrats in office.

The return of the Republicans provided a backdrop for five years of party politics. Demobilization held the center of the stage for much of the period,—demobilization of the armed forces and abandonment of the state of mind which might maintain them, until the security of the United States was left resting on the continuing good will of all nations and the toughness of British policy. Interest in foreign affairs diminished as men genuinely devoted to the League to Enforce Peace subordinated their desire for a new world order to their lust for party power. The domestic program was demobilized as the war machine was scrapped, and the progressive adjustment to changing life which had marked the decade before 1915 was not resumed. There was demobilization of the party bond as pressure groups supplanted party programs in calling the tune for national behavior; demobilization of the behavior itself as new ways of life built up new rules, as elders scoffed at law and as juniors scoffed at elders.

But demobilization, though near the center of the stage, was much less than the whole plot in these five years, 1918–1923. In the wings, waiting for their cues, were the forerunners of a new era. Here, a new means of communication prepared to make a unit of the United States and to make all the countries of the world next-door neighbors; there, new gadgets to embellish life if not always to enrich it; there, also, new controls in science and mechanics to build new fortunes and to accentuate class interests; and behind these, new concepts of welfare to produce their monuments in a rebuilt America and in endowments to prepare the coming generations to live therein.

These new actors in the American drama were clumsy with their cues and sketchy in their lines, yet they promised, if only they should be well rehearsed, a new America, better than the old. For the moment, however, they were in the wings as the dominant party regained its dominance.

*   *   *   *   *   *   *   *

In any other modern country Woodrow Wilson would have been forced out of office after such a parliamentary defeat as he suffered on November 5, 1918. To a different crew, led by a different chief, would have been assigned the task of guiding the nation along a course which constituents were willing to follow. But in the United States, though the supporters of Wilson lost on that day their control of the Senate and the House of Representatives, their leader remained in office, as secure in his tenure of the presidency as though he were still the choice of the electorate.

There is something to be said in favor of the immediate reaction to the public will which prevails in governments of the parliamentary type. But there is also much to be said for the rigidity of the scheme laid down by the framers of the Constitution, which protects the people against their own quick emotion without setting up insuperable barriers to block their settled convictions. It is, perhaps, a wise people who while politically sober protect themselves against their own ecstasy when politically drunk. But the books are not yet closed. Both the parliamentary and the fixed-term systems struggle to survive against the dictators' plan which repudiates them both.

In 1918, the congressional election hobbled the administration of Woodrow Wilson without placing power or responsibility in the hands of those who did the hobbling. In a world of nations which knew their own minds, Wilson knew his mind; but he had lost the power which comes from knowing that the people travel with the leader.

Beaten at the polls, he had still half a term ahead of him, with no possibility that the new majority could take over the reins of executive authority. He might die, but his death would do the opposition no good. It would only bring into the White House the quiet and cautious Indiana politician, Thomas R. Marshall, best known to posterity by a brave attempt to revamp the resistant constitution of his state. Whatever might happen, unless death or partisan impeachment should remove him Woodrow Wilson would remain the constitutional president until March 4, 1921. At a moment when, if ever, the United States needed to know its mind and speak it through a trusted chief, the nature of the Constitution set a screen between mind and action. To make the matter worse, illness intervened. The collapse of Wilson in the autumn of 1919 emphasized what the lingering death of Garfield had suggested a generation earlier—that the United States lacks a method for determining when and if a president is no longer able "to discharge the Powers and Duties" of his office.

The Sixty-sixth Congress, elected in 1918, belongs to the period which preceded it as well as that which followed. It was responsible for the final phases of the war and for demobilization. Yet it lacked the simplicity of motive and performance which characterized the first two Congresses of the Wilson administration. It lacked also the simplicity of the war Congress, during most of whose biennium the common purpose to win the war served as a bond for action. It took office at a time when the need to prepare for peace was as imperative as winning the war had been; yet it lacked authority and pattern. The people and the Congress were nostalgic in the presence of the technical complexities of reconstruction and under the impact of new conditions for the facing of which there were few American precedents. The government was on dead center, with a Republican Congress pulling one way while a Democratic president pulled the other. It functioned in a "lame duck" period in which the executive had lost the mandate of the people and much of his power of leadership. And its deliberations were to be distorted by the quadrennial struggle to elect and install a president. When facing the future the Congress was as inadequate as when it faced the past.

The fighting stopped on November 11, 1918; whereupon, as though the war were over with victory attained, the American Expeditionary Forces were brought home. Only the Third Army, created as the battle of the Meuse-Argonne neared its end, was designated to represent the United States in the march to the Rhine, which its first units crossed on December 13. Under Major General Joseph T. Dickman, it set up headquarters in the old castle of Ehrenbreitstein, opposite Coblenz; and here, under a new designation as American Expeditionary Forces in Germany, this army and its commander, Major General Henry T. Allen, remained on guard too long to please American public opinion. With dwindling numbers, it maintained a token occupation until France moved into the Ruhr in 1923 and the Senate prodded the administration with a sharp resolution calling for complete recall. On January 24, 1923, its last remaining regiment, the Eighth Infantry, hauled down the flag and took train for Antwerp, where the transport *St. Mihiel* waited to bring it home.

Even before November 11, 1918, the War Department had begun to cancel inductions and stop sending men to France. The gears were reversed at once, without waiting for a peace to be concluded.

Germany was helpless from defeat and revolution, and the Allies were ready enough to take over the remaining burden of police at the Rhine bridgeheads. The army camps at home, which on the morning of the Armistice held 104,155 officers and 1,533,344 men, were emptied faster than they had been filled. Pershing had 82,302 officers and 1,898,352 men on his ration strength that morning. He withdrew men from the lines of battle, concentrated them in training areas, set up an army university to occupy their minds, and gave them drill and athletics to send them tired to bed, while they waited for berths on the Atlantic transports. Even at that, the men had time to write doggerel:

> We drove the boche across the Rhine,
> The Kaiser from his throne.
> Oh, Lafayette, we've paid our debt.
> For Christ's sake, send us home.

Pershing rode at the head of picked men in ceremonial parades while they were waiting. The parades passed under the Arc de Triomphe and through Whitehall; and he was himself honored with gown and hood at Oxford. And every month the transports hurried their thousands home faster than they had floated them to war.

The General kept with him, until the last, the earliest of his units to take shape; he elected to make his homecoming with the First Division. Out of this division had been graduated, and back to it had come, a large fraction of the key men upon whose shoulders the management of the A.E.F. had rested.

There was no grand parade on Pennsylvania Avenue, such as that in which on May 23 and 24, 1865, the veterans of Sherman's army, with those of Meade and Grant, had passed in final review before President Johnson, Secretary of War Stanton, and Lieutenant General Grant. That review, indeed, took place only because Pennsylvania Avenue was on the direct route from the last battlefields of the Civil War to the normal places of discharge. In the greatest parades of 1919, the First Division was in line. Fresh from its transports, it marched on Fifth Avenue on September 10 and in Washington on September 17. Its casualty list, nearly as long as that of the division at battle strength, had run to 864 officers and 25,487 men. Pershing, riding at its head, looked the general. He was even more of a leader, however, than people knew, for few who saw him head the parades knew of the battles he had won in council in addition to the armed combat he had directed in the field. Rewarded earlier than Grant had been, he wore four stars which were no longer temporary insignia to be removed on reversion to peacetime rank. He was not to revert. While he was still at sea, Congress revived the office of General of the Armies and the Senate confirmed him in the rank. A Pershing-for-President club had already sprung up in Nebraska.

Wilson was not on hand to welcome Pershing back from the wars. His own war was not yet over, and he had just started west to urge the people to press the senators to ratify the treaty he had concluded at Versailles.

The fleet, too, came home. Germany was under such guard that it could not conceivably renew the war. Its leaders did not yet entertain the myth of the Third Reich that signing the Armistice was a voluntary act, or that the German Army was undefeated. The need for the United States Navy in Europe ceased with the Armistice, whatever the outcome of the peace should be.

The United States dreadnaughts, stationed near British waters and operating as an integral part of the Allied fleets, were ordered home. Ten battleships, under the command of Henry T. Mayo, arrived off Sandy Hook on Christmas Day, 1918. There they were met by the home fleet, to pass in review before the Secretary of the Navy, Josephus Daniels. Daniels was already preparing to urge upon Congress a demand for the greatest of all fleets for the United States, unless an effective League should be agreed upon.

Unlike the army, the navy was not preparing for demobilization and discharge, but for new duty. In the office of the Chief of Naval Operations, the navy equivalent of Chief of Staff, Rear Admiral William S. Benson, was having drawn up the arrangements for a new scheme of national defense, taking into account the disappearance of the German menace in the Atlantic and the actuality of an unguarded Pacific front. His program was put in operation in the summer of 1919, while Pershing was homeward bound. Half the major units of the navy passed through the Panama Canal, to be reviewed by Secretary Daniels at San Diego on August 7. The Pacific Coast lacked most of the installations necessary for the servicing

and support of a modern fleet, but this was a real beginning of
armed occupation of Pacific waters.

As the government called home its armed forces, the American
people turned happily and instantly to a consideration of the domestic front. The legal state of war lasted long after the cessation
of hostilities. It outlasted the signing of the Treaty of Versailles
and the administration of Woodrow Wilson, and came to a unilateral pause only when President Harding, on July 2, 1921, signed
an act of Congress declaring that the war was over. Having entered
the war without commitments to the Allies, who were bound by a
formal agreement signed in London on September 4, 1914, the
United States left the war similarly without commitments, at its
own time and on its own terms. But for the United States, the struggle was not completely over until Germany assented to the termination of the war in a separate treaty signed in Berlin on August 25,
1921; or rather, until the ratifications of this treaty had been ex-
changed on November 11, 1921, three years to a day after the signing
of the Armistice.

A week after that signing, November 18, 1918, it was officially
announced that soon after the opening of the regular session of
Congress on December 2, President Wilson would accompany to
Europe a commission to negotiate peace. A demand for a stern
treaty had arisen as early as September, when Germany began vis-
ibly to crack. There had been increasing discussion of the time,
place, and manner of the negotiations, and of the part which Woodrow Wilson would play in the transaction. As the possibility that
such a commission would be necessary developed into certainty,
there was keen interest in the persons who would represent the
United States.

Under the American system only the president is in a position to
state national policy; and even he is unable to guarantee adherence
to policy by his party, by the Senate or the Congress, or by the
people. In the field of international relations, the more difficult the
problem the more specific is his responsibility for a proper solution.
Early in his administration, with foreign affairs crowded to the
margins of his mind by domestic reform, Wilson had indulged
Bryan's personal desires respecting the business of the Department
of State. When, however, the problems connected with neutral

status became dominant, there could be only one mind in the determination of foreign policy—the mind of the President. When the minds of Wilson and his Secretary of State diverged, Bryan withdrew from the Cabinet, with dignity and decency, and made no disturbing political opposition on the issue of policies which President Wilson had rejected. Wilson had become his own foreign minister, and retained that authority even after Robert Lansing had been appointed to Bryan's post. Thereafter Wilson called the tune and Lansing signed the notes, though the latter filled his private files with memoranda in justification of his differences of opinion with his chief. Wilson never concealed his distrust of the legal mind, and seems to have tolerated a member of the Cabinet who disagreed with him only because Lansing was, after all, a good businessman.

As the United States neared the decisive step to war, it was the doctrine of Wilson, expressed by him in person, which stated American policy and acquired binding force upon the common people of Allied lands. From "peace without victory" he moved on to "force to the uttermost," while his points relating to an honorable and durable peace became frozen as a charter of intent in the Fourteen Points. It was, nevertheless, the intent of only the President of the United States and those who agreed with him, regardless of the appeal it might make to the voters on whom Lloyd George and Clemenceau depended for their continuance in office, or of the power of its ideas in weakening the will to resist among the rank and file of enemy peoples.

As the only leader who had standing among all the Allies as well as influence across the enemy lines, Wilson had become the proponent of a new kind of peace. He had no coadjutors within the United States who could act with even a semblance of right to pledge the public faith. A peace conference to draft a Wilson peace was unthinkable without him; although a peace conference with the President of the United States sitting next to men who were no more than prime ministers had for these ministers too many possibilities to be regarded with complacency. During the war there had been many friendly gestures from overseas expressing the hope that he would find it possible to visit Europe. But Europe cooled off as the time approached when such a visit might be possible. Wilson had seen himself as presiding officer, shaping the terms of the treaty and building the League into it. But Colonel House had had the disagreeable duty of disabusing his mind: "If a neutral country had been chosen [for the conference] you would have been asked to preside." When Paris was chosen as the place of conference, both precedent and preference indicated Clemenceau as presiding officer.

The news that he could be no more than the head of the American delegation reached Washington only a few days before Wilson's decision to attend was made public. The New York *Times* knew its own mind: "The place of the President is here." The *World,* whose Frank Cobb generally understood and approved him, now disapproved, and Cobb wrote a powerful memorandum against it for Colonel House. *The Intimate Papers of Colonel House* (1926–1928), which Charles Seymour edited from the abundant journals of the Colonel, presents a picture of the Paris situation into which President Wilson was projecting himself. At home, George W. Wickersham, late attorney general for Taft, declared in public that the Vice-President would constitutionally become President when Wilson left American shores; but the canny Vice-President, Thomas R. Marshall, maintained complete silence. On the day before the President sailed, Lawrence Y. Sherman, a partisan Republican senator from Illinois, introduced a resolution declaring that Marshall would be Acting President. Others less critical, and less partisan, saw difficulties of time and communication impeding exercise of the authority of the President while overseas. Attorney-General Thomas Watt Gregory, however, advised that the ten constitutional days allowed the President for action on proposed laws might be counted from the day on which the statute reached him. The mind of the President was made up and he prepared to sail.

Whichever way Wilson had decided the matter, he would have had to face criticism, and the personnel of his staff was certain to meet with partisan attack. The Republican party knew what had happened on November 5 even though the public missed the point and the people of Europe continued to assume that since Wilson was still in office he was still able to speak with the full authority of a chief of state.

The membership list of the American Commission to Negotiate Peace was not released until November 29, and even then it appeared sooner than the lists of the principal Allies. Next to the President, it included Robert Lansing, who already disapproved of much of the content and strategy of the American effort, as his *Peace Negotiations, A Personal Narrative* (1921) indicates. Edward M. House, already in Paris as personal agent of the President with the various conferences and war boards, was included. General Tasker H. Bliss, whose role is fully recorded in Frederick Palmer's *Bliss, Peacemaker* (1934), was named. Bliss was learned and steady, and had been well-seasoned by duty as Permanent Military Representative with the Supreme War Council. And last came Henry White, who lacked political importance but was the only Republican on the Commission. His distinguished career, related by Allan Nevins in *Henry White, Thirty Years of American Diplomacy* (1930), entitled him to the thanks of his country, but he had been out of service since the Taft administration. No senator was named, which was a slap even to the Democratic Senate of the moment. The inclusion of White and the failure to name such a Republican as Roosevelt, Root, Hughes, or Taft—not to mention Henry Cabot Lodge, who was already chairman-designate of the Senate Committee on Foreign Relations—was regarded as an insult which justified the Republican party's charge that Wilson was determined to negotiate a Democratic peace. Republicans filled the mails with letters to their friends in Europe, explaining precisely where the President stood, and Lodge endeavored to induce White to leak information to him, regularly and treacherously. Karl Schriftgiesser, bitterly critical, has traced the attitudes of Lodge in *The Gentleman from Massachusetts: Henry Cabot Lodge* (1944).

The five commissioners did not make up the whole group which expected to have a hand in the peace. Journalists, in huge numbers, packed up for Paris. The various war boards sent their agents instructing them to watch. The navy selected a list of intelligence officers to accompany the mission and, like the army, which did the same, felt that military personnel should have a large share in making the peace. The civilians, whom Colonel House had hurriedly drawn into his Inquiry in 1917, and who had been engaged in specific studies with which to brief the conference, went with the

President. In addition to the official delegations and the press, every interest which hoped to turn the conference into a world parliament for the settlement of world grievances sought passports for its representatives.

The *George Washington* sailed from Hoboken for Brest on December 4, 1918, with the President somewhat bewildered by the number of associates who had managed to get aboard. There might have been more peace at home if Mrs. Wilson had not accompanied him, for the rigorous exclusion of other wives from the mission aroused sharp remarks even in quarters which would otherwise have been friendly. There might have been more peace in Paris without her, for her antipathy to Colonel House was far from helpful in the close quarters in which the Americans lived in France.

In Paris, on December 14, with the applause of the crowds still echoing, the Commission was quartered in the Hotel Crillon on the Place de la Concorde, but found no one ready to begin the consideration of the business of peace. Lloyd George was winding up the campaign of a general election, in which his majorities were sustained. Clemenceau was openly expressing his preference for "a system of alliances" as against the notion of a league; and he was to be upheld in this by a vote of 380 to 124 in the Chamber of Deputies on December 30. With the danger of defeat behind them the Allies were looking for salvage and indemnity; Churchill was concerned with the preservation of the dominance of the British Navy; France was convinced, and with reason, that the proximity of Germany made security for France more important than any sort of altruism.

For the European statesmen, the popularity of the American President among the common people was enough to endanger some of the national hopes which had deferred the acceptance of the moderate program of the Fourteen Points. It was not because of hospitality alone that the Wilsons were overwhelmed with invitations to visit the Allied capitals—for invitations delayed business and gave breathing space for consideration of national programs. Paris entertained the visitors, the Sorbonne listened to a state address, the President sat with the Academy when Joffre, Marshal of France, delivered his inaugural; and he received the freedom of the city at the Hôtel de Ville. The Allied delegations were still not named as the holidays approached, leaving Wilson free to kill time with a Christmas dinner among the troops at Chaumont, and with a visit to England to be a guest in Buckingham Palace and to preach in his father's pulpit in Carlisle. There were dinners with royalty, state banquets, and a great luncheon at the Guildhall where he declared—with hope fathering the belief—that "the ground is clear and the foundations laid . . . we have already accepted the same body of principles."

Back in Paris for New Year's Day, there was still nothing to interfere with the visit to Rome, which Italy demanded, even at the cost of several of the precious days before his deadline of February 15, when the need to be in the White House for the crowded details at the end of the Sixty-fifth Congress would force him to start back to Washington. He was once more in Paris on January 7, 1919, to confer with his associates on the paper work which had kept them busy while he was away; but with more days to wait before it was possible even to confer with the premiers of France and Britain on the course of procedure to be followed when at last the delegations of the Allied and Associated Powers should be ready to convene.

When he met the premiers and foreign ministers of the principal Allies in their preliminary caucus of January 12, Paris was crowded with the delegations of the many nations which had cast their lot among the Allies, of the neutral countries whose concern was with the peace, and of aspiring dependencies which hoped somehow to improve their status. Each of these kept its typewriters clicking and its mimeographs rolling off copies of material designed to show the world the importance of its own demands.

At this first meeting, the business of the approaching conference was mingled with that of the Supreme War Council. There were military decisions to be made respecting the terms and continuation of the Armistice agreement, now two months old. There was new business concerning the procedure to be followed by the associated nations and with the share in the business to be allowed to the minor powers whose chief service had been a technical state of war and whose chief advantage had been the privilege of sharing in the loans first authorized by the United States in the act of April 24, 1917. It was agreed that on Saturday, January 18, 1919, the full delegations of the enemies of Germany should meet for organiza-

tion in the Clock Room of the Quai d'Orsay; that a steering committee for the conference should consist of the five belligerent powers with special interests—Great Britain, the United States, France,
Italy, and Japan—and that all differences among the victor powers
should be settled among themselves before Germany should be admitted to the discussion of peace.

The practical need for agreement among Germany's enemies before the opening of a conference delayed the opening of the genuine
Peace Conference until May 7, 1919, when for the first time the
German delegates were seated. The other enemy powers were required to await their turn and the convenience of the victors: Austria finally signed at St. Germain, September 10, 1919; Bulgaria at
Neuilly, November 27, 1919; Hungary at Trianon, June 4, 1920;
and Turkey at last and ineffectively at Sèvres, August 10, 1920.
Although Germany was the only Central Power involved, this Conference has been commonly but erroneously called the Peace Conference. Between January 18 and May 7 it was only a prolonged
caucus which sat in Paris as the victors worked out agreement
among themselves. Germany, and Germany's allies, were left to
wait in uncertainty and disorder. Bad as the delay was for the enemy
lands its consequences were worse for the victors, since lapse of
time and loss of unity went hand in hand. But no other course was
possible, and the period could have been shortened only if the
associates had had fewer and less vital subjects for disagreement.
The clear advantages of a short wait and a quick peace were beyond
attainment. The simultaneous discussions of postwar affairs did
not delay the final preparation of proposals to be made to Germany;
they merely occupied days in the beginning of the period during
which other issues were receiving preliminary examination.

When the first plenary session of the delegations was called to
order on January 18, it was Wilson who nominated Clemenceau
for president, and it was Poincaré, President of the French Republic, who declared that the question of war guilt was settled, that all
the Allies were free from blame, and that the peace must be a peace
of justice. When the Conference proceeded to arrange to issue news
through communiqués and to meet only occasionally, after business
had been cleared in a committee of ten consisting usually of the five
leaders and their foreign secretaries, a hostile and contentious

atmosphere was provided for the whole of the proceedings. When the ten were reduced to eight by the voluntary abstention of Japan, the concentration of authority was even greater. When the eight were reduced to four—Wilson, Lloyd George, Clemenceau, and Orlando—by the elimination of the secretaries, the Big Four controlled the caucus. And these became the Big Three when Italy withdrew Orlando from Paris.

The smaller powers, excluded from discussion except when their special interests were concerned, and forced to do business with committees, were indignant and rebellious. The assembled journalists were outraged at having to work through keyholes rather than in the open. Ray Stannard Baker, selected to be press agent for the United States delegation, and later chosen by Wilson to be his literary executor, did what he could to placate the American press. But Paris became a city of rumor and suspicion as the weeks went on, and as increasing national interest reduced the popularity of Wilson and his program.

With Wilson first things came first. He arrived in Paris to match his wits with those of European politicians whom he had never met, and who, knowing and liking House, muddied the waters of diplomacy by inquiring of House what the President really meant. He came to Paris, filled with his conviction that the peace must be founded on an accepted association of nations. He was certain, and probably correctly certain, that unless the association were built into the actual treaty of peace it would never be attainable. He was looking into the future rather than at the present; ready to ignore the evidence that the world was in danger of falling apart while he contemplated the advantages to be gained through international unity; ready also, in spite of his distinction as a student of government, to disregard the fact that his own Congress was prepared to challenge his authority as leader of the American people. In spite of all suggestions of other courses of action, and he was tragically right in rejecting them, he insisted upon immediate consideration of a proposed constitution for the world. And so great was the personal prestige which still attached to him that his persistence was allowed to have its way.

At a second plenary session of the victors, on January 25, Wilson's proposal that the League receive priority over the peace was approved. The Conference resolved that a league of nations was essential to the maintenance of the world settlement, that it should be an integral part of the general treaty of peace, and that in its structure should be included periodical meetings of the full membership of nations, and a permanent secretariat which should carry on the business of the League between meetings. In anticipation of this resolution the advisers of the American delegation had worked out with the President a plan of organization. The British, French, and Italians had proposals and Smuts of South Africa offered many germane suggestions. Much of what every plan had to include was so obvious if there were to be a league at all, that the matter of origins is unimportant. One of the American advisers, David Hunter Miller, has described in great detail *The Drafting of the Covenant* (1928) without being able at all points to see eye to eye with Ray Stannard Baker. The latter, working under the spell of the President, has recorded the full story of the American effort in Paris, in *Woodrow Wilson and World Settlement* (1922).

President Wilson was named chairman of a committee to draft the agreement for the League,—a committee consisting of two from each of the five major powers, and five others. Before the work of his committee was completed the protests of the lesser nations forced the Conference to raise the five others to nine. The clash of points of view between those nations which needed a safe peace and those upon whose shoulders must fall most of the burden of maintaining it, characterized the work of the Conference and its various committees. It was much the same old clash that has helped to shape every federal arrangement in which the coöperating units have had equal juridical standing but have actually carried unequal weight. Wilson worked his committee under forced draft, both because of his overwhelming concern, and because of his practical need of having something to take back to Washington in the middle of February. The drafting was done between January 25, when his committee was set up, and February 14. On the latter date he appeared before a third plenary session to present the report in the form of a covenant or constitution proposed for a league of nations. His own ideas on the subject had been steadily developing since the spring of 1916 when he stood on the platform at a Washington meeting of the League to Enforce Peace and accepted the doctrine of a league. He had further advanced the doctrine when he described a peace without victory in 1917; and he had embodied it among his Fourteen Points of January 8, 1918.

The draft of the Covenant stopped short of the creation of a superstate. It failed to provide for the military staff and the full control of security which France demanded, but it went far beyond any general agreement for the arbitration of disputes. It contemplated that in some way, through orderly channels, the physical power of the world might be assembled to stop aggression. There was no way in which a member nation might avoid being challenged by the disapproval or force of its co-members, or escape falling under pressure to follow a course of action contrary to its desires. To the periodic meetings of the full membership, and the permanent secretariat, which had been provided for in the resolution of January 25, the draft added an executive council, to consist for the present of nine seats, five of which were permanently assigned to the five major powers. The Executive Council was directed to prepare plans for a Permanent Court of International Justice, so organized as to be able to act upon matters referred to its jurisdiction; and it was expected to meet as often as business warranted, to take note of aggressions or threats to peace, and to recommend the degree of military or naval force which the several members of the League should contribute when it might become necessary to protect the Covenants of the League. Any war or threat of war was declared to be a matter of concern to the League. One of the articles of the Covenant, the tenth, bound "The high contracting parties . . . to respect and preserve as against external aggression the territorial integrity and existing political independence of all States members of the League," and the Executive Council was empowered to "advise" upon the means of fulfilling the obligation.

The draft of the Covenant was not accepted on February 14, 1919; it was merely received as a proposal from a committee, but it was news of such quality that it was put at once upon the cables and appeared in the morning papers in the United States the following day. Senator Lodge, who was certain to be chairman of the Senate Committee on Foreign Relations after March 4, read it into the *Congressional Record*. And before the President reached

Washington to sign the acts passed in the last minutes of the dying Congress, the public debate was under way. Wilson followed the news as rapidly as the *George Washington* could carry him from Brest, landing in Boston on February 24. He arrived too late for his cause. Demobilization was under way. Opinion had undergone change since the Armistice; and new business, immediate, compelling, and more interesting than the peace, had crowded into the American mind. It was to be a rocky road to peace, but for Wilson there was no turning.

Chapter II ★ The Home Front

AMONG THE HUNDREDS of advisers who surrounded the five American commissioners in Paris there were representatives of most of the War Boards. Their service during the nineteen months of war had opened a new chapter in American administration as well as new points of view in their own minds. Even at its best, the problem of untangling the ties with which war had bound the United States to its associates was so technical as to call for all the wisdom there was. The desire to be in Paris during the exciting days of negotiation made it easy to persuade men anxious to get back to work to defer their resignations; and harder to resist the pressure of others eager to be permitted to attend. Their presence, and their pride in their jobs, contributed lavishly to the volume of comment which was to become available to the historian of the peace negotiations. And if most of them finally came home feeling that the work would have been better had their personal contributions been accepted as the basis for the peace, this attitude was only natural.

The Supreme War Council had hardly begun to transform itself into the little group of leaders who were to direct, adequately informed or not, the negotiations before it was clear that besides the obligation to liquidate the war there was new business at hand. Conditions on the home fronts complicated operations on the Paris front.

Few normal activities in Europe had lasted through the four years of war. Even the strongest of the victor countries were so nearly bankrupt that solvency was almost a joke. Each of the victors had its own problems of domestic reconstruction with which the peace must not be permitted to interfere. Business was distorted, and the labor markets were crowded with former soldiers and war workers. The value of money was uncertain. Areas had been devastated, whether through the necessary consequences of war or through the malice of Germany as the enemy armies had been pressed back by Foch. Belgium was full of ruins, and France had the task of rehabilitating the ten *départements* which the enemy had overrun. The French had promised in 1914 that the injury of a citizen should be a charge upon the nation, and faced bankruptcy and politics as the time came to fulfill the pledge. Huge populations, driven from the theaters of war, were crowding neighborhoods which lacked the means for their own support. The enemy countries, beset by both defeat and revolt, were in confusion. Russia had become a world problem.

One of the Allies at the beginning, the Czarist government of Russia had fallen before a constitutionalist revolution in the spring of 1917; and the moderates had fallen in turn when all-out revolution brought the Bolshevists to power in November. The Bolshevist revolution had launched new and positive doctrines upon a world whose bonds and structure were weakened by the strain of war. The new business, forced upon the Allies when combat ceased, was that of fighting both the hunger which made men desperate and the new ideas of proletarian dictatorship which had wide charm for peoples who had nothing left for which to hope. Whatever the nature of the peace which was to be constructed, it was imperative that there should be a Europe left to implement it. The director of the United States Food Administration, Herbert Hoover, was summoned to Paris before the President sailed. Hoover had been converted from mining promotion to relief and had acquired a unique position when his Commission for Relief in Belgium had functioned between battle lines in its labor to keep Belgium alive from 1914 to 1917. As Food Administrator, whether with law behind him, or only public spirit, he had turned American agriculture into war channels. He found the Supreme Council of the Allies ready to assign him the emergency task, as Director of Relief; and Wilson, early in January, cabled to Washington for an appropriation of one hundred millions to support the work.

The call for action in this new field came to a lame duck Congress. The long session of 1918, ending on November 21, allowed weary members to snatch only a brief recess and to collect mileage before the opening of the regular short session on December 2. Already the obligations of American reinforcements were a burden to a people eager to get back to work, and a bargaining weapon to those who wished to examine the hearts of the Allies before extending further aid. The fear had begun to permeate the United States that un-American purposes were gathering strength and that new ideas of Russian origin were dangerous to the American interest. The money was voted for relief in countries which had not been hostile, but it was discussed heatedly. So many doubts were expressed that final approval was delayed until the President was back at his Washington desk on February 25. Penrose, of Pennsylvania, irked because the name of Hoover had been attached to a campaign document urging a Democratic Congress, inquired sharply if Hoover was in fact an American citizen. Congress had become increasingly suspicious as the session advanced, and more disposed to scrutinize the expenditure of every cent already allocated to the special funds of the President, "for the national security and defense, and for each and every purpose connected therewith." Much of the normal business of the session was being jammed at the end, in order that it might be thrown over into the first session of the approaching Republican Congress.

Demobilization had begun. It affected both partisans and patriots. It touched the personnel of the government services and the willingness of the citizen to put up with the costly and irritating restrictions which war had required. With the danger of defeat averted, suppressed demands could now be urged in the open. The congressmen, who had sat in almost continuous session since Wilson convened them on April 2, 1917, were wearied with well-doing and novelty. They were still in session when the election of November had left some of them lame. Too much confused by the sudden return to peace to do business, they then gave up the idea of completing the unhappy tax measure, and left it to be revamped during the short session, as the Revenue Act of 1919. Ever since the passage of the first war revenue act in October, 1917, the committees had been laboring over the next act; and every time they neared agreement on a scale of taxation the demands of war had compelled them to raise their sights and expand their view. Now, as they were about to agree again in the autumn of 1918, the end of hostilities made a case for a lowering of the estimates as war purchases should taper off.

The most significant measure which could be enacted before the recess between sessions concerned wartime prohibition. The Eighteenth Amendment, helped through Congress by the need for conservation of grains, had gone out to the states a year earlier, in December, 1917. The list of approvals was lengthening, and there was likelihood that the legislatures of 1919 would complete the ratification. But not until a year after ratification would the United States be constitutionally dry. In the interval it was now anticipated that military demobilization would occur, and perhaps even a legal state of peace would be established. The latter would terminate the wartime dry laws which had stopped the waste of grain. A bone-dry rider, to be effective July 1, 1919, and thereafter until the end of demobilization, was attached to an agricultural appropriation bill in the autumn of 1918. Passage of the bill was delayed until after the election—an election in which the ability of Alfred E. Smith to carry the State of New York for governor might be lessened if the bill were passed too soon. Smith was no dry. He disapproved of prohibition on principle, and was too courageous to conceal his views. He won the election, and in the next fortnight Congress sent the bill to the White House. Nebraska, the state of William J. Bryan, appropriately enough brought the Prohibition Amendment into force by ratifying as the thirty-sixth state, January 16, 1919.

The war had been fought by a scratch team, assembled out of civil life for unexpected duty. Even in the armed forces only a handful of men had received professional training before 1917. The uniform commonly covered a hurriedly reconditioned civilian; and the removal of the uniform commonly revealed a citizen only slightly changed by war. Dixon Wecter tells the story of the demobilized soldier in *Johnny Comes Marching Home* (1944), and compares the status of the veteran reëntering civil life in 1919 with that of those of 1783 and 1865. The military servants of the United States in this war had been better cared for than the veterans of any other war had been. They could not come marching home, however, until the armed forces were through with them.

The civil servants of the war were free to decide for themselves when their share of the war was over. The President said to Congress in December: "the moment we knew the armistice to have been signed we took the harness off." George Creel, who had imposed part of the harness of war, released the press from the voluntary censorship which had been a credit to it, and the censorship of outgoing mails and cables was immediately lifted. The Four-Minute Men, whose little speeches had been a continuous exhortation to compliance with war needs, disbanded before Christmas. A lifting of the steel priorities opened the way to a prompt resumption of activities curtailed by the war need: structural work, road building, automobile manufacture. Individuals laid aside their personal harness. McAdoo, the first of the cabinet to drop out since the departure of Garrison in 1916, resigned as Secretary of the Treasury and Director of the Railroad Administration. His avowed reason was his financial need to return to the practice of the law; his critics suggested that he wished to be free to groom himself for 1920. Before long he headed for California, a state already overcrowded with presidential possibilities in the persons of Hiram Johnson and Herbert Hoover. Gregory surrendered his post as Attorney General early in the new year. Baruch resigned as chairman of the War Industries Board, and when the negotiations at Paris no longer needed him he slipped easily into an honorable post as elder statesman for the Democratic party. John D. Ryan went back to Anaconda Copper from his post in aircraft production. Charles M. Schwab left the Emergency Fleet Corporation to return to Bethlehem Steel. Men who had been understudies took the posts vacated by the wartime chiefs, while underlings and clerks scuttled home for jobs unless the modest opportunities of the civil service were attractive to them.

It was off with the new and back to the old, as the United States broke from the locked step of war. The United States Golf Association waited only for the turn of the year to announce the resumption of public competition and the great championship tournaments. The Chief of Staff, General Peyton C. March, gave military sanction for the opening of the regular professional baseball season in 1919; which had been threatened in September when baseball as an occupation had been declared nonessential. And Sir Thomas Lipton, still coveting the *America's* cup, forwarded a challenge through the Royal Ulster Yacht Club.

More serious matters than sports were involved in letting go. The railroads, operating as a unit system, were eager for an unscrambling and a settlement of accounts. Those who hoped that the Railroad Administration would be a step toward complete nationalization of the railroads were prepared to fight the return of the lines to the owner companies. Glenn E. Plumb, legal counsel for the railroad brotherhoods, was at work upon a plan for employee management of the roads. Under the control act of March 21, 1918, it would be necessary to return the lines to the owners twenty-one months after the peace. Unless the United States was to return to its prewar railroad status, it was necessary to give early consideration to the railroad problem. It was more difficult now to return to the old system than it would have been to continue in it from the first, for the war had in every direction developed the self-consciousness of labor. The brotherhoods were the most dependable of all the unions, were job conscious, and were determined to improve their status in the system. Other unions were like-minded.

The status of labor in whatever reconstruction there should be, had two sides. The president of the National Founders Association, which met at the Hotel Astor two days after the Armistice, announced that wages must now come down. Part of the price paid for the war was a continuous rise of the wage scale as prices rose, and cost-plus contracts had induced in industry a temporary indifference to labor costs. Government had accepted the idea that labor must not be squeezed between fixed wages and rising prices. From Samuel Gompers, speaking now as head of the American Federation of Labor rather than as labor representative on the Council of National Defense, came quick retort that labor expected to hold the gains in wages and working conditions which war had brought. Women had acquired a share in the new labor status brought about by war, creating new complications for labor leaders. Negroes, too, were in a position in which it was less easy to ignore them than had been possible before the war. The National Association for the Advancement of Colored People had ideas of its own; the National American Woman Suffrage Association had not quieted its agitation during the war and had no notion of discontinuing it after peace.

Under the terms of the Armistice the advance of the Allied columns to the Rhine bridgeheads began on November 17, 1918. Dickman's Third Army, organized for the purpose, had hardly begun its march to Coblenz before New York was considering how to receive the returning soldiers who were no longer needed by the A.E.F. Mayor John F. Hylan, recently installed by grace of Tammany and Hearst, prepared invitations for a huge welcoming committee, through which New York should act as greeter for the nation. A subcommittee under the chairmanship of William Randolph Hearst, was placed in charge of military receptions. The attitude of the Hearst papers before and during the war had incurred the bitter disapproval of the National Security League and the American Defense Society, which had made themselves custodians of patriotism, and which now thundered in disapproval of Hearst. The Supreme Court decided against his journalistic organizations in a suit brought by the Associated Press on charges of news piracy. Wide protest was made against the New York resumption of leadership and against the honor given Hearst, and refusals to accept appointment on the committees came in as the invitations went out. Colonel Henry L. Stimson of the 31st Field Artillery declined to serve with the chairman; Charles E. Hughes refused. Those who protested could not control the stands erected on Fifth Avenue from which the returning divisions were eventually reviewed, or keep Hearst off the stand, where he later stood with Governor Smith, the mayor, and Franklin D. Roosevelt, Assistant Secretary of the Navy. But they could hold a meeting about it. Madison Square Garden was rented, and there a crowd, described by the Hearst paper as a small meeting from which many walked out, listened to denunciations of the publisher by Bishop William T. Manning and John Grier Hibben, president of Princeton.

Whether or not Hearst had been guilty of disloyalty, as charged, the reception episode revealed the uneasiness of many minds, and an irritability left from war. The death of one of Hearst's great enemies, coming at this moment, produced a burst of patriotic expression. Theodore Roosevelt died in his sleep at his home on Oyster Bay, January 6, 1919. Deprived of an opportunity to seek a coveted death in combat, Roosevelt had thrown his last reserves of strength into the support of war, covering the nation on itineraries which might have wrecked a lesser spirit. Never able or eager to conceal his contempt for the man who was occupying the White House, he had been equally unable to go along with that wing of his party which saw a League of Nations as the next step for the United States. Taft, Root, Hughes, and A. Lawrence Lowell of Harvard seemed to him to be supporting a course dangerous to American security. But at the moment of his death he was the likeliest of all members of his party to have been selected as its candidate in 1920. The voices which hailed him as a great American in a class with Washington and Lincoln were in part inspired by the antithesis which he presented to Woodrow Wilson.

The nature of Americanism, the dangers threatening it, and the means of bolstering it, occupied many minds. Here and there it was pointed up by the action of the courts, as in due process the cases of alleged sedition and conspiracy came to their final hearings. The acts on espionage, sedition, and sabotage, passed in a hurry, had been inspired by a fear of danger from these sources, a fear greater than any known facts could warrant. The charges of violation were substantiated in part by facts; in part they arose from war hysteria. Hearings and trials ran their course, as the war, too, ran its course; and judgments in the lower courts gradually placed defendants under bail on appeal, or in jail if they had no means of pressing their appeals. As measures of restraint of dangerous opinion, the laws had completed their work before the highest courts had opportunity to pass upon either the constitutionality and adequacy of the laws or the fairness of the trials.

The case of Tom Mooney, arising from a preparedness parade in San Francisco, July 22, 1916, was in the news at the end of November, when the governor of California commuted his death sentence to life imprisonment. Though convicted and sentenced, the date of Mooney's execution had been postponed while final appeal was made to the Supreme Court of the United States. When the Supreme Court found no grounds on which to interfere, the governor, unwilling to pardon him, was equally unwilling to hang him. Hence the commutation, and the case which made of Mooney a symbol of labor warfare with capital, until the question of his possible guilt was lost sight of by both friends and enemies. The case was by no means ended, and rankled until a later governor of his state gave him a pardon in 1939. Whether Mooney was guilty as charged or merely a scapegoat, whether the trial was fair, or only a frame-up, the case produced a huge literature of controversy, which is an index to the tremendous importance which labor and radicalism had assumed in the American mind.

More prominent persons than Mooney were in the toils. Victor L. Berger, of Milwaukee, the first congressman to be elected as a Socialist, went to trial in the Chicago court of Judge Kenesaw Mountain Landis early in December at the same time as a group of members of the Industrial Workers of the World went on trial in Sacramento on charges of sedition. The fact that Berger had been reëlected to Congress in November gave his case great prominence. Was a convinced Socialist disqualified by his belief for service to the nation? Was a congressman under indictment eligible to be seated? Was Berger guilty of a crime? Berger admitted on the stand that he was a Socialist by conviction and by membership of long standing, that he had opposed the entrance of the United States into the war, and that he believed it to be a capitalists' war. He denied disloyalty or conspiracy and fought the contention of the government that one who supported the Socialist antiwar platform of April 7, 1917, could not be loyal. The jury convicted him early in January, a few days before the Sacramento jury convicted the members of the I.W.W., and Judge Landis sentenced him to twenty years in prison. The force of the conviction was lessened when the Supreme Court quashed the proceedings on the grounds that Judge Landis had used improper language during the trial. But as a component of disturbed public opinion the case cut two ways. To some it indicated a slanting of justice against free speech; to others it indicated a dangerous restlessness and radicalism against which the United States must struggle. When the Congress to which Berger was reëlected went to work, it kept the case alive through long hearings and by a final refusal to admit him to his seat. Reëlected by his district in a special election at the end of 1919, he was again excluded, and his seat remained vacant until in 1920 a Republican sought it and won it.

As the Berger case neared its end, the Supreme Court gave hearing to the appeal of Eugene V. Debs, convicted of violation of the Espionage Act. If anyone was a Socialist by conviction, it was Debs, who had been his party's candidate for the presidency in 1900, 1904, 1908, and 1912. He had opposed the war before entry, had spoken against it after entry, and had received a ten-year sentence upon conviction. The Supreme Court whose opinion was prepared by the great liberal Justice Oliver Wendell Holmes, was unanimous in sustaining the conviction of Debs. He was held guilty under the law; the Court did not enter upon the matter of constitutionality. The abstract right of freedom of speech was not permitted to interfere with the concrete necessity of the nation to defend itself in wartime. Debs was sent to Atlanta. Again nominated for the presidency by his loyal followers in 1920, he polled nine hundred thousand votes. Harding pardoned him at Christmas, 1921. The war was over, peace had been proclaimed, and interest in wartime offenses of thought and speech had run its course. Such offenses in peacetime were to be a different matter.

But the period of the war had brought new ideas into extensive circulation, had developed new techniques in publicity and promotion, and had intensified fear in many American minds. During the decade prior to 1914 those who were satisfied or conservative had been disturbed by the violence of the progressive movement, and by the proposals of the leaders of that movement to extend the activities of the government of the United States into the reform and control of business practice. One Roosevelt had called this reform the "square deal"; another was to call it the "new deal," as though it had begun in his own term. The proposal seemed to those of the extreme right to shake the foundations of American government.

There had also been a growing fear that the waves of immigrants, washed into the United States by prosperity here or by distress abroad, were carrying ideas as well as man power—ideas certainly foreign in origin and perhaps subversive of the traditional order. Three times, before it became a law over the veto of Woodrow Wilson in 1917, a bill for a sifting of immigrants by a literacy test had been stopped by presidential veto. It was an inadequate sieve, since the most dangerous of the subversives were likely to be the most literate; but it attracted the support of such groups in the United States as feared the dilution of American principles or the competition which alien labor might engender.

These groups were aware that the end of the war might bring a sudden swelling of the stream of immigrants. The ideological consequences were the more ominous because of the prevalence in eastern and southern Europe of the Bolshevist experiment and propaganda. The attempt of international Socialists in 1919 to reestablish solidarity called attention to the existence of groups in all countries which professed a Marxian allegiance to class and a subordination of national patriotism to class loyalty. War had disrupted them. Their representatives—those who could get passports, and not including Americans, who had been denied passports —gathered in at Bern to rebuild their structure. The French and German delegates lost sight of their goal of solidarity in a wrangle over the responsibility for the war. Branting of Sweden, the chairman, was suspicious of Bolshevism. Many of the American Socialists, from their vantage point at home, sniffed at the Bern meeting as a German plot. Gompers remained, as always, hostile to labor or Socialist parties. There was little but the name, at Bern, to alarm American conservatives. But in March the left-wing movements acquired a spearhead at Moscow.

The Third International was launched in the Bolshevist capital, with a call for world-wide proletarian revolution and substitution of workers' solidarity for national patriotism. Such reports of the new "Comintern" as leaked into the press had their disquieting side. The United States had come to believe that the overthrow of Czarism was a social revolution rather than a victory for the kind of democracy Americans understood. The excesses of the revolution and the doctrines of Bolshevism were magnified and distorted in transmission. A spark set off the explosion. Friends of the new Russia hired a theater in Washington for a meeting on February 2, at which to tell the "truth"; and a spread-eagle congressman from Illinois made so enthusiastic a speech for the new social-economic revelation that in two days the Senate came into action. It commissioned the Judiciary Committee, which was already investigating German prewar influence in the United States, to look into the spread of Bolshevism. Senator Overman, chairman of the subcommittee in charge, turned his searchlight upon the disturbing doctrine and its adherents. Fragments of the testimony got into the papers in the late winter, and vituperation, as usual overshadowed the facts. The New York legislature, under Republican control, launched a similar inquiry of its own through Senator Clayton R. Lusk's committee. Four great volumes of testimony were printed by the professional investigators who kept proceedings in motion. In due time the "Lusk bills," all restrictive in character, were vetoed by Governor Alfred E. Smith, whose background was Democratic, liberal, Catholic, and Irish. They awaited enactment until Smith's Republican successor signed them in 1921. "The nation today is face to face with an alien misapprehension of its institutions," was the sober comment of the *Christian Science Monitor* on February 11. California, with Mooney in mind and worried by the doctrines of the I.W.W., passed a rigorous law against criminal syndicalism at the end of April, 1919; and in the state of Washington the mayor of Seattle, Ole Hanson, gained a moment of prominence in combat with a general strike.

The Seattle troubles began among the metal trades in the shipyards, where there had been a walkout in January. They were directed by unions which the mayor believed to be full of Bolshevists and led by penetrators from the I.W.W. When the Central Labor Council of the city, in sympathy with the metalworkers, called a general strike for February 6, 1919, the threat of stoppage of service by the utilities and transportation lines brought the mayor into action. He called the strike a rebellion against the government; the strike was the first major demonstration of its kind in the United States. "Any man who attempts to take over control of municipal functions here will be shot on sight," Hanson told the strikers and the press, as he prepared to demand troops from Fort Lewis to put down the insurrection. Called for Thursday the sixth, and called off on Monday the tenth, the general strike brought only limited inconvenience. Hanson, who became a public figure through this strike, took his story around the country, preaching a gospel of resistance to anarchy to audiences almost ready to suspect that social revolution was just around the corner. The mayor's name was soon forgotten, but his temporary prominence was an indication of the nervousness prevalent in the United States.

More successful than Hanson in staying in the public eye was Henry Ford, who appeared in a new guise in January, 1919, with the first issue of his recent acquisition, the Dearborn *Independent*.

Ford was not content to remain merely the successful manufacturer of a cheap automobile, or one of the industrial pioneers of mass manufacture and continuous flow. He had introduced new standards of wage scales in the past, startling his rivals with a five-dollar daily minimum wage in 1914. In 1915 he had been captivated by the idea of a personal intervention to stop the World War; and the failure of his personally conducted tour in the *Oscar II* had not satisfied his craving for public position. He hated war, yet set up an assembly line for Eagle boats in 1917. In 1918 he yielded to pressure to enter the Michigan primary when a seat in the Senate became vacant. Here he captured the Democratic nomination with ease, but was beaten for the Republican endorsement by Truman H. Newberry, who had seen both service in the Spanish War and duty for a year as Secretary of the Navy under Roosevelt. Too much money was spent in the canvass by Newberry's friends and he was elected in November. But he was to be plagued for four years by a contest filed by Ford, by federal prosecution under the corrupt practices act, and by the attacks of Democrats and radical Republicans who made of him a symbol of corruption in politics. The case gained prominence because of the almost even division of party strength in the Senate. Had Ford been elected neither party could, after March 4, 1919, have commanded an absolute majority of the ninety-six Senators. With Newberry seated, the Republican party had a majority of two. It was indicated in December that there would be a long and bitter fight. How long and bitter could not be foreseen, but the appearance of Ford with a weekly of his own aroused more than partisan interest. He had a simple explanation for the war, which was, as the first editorial of the Dearborn *Independent* stated, the "Outgrowth of bad conditions everywhere; the world was simply festering with selfishness." His paper was later to become a carrier of anti-Semitism and a crusader against international bankers. Meanwhile Ford attacked his enemies, selecting as his target the Chicago *Tribune,* which had in 1916 called him an anarchist. The *Tribune* defended itself in a long trial for libel at Mt. Clemens, Michigan; it admitted its guilt and tried to prove the charge. No one among the attorneys on either side, or among the professors summoned to give expert advice, was quite able to define an anarchist, but Ford won his case. The jury on August 14 awarded him six cents damages and costs. Ford returned to his factories, sold more than a million cars in 1922, and indulged himself in the belief that automobiles would spread so much prosperity that they would end wars, since prosperous peoples would not fight. And there were some who said that his car "at a startlingly low price . . . had set back the revolution" for a quarter of a century.

The friends of Soviet Russia were not the only "friends" in the United States whose interest in the outside world added to the confusion of American currents of thought. A group calling itself the Friends of Irish Freedom had been organized in 1916, in New York, on a call spread by George Sylvester Viereck's *Fatherland*. It was just in time to sympathize with the Easter Rebellion and to protest against the iron hand with which England had tried to put it down. Branches of the society spread over the country, where the deep love of the Irish for Ireland had not been inconsistent with equal loyalty to the United States, but where the deep distrust of the Irish for England had long tied American diplomacy to American politics. The rebels in Ireland, financed and sympathized with by their cousins in the United States, kept up their fight after the Easter rising of 1916. In the general election of December 14, 1918, which kept Lloyd George in power after the Armistice, the Irish voted less on the coalition government than on their own nationality, and some seventy-three of the Irish seats in the House of Commons were carried by nationalists—Sinn Feiners, who pledged themselves not to sit in Westminster but to set up an Irish republic in Dublin. Nearly half of the Irish members were in jail when the other half issued their declaration of independence at the Mansion House on January 21, 1919, and named a delegation to represent Ireland at the Peace Conference. Eamon de Valera, New York born, head of the Sinn Fein movement, and survivor of the Easter Rebellion, had already been declared president, but was still in Lincoln prison.

The Fourteen Points had said nothing about self-determination as it might be applied to the internal affairs of Allied countries, but the insistence of Wilson upon this basis for the treatment of oppressed peoples under enemy control suggested an outlet for every dissatisfied group wherever it might be found. The Peace Conference seemed to be the place to press the claims.

Before Wilson had read the draft of the Covenant to his associates in Paris, the Friends of Irish Freedom had taken up the matter of the Irish declaration, and had called on February 22 in Philadelphia an Irish Race Convention at which to marshal their pressure. Cardinal Gibbons there introduced the resolution asking Congress to recognize the Irish Republic, and urging the Peace Conference to see that Ireland got its independence. The various Irish societies in the United States endorsed the resolution in the next few weeks, and passed supporting resolutions of their own; at Paris a representative of the Irish Republic, John O'Kelly, loyally rewriting his name as Sean O'Ceallaigh, suggested that if the Conference failed to assure Irish independence "we can stop ratification" of the treaty by the United States. Few knew the potential weight of the Irish vote better than Henry Cabot Lodge. Before the summer was over the Friends of Irish Freedom were paying for space in the American press to advertise: "Would You Buy Into a Bankrupt Concern? Would You Have Your Country in Partnership With a Crumbling Empire?"

The woman suffragists continued to press their case at home, and their pickets burned the President in effigy before the White House on February 10. They had learned much about pressure since their Congressional Union for Woman Suffrage had kicked over the traces at the first inauguration of Woodrow Wilson, and had abandoned ladylike advocacy in favor of militant attack. It was now fifty years since the granting of woman suffrage in the young Territory of Wyoming had been the opening wedge of the movement, and in fifteen of the states women were now enfranchised. The National American Woman Suffrage Association, deprecating the militants but profiting by their endeavors, was nearly ready to stop agitating and exercise the right to vote. The Congressional Union and the Woman's Party, which had been launched on a national basis in 1916, were counting on an early victory for the Susan B. Anthony amendment to the Constitution. By publicity they had gained prominence; by persuasion they had made converts; by persistence they had worn down all but the most stubborn of their opponents. In the lame duck session, the Senate again rejected their amendment, but only by a single vote on February 10, which would be corrected in the next Congress. The old National

Association prepared to transfer the torch of women's influence to an American League of Women Voters, in which women of the several states should be shifted to full membership as rapidly as they gained the vote. The year 1920 was to be the centenary of Susan B. Anthony and was to be marked by the full accomplishment of her purpose. The Association arranged for the shift in organization at its meeting in March, 1919, and sang its swan song in Chicago a year later. The League of Women Voters took over the last phases of the fight which was at an end when Tennessee ratified the amendment in August, 1920. The successful culmination of the campaigns of pressure for the prohibition and suffrage amendments suggested techniques which other movements were not slow to adopt.

Within a few days of the death of Theodore Roosevelt, the Senate dropped the La Follette case. The Republican party had not been large enough for the full activities of both Roosevelt and La Follette since the fatal year 1904, when the Republican National Convention refused to seat the regular La Follette delegation from Wisconsin and turned its leader into an independent. The death of Roosevelt deprived the party of a likely candidate for 1920, and eliminated one possible source of deep intraparty contention. Even his bitterest enemies could join in obituary eulogy, and did. La Follette, alone, remained to be assuaged.

Robert Marion La Follette had constituted a "case" since the autumn of 1917, when his speech at a stop-the-war convention in St. Paul was made to sound worse than it was by garbling in the press. Attacked as a near traitor—he had been one of Wilson's "little group of wilful men" and one of the half-dozen senators to vote against entering the war—the effort to expel him from the Senate had run a long course through investigation, hearings, and debate. He had been made the whipping boy. His opposition to the war and his loyalty were equally fundamental; and among those who yielded to public pressure and denounced him were many who took covert pleasure in the breadth and incisiveness of his stubborn opposition. But it goes against the temper of the Senate to restrict the freedom of a senator, whether under the dome of the capitol or before the public. It had taken the filibuster of the "wilful men" to drive the Senate into adoption of even a mild machinery for putting a cloture upon obstructive debate. The Committee on Privileges and Elections evaded the completion of a report which would have been expected to recommend La Follette's expulsion. After the election and the Armistice, on January 16, it advised the Senate that no ground for expulsion had been uncovered; and only one Republican joined the Democrats in opposing the quashing of the proceedings.

Through much of the war La Follette had been relatively silent, owing to sickness of his own and in his family. He had come again into activity as the revenue bill was taken up in the lame duck session, for he had not lost the concern for a pay-as-you-go war which inspired him in 1917, or his desire to keep the tax burdens heaviest on the corporations and the rich. No forgiving by his colleagues was likely to lessen the threat which his economic principles offered to party solidarity. When the managers of the bill reported that the tax revenue might safely be cut from eight billions to six billions because of the end of fighting, he attacked their whole proposal as inadequate and offered as an amendment a complete bill drafted in his own office. Never a modest man, he saw nothing humorous in insisting that all but him were out of step. The Senate majority brushed aside his amendment, for he had only a few supporters, and passed the bill just before Christmas. After being kept in conference for nearly another month it was ready for the signature of the President in time for Tumulty to carry it to Boston when he went to meet Wilson at the dock.

Among the clauses of the revenue bill was a second attempt to abolish the abuses of child labor. Early in the progressive period Beveridge had taken a lead in the struggle for child welfare, and Taft had approved the Children's Bureau. The constitutional warrant for a federal eradication of child labor being doubtful, the first attempt had been to control it by forbidding the products of child labor to pass in interstate commerce. The law to "prevent interstate commerce in the products of child labor" was approved in 1916, and immediately challenged in North Carolina. In the case of Hammer *vs.* Dagenhart the Supreme Court declared it to be unconstitutional on June 3, 1918. The five justices concurring in the decision believed that the statute was not one to regulate interstate commerce but was a piece of social legislation masquerading as such. The supporters of the reform divided their strength between attacking the conservatism of the court and devising a more persuasive approach. The taxing clause provided coverage for the second attempt: child labor was to be broken up by a surtax on incomes derived from the use of child labor. Before the attack upon this approach had run its full course, William Howard Taft had become Chief Justice. Taft wrote the adverse opinion, from which no justice dissented. The check administered to the reform illustrates the double difficulty with which the United States executes a change in the direction of its policy. The expediency of the new course needs to be established; but after that the project may be blocked by the inability of the Supreme Court to give effect to any statute which, in its judgment, has been passed in excess of the powers vested in Congress by the Constitution.

Between the date of the Armistice and the docking of the *George Washington* at Boston on February 24, 1919, the voices which sought to express the hope and purpose of the United States had changed their tone. The single-mindedness which pervaded the last few months of war had never been as genuine as it seemed. Public opinion, at best, is the opinion expressed at the moment by those of the public who wish to be heard. The shift from prayer for victory to acceptance of it quieted some of the voices raised during the period of danger and released other voices whose utterances had been restrained. Politics had succeeded war, presenting an external appearance and sound different from that of the autumn of 1918. The government had no master on the spot, no deputy to take the place of the President. None but Wilson could have spoken for either the country or the Democratic party; most of those in the opposition, however they may have agreed with the President, welcomed a disintegration of party strength. Wilson returned to fight his way through a trying ten days, as confusing as any President has had to face. Never again did he succeed in unifying American thought and its expression. On March 4, 1919, the episode of six years of Democratic leadership was due to end. Lodge was to receive his treaty.

The President did not pause in New York as he returned to Washington from Boston. Had he done so, he might have caught a glimpse of specific tokens of a new American period.

A month earlier, on January 25, the Hotel Pennsylvania had thrown open its doors to welcome guests in what, with its 2,200 rooms, it claimed to be the largest hotel in the world. And three days later the claims were challenged by the open doors beneath the twenty-six stories of the Commodore Hotel, where there was an automobile elevator on which guests in their own cars might be carried in privacy from the street level to the ball room. New York had resumed the modernization which had been under way during the last decade when it was interrupted by the war. The Waldorf-Astoria, the New York home of American provincials, was venerable but obsolete. New York luxury was on its way up Fifth Avenue, and opportunity had presented itself for terminal hotels with all the gadgets of another generation.

The great railroads serving New York had fought great battles in finance and engineering in their invasion of Manhattan. McAdoo had built the first Hudson River tunnels, and in 1910 the Pennsylvania Railroad had reached New York in its huge new terminal; across the street it built its new hotel. The Grand Central Terminal of the New York Central lines had come three years later, and the railroad could not have chosen a more appropriate name than Commodore for the hostelry at the terminus of the roads which Vanderbilt had assembled. Throughout the land, schemes of similar character were under scaffolding or on the drawing boards as urban United States rebuilt its plant. The new hotels were forerunners of the material aspects of a new American chapter.

The railroads, with their tunnels, terminals, and hotels, were bringing about a "partial annexation of Manhattan to the continent"; but "along a 150-mile front the Hudson" still remained "a barrier to road traffic." While Wilson was passing through New York in the dark, there was being prepared for Governor Smith a contract to be executed by his state with the New Jersey neighbor for the construction of a vehicular tunnel, which was to be more in harmony with the released spirit of the times than the League of Nations or even the return of the Republican party to power. He signed the tunnel bill on April 11, 1919, and later in the summer Congress gave its willing assent to the agreement between the states. A new phase of American constitutional experience was presenting itself, in which with the blessing of Congress the states were to undertake by agreement projects beyond the powers of any one of them alone. It was still a long way to the Tennessee Valley Authority, or to grandiose schemes for the correction of the flow of all the rivers of the nation, but the United States had started on that way. Whatever its relative importance as a cultural index for the nation, the modernization of the American physical plant so that it might carry, with advantage to all, the loads and speeds of gas-driven traffic was a matter which was to provide one of the strongest and unifying factors for the all-out American effort.

Chapter III ★ The End of the Democratic Interlude

WHEN WOODROW WILSON decided that his duty lay in Paris, there had been reason to hope for a speedy settlement of the problems which called him thither: the negotiation of a peace and the erection of an association of nations. How adequately he read the meaning of the November elections is still uncertain. As a competent professor in the field of American government he had no excuse for failing to see the meaning. After March 4, 1919, the interlude of Democratic control of the United States would be brought to an end by a Congress in which Republicans would possess a safe majority in the House, and probably a bare majority in the Senate. After that date, unless citizens in general should disregard party lines and give him overwhelming support, he must rely upon Republican coöperation for the approval of whatever treaty he might bring home. It was urgent that he bring it while his own party controlled the machinery of the Senate; and this, in December, 1918, did not seem to be impossible.

But the success of his labors was threatened by the equally urgent need that he be back in Washington to assist in winding up the business of the last Democratic session of the Congress. It became clear, as he met with procrastination, hospitality, and cross purposes in Paris, that delay would upset his original timetable; and that the demand for an immediate peace, which should not be postponed by constitutional discussion, would be hard to overcome. By rushing his colleagues he was able to offer at least a constitutional proposal to the plenary session on February 14; and by rushing the *George Washington* he was able to be off the port of Boston on February 23 and to land the next morning. The choice of Boston seems to have been made without malice, but the fact that it was the home of the Republican leader of the next Senate made the landing in Boston look like open defiance of Henry Cabot Lodge. Wilson allowed himself nine working days in the White House, arranging to have the *George Washington* pick him up at Hoboken on the night of Wednesday, March 4.

Plans were made on both sides of the Atlantic for the crowding of these days with a multitude of tasks. The President was already having trouble in his own delegation before he helped draft the Covenant. Lansing was submitting a "lawyer's treaty" for him to brush aside. House was ill. White was inclined to doubt whether Wilson should have come to Paris. As he prepared to sail on February 15 he cabled a request to the Senate to defer discussion of the proposed Covenant until he had had time to explain it; but he might as well have wired the winds. He cabled also an invitation to the members of the Committee on Foreign Relations to dine at the White House for a man-to-man talk on February 26; but it was not encouraging that Borah of Idaho declined to come. Fall of New Mexico declined as well, though this was of less significance, for he carried no moral weight. Lodge let it be known that he would attend, but would ask no questions; and he was putting the last touches on a set speech in opposition which he was preparing for delivery in the Senate two days later. Eventually, and with pride, he was to present his side of the contest in *The Senate and the League of Nations* (1925). Other members of the committee, who accepted without public comment, had already indicated a course of action out of harmony with that which the President desired to recommend.

This course of action had been foreshadowed during the autumn campaign when leaders in the Republican organization—not those who like Taft were heart and soul for a league of some sort—chose to pick up "unconditional surrender" as an issue and to play upon a fear that a President who had once advocated a "peace without victory" would be soft with the defeated enemy. "Unconditional surrender" had the political advantage of seeming to be based upon a patriotism even more aggressive than that of Wilson. Partisan leaders who were concerned with political as well as military victory criticized, further, the personnel of the Peace Commission and the decision of the President to leave the United States in order to have a direct hand in the negotiations. The attack ranged from the sharpest partisan criticism to genuine doubt about the wisdom of curtailing national freedom of action through membership in any international organization possessing power to act.

Hays, chairman of the Republican National Committee, had already called his members together for a Chicago meeting to rejoice in the victory of November, and to discuss plans for 1920, when the death of Theodore Roosevelt removed from consideration the one name which had been most often mentioned and opened the door to the whole range of Republican aspirants. The meeting was held on January 10. A few days later the Senate caucus of Republicans entrusted Lodge with a special committee for the double purpose of arranging to take over the Senate organization and of keeping the radical Republicans on the party line. La Follette had been forgiven, but his power to disturb had not been forgotten.

Lodge, like Roosevelt, had long supported the idea of a league of nations; but, also like Roosevelt, he could not be happy in the presence of such an organization put together by Woodrow Wilson. He had at least had a last-minute opportunity to discuss course and tactics with his old friend. In later years the friends of Wilson convinced themselves of what they could not prove, and what the historian cannot prove unless new evidence comes out of the archives. They believed that the inner leaders of the Republican party were in planned agreement to keep from their opponents and from Wilson in particular, the credit for accomplishing a peace and a new world order. A critical debate on the Covenant was ready to break out as soon as the document appeared in the *Congressional Record* on February 15.

While the *George Washington* was at sea the debate was opened against a background of nervousness over Bolshevism, the I.W.W., and labor unrest, and of a mounting desire to get back quickly to the ways of peace. The day, February 22, was nearing when it was habitual to read and reprint the Farewell Address of George Washington. The Address had a fresh meaning as the President launched the new order.

Poindexter of Washington led the procession of senators whose set speeches pointed two ways: against the proposals of the Covenant, and against that section of Republican leadership which endorsed them. Ex-President Taft was still on tour in his persistent advocacy of a league. From Missoula he welcomed the Covenant and its promise; from Stockton he endorsed it again, bringing the doctrines of the League into harmony with the Farewell Address and the Monroe Doctrine. Some, who disliked the proposals on their own account, disliked them more because they had the support of Taft. The wound made by the progressive split was by no means healed. "Why on earth," asked Sherman, "should I take the advice of an ex-President when I will not take the advice of a real one?" Poindexter argued the need for immediate peace as more immediately important than the need for a league. He feared the new order and the consequences of its "entangling alliances." And he took a slap at the party of the South as he commented on the "sardonic triumph" it was suspected of trying to achieve over the North which had held the union together in 1865.

Poindexter spoke on February 19 and Borah followed him in two days, hastening to the attack because of his desire to challenge the Taft endorsement. Article X of the Covenant was his target because of the possibility that it might bind the United States to fight to maintain all governments in their existing possessions, and in particular the British Empire. As it came before the Conference Article X promised that

The high contracting parties undertake to respect and preserve as against external aggression the territorial integrity and existing political independence of all States members of the league. In case of any such aggression, the executive council shall advise upon the means by which the obligation shall be fulfilled.

Like others who attacked the article, he chose to ignore its limitation to "external aggression," its limitation of the power of the council to advice, and its leaving to each of the members of the League the right to be the judge of its own obligation under the pledge. He noted, as others were to note, that the treatment of each of the British self-governing dominions as an independent state had the effect of building up the weight of the British vote in the assembly from one to five.

It was Frelinghuysen of New Jersey who called up the Farewell Address for printing on the twenty-second; and immediately the Republican critics of the Covenant were reinforced by James A.

Reed, Democratic Senator from Missouri, who had the skills of a great trial lawyer and was conducting a feud with the President. Reed found all of his worst fears realized: Europe and Asia would control a majority of the votes in the assembly; Britain would lead the coalition to the disadvantage of the United States. The League might interfere in matters of immigration, of the Monroe Doctrine, of even the armament which the United States should think essential to defense. As he warmed up later, during the long fight in which he fought the League, it became a "league of black nations" against which he was defending the American interest.

This was on Saturday. On Monday Wilson came ashore, to be escorted to Mechanics Hall where Governor Calvin Coolidge welcomed him as the first important visitor to Masaschusetts in his new administration. Here began Wilson's fight to control American opinion. He spoke generally, stressing the position to which the war had brought the United States. He asserted, without as yet arguing it in detail, that any peace would be futile without a guarantee for its enforcement; and that the United States had a duty to lead in formulating the guarantee. "I say that America is the hope of the world," he declared; and he added, as he started to Washington: "I have no more doubt of the verdict of America . . . than I doubt the blood that is in me."

Every minute of his day had been filled with duties or appointments when the President sat down to ten hours at his desk on Tuesday morning. He had approved the revenue act while on the train, but there was doubt whether the Congress would be permitted to authorize the loan act the proceeds of which were necessary to supplement the funds to be derived by taxation. A filibuster was impending. The European relief act awaited signature, and received it. An act which, after long delay, created a national park at the Grand Canyon of the Colorado River was put off until the morrow. An industrial board was given executive sanction.

The Industrial Board had been proposed by Cabinet members who feared confusion in industry when the hand of the War Industries Board should be lifted from the controls and prices should rise to levels which would deter purchasers. Baruch was already out. The power under which he had operated was less specific than his determination to get the war job done. By persuasion and bluff he had accomplished much; but the public opinion which had backed him while the war was on was softening under the pressure of industry to be free again. It was proposed that, under the Secretary of Commerce, an industrial board should make the attempt to hold back chaos. Through this board the several buying agencies of the government were to control maximum prices of staple commodities by refusing to buy at higher prices. The attempt broke down because the board lacked the power to command coöperation from the buying agencies. George N. Peek, its chief, handed in the collective resignations of its members in May, after a notable failure on the price of steel.

During this day the President found time to direct the Secretary of Labor to approach from a different side the same problem of employment and price which the Industrial Board was commissioned to approach by keeping prices down. He was to organize the localities in an effort to keep employment up. The governors and mayors were summoned to a conference at the White House on the following Monday to consider ways and means. Local authorities were to be inspired with a realization of their own responsibilities for welfare. This was their "primary duty" the President told them when they met, forty-five states strong, in the East Room on March 3; the function of the government in this field was that of counsel and coördination. The mayors and governors proved to be without clear plans for reducing unemployment, but they were ready to discuss the derelictions of the Department of Agriculture, to deplore revolutionary strikes, and to approve by resolution the deportation of radical aliens.

The President met with his Cabinet that Tuesday afternoon, picking up the threads which had been too short to reach to Paris, and learning how completely the lame duck session had failed to pass constructive laws for easing the country back to peace. The session had not even completed its routine work. The appropriation bills were in a jam, delayed in part by a desire in Congress to compel the President to call an early extra session, and in part by a filibuster which the Republican caucus refrained from endorsing but which Republicans conducted. La Follette was to obtain the floor against a federal conservation act and was prepared to assist in talking the session to death. He was insistent, too, upon details of the bill authorizing the fifth loan drive to be conducted during the spring. He lifted the filibuster long enough to let the loan bill go through, but he and his associates hobbled the Congress as the session came to an end.

On Wednesday the twenty-sixth, with less than a week of the session still to go, the President's day was again filled. The Democratic National Committee was in session at the Shoreham Hotel that morning. Vance McCormick, the chairman, then in Paris as the representative of his War Trade Board, had summoned it for the purpose of registering his own resignation and for the selection of a new chairman. Democrats, like Republicans, were deeply conscious that the voting in November had been a prelude to more important voting in 1920; and they, like their opponents, had every prospect of needing to pick a dominant candidate from a field in which none was evident. There were whispers that Wilson might himself consent to run again, in spite of the taboo upon the third term. Homer S. Cummings of Connecticut was chosen chairman.

Wilson managed to get two afternoon hours for interviews at the Capitol with members of Congress, but the dinner for the members of the Senate and House committees on foreign affairs was the big event of the day. It was designed as an important preparation for a friendly reception of the treaty when the Peace Conference should have completed its task and the next Congress had convened. The delays in Paris had destroyed all hope for the completion of the business by a Democratic Senate. There was need to do what could be done to maintain a nonpartisan coöperation in the Senate, and a nonpartisan backing for this spirit among the people.

There is no reason to believe that anyone's opinion was changed by information which the President was able to give his guests that night. He had no secrets the release of which would change the pattern that was forming among those who were still concerned with international matters. In spite of clumsiness in the matter of managing press releases in Paris, and confusion created by the censorships in France, the essential facts were known. What was at issue was their interpretation. At the start of the conversation Wilson placed himself on the witness stand for examination. The questions, so far as they can be guessed, were asked by friends to strengthen their positions, and by critics to bolster their own.

On Thursday the newspapers featured Wilson's dinner party and the caucus of House Republicans. The President was not, however, idle, for he spent two hours marching the length of Pennsylvania Avenue in a parade in honor of returned soldiers of the District of Columbia, and later reviewing it from a stand at the White House. And for two hours more he was at the Capitol in conference. Here he dispelled the hope that if the appropriation and loan bills failed to pass he would summon the next Congress in advance of the time when treaty business should compel it. He put upon the obstructionists the responsibility for a course of delay which might hamper the government, and which, with his calling attention to it, might rebound upon the obstructionists to their disadvantage. The Republican leaders had no desire to suffer this disadvantage, and hoped to get through the House caucus without disruption.

The question of the next speaker of the House provided their business. It was eight years since the last Republican speaker, Joseph Gurney Cannon of Illinois, his wings clipped by the insurgent Democratic coalition, had surrendered the gavel. Cannon still sat in the House, in his twenty-second term, at the age of eighty-two. His leadership had passed. The Republican minority leader, during the four Democratic Congresses, had been James R. Mann, a Chicago representative, whom Cannon was preparing to nominate for speaker when the caucus should meet. Like Cannon, Mann was of the Old Guard. He was an able leader and a skillful, partisan parliamentarian. He was certain to fail to get the caucus endorsement, for during the prewar years he had reflected the views of a constituency whose war spirit was low. His course during these years had made it difficult for wartime Republicans to accept him now, and his selection would be dangerous to the future of the party. During the preceding summer a similar prewar record had disposed of the chairman of the Republican Congressional Committee, Frank P. Woods of Iowa; he had resigned the chairmanship in time to beat a demand for his resignation.

The influence of Will H. Hays, chairman of the Republican National Committee since February, 1918, was believed to have inspired the movement to displace Woods, and was believed to be backing the similar movement to refuse advancement to Mann. Penrose and Smoot, who did not let personal feelings interfere with party advantage, were behind Hays, even at the risk of House resentment at Senate interference. A Massachusetts Republican, Frederick H. Gillett, met the specifications of the party leaders, and was easily selected as the caucus candidate.

No new light upon the proposed Covenant passed from the Wednesday dinner to the public. The President's plea that discussion be withheld until after the dinner had been completely disregarded, lines had been formed, and some of those who had been to the White House felt that they had been invited into a trap.

On Friday Lodge, entirely unswayed by presidential influence, delivered his set oration against the Covenant; and at their desks the senators thumbed the morning's New York *Sun* where they found what was represented as a summary of the Wednesday conversations as collected from the guests on Thursday. As soon as Lodge sat down Hitchcock of Nebraska, who was to be succeeded after March 4 by Lodge as chairman of the Senate Committee on Foreign Relations, rose to protest the *Sun* account as false. The ensuing colloquy turned the result of the dinner conference from neutral to sour.

The *Sun*, with malice, put into the mouth of Brandegee of Connecticut, who did not disclaim it, the conclusion that "I feel as if I had been wandering with Alice in Wonderland . . . When I awakened this morning I expected the White Rabbit to go to breakfast with me." Whatever Brandegee had thought, or even said, he had at least been present and had asked some of the questions. The attention of Borah was caught by a sentence attributed to the President: "Ireland is to be left to the mercies of England"; and he pressed as if in cross-examination of Hitchcock for an explanation of these words. Having declined to attend the dinner, he could not draw upon his own recollection. All that he extracted from Hitchcock, who denied the words, was an admission that the President had several times emphasized that "the league had nothing to do with domestic and internal questions." Borah suggested that if this were properly interpreted its meaning was that of the disputed sentence. Poindexter joined in the attack on Hitchcock, but with reference to Article XII of the Covenant which expressed an obligation upon members to resort to arbitration in disputes which could not be adjusted by diplomatic means. This meant to Poindexter that the United States might be bound to submit to arbitration a dispute with Japan over immigration into the United States. The *Sun* had, on this point, attributed to Wilson the sentence: "Chinese and Japanese exclusion goes out of American control into the hands of league control," which Hitchcock categorically denied; but his denial carried no weight with those who wanted to disbelieve.

While the Senate was in session on Friday—it sat from ten in the morning until fifty-five minutes after midnight—new gossip, with worse results, was in the making. The members of the Democratic National Committee, having completed the business for which they met on Wednesday, were having luncheon with the President. Reports of their discussions leaked out almost at once, to be collected by the newsmen, and on Sunday the Washington *Post* was full of them. The President was reported to be deeply irritated by the impending filibuster, to believe that it was inspired by party spite, and to have made a violent partisan address. Outsiders were told, and Sherman of Illinois who was eager to believe the worst declared, that Wilson had broken loose, characterizing the heads of those who opposed the League as no more than "knots to prevent their bodies from unraveling"; and stating that he "loathed their pigmy minds." What he really said is not reliably recorded, but among the reports were contradictions of interest to those who were thinking in terms of the succession to the presidency. Some thought that he would welcome the time when he might return to the historian's study and that he would not again be a candidate; others thought he expressed a yearning for the opportunity to fight his critics, which could be gratified only by another nomination. Whatever the members of the National Committee were hearing as Lodge delivered his address, and whatever they may have said to the reporters, the rumors embittered a situation already bad. The new chairman, Cummings, made it his business to deny that there had been talk of a third term.

Lesser senators than Lodge, Borah, and Poindexter said their say about the Covenant as they could get the floor on Friday, Saturday, and Monday. And Democrats less important than Reed joined them in denunciation. There were addresses in support of the President from the administration side; and at almost the last minute of the session Porter J. McCumber, Republican from North Dakota, came to the defense of the League. He was driven to it, "notwithstanding the arguments and criticisms" heard from his side of the chamber, by the fear that "the country . . . might be misled into the belief that the Republicans of the United States as a party were opposed" to any sort of a league. He had been a senator for twenty years. But at the next primary in North Dakota his constituents deserted him and sent Lynn J. Frazier in his place. No other Republican in the Senate, in this last week of the Congress, gave such weighty support to the President.

The pressure of speeches on the League reduced the too-brief period in which the Congress struggled with terminal legislation; and when, on Saturday, March 1, La Follette "obtained the floor" there was doubt whether he would permit any business to be completed during the session, for other senators were ready and willing to spell him in a filibuster until Tuesday noon. The Senate took a two-hour recess for dinner and conference on Saturday, and then continued debate until 6:40 A.M. Sunday. It conducted a memorial service during a recess on Sunday, and on Monday at ten resumed the "legislative day" of Saturday, remaining in debate until noon Tuesday, when the last session of the Sixty-fifth Congress ended.

The dilatory proceedings were allowed to be interrupted for fragments of genuine business, but only when the consent was unanimous. It was just before midnight when Lodge rose for "only a moment" to ask unanimous consent for the introduction of a brief resolution. He and his associates had been busy since the dinner at the White House. Brandegee is said to have suggested the course of action; Knox to have helped put it into words. Lodge now read what he desired to introduce:

That it is the sense of the Senate that . . . the constitution of the league of nations in the form now proposed to the peace conference should not be accepted by the United States,

[and]

That . . . the urgent business of negotiating peace terms with Germany . . . should precede the careful and serious considerations . . . [of] the proposal for a league of nations.

As Lodge anticipated, a Democrat objected, thus preventing the introduction of the resolution. He courteously accepted the refusal. He added, as he had the floor for the moment and no one could stop him, merely "by way of explanation," that thirty-seven members who would sit in the Senate after March 4 (they were all Republican) "would have voted for the foregoing resolution . . . if they had had the opportunity." The course of the President in insisting upon the formation of a league before the drafting of a treaty, and the details of the Covenant, were thus met with signed defiance. The "round robin" bore the names of more than enough Republicans alone to defeat any treaty which the President should lay before the next Congress. Other Republicans hurriedly telegraphed that their names be added. Democratic names were not appended only because they were not invited. It was believed that more than fifty senators were opposed to the Covenant in its present form.

When a few hours later the Vice-President was forced by the clock to declare the session at an end, the *Congressional Record* states that he adjourned it *"sine die."* Some of those present thought they heard him say "with bitter emphasis . . . 'adjourned *sine Deo',"* (and thus the New York *Times* reproduced it). Whatever Marshall may have said, or may have wished to say, the six years of Democratic control of the affairs of the United States came to an end at that instant. For the next two years, under the Constitution, Woodrow Wilson continued in office, facing a hostile party control at the Capitol. The American political machine was again on dead center.

And for the moment, in that hostile party, the lion and the lamb were on cordial terms. About noon on that last day Senator Boies Penrose of Pennsylvania drove down Pennsylvania Avenue in his red touring car, carrying as his passenger Senator Robert Marion La Follette of Wisconsin.

Chapter IV ★ The Treaty Draft

A FEW HOURS after the Sixty-fifth Congress adjourned on March 4, 1919, Woodrow Wilson went into action, stating again the course which he proposed to follow in the drafting of the treaty of peace. He stepped out upon the stage of the Metropolitan Opera House in New York, where Enrico Caruso sang the "Star Spangled Banner" for an impressive audience, and where the orchestra played George Cohan's melody the refrain of which was appropriate to the occasion: "We won't be back till it's over, over there." Governor Smith had invited the President to speak in New York; and Wilson, who had not made a major address since landing at Boston, found the occasion made doubly important by the defiant tone of the manifesto of the Republican senators.

Flanking him on the stage was his predecessor, William Howard Taft, hurried back from nearly two hundred addresses on behalf of the League in more than thirty states, and prepared again to speak in detail upon the merits of the Covenant. The structure of the treaty was only in its preliminary stages when Wilson had left Paris with the draft of the Covenant. He was now on his way back to concentrate on the treaty terms, knowing that enough senators to defeat a treaty were already opposed to both his procedure and his aim. He had time before midnight, when he was due aboard the *George Washington,* to state his case.

If he had been confused when he dined with the foreign affairs committees, or violent when closeted with the Democratic National Committee, he was now both clear-headed and urbane. He told his audience, as he had already cabled House, that an "overwhelming majority" of the people favored the League. He accepted Taft's detailed analysis of the Covenant as more than adequate, and confined himself to a description of the setting within which the Conference was at work—the world, the war, and the future—and out of which must come an organization powerful enough to prevent another war. He had no unkind word for any man, but he wondered how in the setting which he described some could think the way they did. He was not afraid that the treaty would fail, nor was he diverted from his course, but declared with confidence in word and tone: "When that treaty comes back, gentlemen on this side will find the covenant not only in it, but so many threads of the treaty tied to the covenant that you cannot dissect the covenant from the treaty without destroying the whole vital structure."

Set to his program, as he was, he may have been fatally tripped that night by a force as dangerous to his success as was the constitutional argument of the objecting senators. The House of Representatives that very morning had, by a vote of 216 to 41, adopted a resolution expressing its hope that the Peace Conference might favor self-determination for Ireland; and in cabling Colonel House, Wilson had noted the "many forces, particularly those prejudiced against Great Britain," which were exerting their influence against the League. When the House was debating this resolution, only Tom Connally, a Democratic Representative from Texas, had seriously fought the drift of sentiment to point out that the Peace Conference was concerned with the problems of the defeated enemy, and could have no jurisdiction over the internal affairs of the Allies. Wilson had agreed to receive, for a few minutes after his address, a delegation representing the Irish Race Convention which met in Philadelphia on Washington's Birthday. But when the delegation appeared it included a New York judge, Daniel F. Cohalan, whose name had been tied to that of von Bernstorff in anti-British intrigue, and the President declined to meet him. Cohalan left the Opera House, and Wilson held an unhappy conference with his associates.

Three delegates of the Irish Race Convention eventually obtained their passports and tried to force their way into some formal reception in Paris. Before Wilson brought his treaty back, Eamon de Valera had been spirited out of Lincoln prison, and had slipped through the immigration laws into the United States—perhaps as stoker on a friendly freighter. He held audiences in the Waldorf-Astoria in June, and was officially received as President of the Irish

Republic by the New York Board of Aldermen and Mayor Hylan. On the very day that the treaty was presented to the Senate, de Valera heard an audience of the Friends of Irish Freedom hiss the name of the President of the United States.

On the ninth day after the New York meeting, Wilson arrived at Brest; it was just a month since he had read the Covenant to the Conference. The conferees, hampered by his preoccupation with other matters of government (as each delegation was at times hampered by the other duties of its chief) had not been idle. Their mutual acquaintance had ripened. Each delegation had learned not only the complications involved in the drafting of a peace, but also the nature of the respective interests which each nation at Paris was bound to defend at all costs. The prestige of the President was such as to make it possible for him to have his way in the priority of the Covenant and in its inclusion in the treaty. But in the four months elapsed since the signing of the Armistice it had become possible for each interested government to stick to its national claims without inviting defeat at home by its own constituents. Within the delegations at Paris there were doubts about the Wilson program, which the Allies were prepared to encourage so far as was safe.

They all knew Colonel Edward M. House. They knew him better than they knew the President, and they had with him none of the embarrassment which they had in challenging the program of his chief. The American critics of the President had used the mails to let their disapproval of his program be known. Whatever should happen to the Covenant, the Allies were eager to end the period of uncertainty; while enemy countries were fighting off disorder and hunger as they awaited decisions which others must make before they could begin to build upon their wreckage. In some of the areas all orderly government was in abeyance.

It has become the belief of those historians who mass themselves behind Ray Stannard Baker, the literary executor of Woodrow Wilson, that during the absence of the President his own delegation gave consent to the postponement of the League in the interest of immediate peace. Mrs. Wilson in *My Memoir* (1939) quotes her husband as complaining before they reached Paris: "House has given away everything I had won before we left Paris." She states that the conference between House and his chief as they traveled from the dock at Brest was the turning point at which success was changed to ruin. Those, however, who trust the House side of the story, have much support for their belief that there was neither conspiracy nor agreement to shelve the League for the sake of peace; and that the concentration on treaty details during Wilson's absence was by his own direction and because he who had presented the Covenant as his last act before leaving Paris was the only proper person to take it up and direct the course leading to its adoption. The newspapers reported that some agreement to defer had been reached; but whatever the fact, Wilson immediately made his own course clear. He cabled Tumulty, and on the day after he reached Paris the White House announced that no change of plan had been adopted and that the League would be an integral part of the treaty. The long intimacy between himself and Colonel House and their dependence on each other, begun at their first meeting in 1911, faded away. It ceased with the signing of the treaty.

The crowded days following the return of Wilson to Paris belong completely to the history of modern Europe. Out of them came solutions which did not solve, and problems some of which defied solution. If the United States had been willing to consent to the treaty which resulted, and to give its continuing support in the operation of the League, these problems would have been unavoidable parts of the history of the United States. They were left in Europe, and for Europe to confront, and only their repercussions crossed the Atlantic. The distinctive American contribution to the final treaty was the Covenant, which, in due time, prevented American consent. The weeks in Paris between March 14 and May 6, when the draft of a treaty was approved by the Conference, were spent in conversations that revealed the full difficulties of the task which Wilson had set himself.

Upon his announcement that the program would stand, all serious attempts to change it disappeared. The conferees concentrated upon a reconciliation of world structure with the broad generalizations of the Fourteen Points. These points, shaped and numbered by the President in January, 1918, to illustrate the sort of peace he craved, were neither self-enforcing nor self-interpreting. They were susceptible to argument by all who had insurable interest in their meaning. For the United States the points were academic: the United States did not desire either territory or indemnity. The measure of universal acceptance which they received outside the United States and before victory was won was more sweeping than it was after the armed power of Germany ceased to be a menace.

Based on a doctrine of self-determination, and thereby gaining passionate support from every racial minority placed next unfriendly majorities on the map of Europe, the Fourteen Points suggested a pattern of reorganization inconsistent with perfection. Before the war the lands extending from the western boundaries of Russia to the eastern frontiers of France had not been divided along ethnographic and political lines; and neither set of lines coincided accurately with natural geographic boundaries. Among the nations whose delegations were drafting the terms of the settlement were Hejaz, Poland, and Czechoslovakia; none of these states had had independent existence when the war began, and all of them received recognition by the Allies, as much to bring pressure on the enemy as to do justice. In areas still technically of enemy character there were many racial groups with claims to area and independence that had no provable relationship to their degree of right or self-sufficiency. It would have been impossible to give satisfaction with a newly constructed map of Europe even if its drafting had been undertaken with detachment in profound peace. To give it now was even less possible in the presence of deep desire to punish enemy countries by curtailment, and to ward off Bolshevism by new political structures to be erected between Russia and Western Europe.

The European Allies, in close union through the Pact of London of September, 1914, had agreed to hold together until victory and to reject any suggestion of a separate peace. Great Britain, France, and Russia adhered to this pact and accepted additional endorsements as the war went on. It was not unnatural that each signer should hope that victory might bring other things in addition to peace, such as security, indemnity, and perhaps territory. The countries had never in the past agreed upon all matters concerning their several interests; they were not likely so to agree in the future. The Russian revolution and the separate peace made by the Soviet government at Brest-Litovsk in 1918, in spite of the Pact, raised a fair question as to the binding force of the agreement upon its remaining partners. The United States had never signed, so that Wilson was the only major leader entirely free from whatever binding force the Pact still possessed.

For Great Britain, the hopes for the future turned upon the status of the German Navy and the control of those German colonies which lay uncomfortably close to British dominions. A somewhat neglected chapter of the World War concerns the effort made by Australia, New Zealand, and South Africa to advance victory for Britain by dislodgment of German neighbors.

For France, the recovery of the lost provinces, Alsace and Lorraine, taken by Germany after the war of 1870, had emotional values too high ever to be challenged. Future security against invasion from the Rhineland could not be disregarded by any French government; the French military authorities were disposed to demand the whole of the left bank of the Rhine as essential to this security. Reparation for the damage done by the German invasion was so vital that it had affected the terms of the Armistice, even adding another to Wilson's points.

The claims for reimbursement from the enemy were huge, depending for their dimension upon what the claimant might hope to get. Those whose areas had been devastated foresaw the heavy costs of reconstruction, which must fall upon their own governments if the enemy could not be made to pay. France, when the private claims came to be itemized, found itself owing substantially as much to its own people as it owed to the friendly associates who had helped finance its war. After the claims for direct property damage came the matter of the intergovernment loans with which the stronger had carried part of the burden of the weaker. These, too, were an item for the enemy to pay. The United States sat through the discussion over reparations, differing from its associates in that it made no claim to reparations from the enemy, but held the notes of the associates to a sum approaching ten billions as the consequence of the policy of loans to the Allies launched in the first war loan act. It had borrowed from Americans in order to lend at the same rate of interest. There were no accepted details respecting the repayment of these loans; and at the time they were authorized they seemed to be essentially a part of the American reinforcement and repayment was not seriously debated. But during the discussions in Paris there was no way to prevent borrowers from believing that repayment to the United States was contingent upon ability to collect from the enemy for both damage done and loans among themselves; and there was nothing in the law or in the disposition of Congress to justify an opinion that the debt of the Allies was not a debt to be repaid. It was a hard technical matter even to appraise the gross reparations. It was quite as hard for the Allies to accept the notion that whatever Germany might pay, the debts to the United States remained an obligation. The devastated provinces of France soon became the basis of a demand that citizens should be reimbursed before any foreign lender should be paid; it was felt that if the latter were insisted upon the former might fail, and that the inter-Ally loans were in fact a military contribution and not a sacred contract.

So long as Russia remained a solvent member of the Allies it could not be indifferent to conditions among the related races of the Balkans; and Russian concern for the right to pass through the straits between the Black Sea and the Aegean was centuries old. With Russia insolvent and in revolution, these claims were in abeyance, and the Conference was indisposed to believe that Russia had rights which it was bound to respect.

Italy gave adhesion to the Pact of London after abandoning its old allies, Germany and Austria-Hungary, in April, 1915; but in doing so, it stipulated for compensation. It was exchanging risky neutrality for dangerous war. At the head of the Adriatic lay the lands which Italy needed: the southern approaches to the Alps at Brenner Pass, with their German inhabitants, and enough of the shoreline of the Adriatic to ensure security. The compensation was promised while Austria-Hungary was the neighbor of Italy; payment was now demanded after a new Balkan grouping had brought into the picture the rights and claims of Yugoslavia.

Japan, breaking with Germany during the first month of the World War, had been inspired by more than altruism or the binding force of its alliance with Great Britain. Its government was concerned with its position in Eastern Asia as well as with its prestige among the nations of the West. Japan cherished the alliance with Great Britain made in 1902 when both countries were nervous about the plans of Russia, and was aggrieved by the unpopularity of its nationals in the United States and in the British dominions in the Pacific area. In 1894 it had emerged as a modern military power, when its decisive blow against China was followed by a race among the great powers for leases, cessions, and concessions at the expense of China. In 1905, the Japanese blow at Russia, whose Siberian railroad and national power had crossed Asia to the Pacific, was again decisive.

The appearance of the United States in the Philippines, by the accident of the Spanish war, had brought new competitions into an area already crowded with complex interests. The United States pressed for a policy of the open door in China—a policy inconsistent with the dominance on the mainland toward which Japan was directing its foreign policy, a step at a time. That advance detached Korea from Chinese influence, and then annexed it, acquiring thereby for Japan a mainland frontier against Russian Siberia. Japan was deeply conscious of the strategic position west of the Korean Peninsula held by Germany on its leasehold at Kiaochow, and of German influence on the Shantung Peninsula. When war broke out in 1914 Japan moved quickly, seizing the German area in China, and proceeding to occupy German islands in the north Pacific, at the same time the British dominions south of the equator sent their expeditions against the other German islands. Japan was permitted to adhere to the Pact of London in the autumn of 1915.

As the World War proceeded, the more powerful of the Allies had found it necessary to bolster the weaker, or the more reluctant, by cash and promise. The various agreements for postwar compensation, made by treaty or through exchange of notes or by less formal understandings, had been imperfectly concealed. Their existence, if not their precise details, had been common knowledge, although when the United States broke with Germany in 1917 it was not known that England and France with the concurrence of Russia—as almost the last act of the Czarist government—were promising Japan the German possessions on the Asiatic mainland and the islands of the northern Pacific. This secret was so well kept that in November, 1917, Secretary of State Lansing agreed with Japanese Ambassador Ishii, that "Japan has special interests in China, particularly in the part to which their possessions are contiguous." This appeared at the time to contain no threat to the territorial integrity of China or to the commercial rights of other nations in China. That Japan might plead it as sealing the secret compact for partition, of which the United States had no knowledge, was a possibility kept under cover until the course of affairs in the Conference brought the agreement and the other commitments into full light.

The secret agreements were hurried into publicity by the Bolshevist government in its desire to uncover the sins of the preceding regime. Texts were found in the imperial archives and were given to the world. The agreements contained so many prearmistice commitments as partly to account for the delay with which the Allies accepted the program of the Fourteen Points. Among the Allies they raised the juridical problem of their binding force after one of their prime endorsers had collapsed and the others had accepted the Fourteen Points as basis for the peace.

The secret treaties confronted Wilson with entanglements so tough that the promotion of the League was, by contrast, almost simple. Where the salvage from the agreements was still useful to the Allies, they tended to talk about their binding quality; where they were inconvenient, the trend was to abandon them. As Wilson settled down to the new aspect of the negotiation, in the new residence he took in Paris, he found conflicts for the solution of which there was no answer in the patient studies of the army and navy intelligence officers, or in the memoranda of the State Department staff, or in the hurried investigations made by the members of the House Inquiry who had briefed him for the Fourteen Points. He was continually compelled to balance what his advisers urged as fair against what the premiers pressed as unavoidable. In the week in which Lansing unwittingly gave a clearance to Japan, Balfour had pledged England to the support of Palestine as "a national home for the Jewish people." No country had escaped commitments, made to ensure solidarity and victory, which set up threats to an agreement upon terms of peace.

The course of the United States in the negotiation passed in these days from crisis to crisis, as the President sought to reconcile the conflicts of purpose with the pattern in his mind. Part of the time he was sick. He was ill during the voyage to Brest, and just escaped the influenza when his doctors put him to bed in April. For some days Lloyd George, Clemenceau, and Orlando sat together in a chamber near the sick room; their work proceeded while messages to the President passed back and forth. Wilson never again displayed the full capacity and elasticity which had marked him as an administrator during his first term in office. He had an additional obstacle in the fact that he was himself forced to ask indulgence from his fellow negotiators.

The "round robin" contained a vital threat to the League as at first conceived, but there was reason to hope that some of the signers would withdraw their opposition if the Covenant were amended at the points which had drawn the heaviest fire. The principle objections to the League were fears that it might interfere with the course of the United States under the Monroe Doctrine, that strictly domestic questions such as related to tariffs and the control of immigration might be dragged into compulsory arbitration, that members might be compelled by League action to undertake the custody of former enemy areas designed as mandates, and that there were no provision for orderly withdrawal from the League. Leading Republican supporters of the League were invited to suggest to the President amendments the adoption of which might help obtain consent by the Senate, and the President acted on the advice thus given, Taft, Root, and A. Lawrence Lowell had a share in the work; but it was the painful duty of the President to reopen the subject in the commission responsible for the draft of the Covenant. When he asked for consideration of amendments, other delegations felt as free to ask for compensation.

France reverted to the conviction that Article X, too strong to please senators, was too weak to produce security for France; but the President found it hard to yield. Eventually, however, he and Lloyd George prepared with France a separate treaty by which Great Britain and the United States agreed to come to the rescue in the event of an attack on France. He found it necessary, too, to resist the plea which Japan pressed again: a plea for the guarantee of racial equality. Consistently, from the early stages of the drafting, Japan clung to this demand, although at the last it joined with "poignant regret" in the vote by which the Covenant was unanimously accepted.

It was difficult to procure the insertion of a withdrawal clause in the Covenant, or clarification respecting domestic policies. The clarification, based on a suggestion by Taft, added the sentence: "If the dispute between the parties is claimed by one of them, and is found by the council, to arise out of a matter which by international law is solely within the domestic jurisdiction of that party, the council shall so report, and shall make no recommendation as to its settlement." But it was very difficult to phrase a sentence which would at one stroke free the Monroe Doctrine without at the same time freeing many other special policies with which some of the Allies were concerned, or to do it without appearing to give to the Monroe Doctrine a recognized status in international law which all the signatories must accept. The Monroe Doctrine, however powerfully the United States adhered to it, was no more than a unilateral expression of national interest, derived not from the consent of others but from the inherent right of self-defense. In its interpretation the United States could admit no interference, and other powers would admit no matter of right. A new article was drafted to allay American fears without conceding too much:

Nothing in this Covenant shall be deemed to affect the validity of international engagements, such as treaties of arbitration or regional understandings like the Monroe Doctrine, for securing the maintenance of peace.

Yielding to the President in matters relating to the League, the delegations permitted the insertion of the amendments for which he had to ask. But the fact that he asked weakened him for the remaining tasks of the Conference, since it was an open admission that he was unable to command a continuing effective support from all the leaders of even his own party. Before the League of Nations Commission gave final approval to the amended Covenant the Italian crowds which, in January, hailed him as a messiah were denouncing him as a traitor. The validity of the emotional and constitutional objections urged against the original draft is beyond measurement. Acute lawyers presented the objections under both heads, but lawyers equally acute opposed them, and the most powerful arguments sustaining the position of the President came from Republicans who could not be accused of desiring to advance a personal triumph for Woodrow Wilson. On March 19 Senator Lodge, "reduced to silence" when the President invaded his home town, was confronted there in a great debate in Symphony Hall by a Republican of standing equal to his own, the president of Harvard University, A. Lawrence Lowell.

The discussions over the amendment of the Covenant dragged along through March and April, interwoven with discussions of other business which was being advanced. March was the "dark period" of the Conference, as the three great powers outlined the terms upon which all of the Allied and Associated Powers must agree before Germany could be admitted to the negotiations. They wrestled with France and its security problem, with Italy and Adriatic issues, with every other nation which had a claim.

The practical control of the deliberations narrowed down to the Big Three leaders, Wilson, Clemenceau, and Lloyd George; stubborn men all, who surrendered little merely for the sake of agreement. The whole membership of the Conference had been obviously too large to do business, and was packed with delegations of a score of nations which had carried few of the burdens of the war and lacked the weight with which to assist in the maintenance of any peace. The council of ten as a steering committee was nearly as unwieldy, for when the ten attended they brought along their technical advisers to act as reference works and made a crowd which always included some who leaked secrets under persuasion. The council of four (when Orlando was present to make the fourth) was workable but was often jammed by Italian insistence. Three men did most of the directing. But one of these three was Clemenceau, who wrote *"très cordialement"* to the President and fought him tooth and nail.

The Italian case was complicated by the fact that at the moment only the German peace was being arranged, whereas the demands of Italy affected Austria (whose peace conference was another matter) and the enlarged Serbia whose king was one of the Allies and had a delegation assisting in the drafting of the German treaty. So it was now the territory of an ally which Italy was demanding. Wilson protested in vain that the secret treaties lost their validity with the default of Russia, and that they were inconsistent with the new world order which was in the making. Italy clung to its claim as its just price, and demanded payment by Britain and France as the still solvent members of the partnership. Turkey was not under immediate consideration, but Italy was concerned in this quarter, as well as in the Adriatic. The partition of Turkey, one of the oldest objectives of European diplomacy, was now in contemplation, and had provided subject matter for the secret agreements. With Russia out of the picture, England, France, and Italy, to say nothing of Greece, had aspirations of contradictory nature; and England was suddenly aware of the position of the Sultan as Caliph. The future of India might be gravely influenced by the treatment of Turkey whose ruler, in the religious world, was the chief of the Moslems.

The Italian controversy raged hottest over the region of the Istrian Peninsula, where Trieste and Fiume were the bottlenecks through which Austria and the northern Balkans found their only access to the sea. What France demanded for safety on the left bank of the Rhine was paralleled by what Italy demanded at the head of the Adriatic and along its eastern shore. And protesting editors complained in many tongues that the legitimate needs of the European Allies were being ignored while the Conference tinkered with the Covenant to please the American Senate.

By the first week of April the President was again ill, and Italy was preparing for a last ditch fight for the Adriatic demands. Too sick to sit among the Big Four, Wilson was not too sick to order the *George Washington* back to Brest for use should he find it necessary to abandon the Conference and leave the conferees in deadlock. But Lloyd George, elastic as ever, gave him enough support to make use of the transport unnecessary. Trieste had been assigned to Italy in the 1915 agreement, whereas Fiume had been held back; and the technical advisers assured the President that Fiume was indispensable to Yugoslavia. He held his ground, and on April 23 appealed to the world over the heads of the Italian delegation, in an attack upon the demands with which Italy was holding up the peace. Orlando, head of that delegation, hurried back to Rome in the crisis, and the Big Three proceeded to go ahead without him or Italy. The Italians came back to the Conference in a few days. In the East, however, where enemy areas would be dealt with later in the Austrian and Turkish treaties, they proceeded to improve their military situation and to maintain their claim.

The Japanese plea for the retention of the areas taken by force from Germany in China, and for the fulfillment of the pledge of support promised in 1917, caused much embarrassment to the conferees. It was only a leasehold which had been seized, but those who are familiar with German policy may guess whether Germany contemplated surrender of the area upon the termination of its lease. The territory could not be confirmed to Japan without requiring the republic of China, an enemy of Germany and with a delegation in the Conference, to pay for the defeat of Germany. The conferees were squeezed between the persistent pressure of Japan and the equally determined opposition of the President to both the coercion of a Chinese population and the validity of the secret treaties. Meanwhile China spoke through an outraged delegation in bitter protest. The situation was made worse by the necessity to reject the other major contention of Japan, for the guarantee of equal treatment of its nationals within the territory of other signatory powers. The latter contention was not a matter of the peace with Germany, but was one of prestige to Japan which invaded the domestic affairs of other members of the League.

On both counts the Japanese plea reached its crisis almost at the time when other matters were at their worst. Orlando led his Italian delegation back to Rome on April 24. The German delegation began to assemble in the hotels reserved for it in Versailles on April 25. The Covenant was presented to a plenary session of the Conference and voted into the treaty on April 28. Two days later Japan's face was saved by permission to remain on Shantung after Japan had given a secret promise to withdraw on its own initiative. On May 4 Italy's face was saved by a cordial invitation to return, extended by the Big Three; and Italy was eased back into the work.

Compromise and something resembling legal fiction were the price which Wilson had to pay for the acceptance of his program. His determination that the Covenant must come first and be an integral part of the treaty never wavered. He was in the painful presence of the fact that when in a group of equals there develops a fundamental clash as to the course of action to be taken the individual, however right he may be, must choose between leaving the group and abandoning the project, on the one hand, and accepting the best attainable compromise, on the other. It is that or nothing. It is perhaps remarkable that the draft which was finally prepared bore as much resemblance as it did to the Fourteen Points.

Wilson's regret at compromises inconsistent with his interpretation of the Fourteen Points was assuaged by a belief that a workable league would provide a forum for continuous reconsideration of the treaty and for readjustment of burdensome conditions. Article XIX of the Covenant had a specific provision for this:

> The Assembly may from time to time advise the reconsideration by Members of the League of treaties which have become inapplicable and the consideration of international conditions whose continuation might endanger the peace of the world.

Article XI had an even more sweeping safeguard clause:

> Any war or threat of war . . . is hereby declared a matter of concern to the whole League, and the League shall take any action that may be deemed wise and effectual to safeguard the peace of nations.

Among the knottiest problems before the Conference was one concerning the treatment of former enemy areas which had been taken by Allied force, and which the opinion of the Allies would not permit to be returned to the prewar sovereigns. The mandates represented the attempted solution. They were a sort of legal improvisation, to avoid handing them back to their former owners without seeming to distribute them as conquests among the victors. After earlier wars there had been little in the way of ideological obstruction to the acquisition of territory by conquest, although in 1898, in the United States, the anti-imperialist movement had begun the formulation of principles challenging it. In the World War the doctrine of the rights of small powers and subject peoples was spread by the sounding board of the Fourteen Points, until it became necessary to reconcile national desire for the control of territory with the opinion denying the rightfulness of territorial gains made without the consent of populations concerned. Jefferson's revolutionary pronouncement that governments derive "their just powers from the consent of the governed" had gained world stature. It had become difficult for those Allies which were colonial powers to justify their holdings as "a decent respect to the opinions of mankind"; it was more difficult to justify new conquest.

In some of the areas where the question of disposal arose the Conference provided plebiscites as a means of determining popular preference. In others the mandates were instituted, to avoid returning them to former enemies, to avoid a transfer of legal title to a victor, to enable a victor to exercise actual control in appropriate areas, and to lessen rivalries among the Allies which might have followed transfers of title.

From the very beginning of the deliberations in Paris it was agreed that former German colonies should not be returned to Germany, and that the Turkish Empire should be broken up. There was pressure upon the conferees to arrange for distribution among themselves before framing the Covenant. The United States wanted none of the German colonies; and in the fifth of the Fourteen Points the principle had been laid down that there must be an "impartial adjustment" giving full weight to "the interests of the populations concerned." The draft of the Covenant which Wilson read to the Conference on February 14 contained an elaboration of this principle in its Article XIX, beginning with the assumption that the colonies had ceased to be "under the sovereignty of the States which formerly governed them." It classified them in three groups: those so far advanced in institutions as to be able with moderate guidance to stand alone, those in which there was need for a complete government to be operated for the benefit of those under it on terms of the open door for members of the League, and those, backward and scattered such as the Pacific Islands, in which it would be appropriate to administer as though they were territory of the trustee nations, but under the eye of the League. Wilson was ready for the United States to accept a mandate over Armenia, where no one of the European Allies was eager to have another undertake it. He promised in his New York address that "many threads of the treaty" would be tied to the Covenant. The system of mandates fulfilled the promise, for their status was established in the Covenant and their custody was assigned to members of the League who were responsible to it. With the slightest of changes, the article of the February draft became Article XXII of the Covenant which the Conference approved for insertion in the treaty on April 28.

But all of these matters, in which the principles and the flexibility of Woodrow Wilson were tested between March and May, were taken up and determined in the caucus of the Allies, as they prepared for the Peace Conference. Meanwhile, the Germans, wrestling with the consequences of defeat and uncertainty, were framing the Weimar constitution, struggling with internal revolt, and preparing to turn the provisional government into an orderly republic. As one by one the decisions reached in the caucus came to public attention they gave rise to problems, the most disturbing being the willingness of Germany to accept the treaty. The armies, particularly that of France, were held in readiness to meet refusal. Nearly every agreement reached by the Big Four meant a denial for some one of the Allies and was criticized as a betrayal.

The German delegation to the Peace Conference was not permitted to come to Paris until the Allies were reasonably certain that an agreement could be reached among themselves. Permission was given in mid-April; and when the delegation came it was assigned hotel space and a restricted area at Versailles.

On May 7, 1919, the German commissioners were admitted to the presence of the Allied delegations in Versailles. At this moment what may properly be described as the Peace Conference began its work. It contained little of peace, for the German delegates, about to be handed a draft treaty as an ultimatum, knew that if they conceded too little the terms would be made harsher, whereas if they conceded too much the wobbly government which they represented might not stand the strain. It contained little of conference, for the twenty-seven Allied nations had decided against oral argument. Discussions and explanations were to be in writing. Germany was given fifteen days to submit written comments on the terms.

The 440 articles of the draft treaty made a substantial volume which the Conference had decided not to release to the press. But the Germans could not be prevented from reprinting from their own copy, and the Peace Conference could not control the extra copies printed for the private use of the several delegations. The world soon knew much about the terms, and debate broke out as though they were final, as debate had arisen upon the first draft of the Covenant. In the United States the Congress had been in session to provide a channel for the discussion of the Covenant. It was now in recess; but as the Germans were given their draft treaty the President summoned the Sixty-sixth Congress to meet in special session on May 19, 1919. He would have been forced to call a special session to pass the appropriation bills, even if he had not anticipated having the treaty to present to the Senate. The American opposition could hardly wait until the new Congress was called to order.

Chapter V ★ Interests Resumed

O N THE DAY of the great German drive to the Marne, May 27, 1918, President Wilson declared politics to be adjourned. He was hopeful, and in large measure he was right, for through the approaching summer the war and its problems constituted the chief interest of most Americans. But upon the end of combat politics resumed its grip on American affairs; and a year after Wilson's pronouncement it might have been asserted with even greater emphasis that American interests had been resumed.

The American newspaper readers, during the spring of 1919, kept one eye on the front-page news of the proceedings in Paris, and the other on the inside pages where were featured the day-to-day details of national life. Historians, working over the themes upon which they could concentrate their labors now that the war was won, hurried to cover the years since the beginning of the century. More than ever before, the years of an immediate past invited and received attention, and there was unwillingness to let politics and war give the impression that they, and they alone, were history.

Mark Sullivan, whose career as fighting journalist had covered two decades, and who was to cover more decades as observer of events, soon directed his thoughts to *Our Times* (1926–1935), whose six solid volumes were to be ten years in the making, as they followed their opening volume on "The Turn of the Century." Charles and Mary Beard went farther back for their beginning, but always with their eyes fixed on the present, as they told the whole story in *The Rise of American Civilization* (1927). Dixon Ryan Fox and Arthur M. Schlesinger began to assemble co-workers for their monumental *History of American Life* (1927–1944) in a dozen volumes from Priestley's *Coming of the White Man,* to Slos-

[69]

son's *Great Crusade and After*. Whether the scholars were inspired by the narrative of events which they could comb into shape, or by the life of the American society to which the events gave point, they felt a new urge to relate in some way the trend of history with the trend of society. They could not quite prove their case. The causal relationship which obviously exists between social habit and group activity becomes a baffling problem to the historian who tries to prove it. Yet the culture of America was what it was, always at hand, and still at hand when for the moment the major attention was diverted to domestic politics, to war, or to world affairs. The reader watched from day to day the proceedings in Paris but did not forget that the Kentucky Derby was to be run in May, or that the major baseball leagues would begin to play in April.

Interest in world affairs was a novelty for most Americans. The solidarity of opinion which supported the reinforcement of the Allies, and the war measures made necessary by the military effort, were the more unusual because the scene of action was remote. By a sheer power of imagination the United States was led to project its weight across the ocean. Action and reaction balancing themselves, it was not strange that with the defeat of the enemy the remote danger should be crowded from the American mind by the normal habits which had temporarily lost their precedence.

It had been feared by the fans, when the world series ended the day before the action at St. Mihiel, that there would be no professional ball games in 1919. It was hardly worth while to arrange a schedule if crowds were to be no better than in 1918, and impossible if the players were to be needed by the armed forces. The Boston Red Sox of the American League had fought out the 1918 series with the Chicago Cubs; and the dual-purpose wonder of the Boston team, George Herman (Babe) Ruth, who could pitch as well as bat, pitched the winning game for the Red Sox although he failed to hit. The sports writers sounded "taps" for the duration; but when the war was over the Red Sox were able to open the 1919 season on the Polo Grounds in New York, where the Yankees were defeated and Ruth delivered the home run which his admirers had come to expect. Ruth was too valuable a property to be left in Boston, for his showmanship was equal to his batting average and his intractability, and the Yankees bought him for use in New

York in 1920. Here the American League team shared the one ball field with its friendly rivals, the Giants of the National League; but this field became inadequate when the crowds attracted by Ruth could no longer be accommodated there. Around his prowess his owners built the new Yankee Stadium, near Harlem River, admitting it to be the biggest in the world. Its three-decker stand held nearly 75,000 spectators at its dedication in 1923, when the "king of swat" did the expected, as the leading figure in his trade. Sport had, more than ever, become business.

Within a few days of the opening of the 1919 season New York lifted the lid which had held baseball to six playing days a week. The Sunday laws, restricting movies as well as baseball, still made unavailable the one afternoon when the largest number of possible patrons was available. After open hearing, and loud protest from those who lamented the desecration of Sunday, Governor Smith signed a local option bill permitting local authorities to determine the matter. The aldermen on Manhattan took prompt advantage of their freedom and on May 4, three days before the Germans received the proposal for a treaty, the first legal Sunday game was played in New York. Massachusetts, under similar pressure pro and con, evaded action in 1919; but in 1920 Governor Coolidge yielded to the pressure for a greater freedom.

It took months for the world of sport to adjust itself to the new popularity which came to it as war was replaced by peace. The "stadium building era" (the restrained words of the *Christian Science Monitor*) was sweeping the country. It was indeed sweeping the victors' world. In France, on June 22, 1919, Pershing assisted at the dedication of a stadium bearing his name, and built near Paris with funds provided by the Y.M.C.A. It was left to the French as a memorial, on the second anniversary of the arrival of combat troops of the A.E.F., and became at once the scene of the Inter-Allied Military Olympics. Plans were already under way for a revival of the international Olympic Games, which were assigned to Antwerp, where in August, 1920, the athletes of twenty-seven Allied nations paraded before Albert of Belgium. The Rose Bowl at Pasadena became the site of a well-advertised postseason football game. England, as it prepared for an Empire Exposition in 1924, drew plans for an Empire Stadium at Wembley.

The normal movement for war memorials, accelerated as the veterans came home, invested the promotion of many of the stadia with a public interest. As memorials they drew subscriptions from sources indifferent to sport as such. Harvard and Yale, ever in the front in education, had provided themselves before the war with Soldiers Field on the Charles, and the Bowl at New Haven, setting a standard which higher education throughout the country tried to surpass. The techniques learned in the war loan drives taught the promoters much, and promotion itself, on a percentage basis and for any cause, became a trade. In Philadelphia Franklin Field of the University of Pennsylvania was rebuilt to postwar dimensions. Stanford had a "memorial stadium" ready in 1921 for its "big game" with California, and California, victor in the game, was victor again when it dedicated its own stadium in its "homecoming" game in 1923. Between the coasts, the athletic enthusiasm of educational institutions matched the swelling figures of undergraduate enrollment. War was followed by a rush to college. Whereas in 1890 there was only one American per thousand of population in college, there were two in 1910, and nearly eight in 1930. Every campus in the country groaned under its load; the athletic needs, at least, met with cheerful recognition.

Society was touched at many levels by the games, which were reported with meticulous care by a growing school of sports writers who tended to believe that sport existed for the journalist rather than for the spectator or the player. When the games became spectacles which gathered crowds, the crowds themselves became news. So it was at Churchill Downs near Louisville, where on May 10, 1919 Sir Barton won the Kentucky Derby. It was the forty-fifth running of a famous mile and a quarter race for three-year-olds, and burst from the background of war with a glitter never before attending it. There were gathered for the few minutes of suspense a local clientele, the gamblers, the sporting folk who came like the horses in private cars, and the breeders whose pastures in the famous blue-grass region were filled each spring with foals whose future might be anything. Most distinguished of the colts of 1919, though he rarely raced, was Man O' War, who was described in 1920 as "the best three-year-old that ever looked through a bridle." His owner ran him only enough to show his quality, and then put him to stud on a farm near Lexington. Here Man O' War bred a lion's share of winners; and twenty years later the old horse in his paddock was perhaps the most distinguished citizen of Kentucky. And the race tracks, working their way through the legal obstacles to public gambling, were spreading as rapidly over the land as the stadia.

There were profits as well as entertainment in sports, for there were cities full of patrons for every show. John L. Sullivan, greatest of the fistic heroes, and honored in his old age by acquaintance with the great, had died in 1918. Nearly thirty years earlier, as the poet has it, he "Broke every single rib of Jake Kilrain." He had been succeeded by a long series of "champions of the world" whose glory grew dimmer at every transfer of the title. He had fought where he could; and he fought to fight, dodging the sheriffs with their unfriendly law. It took a new promoter to bring the game again to life, and a new fighter to make it pay. Tex Rickard turned the trick.

Sensing the financial possibilities of fight promotion, Rickard had in 1910 produced a Negro heavyweight, Jack Johnson, and persuaded a former but now obsolescent holder of the title, Jim Jeffries, to fight once more. They fought at Reno, after they had been excluded from California by the governor of the state. Five years later Johnson fought in Havana, since he was kept out of the United States by federal law, and lost the title to Jess Willard, who was ready to retire upon his share of the gate. Now, in the spring of 1919, Rickard dragged Willard back into the ring to face a new contestant. Willard was too old for the fight, and knew it, but there was money for the loser. And after three rounds at Toledo on July 4 Willard quit. William Harrison (Jack) Dempsey emerged before the alleged $600,000 gate as not only an authentic champion but also as forerunner of the wave of popularity of fistic entertainment. In December, 1919, Gene Tunney, champion of the A.E.F. at twenty-three, turned professional and started up the climb for Dempsey's title. Babe Ruth, Man O' War, and Dempsey were cultural indexes to a period of American life then unfolding. Unmatched in their respective fields, there could be built around them an organized industry for purveying sport. And outside their arenas sport for the player spread on a scale to match that of the professionals.

A few days after Dempsey took his title from Willard, a young French woman, Suzanne Lenglen, won the women's singles in the English championship matches at Wimbledon. Lawn tennis, nearly forty years after the first American association had been formed, became news as well as sport. It produced its heroes who remained amateurs until promoters learned that it, too, might be made to render profits. A California girl, .Helen Wills, learning the game on Berkeley courts, was not to make her place as junior champion for two more years, but was to continue, on even greater scale the tradition of the other California girl, May Sutton. A young Philadelphian, William T. Tilden, Jr., playing in the finals at Forest Hills in 1919, missed the title in men's singles. In 1920 as American champion he gained the English title on the Wimbledon courts. Tilden and Wills were, in their way, as authentic indexes as were the professionals. And that for which they stood produced a network of tennis associations and regional tournaments which covered the country.

Spotted again was the United States by the golf courses which retrimmed their fairways after the war, enlarged their nine-hole courses to eighteen or more, recruited new members, and blossomed around the club houses on the edge of town. These club houses began as locker rooms and grew to be social centers for their fractions of the community. Golf had been a tournament game in the United States only since the mid-'nineties. As it spread it brought relaxation to middle age and occupation to boys who, beating their fathers, did not hesitate to take on the "pros" who taught them both. In the national amateur games of 1919 an Atlanta "golf phenomenon," Robert T. (Bobby) Jones, worked his way into the final match, only to be eliminated by another. He kept at it, being only seventeen. In 1923 he won the national open and the next year won the national amateur tournament. He finished the decade with a standing which yielded nothing to any of the other kings of sport. By 1923 the Boston *Transcript* told the "future historian of American social manners" that it was his duty to "give a prominent place to golf." The game had not spread as far as baseball had, from the ball parks to the corner lots, but it had spread from the social register to the public links; and in 1922 the first of the public links national tournaments took place.

The habits of peace which reëntered the American picture at the end of the war became particularly conspicuous for two reasons. Restricted and obscured by the war for two years, they returned upon a larger scale and with a greater momentum than before the war. Few of the habits of 1919 were new, and most were not shaped by the war itself. The nation was ripe for a shift in emphasis, war or no war, as it had been half a century earlier when a railroad system and a growing industry were ready to show that the whole is sometimes greater than the sum of its parts. Put together, they bred a new nation, whereas the Civil War merely obscured the transition. Behind the deterrent influences of the World War controls American forces had been dammed up between 1917 and 1919. They broke from the controls in unavoidable disorder.

Members of Congress, who were to steer the United States into what was to serve as peace, were conscious of pressures other than those for the establishment of peace. They, too, read the papers, and they read their mail. A few hours after the Sixty-sixth Congress assembled, the new chairman of the Senate Committee on Post Offices and Post Roads held a conference in his office to establish a highway program. He had made himself sponsor of this while a minority member of the committee in the preceding Congress.

Townsend of Michigan had just presented his new colleague Newberry to the Senate. He had supported him in the canvass, and was to continue to support him until 1922, when the "Newberry case" wrecked him. But he understood the business in which Newberry's rival in the 1918 election, Henry Ford, was the leading American figure. He had made the highway movement his own. When the lame duck session met in December, 1918, the pressure for highway legislation broke into publicity. A meeting of interested supporters had been held in Chicago, with the patronage of the Bureau of Public Roads of the Department of Agriculture. A Federal Highway Council was organized there in April, 1919. The time was appropriate for such pressure, for the experimental Federal Highway Aid Act passed in 1916 had developed defects to be cured, its five-year period of subsidy would soon expire, and its funds were but a token contribution to the task. In 1919, the first year after the war, nearly two million cars and trucks were to be added to the American fleet, far more than were in operation when

Wilson took office in 1913 and the registration figures revealed 1,258,062. The cars were ready, and more were coming from the assembly lines with increasing speed. The year 1923 was to double the output of 1919. Every owner and every driver was subsidized by his interest to be a promoter of highways fit to carry cars.

Apart from its virtues as a binding agent for the nation, and as a carrier of traffic, the American railroad net possessed defects. Its very adequacy had hindered the development of traffic on the roads, and of roads to carry traffic. The cities had been joined, the range of competitive business had been extended, the people had been concentrated in urban groups, and the United States had come to think of transportation and geography in terms of railway terminals. In the great cities monumental terminals had been built as though the railroad dominance was to last forever. The people had nearly lost the awareness of topography and the surface highway which had been in the making when the railroad movement interrupted this process of acquaintance. In the cities and their suburbs the stations were points around which life was organized. In the country life was determined by the effective radius of horse-drawn vehicles from freight and passenger depots as the centers. Road construction had commonly been left in local hands, as a charge upon the local community, with the states slow to help the counties in matters of finance or construction. Roads had been constructed for horse-drawn traffic but at the turn of the century the bicycle, with its riders organized in the League of American Wheelmen, presented new demands. Only in cities and their well-to-do suburbs were hard-surface roads likely to be found, and the highway engineer was not yet a specialist drawn from the ranks of civil engineers. Three million miles of roads, most of them dirt, undrained, and unimproved, were shown on maps when the first automobiles began to run. And in many parts of the United States there was no passable road between adjacent county seats. Everyone traveled by train. Country driving was an experience for the first automobile owners. Cross-continent driving was a major adventure. The possibilities of the automobile were limited by ruts and mud. The demand for hard-surface roads had been raised before the World War, but compliance with it was delayed not only by the war but by the slow acquisition of a new habit of locomotion.

The first step toward the creation of a national system was taken when the Highway Aid Act was passed in the summer of 1916. This, in the light of the future, was perhaps a more significant preparedness measure than any of the other laws hurriedly passed in that summer of preparedness legislation. The Department of Agriculture, which had shown mild interest in rural roads since 1893, not only blessed the new law but prepared the way for it by assisting in the organization in 1914 of the American Association of State Highway Officials. The fact that there were few of these officials eligible to membership is a measure of the backwardness of road building. The demand for a policy had been pressed by the automobile manufacturers, the automobile owners, the tire makers, the local boosters, the road builders and the makers of concrete and of dirt movers. It fell upon Congress with such a backing as has rarely prevented that body from evading a costly undertaking. It was not the earliest coöperative undertaking by which the United States, paying half the cost, obtained a share in the internal policies of the states, but it was the most important thus far. For a five-year period the United States agreed to provide funds, to be covered by state appropriations, and to be split three ways: one-third by population, one-third by area, one-third by mileage of rural post roads. In their next legislative sessions the states scurried to bring into existence highway departments to meet the requirements of the law, and there were nearly forty of these departments represented in the Federal Highway Council of 1919.

This was a trial and error measure, for none knew as yet how fast an automobile could move, what surface could carry the loads, or what the loads would be. The carriage of freight, except on short hauls from farm to market, was not yet in the picture. The race between the road builders and the automobile designers had begun, with each improvement by one compelling a readjustment of plans by the other. It was important that out of the federal aid there should emerge an adequate federal network, not too greatly distorted by local greed, but in this the first law was ineffective. And money was needed, most of all: from Congress to cover appropriations, from the states to match the federal contributions and to meet the rising local demand for local roads. Every automobile dealer became in a way a lobbyist.

Named highways—the Lincoln Highway, first of all—were spearheads of the booster movement, which no chamber of commerce or local automobile owner could fail to encourage. A Jefferson Highway, creature of the New Orleans chamber of commerce, was dedicated at a terminal marker in New Orleans in January, 1919; and when the roads had dried off a group of Louisiana cars made a run to Winnipeg in the summer, along a route which they guessed the highway might some day follow. There were as many such plans as there were communities to press them, but the improved roads of which their proponents dreamed were nonexistent. The railroads failed to see what was happening as the movement broke into action.

The military, thinking of postwar strategy, were interested in highways, too. In the Civil War the United States had been the first to use rail transport in the large strategy of war, and had used it without full realization of the new weapon which had designed itself. Army men now, conscious of the motorization which had taken place on the Western Front, were fully aware of the antipathies between motor trucks and mud, and of the place which roads must hold in any future mobilization or defense of the United States.

The Army Motor Transport Corps, newly created to deal with the new problem in logistics, took part in promotional work in the summer of 1919. Partly to satisfy itself concerning the ability of a motorized unit to operate over long distances, and partly to bring to notice the condition of American roads, it outfitted a test and demonstration train to cross the continent. The nearly eighty vehicles, manned by nearly three hundred officers and men, included trucks and touring cars, and carried camping, repair, and hospital equipment. The route selected was close to that of the most famous of the continental roads: Cumberland Road, National Road, and the central western trail. Publicity was contributed by the Lincoln Highway Association, which had organized the towns along the same route for its own project, and which planted terminal markers at either end of the 3,242 miles between the White House and the Presidio of San Francisco. Leaving Washington, where Secretary Baker saw it off on July 7, 1919, the train made some fifty miles a day, reaching its western destination on September 6. As it crossed Nebraska, a Pershing Highway movement was getting under way in Lincoln; and Pershing had just come home, a four-star general, as the trip ended. The train had left the paved roads when it left the East, finding only occasional stretches of brick or concrete in the Middle West. Beyond the Missouri there were no more traveled roads. Every shower made mud to hold the trucks back; or they met sand, where traction failed. The crossing of the mountains, where roads were merely trails, made an adventure of every mile. The roads continually forded the streams, a situation which was at times of less inconvenience than when there were rural bridges, for more than a hundred bridges gave way under the heavy trucks.

The requirements of a new system of highways were brought into the open. Military studies could not whittle down much below three hundred thousand miles the roads which strategic necessity would require. The roads must be wider and stronger than even the paved roads proved to be. The locations must be determined after a reconsideration of the road map and must bypass momentary local needs. The engineering and financial problems incidental to a minimum program were still to be solved, and the administrative set-up and the trained personnel still to be worked out. There was no likelihood that Senator Townsend's conference could satisfy the demands or solve the problems at a single sitting. But a new chapter in the development of the physical plant of the United States was in its initial stages as the troops came home.

The Army Air Service, like the Motor Transport Corps, represented a development forced by war which was to entail new problems in time of peace. Air enthusiasts came home, after Major-General Charles T. Menoher was brought back from France to be chief of the service in January, 1919. They were filled with enthusiasm for the future of air travel, whether for army, navy, civilian, or commercial flying. They knew, at least, how to get into the air; but in the United States the hazards in getting back to the ground were far greater than all other aviation risks. Without landing fields there could be little opportunity for air development. These had not yet caught the attention of budget makers or civilian planners, and the military landing fields were few and poor. Military flying during the war had been mostly above the battle lines or immediately behind them. Prewar flying had been chiefly circus stunting, from the race-track enclosures of county fair grounds. The navy had been limited to the use of hydroplanes, rising from the water, though there had been instances in which planes had managed to take off from ships, and to land on improvised flight decks. The first of the American carriers, the *Langley,* was still serving as the collier *Jupiter,* although the current appropriation bill carried funds to recondition the *Jupiter* with a flight deck.

The airmen were allowed to show their powers in the autumn of 1919, in an aerial derby designed to test flyers, planes, take-offs, and landings in a grueling race. The course was set between the army field at Mineola, Long Island, and the little field at the Presidio in San Francisco, which had as yet no name. It received a name in honor of one of the starters in the race, Major Dana Crissy, who plunged to death on the army field at Great Salt Lake. The lists were restricted to military flyers who were to attempt a circuit, field to field and back, with victory to be determined by hours and minutes in the air. Menoher was on hand at the Presidio field when the derby started on October 8; and with him when the first of the eastern entrants reached the West were Hunter Liggett, who had commanded the First Army in the Meuse-Argonne, and Major Henry H. (Happy) Arnold, who later was to wear more stars than Liggett. Carl Spaatz was one of the starters in the race. Of some sixty starters, only eight managed to complete the run, and ten at least were killed. The disasters of those who failed taught airmen more than did the experiences of the winners.

Before the air above the spreading highway system could be brought under control there were to be years of work and planning. A network of airways was to be surveyed, charted, and marked, a multitude of landing fields to be developed as planes took on new speed and weight, landing mechanisms had to be designed, and a complete redrafting of the planes themselves was necessary. A new technique in meteorology was required in order that the flyer might know the condition of the air ahead of him. Here was another new industry at its starting post, similar in many of its requirements to that of the highway network, providing new scope for labor, capital, and technical skill, and more news to fill the American mind with the business of the nation.

The President remained in Paris long enough to receive and congratulate the winners in a navy flight which added still another pointer to the future. The development of naval aviation had produced planes with a range and dependability which encouraged ideas of cross-ocean flights. The fighting was over before the planes were ready, but the cessation freed surface ships so that the test could be made under conditions of more than normal safety. A crossing of the Atlantic was charted, from Rockaway Beach, Long Island, to Plymouth, England, by way of Newfoundland, the Azores, and Lisbon. The water was patroled by small surface craft, to be on hand should the planes fail, and three seaplanes were specially commissioned for the trip—NC-1, Bellinger; NC-3, Towers; NC-4, Read. Assistant Secretary Roosevelt read them their orders on May 3. They proceeded to Trepassy Bay, Newfoundland, for the take-off during the next few days, and started overseas on May 16. The first of the craft was forced down and lost at sea, but its crew was taken to port by a rescue ship. The second, whose skipper, Commander John H. Towers, was senior in the fleet, was forced down but proceeded to the Azores under its own power. The third, NC-4, flown by Lieutenant Commander Albert C. Read, completed the mission and with it the first trans-Atlantic flight. Read made the Azores in fifteen hours in the air, flew to Lisbon on the twenty-seventh, and came down at Plymouth on the last day of the month. Four days later the President in Paris did him honor and received as well the associates whose machines had failed them.

As Congress met for its special session on May 19, the logs of the navy airmen filled the papers. The day before, another attempt had been made to cross the Atlantic, but by the northern route and a nonstop flight. To encourage this the London *Daily Mail* had put up a prize of £10,000; and among the contestants gathering around St. Johns, Newfoundland, were two British teams who were soon to be in the air. Harry G. Hawker and Mackenzie Grieve had for weeks been watching for good weather, while John Alcock and Arthur Whitten Brown with a Vickers-Vimy bomber, were waiting for a start.

Hawker got into the air on May 18. It was a one-plane attempt with no attendant rescue ships, a hazardous acrobatic stunt rather than a military effort with calculated risk as was the endeavor of

the NC ships. He flew east from St. Johns, but as the days passed
without news of a landing at his destination he was written off as
probably lost at sea. He came down, however, in the path of a
Danish cargo ship, homeward bound and without means of announcing the rescue until she reached British waters. A British
destroyer was sent to fetch him to London just as the NC-4 was
flying the leg of its trip from the Azores to Lisbon. He was welcomed in England as though he had succeeded, but his Sopwith
plane, found afloat, was brought to port by an American ship.

More nearly successful than Hawker were Alcock and Brown,
who struggled into the air on June 14, were forced to come down
before they were ready, but managed to reach land on a bog in Ireland, were knighted by the King George on June 20, and were
accepted by the *Daily Mail* as entitled to the prize. Alcock crashed
to his death in France before the year was out, Hawker fell in flames
in 1921. The hazards of flying as a major sport were unwarrantable,
but the accomplishments made it clear to anyone who could read
that the air age was coming.

The demonstration of this coming was completed in July by
R-34, a British dirigible, which calmly sailed from the East Fortune Aerodrome near Edinburgh on July 2, was moored four days
later at temporary anchors on Roosevelt Field at Mineola, Long
Island, and was back on its own field on July 13. Its test cruise had
been held back until the acceptance of the treaty by Germany made
such adventure appropriate. Among its passengers, as observer,
was Lieutenant Commander Zachary Lansdowne, U.S.N., who was
to be lost with the *Shenandoah* in 1925. This dirigible, ZR-1, was
built at the Philadelphia Navy Yard from German blueprints—for
the victors had to learn about lighter-than-air craft from the enemy.
It was assembled at a new Navy Airship Station at Lakehurst, New
Jersey, made its first flight in 1923, and crashed in 1925. Germany,
meanwhile, in compliance with the treaty, built for the United
States the ZR-3, which Dr. Hugo Eckener flew safely from the shop
at Friedrichshafen to Lakehurst in the autumn of 1924. When Secretary Wilbur announced an American name for ZR-3, the *Los
Angeles,* he spoke feelingly of it as an emblem of peace on earth.

The spectacular feats of the airmen were spread on front pages
and in the sporting sections, and those who were to take to the air

were busy in their offices with their planning. Otto Praeger, the Second Assistant Postmaster General, had a new activity on his hands after the first flight of army-run mail between New York and Washington on May 15, 1918. Commercial flying, differing from military, called for no stunts in the air and no records for speed, but demanded safety and regularity. The requirements of the Post Office differed from those of the armed forces but made the same immediate call for charted routes, landing fields, and service stations. Night flying had to wait for instruments, but the gyro-compass was making progress in the laboratories. The wedge was tapped in, to be driven home by public demand and departmental pride, and to be supported as Congress, step by step, could be persuaded to provide the funds. No one of the three thousand-odd counties of the United States failed to find some new improvement to be worked for—road, landing field, or post office—whether it had been delayed in coming or was demanded to meet a new need.

By 1920, without waiting for night flying, an air and mail route was opened across the continent, New York to San Francisco; and men who had been brought up as boys on the fantasies of Jules Verne and H. G. Wells realized that these prophets had underestimated the future. The thirty-seven hours' scheduled time for the continental air route put to shame railroad timetables, and reduced the record of the pony express (seven days plus between the Missouri and Sacramento) to the dimensions of a noble gesture. Boys who had ridden relays on that post route, when it was a wonder of the world, were still alive; W. F. Cody, the best advertised of them, had lived until 1917. The transcontinental airmail route, like those of the army motor train and of the Lincoln Highway, kept close to the tracks of the first continental railways, as this had in its turn followed the trappers and the route of the 'forty-niners.

The planning within the armed forces aimed at the preservation of lessons learned in war, and at a scheme of organization for applying them to the uttermost. A fresh equilibrium was to be established between the new and the old, with air enthusiasts in the army pressing against the claims of the ground forces, with those in the navy arguing the relative values of planes as against dirigibles and the usefulness of surface ships against either, with those of both forces debating whether the air force should be coördinated with army and navy or be merely a service agency for both. The army had sent Assistant Secretary of War Benedict Crowell to Europe in the spring of 1919 as head of a study commission. On the day that Pershing rode in the victory parade in London, July 19, Crowell reported in favor of a Department of Aeronautics, to serve army, navy, and commerce. Secretary Baker disapproved the report, but released it to the press. The New York *Times* ventured into prophecy: "Any future war will inevitably open with great aerial activity far in advance of contact either upon land or sea."

It had been more or less a military secret during the war that wireless telegraphy had been implemented by a practicable radio telephone, but when the need for secrecy had passed Americans were told how Secretary Baker had talked from the ground to aviators in the air. Secretary of the Navy Daniels outdid him. On February 22, 1919, while the *George Washington* was still some nine hundred miles east of the capital, he called up the President for a talk and assembled a navy group to watch him do it. The inventor of the Alexanderson Amplifier (which was still a key instrument in the transmission) looked over his shoulder as he spoke; the General Electric Company, which controlled the amplifier, pondered upon the future of the air as a medium of communication. The President's point on the freedom of the seas had been cast into the discard by the Allies. Marconi's Wireless Telegraph Company, Ltd., of England, through its ownership of an American affiliate, had a fair chance of dominating international air. The navy continued to control the American air under the war powers of the government, operating all stations including Marconi's, with private stations sealed for the duration. Daniels was ambitious to retain the control in time of peace. What such control would come to mean, few of the dreamers but David Sarnoff were visionary enough to see. But the great electrical manufacturing companies, as war contracts were ended, had their eye on future business.

Wireless telegraphy, since that day in 1902 when Marconi received at St. Johns the letter "S" from his Poldhu station in England, had been developed to supplement or rival the wire-borne service. It had gone to sea, when law made it a part of maritime equipment, and had been made real to the public when, on January 23, 1909, Jack Binns tapped out the call for help as the *Republic* sank off

Nantucket. There was even greater publicity when in 1912 the maiden voyage of the *Titanic* was turned into tragedy as the liner hit an iceberg, and its wireless summoned all aid within reach. Congress at once vested initial jurisdiction over wireless in what was to become in 1913 the Department of Commerce, but it was fifteen years before the law caught up with even the frontier of the new interest.

Until 1920, said Herbert Hoover, as Secretary of Commerce, "we were dealing with a scientific toy." "Up to now," commented the editor of the *Radio Amateur News*, which made its bow in July, 1919, "radio has been more or less a plaything." Listeners were still wearing a heavy headphone, and were still operating their receiving sets with batteries; but they were listening in numbers gratifying to manufacturers. Science and invention were developing new techniques and adding new gadgets the advertisements of which kept a new radio journalism out of the red. But few realized that point-to-point communication was only a small part of the radio promise. The American Telegraph and Telephone Company was developing a business in the production of transmitting devices, and saw the way in which wireless could reach not only ships at sea but islands still beyond the oceanic cables. The General Electric Company, from its laboratories at Schenectady, was devising apparatus to permit voice transmission. Westinghouse Electric was turning out receiving sets suitable for use by amateurs. But the United States had as yet no administrative machinery with power enough to control the channels of the air.

There is persuasive testimony to the effect that Woodrow Wilson sent a naval officer back from Paris to urge General Electric to keep in American hands the basic inventions which it controlled. The direct action by the Assistant-Secretary of the Navy in this direction offers better proof. By April, 1919, the problem of making a pattern out of the jigsaw parts was in the hands of a master of negotiation and organization. Ida M. Tarbell has preserved part of the story, in *Owen D. Young: A New Type of Industrial Leader* (1932), for Young undertook to fight off foreign control of American wireless, to prevent nationalization at the hands of the navy, and to dodge at the same time the provisions of the Sherman Act respecting "conspiracies in restraint of trade." Something resembling a monopoly was required to protect the trade, for the open air provided all the channels, and the only possible result of complete freedom in its use must be complete confusion as efforts to use the air brought about a hopeless tangle among the corporate broadcasters and the private operators. Young and his associates and rivals were still thinking chiefly of an enlargement of telegraphic communication and of the profits to accrue from the manufacture of sending and receiving apparatus.

Young, a Boston lawyer, had been trained as counsel in the construction and utility fields, and in litigation against General Electric which added him to its own staff in 1913. He arranged, through the summer of 1919, to have General Electric take over the interests of the American Marconi Company, thus cutting off the tie to England. He displayed to the American rivals of his corporation the advantage to be gained by pooling their respective patents and creating a marketing agency which should serve all of them. On October 17, as the result of his business diplomacy, a charter was issued in Delaware to the Radio Corporation of America. The danger of navy control was prevented when the President signed in July an act directing the return of the private communication lines to their private owners. And on March 1, 1920, when the railroads were turned back to the owner companies by the United States Railroad Administration, the navy released the wireless stations from war control, enabling R.C.A. to send its first messages as agent for a partly pooled industry.

The new activity, occupying the attention of more minds than the public realized, was ready to leave its status as either "plaything" or "scientific toy." But before the R.C.A. had completed its first year of operation one of its backers and co-owners, Westinghouse, stumbled into the future. To encourage a market for receiving apparatus, and to advertise its wares, it built a sending station at Pittsburgh, received from the Department of Commerce the designation KDKA, and on election night, November 2, 1920, sent out what is commonly regarded as the earliest effective news broadcast. What it announced was the landslide electing Harding as President; what it revealed was the impending landslide of interest in radio with a market in every home, and a new influence which was to affect every problem of the world.

Chapter VI ★ Pressure

War ceased to fill the American mind, but the negotiation of a peace failed to occupy the space released. New interests and old interests crowded into this space with a zest greater because of the temporary eclipse which war had brought about. Those interests which were cultural were none the less real because they were cultural. Those which were grounded in nervous apprehension were effective, whether warranted or not. Those which were economic were better organized than ever because war had taught much respecting organization and propaganda. Those which promised advantage to some special group were aided by this same war experience, and found notable precedents for effective pressure in the achievements of the suffragists and the prohibitionists. Party, as party, had become so tied by its structure that it was less effective in promotion than in opposition; and promotion tended to fall into the hands of single-purpose groups with nonpartisan membership. Pressure politics began with the Armistice to alter the technique of the American process.

In the absence of legislation directing the course to be followed in the shift of American life from war to peace—the lame duck session had given no guidance in the winter of 1918-1919—two extralegal attempts were made to lessen the shock of transition. They provide terminal dates for a summer seven months long, during which pressure and controversy raised problems more immediate to many Americans than the structure of the peace itself. The earlier of the attempts was that of the President, through George N. Peek's Industrial Board, and under the supervision of the Secretary of Commerce, to project beyond the war the stabilizing influence of the War Industries Board. Created in February, the Industrial Board was disbanded in May, broken down by the refusal

[87]

of the Railroad Administration to let it fix a price for steel. More fundamental a cause of failure was the lack of legal authority. The War Industries Board had lacked such authority in many cases, but Baruch had had behind him a driving public opinion to support the war, whereas there was no such opinion to give sanction to the efforts of Peek and his associates. The later attempt was through an Industrial Conference, called by the President for October 6, 1919, in the hope of harmonizing the divergent demands of labor, capital, agriculture, and the general public. The need for harmony was greater than it had been at any time since the creation of the Industrial Board; but when the Industrial Conference finally met there were no agenda ready for it, and Wilson was in the sick room and unable to have more than a technical share in the procedure. Labor and capital proved to be equally insistent and uniformly in opposition to each other, so that after a fruitless fortnight labor withdrew and left the conference wrecked.

It would have been difficult, even in complete dispassion, to adjust the contradictory claims of various American groups for a larger share of the output of American productive labor. Violence and outlaw strikes made it more difficult. The nervousness of the winter, when fear of a spread of Bolshevism contributed to the "red scare," continued as the year advanced. None could draw a line at the point where proper activity of labor stopped and the violence of revolutionaries—or hoodlums—began. The I.W.W. were not gentle either in their expression of syndicalist philosophy, or in their behavior. When bombs began to be mailed to persons who were opposing either labor demands or violence, there was reason to worry. When they began to explode at their destinations, in spite of the care with which postal inspectors caught them in transit, it was worse. As a May Day demonstration some dozens were mailed, but they were detected before they reached such prominent persons as Senator Overman who had investigated Bolshevism, Judge Landis who had sentenced a flock of members of the I.W.W., the attorney who had prosecuted Tom Mooney, or the Attorney General of the United States, A. Mitchell Palmer. On the night of June 2 the front was blasted off the R Street residence of Palmer.

Months before the bomb outrages of May, the executive mansion of the Governor of California, William D. Stephens, had been blasted from the rear, and a mass trial of I.W.W. at Sacramento resulted. When Stephens was reinaugurated in January, 1919, he denounced "these skulking wielders of the torch," and demanded a law which could control them. He signed the resulting law on criminal syndicalism on the last day of April, and officers of the law proceeded under it to treat as a felony mere membership in any organization whose official creed advocated the use of violence. It became a nice matter for the courts to determine, from the loose language, which radical organizations used in stating their objectives, whether the words were excited rhetoric or indication of deliberate intent. A well-to-do and kindly woman of Oakland, California, Anita Whitney, was presently in the net as a member of a Communist society, and provided a long-drawn-out case which rivalled that of Tom Mooney as a social provocative. Miss Whitney was no hoodlum, but came of a family so well placed that her radicalism was the more notable. In the end, nothing but a pardon from a later governor of California saved her from serving her sentence.

The leaders of radical movements stood upon their constitutional rights, defying restrictive laws, and receiving considerable moral support from such liberal journals as the *Nation*. The confusion of readjustment provided an atmosphere fertile for agitation. Labor, nursed through the war for the purpose of keeping war production active, had received wage adjustments which employers could pass on to the public or to the government. With the cancellation of war contracts there was fear that gains, won in the war, might be lost. The American Federation of Labor, larger than ever, hoped to go forward rather than backward. Moderate liberals, announcing that "the future of civilization" was at stake, gathered together a Committee of Forty-Eight, to do something about it in a political way, and radical labor, with an aim at the political organization which the American Federation had consistently opposed, laid plans for a National Labor party to be formed in Chicago. The Socialist party, which split over the issue of war in 1917, sought to reassemble its handful of adherents.

Before Pershing came back with his First Division, the tendencies and the discordancies of radicalism had received full display. On August 30 a national emergency convention of the Socialist party met in a Chicago hall, with its delegations as badly split as in 1917, and with its "left-wingers" determined to capture the organization. Debs, traditional leader of the party, was in jail. The Lusk committee in New York had investigated the party, and had raided the offices of the Rand School in the hope of finding evidence of specific subversive activity. The rebellious foreign-language Socialist groups were in bad repute with the party leadership, and on the second day of the convention Victor Berger with difficulty held physical possession of the hall for the regulars, while John Reed led the radicals out to caucus elsewhere.

A convention for the organization of a Communist party had already been called to meet in another Chicago hall on September 1, and to this convention the Socialist seceders made overtures for fusion. They were less than welcome, for they were more radical than the Communists, and their foreign-language leaders were a visible target for all who were attacking radicalism as the work of unassimilated European agitators. The alleged connection of the movements with the Third International of the Bolshevists provided a basis for the charge that they were international revolutionists in intent and act. Failing of their welcome among the Communists, the Socialist "left-wingers" moved on, and on September 2 gave birth to a Communist Labor party. The various manifestoes which emerged from the three conventions indicated that there were variations in radicalism respecting aim and method. The Socialists, hoping for the future, were willing to participate in the existing government. The Communists were unwilling to have a share in a government of which they disapproved, but were less than clear how their new order was to be brought about. The Communist Labor group were revolutionary Socialists in profession, prepared to overthrow "the present system of production," and to go the whole way to a proletarian dictatorship. The degree to which the professions of a party platform were a fair juridical index of the intentions of a party member became a matter for the courts to decide as cases under the new laws came to trial.

In the federal sphere, part of the law was already clear. The act which had imposed a literacy test for immigrants in 1917 was specific in directing the exclusion of anarchists and all who advocated overthrow of the government by force, or unlawful destruction of property. This act had been implemented by a deportation act in October, 1918, whereby, on warrant of the Secretary of Labor such aliens might be sent back to their lands of origin. Pursuant to duty imposed by the deportation act, Secretary William B. Wilson ruled in 1920 that the language of the Communist platform made membership in the party a deportable offense for aliens; whereas that platform of the Communist Labor party, just missing incitation to violence, failed to warrant this deportation for its alien members. Collecting evidence of membership and belief from sundry sources, and conducting hearings, with Palmer's Department of Justice annoyed at a lack of prosecuting vigor, Secretary Wilson assembled a group of deportable persons at Ellis Island, and invoked the good offices of the State Department and the army transport service. On December 21, 1919, the army transport *Buford* sailed with 249 Russian aliens, for the port of Hargo, Finland, which was as near to Russia as it could hope to dock. Many of the passengers on the "Soviet Ark" were reluctant to go, some like Emma Goldman and Alexander Berkman were unquestionably anarchists, all were uncertain of the reception they would have in Russia, whose government the United States had not recognized.

The first national convention of the American Legion, meeting in Minneapolis on Armistice Day, November 11, 1919, approved the deportations, and urged that Victor Berger, though long a citizen, be added to them. Its inauguration marked the appearance of another force among the crosscurrents of American interest, and one disposed to challenge radicalism.

The long career of the Grand Army of the Republic set a precedent which made it impossible that veterans of the World War should fail to unite, but did not provide a functioning organization into whose ranks the veterans could step upon discharge. As early as March there had been a Paris conference on organization which had been dissuaded from acting. The leaders pointed out that fully half the armed forces had never reached Europe, that military rank made it impossible for enlisted men to have their full share of influence in a society formed while they were within the army, that the discharged veteran must be the unit regardless of rank. The World War had not brought about the distinctions between officers and men which, after the Civil War, had left the officers heroes and had for a generation sent them up in politics and on to Congress.

On May 8 (the day after the draft treaty was handed to the Germans) St. Louis was the scene of an organizing caucus, with a plan of procedure, and with two self-denying sons of distinguished fathers—Colonel Theodore Roosevelt, Jr., and Colonel Bennett Clark—active on the floor. The agenda called for a temporary organization and for the setting up of local groups whose delegates should come together in a formal convention in the autumn. The director of the Bureau of War Risk Insurance in the Treasury, Colonel Henry D. Lindsley, was made chairman at St. Louis and became head of the interim executive committee. Lindsley was already at outs with his chief, Carter Glass, Secretary of the Treasury, because of his complaints respecting narrow interpretations of the law, and he was to be out of the bureau in ten days more. There was significance in the connection between the Treasury and the Legion, as there had been in that between the Grand Army and the Pension Bureau; and the Hearst papers were preparing to run a campaign for a six-months pay bonus to veterans to supplement the formal sixty dollars allowed them on discharge. The pension attorneys had managed to have an active hand in the affairs of the Grand Army; lacking these attorneys now, the hope for a bonus was one of the unifying forces on the new membership. The veterans, best paid and best guarded of soldiers of all armies, were nevertheless fully conscious of the rising wages with which those who did not fight were cheerfully rewarded; not only had these received high pay, they still held the jobs.

The new Legion, critical of labor, was hostile to radicals. On Armistice Day, when the delegate convention opened, the members who remained at home took part in local commemorations. One of these, parading the streets of Centralia, Washington, met with tragedy. As the marchers passed the hall of the local I.W.W., shots were fired and four service men were killed. Although the courts, in a community hostile to the I.W.W., were satisfied that the Legion members had been lawlessly attacked, the evidence concerning responsibility was inconclusive. Passions were dangerously close to the surface. However, the law turned against the I.W.W., one of whose sympathizers had been taken from the jail and lynched;

eleven others, pleading self-defense, were brought to trial. Seven of these were in 1920 convicted of second-degree murder. The American Legion had meanwhile completed its organization at Minneapolis and had set up an agency to guard the interests of veterans.

The Plumb Plan League made its appearance among the American pressure groups during the summer of 1919, and claimed that three million buyers of its lapel buttons had paid three dollars apiece for the privilege of association. The time was approaching when something must be done about the United States Railroad Administration. McAdoo had been given charge of the railroads by executive order during Christmas week, 1917, and Congress had in the following March fixed the war relations between the owner corporations and the government. Federal operation was an emergency measure, surrounded by the suspicion and opposition of the owners, by the hope on the part of liberals and labor groups that it might become a step to nationalization, and by interest within the Railroad Administration in the experiment of unified operation. McAdoo, retiring from his positions, had hoped that the experiment might continue long enough in peacetime to establish the limits of its usefulness. All concerned were drafting schemes to be tried when the war powers should cease, among them, John J. Esch of the House Committee on Interstate Commerce. Within the ranks of labor, and especially among the great railway brotherhoods, a chance to make a gain for labor had been seen.

The prewar railroads had been brought under federal and state control in such a way that the rates which they could charge were frozen by the law. But all that they had to buy—labor, construction material, fuel, working capital—they must buy in a competitive market; and in the squeeze between the ceiling on charges and the rising prices the railway systems had suffered. Labor, seeing no possibility of larger pay funds in the narrowed earnings of the roads, had turned to the possibilities of strikes and politics. In the autumn of 1916, with preparedness under way, as well as a presidential campaign, the brotherhoods had called a strike for Labor Day, and were bought off by congressional intervention which, in the Adamson law, fixed the length of the basic day and established the right to time and a half pay for overtime. The Railroad Administration had, as a war measure, adjusted wages as needed; but the return of the roads to owner companies which must balance their books carried a threat of wage reductions.

Glenn E. Plumb, a railroad lawyer who had become counsel for the unions, had a scheme in mind, and back of it a fear of revolution. He described his new order in *Industrial Democracy: A Plan for its Achievement* (1923), after he had prepared for the brotherhoods a proposal to avoid either the return of the railroads to their owners or direct operation by the nation. He launched a demand for a share in management and a share in the profits of operation. The nation, with an issue of bonds, was to buy the roads and to entrust their operation to a corporation whose directors should represent equally the government, the operating officials, and the employees, with net profits to be split between the government and labor. In urging his plan he took full advantage of the old complaints against railroad management, the distrust of railroad finance, and the distaste for speculation in railroad securities, all of which had been grounds for attack before the war. He added a demand which was relatively new in American thought: organized labor as such should share in the management of the plant in which it worked. The brotherhoods liked the plan, the American Federation of Labor, meeting in Atlantic City in June, was friendly to it, and Congress in August was formally urged to make it the basis of the impending law.

With each month, as the Plumb Plan was discussed, American labor became more uneasy. Prices ran riot, with their heaviest impact upon wage-earning classes, and upon the middle class which was coming to be described as "white collar," and which lacked effective organization. Unemployment and confusion were resulting in decline of union membership, and union officials were finding it increasingly hard to keep their membership in check and to fulfill their contracts. The Railroad Administration had a growing doubt of the validity of war powers in the face of peace disturbances.

For a brief day the Plumb Plan was the emblem for liberal labor thought, and in proportion as it attracted labor it antagonized the forces of conservatism. It not only did away with railroad securities for investment, substituting low-rate government bonds for the chance of profitable dividends, but it looked like a first step toward general confiscation and nationalization. When it was denounced as a Bolshevist proposal it was linked to the other dangers thought to be coming out of Soviet Russia. And when the Plumb Plan League threatened to follow the procedure of the Anti-Saloon League in a campaign of pressure, the new industrial democracy was denounced as thoroughly un-American and undemocratic. When Plumb told the Committee on Interstate Commerce in August that with the passage of time railroad men might cease to serve, and quoted those who feared that revolution was at hand, his proposal was treated as threat and blackmail.

Only a few days before Plumb testified at the committee hearing, the President had conferred with representatives of a group of minor railroad unions which had prepared a strike referendum and announced their determination to fight for the proposed change. National guardsmen were patrolling the streets of Chicago, where Mayor William Hale Thompson had asked them to keep order in the presence of race riots, white against black. The trouble had broken out at one of the lake bathing beaches late in July, and the Negro quarter of the city, where Thompson was building up a powerful political backing, was substantially in a state of siege. The disturbing episode was a reminder that roughly one-tenth of the American population was black, and that Negro labor, shifted north for war jobs, was disinclined to drift back south. In New York, by the middle of the month, the subway and elevated railway employees were ready to go on strike, following the Brooklyn employees who struck on August 6. The street railways over the land were caught in as tight a pinch as were the railroads. In New York the mayor denounced all efforts to increase income by raising fares above the traditional five-cent level as a "state-wide" plot, and there as elsewhere the motor bus was taking advantage of disordered service to enter into competition with the rail lines. At a less disturbing level, the Actor's Equity Association was laying plans for a general theater strike, and pessimistic observers feared that both the Lambs and the Friars clubs might be disrupted as a consequence.

The rising cost of living was behind the demands of labor and of the Chicago shopmen whose irregular strike began on August 1.

Behind the demands, too, was a belief that employers were in a conspiracy to wreck the unions and to recover ground surrendered for
the pursuit of the war. The international unions repudiated the
Chicago strike, but the men were out; and nervousness was such
that Wilson interrupted his major duty with the Treaty in order
to work for domestic peace. The Congress had hoped to get a brief
vacation, but letters came from the White House urging leaders to
wrestle with the new problem, and the legislators in compliance
abandoned the idea of a recess. In a few days, August 7, 1919, the
President appeared before them to urge a line of action in attack
upon the "high cost of living." He told them only what they already
knew: that rising prices and radical demands went hand in hand,
and that wage increases without a check on prices would only raise
the prices higher. But he struck a popular note in his insistence
that "there must be no threats." He was less popular with his
political opposition when he connected the whole problem with
the long postponement of the peace. The Senate was still holding
hearings on the Treaty, and until ratification could be brought
about there could be no hope of peace abroad or a return of peace
conditions at home. Wilson was preparing to take the matter of
the peace directly to the people; but meanwhile he urged the Congress to face the problem of prices and supported the ruling of the
Director General of Railroads, Hines, that the shopmen's demands
could not be considered while they remained on strike. They must
return to work. The men abandoned their strike on August 18,
while their leader, Bert M. Jewell, who had spent the war organizing workers in shipyards and war plants, took their case before the
adjustment officers of the Railroad Administration.

Worse trouble impended. The radical and socialistic parties
flew their flags of defiance at the end of the month, and one of
their leaders, who had been identified with the I.W.W. for a decade,
William Z. Foster, completed his plans for the organization of the
steelworkers and for a blow at the steel plants.

The steel industries, blossoming out since Andrew Carnegie converted his iron mills to steel during the depression of 1873, had
managed to head off the general organization of their workmen.
Employing immigrant labor in increasing numbers as they expanded, their labor supply, like that of the mining industries, had

been hard to organize because of the medley of races and tongues. The Amalgamated Association of Iron and Steel Workers had been unsuccessful in extending unionism in the face of refractory labor groups and company opposition. Like most of the craft unions its scheme was built around skilled labor, and failed to reach the larger number of common laborers.

The Homestead strike against the Carnegie plants in 1892 had been a fizzle, with opinion turning against the unions because of violence in the Pittsburgh area. Trying again in 1901, the Amalgamated Association had been outfought and outgeneralled by the United States Steel Corporation. The steel merger, with financial backing from the house of Morgan, included every type of plant, some union, some open shop. The corporation declined to recognize the union as a general bargaining agent, and met the strike in the organized plants by closing them down and continuing operation in the nonunion mills. The complete organization of the industry and recognition of the union by the employers continued to be a goal for labor, to be fought for once more in 1919.

William Z. Foster had counseled a policy of "boring from within" before he became secretary for the labor committee which undertook to organize the steelworkers. He had learned about syndicalism by traveling in France to study it, and he now picked as his target a dozen principal open-shop plants, most of them in the Steel Corporation. Twenty-four struggling unions were behind him. Directly before him was the firm refusal of Judge Elbert H. Gary, head of the Steel Corporation, either to argue with him or to concede a right to unions in the open shop. The American Federation of Labor had, at its annual meeting in 1918, directed its executive officers to create the organization necessary for "one mighty drive to organize the steel plants of America," and Gompers had presided at the conference which formed the National Committee for Organizing Iron and Steel Workers. After Gompers had launched the committee he turned its chairmanship over to John Fitzpatrick, president of the Chicago Federation of Labor, who was later in 1919 to assist at the birth of a National Labor party.

The recruiting of the workers proceeded on the principle of federating the trades rather than working plant by plant, or craft by craft, or by disregarding the crafts to form an industrial union.

The organizers met with welcome at the workers' level, and with opposition from employers and from local governments where company influence was strong. There was much complaint of interference with freedom of speech, meetings were banned as likely to disturb the peace, violence was sometimes met by violence. But the Organizing Committee proceeded with its preparations during the early summer of 1919. Judge Gary, who was directing the defense of the companies, received friendly treatment from Ida M. Tarbell in *The Life of Elbert H. Gary: A Story of Steel* (1926). Foster painted a different picture of him in *The Great Steel Strike* (1920). To the workers Gary was an advocate of their wage slavery. On September 10 the strike was called.

Woodrow Wilson, drawn into this contest, as he had been drawn into that of the Chicago shopmen, urged that the strike be deferred until after his Industrial Conference in October should have given consideration to the whole problem of labor and living, but with angry determination on both sides the men walked out on September 22. How many walked out, how many others were deprived of work through lack of steel, and how many and how quickly they walked back, are variously reported, although Foster's figures fix the original walkout at 365,600. The steel companies continued to produce while disorder milled around their gates. The Pittsburgh mills and those at Gary, Indiana, were the foci of the strike. Again the men lost out. By mid-October the only uncertainty was the date at which failure would be openly admitted. In January the strike was called off. The battle was lost, but in the larger war of labor against capital there were gains. The principle of unionism, gaining wider acceptance, made it increasingly difficult for groups to decline collective bargaining. Foster himself moved on in radical circles until his name became to his opponents a synonym for attempted class revolution. In 1923, it was only by a divided jury that he escaped conviction on a charge of Communism under a Michigan syndicalism law.

On the day before the call was issued for the steel strike, trouble broke out in Boston, presenting a new aspect of the labor problem and contributing to the fears of those who saw back of the disputes the beginning of revolution. The Boston police, organized as a local of the American Federation of Labor, left their posts.

The strike did not come as a surprise. Like other strikes, it had been preceded by promotion and publicity, each stage in its coming serving to crystallize opinion upon it. It was not unusual for Boston police to be poorly paid. Most civil servants were in the same position, and most were sorely pinched by H.C.L., as the high cost of living came to be known. By tradition rather than by specific law, there was a general assumption that the nature of the duties of the police compelled them to forego the right to strike. By the nature of its mission the American Federation felt bound, wherever it found them, to bring new bodies of wage earners into membership. The Boston police commissioner, as the issue was formulating, ruled that membership in a union was inconsistent with continuance on the force. The mayor of Boston named a citizens' committee, with which to take counsel in crisis, and the commissioner called before him for a hearing the patrolmen who had publicly offended by becoming officers of the union. The decision to suspend them was reached on September 8, whereupon the *Transcript* declared: "the die is cast." Eleven hundred members of the force voted to strike, and took off their uniforms on the afternoon of September 9. The Central Labor Union of Boston endorsed their action, and there was some talk of a general strike.

There were other cities where police unions had been formed, but nowhere else had the issue been so clearly joined. The question of public safety was raised at once, and the worries of the police commissioner spread from his office to that of the mayor of Boston, and thence to that of the governor of the commonwealth, Calvin Coolidge. Coolidge withheld action until violence had appeared, the *Nation* saying that he ran from it "as a singed cat from fire." He was, however, commander in chief of the militia, with a responsibility not to be evaded when Boston mobs proved to be more ingenious in making trouble than voluntary patrolmen were in checking it. The mayor called for military protection, and the National Guard was put to work, while political leaders wrestled with the hot issue. The refusal of the police commissioner to reinstate the strikers pending trial made compromise impossible. In Washington senators denounced Bolshevism, and Wilson, speaking at Helena, Montana, stressed the obligation of the police. Gompers urged reinstatement upon Governor Coolidge, pending arbitration;

but the commissioner talked of filling the vacant places of the strikers. On September 14 Governor Coolidge replied to Gompers in words which brought a new name into the American political arena. He had risen, post by post, in the services of Northampton and the state, had been elected governor in 1918 and was a candidate for reëlection in 1919. Replying to the head of the American Federation he denied the right of the police to unionize, and went beyond mere denial: "There is no right to strike against the public safety by anybody, anywhere, any time." The New York *World* took comfort from his words. "Forty-eight Coolidges properly distributed among the State Capitols would settle every question of law and order," it said after he had been reëlected in November, "and the economic fermentation of the country could be safely left to clarify itself."

No number of Coolidges could have adjusted to the satisfaction of all concerned those controversies of economic balance raised by the developments in industry and aggravated by the letdown from war. Each had to work out its own equilibrium. The United Mine Workers of America had opened their convention in Cleveland just as the Boston police commissioner disciplined his force. The delegates who gathered there were worried by high prices, by the huge number of part-time workers and marginal mines the potential output of which was beyond the capacity of the United States to consume, by the increasing use of fuel oil and the threat of hydroelectric power, and by the early need to negotiate a new contract for the soft coal mines. They were persuaded of their privilege to declare the existing contract ended on October 31. Professional leaders guided them. John L. Lewis, acting president, had been in their service for a decade. William Green, secretary-treasurer, had served in various ranks since the beginning of the century. Their session ended just as the steel strike began, with an announcement of a bituminous strike to begin on November 1.

The Fuel Administration had been liquidated during the spring of 1919, but such powers as had been delegated to it remained legally active until the peace. Its staff had been dispersed. Its wartime chief, Harry A. Garfield, president of Williams College, was recalled by President Wilson to resume his duties and to see to the rationing of the coal already above ground. In coöperation with the Railroad Administration new rules of conservation were at once set up.

President Wilson tried in vain to persuade the United Mine Workers to defer the strike and seek adjustment through orderly channels. Next he asserted that the strike would be in defiance of the war powers vested in him by the Lever act of August 10, 1917, and that he would enforce the law. On the last day of work, upon application of the government, a restraining order was issued by the federal court in Indianapolis, directing the officials of the United Mine Workers to desist from their connection with the strike which they had called. It was too late to prevent a stoppage of work, and some 400,000 miners were out on November 1, but the officials heeded the restraining order and prepared their case for hearing and argument a few days later. On November 8, after the hearing, Judge A. B. Anderson, to whom the appeal had been made, further directed the officials to withdraw the strike order. He agreed with the President that the strike was in violation of agreements entered into by the union with the Fuel Administration under the law of 1917, and believed that it was a conspiracy against the United States. Gompers made lengthy argument against the order, for nothing was dearer to labor than its right to strike, but the United Mine Workers, recognizing the power though they denied the right of the government, obeyed the mandate. The dispute was passed into debate before a coal commission and serious interruption in the mining of soft coal was avoided. The old controversy over the right to strike and the use of injunctions in labor disputes was left embittered and provocative.

Labor had gained greatly in official and popular recognition during the war, and clung to a hope that the gains might be carried over into peace. Agriculture, too, had made gains and had acquired hopes. The American aid which had consisted in supplying the armed forces and the Allies with food led to the passage of the Lever food and fuel control act and to the ensuing effort of the Food Administration to increase food output. It had been patriotic duty for labor to stay on the job and for the farmer to increase his crop. It had also been profitable to both.

In a technical way agriculture was at the point where change was imminent. New knowledge, new machinery, and wide use of tractors, were about to increase the output per acre and per farmer. Farming had completed a generation in which the agricultural college, stimulated by land grants and federal cash, had been converting its processes into industrialized science. New seeds, new knowledge of soils, new understanding of genetics, had helped to increase the crop. Every new technique was called upon to increase war production while war prices, generally uncontrolled, had brought rewards to the farmer. The cultivated acreage was expanded under the pressure, and a rising price for farm land kept pace with the rise in food prices. For the farmer the end of the war meant curtailment of the extraordinary demands for food. It left him overcapitalized in plant and equipment, filled with new desires bred by prosperity, and bound to sell his produce at falling prices because of overproduction.

The numerous farmer movements in American politics had generally been local and temporary. They had warmed in time of depression and cooled in periods of prosperity. The farmer was an individualist, hard to organize and indisposed to make trouble in good times. A new principle of organization, in which the farmer was organized by others instead of organizing himself, had made its appearance just before the war. More than ever before, and on a more permanent basis, the farm influence in 1919 was ready to exert a constant pressure upon the conduct of government. Frank R. Kent, describing more than a hundred pressure groups whose stockades surrounded the Capitol in Washington, in *The Great Game of Politics* (1923), was to characterize the new farmer organization as "probably the most effective and formidable of these groups."

The germ of the new organization was derived from a discovery that agricultural education was fundamentally a matter of adult education. The agricultural colleges, spreading since 1857, and endowed by the Morrill act during the Civil War, had slowly built up a curriculum suited to prospective farmers, only to discover among their graduates a pronounced tendency, once educated, to go to town. The laboratories of the colleges, producing new discoveries useful to the farmer, were learning that to gain results these must be taken directly to the farm. In a Smith-Lever act of 1914, Congress was induced to finance a coöperative, fifty-fifty system for advancing agricultural experimentation and agricultural education. The placing of agents of the Department of Agriculture in the counties was a consequence of the new policy; and around the agents, who numbered nearly 2,000 as the war ended, local farmers were enrolled in farm bureaus for the purpose of spreading knowledge through demonstration on the ground. The farm agent, publicly financed, became an organizer for his constituents; and his constituents, once organized, began to think of pressure.

The grouping of these farm bureaus into state federations was both in harmony with American habit and useful to the cause. There were a dozen federations before the Armistice, and war needs multiplied them in 1919. In compactness of organization they went beyond the other efforts at a grouping of the farmer interest: the National Board of Farmers' Organizations, the Farmers' National Council, and the National Grange which had survived for fifty years. All of these had grown from the farm up, rather than from government subsidy down. From state federation to national federation was the next and natural step. Early in 1919 a conference at Ithaca proposed a permanent national organization. A home in Washington was bought to be an observation post near Congress. More than thirty states had representatives at an organizing convention in Chicago in November; and in March, 1920, the constitution of the National Farm Bureau Federation went into operation. Obscured somewhat during its period of genesis, because farmer news received little attention from the urban press, and because of the more exciting news about strikes and radicalism, the new Federation testified to the rearrangement of American ideas and interests which was in process during the critical year of demobilization.

The National Industrial Conference had meanwhile held its meeting and passed into history. It was Franklin K. Lane, Secretary of the Interior, who suggested it to Woodrow Wilson who was facing at the same time the objections to the Treaty and the disturbances of the nation. As the President started on his western trip he issued the call to employers, labor, and the public, to meet in conference and search for "fundamental means of bettering the whole relationship of labor and capital." Before a program had been outlined, the western trip had been cut short by his collapse, and the delegates invited by him assembled in the Pan-American

Building without organization or agenda on October 6. They came in an urbane mood. Judge Gary was polite to Samuel Gompers. John D. Rockefeller, Jr., smiled on Ida-M. Tarbell, in spite of her exposure of the Standard Oil Company. Charles William Eliot was there, still a citizen of the world at eighty-five. After two days of discussion of procedure in committee and on the floor, the conference took shape as three estates—labor, employers, and the public—worked as unit groups; all business was cleared in a general committee before it was discussed. They presented, in·spite of themselves, a fair summary of the bewildered American mind.

The conference sat for three weeks, displaying only the intricacies of a problem the solution of which was not yet in sight. And while it sat, the papers brought every day the news of a disturbed society. The New York printers were on strike, driving many publishers to out-of-town presses; for four weeks the *Literary Digest* appeared in typewritten pages—done, as it proudly advertised, "without the aid of typesetters." The men on the New York ferries were on strike, and the longshoremen. The soft coal conference was in protracted deadlock; the Railway Express had a walkout. General Leonard Wood was policing Gary, Indiana with federal troops and being suggested for President as a defender of the Constitution. The Senate Committee on Interstate Commerce was writing an antistrike clause into its pending railroad bill.

The rocks on which the conference foundered were arbitration and the right to strike. Labor was stern in rejecting any scheme of compulsory arbitration because no such scheme could operate without canceling the right to strike. Employers were equally adamant in opposition to the labor demand for a clear recognition of labor's right to free organization, collective bargaining, and representation in negotiation by agents of its own choice. No formula from the public representatives could bring the groups together, and on October 22 Gompers led labor out of the conference. The employer group withdrew the next day, leaving only the representatives of the helpless public to bring the conference to a formal end. As the conference dissolved the United States Senate was at long last nearly ready to bring the Treaty to a vote, if means could be found to prevent an unlimited filibuster by its irreconcilable opponents.

Chapter VII ★ "... the Advice and Consent of the Senate"

T̲HE UNITED STATES SENATE holds a whip hand over foreign affairs. It is conscious of this, and is jealous because the full extent to which it makes a claim is not precisely justified by the Constitution. The historical reasons for giving to the Senate a share in treaty making are clear enough. In the House, the basis of representation being population, the possibility of the coercion of the agricultural states by the populous states, when there were only thirteen in all, was sufficient excuse for denying the authority to that body. In the Senate it would still have been possible for a coalition of large states to oppress the smaller had the vote been by mere majority. But by fixing the requirement at two-thirds of the senators present it was made unlikely that the large states could swing Senate consent without the concurrence of several of the smaller states. The result of the compromise worked out in the Constitutional Convention was to leave the House irritated because it had no clear right in foreign agreements, and to leave the Senate dissatisfied because the language of Section 2 of Article II was less than clear.

The treaty power is defined in the article dealing with the President. The concurrence of "two thirds of the Senators present" is specified; but to the President is assigned "... Power, by and with the Advice and Consent of the Senate to make treaties." The point at which "consent" shall apply is obvious. The point at which the "advice" shall begin to function has been under debate since the organization of the government. Occasionally a president, even Washington, has consulted the Senate while a treaty has been under negotiation; more often he has merely transmitted an accomplished

[105]

fact. And senators, jealous of their constitutional privilege, as they were designed to be, have insisted on their right to have a hand in every phase of a negotiation. It has hurt them when a president of their own party has taken the lead; to have the right to the lead assumed by a president of a different party has tended to enrage them.

The American Commission to Negotiate Peace, named by Wilson without regard to this sensitiveness of the Senate, became a kind of symbol of defiance which senators resented. As the vague picture of a League to Enforce Peace was brought into focus in the text of the Covenant of the League of Nations, the conditions precedent to any effective league were magnified by senatorial jealousy. No league without a measure of authority over its members could hope to do its work. No member could hope to have retained a full and complete sovereignty after having admitted, in the language of the Covenant, that "any war or threat of war . . . [was] a matter of concern to the whole league." It became a case for a nice balancing of the advantages of unshaded independence against the advantages of effective insurance against war. This was a balancing difficult even if undertaken in nonpartisan cold blood, but hardly to be hoped for in the midst of partisan politics among a people whose fear of defeat had been displaced and whose interrupted domestic affairs filled their mind. On the evening before the new Congress met, a first-term senator from Ohio, Warren G. Harding, told an audience in Carnegie Hall in New York that "at the present time the preservation of American nationality rests with the Senate in the United States. And . . . the Senate is not going to fail you."

The Sixty-sixth Congress met on May 19, 1919 with its Republican membership able to take control of the organization of both houses. Gillett, senior in continuous service, was made Speaker as the caucus had agreed in February. Victor L. Berger, under conviction and sentence by a United States court for violation of the espionage act, was denied the right, pending an investigation, to take the oath as a representative from Wisconsin. In the Senate, Truman H. Newberry, over whose credentials hung the claim of Henry Ford, was seated without immediate objection. Lodge took over the leadership of the Senate and the chairmanship of the Committee on Foreign Relations, and Fordney of Michigan was installed as chairman of the House Committee on Ways and Means. The progressive Republicans in the Senate acquiesced reluctantly to the elevation of Boies Penrose as chairman of the Committee on Finance, and were but partly comforted by the selection of Albert B. Cummins of Iowa as president pro tempore.

It was nearly five months since Lodge had deserted the idea of a world organization. In 1916, at the meeting of the League to Enforce Peace, he had supported it with an eloquence as great as that of Wilson. In the next two years he had "reflected upon it," and had come to believe that "in trying to do too much we might lose all." Since Wilson had gone to Paris, he took counsel with Roosevelt; and just before Christmas he served notice to the President and the Allies that the Senate must pass on any treaty made in Paris, and that senators had means of letting Europe know their thoughts as the negotiation progressed. He spoke in the certainty of being soon in a position to shape those thoughts, and warned the negotiators of the danger of putting treaty and league into the same document. He managed to have practically a death-bed conference with his old friend Roosevelt upon his tactics.

Lodge found many associates in the Senate who feared the Wilson treaty, and many outside. In some the sense of nationality was outraged, in others the sense of party advantage. Beveridge feared that the prestige of a treaty would make it impossible for Republicans to elect a president in 1920. A barrage of criticism was opened as the Paris Conference met, and Lodge reinforced it with a ferocious attack on the proposed Covenant at the end of February. As the new Congress convened in May, and he found himself chairman of the Committee on Foreign Relations, he thought that the "interests and safety of the United States might be so protected by amendments and reservations that a large majority of Republicans could vote for" the Treaty. In any case, he was certain that an "attempt to defeat the Treaty of Versailles with the League by a straight vote in the Senate, if taken immediately, would be hopeless even if it were desirable." When he came to describe the struggle over ratification, in *The Senate and the League of Nations* (1925), he wrote as if he wanted the reader to believe that he was anxious for a proper league, but saw no chance of obtaining it without a surrender by Woodrow Wilson. He conceded grudgingly that Wilson might be able to place the nation above the party, but was sure that his opponent placed himself above both. He wrote as one who found it necessary to keep Republican senators working as a team in order to avert disaster.

There was as yet no Treaty to discuss. The draft of May 7 was still under discussion, with six weeks more to go before the final document could be signed. Not even the draft was available, since the Peace Conference had treated it as a confidential document. However, it soon became available through private channels, and in a fortnight Lodge admitted that he had seen a copy of it in New York, whither it had been brought by Americans returning from Paris. On June 3 Senator Borah charged on the floor of the Senate that Wall Street could see the draft yet it was kept from the Senate. He launched an investigation of the channel which permitted the leak, and his colleagues passed a resolution offered by Senator Hiram Johnson calling on the President to transmit the draft. The resolution, relayed to Paris for answer, came to nothing, for the American delegation kept the pledge of secrecy; but the draft was forthcoming. By Wednesday, June 11, the eastern papers carried the boastful advertisement: "The *Chicago Tribune* Scoops the Earth with the Peace Treaty." It was not the Treaty, but the draft, which Frazier Hunt had carried out of Paris and turned over to his paper for publication on Monday morning. The same day Borah rose in the Senate with the text in his hand—the English text filled 264 printed pages—and threatened to read it into the *Congressional Record* unless his colleagues gave him leave to print. They surrendered; and with the text before him Senator Philander C. Knox moved to separate the Covenant from the Treaty. Before the Treaty of Versailles reached the Senate in official form most of the senators were firm in the convictions which ruled them through the next nine months.

The course of the Peace Conference, from the delivery of the draft until the end of June, prolonged the period in which Europe might fall apart and American lines of thought might be frozen. The President found time to visit in Belgium, to receive the crew of the NC-4 and their less successful associates, and to give an appointment to the hopeful deputation of the Irish Race Convention a few days before de Valera appeared openly in New York. The leaders gave part of their time to the consideration of the secondary Treaty of St. Germain. The Austrian delegation was admitted to that conference on May 15. Austria was broken up before its conference met, for Hungary had withdrawn and the Allies had recognized Czechoslovakia and Yugoslavia while the war was on. The leaders listened to German complaints upon details of the draft treaty, but handed back the same printed text with only red-ink modifications on the margins. They ignored the German protest that the Treaty would be one of violence and not of justice. They fixed tentative dates for the final ceremony of signing, meanwhile the Weimar government, having no alternative but to sign, hunted for a deputation the members of which would be willing to place their names upon the Treaty. American divisions sailed west across the Atlantic, and Foch held his forces in readiness for a possible breakdown of negotiations. When they finally decided to sign, the Germans scuttled their captive fleet at Scapa Flow. At last, on Saturday, June 28, 1919, the Peace Conference concluded its work. That night the Wilsons took the train for Brest, and on Sunday afternoon the *George Washington* put out to sea.

The termination of the Peace Conference also brought to an end the mysterious close association of President Wilson and Colonel E. M. House. House traveled with his chief to Brest and never had a chance to speak to him again. Nine years later he wrote to the editor of his papers: "My separation from Woodrow Wilson was and is to me a tragic mystery, a mystery that now can never be dispelled, for its explanation lies buried with him. . . . Until a shadow fell between us I never had a more considerate friend, and my devotion to his memory remains and will remain unchanged." Their contact ceased, their correspondence dwindled, and no word from Woodrow Wilson offered an explanation.

The peace mission of the President ended when the *George Washington* docked at Hoboken on July 8. Perhaps he came back a changed man; certainly he landed in a country which had changed since March, and which had even then changed since November when the Armistice was signed. When he reached home, Hiram Johnson was thundering in Faneuil Hall against the Treaty which the President carried. He delivered the document formally to the Senate at an open session, on Thursday, July 10.

The tactics of the Senate were the tactics of the Committee on Foreign Relations, guided by the firm hand of Henry Cabot Lodge. When the new Congress filled the vacancies in its committees, and shifted the control to match the new majority, the seventeen members of the Committee on Foreign Relations included seven Democrats. Among the ten Republicans were eight whose names were attached to the Knox-Lodge manifesto of March 3, and a ninth who, being away, had wired to have his name appended. Five of the committee were irreconcilable, and could count on consistent support from the fourteen senators whom they represented: Borah, Brandegee, Fernald, France, Gronna, Johnson (Cal.), Knox, La Follette, McCormick, Moses, Norris, Poindexter, Sherman, and a single Democrat, Reed of Missouri.

Long before the Treaty was ready, Lodge had conferred with Borah, "the original irreconcilable," as Claudius O. Johnson has described him in *Borah of Idaho* (1936). They were in disagreement. Lodge professed that it might be amended so as to be safe; Borah rejected it. They agreed that the thirty-three votes necessary to defeat it in a full Senate, were not available, and that they had a common interest in prolonging discussion until opinion might change. To this end, Borah agreed to direct the votes of senators who thought with him into support of such amendments or reservations as should be presented, so long as the Treaty was merely under consideration and not up for final consent. He retained for them the right to vote against the Treaty, though supporting modifications to improve it.

Lodge knew the treaty process, and was aware that any amendment to the text of the document would make it necessary to re-submit it to the whole group of signatory powers and to the enemy, which was substantially the same as a rejection. But he saw the tactical value of considering all suggested changes in full, or giving free hearing to all who criticized, of using ample discussion as a means of spreading doubt, and of putting off the final vote. So far as consent was concerned, if a two-thirds vote should survive the debate, he accepted the method of reservation as sufficient; for a reservation stated at the time of exchanging ratifications would safeguard the American interpretation of the meaning of the Treaty, and would be as good as an amendment unless some other signatory should challenge it. He was not an irreconcilable, but unless he could attach reservations to the Treaty of Versailles he preferred to have no treaty. He told Borah that "The great mass of the people did not understand the treaty at all . . . [They want] peace as quickly as possible. The . . . vocal classes of the community [clergymen, educators, editors, public speakers, and writers] were friendly to the League as it stood and were advocating it." Lodge and Borah agreed that time, group interest, racial affection, and diversion owing to other lines of thought, might work a change. The Committee on Foreign Relations received the Treaty on July 10, had an English text ready on July 14, and began to hold public hearings on the last day of the month.

Two days earlier, the President had laid before the Senate the brief treaty of protection with which the demand of France for security had been met. This promised that the United States would come "immediately" to the assistance of France, "in the event of any unprovoked movement of aggression against her being made by Germany." The Treaty of Versailles included stipulations designed to demilitarize the left bank of the Rhine, over which any German attack on France must pass. England and the United States, "in similar terms," had through their leaders agreed to insure France against attack, and to implement the demilitarization.

The Treaty was reported back to the Senate two months to the day after Wilson had delivered it, two months of a summer in which disturbing events drew the attention of the friends of the League to matters of more immediate concern, but during which those who opposed it fought desperately to get their case on record. For more than half the time, July 31–September 5, the committee members kept up their quorum and sat through hearings in which the bulk of the testimony was adverse. The hearings began with Bernard M. Baruch, an economic adviser of the Peace Conference, on the stand. They ended, in a special delayed sitting after the Treaty had been reported back, with William C. Bullitt giving his version of a mission to Russia which brought dissatisfaction to him and to the President. The transcript of the hearings—1,297 pages in a Senate document—reveal the diligence with which the Treaty clauses were combed and the discontents were mobilized. In other meetings, crowded into the busy summer, the committee gave friendly attention to every suggested amendment, and to the points to which reservations to protect American interpretation might be applied. At the regular sittings of the Senate the flow of oratory continued, with the critics having every advantage over those who, supporting the President, could do little more than paraphrase him, as nearly as they understood him. There was no group of authoritative statesmen to expound the Treaty with a finality such as *The Federalist* had thrown into the debate over the ratification of the Constitution of the United States.

The testimony, and the accompanying documents laid before the committee, reviewed the debates in Paris, and the compromises made there in the interest of a Treaty which could be signed. The new states of middle Europe, all of which had their children among the citizenry of the United States, came in for attention: Estonia, Latvia, and Lithuania, along the Baltic; the new Poland with its corridor to the Baltic west of Danzig; Czechoslovakia, Hungary, and Yugoslavia farther south. Dependent communities, too, whose affairs had no business in the negotiations between the Allies and the enemy, received their hearing. The case of the Ukranians of America was presented, as well as that of India, Ireland, and of Negro populations in whatever country. The mystery of Soviet Russia was probed, and China told a long story of Japanese aggression.

Best organized among American groups with foreign interests were the Irish; completely assimilated in the United States, yet without having wavered in old affections or dislikes. On August 30 the committee heard Judge Daniel F. Cohalan of New York, whom Wilson had declined to receive at his meeting with the Irish delegation after his Metropolitan Opera House speech. Cohalan, speaking he said for the twenty million "of the Irish element," laid down the best-knit pattern for the opposition. They objected to the League because it was a superstate infringing upon the sovereignty of the United States, because it was an affront to the United States for England and the Dominions to have six votes when the United States had but one in the Assembly of the League, because the American doctrine of the freedom of the seas had not even been considered and England had been left in "control of the oceans of the world," because under Article X, freezing the boundaries, the

United States would be bound to support Britain and Japan in defending ill-gotten empires, and because England had a long record of brutal repression of the Irish. No Germans could have attacked "perfidious Albion" with greater bitterness; but the Germans in the United States, more than eight million of German birth or parentage by census count, were in no position to make a formal case. The German-American Alliance had been liquidated early in the war. Its successor with a safer name, the Steuben Society, though launched, had not yet gained authority.

The examination of the compromises made in Paris brought the committee into contact with the secret treaties made among the Allies before American entrance and in part maintained at the Peace Conference. It would have been useful to have been able to summon the President to explain every modification of a demand which he had proposed, but the committee had no authority to compel his presence. Wilson solved this deadlock by inviting the committee to visit him for "a frank and full exchange of views," and received the members at the White House on the morning of August 19. The conference was frank and full, but produced a mystery for which no convincing explanation has been found. The texts of the secret treaties were now generally known, released as they were by injured or revolutionary governments. Their secrecy suggested bad faith toward the United States, particularly bad if they had been concealed in April, 1917.

It was Senator Johnson who asked the key questions. "Was the United States Government officially informed, at any time between the rupture of diplomatic relations with Germany and the signing of the armistice, of agreements made by the allied Governments in regard to the settlement of the war?" Wilson answered, "No; not so far as I know." Johnson asked again, listing the specific treaties: "of these did we (and when I say 'we' I mean you, Mr. President) have any knowledge prior to the conference at Paris?" And Wilson replied, "No, sir. I can confidently answer that 'No,' in regard to myself." The mystery arises from the fact that some of the agreements were commonly known to exist before American entry, some of the texts were printed before the Conference assembled, and the aims and commitments of the Allies had occasioned concern in Washington shortly after the declaration of war.

That Wilson could have meant only a technical official knowledge would have been a frivolous evasion; that he was completely uninformed runs counter to abundant testimony; yet he said and repeated "No." It is as difficult to believe that he went to Paris in the dark as it is to believe that he should have told an obvious untruth. Those who believe in the essential honesty of the President remain baffled; but those who were fighting him added dishonesty and evasion to the other crimes which they alleged. In every case where he had permitted a compromise, the opposition insisted that he had betrayed someone. It was the power of the League to correct mistakes which had reconciled him to the compromises which the moment had forced upon him. Only a reckless and partisan opposition could have assumed that it was in his power to dictate a peace to the world.

In the discussion of the Treaty the fourteen irreconcilables led the attack. They were tough and experienced fighters, and some of them gloried in combat. Although they were far apart on other matters (as Borah, Johnson, and La Follette were from Brandegee, Knox, and Moses), they were in agreement as they labored to defeat consent. It had been intimated before Wilson left Paris that he might go to the country on the issue, and Joseph P. Tumulty, his devoted secretary, tells in *Woodrow Wilson As I Know Him* (1921) of the attempts to dissuade him. Wilson was stubborn in his belief that in spite of the political overturn of November, 1918, the matter was nonpartisan and that the people would compel their representatives to support his effort. Never a stalwart man, he was tired, but he felt he must explain to the people face to face the need for the Treaty, the necessity for keeping the League a part of it, and the virtues of the compact. He felt that the only Treaty which could be signed at all was one which all would sign and this was it. Talk of a speaking trip was resumed while the senators examined and dissected. It must be a western trip, for it was in the interior and beyond that the public seemed least convinced.

Lines were clearly drawn within the Senate before the open hearings on the Treaty were concluded. Approval would call for sixty-four assenting votes in a full Senate, making it obvious that the assent must be bipartisan. The forty-seven Democrats, even had they all agreed, were not enough. Only thirty-eight of them, as the final vote proved, were willing to ratify without condition. There were thirteen Republicans for whom nothing could make the Treaty acceptable. The remaining forty-five ranged from mild to harsh as they demanded amendments or reservations, yet twenty-seven of them must be brought into line. It was still uncertain whether the President would yield enough in the way of reservations to attract them. If he yielded nothing, the Treaty was already lost; if he could revive the 1918 enthusiasm for the League it might be saved.

Late in August Tumulty released the itinerary of the President, and the irreconcilables announced that some of them would trail the presidential train to combat his arguments. The West Coast was his objective, where dates had been arranged in the state of Hiram Johnson, whose friends had already announced him as a candidate for the presidency. Wilson expounded the Treaty as the train rolled west. At Columbus, where he spoke the first day out of Washington on September 4, he tried to clarify the issue and to persuade his listeners to press their senators to ratify the Treaty.

Advancing west from Indianapolis, Wilson spoke in St. Louis and Kansas City, the home country of his chief Democratic opponent, James A. Reed. Swinging north through Des Moines, Sioux Falls, and Omaha, on his way to St. Paul, he defied the "pro-German element" which had again "lifted its head." As he proceeded to Bismarck and Mandan the Treaty was reported to the Senate, the Boston police went on strike, and the steel strike was called; and behind him, Borah, Johnson, and McCormick were at work. At Billings, Montana, where the I.W.W. was a fighting subject, he warned radicals to be orderly, denounced the "apostles of Lenin in our midst," and informed the Boston police of their duty. Spokane, Tacoma, and Seattle were among his stops, and at the last he was taken aboard the old *Oregon*, whence he reviewed the Pacific fleet. He had been delayed too long to receive it at San Diego after its passage of the canal. In Portland he cited Lodge's reversal of opinion on a League. In San Francisco on September 17 he was beginning to curtail the elaborate programs which local committees had loaded upon him, but here he explained the Shantung settlement for the benefit of Johnson, and Ireland for Phelan. After Oakland, he spoke in San Diego, quoting Theodore Roosevelt, who had once like Lodge advocated a league; and here he had the novel experience of using an amplifier (defective) in the stadium. After Los Angeles, where it was not yet the custom to decorate the stage with movie stars, he headed back through Sacramento to Reno, Salt Lake City, Cheyenne, and Denver.

His audiences were large and cordial, as cordial as they always are to a president, and as little indicative of frame of mind. Any president is a spectacle wherever he appears, whatever he has to say. The wrecking squad had similar audiences with similar and equally unmeasurable enthusiasm. Out of Denver, Wilson paused at Pueblo to deliver the fortieth speech of his campaign. He returned to his train, weary and in discomfort, and that night, en route to his next stop at Wichita, he collapsed. Admiral Grayson, his physician, who had deprecated the trip and who had watched his every movement, reported him to be nervously exhausted, canceled the itinerary, and brought an invalid back to the White House as fast as the train could move. David Lawrence, who was among the correspondents, believed that the western speeches were Wilson's best work, but that they missed their influence upon the East because the difference in time made it impossible to report many of them completely in the eastern morning papers. Whatever their influence Woodrow Wilson's work was substantially done.

For the remaining months of his term in office the President was in varying degrees an invalid. The White House physician kept close watch at the door of the sickroom, while Mrs. Wilson guarded her husband. Tumulty had only limited access to his chief. Occasional visitors were permitted entry. King Albert of the Belgians saw him for a few minutes, as did the young Prince of Wales. Even a delegation from the Senate, Hitchcock and Fall, sent to see how sick Wilson really was. Fall is said to have prayed for him. Lansing, chief of the Cabinet, ventured to assemble his associates to discuss the course which they might follow during the President's absence from the conference room. The degree to which Wilson was able to discharge his powers and duties was much questioned though never formally challenged; yet of necessity what came to his attention was less than what gravely needed his attention and full power. "I, myself, never made a single decision regarding the disposition of public affairs," wrote Mrs. Wilson. "The only decision that was mine was what was important and what was not, and the *very* important decision of when to present matters to my husband."

The Senate, "as in Committee of the Whole and in open executive session," was in the midst of eleven weeks of Treaty debate when the President was hurried back to Washington. It was indeed more nearly eleven months of such debate, for discussion had been endemic since the beginning of the year. During the two months while the Committee on Foreign Relations considered and revised, members of the committee had left the sittings to resume the consideration on the floor of the Senate. The flexible rules of the Senate, tolerating much in the way of eloquence, permitted comments on the Treaty to be interjected anywhere at the pleasure of a senator.

The committee, following the course drafted by its chairman, proposed forty-six textual amendments and four basic reservations when it reported the Treaty back to the Senate on September 10. It presented a volume of 542 pages as *Senate Document* 85, 66th Congress, 1st Session, with French and English texts on facing pages, and with the amendments in italic type. The reservations covered the right to withdraw from the League, a refusal to assume military obligations in connection with the guarantee expressed in Article X, an assertion of exclusive right in the determination of domestic questions, and a specific refusal to submit the Monroe Doctrine to arbitration. There was bitter argument in committee and on the floor over the necessity for these, with friends of the Treaty maintaining that the dangers alleged to justify the reservations did not exist. When the debate was transferred to the Senate the committee reserved its right to submit additional reservations as they might be needed, and exercised the right to add ten more before the final vote. The amendments, however, earnestly presented, were to have no chance of acceptance by the Senate, even by the mere majority vote which was all that was required to attach them to the Treaty. The two-thirds vote was necessary only for the final act of ratification; the modifications were considered "as in Committee of the Whole."

The forty-six proposed amendments were less impressive than their number suggested, although they changed the whole nature of the League and the Treaty. Most of them were merely verbal, striking out "United States" where it was named as functioning on committees and "Associated Nations" where the term was used. Those which were substantial played up, for the purpose of display, the possible costs of participation in an effective League. They were "the work of Senators organized for the purpose of destroying the league and, if possible, defeating the treaty," complained the Democratic minority members in a dissenting report. What the opponents failed to do in belittling the compact was done for them outside the Capitol. Hearst's New York *American* jested editorially at the "constitution of the league of nations. . . . Properly toasted and shredded . . . it would be an invaluable food for infants . . . carefully diluted with flour paste and insect powder, it would create havoc with cockroaches . . . it would infallibly check the ravages of bedbugs . . . it would baffle the most-determined and blood-thirsty cootie."

The first of the proposed amendments had teeth. No detail of the Covenant stirred the racial groups in the United States so profoundly as the voting privilege accorded to the members of the British Empire. That empire was passing through basic change in a long process, well-indicated by David Lloyd George, when he described George Washington as the "founder of the modern British Empire." It had reached the point at which Britain had been forced to recognize the self-governing dominions as constitutionally independent. The Covenant and the Treaty of Versailles recorded the development by assigning to each of the four dominions and to India a vote in the Assembly in addition to the vote of England. The first amendment proposed for the United States a voting strength equal to that of any power plus the Dominions which were members of the League. Critics insisted upon regarding the British Empire as a unit, however internally divided it might declare itself to be. The possibility that the independent states of Hejaz and Persia might be no more than additional votes in a British bloc added to the tactical strength of the amenders and to the bitterness of anti-British groups. There were half a dozen states in the Caribbean area which might as reasonably have been regarded as a bloc to be controlled by the United States.

The second proposed amendment reinforced the first. It provided that when a case should arise involving a member whose dominions were also represented in the Assembly, neither the "disputant member" nor its dominions should have a vote.

A group of six amendments (39–44) reflected the dissatisfaction respecting the Shantung settlement. No part of the Treaty, indeed, had dissatisfied the President more than this; and he had yielded his objection only upon the pledge of Japan that, once its face was saved, it would of its own initiative withdraw from Shantung. The Treaty provided for German renunciation of its rights relating to Kiaochow and the Province of Shantung, and their transferral to Japan. The amendments substituted China for Japan.

As the debates proceeded, there came a flow of proposed additional amendments to the Treaty and to the committee reservations. Individual senators, like lawyers in court, argued their points and filed their objections in the form of amendments. These came alike from irreconcilables and from senators who were willing to accept the Treaty as it stood. The opponents, by their speeches and their amendments, showed that they understood delaying tactics and the temper of groups among their constituents better than the historical background of the situations to which the Treaty clauses related.

In October, with no cessation of the debate in sight, Lodge brought the committee amendments to a vote. On October 2 the roll was called on the first of the nearly forty textual corrections which bore the name of Senator Fall. The tenor of these was the separation of the name of the United States from the commissions created in the Treaty. Each of Fall's proposals failed of a majority, and after roll calls on a few the remaining ones were rejected viva voce. On the first vote there were thirty yeas, fifty-eight nays, and eight not voting (paired or absent). The thirty yeas included some of the Republican reservationists, grouped around twelve of the thirteen Republican irreconcilables; but nearly a score of Republicans joined the Democratic supporters of the Treaty in rejecting the amendment. There were not enough votes available for a rejection of the Treaty.

Senator La Follette closed the debate on the six Shantung amendments, which reached a vote on October 16. He denounced the "rape of China," and the Treaty for countenancing it and promised: "Adopt this amendment and the moral power of that act alone will compel Great Britain, France, and Italy to reconsider ratification of this treaty." Hiram Johnson had supported the amendments; as did George W. Norris (whose shift from the first Roosevelt to the second has been documented in Richard L. Neuberger, *Integrity: The Life of George W. Norris* (1937). Norris was one of the "little group of willful men" and one of the six senators to vote against the declaration of war. He justified his vote: "I am going to cast . . . every possible vote that I can cast anywhere along the line in the hope of defeating" the Treaty. Borah, too, had defended himself against the charge of inconsistency in voting to amend a document in order to destroy it. Brandegee and Knox were among the supporters of the Shantung amendments, which were lost by a vote of fifty-five to thirty-five.

Johnson's own amendment, number one on the committee list, was rejected October 27 by a vote of forty to thirty-eight. A number of Democrats who would have joined in the negative were caught napping. It was repeatedly pointed out by senators who voted "no" that they were in sympathy with the end sought but believed that procedure through reservation was the only way to reach it and yet save the Treaty. Two days later the Moses amendment, number two on the committee list, was defeated by a vote of forty-seven to thirty-six, with a dozen of the Republican irreconcilables still holding together for the affirmative. This was the last of the committee amendments and, all of them having been rejected, Lodge announced that the Treaty was now open to amendments to be offered by individual senators. These were offered and debated, and continued to increase in number, until on November 6 the chairman of the Committee on Foreign Relations presented to the Senate the committee resolution on ratification, now carrying fifteen instead of the original four reservations. As amendments had been rejected the committee had drafted new reservations to accomplish the same result by a different process.

The discussion and voting on the reservations continued until November 18. Only two of the committee proposals failed to pass; three were added from the floor. In the voting, still in Committee of the Whole, the full Republican membership of the Senate was generally brought together, reservationists voting "yes" because they wished the Treaty to pass, irreconcilables voting with them to make the Treaty more obnoxious to Democratic senators. A few of the latter showed no sign of willingness to end the debate, and the more intent of the irreconcilables never reached the end of their objection. Twelve of the irreconcilables and four Treaty friends made up the sixteen votes which were overridden by seventy-eight senators to force an end.

The cloture, written as the twenty-second rule of the Senate, after the "willful men" of 1917 had outraged the Senate and the country by their opposition to the armed ship bill, permitted sixteen petitioners to force a vote to stop debate on any pending measure. Upon filing of a cloture petition it became mandatory on the next day but one to call the roll. Upon approval of the petition, a limited debate under the five-minute rule was all that could postpone final action on the pending business. The cloture in this case —now invoked for the first time—was filed in the Senate November 13 and carried on November 15. On the following Wednesday, November 19, the vote was taken with McCumber, the lone Republican willing to approve the Treaty as signed, saying the last word. During the debate on that last day a letter from the President to Gilbert M. Hitchcock, Democratic manager of the Treaty, was read to the Senate. The President did not hesitate to say that the Lodge resolution with its "many reservations . . . does not provide for ratification but, rather, for the nullification of the treaty. I sincerely hope that the friends and supporters of the treaty will vote against the Lodge resolution of ratification." The party bond was strong. Only five Democrats broke away from compliance with the wish of the chief to join thirty-four Republican reservationists in voting "yes." Ratification was prevented by the junction of forty-two Democrats and the thirteen Republican irreconcilables. On a second vote, on a Hitchcock resolution with five reservations, the same thirteen joined thirty-eight Democrats to make up the fifty-one who outnumbered forty-one reservationists. And on a third and final test, for ratification of the Treaty as signed, fifty-three negative votes cast by the thirteen, the Republican reservationists, and seven Democrats, swamped the thirty-eight affirmatives. It is unusual to have a matter of admitted partisan character in which the lines of party are drawn more sharply than they were drawn at this time.

Human motive is hard to measure or to prove; even harder when humans have stated it at length. The tactics of Senator Lodge were successful in preventing the ratification of the Treaty which Wilson brought back from Paris. The tactics of the irreconcilables were successful in preventing ratification in any form. Whether Lodge really desired to engineer defeat, or could have been satisfied with any reservations acceptable to the White House, cannot be proved. He at least succeeded in steering his narrow and divided Republican majority through the long debate and in keeping it together on the final vote.

The special session of the Sixty-sixth Congress adjourned immediately after ratification of the Treaty was prevented, and members took comfort in a brief recess before the opening of the regular session on December 1, 1919. The Treaty, not yet killed, remained in the hands of the Committee on Foreign Relations subject to such positive action as the committee or the Senate might later take. It was not yet killed among the members, for a majority of them wished for some sort of treaty and some sort of league, and the opponents wanted to make it clear that the Democrats and the President were responsible for its failure. Although the peace arrangement did not dominate American minds as the war had done, or as the League had done in 1918, the vocal sections of the population were largely for it.

When the Congress reassembled a formula of compromise was sought by moderate men in both parties, a compromise so generally acceptable that the irreconcilables could not block it. A bipartisan conference labored informally through January, finding the same old stumbling blocks at Article X, the Monroe Doctrine, and the equality of voting in the League, and finding no way to bring Lodge and the sick President together on a reservation. On February 10 the committee again reported the Treaty to the Senate. New reservations were drafted in the Committee of the Whole, and a new resolution of ratification was prepared for submission to the Senate. It was defeated on March 19, 1920, by a vote of forty-nine to thirty-five. It would have taken a shift of seven votes to have met the constitutional requirement of two-thirds. This time the failure was final. Upon motion of Lodge the return of the proposed Treaty to the President was ordered.

The Congress turned its attention to matters of domestic business, long interrupted by the debate. The case of Truman H. Newberry on trial in federal court for corrupt practices in the Michigan primary of 1918, had just gone to the jury at Grand Rapids. General Leonard Wood was taking leave of absence from the army to be an active candidate for presidential nomination in 1920. A new railroad law had aggravated controversy instead of silencing it. Reducing the armed forces to a peace basis could no longer be put off. And the United States, sixteen months after the signing of the Armistice, was still at war with Germany.

Chapter VIII ★ Dead Center Government

MEASURES DESIGNED to bring about an orderly demobilization had failed of passage in the lame duck session of 1918–1919 when for the last time the Democratic party was in full control of the machinery of government. They were avoided again during the special session of the Sixty-sixth Congress when the government found itself on dead center.

Even when a dominant party has continuous control of the legislative agencies, the different terms of president, senator, and representative create different forms of political responsibilities for each. Once elected, they must strive to be reëlected. They may not disregard either the temper of the party which put them in office, or the changing temper as revealed when the next elections approach. There are always some in office who no longer fairly represent their constituents, some whose constituents have not yet arrived at an approval of their views. There is always, under the best of conditions, some inexactness in translating the will of the people into action.

When, however, the drift of public desire takes the control of one or both of the houses of the Congress away from the party of the president, the ability of president, senator, and representative to carry out the will of the people is gravely impaired. Under this condition, which grew more apparent after William McKinley and Marcus A. Hanna took over the organization of the Republican party at the turn of the century, the United States became politically impotent unless led by a president with power of imagination and a gift for making his ideas clear to the average voter and with organized congressional votes marshaled behind him. Wood-

[124]

row Wilson still possessed the imagination when the Sixty-sixth Congress met. Through the failure of his health his power to interpret and persuade was blunted. Upon the loss of the control of Congress, his ability to implement either imagination or persuasion had been taken from him.

This condition of dead center lasted through the life of the Sixty-sixth Congress, 1919–1921. The protracted fight over the Treaty of Versailles diverted duty from the ordinary business of the government, and the conflicting problems of 1919 pressed until they crowded the Treaty into a place of secondary importance in the public mind. The special session of 1919 did little more than the lame duck session had done to break the force of impact, as the United States passed from combat into peace. The regular session, beginning in November, 1919, did less than was needed; and the impending presidential election of 1920 threw the Republican Congress into partisan opposition to the Democratic President.

If information had been all that was needed for the development of an American policy the task imposed upon the dead-center government would have been lighter. Few subjects of debate have been covered more thoroughly than the Treaty was covered by the combined efforts of the Congress, the private agencies which were lined up on one side or the other, and the press. Fact and fiction as well as hope and fear were displayed and argued, without developing a commanding opinion in favor of ratification. The agencies of propaganda were better served than they had ever been.

The coverage of the debate by the press was thorough and reached all the levels of society. The old *Nation* and the young *New Republic* agreed, though for different reasons, that no treaty at all was better than the only one at hand, and the latter thought that the country was too wearied by debate to care. The New York *Times* consistently supported it, the *Christian Science Monitor* was hesitant. The Hearst papers and the Chicago *Tribune* played up to the fullest every line of opposition. Conservative and radical opinion not agreeing which was which, had fought it out. Just before the special session met the *Review* entered the arena, founded, its prospectus said, "to combat unthinking radicalism," and selecting the *Nation* and the *New Republic* as the worst offenders. A year later, from the other wing, came the *Freeman*, aiming while it lasted "to sweeten radicalism with wit and irony." These periodicals and newspapers enlivened the debate and helped to prevent it from reaching a conclusion.

In the field of the dailies, coverage of the news improved and special correspondents increasingly supplemented the service of the press associations. The last of the great independent editors, Henry Watterson, chose this moment in *"Marse Henry"; An Autobiography* (1919) to protest against "the timorous, corporation, or family owned billboard of such news as the ever-lasting censorship of a constantly centralizing Federal Government will allow." And Upton Sinclair, who had made a novel, *The Jungle* (1906), do political work at the crest of the muckraking era, tried again in *The Brass Check* (1919), whose shaft he directed at the press.

The newspaper as an industry had become more powerful as it improved in the collection of the news. It had worked economies by merging. The afternoon issues had grown in influence, in the advertising fields at least, because of the wide reading received by the home-read paper. The battlefields of the World War were conveniently placed geographically for the afternoon papers because the difference in time enabled them to print much European news the day it happened. The morning-evening combination became common, whereas many morning papers were strangled or bought and scrapped. Frank A. Munsey, who had extinguished the Dana tradition when he bought the New York *Sun* in 1916, extinguished that of the Bennetts when he acquired the *Herald* early in 1920. "Dealer in Dailies," Oswald G. Villard called him. Speaking more specifically the "sage of Emporia," William Allen White, stated that Munsey "contributed to the journalism of his day the talent of a meat packer, the morals of a money changer and the manners of an undertaker." The elder Scripps had almost completed the linking of his chain of minor papers and Roy W. Howard was preparing to take over the management. William Randolph Hearst, building his castle at San Simeon, was still engaged in adding titles to his list. One of the McCormick kin, Joseph Medill Patterson, broke away from the offices of the Chicago *Tribune* to invade New York with a new experiment in journalism. After running a publicity competition to find "the most beautiful girl in Greater New York," he brought out the first issue of the first great tabloid, the

Illustrated Daily News in June, 1919. If its buyers could not read they could at least look at the pictures, and the page was small enough to be handled in a crowded subway train. The tabloid carried a threat to urban newspapers, and a promise of profits which soon brought into publication the *Daily Mirror* and the *Daily Graphic*.

The American reader, bombarded by editions of newspapers, was softened up for the less frequent attack of the periodical press. Before the Sixty-sixth Congress adjourned the twenty-nine leading monthlies and the seven principal weeklies (excluding those having a circulation of less than a mere half million) were distributing some fifty-six million copies a month. They aimed at every class able to read and with a nickel or dime to spend. Topping the lists in both monthly and weekly fields was the output of the editorial genius of Cyrus H. K. Curtis, whose *Ladies Home Journal* and *Saturday Evening Post* sold more than ten million copies every month. Curtis' right-hand man told his personal story in *The Americanization of Edward Bok. An Autobiography* (1920), and prepared a life of his chief in *A Man from Maine* (1923). Curtis had acquired the Philadelphia *Public Ledger* in 1913, and was to add the New York *Evening Post* in 1923.

Servants of the public, as the publishers proudly claimed to be, they did not fail to serve themselves. They were faced in 1919 with a new postal law which threatened an old subsidy. Congress had in 1885, because of the educational value of the press, granted the papers a flat postage rate of one cent a pound. The war revenue act of 1917 had modified this rate, under pressure for greater revenue and egged on by the rural and local press which claimed that the generous rate discriminated in favor of the great urban issues. A system of zone postage was substituted for the flat rate. The publishers, attacking with their American Periodical Publishers Association as spearhead, opposed the new system, and in their fight they confused freedom of the press which sheltered them and the privilege of having their product delivered by the government below cost. They were similarly sensitive to suggestions of customs duties on pulp and print paper, for the timber stands of Canada had become a principle source of their supply.

There was plenty of information passing from press to people, and presented more accurately and promptly than ever before. By its very abundance, and its contradictions, it added to the difficulty of charting any course of action. The need of the press generally to live at peace with its community made it hard for the press to give fair treatment to proposals which seemed likely to make the community suffer for the sake of a broader public advantage. There were genuine doubts as to what constituted public advantage in nearly every important aspect of life.

The complexity of the problem, rising with the industrialization of the United States, and attacked by the leaders of the progressive movement in the early years of the century, was revealed with new clarity just as the partisan jam decreased the ability of the American government to function. The voters of Illinois, on election day 1919, chose delegates to sit in a convention to revise a state constitution which was badly out of date. Nebraska, still living under its "grasshopper" constitution of 1875, met in convention in December to revise it. In Pennsylvania a commission had sat through the year receiving proposals for change in the antiquated constitution of 1873. Massachusetts hoped and believed that it had made a revision when the voters approved the work of a convention in November.

The American method of continuous constitutional construction had bogged down. From the formulation of the first state constitutions in the revolutionary period until the completion of the statehood process by the admission of Arizona in 1913 each state had framed its basic law, and enough had remade them to suit new conditions, to build up a list of nearly one hundred and fifty constitutions which provide a documentary basis for the history of American political ideas. The attempts which had failed of ratification raise the total number a score or more.

With the shift in demands following the growth of industry and transportation, concern for social welfare, emergence of corporations, and zeal for the bill of rights, the framing of new constitutions had become more experimental and ratification had faced new hazards. In the autumn of 1919, fearful lest the Constitution of the United States be endangered by new ideas, and alarmed by social-economic ferment, the National Security League had insti-

tuted Constitution Day (September 17) to commemorate the signing. Careful-minded conservatives were already in the habit of
voting "no" on principle when new constitutions were brought
up, thereby adding their votes to those of groups with special
grievances.

In recent years New York had drafted a new fundamental law
in a convention under the presidency of Elihu Root, and aided by
the deep understanding of Alfred E. Smith. The people had rejected its work in 1915. Massachusetts had sought to evade the
rejection by offering a long series of amendments, each to be voted
on separately; and each proved to command an adequate majority.
The old constitution, as modified by amendments, was approved
in 1919, only to be set aside by the Massachusetts courts. The Pennsylvania commission received suggestions, drafted a proposed constitution incorporating them, submitted the proposal in the form
of a referendum in 1921 on the calling of a formal convention to
act upon the draft, and the people rejected it. The Illinois convention met early in 1920, sat through two years in which it discovered
the craving for power of Chicago challenged by the jealousy of
down-state Illinois, and submitted its work in 1922 only to have it
rejected. Nebraska, proceeding by the method of separate amendments, gained acceptance for a revision. The clash of hopes and
interests which was making the modernization of state constitutions nearly impossible permeated the United States at every legal
level.

The United States went dry, in law at least, before the Treaty
reached the Senate. The prohibition amendment to the Constitution, ratified in January, 1919, was to become operative in January,
1920. The war laws, meanwhile, for the avowed purposes of conservation, had stopped distilling, brewing, and the importation of
alcoholic beverages, the last of the restrictions becoming operative
on July 1, 1919. The new amendment provided that the Congress
and the several states should have "concurrent power to enforce"
it, but none had as yet explained the full bearing of this concurrence, and no federal law as yet enforced prohibition under either
the war laws or constitutional prohibition when it should arrive.
An Association for the Repeal of the Eighteenth Amendment had
already acquired a letterhead.

Quite as difficult as the matter of enforcement was that of de-
fining the "intoxicating liquors" at which the amendment was
aimed. Police departments had of necessity developed rule-of-
thumb definitions in dealing with drunks, but there was nothing
resembling medical or scientific exactitude by which might be established the percentage of alcoholic content which the law should
permit as nonintoxicating. To implement the laws, and to please
those for whom prohibition had been a great crusade, an enforcement bill was brought into Congress by a Minnesota Representative, Andrew J. Volstead. His act construed "alcoholic" as one half
of one per cent by volume, and vested investigation and report in
the Bureau of Internal Revenue in the Treasury. It was made the
duty of the Attorney General to prosecute offenders under the
amendment. The House passed the Volstead act by nearly three to
one in July. It was accepted by the Senate in September without a
record vote. And in October it penetrated the sick room where the
President was permitted to do a little work. A sharp veto message
of October 27, 1919, protested against the inclusion in one bill of
provision for enforcing wartime prohibition, which was temporary,
and constitutional prohibition, which was not yet operative. The
Volstead act was immediately passed over the veto, and in the next
spring the Supreme Court found no difficulty in upholding the
constitutionality of the enforcement act.

If prohibition and its enforcement were contentious and experimental, so was every other proposal which aimed at a new pattern
and involved change. Proponents with a vision, unchastened by the
facts of experience, were more insistent than they had a right to be.
Opponents, with either honest principle or personal interest at
stake, were disposed to overestimate both novelty and inconvenience. The matter of a permanent railroad policy continued to
face the government.

McAdoo, busy and competent, had made an emergency administration for the railroad system, and upon retiring from government
service had recommended a five-year experiment with government
management in time of peace. The investors in railroad securities
had different ideas, as had both the operating officials and the railroad unions. The public listened to a debate in which the advocates
of national ownership or operation were confronted by conserva-

tive thought to which the mere name of socialism was an irritant. The states were sensitive lest they lose their right to control and to tax. In the President's last word with Congress before he sailed for Europe in December, 1918, he had left the railroad policy with the people: "I have no confident judgment of my own." A year later he had gone no farther than a decision to exercise his privilege under the act governing the use of the roads in time of war. In a proclamation issued December 24, 1919, he returned the lines to their owners, effective March 1, 1920. If anything was to be done about a policy, Congress must initiate it.

The return of the Republicans to power had elevated to the leadership of the committees on interstate commerce Representative John J. Esch of Wisconsin, and Senator Albert B. Cummins of Iowa. Both had been seasoned through the Progressive movement and both came from the region where the railroads had been continuously distrusted since the Granger movement of the 'seventies. They and their committees listened through the summer of 1919 to suggestion and argument. They were told that the Railroad Administration was both a huge success and a total failure; that the railroads had been nearly bankrupt in 1917, yet rich enough to carry heavy taxes; that government ownership was a logical next step, and that it was a denial of private initiative. They might have agreed with the President, who had not seen "any general scheme of 'reconstruction' which I thought it likely we could force our spirited businessmen and self-reliant laborers to accept with due pliancy and obedience." In midsummer they were faced with the demand of railroad labor for a share in management and profits in accordance with the Plumb plan. It was Esch whose committee bill began to receive serious consideration in November and Cummins whose modifications of the bill in the Senate sent the measure to conference in February, with each day bringing the deadline of return nearer. The conference report was debated in the presence of threats that labor would punish at the polls those who voted for the measure, with Congress less responsive to the threat than "swayed by the situation as it exists on the outside," and indisposed to yield to radical demands.

The Esch-Cummins act, more formally known as the Transportation Act of 1920, was a compromise the terms of which left discontented groups on all sides. It vested in the Interstate Commerce Commission the positive power to initiate rates, which was an advance from the limited right to review rates made by the carriers; and steps were in the making for a valuation of railroad property to serve as a basis for reasonable rates. These plans contemplated a regrouping of the railroads in great systems with similar average earning capacity, and contained an assumption that any profits in excess of six per cent were excessive and were to be recaptured by the government for general railroad advantage. These provisions gave no satisfaction to the owner companies or to investors.

By discontinuing federal operation the act displeased those who were pressing for nationalization; and those who were impregnated with hostility to the operating companies saw in the six per cent maximum earnings a guarantee of six per cent which was not there. Labor was further embittered, not only by the disregard of the Plumb plan but by the continuance of adjustment machinery which had, during the war, been used to prevent interruption of service due to strikes. A Railroad Labor Board was created, with a membership spread among the workers, the operators, and the public, with appellate jurisdiction over labor disputes. It had no power to determine the dispute but only to display it before the public in the hope that public opinion might apply coercion where it was needed. Its jurisdiction stopped short of the power to compel, but it struck close enough to organized labor's cherished right to paralyze industry by the strike to leave labor in harsh opposition. Such as it was, it was passed through conference in time to receive the signature of the President on February 28, 1920, just one day before the period of federal administration ended.

Three days before the Esch-Townsend act became a law, the President put his name to a delayed measure of conservation which had been under intermittent discussion since Congress, in 1910, legalized the withdrawal from entry of public lands suspected of containing oil deposits. The somewhat arbitrary creation of national forests by Theodore Roosevelt, and the withholding of areas of mineral content from entry under the general laws, had emphasized the inadequacy of legislation governing the public lands.

From the first creation of the national domain the basic policy had been the transfer of title to citizen farmers in order to create new homes. The law had given little attention to the treatment of mineral lands, timber lands, and lands controlling water power. By a twisting of the homestead laws it had been possible for much nonagricultural acreage to pass into the hands of corporate exploiters. In spite of the efforts at conservation, the law had not caught up with the fact, which was that substantially all of the public domain suited for development by the standard farmer had passed out of the ownership of the public before the conservation movement was inaugurated. In 1910 Congress had legalized the reservation of the oil lands, as the navy turned from coal burners to oil burners, but general legislation to regulate the remaining national resources in the public interest had lagged. The lagging had been encouraged by honest doubt respecting wise policy as well as by the hearty opposition of those for whom the twisting of the intent of the homestead laws had been profitable. This was the decade in which the exploitation of minerals, oil, and water power had become big business. The need for regulation, and the fight against it, had developed with the years.

The new law, dealing specifically with public lands containing coal, phosphate, oil, gas, and sodium, placed this public property under the control of the Interior Department, subject to leasing for private development. The naval oil reserves were left under the Secretary of the Navy, since the theory of the moment was that this oil had better remain in underground, natural storage until necessity should call it forth.

The same pattern of conservation was to be found in the problem of water, newly important because of the development of hydroelectric power. The United States had become an industrial nation largely on coal, the supply of which had passed easily into private hands. Oil and natural gas were now offering destructive competition to coal, and these untouched resources were in many cases concentrated in the public domain as property of the nation. The very roughness of terrain which removed the mountain West from agricultural use conserved the winter snow pack, so that the dammed flow-off could be stripped of its electric power as it fell to the sea, and yet be available for irrigation and civic use when it reached the bottom lands. Private initiative was increasingly active in seeking out sites where water could be impounded, and in acquiring title to adjacent land the ownership of which would permit the erection of the necessary dams and power houses. The owners of public utilities made common cause against community owner ship and public control, and the debate ran through as many years as the debate over the oil lands.

The extent of the federal interest in water power was as yet untested. Navigable streams fell naturally within federal jurisdiction; but it required high power of imagination to conceive of the mountain streams as navigable. Congress had, however, placed the control of navigable streams in the War Department, whose engineer officers directed the expenditure of public funds in the improvement of the Mississippi and Ohio rivers and in the control of floods. The annual rivers and harbors appropriation bill had become a federal "pork barrel," while Congress retained its direct control over bridges across navigable streams, passing special bills of authorization as they were demanded.

Nonnavigable streams were at the disposition of the owners of adjacent lands and thus outside the direct power of the United States except as owner. But within the public lands, where the government retained its title, Congress possessed the power to control the running water. Perhaps half the undeveloped water power thus fell within federal jurisdiction; of this, four-fifths flowing through the national forest had already been entrusted to the Department of Agriculture, whereas the remaining fifth fell to the Interior Department as custodian of the public lands. A Federal Water Power Commission was given control of federal water by an act passed in June, 1920, and the three Secretaries of War, Interior, and Agriculture were entrusted with the duty of preserving the public interest through the issuance of licenses to users.

The state of New York at once challenged the right of the government to intrude upon what it regarded as its own exclusive ownership of its half of the Niagara River. The seven states of the Southwest whose water was drained away by the Colorado River took steps to organize by compact or otherwise a unified beneficial control of the Colorado basin. That a river basin possesses an essential unity regardless of the acts of man in ascribing opposite banks to different states or private owners, was becoming clear. The Constitution makers had imagined a possible need for special arrangements when they authorized interstate compacts made with the consent of Congress; but a new chapter in the use of the authority was beginning to be written. Congress had in 1919 approved a New York-New Jersey agreement for the Hudson vehicular tunnel. The same states were now involved in the preliminary discussions respecting a joint control of the waters around Manhattan Island and along the Jersey shore, which were soon to bring forth in the Port of New York Authority a new type of American control which was not quite state, not quite federal, yet partook of both.

But these matters had been debated to the threshold of enactment even before the war and the government, though on dead center, found it possible to reach a compromise agreement on them. When it came to new business, planning for what the future might be expected to be, agreement was more difficult and decision was blurred by interest and politics, by fact and hope. In no range of action was policy more bewildering than in the field of national defense and self-sufficiency. Here the war had brought into existence a specific and temporary objective which was to win the war. There was left a huge army which must be reduced to a peacetime basis, a new naval program contemplating a navy "second to none" which was intended to be in commission by 1921, and a new merchant marine to ensure the carriage of American freight under the American flag. The time was not ripe in 1919 for decisions upon these matters. It was not yet ripe in 1920, but some sort of decision had to be reached before the appropriation bills could be passed.

The United States had used the Emergency Fleet Corporation as its agent to build the merchant ships and the War Trade Board to determine what the ships should carry and whither. The Treasury had borne the costs as a war measure, without reference to the ability of the ships to pay for themselves out of earnings. The procession of new cargo ships began to leave the yards where they were put together, about the time of the signing of the Armistice. Nineteen months had been too short a period to permit the selection of the sites, the designing and building of the yards, and the fabrication and fitting of the vessels. Too late to affect the service of the war, the ships were now tied up in long lines at safe anchorage. Unless they should prove useful enough to serve the peace they must be written off as total loss.

The emergency ships had been built to a pattern suited for quantity production, and were in many cases unfit for competition with ships specially designed for ordinary trade. Whoever should operate them must call upon the government for subsidy, for they were wasteful in design and made costly by prewar law. Their mere existence was so much a threat to private builders, who must pay their way, that they were a barrier to initiative. Business had impeded the authorization of their construction for two years after the emergency need arose in 1914; business was now hostile to their continued operation by the government.

If they should be manned and sent to sea, their labor conditions were not determined by free competition in an international carrying trade, but were forced to a pattern set up under labor pressure. Andrew Furuseth had made the improvement of the conditions of marine labor his lifework, and Congress had passed a regulatory law in 1915. This, the Alexander law, was indeed a charter of rights for the seamen, but it cured the disease by preventing employment since the costs of operation under the American flag were made prohibitive at a time when other nations held to competitive wages and the immemorial abuse of men who go to sea. The United States had, moreover, bound itself by commercial treaties which stood in the way of an effort to build a peacetime merchant marine by means of preferential legislation.

The business elements within the Republican party would gladly have knocked the ships down to the highest bidder, or scrapped them, and have the government withdraw from the business. With La Follette still in the Senate it was impracticable to pass any law interfering with the new rights of American seamen for the sake of profitable operation of ships. It was La Follette who had directed the drive for the seamen's act. To abrogate all commercial treaties so as to be free to discriminate against ships of foreign flags which would not comply with American standards would have thrown the whole business of foreign trade into confusion. But this abrogation was ordered by the Jones law, which was enacted in June, 1920, and in which a reorganized Shipping Board was continued in the experiment of federal operation. The President signed the law, but he flatly declined to abrogate, and challenged the right of Congress to force him to it. The war merchant fleet continued at its moorings to rust its way to the scrap pile, and the few which seemed likely to be self-supporting were only an ineffective gesture at a revived American merchant marine.

"The most serious trouble with the navy now, as it has been in the past, is Congress," said the New York *Times* as it commented in June, 1920, on the new appropriation bill which directed an interim reduction of naval strength. But it was the people, more specifically than the Congress, whose zeal for defense appropriations had cooled, and whose readiness for peace had been insufficient to force the ratification of the Treaty and the Covenant. Secretary Daniels had done his best to balance the need for a large navy against an effective league and to persuade Congress that the United States must choose between them. The Assistant Secretary, Franklin D. Roosevelt, had been persistent and persuasive before the committees, yet without converting the Congress.

The problem of the navy, apart from its relation to any new world order, was different from that of the army which could and did discharge its soldiers. Even if naval forces were demobilized, the vessels and the shore installations remained to be provided for. Their minimum custody implied a personnel larger than in the prewar past. The question of continuing upon the expansion program of 1916 was tied into the future of world organization, but the question of profiting by the lessons of the war and keeping the navy up to date called for an early answer.

The battleship, most impressive of naval units, was challenged on the surface, in the air, and under sea. After the Battle of Jutland it appeared that there was imperative need for a capital ship faster than the dreadnaught and as heavily armed, with the result that the preparedness act of 1916 made provision for six battle cruisers so designed, in addition to the ten new dreadnaughts. The submarine challenged the future of the battleship, though less convincingly than before convoy, destroyer escort, and mine barrage had lessened the effectiveness of the German undersea fleet. The advocates of air power were convinced that if they could have a chance to prove their case they could show how helpless any surface ship would be under air attack. In any new building program, or in the continuation of the program already on the statute books, the full weight of war experience needed to be measured. And among the minor devices there were many new ones to be tested before they could be either adopted or rejected. After the Civil War the United States had accepted the navy of 1865 as adequate, and had permitted it to rot without replacement until by the end of twenty years a new navy had to be built from scratch. The world of 1919 was unlikely to wait for a country to build its fleet before it fought.

Consideration of the navy appropriation act for 1919–1920 was begun while the outcome of the conference in Paris was still in doubt. The legislative deadlock of March, 1919, deferred the passage of the bill until the treaty session of the Sixty-sixth Congress was convened. It was still uncertain which of Daniels' alternative courses would be accepted, and every month made it less likely that either would command public or congressional support, meanwhile professional uncertainty as to relative values contributed to delay. Before going to Europe to inquire into the matter, Daniels discontinued work on the six battle cruisers in the spring of 1919. They had already been retarded, like the ten dreadnaughts and the ten light cruisers, by the pressure of other naval construction on the building yards. The earliest of the dreadnaughts, the *Maryland,* was not ready for commission until July, 1921; the *Omaha,* first of the cruisers, was delayed until February, 1923.

The navy funds for 1919–1920 had not been voted before the new fiscal year began on July 1, 1919. It was with difficulty that permission to continue work on the ships authorized in 1916 was kept in the bill, which restricted the enlisted navy personnel to an average of 201,000 for the year, but the act was at last ready for the President to sign the day after he delivered the Treaty to the Senate. Consideration of the bill for the following year, which was to become law on June 4, 1920, was colored by hostility to the administration and zeal for economy; and was obscured by preoccupation with treaty matters. It was affected also by uncertainties at technical points which could be alleged as excuse for delay or curtailment of the navy estimate. At the end, it was hurried into form by the desire of Congress to adjourn in time for the nominating conventions.

The Republican floor leader, Frank W. Mondell of Wyoming, declared when the bill was introduced that the committee had been "economical to the point of parsimony," and had curtailed the navy request by approximately one-third. The manager for the House, when he came to urge acceptance of the final conference report, providing 453 millions, apologized for the carefully restricted fund allowed for naval aviation. He admitted: "I know but little about [it] and I deal largely with it as I do with the sick and disabled people—rather lean toward its side in order that aviation may be developed." Daniels deplored the failure of the bill to meet his view of minimum needs, and regarded the studied neglect of aviation as a grave defect. He was disappointed at the absence of funds for shore bases on the Pacific, which had been the subject of serious navy inquiry. He lamented the failure to authorize any new ship, although provision had indeed been made for work on the ships actually under construction. He found that the appropriation was insufficient for the current maintenance and repair of such vessels as the navy must keep in active service. But Mondell had defended caution, because "nobody knows whether the capital ships . . . are going to be of any real value after they are built and paid for."

The army had demobilized four-fifths of its war strength before the appropriation for its support in 1919–1920 was made. More than three million men had been discharged. The seven hundred thousand who remained, seven times as many as were in uniform when the World War began in 1914, were more than the army was prepared to urge or Congress to permit to remain in the service. The decision upon future military policy was further hindered by cleavage of opinion within the army. Officers who had been kept in Washington, as they worked upon necessary amendments to the basic National Defense·Act of 1916, derived conclusions on size, organization, and overhead control from their experience in recruiting, training, and supplying the A.E.F. Their views did not coïncide with those of the officers who, with Pershing, had commanded forces in the field, and who were over-ready to assume a professional superiority. They had, indeed, seen combat. But too many of the best men in the regular army had been kept at home to permit an assumption that the brains of the army were overseas.

A minor complication, during the discussions of military policy, was the absence of Pershing, who did not reach Washington until after the appropriations for 1919–1920 were passed. This complication was not lessened when he was at last installed as General of the Armies in offices next to those of the Secretary of War. His rank too high for any duty except at the top, was also too great for any ordinary assignment in time of peace. It was with difficulty that the United States had in 1903 rid itself of the "General Commanding the Army," and channeled the command through the office of a Chief of Staff. The relations between the General of the Armies and the Chief of Staff, Peyton C. March, in 1919, were strained. There were more complications arising from Republican willingness to believe that Major General Leonard Wood, who had been kept at home, had been made a martyr to Democratic politics, and that officers and men of the National Guard had been victims of persecution by the West Point and War College clique.

Hope, rather than confidence, led many officers to believe that the United States would now, having abandoned the tradition of an army of volunteers, convert the Selective Service Act into a plan for compulsory military training in time of peace. Realists, however, worked for an arrangement in which a regular army of moderate size, supplemented by the National Guard, should in time of war be expanded by troops raised directly from civil life. Studies for a revision of the draft act, so that it should be ready for passage if another war should come, were begun at once in Washington. This was a problem different from that which concerned the size of the peacetime army, its relations to the National Guard, and the structure of the General Staff. A demand that the air services should be made an independent department vexed the planners in both army and navy.

The officers who had entered the army through the National Guard returned to civil life soured on the regular army. Through the American Legion and the National Guard Association they demanded status for the civilian soldier. Few of them had been allowed to rise above the rank of colonel. Few were qualified to rise higher; and many had been irked by duty under young officers of the regular army to whom war had brought a temporary promotion in rank. It was widely believed by members of the National Guard that they had been discriminated against, contrariwise officers of the regular army often thought and said that the National Guard was incompetent. The states had a legitimate concern in the status of the National Guard which, as their organized militia, had local duties in addition to those brought about by war. The whole membership of the National Guard, upon being mustered into the United States Army in 1917, lost connection with the states. Upon being discharged they did not revert to their former status, but became civilians. Until a new National Guard should be organized there would be none.

The War Department proceeded to the discussion of the appropriation for 1919–1920 hoping for authorization of a regular army of half a million. Opinion was divided on whether to re-create the National Guard or replace it with a federal reserve. The public was not greatly interested in either plan. The resulting appropriation was no more than an interim statute to provide for a period between demobilization and the adoption of a reorganization act. The National Guard was left in place, and new units were created under the old laws. There were funds for an average strength of about 325,000 in the regular army for the fiscal year; but the number in uniform on July 1 was so great that in order to keep to the average it must be reduced to about 225,000 by October 1, 1919. General March acted as soon as the tenor of the law was known, ordering slashing reduction in enlisted personnel and discharge of emergency officers during the next three months.

Hearings on the appropriation for 1920–1921 were held through the summer of 1919, and were as comprehensive as any American military problem had received. They uncovered the snags, functional and organizational, professional and amateur, until they revealed once more the great difficulty of reconciling the constitutional power of the states over the militia with the constitutional power of the United States to maintain an army. The reorganization act, signed June 4, 1920, was a compromise, as was the navy act of the same day, and the merchant marine act of the next day.

From the average of 325,000 for 1919–1920, the army was cut down to an average of 298,000 officers and men for 1920–1921. They were, except for the professional officers, to be generally new troops, for when the emergency soldiers were discharged it had been made possible for enlisted men of the regular army also to procure release. The General Staff proceeded to plan the distribution of the

reduced force so as to serve the need for garrison duty in the overseas possessions and yet retain something of an army in the United
States, rather than to make a list of assignments to duty at the several posts. "The old division of the country into territorial or
geographical departments was abandoned," the Secretary of War
later reported; and a tactical organization was created for the first
time. The United States was divided into nine corps areas serving
three tactical—if paper—armies whose headquarters were at Governor's Island, New York, the Presidio, San Francisco, and Fort Mc-
Pherson, near Atlanta, Georgia. It was planned that within each
corps area there should be maintained an army corps. There was
to be a regular army division, of as nearly full strength as possible,
present within each of the nine areas. The army corps was to include National Guard Divisions as they might be organized among
the states comprising each area. There was to be also a "paper"
reserve division staffed with reserve officers who should be ready to
take into the ranks the troops which emergency should summon.
Major General William G. Haan, chief of the War Plans Division,
described this scheme in September, 1920, as constituting a balanced peacetime force.

The balance might have come about if the next appropriation,
for 1921-1922, had not reduced the total by 50,000 men, and that
for 1922–1923 had not further cut it to 137,000. By the time the
army prepared to give public test of its plan for mobilization in
September, 1924, a National Council for the Prevention of War
was in arms against any military demonstration, church organizations resolved against it, and one of the governors who declined to
let his National Guard take part in the test denounced it "at a
time when all the people of the civilized nations of the world are
demanding reduction of armaments."

The shift in the direction of American opinion was felt strongly
as the Republican Congress clashed with the Democratic President
during the period of dead center government; and where clash prevented the passage of even compromise laws there was an open
deadlock. There was deadlock over reforms which were long due.
One of these called for the enactment of a federal budget system
whereby appropriation should be kept within income and it should
be made more difficult for irresponsible private schemes to be voted

without taxes to support them. As the Republican leaders worked it out the proposal called for an executive budget to be presented annually and to be constructed with reference to funds in sight. Expenditures should be watched by a new office, under a comptroller-general. The proposal called upon each house to rearrange its business and to channel appropriations through a single committee instead of permitting every committee to introduce them according to its desires. It had, in principle, the approval of President Wilson.

The budget bill was sent to the White House near the end of the session in 1920, to be returned with a veto by a regretful President. In a desire to protect the comptroller general against the president he was given a long term in office; but to maintain for Congress a control against the budget it was provided that he might be removed from office by a concurrent resolution, in which the signature of the president would not be needed. Wilson vetoed the bill on constitutional grounds, maintaining that the constitutional method of impeachment was designed for the use of Congress, and that under "the accepted construction of the Constitution . . . the power to appoint officers of this kind carries with it . . . the power to remove." The provision was an intrusion on the prerogative of the presidency, and Wilson was not too sick to safeguard his office.

Less friendly than the disagreement on the federal budget was the clash over peace. Upon the rejection of the Treaty on March 19 both houses had taken up the matter of the continuance of the legal state of war. The Treaty had been ratified by enough of its signers to become effective, and the Council of the League of Nations had been organized in January. The United States was still in the status which it had assumed on April 6, 1917. Senate and House differed upon the procedure for restoring peace without a treaty with the enemy, one preferring an affirmative statement that peace had superseded war, the other desiring merely to repeal the declaration. Toward the end of May Senator Knox worked out a form with which the House concurred, in which the United States repealed the declaration of war and asserted its right to all the advantages which would have accrued if it had ratified the Treaty of Versailles. It outraged the President who returned it with a veto on May 27. He disapproved it "because I cannot bring myself to become party to an action which would place ineffaceable strain upon the gallantry and honor of the United States." The peace which it would restore, he wrote, "ought to be inconceivable, as inconsistent with the dignity of the United States, with the rights and liberties of her citizens, and with the very fundamental conditions of civilization." Although a majority in each house favored peace by resolution, the two-thirds necessary to pass the Knox resolution over the veto were not available. The United States remained at war; and upon this note the session ended on Saturday, June 5, 1920.

As the Congress adjourned, President Wilson released to the press a comment on the session. "It must be evident to all," he said, "that the dominating motive which has actuated this Congress is political expediency rather than lofty purpose to serve the public welfare." He had long since declared that the approaching election should provide "a solemn referendum" upon the Treaty and the Covenant. The referendum was now at hand.

Chapter IX ★ The Solemn Referendum: 1920

T

HE DEBATE upon the Treaty and the pursuit of public duty in the dead center Congress were intricately snarled in party politics. As the session opened the Republican National Committee, shepherded by the ever cautious Will H. Hays, met in Washington on December 10, 1919 to select the time and place for the meeting of the National Convention in the following summer. A month later, January 8, 1920, the anniversary of Jackson Day brought the Democratic National Committee to Washington for a similar purpose. Both parties were troubled over candidate and platform, but both were obliged, as major parties always are, to enter the canvass with the candidates who could be nominated, and the platforms upon which agreement could be reached. The duty upon the party organization was to attract enough votes to carry the election.

Woodrow Wilson was not well enough to dine with his National Committee, or to address it. Instead, he wrote to Homer S. Cummings, the chairman, and called the tune. His mind, on January 8, was filled with the fight for a second vote on the treaty, with Republican insistence upon reservations, and with pressure from Democrats who hoped that he would yield enough in the matter of reservations to swing to the treaty the few marginal votes needed to ensure its acceptance. He was in no mood for a compromise on matters of moment. "We can not revise this treaty," he wrote. "We must take it . . . or leave it . . . If there is any doubt as to what the people of the country think on this vital matter, the clear and single way out is to . . . give the next election the form of a great and solemn referendum."

[145]

The proposal of the President cut sharply across the intention of the Republican organization to marshal every dissatisfied vote needed to make a majority in November. There were complications in both programs. For the party of the President it was fundamental that his Treaty and his Covenant be endorsed, for if the party denied this it would lose all hope of retaining the votes of nonpartisan advocates of the League. The opposition, however, could not hope to win if it lost the votes of either the Republican advocates of the League or the bitter irreconcilables. The campaign called for cautious management on both sides; and in the end the presidential election was turned into the conventional channel, where it provided a president-elect without giving a positive answer to any single question of program.

The personal candidacies which had emerged even before the National Committees met had little reference to that need to catch and hold the vote with which the party engineers were concerned. Their names had been sounded even before the fighting stopped. A boom for Leonard Wood arose in the spring of 1918 when he was sent back to camp to train another division after the Eighty-ninth which he had built at Camp Funston, Kansas, was sent to Europe. He had been passed over for the command of the A.E.F. in favor of Pershing. Pershing did not want him in France at all; but the President was held responsible for a military martyrdom. The death of Theodore Roosevelt, with whom Wood had been associated in the war with Spain, and the long friendship of the two, helped the boom as it became possible to think of Wood as a continuator of the Roosevelt tradition. A native of New Hampshire, Wood was a favorite of the senator from that state, George H. Moses, who described him in May, 1919, as "the rightful heir, with the strawberry mark on his right arm." Major Frank Knox, publisher of the Manchester (N.H.) *Union and Leader,* who recalled the days when he had been a Rough Rider under Wood and Roosevelt, endorsed the candidacy. A year later Major General Wood, on leave from the army while he worked for delegates, returned to duty in Chicago as commander of the Central Department of the army to maintain order during the summer strikes. There was admiration behind his candidacy, and money coming from the capacious pocket of an Ohio soap manufacturer.

Leonard Wood was not the only inheritor of the Roosevelt tradition, strawberry mark or not. Contestant for the inheritance was Hiram Johnson who as governor of California had been bracketed with Roosevelt on the Progressive ticket of 1912, and who had since come into the Senate as a stubborn individualist. Wood had no reputation as a progressive, but Johnson, apart from his individuality, had nothing else. There was extant a letter from Roosevelt saying that "of all public men in this country he is the one with whom I find myself in complete sympathy"; and there was no way to discover whether this sympathy had endured until the death of the writer. At any rate the two were in agreement upon the danger inherent in the Wilson devotion to a league of nations. There was even a legend that in 1879, as a schoolboy, Johnson had recited "Sheridan's Ride" in the presence of General Grant, provoking the prophecy: "My boy, our country will hear from you yet."

The country had heard from Johnson at every stage of treaty negotiation, and was to hear more when he trailed the President to counteract the impression made by the advocate of the Treaty. His friends in San Francisco, and many who had never been his friends, held a great dinner in June, 1919, to present his name as a candidate. In December, after the convention had been called for Chicago in June, 1920, Senator Johnson announced "I am exercising what is every American's birthright," and set out to capture delegates at the primaries.

Both Wood and Johnson aroused the interest of large groups of Republicans without impressing the managers of the party. Wood, a professional soldier, was an outsider in politics, and the sort of candidate that the worker in the precincts or on the state committees hoped to escape, the sort of candidate whose victory might turn the rewards of success to men who had not labored long in the field. At all times through the two terms now ending, the Democratic workers were irked by the influence of "original Wilson men" in the administration. Champ Clark, wheelhorse of the party, who died as the Sixty-sixth Congress reached its end, never forgave the outsider, or Bryan who had made Wilson possible.

Johnson, still in his first term as senator, was still a remote westerner, outside the range of vision of eastern Republicans, even if he had not been distasteful to some as a Progressive and to others as an irreconcilable.

There was less professional or doctrinal objection to Frank O. Lowden. As war governor of Illinois he had done well. Before that he had been a professor of law, a member of Congress, and a member of the Republican National Committee. As governor he had directed a simplification and reorganization of the business of the state, and had experimented with a state budget which was forerunner of the demand for a federal budget. He was in big business, having married into it when he became husband of the daughter of the founder of the Pullman Palace Car Company. His connection with business and his success as a businessman in politics, which gained him supporters from one side, was an impediment on the other side. The Pullman Company was in bad repute with labor, for labor had not forgotten the strike of 1894, the troops in Chicago and elsewhere, and the federal injunctions which struck at Eugene V. Debs. Jailed then for contempt of court, Debs was now in the federal penitentiary convicted of a war crime. The name of Lowden could not be made attractive to labor. Like Wood, however, Lowden had money behind his candidacy; and the costs of the direct primary put at a disadvantage all aspirants who lacked large financial backing. Lowden filed for the Dakota primaries in December, 1919, and won the delegation of his own state in direct contest with General Wood on April 13, 1920.

At any time the aspirants for the Republican nomination would have ranked higher than any politically minded party worker, for each stood for something and none was surrounded by the taint of scandal. While their adherents were building preconvention organization a different sector of American thought turned to a nonpartisan humanitarian. Herbert Hoover of California came back from Europe with praise for his work ringing in his ears.

Hoover, self-made, and a graduate of Stanford University in the "pioneer class," had minded his own business while he assembled a fortune in the international promotion and development of mining. He became a public figure only when, in 1914, Walter H. Page found him temporarily at loose ends in London and put him to work. His Commission for Relief in Belgium made him a world figure. His direction of the United States Food Administration brought his name into every American household. As Director General of Relief he had helped bind up the wounds of war, and upon returning to the United States in the autumn of 1919 he announced "I am through with food." For several months he was unwilling to state publicly what he would do with his growing popularity, but his candidacy developed of itself. He knew the world, thought well of mankind, had no grievance against the businessman, favored the ratification of the Treaty, and was not a professional politician. On each of these counts his name had an appeal. The *Saturday Evening Post* came out for him. The *New Republic,* which was dissatisfied with the Treaty, thought him "the man best fitted to be President." The New York *World,* the most solidly Democratic paper in the country, formally endorsed him on January 21, 1920. The bubble burst. It was only a bubble, for the groups admiring Hoover had little influence in the making of party slates. When at the end of March Hoover broke silence to admit a willingness to accept the Republican nomination his Democratic supporters fell away, and the Republican leaders were unwilling to move over to make room for him. In the California primary on May 5 the other California aspirant, Hiram Johnson, swept the state, receiving the twenty-six votes of California when the convention balloted on their candidates.

Hoover, by admitting membership in the Republican party, destroyed his availability as a nonpartisan without establishing himself among the major aspirants or in the approval of the party leaders. His status was above that of favorite sons, put forward from local vanity or to keep a delegation free for a good bargain at the right time. Somewhat more than a favorite son, too, was Calvin Coolidge of Massachusetts, whose words during the Boston police strike had evoked commendation from the Democratic President and admiration from nerve-wracked Americans. The Republican Club of Massachusetts endorsed the governor just after Congress adjourned, when he had been easily elected for a second term; and a wealthy merchant of Boston, Frank W. Stearns, played Hanna to his McKinley. Coolidge disclaimed a willingness to contest for the delegation from his state, but his supporters opened headquarters at Chicago and announced him as a law-and-order candidate.

The Republicans discussed the personnel of their ticket as though it made no difference what happened in the party of the administration. They had lost the presidency by accident in 1916, had drifted back to control of Congress in 1918, and expected to consolidate a position as dominant party in 1920. President Wilson was unlikely to be a candidate himself, even if the third-term taboo was no deterrent, and there was no other established leader in sight to command the Democratic nomination. The degree to which the ranking members of any party are subordinated when their leader is in the White House had been heightened by the war and the centralization of authority necessary for winning it. Bryan, eased out of his commanding position by Wilson, was now only a voice, more interested in the enforcement of the prohibition amendment than in anything else. McAdoo, no longer in government office, had been an "original Wilson man" and was less than acceptable to party workers even if he had not weakened himself politically by marrying a daughter of the President. Republican sneers at his name as that of a hopeful "heir apparent" were a political burden which his ability and industry could not overcome. The Attorney General, A. Mitchell Palmer, who had been Alien Property Custodian during the war and had been shifted to the Department of Justice upon the retirement of Gregory, had hopes of the law-and-order support for which Coolidge forces were reaching. He had pressed the war crimes cases and the deportations. The "Soviet Ark" sailed with its Russian radicals just before Christmas, and Palmer came out formally as a candidate a month before Hoover declared himself to be a Republican.

As the spring of 1920 advanced, with legislation lagging, and pressure groups made vindictive by every compromise which cut across their desires, the troubles of both party and nation arising from the illness of Woodrow Wilson increased. The world was not yet at peace even though the Council of the League of Nations, from its temporary home in St. James's Palace in London, had invited Elihu Root to sit with the jurists who were to frame the statute for the creation of the World Court. The Senate was tied up in a last vain attempt to bring about a compromise ratification of the Treaty. The House Democratic caucus had just declined overwhelmingly to accept the principle of universal military training which the President had asked for. Polish troops, under the Treaty, had just occupied the corridor west of Danzig and watched a ceremonial marriage of Poland with the Baltic. Northern Schleswig had just held its plebiscite and voted for a reunion with Denmark. On Lincoln's Birthday, February 12, Lansing presented his resignation by request.

On October 14, 1919, while Woodrow Wilson was believed to be hovering between life and death, the members of his Cabinet had been functioning for nearly three weeks without a head. On that day, at the instance of the Secretary of State, they had met to consider what was open for them to do in the absence of their chief. The President knew of the meeting, may have informed the secretaries through Admiral Grayson that he was "in full possession of all his faculties," and may have asked acidly "what business is it expected might be transacted at a Cabinet meeting without his participation?" The answer to his inquiry, if indeed it was made, was of course "nothing," for the United States Cabinet does not take formal or binding action even when the President is present. It discusses matters which he is willing to have discussed, and listens to what it is told. Its members may, indeed, return to their diaries to make record of their grievances, but there are no minutes. No usurpation of authority was contemplated by the Secretaries on October 14, and none occurred, though the departments were under heavy pressure for decisions which could not be made. On February 7, the day before the President offered the "solemn referendum" at the Jackson Day Dinner, Wilson took up with Lansing the matter of the Cabinet meeting, treating it on constitutional grounds as an impairment of his prerogative. Two days later Lansing admitted that he had "frequently . . . requested the heads of the executive departments . . . to meet for informal conference." Two more days later the President again deplored the meetings and the "assumption of presidential authority" and expressed further regret that Lansing had, even in Paris, accepted his "guidance and direction . . . with increasing reluctance." He now welcomed an "opportunity to select [as Secretary of State] some one whose mind would more willingly go along" with his own. Lansing resigned the next day, and Bainbridge Colby took his place. The episode inspired Fremont Older, the crusading journalist, to make the comment that "President Wilson is making it very difficult for the historian." He was clearly making it difficult for those who served him, despite the assurance of his physician that he was making steady improvement in his health.

The necessity for the Democratic party to select a candidate who would uphold the policies of Woodrow Wilson was matched by the necessity placed upon the Republican party to avoid a candidate who, by the precision of his ideas, might alienate the necessary groups of anti-Wilson voters. The leaders worked through the spring for a united convention, avoiding action which might be interpreted as an endorsement of any aspirant. They were warranted by a belief, easily reached by any student of nominating conventions, that prominence before the convention meets is an excellent way of escaping nomination. The enthusiasm of delegate groups for their several candidates comes first. Then comes the determination to prevent the selection of any rival aspirant. After this, a tired convention needs to be offered a relatively new name, not bandied in preconvention fights, not ticketed to a specific policy. The vigor of the struggle for delegates increased as spring advanced, and with it increased the likelihood of a deadlock in the convention and the selection of a compromise candidate.

Such a candidate had been presented from Ohio by a skilled and professional politician, Harry M. Daugherty, acting as much from affection as from political strategy. His candidate was Warren G. Harding, now in his first term as United States Senator. Harding was named early in 1919 in the lists made after the death of Theodore Roosevelt forced a reconsideration of the field. The Harding boom was begun before the Republican National Committee met, was formally admitted in December, and was developed with restraint lest by being forced it might be caught in the anticipated deadlock. No one disliked Harding, and no one knew precisely where he stood. If he was involved in the unsavory politics of his state, he did not differ greatly from other sons of Ohio who had given useful service. He had not risen high enough to incur deep animosities, and it was not easy for opponents in the other party or factionists in his own to make him a target. By profession a journalist with a small city newspaper, he had been no more than lieutenant governor of his state before he was defeated for governor by a Democrat in 1910. He went through the year of the Progressive schism as a "regular" without making enemies, and took his seat in the Senate from Joseph Benson Foraker in 1914. The Republican managers, looking for a safe and tactful keynoter for the convention of 1916, selected Harding and were not disappointed. He made an impressive picture on the platform, his voice was good, and he was as kindly as McKinley. He was, above all, a senator, proud of that body at a time when it was deeply jealous of the President.

By the time the Republican National Convention met on June 8, 1920, certain that Senator Lodge was to be both temporary and permanent chairman, there was a stronger hope for Harding among the inside leaders than the public knew, and a growing preference for him as second choice among those whose first devotion was pledged to some leading aspirant. Among his backers was George Harvey, once promoter of the destiny of Woodrow Wilson, who crossed to the opposition when his affections were rebuffed, and whose personal sheet, *The Weekly*, was venomous. Harvey was as zealous for the defeat of the Treaty as any of the irreconcilable senators, although he held no office. The story of his transit across the party frontier is documented in W. F. Johnson, *George Harvey, Passionate Patriot* (1929), and his convention strategy is described in the sixth volume of Mark Sullivan's narrative. Eventually Harry M. Daugherty put his name to *The Inside Story of the Harding Tragedy* (1932). Harvey may have had the power of prophecy, for no one may claim foreknowledge of the behavior of a convention. His biographer tells of a Long Island dinner party in 1919, at which the hostess made a guessing game of the approaching nomination, still a year away. Harvey refused to guess because, he said, "I know"; and he wrote and sealed a name while the diners jeered at "just a piece of George Harvey's fooling." The name he wrote was that of Harding.

The writers of the news, and the readers, lacked Harvey's certainty when the Chicago convention cleared the credentials of its 984 delegates, listened to the decorative oratory of the occasion, and plunged into the major decisions which it must make. The platform came first, lest by naming the candidate first the delegates might be compelled to make the resolutions suit his taste. The convention leaders did not wish either the platform or the nominee to cost the party votes. The New York *Times* greeted the meeting with bitter reference to the recent wrangle over the treaty, in which "the very soul of the Republican Party shrunk and shriveled almost to the point of disappearance." But Will Hays declared "The great party of the Union has become a unit."

The steadiness of the committee on resolutions was insured by the selection of Senator James E. Watson of Indiana as chairman, a stalwart who, in the convention of 1912, had helped to steer the "steam roller" over the Roosevelt supporters. He had signed the round robin in 1919, and now had the tactical task of keeping the platform from driving out of the party either the irreconcilables or the advocates of the League. They talked it out in the committee room on Tuesday and Wednesday, building at last on a plank drafted by Elihu Root, and presenting the resolutions for adoption by the convention late on Thursday, the third day of the meeting. Watson told the story as he recalled it in *As I Knew Them* (1936), and the Chicago *Tribune* the next morning described the platform as a compromise, in interpreting which "any President will necessarily choose his own emphasis." The careful words of the Republican statement approved the rejection of the Treaty as submitted, reproved the President for his "insistence" upon his own view of it, and pledged the party to "agreement among the nations to preserve the peace of the world."

With split over the platform avoided, the convention turned to the nomination. The aspirants had meanwhile suffered disappointments. Johnson had found that his pledged delegates were substantially all that he might hope to receive. The other two had been so "smeared" as to be injured as candidates. Arizona yielded to Kansas, on the call of the states, for the presentation of the name of Leonard Wood, but there were rumors on the floor that oil gamblers had put up money to advance his cause. A Senate committee, created on the motion of Senator Borah for the investigation of campaign funds, had uncovered the financial dimensions of his backers' support. Arkansas yielded to Illinois for the nomination of Frank O. Lowden, but the same committee had discovered misuse of Lowden funds by workers for him in Missouri. No scandal reached the actual candidates, but the backers of each, as partisans will, exaggerated the sins of the backers of the others.

After a day of fulsome oratory, as delegates named their men, or seconded the nominations, the roll of the states was completed and the convention began to ballot. Four ballots were taken before adjournment, and on each of the four the three leaders stood at the top of the fifteen names for whom votes were cast. Together they commanded 632 of the 984 votes on the first ballot, and 744 on the fourth. Wood began and continued in the lead; Lowden held his place as second. Johnson failed to pick up votes when delegates, having paid their compliment to favorite sons, began to search for a winner to support. New York, of whose 88 delegates 68 had played safe with Nicholas Murray Butler on the first ballot, had 20 who were still voting for Butler on the fourth. The party managers had still more doubt of victory under either of the two leaders than Boies Penrose, who had been quoted as saying that "Any good Republican . . . can defeat any Democrat." Penrose, in Philadelphia, was too ill to attend the convention but was informed of events by telephone.

The steersmen conferred that night upon their tactics, convinced that the only possible result of the convention, if unbossed, would be the naming of a candidate who could not win. They gathered in the rooms of George Harvey in the Blackstone Hotel—in whose dining room Roosevelt and Taft had staged the great reconciliation in 1916—and came and went through the night as they sought information and fetched news. It may have been plotted, or it may have merely happened, but the result was that Harding was to be pushed upon the convention as soon as the supporters of Wood and Lowden were severally convinced that they could not win, and when it was apparent that neither of the two groups could command the total vote. Harding himself, a delegate from Ohio, having little ambition for the presidency, and preferring to file for reëlection to the Senate in November, was called into the conference. He was asked whether there was any reason "arising out of your past life" to prevent confidence in his candidacy; and after a few minutes of private thought he replied firmly "Gentlemen, there is no such reason." The situation foretold by Harry Daugherty had come to pass. As early as February Daugherty had told the newsmen the substance of the quotation which was recalled on Saturday afternoon: that after the leading candidates had canceled themselves out of the picture "some fifteen men, bleary-eyed with loss of sleep and perspiring profusely with the excessive heat, will sit down in seclusion around a big table," and select the nominee. The only thing to be done on that last day of the convention was to pick the minute at which to steer the votes.

The deadlock continued through the Saturday morning session and four more futile ballots. Then, after a recess, the Lowden votes scattered so that Harding took a lead on the ninth ballot and on the tenth became the Republican candidate for the presidency. It was not the first time, nor the last, that the party leaders directed the choice for a divided convention. It is possible that no candidate, widely known or sharply identified with any of the issues which cut across American opinion on their several planes of cleavage, could have been elected. The New York *Times,* disgusted, could say nothing better than that Harding was "a very respectable politician of the second class." The *Nation,* opposed to all the leaders, could only say Harding's nomination "prevented something worse." Mrs. Harding had been quoted before names were even presented to the convention: "I can see but one word written over the head of my husband if he is elected, and that word is 'tragedy'."

Almost as an afterthought, the convention proceeded on Saturday afternoon to the nomination of a candidate for Vice-President. Lodge was not even in the chair when the rank and file broke loose. The leaders had agreed upon another senator, Irvine L. Lenroot, who had begun his public life as a supporter of La Follette in Wisconsin. But the irritated delegates would not listen to the nominating speeches. One of them, McCamant from Oregon, who had defied the preference of his state for Johnson and cast his vote for Wood, defied the steersmen and shouted the name of Governor Calvin Coolidge, which the convention accepted by acclamation and in disorder.

The name of William Gibbs McAdoo led on the first ballot when the Democratic National Convention, meeting in the Civic Auditorium in San Francisco, began the test of strength of the rival aspirants for the nomination. San Francisco was an inconvenient place for such a test, for the difference in time made it impossible to report in the eastern morning papers the outcome of the long evening sessions; but the correspondents were all on hand. Among them was "Godfrey Gloom," self-identified as "a prominent paw-paw grower of Amity, Indiana," who avowed that he had first voted for Douglas in 1860, and who expected "to see a good many mistakes made in this convention. The Republicans set a high standard for us to aim at." Behind the pseudonym was Elmer Davis. It was, he wrote, "the scaredest convention ever convened."

Senator Carter Glass was there, picked to be chairman of the committee on resolutions, and carrying the draft of a platform which he had checked with the President in Washington. Bryan was there, with his passion for peace and his devotion to prohibition enforcement. The name of the President was there, but no more than rumors of a third-term possibility. McAdoo, under the burden of the epithets "heir apparent" and "crown prince," had specifically withdrawn his name ten days before the convention met, and had in February declined to be a candidate. But among the bewildered and leaderless delegates his name would not down, the opposition declaring his renunciation to be only tactical. The party managers were there as well—Murphy of Tammany, Taggert of Indiana, and Brennan of Illinois—determined to uphold the renunciation which McAdoo announced. The name of Governor James M. Cox of Ohio ran third on the first ballot, supported by the political prestige of having three times been elected to his office in a notably doubtful state.

Cummings, chairman of the Democratic Committee, and temporary chairman of the convention, declared that "the [Republican] meeting in Chicago was not a convention but an auction" when he opened proceedings on Monday, June 28. Senator Joseph T. Robinson of Arkansas, as permanent chairman, took command on the second day, when the convention declined to enforce the unit rule and confirmed the report of the committee on credentials which excluded from the convention Senator James A. Reed of Missouri.

Like the Republicans, the Democrats found it necessary to clear the platform before they named a candidate, and in the absence of a report on the platform the third day of the convention was given over to eight hours of presentation oratory. More names were presented on the fourth day, until sixteen were on the list, and still the committee on resolutions was not in agreement. Tammany included in the list the name of Governor Alfred E. Smith, which was seconded, from outside Tammany, by Franklin D. Roosevelt, with the words: "I love him as a friend, look up to him as a man, and am with him as a Democrat."

Glass brought in the platform on Friday morning, with Bryan overridden in committee and waiting to continue on the floor of the convention his fight for a bone-dry plank. Not until Friday evening did the convention accept the platform, after rejecting both the Bryan amendment and that of W. Bourke Cockran which proposed an endorsement of light wines and beer. The first two ballots were taken that evening. Under the ancient two-thirds rule the votes of 729 of the 1,094 delegates were required for a nomination.

McAdoo and Palmer were easy leaders on the early ballots, but faced the same ganging-up tactics from which the Republican aspirants had suffered. Twenty-two ballots on Saturday brought no important change in the alignment. Another fourteen, equally without a break, were counted on Monday, before the convention allowed itself a brief recess; and in a night session the roll of states was called again, for a thirty-seventh attempt. Delegates had begun to drift out of the hall, and spectators had thinned the galleries, when after the thirty-eighth roll call Palmer released his delegates. The New York *Times,* getting its news late, and over wires detouring through Canada at that, put its Tuesday edition "to bed" before that time, and failed to present the picture of the exciting morning hours when the bonds relaxed and the delegates drifted to the support of Cox. There was stampede and victory on the forty-fourth.

The convention had, as usual, given little thought to the Vice-Presidency—quite as little as the Republicans had given. There was not even a preference among the professional politicians. When the ballot-weary delegates were held to the completion of their work in the small hours of Tuesday morning, eight names were put forward. They were named without enthusiasm on the part of nominators or candidates. Governor Smith made a warm second to the name of Assistant Secretary of the Navy—Franklin D. Roosevelt, though he had for a decade been a thorn in the flesh of Tammany. The name caught hold. The other seven names were one by one withdrawn until only that of Roosevelt was left, and he was given the nomination by acclamation.

It would not have been a normal American election if the two tickets of Harding and Coolidge, and Cox and Roosevelt, had been permitted to divide the vote. The "third parties," several of them, put their token tickets into the field to advertise a principle or to register a discontent. These tickets revealed as great a lack of precision and purpose as prevailed in the membership of the major parties. Nearest to having precision and purpose was the Socialist party, which undertook to re-form its ranks in the Chicago convention of August 30, 1919, and there parted company with the Communist party and that of Communist-Labor. The Socialists, not waiting for the majors to show a hand, had met in New York in May, 1920, to adopt a moderate program, neither antichurch nor proletarian, and to name Eugene V. Debs for the fifth time. Their delegation, sent to the White House to ask the release of their leader that he might campaign, had met with rebuff, but Debs was a stronger candidate in the penitentiary at Atlanta than he would have been outside. He gained votes of sympathy which he could not have commanded with his doctrine. His was frankly a party of protest, expecting no more than its handful of doctrinaires, and a group of the dissatisfied, to ballot for its ticket.

The Committee of Forty-Eight went to Chicago, shortly after the Democratic Convention adjourned, to attempt a fusion of the liberals. It looked longingly at labor, at the farmer, and at the single-taxers. Its fusion with the last of these failed because it looked also at La Follette as a nominee, whereas the single-taxers would not have him. It was more hopeful of labor, for the National Labor party, taking a name in November, 1919, had called its own convention for July 11 in Chicago, the day after the Committee of Forty-Eight convened. Confusion of ideas and personal jealousies prevented the fusion. The convention of the Committee of Forty-Eight was captured by western radicals who put Parley Parker Christensen of Utah in the chair, and who resented an assumption of leadership by eastern intellectuals. After days of wrangling between the two conventions most of the Committee of Forty-Eight lost hope, and Christensen moved over into the Labor convention, from which he emerged as candidate under the title of Farmer-

Labor, and with a platform so radical that La Follette had no interest in it.

The Prohibitionists, not satisfied that the Eighteenth Amendment had completed the crusade of which it was a part, met in Lincoln, Nebraska, toward the end of July. They were now concerned with matters of enforcement. Some of their delegates aimed their sights at William Jennings Bryan; others sought the evangelist Billy Sunday as their candidate. The convention contented itself with the Rev. Aaron S. Watkins of Ohio.

The various minor tickets in November commanded some 1,400,000 votes out of a total of some 26,700,000—too few to do more than relieve the minds of the citizens who cast them. It is impossible to give with precision the vote for any candidate because of the requirement that the votes be cast for presidential electors rather than for individuals. The ballot of an elector in the electoral college, if he has received the smallest number of popular votes cast in his state for a winning elector, is just as good as if he had received the largest number. Occasionally the electoral vote has been split by the "scratching" of names, so that the weakest names on the winning slate have received fewer votes than the strongest names on the losing slate. No state was so divided in 1920; but no one may say with certainty how many voters supported any candidate, and how many, by splitting their ticket, may have supported both. Even the approximate totals, as they are quadrennially assembled, are brought into one table only through the diligence of the press in copying them from the records of the several states.

The uncertainties of the impending canvass were increased because the total vote was in 1920, for the first time, to be swollen by the votes of women throughout the nation. Managers could only guess how the women would divide. It had been assumed that woman suffrage, doing more than mere justice to women, would bring some change into American elections and politics. The proponents of the reform had promised, among other things, to bring correction to a man-ruled world. In this campaign they had their chance. The National Woman Suffrage Association made its plans in 1919 to retire from the field. When in February, 1920, the League of Women Voters took its place, thirty-one states had already ratified the Susan B. Anthony Amendment. The fight for the five more states needed in order to bring the new amendment into force in time for the elections of 1920, was pressed with enthusiasm. The proposal of the amendment, calling for a two-thirds assent in each of the houses of Congress, had received priority when the Sixty-sixth Congress met, and the amendment went to the states when on June 4, 1919, Senate reluctance was at last overridden. Both major parties urged the completion of ratification; those who opposed the vote were nearly as eager to get rid of the question as those who advocated it. Tennessee became the thirty-sixth state to ratify, which made it possible for the Secretary of State to proclaim the Eighteenth Amendment as part of the Constitution of the United States on August 26, 1920.

Since the voting machinery of the states did not tabulate separately the votes of men and women, it becomes only guesswork for the historian to try to measure the influence of votes for women. They at least helped to increase the number of votes cast, from totals of 15,000,000 (1912) and 18,500,000 (1916) to 26,700,000 in 1920. The politicians could not avoid the attempt to forecast the influence of campaigning upon the new electorate. Some of those on the Republican side weighed the advantage of giving publicity to the fact that Governor Cox had been divorced many years before. The advantages disappeared when it was learned that an early divorce of Mrs. Harding was receiving similar consideration from the Democratic side. The matter was dropped.

The Democratic candidates made an early formal call upon the titular head of the party in the White House and received his blessing. George Harvey, full of advice, moved to Marion, Ohio, where Harding took up his residence in his home town as soon as he could leave Washington. It was the determination of the Republican managers to repeat the front-porch campaign which had been so successful with McKinley in 1896, and the hope of Harvey and the other close advisers was to steer the candidate away from utterances which, by seeming too friendly to the Treaty, would wreck him with the foes of the Treaty. When Senator Harding spoke of his desire for an "association of nations," anyone might interpret the words to please himself. His four words of the campaign which had clear meaning and wide appeal had been spoken in Boston before the conventions met: "not nostrums but normalcy."

The Republican candidate, pressed from both sides, thought he kept close to the compromise line of the party plank, and was consistent "in complete opposition to the Wilson League" but kindly to "an association of nations based upon a rule of justice." Perhaps, he lamented, "I have not been able to make the country understand me." His "complete opposition" crowded pro-League members of his party into a corner between their sincere desire to make the League a fact and their partisan hopes. On October 14, helped to it by the verbal ingenuity of Elihu Root, they found a way to serve both ends. The president of Cornell University, Jacob G. Schurman, released a manifesto in which thirty-one Republicans of high distinction endorsed Harding as the best possible means for getting the United States into the League of Nations. Hoover, Hughes, and Root were among the signers; Nicholas Murray Butler, A. Lawrence Lowell, and John Grier Hibben; Lyman Abbott, Henry L. Stimson, and William Howard Taft. Any of their names would have looked better at the head of a ticket than either of the leaders; but any of them would have divided the vote of the party without drawing support from Democrats. George Sylvester Viereck formed a committee of German-Americans to support Harding. While the canvass was at top heat Terence McSwiney, Lord Mayor of Cork, died of a hunger strike in Brixton prison, a martyr to the cause of the Irish Republic and citizens of foreign blood, Irish and German, Italian and Austrian, voted with anger in their hearts—at the Treaty or at England. Professor Irving Fisher, who made a statistical examination of the election returns, declared that they so reinforced a tide already running strongly against the party in power, as to turn Democratic defeat into a Republican landslide.

The vote came on November 2, 1920. The Republican ticket received 16,100,000 votes against 9,100,000 for the Democratic candidates, 404 electoral votes against 127. Cox and Roosevelt were supported by only eleven states, of which only Kentucky was outside the Solid South. Harding, first candidate since the Civil War to break into the Solid South, captured the dozen votes of Tennessee. Far from being a "solemn referendum" on the Treaty, it was a free-for-all the outcome of which threw no new light upon the issue which Woodrow Wilson had posed. If the vote meant anything beyond mere shift in the controls of government it revealed a craving for what was described as a "return to normalcy."

Chapter X ★ American Wherewithal

NORMALCY, by its very nature, is an after thought. Few who are alive can bring themselves to think that the times in which they live are so nearly perfect as to be beyond improvement. When man thinks or speaks of normalcy, and yearns for a return to it, he is driven by immediate annoyance, and tends to idealize the past. Old men have a nostalgia which drives them to recall a happy past—which could never have recognized itself from their description. Old countries and old parties have some of the same nostalgia when they are vexed by present-day life and its problems. This tendency makes for conservatism in the management of the body politic, and provides a useful brake against the enthusiast for an untested new order, but it does not lead to the drafting of a road book or a sailing chart. Its virtues become a cloak for those who shirk new issues or fear their cost, and for many whose title to the enjoyment of what they have is suspect, and who would evade discovery.

Never before the World War had the United States given much heed to its morrow. Nature was bountiful, resources were abundant, and no enemy threatened to disturb the exploitation of either. Encouraged by the fact of individualism, and the doctrine, men grabbed without restraint advantages of which law had not yet taken notice. The land passed into private hands, the resources beneath the land, and intangibles in the form of franchise to exploit the public interest. There was a safe twilight zone, where the state could not interfere, and which the nation had not yet reached with regulatory law. But the people and the states and the nation never took account of stock. Theodore Roosevelt pointed to abuses, and proclaimed them in *The New Nationalism* (1910). He found many to support him in all seriousness, a marginal group which

[163]

he characterized as "the fringe of lunatics," and a rigid group from which came quibblings over method or out-and-out denial. The World War brought to a pause a period of modernization of American institutions. There were many who hoped it would never be revived.

It was too obvious to be denied that the frame within which American life might proceed was determined by the fluid wealth available to be enjoyed. Only as men or nation produced could they consume. Only as production was increased could the rich have much or the poor have more. The American continent was now largely inhabited and its untouched resources were not unlimited, even if they had never yet been accurately tabulated. The open frontier, which had helped to free the American spirit from the beginning, was now gone; and within fixed boundaries the growing population was showing signs of crowding.

The presidential year, 1920, was census year as well. The decennial census, built into the Constitution to provide a statistical basis for representation and the apportionment of direct taxes, was taken for the fourteenth time. Its enumerators, not required in the beginning to notice more than the color and the status of the "persons" whom they counted, now asked questions covering many aspects of life and livelihood, and the census office had acquired elaborate machines with which to count and tabulate. The official count showed 105,710,620 persons in continental United States, forty-three million more than in 1890, when the open frontier was declared no longer to exist.

Any breakdown of the census figures makes it clear that although "created equal," in the language of the Declaration of Independence, the Americans lost some of that equality as they materially advanced in their various pursuits. They were a group of agricultural communities when the Declaration was drafted as the manifesto of fewer than three million of them; more than forty-two million of them, in 1920, still lived on or near the farm. They had less than the community organization which might be expected to exist in incorporated places of 2,500 population. More than a quarter of the people—some twenty-seven million—lived in cities of 100,000, or more. The people were equal and alike in that they possessed the same civil rights, they had much the same access to the news, were capable of desiring and enjoying much the same pleasures, and all needed the necessities of life. But in access to opportunity they varied.

The urban-rural cleavage was matched by other cleavages. Nearly fourteen million of those counted in 1920 were foreign-born, and were on this account different from their fellow residents. More than ten million, even more different, were black. The American social-economic pyramid, at the apex of which the luxury hotels glittered, with shiny cars and showy homes as additional decorations, had a great and visible height. It towered above a base broader in extent and farther below the apex than American thought commonly recognized.

It was still conventional to think of the forty-two million who were in immediate contact with the soil as farmers of the single-family farm. History was being taught as the history of the free farmers, whose advancing homesteads had cleared the continent, and whose experiences had shaped not only their own American character, but also that of region, state, and nation. This was substantially true, with respect to the first century after independence, but it told only part of the truth in 1920. The single-family farmer still existed, but farming had become a business and had lost much of its character as a way of life. The farmer was a businessman, producing for a market, using commercial credit when he had collateral, operating elaborate machines, and being brought every year closer to the pattern of the city dweller. The southern plantation no longer survived on its antebellum basis. In many regions great farms had appeared, which were to all intent food factories operating on the soil. Most of the ten million Negroes were laborers, or small farmers, living the precarious life of those who lacked ownership of either farm or of tools with which to work it. Tenancy was increasing as ownership declined, and ownership was often less than real because of the mortgage burden on the farm. Agrarian America was different from urban America; with fewer advantages, but more conscious than ever of what life offered for those who could command them. Economists were beginning to wonder whether peasant status might not be the necessary condition of those who tilled the soil. Only through the profitable disposal of the surplus which the farmer could not eat could he hope to raise the level of his living. Henry Clay had stated the fundamental problem a hundred years before. No answer had yet been found.

Even the city dwellers lacked uniformity and were in the lower economic brackets. The visible throngs on the streets, in the churches, at the ticket windows of the movie theaters, looked much alike. But they owed their similarity to the ingenuity of the clothing manufacturers and the national advertisers. Their clothing was cut from much the same pattern, and quantity production brought fashion to the level of every budget. The people looked so much alike as to encourage a belief that they were a homogeneous group, but most of them were wage earners, only partly organized in their unions, and never far away from inconvenience and disaster if the job was lost. The American standard of life was much admired, as though it was uniform, and without consideration of the fact that any average standard of living presupposes life below the average for most of the people. The extent of opportunity for Americans, at the bottom of the pyramid as well as at the top, was in 1920 just beginning to be a matter of available measurement.

The best guesses of the economists—who were getting better at it all the time—put the average income of Americans at twice that of Germans, and half again as large as that of the British. There appeared in 1921–1922 the two modest volumes on *Income in the United States: Its Amount and Distribution, 1909–1919,* as the result of a coöperative investigation directed by the privately organized National Bureau of Economic Research. The statisticians who must argue public welfare from dependable figures had been enabled, by gifts from philanthropic foundations and private donors, to pool the skills of labor economists and bankers, employers and engineers, in an attempt to assemble tables free from the bias of special interest. The statisticians had studied the figures of production, for all income is derived from production at some level, and the figures of income, for that is all that people have to spend unless willing to deplete savings. When they compared the work of the two teams of investigators and found that the two totals were within seven per cent of each other, they felt that a useful approximation had been reached. So thought Sir Josiah Stamp, who was skilled in such estimates and had recorded his belief that estimates within ten per cent of perfection were as good as the best.

Other groups of statisticians, official as well as nonofficial, were being directed to this estimate of income. Statistics had been much talked of during the war, abundantly collected, and not too greatly used. Most of the war boards had had sections for similar studies. Dean Edwin F. Gay of Harvard had been made chief of a Central Bureau of Planning and Statistics for the preparation of complete progress charts, simple enough for the President to read and understand. A decade later Robert S. Brookings, a St. Louis merchant whose duties on the Purchasing Commission for the Allies had taught him the inadequacy of most statistics, provided funds to establish the Brookings Institution in Washington, D. C., "to aid constructively in the development of sound national policies." In this work young men were trained, some of whom in another decade were to reach confidently for a power of prophecy, in the belief that from their tables they could devise a planned economy which would be workable. For the moment they were working on the past, with little more than a hope that it might serve the future.

Their studies of 1920 took the year 1913, the last year of general peace, as a base. National income for that year, as Willford I. King revised it in *The National Income and Its Purchasing Power* (1930), was estimated at 35.7 billion dollars, giving a per capita average of $368. Checking against this, and giving heed to the rising prices which during the war lessened the buying power of the dollar, it became possible to state the income of following years in terms of both current dollars and dollars of the value of 1913. For the census year 1920 the dollar income had increased to 73.9 billions, without any important change in real income, for when by use of the price index the income was translated into dollars of 1913 the total was only 37.5 billion.

In dollars of 1920 from which Americans must derive their maintenance after deduction for costs of government, the income of 1920 meant $695 per capita. In terms of families, assuming, as the census did, that these consisted of 4.22 persons on the average, the twenty-five million families in the United States might have expected an average family income of a trifle under $3,000, if the national income had been divided evenly. The difficult question of whether the total income would have been as great if it had been shared evenly, remains unanswered.

Out of these incomes came the income tax, which had been an increasing source of federal revenue since the first schedules were voted in the Underwood-Simmons act, and which had been first collected from the incomes of the latter part of 1913. The theoretical per capita or the average family income is of consequence chiefly as it suggests the huge number of American families whose dollar incomes were kept below $3,000, since every income above the average must be compensated for by incomes under that amount. The figure is misleading, since it suggests an even geographical distribution. When the per capita average of 1920 came to be broken down among the states and sections, three states, New York, Nevada, and California proved to average above $800; the old South, omitting Texas, fell below $400. The real income was somewhat larger than the dollar averages suggested, and the spread between urban and rural incomes somewhat less broad, because of two items which the statisticians were unable to approximate. In nearly every family the working housewife made a genuine, if forgotten, contribution to real income. And on nearly every farm the farm household consumed part of its own production, without an accounting. Sectional conditions as well as those of blood and color and occupation showed inequalities in fact despite American equality before the law.

The federal Collector of Internal Revenue, reporting on personal incomes of 1920, declared that only 7.2 million persons (or fewer than one for four families) had been required to file a return of income. Nearly three quarters of these had net incomes under $3,000, and paid no income tax. Only some two million of the 105 million counted by the census enjoyed net incomes above $3,000 in that year. This two per cent of the American population received 13.5 billions of the national income of 73.9 billions.

The American wherewithal, inflated in dollars but in real buying power nearly the same as in 1913, was the most abundant in the world. Yet generalizations based upon the visible level of persons in the comfortable and higher income brackets were far from true, and the national advertiser tended to stress goods manufactured for the few as though they were in fact within reach of the millions. But the millions could crave and hope. American attention had not yet been realistically directed to the standard of life of the ninety-three Americans in every hundred from whom no income tax return had been demanded. Much of the confusion of the postwar years derives from the contradiction between the picture of what might be had and the frame of resources which enclosed it.

Whether recognized or not, the national income of 73.9 billions in 1920 enclosed the American dream within a rigid frame. Only by improved production could the frame be enlarged. Only by successful marketing could the production be turned into effective income. Only by a struggle among classes of society could the share of any class be increased; and at any given time the increase of the share of a single class involved diminution for another class.

All the forces contributing to prompt acquaintance with the news of the world, all those forces of publicity which brought into the news the increasing range of the details of life, and all the statistical agencies which were making fairly accurate measurements of resources for the first time in history, burst into new activity with the Armistice. None were entirely new, but the difference in the degree of their activity was so great as to constitute a difference in kind. Most of the world felt the impact of these forces. Nations were on the defensive or "on the make." Classes were newly hopeful, or deeply apprehensive. The overturn in Russia was a consequence of a new class consciousness and the Soviet government, instead of collapsing upon itself, repelled its closest enemies and showed signs of the power to survive. The dictatorship of the proletariat, which spoke as though it was the people, was relentless in its advancement of a program derived from Karl Marx.

Within the limits of the fixed frames of resources, as these enclosed national or social groups, the possible advantage of any class was limited by the tenacity with which other classes defended what they had. A social-economic shift of balance was in the making, as a political shift had, a century before, carried the franchise perceptibly in the direction of manhood suffrage. The masses of the people were becoming literate and desirous, and as they groped for improvement in status new organizations came to life to advance their cause, or to block it. Asia was becoming conscious of a rivalry with the Western world, and resentful of a domination which would not admit it to equality. Japan had gained much at Paris, wanted more, and indulged the vision of mastery of eastern

Asia and the western Pacific. Italy, inferior in resources and frustrated in its hopes for gains at the peace table, was ripe for upset. Already the "black flag of Fascist revolution" had been raised and the date March 23, 1919, was on its way to being celebrated as the holy founding date for a new order which should checkmate Bolshevism and restore the glories of ancient Rome. The name of "Professor" Benito Mussolini was coming to be recognized as that of its most coherent leader. The world was still able to jest at the castor oil with which his followers purged their opponents. But they had worse than castor oil in their arsenal.

If Italy, one of the victors, was dissatisfied with its share of the world's goods, and ripe for revolution, the case was worse in Germany, where defeat had been real, though less real than was commonly thought. The war had been kept substantially off German soil, and the German armies had been allowed to march home after the Armistice with their organization intact. Here big business feared the policies of the Socialist republic while the army hated them, and both groups were ready to rock the shaky German experiment in democratic government. Both welcomed the rioters of the National Socialist party in their brown shirts (those of Mussolini were black) to do the rough work. An Austrian corporal named Hitler was developing power over the discontented and an authority in Bavaria which was disturbing to the friends of order. His Nazi followers were to join him in celebrating February 24, 1920 as the birthday of his party program. The black shirts wished to restore to Italy the glories of the past; the brown shirts sought for Germany a new hegemony of Europe, based on nationalism, Nordic superiority, hatred of Bolshevism and Russia, and of the Jews.

The ferments of the world pressed against restraints. In India the pacifist leader, the Mahatma, Mohandas K. Gandhi, brought more trouble to Britain than open violence would have caused. His preaching of passive resistance and civil disobedience made a backdrop for the demand for independence. In Ireland the resistance to British rule was in the open, with independence as its goal. And in the United States notice was being taken of a movement inconsistent with the democracy in which Americans placed their trust.

It was Stanley High, reporting on the activities of the new Fascisti, who described the movement led by Mussolini as "a militarized Ku Klux Klan." This alliterative name of the Knights of the Invisible Empire had passed into history forty years before the order was revived in Atlanta in 1915. The Ku Klux Klan had been among the phenomena of the reconstruction of the South after the Civil War. Its masked riders had carried to the freedman the idea of unalterable white supremacy. By intimidation the riders had reinforced the fraud at the polls whereby white majorities were maintained in spite of the extension of the suffrage to the Negro. Better ways than this were found to eliminate the Negro vote as the century ended; literacy tests, and property and residence require- ments for the suffrage, and the "grandfather clause" which Louis- iana devised to protect the illiterate whites in a new constitution adopted in 1898.

When a new constitutional convention was voted for again by Louisiana in 1920, it was noted that the Ku Klux Klan was once more riding, and again in white. Among the matters up for action was, once more, the Negro vote. The Supreme Court had shown an unwillingness to regard the "grandfather clause" as constitutional under the Fifteenth Amendment. The revived order avowed the highest patriotism, sold its memberships, and ritual, and robes with considerable profit to itself, and preached aggressive Americanism. Its fantastic titles—Imperial Wizard, Imperial Kleagle, Imperial Klonvocation—concealed officers and agencies whose doings were swathed in ritual and secrecy. The menaces which it purported to fight were most commonly the Negro, the alien, and the Catholic Church.

The Klan spread again through the South, into the border states, and across the Ohio as a revival of the nativisms which had more than once intruded upon United States politics. In the regions of its influence it gained members through their caution; politicians who cared nothing for it felt a need to join if they wished to stay in politics. Its public gatherings, assembled to impress the public, were heralded by flaming crosses on the hilltops. Its masked and draped members walked the streets in silence. Its marginal activi- ties were whippings, burnings, and occasionally murder. No one could tell where the actions of the Klan stopped, or where those of individual Klansmen began, or where the vestments of the order were used to cover private malice. It was one of those movements for which unhappy peace had given opening throughout the world, whether for the maintenance of the status quo or for the forcing of some new equilibrium upon society. Not all of the adventurers wore masks. In Louisiana, as the constitution underwent revision, Huey P. Long of the State Railroad Commission was fighting the anti-Klan governor. Long was, as the judge who fined him for libel stated, "of an impulsive nature, given to indiscreet and ill-advised utterances." But the inventors had not yet provided for him the sound truck with which to carry a message to the people, and he had not yet thought of the slogan which he was in later years to broadcast: "share the wealth."

Within the limits of the wherewithal of 1920—the 73.9 billions of national income and the resulting per capita average of $695—the people of the United States must live until such time as the gross income might be increased by new methods of industry and better organization of production. Those whose incomes fell within the lower brackets were not made more content by what was the increasingly visible comfort of the upper brackets. The per capita average, varying as it did from class to class, and region to region, tells only part of the story of what anyone had to spend. There were taxes to be paid. Some of these, like the tariff duties, were concealed within the price of commodities. Some, painfully open, were paid directly to local governments or to the United States, and were on record as income tax or property tax on the stubs of every checkbook. Until these were paid the citizen was not free to spend the rest of his income on his needs. In addition to the costs of government services all had to meet, by insurance or by direct outlay, the costs of sickness, death, and disaster. The available individual income was far below what the average per capita suggested. This has always been true of every society. Its measurement was now, for the first time, becoming public property.

After the Civil War the protests of those who paid taxes in order that the government might play fair with the creditors who held its war bonds had heavily affected politics. The movement for paper money and the open attack upon "bloated bondholders" had disturbed the major parties and had even given rise to a third-party attempt. The Greenback party put Peter Cooper into the contest for the presidency in 1876, and gathered a protest vote for General

Benjamin F. Butler in 1884, in addition to providing a candidate for the Populist party, General James B. Weaver, in 1892. Its pressure drove the Treasury into the purchase of cheap silver bullion in 1878, as its adherents clamored for the restoration of "the dollar of their daddies."

The demand for an inflation of the currency for the sake of raising prices had risen almost invariably in the newer regions of the United States when any of those sections was caught in an economic squeeze. Open inflation by means of fiat money was avoided in the World War, but there occurred an inflation of credit and a rise in prices. The pressure campaigns during the Liberty Loan drives had disposed of some twenty-one billions in bonds to some seventy-five million buyers. It was the hope that buyers would save to pay and thus both finance the war and reduce the free cash which might otherwise tend to inflate prices. The purchasers, however, borrowed so frequently from the banks that the financial result was largely an increase in bank credit backed by government bonds as collateral. "We . . . maintained the Union half a century ago by a war financed extensively by paper money inflation," said Edwin W. Kemmerer in 1920, and "we have just preserved our political heritage by a war financed . . . largely by deposit currency inflation." Money in circulation had been increased by this inflation, price controls were few, and prices had risen. The increase in war wages had been passed on to the consumer, and when continuing rise in prices made the increase insufficient to balance wages with cost of living the wages were advanced again. The economists differ in the method and the weighting of the price indexes, but they are in substantial agreement that, taking the prices of 1913 as a base, the prices of 1918 were twice as high. War scarcity had contributed to this rise in prices. The irregularities among them, concealed in the averages of the indexes, had profited some and penalized others. Those whose incomes were fixed in dollars suffered most.

It was impracticable at any time to increase the amount of national income, whether in dollars of 1920 or (corrected by the indexes) in dollars of prewar value. What the citizen received in real buying power varied with his station and his needs. The boundaries between the income groups were variable and their shiftings were beyond control. The people as a whole owed money to some of the people; and although those who were the creditors of the nation paid, in general, the heaviest taxes, the obligation to repay them was spread over and shared by all. The end of hostilities and the lifting of the war restraints found savings ready to compete for goods which war had made scarce. Competition among the buyers drove prices higher. By May, 1920 the index of the United States Bureau of Labor Statistics for wholesale prices stood at 272, in comparison with the 1913 index of 100. By December it had fallen to 189 and new troubles were on their way.

The high cost of living brought the President before Congress to demand remedies in August, 1919, and was a disturbing element through the last months of his administration. It was more disturbing than the facts warranted because of human tendency to concentrate attention upon high prices as a grievance and to overlook income increases which had, to a real extent, matched them. Where price and income had risen hand in hand there was little change in equilibrium. But there were enough fields in which income had failed to advance with price to bring the sense of grievance into action. When the war ended the wage adjustments stopped, and the flood of savings was released. There was unemployment, too; and for those who had no jobs the high prices and the high cost of living were the same. Sugar had risen from five and a half cents a pound before the war to nineteen cents a pound in 1920.

A new word was working its way reluctantly into the American vocabulary. In the massive index of the New York *Times* for the first quarter of 1920 there was only a dummy entry for "Unemployment," and the searcher was referred to "Insurance-Unemployment" where there were two lines of reference. In the first quarter of 1922, two years later, there was still a dummy entry, with a cross reference to "Labor-Unemployment," where, however, the references filled more than three columns. It had been a general American assumption that in the United States there was no unemployment if a man was willing to work. Being out of a job was considered, more completely than was justified, evidence of indolence or incompetence. It was known in a general way that, with the changes in industry, there was a certain interval between jobs which brought about temporary leisure without putting the workman into a category of the unemployed. Even in periods of depression after the great panics, the bread lines which evoked charitable intervention were regarded as temporary and not indicating fundamental lack of work. There had been recognizable unemployment in 1919, as men were discharged from the army or their war jobs; but this, too, was no more than a temporary maladjustment. The figures of total unemployment in the United States were undependable, partly because they were not collected, partly because of the difficulty of separating into accurate groups the full-time workmen, the part-time workmen, the occasional workmen, and the men and women who, not normally holding jobs, were attracted by the high wages of wartime. It was only by sampling and guesswork that the Bureau of Labor Statistics, driven to it by the obvious fact, began in the autumn of 1920 to make an estimate. There was no agreement upon the fraction of regular full-time workmen who might be expected normally to be out of work between jobs.

As 1920 advanced it had become clear that men were out of work because there was no work for them to do, and the word "unemployment," too well known abroad, came into use. The estimates for unemployed employables ran close to four million at the end of the year. The American Federation of Labor thought the number was larger and none could say how many suffered because one man was jobless, or how long family savings would put off a day of hunger. The index for employment stood at 83 in December (with 1913 as 100). The case for compulsory unemployment insurance began to be stated, a decade after the case for workmen's compensation called for legislation. The unevenness in the distribution of American opportunity received a new emphasis.

The high cost of living, inducing the futile appeal of the President to Congress in 1919, produced a futile public demonstration in the spring of 1920. The southern towns carried the torch in an attack upon high prices, while Samuel Gompers commented calmly: "The cost of living has become a paramount issue." Tampa seems to have begun it, and with such success in promoting a buyers' strike that the retail stores pressed the local papers to refrain from noticing the "return to overalls." Jacksonville, Birmingham, and Chattanooga joined in the formation of overalls clubs, with the slogan "don the denim." The idea took hold and was handled with a light touch, but the witticisms of reporters did not conceal the fact that there was bad temper among the buyers. As "The Overalls Spasm" it reached the Pacific Coast. A Georgia representative appeared in Congress wearing jeans. The President of the New York Board of Aldermen, Fiorello H. LaGuardia, took the chair in his army khaki shirt, in limited protest against extravagance. Governor Calvin Coolidge, perhaps with his eye on the votes, donned overalls to plant a tree on Arbor Day. Vice-President Marshall, in New York near the end of April, spoke of the "denim revolution," although without dressing for it. As he spoke preparations were under way for a huge parade on Fifth Avenue to advance the cause. Mayor Hylan, heeding the retailers of the Fifth Avenue Association, ordered the parade to another street, and gave it Broadway, in whose theatrical neighborhood a perhaps mythical "Cheese Club" was leading in the planning. The open revolt was over before the parade formed on April 24, 1920, and the crowds of the curious had little reward for their patience. It was, said the New York *Times*, "flatly a failure." But in the autumn the New Orleans *Times-Picayune* printed an advertisement of an overalls maker who proudly asserted that, tied end to end, the annual output of overalls would stretch for fifty thousand miles, or twice around the earth.

The political field in the United States on election day, 1920, was ripe for harvesters who could persuade followers to believe in panaceas. The captains of industry and finance, with incomes in the highest brackets, were to be taught that they owed the advantages of their position to the compliance of the people. Americans who lived on incomes which someone else had earned were to be obliged to justify their existence. The measures to teach the rich were on the way. The income tax, with its progressive surtaxes, was to be developed by representatives of the people to lower the incomes of the rich. The inheritance tax was to reduce, for the next generation, the number who would live on inherited wealth as well as the amount they would inherit. The politician was to promote public services by offering the attractive guarantee that they could be charged by surtax to the unduly rich, and thus be at once a profitable fiscal device and a proper punishment for being rich. And just beyond the horizon was recognition that old age and obsolescence had a greater claim upon national income than had as yet been recognized.

The high prices began to break in the spring of 1920, bringing as they declined maladjustments which were as painful as those accompanying their rise. Uneven as they rose, prices were uneven as they fell. When their index was analyzed, as the Department of Agriculture analyzed it, it appeared that the price of what the farmer had to sell declined more rapidly than the price of what he had to buy. At the beginning of the year the indexes for buying and selling were nearly the same, close to 205 in terms of the 1913 base of 100. By December what the farmer had to sell was down to 116; what he had to buy was at 156. Here was the start of another inequality within the frame of national resources, one which threatened the success of the administration of Warren G. Harding even before he took the oath of office.

Chapter XI ★ Interim: November, 1920-March, 1921

THE SIXTY-SIXTH CONGRESS resumed its work on Monday, December 6, 1920, to mark time until the lapse of weeks should bring a new administration into the White House. Its first business, after notifying the President that it had assembled, was to listen to the valedictory of the President-elect. Senator Harding had not yet resigned, although the Democratic governor of Ohio, whom he had defeated in November, had been courteous. Cox had offered to name as Harding's successor for the short session the senator who had been chosen to succeed him on March 4, 1921. "No member of this body could be more reluctant to leave it than am I," said Harding; and there is no reason to doubt his complete sincerity. "Peculiarly sensible of the obligations of the Senate," he begged for its coöperation through the four years to come. He left cards of courtesy at the White House and withdrew to Marion for rest and conference. He surrendered his seat as of January 15. The day after his valedictory Woodrow Wilson sent to the Congress his annual report on the state of the nation.

Sick, and his purpose defeated by the failure of the "solemn referendum" to settle anything, Wilson was still undaunted. He had not yet given up. The day before he died, in 1924, he is said to have told his wife and daughter that it was well for the League to have been rejected, that the people were not yet ready for the sacrifices which it entailed, and that although a League must some day come it ought not to come until the nation was ready to accept it. But he urged in 1920 that the United States now set an example of internal reform, and that it show its sincerity by giving freedom to the Philippines; he had faith in the mission of the United States to bring

[178]

about in the world a "new order . . . in which reason and right would take precedence of covetousness and force." The Congress, to which the message was read, paid no attention to it, took up the threads of public business, and found them worse tangled than when the houses had adjourned for the conventions in June. The Republican members kept an interested eye on the doings of Harding who was on vacation.

Wilson had indulged himself in a brief vacation in Bermuda after his election in 1912 and before he took up in seriousness the major business of a president-elect. Hoover, in a similar period, was to visit the American republics to the south. No president-elect can escape the fact that after the fatigue of a successful campaign, and before he takes the oath of office, he must perform as a private citizen a task which may break or make his presidency. The selection of a Cabinet, whose names must be ready for presentation to the Senate as soon as he takes the oath, is a thankless job, one that is likely to make more enemies than friends. Every section of the land, every faction of the party, every creed and every race, feels an interest in the choice of the secretaries; and although these have little status of their own, being the personal servants of the President, their distribution and their affiliations may bring triumph or disaster to an administration.

Few Cabinets have been so casually selected as that of Woodrow Wilson, for Wilson was new to Washington, and hardly knew even the leaders of his own party. Harding knew them all, and had a kindliness of heart which made it hard ever to say "no" to a friend. In addition to the reasonable claims which a president-elect must reconcile with the public service there are also the personal claims of those who, from past association or from direct aid in nominating or electing him, feel themselves entitled to reward. Harding put off the day of hard decision, and went fishing in southern Texas; but those who were in his party, and those whose hospitality he accepted, were significant. Daugherty, his preconvention manager, was there; Frelinghuysen, Elkins, and Hale—intimate friends and senators all; the family doctor, Sawyer, who was to be made a reserve general and assigned to duty at the White House; and the son-in-law of a late bonanza miner, Edward Beale McLean, whose Washington mansion was a place of boundless entertainment.

The Harding party started south on the Saturday after election, in time to make a public appearance at Brownsville on Armistice Day. Declining the offer of a warship for the trip, the President-elect proceeded to the Canal Zone on a steamer from New Orleans. After an inspection of the Canal and the fortifications—Hale was chairman of the Senate Naval Committee, and Frelinghuysen of that on Coast Defense—the party touched at Jamaica before returning to Newport News and Norfolk. Here Harding made five speeches in one day, and kept an engagement which had in part shaped his trip. On Sunday, December 5, as a member of Marion Lodge 32, he delivered a long-promised address at the Elks Memorial Home at Bedford, Virginia; and on the following day he bade farewell to the Senate.

Harding was, among other things, what the successful publisher of a small-town paper needed to be, a "joiner." He took in all good faith and seriousness his fraternal relationship with the Elks and allowed the Masons at Columbus to put him through the high degrees. His wife was proud to admit that they were "just folks"; and both lived in fellowship with that sector of American life which Sinclair Lewis had recently lampooned in *Main Street* (1920). No American leader is safe for himself or for the people if his mind resides too far off Main Street for even the level of Main Street is so far above that of most Americans that its habits and ideals are lived and emulated by many of them.

It was, in a way, Main Street which was about to be commissioned with responsibility for the government of the United States. It was a Main Street which admired big business, its successes and its profits and yet was jealous. Its consciousness of the side streets and the slums was growing, without as yet driving it to violent effort to correct them. The Benevolent and Protective Order of the Elks, for which Harding had affection, was a symbol of a Main Street process. The Elks had become a national order in 1868, based on fellowship and mutual protection. The Loyal Order of the Moose had followed it in 1888, and had a director-general who did not yet know that he was on his way to the Cabinet and the Senate. The Order of Eagles joined the group of associations in 1898. Their club houses were visible across the land, not too far from Main Street for their associates to get together easily. They were all less serious than the Masonic Orders, or than the Knights of Columbus (1882) with which the Catholic Church had undertaken to provide for its communicants the social advantages of Masonry. Marshal Foch was made the millionth Knight at Chicago in 1921. All these orders were burgeoning with new residences and growing memberships as the United States moved from war to peace; and within their ranks there was a spread of information on a basis of mutual confidence. They learned of matters, often to public advantage, in a manner comparable to that which the committees of correspondence had provided in earlier generations. Nonpolitical in character, their members went along with their several parties without losing the concern for private welfare as their principal interest.

Around the orders, with overlapping memberships limited only by the capacity of citizens to be "joiners," organizations of a different type were making an impact on social life. On the highways, at city limits, signs were appearing, bearing an emblem, and stating the day of the week on which the luncheon clubs met, and the hotels in which they met.

Some of the loneliness of business life had been translated into a sort of fellowship. The small businessman (and most American businessmen were small), harassed between his customers on one side and his employees on the other, saw little of his kind. When he traveled on business, within the huge American dimensions, he was often away from home for a long time. The familiar Gideon Bible in his hotel room was an attempt to mitigate his loneliness. It was this loneliness which drove Paul Harris, brooding over it in his Chicago hotel, to become the Father of Rotary.

The dream of Harris was of a social contact in every town, to be made real by the creation of a chain of clubs with which any member might anywhere make contact. They were to be selective clubs, meeting for weekly luncheons, and noncompetitive. Their members were not to eat with their rivals, for a typical membership list was to include only one representative from each recognized activity; but for an hour each week they were to get away from business. The first Rotary Club came into existence in 1905. A National Association was organized in 1910; and two years later, as the idea spread, it became Rotary International. More than a thousand clubs were functioning by 1920 and their members, thinking of themselves as "key men" in their several lines of work, were conscious of more than fellowship at luncheon. There was plenty of fellowship, horseplay, and song, as well as deliberate equality. There were also adoptions of useful public tasks. The meetings provided audiences for speakers who passed through town, for public figures who wanted to be heard, for promoters in search of converts. From various lips, in the minutes left between dessert and going back to work, the spoken word often put a fresh interpretation upon the doings of the world. The level of interest was the level of Main Street.

The "key men" concept of Rotary of necessity put on the defensive all who missed an invitation to join. But these could at least seek a charter for a new club, or affiliate with one of the rival chains which followed Rotary. Gyro International was organized, in 1912. Kiwanis International joined the list in 1915. An International Association of Lions Clubs made its appearance in 1917; and in 1920 the Civitan International spread the movement into the South. Overlooked by the men, the women in business started in 1920 what became an American Federation of Soroptimist Clubs. An Optimist International had been launched in 1919.

The members of the clubs were all closer to the people than were the few who enjoyed the most abundant life. They were giving voice to the interests of an American middle class. Out of their ranks came many of the men who held local offices and helped to operate the parties at the voting level. Many were capable of rising to large responsibility when occasion came; many wore buttons indicating their eligibility for membership in the American Legion. If they were as human as men must be, they were nonetheless representative of an America well above the middle. H. G. Wells, turned by the war from the future to the past, had just provided for the middle class *The Outline of History: Being a Plain History of Life and Mankind* (1920). His work was fanciful as well as plain, but it reduced the past to a recognizable pattern, and had influence in the innumerable clubs which women joined.

The last session of the Sixty-sixth Congress reflected the attitudes of an uneasy middle class, irked by war, strained by its effort in a new sort of coöperation, fearful of violent change, and hopeful for a return to old times which, because they were past, seemed to have been good. It was unlikely that new business would have much chance with the dead center prevailing in government and the President at odds with Congress, but a beginning might be made respecting matters whose completion would have to wait for the inauguration of the new administration.

There were echoes of oratory in the air as Congress met, for the English past and the English present were under discussion. The three hundredth anniversary of the landing of the Pilgrims was being celebrated, and Parliament was putting the finishing touches upon an Irish home rule act. The occasion was taken by the Friends of Irish Freedom to convert the organization into an American Association for the Recognition of the Irish Republic. Mr. *Punch* was driven to wish that he could "believe that the United States is really a melting-pot. It seems to me that your German remains a German, that your Irishman remains an Irishman. You never seem to get together as a nation except when you go to war." The Germans had, indeed, got sufficiently together to form a German-American Citizens League, and to send an envoy to the President-elect to suggest the inclusion of an American German in the Cabinet.

It was just a century since Daniel Webster had commemorated the arrival of the Pilgrims, their anchoring off Provincetown where they signed the Compact on November 21 (N.S.), 1620, before landing a month later at Plymouth. Henry Cabot Lodge was now the orator of the day, combining praise for the transplanted virtues of England with praise for the isolation of the United States. Hecklers in New York had recently howled a similar speaker from the stage, and Carnegie Hall had been picketed by "American Women . . . for the Enforcement of American War Aims." The elevation of William T. Manning to a Protestant-Episcopal bishopric had been attacked because of his vocal efforts on the side of England against the enemy. And there were Protestant clerics who feared that the United States was being turned into "A Roman Catholic Irish Republic."

But the Plymouth Tercentenary was conducted with propriety and Governor Coolidge, who presided, revealed his ability to speak with brevity. Oxford University seized the moment to select a Harvard historian, Samuel Eliot Morison, as its first Harmsworth Professor of American History. The associates of the Anglo-American Sulgrave Institution proceeded with their plans to convert Sulgrave Manor, one of the ancient homes of the Washingtons in England, into a historic shrine.

The Assembly of the League of Nations met in November, exchanging greetings with Woodrow Wilson and confident that the League could function without the United States. The Council had already come into action, and the Secretariat had been recruited. A commission of jurists, Root among them, had drafted the statute which, reduced to treaty form, should create the World Court and define its relations to the League. Business was awaiting action by the League.

The Peace Conference completed its basic work with the Treaty of Sèvres in August and its members had been recalled to their homes. Part of what was still left to be done had been entrusted to the League; part, in the form of unfinished business, passed to a council of ambassadors representing the major nations. In middle Europe, between the frontiers of Germany and Russia, both redrawn, there was still confusion. Italy and Yugoslavia had just reached at Rapallo a compromise agreement upon their territorial problems; but this, like other agreements in the making of the new map of Europe, was far from stable. Armenia, whose independence had been recognized, and for which the Allies wished to make the United States the mandatory power, was being pulled two ways. Both Russia and the nationalist Turkish government of Kemal Pasha claimed it, yet out of Armenia itself came a voice declaring it to be one of the affiliated Soviet republics. The United States had just been caught napping by the assignment of the island of Yap to Japan as mandatory. Here, on a former German island, was an important cable station on the line to the Philippines and to China. It seems not to have been noted until too late that the tiny isle lay to the north of the equator, in an area of the western Pacific over which Japan was to be assigned control. The nervousness over this assignment was not lessened by the fact that the prewar alliance between Britain and Japan, which had been renewed in 1911, still had a year to run.

It was too soon in 1920 to appraise the power of the League to prevent wars, but there were movements within the United States which approached the matter of peace by other routes than through the League. Borah was ready, when Congress met, with a proposal to negotiate disarmament. The appropriations for the fiscal year 1921–1922 were the natural business for the short session. They involved some answer to the question posed by Secretary Daniels in 1919 and 1920: if the League should fail, could the United States avoid the need to maintain complete national defense? The ships authorized in the act of 1916 were still uncompleted. Some were not even begun. Borah proposed the negotiation of a holiday during which the powers should agree to peg, and keep pegged, their existing naval strength. His resolution suggesting the negotiation to the President was introduced on December 14. Japan, desirous of being left alone in the Far East, was for it. England was in too poor a financial state to wish to resume naval construction on a large scale, or to run a race in armament with the United States. The Senate was persuaded in January to direct its Committee on Naval affairs to inquire into the practicability of suspending battleship construction, pending new study of the values of the several types of ships, and pending further discussion of an international agreement for the reduction of armament. The navy appropriation bill went over into the new administration, and did not become law until after the new fiscal year had begun. But Borah's movement was launched. The army bill had better luck, but the debate on it was interrupted by the passage of a mandatory resolution requiring the Secretary of War to discontinue new enlistments until army personnel had been reduced to 175,000. A veto by the President, who saw nothing at home or abroad to justify the bill, was promptly passed over his veto in February.

Representative Isaac Siegel of New York, chairman of the Committee on the Census, had ready for introduction as Congress met the usual bill for a reapportionment of representatives, in compliance with constitutional requirement, and based on the enumeration of 1920. That the bill would raise difficult questions had been foreshadowed when the returns indicated such uneven population trends among the states as to force a decision between an increase in the size of the House and a reallotment which would reduce the representation of several states. The great cities had drawn more population into centers which were already congested;

new industry had turned Detroit into a new major center; migration had shifted new residents into southern California and changed the balance of the state. If the existing number of representatives was to be continued at 435, at least three states must surrender two apiece, and seven others one.

The size of the House of Representatives had steadily grown since the Constitutional Convention and had fixed its membership at sixty-five, subject to reapportionment after each census. As the states grew in number and population the membership in the House had been increased at nearly every reapportionment, for Congress hesitated to take from any state a single representative, yet could not deny to any state the increase called for by the census enumeration. The ratio of population to representative had grown from 30,000 to one, to 218,986 to one. In 1911, with the end of the statehood process in sight, it had been provided that upon the admission of the last two, New Mexico and Arizona, the membership should stand at 435. The representatives were at last so numerous that a reconstruction of the Hall of Representatives was undertaken so that members might have room to sit, and office buildings were put up near the Capitol so that each of them might have a place in which to work.

The new proposal was based on an increased membership, 483— "the smallest possible number for no State to lose a Member"—and Siegel promised to promote a Constitutional Amendment fixing the maximum size of the House at 500. Before it passed the House in January the debates renewed old sectional recriminations. It was demanded that the South be cut down proportionally to the number of citizens excluded from the franchise, and that the North should not be allowed the inflated representation arising from the great number of aliens, counted there by the census but not having the right to vote. Sectionalism appeared, which was to prevent any reapportionment until after the next census in 1930. Apart from the shifting of population from state to state and the varying rates of increase, the drift to town intensified the rivalry of city and country. When the states should in turn redistrict under a new apportionment the cities would gain and the country lose. The greatest of the cities were already under attack in their several states, the rural legislators of which fought to retain a control by the farmlands which the distribution of population did not warrant. Illinois and New York were continuously rent by the feud against their metropolitan areas. The metropolitan areas were, moreover, almost consistently "wet" and giving moral support to a recently incorporated Association against the Prohibition Amendment. The small towns and rural areas were likely to be "dry" and had some right to fear that an increase in the representation of the cities would endanger prohibition. The Democratic South, where prohibition was linked with the race question, had additional reason for its fears. The apportionment bill passed the House, with heavy support from urban areas. The Senate, in which population did not count, failed to pass it. The growing deviation of attitudes of city and country prevented for another decade a compliance with the constitutional mandate for decennial apportionment.

The seven and a half million aliens who aroused the concern of the South because though they were ineligible to vote they were nevertheless counted for Congress, were fewer than the ten million Negroes who, though citizens, were largely deprived of the vote and thereby distressed the North. But the aliens worried others than the South. More than 400,000 had been added in the year ending June 30, 1920; twice that number followed before another year elapsed. The more depressed by war and poverty the European homelands were, the greater was the eagerness of those who could manage to get away to seek opportunity in the United States. The presence of millions of foreign-born residents who had not sought naturalization was a grievance in the labor market, and was not without a bearing upon the process of Americanization. The coming of more millions threatened to increase competition among the workers at the very time when the unevenness of price decline was placing farmers at a disadvantage. The possibility that many of them, coming increasingly from central and southern Europe, might be Bolshevist at heart made them unwelcome for reasons other than competition. Albert Johnson, of Hoquiam, Washington, had a bill treating the flood of immigration as an emergency, and setting up a temporary barrier behind which the United States might deliberate upon a permanent policy.

Representative Johnson was a member of the Sons of the American Revolution, a son of a Civil War veteran, and had been a reserve captain in the World War. His state was unfriendly to radicalism, and at Centralia it had seen the clash of the American Legion and the I.W.W. in 1919. Like most of the West Coast, his region was peculiarly sensitive to the presence of Orientals among its population. His proposal, which the House passed at once, called for a suspension of immigration for a year.

The Senate amended the Johnson bill, incorporating in it ideas which had been under consideration since the passage of the literacy test in 1917. Similar ideas, based on race purity, had been abroad since Gobineau developed the idea of the inequality of human races in 1853 and Darwin had launched *The Origin of Species* in 1859. A senator from Vermont, William P. Dillingham, was mouthpiece for those who were interested in the effect of immigration upon the American melting pot, and who were disturbed by the volume of its flow as well as by the increasing percentage of southern Europeans which it was adding to the population. Pseudoscientific theories of eugenics were being utilized for political reasons in an attempt to prevent further changes in the proportions among the races comprising the American people.

As the Johnson bill became by amendment the Johnson-Dillingham bill, and was finally sent to the White House, the principle of suspension was dropped, and quotas were set up to preserve the proportions among the races. No countries for the next year—it was still a temporary act—were to be permitted to send to the United States more than three per cent of those of its nationals who were found in the United States by the census of 1910. The figures of 1920 were not yet available, and the proportions of 1910 antedated the war-driven arrivals. Labor liked the idea, in spite of the proportion of immigrant stock within its ranks. Old-line Americans, nervous on race questions, were likely to be for it. The opposition— the employers of labor and those who were themselves immigrants or children of immigrants—was bitter against it. The New York representative, Siegel, led a delaying fight from the Republican side. Adolph J. Sabath of Illinois, born in Bohemia, gave him support from the Democrats. They joined in charging trickery in the parliamentary tactics whereby the Johnson proposal had been hurried through the House. Wilson, who had twice vetoed the literacy test, received the measure in the last hours of the session and of his term in office. He failed to sign it, and the proposal to erect a barricade against the immigrant was passed on to add another problem for the new administration.

The sweeping exercise of federal power made necessary by the war paved the way for an increasing tendency to turn to Congress for protective legislation. It would have been strange if the return of the Republican party to control of the Congress had not been followed by renewed discussion of the protective tariff, for the sake of protection and for defense against the dangers of postwar competition. Few of Wilson's Fourteen Points had aroused more partisan resentment than the third which called for "the removal, so far as possible, of all economic barriers. . . ." This had been interpreted as an open attack on the principle of protection which, more than any other, had been the mainstay of Republican policy for a generation. The Underwood-Simmons (1913) tariff was indeed in need of revision because of lapse of time; but immediate and urgent revision was now pressed upon Congress. Joseph W. Fordney of Indiana, sitting in his eleventh Congress, and elected to a twelfth, had the Republican case in hand, as chairman of the Committee on Ways and Means.

The Fordney proposal for an emergency tariff on agricultural products was to be "key log" in the legislative jam which brought the short session to an end. How critical the farmer situation was, was indicated by the prompt action taken in a related field upon a resolution from a North Dakota senator, Asle J. Gronna. Gronna's constituents knew that agricultural depression was at hand. The break in prices had reduced the farmer's receipts without proportionately lowering the prices which he had to pay. In the analysis of the incomes of 1920 only North and South Dakota were in the class of the South, with per capita averages under $400. The people were poor and distressed and were normally Republican even if they voted the ticket recommended by their Nonpartisan League. In 1915 this league had been set up among them in the interest of "a square deal for the people of this state." Its official organ, *The Nonpartisan Leader,* had then asserted that the members were "not angry at anybody"; but they were angry now. They were angered by the continuance of loans to the Allies, two years after the end of the war, and the Secretary was driven to assuage them by promising to lend no more without approval from Congress. The preamble to the Gronna resolution summed up their case: the prevailing prices for their output would not even meet "the cost of production," Europe though in great need of their foods was too poor to finance their purchase, and the very agency of Congress which had been created to finance exports, the War Finance Corporation, had suspended action.

The War Finance Corporation, a government-owned creation of 1918, had done business in accepting as collateral for loans the paper of banking institutions whose customers were making exports. It was due for liquidation six months after the war, but when the legal state of war lasted long after the fighting ceased the Treasury had brought about a discontinuance of activity and a liquidation of outstanding loans. The Committee on Agriculture backed the resolution which directed the rehabilitation of the War Finance Corporation that it might lend assistance to agricultural exports, and also to direct the Federal Reserve Board to extend to farmers the most "liberal extension of credit" consistent with the law. Bank failures were sweeping over the Dakotas, as prices of food fell and land values declined. Worst there, the conditions were bad in much of the West. Frozen assets clogged the banks which could not dispose of notes and mortgages when market values fell below the face of loans; ultimate foreclosures threatened the owners of the land.

There was real doubt as to the sufficiency of the remedy to the existing conditions, but there was no doubt that western Republicans, with much southern backing, were in earnest. The Gronna resolution passed the Senate a week after the session opened. In five days more it passed the House; and the President received it before Christmas. The houses joined in passing it over the sharp veto with which Wilson rejected the measure on January 4, 1921.

Two days later, Boies Penrose, after a long illness back in the Senate in a wheel chair, experienced a political change of heart. He knew the tariff and its implications from the days of Nelson W. Aldrich, knew it by hearsay from the time of his mentor Matthew Stanley Quay, and knew how in 1888 the Republican party had promised to put a protective tariff on agricultural products to allay the suspicion of the western farmer. In December he had deprecated the idea of the tariff as a remedy, for he was aware that a country chiefly exporting food could do the farmer little good by taxing the importation of food. In January he knew that it must be done whether it was helpful or not.

The Fordney emergency agricultural tariff bill had passed the House before Christmas. It delayed other business through January, for it met a stubborn filibuster in the Senate. Penrose was himself induced to attempt to force a vote by presenting a cloture petition on the last day of January, but he could not command the necessary two-thirds, and the debate continued until the Senate accepted the bill on February 16. Delay in conference kept it from the White House until March 1. Senator Moses, more brutal in statement, but as well-informed on tariff matters as his Republican associates, refused to join Penrose in voting for the bill, describing it as a brat "with congenital economic rickets." The veto message, reaching the House a few hours before the end, was similar in meaning though more polite in language. It closed the administration on the note that "this is no time for the erection here of high trade barriers." There were too few votes to pass it over the veto. It, too, was saved for Harding.

Senator Harding was back in Marion on December 8, fresh from his vacation and prepared to confer, as he had promised, with the "best minds" upon the problems of a president-elect. The daily press informed him of the utterances of some of the "minds," best or otherwise. With these he must make his peace if he hoped to have it after his inauguration. By character and political habit he preferred peace. It was to his credit as a man that he rarely cherished rancor and gained little satisfaction from acts of defiance. It was his handicap as statesman, at his new elevation, that as he listened too readily he believed too much. The deep personal loyalties which marked his character often made him slow to realize that he was receiving bad advice. It was his misfortune that he was to die in the midst of democracy in agitation, in the clash of contradictory interests beyond the hope of instant reconciliation, and at a moment when the organization of his party had come into such bad repute that it welcomed a scapegoat who could not talk back. The precise nature of his attainments is buried under the epithets of those whose aims could not be achieved, and of those who were

shifting blame. No personal archive has yet appeared upon which
a measured estimate of his presidency can be based. The most
formal of his biographies, Samuel Hopkins Adams' *Incredible Era:
The Life and Times of Warren Gamaliel Harding* (1930), owes
more of its color to the temper of the times and to the disillusion-
ment of a decade than to the documented picture of a man.

The path to Marion was beaten by many feet. There had been
nothing like it since Republicans had gone to Oyster Bay to inform
Theodore Roosevelt concerning the inadequacies of William Howard Taft. All through December the President-elect sat and listened. He continued to listen after he went to Florida in the latter
part of January, to be a guest on the houseboat of Senator Frelinghuysen, and to combine a final vacation with a final balancing of
Cabinet claims. Many and contradictory forces sought to shape the
Cabinet to their several desires. There were the party leaders who
had led in the past, to be recognized in fair proportion to their de-
serts. "This," said Harding, "is going to be a Republican Cabinet,
you may count on that." Taft, the last Republican President, had
a wide influence, and had never been advanced to the Supreme
Court—where the Chief Justice whom he had himself named, Edward Douglass White, was nearing the end of a career. Hughes, the
nominee of 1916, had legal talents which might justify his restoration to the Supreme Court and a high position in the party. Lowden and Wood, leaders among the aspirants in 1920, had as good
title as most candidates. Root had assumed the post of elder statesman, and wanted nothing. Hoover represented a body of opinion
too important to be disregarded but, having discovered himself to
be a Republican, had destroyed his chance for a nomination by
either party. George Harvey, having boxed the political compass
and come into the Republican party, knew his own desires and his
numerous distrusts. Harding listened to arguments, pro and con,
respecting all.

There were doctrinaires to be heard, those who hoped Harding
would accept the League, and those who wished him to bury it.
There were senatorial associates, Fall and Weeks, and Harry S.
New of Indiana, key man in Senate politics. Some of the advisers
were still progressive-minded, but to others the Progressive party
was anathema. There were the Irish who demanded a Cabinet seat

in recognition of their race, and the Germans, too. And at last there were the party workers, beginning with Will H. Hays, whose skill as a mollifier had helped to hold together the opposition to Woodrow Wilson. And there was the old friend Harry Micajah Daugherty, to whom the Harding candidacy owed much. It was, in its way, as rough a path to peace as Wilson walked in Paris. Every day the news dispatches from Washington revealed the discordant notes in the Republican chorus.

The prevailing fears and hopes respecting the Treaty and the League made critical the choice of a Secretary of State. There is reason to believe that Harding at one time offered the post to George Harvey but that he really preferred for it his old friend Albert B. Fall of New Mexico, although he hesitated to override the prominence of the pro-League group. The irreconcilables desired to see Philander C. Knox restored to the post he had held under President Taft. Charles E. Hughes was less offensive to them than some, and had owed his nomination in 1916 partly to his ability to avoid breaches with discordant factions. As a signer of the Republican pro-League manifesto in October he had aligned himself with the group which, through the canvass, had struggled against the pressure of the irreconcilables to force the candidate into explicit opposition. Just where Harding stood in the matter was still in doubt, concealed among the balanced statements which he retrimmed from day to day, after each most recent conference. Rumor had it that Harding defied Penrose as he turned toward Hughes. His mind was set on Hughes before he went to Florida, and the intention to make this first cabinet appointment was announced formally on February 19.

Disappointed by the survival of Hughes, Penrose turned to the Treasury, where Wilson's appointees—McAdoo, Glass, and Houston—had been definitely not of the big business group. Here Brigadier General Charles G. Dawes was west of Wall Street, but competent. The financial services of this Chicago banker had been distinguished in the supply of the A.E.F.; and when he, with his unimpeached Republican standing, turned against the partisan search for scandal in the administration of the war, in February, 1921, he brought it to an end. Appearing before one of the many investigating committees set up by the Sixty-sixth Congress, he turned upon his inquisitors: "It was a big job . . . We would have paid horses prices for sheep if the sheep could have pulled artillery to the front." Whether the mild profanity which emphasized his disgust was "What the hell," or "Hell, Maria," is somewhat uncertain, but his violence was well-timed and adequate. It was, however, a Pittsburgh banker, Andrew W. Mellon, whom Penrose pressed the more forcibly because of the success of Hughes. Mellon had, with almost perfect anonymity, gathered one of the great American fortunes without being labeled as of Wall Street. Harding accepted him for the Treasury, and used this compliance to back his own preference for other seats.

The war and navy appointments, with the problems of reorganization at hand, were highly controversial. Backers of Major General Leonard Wood, for Secretary of War, were faced by an American preference for civilian military secretaries, in which Harding joined. One of the senatorial associates, John W. Weeks, had turned banker after training at Annapolis for naval service which he never saw. He was graduated at a time when a dying navy could not use its whole output of midshipmen; yet since he was a member of the same class as many of the ranking admirals in 1921, he had no reason to be eager for the Navy Department. Weeks accepted the post of Secretary of War, leaving a Secretary of the Navy to be hastily named in the last days of Cabinet selection. The choice fell, for no explained reason, upon a Michigan manufacturer, Edwin Denby, who had been a gunner's mate in the navy in the war with Spain, had sat in three Congresses, and had been accepted as a private in the Marine Corps in the World War. He was overage and overweight; but his talents in the building of morale had made him a major in the Marine Corps.

After these appointments there were six more to be made, but only one of them, that of Secretary of Commerce, was a matter for a major clash. It went to Herbert Hoover, to the distress of Penrose and Lodge, for Hoover, as Food Administrator, had endorsed the plea for the election of a Democratic Congress in 1918. His reputation was entirely nonpartisan. There had been a suggestion of assigning him to the Department of the Interior, whose conglomerate of disconnected bureaus offered a chance for the work of an organizer as secretary, and whose duties in the Far West made the

post appropriate for a westerner. But the Department of the Interior went to Fall, senatorial associate and oil man, who was tied
too closely to the Mexican problem to have been useful in the State
Department, and not known to be in sympathy with the policies
of conservation.

The posts in Agriculture and Labor were similar in that the
specialized nature of their work had developed a habit of naming
secretaries whose background was of the field of departmental activity. They were different in that while labor had a program which
it was organized to advance, the farmer was not yet able to present
one. The appointments were of consequence because of the need
to keep the peace with two large classes of citizens, each of which
could, by a withdrawal of support, bring about the defeat of Republican policy. The former was filled from the office of *Wallace's
Farmer* in Des Moines, Iowa. Here was the center of the agrarian
West, and the farm paper was in the hands of the second generation
of family editors. The present editor, Henry C. Wallace, had been
a farmer and a professor of dairying in the Iowa College at Ames.
He was unpopular enough with the Chicago meatpackers for his
appointment to be popular with the farmers. The Federal Trade
Commission had taken notice of the trend whereby the slaughter-
ers of cattle and the processors of meat were expanding their activities in the direction of a food monopoly. The farmers had noticed
it too and Gronna had already driven through the Senate a bill to
regulate the packers and separate the marketing of meat from other
lines of business.

Labor was disposed to think that the Secretary of Labor, instead
of being an officer of government specially charged with labor
problems, should be in substance an ambassador and attorney for
labor at the Capital. It would have preferred the naming of a professional labor organizer, and was less than content with what it
got. James J. Davis of Pennsylvania, though he encouraged the
survival of his nickname "Puddler Jim," had not been a union
workman so recently as to have maintained an active labor status.
He even believed that arbitral awards in labor controversies ought
to be made enforceable and was, in the eye of labor, the sort of a
secretary that employers wanted. For the past dozen years Davis
had been director general of the Loyal Order of Moose and founder

and governor of its elaborate home for widows and orphans of members at Mooseheart, Illinois.

The expectation that the Post Office would be assigned to the chairman of the Republican National Committee was warranted. This had happened in so many cases that it was almost taken for granted, and Hays deserved well of his successful candidate. He was too poor to hold a public office long, but until the motion-picture industry called him to another mediating job, between the industry and the critics of its standards, he left most of his politics outside his office. It was equally expected that the President-elect would indulge himself in one appointment entirely personal; in this spirit McKinley had brought Judge Day to Washington. Harding surprised no one when he selected Harry M. Daugherty and made him Attorney General. There were grave doubts concerning the legal fitness of a small-town lawyer for the job ahead. There were even greater doubts concerning the company he had kept on his way up with his chosen candidate. His loyalty to the President, as he defined it, was complete. But the unpleasant aroma associated with the name of the "Ohio Gang," clung to the Attorney General through his term of service. The attacks made upon him in anticipation of his appointment brought the loyalties of Harding into action: "The opposition to him has more than ever convinced me that I would like to have him in the Cabinet."

The Cabinet slate was completed on the Frelinghuysen boat and while Harding lingered through the last days of his vacation at St. Augustine. It was constructed, as always, under conditions whereby the "best minds" which can be included are those who will accept appointment and those whose inclusion will not arouse resentments so great as to wreck an administration. It contained at least three names of great distinction. In the last week of February the list was made official. By the end of the month Harding was back in Marion, ready for his presidential journey to the Capital. He declined a showy inauguration. On March 4, 1921, the outgoing President summoned his strength to ride to the Capitol with his successor, to sign the last-minute bills, and to withdraw from the White House to a new home at 2340 S Street, where he ended his days. The Democratic interlude was of the past, and the interim between election and inauguration was ended.

Chapter XII ★ Extrication

I T IS UNLIKELY that any private citizen, even though he be a president-elect, has fully realized the strain and pressure upon the Chief Executive. The oath of office, by a fraction of a minute, throws the successful candidate into an unfamiliar world. He passes out of an atmosphere of party adulation, the necessary atmosphere of a partisan canvass in which his associates have supported the ticket whether because they endorsed it or because if it should be defeated they would themselves be lost. He moves into cold isolation, between contradictory programs and competing politicians.

There was a chance for adjustment to this new experience in the old century. There had once been nine months of freedom from direct congressional pressure, between the adjournment of a Congress on March 4, and the opening of the new Congress in its first session on the first Monday in December. But this old order had changed since William McKinley called Congress in special session immediately after his inauguration to carry out a program to which he had pledged his party. Each time the party changed thereafter, the long recess was canceled. Taft, in 1908, was given peremptory mandate to advance the "Roosevelt policies," and began without delay. Wilson dared lose no time in seizing the advantages accruing to his party from the Republican split of 1912. Harding was driven head on into the clash of desires by the demand to liquidate what was left of the war, and to extricate the United States from foreign and domestic complications. But he differed from his predecessors in having received no clear mandate on other matters. The election of 1920 merely served as a writ of ejection upon the existing administration. The "solemn referendum" answered no questions, though it commissioned the Republicans to find the answers.

[197]

"Our eyes will never be blind to a developing menace, our ears never deaf to the call of civilization," said the new President in his inaugural address; "we seek no part in directing the destinies of the Old World. We do not mean to be entangled. . . . We are ready to associate ourselves with the nations of the world . . . for conference, for counsel . . . [but] a world supergovernment is contrary to everything we cherish and can have no sanction by our Republic. This is not selfishness; it is sanctity." Between the two extremes of isolation and internationalism he proposed to find a course. Hughes was to be allowed a relatively free hand in arranging the details: George Harvey was sent to London to interpret them.

No post from which to watch for the dangers of entanglement was better than the Court of St. James for a man who had devoted himself to the campaign against the Treaty of Versailles. The President's intention to make Harvey the ambassador was announced before the Sixty-seventh Congress met on April 11, 1921, and was received with violent disapproval from the friends of the Treaty. *Harvey's Weekly* said its valedictory on April 23, its work accomplished now that Woodrow Wilson was out of office; and its editor was in London and ready for a welcoming dinner from The Pilgrims on May 19. In his court costume, with the regulation silk breeches, Harvey could never have been recognized as an American had he not worn as well his heavy identifying spectacles. But when he drove his own Ford car through Hyde Park there was no doubt. Nor was there doubt when at the Pilgrims' dinner, he avowed "deep and true . . . affection for the Mother Country." As an "undiluted American," he assured his hearers that the American proffer of a helping hand was not "attributable to a tender susceptibility." We sent our armies to France "solely to save the United States of America, and most reluctantly and laggardly at that. . . . We were afraid not to fight."

One of the debts of the President was paid when Harvey became a mouthpiece; another was payable when on the day of the Pilgrims' dinner the end came for Edward Douglass White. There had been caustic comment in 1910 when Taft elevated to the post of Chief Justice of the United States one who was at once a southerner, a Democrat, a Catholic, and a former soldier of the Confederacy; and at a time when Taft's only deep regret was his own failure to have sat upon the Supreme Court. The ex-President was nominated to succeed White on June 30 and was confirmed at once, only four senators speaking and voting against him: Borah, Johnson, La Follette, and Thomas E. Watson of Georgia.

It might have been difficult to procure a confirmation if the choice had fallen upon Hughes, for early in the winter Hughes had led the counsel for Truman H. Newberry in the appeal from conviction under the federal corrupt practices act. The charge, an overlavish use of funds in the Michigan primary of 1918, was sustained by a federal jury at Grand Rapids, March 20, 1920. But the Supreme Court was convinced by argument that the constitutional power of Congress over elections did not extend to a control of the primaries at which candidates were named, and that conviction had been annulled by a five to four decision on May 2, 1921. The Democratic senators, with much support from those with Progressive leanings, were outraged by the reversal. They had no intention of giving up their fight against the senator from Michigan, and the Committee on Privileges and Elections was already making further study of the case, and considering the possibility of an expulsion, when Taft became Chief Justice.

There were other gestures to be made by the President in the direction of men who stood well in the opinion of his party. Two of them were military. Pershing had not been fitted into the practical workings of the army although he had received all the promotion in rank at the disposal of the government. Wood, a double martyr in having been confined to commands within the United States and in having been indiscreetly financed as a candidate, was still in charge of a corps area at Chicago. Wood came first.

The independence of the Philippine Islands, promised by the Democratic platform of 1900 and promised again in the Jones act of 1916, had been demanded consistently by native parties since the cession of the islands to the United States. In the Wilson administration the "Filipinization" of the insular government had been advanced in anticipation of the date at which independence should become a fact. The Republican party, in office or in opposition, had admitted the principle of ultimate independence without being ready to discuss a date. Those who had set up the original island government before 1913, and those Americans who resided there, doubted the readiness of Filipinos to control their own affairs.

The war had made the matter more difficult. The Wilson policies had strengthened everywhere the principle of self-determination, which had sent missions from Manila to present the demand to the nominating conventions of 1920. But even the Democratic administration sensed a realignment of power in the Pacific and the new status of Japan. The dispute over the control of Yap made it more real. The shifting of a fleet to the Pacific showed recognition of a new problem in American defense, and the security of the Philippine outpost seemed to involve something more than the mere capacity of Filipinos for self-government. A new governor general to succeed Francis Burton Harrison was certain, whatever should be done with the independence issue.

Within a few days of the inauguration, Harding let it be known that before naming a successor to Harrison he proposed to resurvey the Islands. General Wood was to be sent to the Philippines at the head of a commission to investigate. Wood, who was considering accepting the presidency of the University of Pennsylvania, put off his entry upon academic life, and sailed on an army transport early in April. He paid a formal visit to Japan en route to Manila, where he was greeted by a separatist parade the banners of which read "We want independence." The result of the survey of island conditions was that the time had not yet come to grant independence. In the autumn Wood retired from the army, secured release from the university, and was confirmed as governor general. In this post he was in almost continuous controversy with the assembly, the Filipino leaders, and their partisan supporters. Here he remained, an able administrator, personally popular, and politically objectionable, until his death in 1927.

The General of the Armies, John J. Pershing, had had few duties since his return from France. There was no command for him equal to his rank, the business of the army passed from the Secretary of War through the Chief of Staff in spite of him, and Congress did not accept his experience and opinion as the basis for its acts. In the spring of 1920 he suggested retirement for himself. As Wood began his Philippine inquiry in May it was announced that on July 1 Pershing was to become Chief of Staff. It was further stated that in this office, where no soldier would even technically outrank him, he would concentrate upon the new attempt at a field army organization, and while the routine administration would fall upon the shoulders of his principal assistant, Major General James G. Harbord. The appropriation bills of 1921 cut most of the reality away from the National Defense Act of 1916, and even from the more recent act of 1920.

The initial appointments, so far as usefulness could be forecast, commanded general respect, however far they may have fallen below the standard Harding set for himself: "to hold them up to Lincoln, to Roosevelt and to the teaching of the Scriptures." It was not to these officials that he was referring when, in the autumn, he facetiously replied to Will Rogers who was calling at the White House. Said Rogers, if his standing as a humorist makes him credible, "I would like to tell you all the latest political jokes"; said the President, "I know 'em; I appointed most of them."

Before the new incumbents, large or small, were adjusted to their positions, the Sixty-seventh Congress was at hand. Its convening in special session was unavoidable because its predecessor had left undone work needed for the approaching fiscal year. It was faced by measures so nearly agreed upon that they could be cleared away with speed. It was confronted by the larger matters of policy upon which a government on dead center could never have hoped to agree. And, before it could go far, it and the new administration must somehow bring about the extrication of the United States from the clash between war laws and the fact of peace, and from the anomalous diplomatic status of a country still legally at war twenty-eight months after it had ceased to fight.

Extrication, rather than reconstruction, came first. This called for acts and policies designed to bring back peace—peace with the enemy and the removal of barriers to friendly relations in the western hemisphere. Next to be adjusted were relations with the Allies and the Associated Powers, for the war was over, what feeling of gratitude had existed had cooled off, and the debts remained. M. Jules Jusserand, long ambassador from France, once said with bitter truth that the bond between debtor and creditor is not "urbane." At home the red tape of war must be unwound. The unwinding had already given disappointment to many in the case of the Esch-Cummins act, and was certain to give more disappointment before the emergency personnel were laid off, emergency offices discontinued, emergency power handed back to Congress. Temporary power, justified only by the needs of war, had begun to "set"; some of the new ventures in government had acquired friends as well as critics. Harding stepped out upon this delicate task while the Senate, in special session to confirm the new Cabinet, was still in Washington in March. He sent to it, on the sixth day of his administration, a treaty with the Republic of Colombia upon which he asked prompt and affirmative action.

It was nearly twenty years since the abrupt recognition of the Republic of Panama created a sense of grievance on the part of Colombia and deepened the Latin-American suspicion of the purposes of the United States. Insult was added to injury when the United States justified its prevention of a recapture of the seceding Colombian state of Panama by reference to a treaty of 1846. This treaty bound the United States by a stipulation to keep transit between the oceans free from interruption or embarrassment; and on this ground the Colombian naval expedition was kept from landing in Panama. Yet an additional stipulation in the same sentence of the treaty was ignored: this guaranteed the "rights of sovereignty and property" which New Granada, the predecessor of Colombia, possessed in Panama. "I took the Isthmus," said Theodore Roosevelt, when he defended the propriety of his action.

The action of the United States, justified officially as in the "interests of civilization," put the American government on the defensive south of the Rio Grande. Roosevelt came to appreciate its consequences and sought a formula whereby the grief of Colombia might be assuaged by cash. Root negotiated for him a proposal which came to nothing. Taft, through Knox, continued "the policy of restoring good relations with Colombia," and failed again. Bryan resumed it in the Democratic administration, sending to the Senate in 1914 a treaty which threw the friends of Roosevelt into violent opposition. A "sincere regret," stated in the text "that anything should have occurred to interrupt or mar the relations of cordial friendship" was twisted into an apology for the intervention of 1903, and denounced as such. Not for three years, and not until the near apology had been softened, was the Bryan treaty even reported to the Senate by the Committee on Foreign Relations. It failed of ratification during the war, but was amended again and reported again, unanimously, and by Lodge as chairman, in the summer of 1919. The "regret" had been eliminated, and the compensation for property rights fixed at twenty-five million dollars. Root and Knox, as well as Lodge, had a hand in the new phraseology, and Roosevelt had expressed himself as well-disposed to compensation. Lodge had relied, too, on Senator Fall, "whose extraordinary knowledge and familiarity with all South American questions" had been freely drawn upon. Action on the treaty was delayed in 1919, and delayed again after still another favorable report had been made just before the conventions met in 1920. Still pending before the Senate, its ratification was urged by Harding; and Lodge opened the debate on April 12.

As a devoted friend of Theodore Roosevelt, Lodge was obliged to urge ratification as an act to "invite added confidence in our Government," without in any way admitting blame on the part of the United States. He defended Roosevelt with all his oratorical power, and defended compensation on its merit. He advanced more than merit for the measure when he pointed out the strategic reasons for friendly relations in the vicinity of the Panama Canal and its approaches. He spoke, too, of foreign commerce in which the competition was no longer among individuals and corporations, but among governments themselves. "The most conspicuous instance of this sort is in regard to oil." He displayed as an exhibit an elaborate list and diagram of the holdings of Britain through the Royal Dutch-Shell combine. Fall had briefed him on the importance of American access to the oil reserves of the world, and the need for cordial relations with Colombia, whose oil resources were in process of development.

Many of the other friends of Theodore Roosevelt declined to go along with the party leaders and thought the compensation quite as bad as the apology. Johnson declared that "every defamer of Roosevelt is its advocate"; Borah wanted an amendment by which blame on the part of the United States should be specifically rejected. And both suggested that oil concessionaires rather than good faith were behind the demand for ratification. On the ninth day, April 20, 1921, the Senate gave its assent by a vote of 69 to 19.

There were, indeed, oil concessionaires who hoped that with Colombia appeased they would have an increased chance to compete with European exploiters in the development of South American oil fields. The world was to show an intense interest in oil in the approaching period. The oil industry had come a long way since Colonel Drake drilled for petroleum and found it at Titusville in 1859. Oil had opened new eras in technology and business, and in social habit. Refined as kerosene, its product had as an illuminant lengthened the day for much of the world. Its profits had been susceptible to capture by those who could control refineries and distribution. They were large because the market was both world-wide and free. The inner organization of near-monopoly in the production of kerosene had managed to keep ahead of controlling laws, in spite of rising hostility to combinations and trusts; and John D. Rockefeller had, by the turn of the century, come to symbolize all that was unsavory in business competition.

But kerosene was only the beginning. As the American oil interests reorganized to avoid too open conflict with the law and yet retain control of their industry, the industry itself took on new shape. Gasoline found a market as the fuel for motor transport; and the heavier oils entered into fierce competition with coal. The waste products of the earlier period became the foundation of the new. There hung over the industry the possibility of ultimate exhaustion of the oil deposits, the distribution of which around the world was haphazard. This led to persistent search for new fields, a quest in which the domestic resources of the United States were richer than those of most of the industrial nations, and one in which success might turn a Cherokee Indian into a millionaire overnight, or a Persian ruler once more into an important monarch. There was a broad incentive to acquire new fields for use or to prevent others from acquiring them. The war had revealed new possibilities in motorization, hence oil and military power were tied together for the future.

In the competition for the oil fields, the American producers were restrained by a type of law against conspiracy from which nationals of other countries were commonly exempt. Those nations which had insufficient oil at home became competitors in the international market, until the odor of oil pervaded the diplomatic

world. How far the ratification of the Colombian treaty was an act
of equity, and how far the pressure for ratification came from the
hope of national or private profit, is uncertain. But it is certain
that the United States could not be indifferent to the depletion of
its own supplies or to new situations set up by the passing into alien
hands of near-by fields. Oil had replaced coal in the newer ships of
the navy, and oil had become a munition of war. The reserves
which had been set aside for navy use by Roosevelt, and legalized
under Taft, were an insurance for the future. Fall, an old miner,
was close to the oilmen; and these were keenly interested in navy
oil, in Colombian oil, and in oil wherever it was to be found. There
was some technical opinion that permanent storage of oil in its
native pools would fail to conserve it for the future; that the navy
fields, surrounded by oil lands which had not been reserved, were
subject to drainage from outside wells.

There were mixed motives in oil promotion, derived from patriotism and scientific opinion; derived, too, from greed, although
courts, juries, prosecutors, and senators divided widely over the
point at which greed became corruption. In the navy the technical
advisers were at loggerheads over the best method to conserve the
precious oil. At the end of May the Assistant Secretary of the Navy,
Theodore Roosevelt, Jr., carried to the White House the draft of
an executive order believed by the Secretary of the Navy to be in
the interest of that conservation. The order provided that the management of the oil reserves, confided to the navy by the act of 1920,
should be shifted to the Department of the Interior, whose normal
business had built up appropriate technical knowledge in the
General Land Office, the Bureau of Mines, and the Geological
Survey. Neither Denby nor his assistant knew how far advanced
were the plans for a leasing of the drilling rights in the reserves at
Elk Hills and Teapot Dome; or how far Secretary Fall was agreed
to the idea of putting the oil into storage above ground; or how
part of the royalty fees were to be commuted into tankage at Pearl
Harbor so that the oil might be kept where the navy needed it. Not
until Fall had left the Cabinet, or while Harding was alive, did the
storm break over the heads of those associated with the handling of
the oil reserves. Those who, at the moment, knew of the executive
order and objected to it included some who had confidence in un-

derground storage, some whose past was one of antagonism to large corporations, some who were in the minority within the Republican party or in the opposition. The act of extrication which lessened the grievance of Colombia helped to create an entanglement which brought unhappiness to the administrations which followed that of Harding.

On the day before the approval of the Colombian treaty, which happened to be the anniversary of the Battle of Lexington, the President was in New York, accepting a statue of Simon Bolivar which Venezuela had presented to the United States. It was a day on which an expression of cordiality toward the republics of the south was appropriate, and liberation and independence of the New World might well be stressed. Each emphasis had its application to the next steps in American policy. Harding wished that this day might have an added significance for the future, as marking "the mutual trust in the fellowship of freedom and democracy" in the Americas. He believed that if Washington and Bolivar could advise they would counsel the hemisphere to go forward as it had gone, and to hold fast to independence. He stressed the new world's experience in arbitration as a means of lessening the danger of war, and felt assured that this experience would justify an invitation "to present day civilization to cast aside the staggering burden of armament." There was nothing in his words to indicate that the Treaty was still alive. As he spoke, the Committee on Foreign Relations was preparing to aid him in the task of extrication by means of a favorable report upon a resolution terminating the state of war between the United States and its two opponents, the Imperial German Government and the Royal Austro-Hungarian Government, neither of which had survived to have a hand in the ending of the war.

Having failed to ratify the Treaty of Versailles the United States was outside the peace, which became effective for the signers upon their exchange of ratifications on January 10, 1920. There was no longer a serious movement to bring about an adherence by the United States to this document. Harding, addressing his special session, had been explicit. "In the existing League of Nations, world-governing with its superpowers," he said, "this Republic will have no part." But this sort of isolation had its discomforts. It deprived the United States of a share in controlling German compliance with the treaty terms, made uncertain the recovery of the costs of the army of occupation, and weakened the influence of the United States in the final adjustment of territorial matters which had been left after the Peace Conference in the hands of the victors. It provided no basis for a resumption of relations with the enemy powers.

It is unusual for a war to end except by a treaty between the belligerents; but Congress had attempted such a step in the resolution which President Wilson vetoed in May, 1920. It is impossible, in theory, to end war by unilateral action. There was no likelihood that Germany would resume the war, but until Germany was a party to it peace could not be real. It was without precedent, too, for Congress to detour around the diplomatic authority of the President, and to make a peace itself. Harding, however, had assented to this procedure in his speech of acceptance, and had assented again when the session was begun. The Knox resolution, which was to be the basis for unilateral action, proposed to repeal the war declaration of April 6, 1917, to declare the existence of a state of peace, and to reserve for the United States all rights respecting the enemy which might have accrued had the United States assented to the Treaty of Versailles. When the resolution was reported back from the Committee on Foreign Relations it had been broadened to include Austria-Hungary, and the Senate entered upon debate on April 28.

The Knox resolution, virtually unfinished business for the Republican Senators, was passed two days later by a vote of 49 to 23. Friends of the Treaty spoke and voted against it. They urged that the war was a fact which no joint resolution could destroy; that it was bad enough to vote to establish peace by law without the self-stultification involved in a repeal of the declaration which Congress had passed in 1917. But the proponents clung to the theory that the way to end the state of war was to repeal the resolution which had created it. And they had the votes.

In the House, never too happy about the power of the Senate in treaty making, and not satisfied by the procedure indicated for the Senate, an independent resolution was already under consideration. Porter of Pennsylvania, chairman of the Committee on Foreign Affairs, had introduced this resolution, and when the Knox resolution was received by the House it was amended by the substitution of the Porter formula. On June 11 the House was asked to expedite its passage by means of a special rule which deprived the members of anything but a choice between the Knox and Porter phraseologies. No amendments to either were to be entertained, since the Republican steering committee was determined that minority members should be held in check.

The Porter substitute said nothing about repealing the war resolution, but stated bluntly that the war declared on April 6, 1917, "is hereby declared at end." Like the Senate version, it made reservation of such rights as the United States had before the war, as it acquired during the war, and as it became entitled to by victory. The House and Senate words differed in detail, but were alike in their effort to retain for the United States the advantages which would have followed from an approval of the Treaty of Versailles. Neither body showed an interest in ascertaining the disposition of the signers of the Treaty toward the American contentions which the reservations sought to protect. Bourke Cockran complained that the public was indifferent: "Accounts of our proceedings are not accorded in the newspapers today as much space as a ball given by a fashionable woman." Meyer London, the sole Socialist sitting in the House, laughed at the majority party as "afflicted with elephantiasis." Its members in the House were rejecting the Senate formula for seeming to apologize for the war, and yet were so confident of the soundness of their substitute as to forbid even the proposal of a modification. "Any fool can enter war," London said. "It is hard to lay the foundations for peace." Pou, of the minority from North Carolina, complained "You have done the asinine thing of making peace, and then saying that all American rights shall thereafter be safe-guarded and protected."

June 11 was a Saturday. The debate on the alternative methods of terminating war, after a disciplined majority had passed its special rule, carried over until Monday, with much discussion of the "apology," of the unilateral character of the proposal, of the constitutional right of the Congress to establish peace by statute rather than the right of the Executive and the Senate to establish it by treaty. There was discussion, too, of the importance of the trade already reopened with Germany in spite of technical war, and of the effect of the proposed action upon German property held in the United States by the Alien Property Custodian. Connally of Texas could not deter the majority by his attack on the "vicious and harmful" precedent and the "political strategy" which dictated "a departure from constitutional processes." By a vote of 304 to 61 the House adopted the Porter substitute.

It was more than two weeks before the committee on conference ironed out the difference of opinion between the two houses, but when the President threw his weight to the Porter formula the Senate conferees surrendered. The reservation of rights was made more specific in its provision that all German property which had been seized by the United States should be held until the former enemies had made suitable provision for the satisfaction of claims against them, and had assured to the United States the "most-favored-nation" treatment; and it retained the claim of the United States to all the rights which ratification of the Treaty of Versailles would have established. Both houses accepted the compromise in time for the Porter-Knox resolution to reach the President on Saturday, July 2, 1921. He was visiting on that week end with his friend Frelinghuysen at Raritan, New Jersey. Signed—perhaps between two rounds of golf—the "Peace of Raritan" advanced extrication to the point at which only the assent of the enemies was needed, and only the negotiation of fresh treaties with them was a condition precedent to the enjoyment of normal relationship. But the Sunday papers were less interested in the peace than in doings in Jersey City that Saturday. Here Jack Dempsey knocked out Georges Carpentier and kept the heavy-weight championship of the world in American hands.

A personal representative of the President, Ellis Loring Dresel, was sent to Berlin to invite the German government to assent to peace on the terms stated in the Porter-Knox resolution. He found there a "cabinet of surrender," which Dr. Joseph Wirth had formed in May, with the avowed intent of hastening recovery by withdrawing obstruction to Allied demands. Germany was not accustomed to parliamentary government, and Wirth functioned between the pressure of former enemies and the pressure of dissatisfied groups within the Reich. He lasted some seventeen months, before the

Socialists abandoned him, and William Cuno, director general of the Hamburg-American line, took over the government. In France, meanwhile, Briand had been replaced as president of the council by Raymond Poincaré who was determined to maintain the security of his country and make Germany pay the reparations in full. France was now seriously at work upon the reconstruction of the devastated regions and the reimbursement of the citizens who were the victims of enemy damage. Success was based upon the payment of reparations, and in the French mind reconstruction was a more essential duty than the repayment to Britain and the United States of the loans which had helped to carry France through the war. There was beginning to be a readjustment of ideas, in which the obligation to pay the foreign debts would be morally canceled if Germany should be allowed to default.

Before Dresel reached Berlin the deviation of the United States from the course of the other Allies had raised a new hope in Germany. It was possible that by playing one set of former enemies against the other the outcome might be made happier for Germany. The Supreme Council of the Allies—on which the victors were now often represented by their ambassadors—was working on the details of reparation and boundary adjustments, and until these were fixed there could be no certainty in German affairs. Whether the reparations, once fixed, would be within the ability of Germany to pay, was yet another question. George Harvey was sitting with the Supreme Council, under instruction to take part only in the discussions concerning matters of specific interest to the United States and to make it clear that he was sitting only in consequence of the position of the United States as a victor power and without reference to the Treaty of Versailles.

The President's commissioner found the German government ready to make peace on American terms, and to embody in the text of a treaty the very words of the American resolution. The agreement was signed without ceremony on August 25, 1921, and was forwarded to the Senate on September 21. It might have been presented sooner, but Congress had taken a recess the day before the signing and had reconvened only upon the day on which the Senate received the Dresel treaty.

Senator Lodge was now as certain that peace would not be complete without the treaty as he had been that peace could be made by unilateral action. He found it hard to induce his colleagues to take it seriously, for they had greater interest in other legislative matters. When he called up the treaty, which was considered in open executive session, the Senate chamber thinned and it was necessary to interrupt the debate while enough senators were rounded up to make a quorum. At the end of September he procured an agreement to vote, after the Democratic minority had decided not to make a party issue of it. A day was set upon which the treaty should have priority; but still the Senate was evasive. Consent was at last given on October 18, after the Senate had once more interpreted its assent by a reservation which reiterated the assertion that the treaty protected all the rights to which the United States was entitled as a victor, and which directed the American government not to participate in any "body, agency, or commission . . . unless and until" Congress should have given specific consent. Exchange of ratifications took place in Berlin on November 11, 1921.

The reimbursement of the United States for the costs of the army of occupation, which still held the bridgehead at Coblenz, was a matter for discussion with the Allies since the German obligation to reimburse was based on the Treaty of Versailles. It was tied to the larger matter of reparations, which the Treaty left to be reduced to terms at a later date, and upon which the Commission on Reparations was at work. The United States did not demand a share in the reparations, and its share in occupation costs was distorted because no other occupation army cost so much per man per day. The Allies had no disposition to give this reimbursement priority over reparations payments, which were a first charge on German resources, and they were despairing of getting from Germany enough reparations in money and kind to meet the liability which Germany had assumed in the Treaty. Negotiations to protect the American interest on this count had to be conducted directly and separately with the Allied powers. It was not until the spring of 1923 that Eliot Wadsworth negotiated with the Four Powers for an agreement which recognized the rights of the United States but did not provide the funds for payment.

American troops began to be withdrawn from Germany after the ratification of the Dresel treaty; and as the pressure of the Allies upon Germany, through 1922, took a form which was unpopular in the United States, the demand for the recall of the whole force became impressive. Many of the troops had been recruited after the Armistice and sent to General Allen so that he might release veterans for discharge. At the end of 1922 France, believing Germany to be in default in payments in kind, and sensing German reluctance to pay at all, threatened to act alone, occupy the Ruhr, and hold the industrial area as hostage. The European Allies were divided. England, where the Conservatives had deserted the coalition government of Lloyd George and taken command under Andrew Bonar Law, opposed an intervention in Germany and suggested a moratorium in the exaction of reparation payments. Balfour, who had gone out of the Foreign Office on the fall of Lloyd George, had already intimated to the Allies that Britain would ask in the repayment of intergovernment war debts only what the United States should demand of Britain in satisfaction of the American loans. The proposal for mutual cancellation of these debts had become increasingly attractive to the debtor nations. Germany was, however, declared to be in default; and a new voice from Italy, that of Benito Mussolini, joined France and Belgium in upholding the justice of occupation.

The German mark collapsed as France moved an armed force into the Ruhr cities in January, 1923, and in Washington the Senate advised the President to order home the American troops and get out of Europe. Constitutionally the Senate had no power in the matter, but the political weight of a 57 to 6 vote was great. The token force, already down nearly to a thousand, was called home at once; and on January 24, 1923 the United States flag was hauled down at Ehrenbreitstein.

The ratification of the Dresel treaty had been followed, early in 1922, by the appointment of a representative from New York, Alanson B. Houghton, as ambassador to Berlin. If nothing could be done directly with Germany in the matter of army costs, it was at least possible to make the preparations necessary for adjusting the financial claims arising from damage done to American citizens. An agreement covering such claims since July 31, 1914 was signed on August 10, 1922. The next day Harding named Justice William R. Day to be umpire for a board on which the United States and Germany had each a commissioner. Day died before the mixed tribunal began to function, but his resignation from the Supreme Court made room for the appointment of Pierce Butler, a conservative from Minnesota, who was thoroughly offensive to the Progressive wing of the Republican party.

The passage of the Porter-Knox resolution, a step in the extrication of the United States from war, was also a step in extrication from most of the network of war laws whose powers had continued to be invoked after the Armistice. These laws were now gone except in a few instances in which they were overlooked, or in which summary repeal would bring snarls into the management of affairs which should be continued to their end. The policy to be followed with reference to the loans to the Allies—another entanglement— with which the United States had reinforced the common effort, was not ripe for determination in the summer of 1921; nor was the implementing of peace which Harding had repeatedly promised when he urged an association of nations rather than the League.

There remained the steps to be taken to bring the war-enlarged government back to peace dimensions and to introduce new methods of doing business. There remained, also, the working out of some articulation of new Republican policies with pre-Wilson Republican policies. Absorbed in disentanglement and new policy making, the Sixty-seventh Congress and the people had been too busy to give much heed to the ending of the state of war. On the new policies, agreement was long in coming; but the leftover business— immigration, agricultural tariff, budget—could be hurried into law, and it was.

Chapter XIII ★ Republican Policy, 1921

THE BONDS of party loyalty among the Republicans who were brought together in the Sixty-seventh Congress on April 11, 1921 were weakened by the extent of the political landslide of November, 1920, to which they owed their seats. Of the 435 members of the House at least 300 were listed as Republican. They lacked the tendency to hang together and to take direction from the steering committees, as happens when the two parties are nearly equal in strength. In every district the issue on election day had some peculiar local slant, so that the common characteristic of the successful Republicans was the fact of having defeated Democrats. Some ninety of them were new to the House, new to Washington also, and as first-termers were highly undisciplined. Every measure brought into the Congress was affected by the lack of cohesion among the majority and as each was passed into law it bore marks of the compromise necessary to ensure enactment.

Included in the unfinished business by which the Republican policy of 1921 may be judged were the three measures which had been cleared by the preceding Congress but failed to receive approval. The immigration bill, disliked on principle by Wilson, had been ignored, and thus died by pocket veto. The emergency tariff had been sent back with explicit objections. The budget bill had been rejected on a constitutional detail in June, 1920. All were revived at once, and neither the Colombia treaty nor the Porter-Knox resolution was allowed to turn the real interest of the Congress away from these matters of domestic business.

Johnson of Washington had the immigration bill ready for reintroduction in nearly the form in which Wilson had ignored it.

It had become Dillingham's bill rather than his own, but he was ready for "any kind of legislation to restrict immigration . . . until we have cleaned house here." Its passage took only four hours' debate in which he had the support of another West Coast representative, Raker (Democrat) of California, and in which the helpless opposition was led by Siegel and Sabath, both eastern, and one from each party. As it went to the Senate on April 22 it carried a clause exempting from the limitation those immigrants who were "actually subjects of religious persecution." The Senate struck this out, and passed the conference report without a roll call. The House accepted it, 276 to 33. The bill was frankly a stopgap, but the permanent measure which was to replace it was delayed until 1924. As in the earlier proposal, the annual maximum was stated at three per cent of the persons born in each country, according to the census of 1910. Immigrants from the American continents were exempted.

The legislative consensus in favor of cleaning house in matters of immigration was helped by noisy racial debates. The rebound from war restraints and loyalties brought these to prominence. On one of the fronts of public argument the share of the immigrant and his children in the making of the United States was stressed as a reason for continuing to leave the door open. The mutterings and worse of the Ku Klux Klan were disturbing the nerves of newer Americans. The pathetic condition of wives and children left stranded at home after the father had become an American citizen, was displayed at length. Foreign families had traditionally come to the United States, wage earner first. The public preference for immigrants from northern Europe over those from southern Europe was attacked by citizens who had come from the latter areas. The preference was defended as in the interest of Americanization, and those employers who demanded free immigration to maintain their supply of common labor were singled out for special attack. Race consciousness had increased as the war doctrine of self-determination had been stressed.

The strong feeling of the American Irish contributed to one of the debates in which the policies of England came under heavy attack. The government of Lloyd George, determined to work out some sort of peace with Ireland without conceding the independence demanded in the name of the Irish Republic, aroused the American members of the association formed to promote the recognition of that attempt at self-determination. Borah presented a memorial in the Senate early in the session. It begged for recognition and cited the Irish vote in the December elections of 1918 as justifying it. But England, aware of the demand from Dublin, was equally aware of the resistance to it from Belfast where the northern counties of the Ulster area were in bitter opposition. A home rule bill had been put through Parliament late in 1920, under which each of the two Irish regions (the six counties of Ulster, and the rest of Ireland) was permitted to proceed to dominion status. Demanding independence for itself southern Ireland demanded also the whole of Ireland and denied equal right to self-determination for the northern counties. Racial sentiment, religion, ancient wrongs, and bitter intra-Ireland dissension all played a part in the controversy.

While southern Ireland remained rebellious, Ulster proceeded to an election under the home rule act, and in April, 1921, the unionists carried the seats for the new parliament, voting down the Sinn Fein of northern Ireland by more than three to one. While Lloyd George continued his negotiations over the status of southern Ireland, the King and Queen went to Belfast in state to attend the formal opening of the North Irish Parliament on June 22, 1921. Sir James Craig was set up as Ulster premier to face de Valera at the head of the Irish republicans.

The prospect of an adjustment whereby Ireland would be shared by two jurisdictions carried the debate over the structure of the British Empire into the United States, where many of the American Irish were more Irish than the Irish themselves; for in southern Ireland an unknown fraction of the supporters of de Valera were ready to accept compromise with England and less than complete independence. The American debate was enlivened by incidents which added to its bitterness. In the most notorious of these the uncontrollable tongue of Rear Admiral William S. Sims made its contribution.

Sims, in command of the United States Navy in European waters during the war, had been greatly irked by the political atmosphere in southern Ireland. He had said as much in *The Victory at Sea*

(1920), which received the Pulitzer Prize in 1921. Always a rebel, he was again in trouble. He was back in England in the spring of 1921, coming to receive an honorary degree at Cambridge, and was met at sea by a courtesy fleet of British destroyers. He warmed to the ovation and on June 7, at a luncheon of the English Speaking Union, reëxpressed his feelings concerning Ireland and its anti-English sentiment of the war period. He charged the Sinn Fein with obstruction of the Allied naval effort, and then described them and their American supporters: "They are like the zebras, either black horses with white stripes or white horses with black stripes. But we know they are not horses—they are asses; but each of these asses has a vote and there are lots of them." Secretary Denby ordered him home on the next boat. He paused in Washington only long enough to receive a formal reprimand before resuming his duties as president of the Naval War College at Newport. "I got what I deserved," he admitted ruefully. "It was the same old thing."

It was the same old thing for the American Irish to come into action to influence American policy whenever it was closely parallel to that of England. The American debate was given a different slant when evidence of sentimental teamwork arose from another quarter. On the day before George V opened the Ulster parliament, Sulgrave Manor, an old country house in Northamptonshire, was dedicated as a shrine for Americans. This had been a home of one of the strains of the Washington ancestry, and had survived in good enough repair to be susceptible to restoration as though it had been the Washington homestead. In 1539, as confiscated church property, it had been sold to Laurance Washington. His descendants had left it half a century before his great-great-grandson, John, emigrated to Virginia; and it was three quarters of a century more before George Washington, great-grandson of John, was born at Wakefield in Virginia. The antiquarian Rosenbach had not yet in 1921 uncovered the documents which were to make it possible to build a new Wakefield house on the old site and to emphasize the fact that Washington, a younger son, had not been born to be a master of the mansion at Mount Vernon. The connection between Washington and the residence of a sixteenth-century ancestor was slender at best, but the Sulgrave Institution was devoted to the strengthening of ancient ties. What was said about it was highly irritating to those who resented the bond between the United States and the mother country. The Germans in America were convinced that they had helped in the shaping of the United States; the Irish were certain that it was their good work which had broken the British bond. By counting the Scotch-Irish—the Ulstermen—as though they were really Irish, the Irish historians were making it appear that they had saved the American Revolution.

The Hearst papers, always on the alert for English plots against American independence, took up the issue. A feature writer, Charles Grant Miller, claimed to have discovered a plot to rewrite the history of the United States so as to clear England of all blame, and kept up a running fight for several years in support of what he called "The League for the Preservation of American Independence." He had much to say about "treason to American tradition." The Knights of Columbus were inspired to offer a prize for "true" books on American history, and at their San Francisco convention in August, 1921 they created a National American History Commission to "make American history safe for Americans," and to make it "propaganda proof." The appeal to the traditional story of the past was to be useful whenever the anti-English groups within the United States feared the coming of a too-close *rapprochement* between the United States and British governments. It brought the historian once more under pressure to relate the past so as to please the present; and in several of the states it was attempted by law to protect the image of the past from reëxamination in the light of evidence.

The background of 1921 was one of controversy in which to the claims of rival regions, groups, and classes there was added the clash between loyalties to the nation and hangover loyalties to some different national past. This was a clash of significant dimensions now that the Americans of pre-Revolutionary stock were no longer in the majority, and now that the newer Americans were growing to dignity and influence in their new environment.

Against the background of conservatism versus radicalism, labor versus employer, court versus the claim of justice, an issue was raised on the last day of May, 1921 which was significantly related to the whole controversy. Nicola Sacco and Bartolomeo Vanzetti went to trial at Dedham, Massachusetts, on a charge of robbery and murder. The crime, in which a paymaster had been robbed of his pay roll and killed, was already a year old; and the case, like that of Tom Mooney, was on its way to fame as a symbol of social clash. In its essentials it was robbery and murder, but in its larger aspects it appeared to be society versus revolutionary forces and alien dangers. The defendants were admitted radicals, whose previous record as agitators and whose extreme utterances were used against them. As in the Mooney case, the identifications necessary to a satisfactory conviction were imperfect, so that suspicion of a "frame-up" was given room to rise. In a procedural way, flaws could not be found for a reopening of the conviction which was announced in July. Through the next half dozen years, while those who believed injustice to have been committed sought every legal device to prevent the execution of the death sentence, the passions arising on both sides made it more difficult to reach a fair solution of any of the problems incidental to the case. In the end Sacco and Vanzetti became for their believers both symbols of conflict and martyrs to a cause.

None of the larger problems connected with the new American equilibrium which was in the making could be solved by act of Congress. But upon the immediate proposal to restrain the new drift of immigration the agreement was wider than either party and irrespective of intraparty factions. The immigration limitation bill, as an amendment to the act of February 5, 1917, was signed on May 19, 1921.

The emergency tariff came next. Republican leaders, who in December, 1920 had seen no need for action before a comprehensive tariff revision could be made, saw a new light after the holidays and gave their backing to a temporary agricultural tariff to satisfy farmers in their immediate emergency. The switch of Penrose from opposition to support was definitive. As chairman of the Committee on Finance he could influence or block any legislation; but he could not carry any through to enactment without the votes of those western Republicans whose antipathy to the eastern party leaders was chronic and who, after hard times, had more than once gone into temporary opposition. The western farmer was caught by the uneven decline of prices in 1920, after war conditions had opened before him vistas of new opportunity and prosperity. Agricultural prices went down, farm values slumped, and the farmer's equity in his farm too often disappeared. Western country banks, loaded with frozen paper, were failing in distressing numbers. To keep peace in the party, if for no other reason, the Congress must make a gesture for farmer benefit. Penrose announced support for the measure of relief which Fordney had worked through the House before Christmas, and word was passed around that eastern Republicans were to support the bill. This they did, only Moses among their number was outspoken against it.

What the farmer demanded, and what the Fordney bill proposed to Wilson at the end of his administration, was the raising of the tariff rates on a long list of agricultural products, raw or processed. Wheat and flax, products of the Northwest, were subject to some competition with Canadian wheat and flax. In both countries the basic price was fixed by the world market price which the surplus above home consumption could command; in neither would the crop in its entirety be consumed at home. Wool was in the picture, for large stocks of foreign wool, kept in storage through the war from lack of transport, were believed to be about to invade the United States. The levying of a protective tariff was what the farm producer asked. It was what his leaders must support, and what was offered to Wilson in the bill which he refused to sign.

During the recess between March 4 and April 11 it was decided that the same bill should be reintroduced, and passed with a minimum of discussion, merely in order to satisfy the western Republican. A high tariff rate upon a commodity which is not imported to a considerable extent has little bearing upon the condition of the home market. But the program was accepted, with its management entrusted to spokesmen of the disaffected regions. Fordney went to work upon a permanent tariff, putting Young of North Dakota in charge of the emergency bill; while in the Senate Penrose assigned it to McCumber of North Dakota. In both houses there was tacit agreement that Democrats should be allowed to do most of the talking and Republicans the voting. It was a notable point at which policy was determined by compromise.

The measure lost its character as farmer relief and nothing else when the Young proposal was worked over in the House. The protectionist, who accepted the act as a gesture, had small confidence in its usefulness. In its larger theory, protection held that the benefits of the policy were in connection with manufactured or processed goods; that in the field of raw materials the United States could hold its own. But the House majority was aware of emergencies other than those of the farmer, and which might be met by rearrangement of the import duties. One of these had to do with dumping; one came from the chaotic condition of money in the countries from which imports to the United States must come.

Dumping had acquired a bad name in parts of the United States because of the belief that big business, protected by high tariff walls, was in the habit of selling goods for export at lower prices than were charged at home. The defense of this practice, when it was admitted, was that the ability to dispose of the full productive capacity of American factories made it possible to reduce prices even in the United States; and that the sale abroad at still lower prices was a means of building up foreign markets from the business of which all Americans would profit.

The manufacturer, hoping for a general revision of the Underwood-Simmons tariff in the near future, was afraid that damage might be done him while he awaited action. Whereas the farmer had goods whose marketing abroad was necessary, the manufacturer faced intrusion upon his home market by the same process which he had used in part of his export trade. There was a chance that European goods would swamp the American market at prices which the home producer could not undersell. The low wage and living standard of the European worker had always been a basic argument for protection. There was now a possibility that in their critical need for export business and the foreign exchange resulting from it, the European countries, particularly Germany and Italy, would sell to the United States even below the cost of production. The new sections added to the Young bill in the House were directed at this kind of dumping; the rates in such cases were to be adjusted so as to keep dumping from being profitable abroad and injurious at home.

The condition of foreign money added to advantages which might be taken injurious to the American manufacturer. Ever since 1894 it had been provided that the relative values of foreign and American money, in terms of gold, should be published by the Director of the Mint, so as to permit accurate translation of prices for customs appraisal. It had been provided also that when the values of the two currencies were deflected by balance of trade into a difference from their gold values, the import valuations should be adjusted in the light of such variation. The German mark, with a nominal gold value of about twenty-three cents, was in fact paper and in value below two cents in terms of dollars. However far money inflation lowered the value of the foreign money, its value for purchase at home was considerably in excess of its value in exchange. And in Germany and elsewhere the local law fixed a price for export above the price at home. The House worked out a scheme for the adjustment of duties so that the foreign country should not profit at the expense of the United States by this juggling of money values for export purposes.

The Young bill, with its anti-dumping and exchange clauses added to the agricultural duties, was approved by the House in the first week of the session. "Those of us who come from the West would rather be considered selfish than foolish," said Young, when in the brief debate the West was attacked as selfish in demanding more protection and higher prices, and as foolish in supposing that import duties would help the farmer. He thought they were neither. He pushed his measure through under a special rule.

McCumber carried the bill through the Senate, with Penrose helping to hold the East to the agreement. The two authors of the last general tariff, Simmons and Underwood, now in helpless minority, were in the Senate to lead in what attack there was. Harrison of Mississippi quoted against the leaders the words of Moses who refused to go along with them: "It is the offspring of a union between the cotton-field, the sugar-cane brake, the rice paddy of one section of the country, and the sheep run, the cattle range, and wheat field of another section." "It may be," said Harrison with hope dominant, "that this marks the death knell of the Republican Party."

Admitting their regret that the House had extended the scope of the emergency tariff, the majority leaders accepted the changes and rephrased them. The import duties were made to fall upon whichever was higher—the price of the commodity in the market from which it was to be exported or the price fixed by the country of origin for the export trade. The leaders added a clause of their own to protect a new industry, accelerated by the war, with roots in the foreign owned patents which had passed through the Alien Property Custodian into American hands. The importation of dyestuffs, explosives, and coal-tar derivatives, which German chemists had ingeniously created, was forbidden. The powers of the War Trade Board, essential for the exclusion of the output of the German chemical trusts, were shifted to the Treasury Department, when the War Trade Board should be liquidated by the repeal of the war laws.

The western interests to which eastern Republicans yielded for the sake of party solidarity, included some in which the effect of agricultural tariffs was more clearly visible than in the case of wheat or flax or cotton, where normal exports were far in excess of imports. The protection of citrus fruits against the competition of Italy and Spain brought unity regardless of party in sections where these industries were at work to capture and enjoy the whole American market. New organizations for pressure had appeared in connection with certain agricultural commodities. It had been found possible to create marketing associations without running afoul of the Sherman act, because in the Clayton act of 1914 such agricultural association was exempted from inclusion among the forbidden conspiracies in restraint of trade.

The California Fruit Growers Exchange demanded two cents a pound on lemons, and received it. The associatioris were well started for the organization of producers for the marketing of their crop through central handling agencies, and for pressure for such assistance as might be obtainable from Congress. By maintaining standards in grading, packing, and shipping they were protecting their market from the competition of unorganized producers and were increasing their own profits. The Sun-Maid raisin had spread its trade name by advertisement and brought home gains. The Sunkist orange was pushed by the same technique. Prunes and apricots struggled for recognition in the market as did peaches, olives, almonds, and walnuts. The representative from the Santa Clara district where prunes were a staple, procured a film of Secretary of Commerce Hoover eating a prune, and had hopes of getting one of the President himself. At Petaluma, where chickens throve, an "Egg Day" was celebrated in the summer of 1921, and funds were raised to the end that in the next tariff the access of the Chinese egg to the American market should be restricted.

Not every agricultural product was in a position to capture a market from foreign trade, but such as were so situated were throwing into politics a form of pressure which had heretofore been largely restricted to industrial promoters. In the regions where soil and climate made possible the production of foods which had commonly been imported from other climes, and whence the new systems of transportation made possible their wide distribution, the organizations for marketing were building up new forms of social consciousness. The "harvest home" picnics of eastern agriculture were far removed from the celebrations of the special crop communities, with their entertainments and "queens" and "days" proclaimed by governors who welcomed the chance at a new type of public appearance for themselves.

With the emergency tariff signed on May 27, 1921—it was effective for only six months in the hope that by that time a permanent tariff would be complete—the reorganization of financial methods was taken up in Congress. The budget bill was revived.

The pressure for the adoption of an orderly procedure in the expenditure of public money was essentially not political. It did not originate among politicians, and although it met with less open resistance from them than did the earlier movement for civil service reform they accepted it without full devotion or understanding. Taft had recommended a budget to Congress without result, but in the next administration businessmen and economists took it in hand. The broadening scope of government increased its importance. The shift from the tariff on imports to the income tax, as the basis of federal revenue, induced a solicitude for economy among those whose incomes paid the heaviest surtaxes. Deficit finance, prevailing through the war period as the United States borrowed for military needs, gave the budget emphasis; and both parties endorsed it in 1920.

The authority of Congress to raise and appropriate public money is complete under the Constitution, and the exercise of the power is limited only by the self-restraint of the two houses. All attempts to maintain a balance between receipts and expenditures, which was once a duty of the Committee on Ways and Means, had broken down by 1885. During the half century before 1917 total income ran well ahead of total outlay, and in forty-one of fifty-two years there was a surplus of receipts. Departments and bureaus lobbied directly before the committees in each house which had the power to initiate expenditures in a period in which there was happily nearly always enough money on hand to pay the bills. The government of checks and balances, as one writer punned it, was one of "more checks than balances." In response to the demand for a reform the budget bill which failed in 1920 had provided for two new offices: one to prepare for Congress an annual picture of resources and needs which it might be hoped that the Congress would follow in its lawmaking; one to keep the accounts of money spent and to watch the innumerable spending agencies which the expanding activity of government had brought into existence.

President Wilson's view of his authority led him to veto the bill of 1920 without convincing Congress that his point was well taken. The Senate, however, was willing to avoid the deadlock in 1921. McCormick of Illinois, with a unanimous committee behind him, brought up the revived bill in April; it still provided for two new offices. The Director of the Budget, under the Secretary of the Treasury (whom Congress was disposed to regard as its own officer quite as much as adviser to the President) was to submit annually his summary of receipts and expenditures for the preceding fiscal year, his expectation for the current year, and a weighed estimate for the approaching year. The General Accounting Office was to be under a Comptroller General, with a seven-year term, so that he need not enter and leave office within a single administration. He was made removable by either the constitutional method of impeachment or by a joint resolution requiring the signature of the President or a two-thirds vote of the Congress to pass over a veto. The idea of removal by the two houses alone through concurrent resolution was dropped. Two days were sufficient for the passage of the bill.

The House had ideas of its own. Differing from President Wilson, it adhered to the method of removal of the comptroller general by concurrent resolution; but it agreed that the General Accounting Office was to be watchdog for Congress and independent of the

President. Differing from the Senate, it insisted that only the President could properly form and submit the budget estimates, and it pointed to the obvious difficulties within the Cabinet if the secretaries, completely subordinate to the President, should be made subordinate also to the Secretary of the Treasury. This secretary, it was said, had enough difficulties in connection with the collection and custody of federal revenues. The Director of the Budget would be required to scrutinize and pare down every request that funds be asked of Congress: "it will try the fiber of the best man the President can secure." But the House passed its version of the bill on May 3, one week after the Senate had acted.

The differences of the houses were ironed out in conference, each house receding in part. The Senate was satisfied when the Comptroller General's term was lengthened to fifteen years, subject to removal by joint resolution; the House won its demand that the Director of the Budget should function as the agent of the President.

Harding signed the Budget and Accounting Act on June 10, 1921, and had already in mind, as the best man he could secure, Brigadier General Charles G. Dawes, of "Hell and Maria" fame. Entering the new office on June 23 he had, in less than a week broken one precedent and established another. He gathered "the entire business administration" of the government—all the more than four hundred officers and business heads—in the Interior Department auditorium and read them the riot act. The President presided at the first business meeting of the government in order to make clear the extent of the authority which had been conferred upon the Director of the Budget. The Cabinet, said Dawes, "seemed to subscribe to it."

The two houses prepared for coöperation by concentrating in single Committees on Appropriations the authority to present bills calling for expenditure, leaving the responsibility for revenue bills in the hands of the Committee on Ways and Means and the Senate Committee on Finance. The rules were revised so as to allow the passage of enabling laws, authorizing activities to be undertaken whenever funds should be appropriated, and thus leaving in the Congress the general power to control the direction of financial policy. As time wore on it became clear that a new, and nonpolit-

ical, arbiter of policy had been created. Proponents of appropriations were obliged first to convince the Director of the Budget, in
order to secure the inclusion of a measure in his estimates. Once
this was secured, and the funds made available, the General Accounting Office and the Comptroller General exercised a scrutiny
over compliance; a scrutiny which tended to demand of the offices
authorization before expenditure as well as audit afterwards.

Dawes took the budget office for a single year, made an immediate
survey of the funds and demands for 1921–1922, with the idea of
saving a considerable fraction of the appropriations already made,
and set to work upon a budget for 1922–1923 which would permit
a surplus and terminate the period of deficit finance. "The first
budget is before you," wrote Harding when in December, 1921, he
laid before Congress the estimate recommending appropriations of
$3,505,754,727. There was, in fact, a surplus when the books were
closed at the end of the fiscal year on June 30, 1923. From his office
in the War Department, where Pershing gave Dawes desk room at
the start, the Director of the Budget pushed his inquisition into
every branch of government, and bombarded the President with
memoranda on reorganization and economy. He established his
right to assemble even the members of the Cabinet for budget discussions while the President soothed them by requiring that these
meetings be held in the Cabinet room in the White House. At the
end of his year Dawes returned to his Chicago bank, convinced
that a great reform had been launched; convinced, too, that the
only hope "for a permanent reform in the government business
system" lay with the President, whom he described as an "ideal
chief . . . Clear-headed, a natural leader, sympathetic and understanding." The time was not yet ripe for a general reorganization
of the services of the government, much as they needed it, although
Congress had a committee at work upon it, and it had been under
consideration since the days of Taft. Dawes underestimated the
effective determination of departments to have their own way, and
the ability of bureau heads and chief clerks to outwit reform; but
he wrote a book about his crusade, *The First Year of the Budget
of the United States* (1923), which reveals the intricacy of the problem to which he gave his energies. His Republican associates would
have been less than human, or political, if they had not attributed

the sharp reduction in federal costs to their own efforts at economy rather than to the return of peace.

The goal of economy, at which the budget reform had aimed, and the complications attending the budget administration, had a direct bearing on the problem of the veteran. The American Legion became, almost from its birth, a sounding-board for demands that a bonus be given to the veteran, a demand the justification of which was the high and protected wage allowed to those who had not been called upon to fight. The discharge of nearly four million soldiers crowded the job market, already congested by the release of a similar number of war workers. Nothing but words had been offered as a cure for unemployment. Hoover, Secretary of Commerce, was outlining a plan for a conference at which he and the President met a group of businessmen, labor leaders, and economists at the end of September. The labor men thought that nearly six million were out of work; the administration admitted more than three. The President and the Treasury thought of it in terms of the cost of a dole, should the United States be driven to this, and foresaw the possibility of a collapse of their efforts for a balanced budget. The economists hurried their studies of business cycles and unemployment and began the drafting of tentative bills for insurance against the latter. There was depression, if not acute panic, in the air; industry was slackening and increasing the unemployment which, in its turn, was curtailing buying power and forcing industry to slow down. The paradox of the 'twenties, confusing to those who lived with it, to those called upon to meet its challenge, or to those who reëxamine it, revealed luxury in the upper and urban levels of life and frustration and deprivation at the lower levels. It was at once desirable to hold appropriations to budget limits and to see to it that those of the veterans who had valid claim upon the public should receive their due. It was impossible to prevent the idea of a cash handout from interesting some of the unemployed, or to prevent the political use of the idea by the politician.

President Harding had for three months refrained from too much intrusion upon the deliberations of Congress, but on July 12 he appeared in person to block the passage of a bill upon which the Senate was in debate. The first bill introduced in the House when the session opened had been for adjusted compensation, and members of both houses were under pressure from veterans and constituents in favor of some such action. The Senate bill, which became the text for debate, called for an allowance of one dollar a day for military service (one and a quarter, if overseas), payable in cash in quarterly instalments of fifty dollars, or to be commuted to a twenty-year insurance policy at a face value forty per cent above the allowance. The demand for adjusted compensation was confused with demands for a more conscientious observance of the duty of the United States to care for the wounded and diseased, and to reëducate those whose partial disability called for reëducation. Dawes had had an assignment in the spring in connection with these duties, and had recommended an administrative reorganization of the services having to do with hospitals and rehabilitation.

The insistence upon a cash bonus cut into the program of retrenchment and revealed the futility of the effort made in 1917 to avoid a pension system such as had followed the Civil War. The World War soldier, better paid than his fellows in the other armies, was less well paid than the carpenters who built his cantonments or the workers in the war plants. For his benefit the law had offered cheap insurance, made allowance to his dependents, and assumed for the nation the obligation to care for him if he should become a casualty. The costs of the bonus now being demanded threatened to overshadow the costs of the pension system.

Harding begged the Senate to desist, although he admitted the full obligation of the United States to the men who had fought. Mellon, from the Treasury, protested against the threatening new obligation which would wreck his plans for the restoration of financial balance in the government. The President agreed that in this restoration the necessary first step was the protection of the institutions of business which created jobs. In spite of strong words in the columns of the *American Legion Weekly* and the other publications of soldiers' associations he was explicit: "It is unthinkable to expect a business revival and the resumption of normal ways of peace while maintaining the excessive taxes of the war." On motion of Penrose, the Senate returned the bill to committee, and the passage of bonus legislation was postponed for at least that session. On the vote to recommit, the forty-seven yeas included the stalwart supporters of the administration; but the Democratic senators and most of the western Republicans were in opposition or silent.

There was no difference of opinion in party or faction on the need to simplify and extend the agencies of soldier benefit. The several protective measures had been hurried into law during the war and after, until they had become, as Barkley of Kentucky said, "a sort of fungus growth upon other acts which had already been put into effect." The original law for soldier insurance had received its name from and was grafted upon a Bureau of War Risk Insurance created only to protect merchant ships against war damage. This had compelled the Treasury, to which the bureau was attached, to set up books and accounts for every person on the military rolls. The records of military service, upon which all claims must be based, were available only in the files of the Adjutant General of the Army. Responsibility for hospitalization was largely in the hands of the Public Health Service of the Treasury (created to keep epidemics from entering the country with foreign imports); and rehabilitation had been entrusted to the Federal Board of Vocational Education—a dollar-for-dollar creation of 1917, whose contemplated function was coöperation with the states in the preparation of young people for life. The Dawes committee had confirmed the President in his duty to reorganize the services; the legislative committee of the American Legion confirmed Congress in the belief that failure to reorganize might have uncomfortable political consequences. This burden of overlapping jurisdictions was no worse in veterans' affairs than in other sectors of government activity, but the veterans had honor, sentiment, and politics in their favor.

The Sweet bill, which Harding signed on August 9, 1921, had been under consideration in the Sixty-sixth Congress, as well as in the current session. It came before the House on June 2, with a unanimous report, and was passed a few days later, 335 to 0. The Senate took it up on July 20, with another unanimous report, and passed it on the same day without roll call or audible objection. Little more than phraseology was revised in conference, and the Veterans Bureau, as an independent office under the President, was given custody of the activities hitherto distributed among overlapping agencies. New business for it to administer was an expansion of hospital facilities, for which provision had already been made, but which were not yet in being. The President entrusted the bureau to Colonel Charles R. Forbes, who was already chief of the Bureau of War Risk Insurance.

Harding lived long enough to replace Forbes with an able and distinguished chief of the Veterans Bureau, General Frank T. Hines, but not long enough to face the full scandal which was later associated with the name of his first choice. He had not overcome the charm which vigorous and attractive personality exerted upon him. Rumors of bad judgment, graft, conspiracy, and misbehavior arose before the change was made. Suspicion of corrupt sale of excess hospital supplies reached the White House. Executive investigation and congressional inquiry followed upon suspicion, until in the winter of 1924 Forbes was sent to trial and convicted for fraud and conspiracy. With the best of interpretations, the appointment of Forbes reflected upon the President who named him; with the worst, it enabled the opposition, as another presidential election approached, to paraphrase a popular song, and chant:

> But how'n the 'ell kin the country tell—
> 'You ain' gwine steal no mo.'

The special session of the Sixty-seventh Congress, with its business of extrication and reorganization, stretched from April 11 until November 23. Before the Veterans Bureau was launched, and before the conference on unemployment met, it was clear that the inner, eastern command in the Republican party had the ear of the President and that the western wing of the dominant party had taken up the role of critic where the Progressive party had dropped it. Before the session passed into its last four months the wish of Borah had become the action of the United States. On the day before Harding asked the Senate to recommit the bonus bill it was known that the principal Allied and Associated Powers, Great Britain, France, Italy, and Japan, had been invited to sit in conference with the United States to consider the limitation of naval armament and the problems of the Pacific. The Washington Conference provided occupation for the minds of those who, seeing no chance of participation in the League, or wanting none, were anxious for another approach to the problem of permanent peace.

Chapter XIV ★ The Washington Conference: 1921

GEORGE HARVEY went to Chequers, the country residence of the Prime Minister, on Sunday, July 10, 1921, bearing an informal invitation to a conference on limitation of armaments. No suggestion could have been more acceptable to David Lloyd George, for if Harding was having difficulties with sections and pressure groups in Washington, Lloyd George was having worse trouble with similar groups in Britain, and was at the same time facing new problems now that the self-governing dominions had been recognized as co-members of a British Commonwealth of Nations. The insistence of these dominions upon their right to independent membership and representation in the Assembly of the League of Nations had been too difficult for the irreconcilable senators to accept; it was equally difficult to accept for a Prime Minister who, like an able successor, had no disposition to liquidate the British Empire. Lloyd George hurried to Commons on Monday to announce the invitation, and accept it.

This was a busy week on both sides of the Atlantic; and beyond the Pacific Japan was ready to welcome a limitation of the naval armament of those western powers whose fleets might be strong enough to extend their influence in the waters of eastern Asia. The English dominions, conceded to have the right to be as free as they chose to be, were sitting in London in an Empire Conference determining policies. The North Ireland Parliament had recently been opened. From South Ireland de Valera had agreed to come to London for a man-to-man discussion of future status, while a truce to endure through the discussion had been agreed upon between the British authorities and the insistent Irish Republic. The

truce became effective at noon on Monday, July 11. The Anglo-
Japanese alliance was to reach a climacteric on Wednesday. Last
renewed on July 13, 1911, its ten-year period would terminate; but
the alliance would endure unless, after twelve months' notice, it
should be abandoned. It had become a thorn in the side of the
Pacific dominions of Britain, and a source of worry in Washington
lest in the event of a Japanese war with the United States England
should act as ally of Japan.

It was a busy week in Washington. Harding was due to make his
appeal against the bonus on Tuesday and to sign the navy appropriation bill. What the next navy bill should carry was at stake,
for the completion and enlargement of the program of 1916 would
be a threat not only against peace but also against the budget; and
the proper shore establishments for a Pacific fleet would add to the
financial threat. The House had just received from the Committee
on Ways and Means the first draft of a protective tariff upon which
Fordney and the Republican members had been laboring since
January. The Democratic members of the committee, as was usual,
had not been allowed to see the proposed schedules of duties until
the bill was introduced, but they were prepared to break into violent attack upon a reversion from the philosophy of the Underwood-Simmons bill to that of the Payne-Aldrich. The Republican
members of the House were none too happy about it, and during
the busy July week they were to caucus upon party procedure. The
votes to pass a tariff were more than half western in each house, but
the party high command, as indicated by chairmanships reached
through seniority, was more than half eastern in both. The fate of
Fordney's bill was likely to be indicative of the future of the Republican party. That future was long in the uncovering, for the
tariff revision did not become law until after fifteen months of increasingly disastrous debate. But this second week of July, 1921 was
pivotal in the establishment of the route to normalcy, upon which
the Harding administration was set.

The first step in the direction of a conference on limitation of
naval armament, announced on Monday, July 11, 1921, was snarled
in the same Republican tangle which had already shown itself in
the debates on the emergency tariff, and which was to embarrass
the party while it constructed the permanent tariff. The western

wing, following the lead of Senator Borah, and supported by many Democrats, was forcing the hand of the President, and intruding upon his responsibility for the conduct of foreign relations. No sooner had Congress assembled for the short session, in December, 1920, than Borah presented a joint resolution requesting the President to confer with Britain and Japan upon an agreement to lessen naval strength. There was rumor that this was the direction in which Harding would move in his search for an alternative to the League of Nations. Opponents of the League favored the approach; pacifists endorsed it; many friends of the League thought it better than nothing. James F. Byrnes, then a representative from South Carolina, had heard that some such conference would sit "before harvest time in Pennsylvania or cotton-picking time in the South." But gossip had it, also, that Harding did not care to take direction from Borah, to have his constitutional discretion pressed, or to talk limitation until a navy appropriation had been passed. Borah persisted in urging his resolution, and at the end of the short session the Senate attached it as a rider to the navy appropriation bill.

In the special session, Borah reintroduced his joint resolution while outside Congress there was growing hope that disarmament offered a practical route to peace. As the proposal became a text to be used in opposing the administration's recommendation for continuation of the navy program of 1916, Congress was confronted with the alternatives of navy expansion or navy limitation. It was frequently forgotten that unilateral curtailment, without any international agreement, would destroy the position of the United States in bargaining. Motives other than love of peace were brought into the debate. Real doubt of the future usefulness of battleships was expressed, as reason for opposing new construction. Some, like La Follette, believed the United States to be safe behind its coast defenses. The profit accruing to the manufacturers of armament was stressed, as it had been stressed in 1916, to suggest that preparedness was a plot of big business. Whatever the reason advanced, it was clear that public interest in the navy was declining while confidence in disarmament was increasing. Borah's proposal had a limited objective, applying to navy strength alone; as the House discussed the navy bill the preference was for an endorsement of general disarmament, on land as well as on sea.

The substance of the Borah resolution was put into the navy bill as a rider amendment late in May, and the word circulated that the President was no longer opposed to its adoption. He had, indeed, already begun informal inquiries about the attitude of the powers concerned and had found England and Japan, each for its own reason, hoping for the economies which limitation would make possible; hoping too for the abandonment by the United States of its program of a navy second to none. When the House showed a disposition to insist upon a limitation more sweeping than Borah proposed, Harding wrote to the Republican floor leader, Mondell, approving an expression of the "favorable attitude of Congress," and denying interest in the form which it should take. The House, gratified by the cuts which the Senate had permitted in the navy bill, yielded the point, accepted the bill with the Borah rider, and sent it to the White House. Here there was some satisfaction in the fact that though the bill in which he was "authorized and re-quested" to initiate disarmament discussion became a law on July 12, his invitation had already been delivered, and publicly ac-cepted in England the day before. Initiation of a discussion was a matter within his prerogative; authority for calling a conference—the law required the consent of Congress in advance—was found to be already existent in a clause of the 1916 act for naval prepared-ness. The formal invitations to meet in Washington on November 11, 1921 went out on August 11, after the powers concerned had indicated their willingness to accept.

The language of the formal invitations was phrased to please even those who desired complete disarmament at once. Its broad inclusiveness spoke of "Limitation of Armament, in connection with which Pacific and Far Eastern questions should also be dis-cussed." It was addressed, in the first instance, to Great Britain, France, Italy, and Japan who, with the United States, had made up the Big Five at Versailles. A special invitation of the same date was addressed to China because of the need to remove "causes of mis-understanding," as well as to reduce armaments; and it was hoped that China would join in the discussion of these matters. Later in the autumn, October 4, still other invitations were sent: to Bel-gium, to the Netherlands, and to Portugal, these countries were to join the other six in a broadened program designed to cover "such common understandings . . . as may serve to promote enduring friendship." The invitations were phrased as though the League of Nations were nonexistent. Hughes was promptly named to head the delegation of the United States, and from his office a tentative agenda was circulated in September. The agenda embraced navy limitation, new weapons, land armament, and Far Eastern questions listed as those of China, Siberia, and the mandated islands.

The opening of the Washington Conference was delayed by a single day. Called for November 11, the third anniversary of the signing of the Armistice, the convening gave way to the use of that day for memorial purposes. France had recently added to the Arc de Triomphe, with its memories of the grand days when Napoleon dominated Europe, a tomb for an unknown soldier and an "eternal flame" which were to constitute a memorial to those who died in the war of 1914. England made room in Whitehall for a cenotaph to "The Glorious Dead." By act of Congress the National Cemetery at Arlington had been designated, and hither in the autumn of 1921 a nameless body was brought back from France for ceremonious internment. Pershing, one of whose duties was the care of American graves abroad, had carried to Paris a Congressional Medal of Honor to be placed on the tomb at Paris; in Washington everything paused during the dedication at Arlington. The conference opened on November 12.

The broad terms of the suggested agenda had not been narrowed or defined during the autumn, in spite of curiosity among the invited nations, or in spite of England's desire to confer with the dominions before entering upon discussions. The self-governing commonwealths were not invited, although Australia and New Zealand, as well as Canada, had interests in the problems of the Pacific. These interests were in the custody of England. The American delegates kept their program to themselves, and were chosen with reference to the sensitiveness of the Senate as well as to skill and standing. Hughes, their leader, was reinforced by Elihu Root, and together they represented the elder statesmen of the administration. From the Senate came Lodge and Underwood, leaders of the two parties. The official *Conference on the Limitation of Armament* (1921) prints the names of advisers and members of technical staffs who hovered in the background.

The British Empire treated the conference as a major enterprise, with Arthur James Balfour presiding over its delegation, and with Prime Minister David Lloyd George named as member though he was detained in England by domestic business. The Irish negotiation with de Valera had failed; but the solidarity of South Ireland had broken down too, and Lloyd George was now in the last stages of an arrangement with those of the Irish who abandoned the stubborn lead of de Valera. On December 6, England and a faction headed by Arthur Griffith agreed to a treaty, in fulfillment of which the Irish Free State was launched as a dominion a year later, and Timothy Healy was sent to Dublin as Governor General. Winston Churchill as Colonial Secretary issued a general amnesty for political crimes committed before the truce of July 11, 1921. Ireland continued in a state of guerrilla warfare, but enough had been yielded on both sides to make something of a peace.

Aristide Briand, President of the Council, led the delegation of France to Washington, although he remained in America only long enough to state his case. When he returned to France, to resume with Lloyd George the long drawn out discussions upon the affairs of Germany, and to be replaced as premier by Raymond Poincaré, he left as active protector of the interests of France former premier René Viviani who, like Balfour, had worked in Washington with the mission of 1917. China and Italy sent lesser delegates, among whom V. K. Wellington Koo was already well known in Washington, and Ricci was already the Italian ambassador there. Japan contributed its Minister of the Navy Kato, its Minister for Foreign Affairs Hanihara, its President of the House of Peers, and its Washington ambassador Shidehara. All delegates came to America with national interests crowding general principles, while those from Japan carried the heavy burden of sensitive and recently acquired dignity. In California the West Coast distaste for Orientals had in 1920 brought overwhelming approval for an initiative measure tightening the law which forbade aliens "ineligible to citizenship" to own land; and in 1922 the Supreme Court was to declare that Takao Ozawa, not being a "free white," was ineligible for naturalization.

Whatever hopes or reservations the visiting delegates may have brought to Washington, there was no doubting the intensity of interest in the proposed negotiation among all the peoples of the world. Distaste for war was nearly universal. Belief that war could be prevented by disarmament derived from wishful thinking, if not from reason. Financial trouble everywhere made the cost of armies and navies look like waste. The costs of past wars, still to be met, limited governmental freedom in every direction. Statesmen with budgets to balance had legitimate uses for the money which might be released if military appropriations could be cut down. Promoters searching for money for new enterprises coveted the funds which might be saved. Pressure for an approach to peace along the route of disarmament increased as Borah urged the cause, until many who had reproached him as an irreconcilable hailed him as a prophet. Before the conference was called to order the more hopeful advocates of peace and economy—no one ever could prove how much of either—were demanding complete disarmament by international agreement. The tentative agenda did not go far or fast enough for these people, and they rushed the President so that in October he felt it necessary to warn them that "reasonable limitation"—"something practicable that there is a chance to accomplish"—was all for which they might hope.

The leading newspapers joined in the agitation for disarmament, driven to it by customer pressure; except for the Hearst papers which remained "vicious and bitter" in their opposition and which pictured the menace to the United States from the two potential enemies, Great Britain and Japan. The Chicago *Tribune* claimed to have led in advocating disarmament. The New York *World*, the Baltimore *Sun*, the Des Moines *Register*, and the San Francisco *Chronicle* spread journalistic support across the map. *Collier's* and the *Saturday Evening Post* helped to make the urge national in scope. The clergy prayed for success, and civic organizations joined in demanding that the world disarm at once. A demand that the National Women's Party make disarmament its major issue split party unity, but did not prevent a group of members from operating a Women's Committee for World Disarmament. The National League of Women Voters, nonpartisan on principle, joined in the promotion, by the side of the Parent-Teachers Association and the American Farm Bureau Federation. Professional pacifists turned from generalities to specific demands, launching a new federation in a National Council for Limitation of Armaments. Petitions, public meetings, interviews, chain letters, and heckling made it necessary for the administration to give a broad interpretation to the "reasonable limitation" toward which Harding aimed his effort.

How broad an interpretation, and how specific, was still a well-kept secret on November 12, when the conference met in Constitutional Hall of the Daughters of the American Revolution, and President Harding turned it over to Charles Evans Hughes. The address of the Secretary of State was courteous, hopeful—and jarring. He passed quickly from generalities to business, declared that the only place at which to begin to reduce was the place at which the several naval powers stood, and that they should agree to peg their relative naval strength at their approximate strength on November 12, 1921. He knew how strong they were. His navy technicians provided data on ships in action, ships in retirement, ships in prospect; and on their guns and tonnage. As they stood that day, Great Britain and the United States were substantially equal, Japan at least forty per cent below either, France and Italy at little more than half the power of Japan. Hughes proposed a pegged ratio of 5:5:3 for the three major powers, and proved to be willing to accord status at 1.75 to Italy and France, whether they had the ships or not. He proposed that the strength in excess of such a ratio should be scrapped, that obsolete ships should be scrapped, and that for ten years no new replacement tonnage should be laid down. Mark Sullivan, who was present with the newsmen at the opening session, and who was about to assemble his notes in *The Great Adventure at Washington* (1922), was deeply impressed by the President whose "strong and full-throated" voice was reassuring, and whose hatred and loathing of war were manifest. He was impressed, too, by Hughes who, as Secretary of State, had emerged from a cloak of austerity which had perhaps prevented his being elected president in 1916. And he was startled when generalities in the Hughes address gave way to a "stern note of imperious demand." Taken by surprise like the delegates, the onlookers, and the world, he gasped at the demand for specific and immediate action.

The delegates gasped, too; met by peremptory demand for an immediate decision, they could do no more on that first day than reply politely and consult their governments. Mingled with their surprise was worry about what an immediate naval ratio and naval holiday would mean for them. What ships might they have to scrap? What new programs must they abandon? What would become of ships already partly built? Hughes provided them with data on their own strength, which they found to be accurate when they checked it, and he told them what he proposed to have happen to every naval unit. He named the "four new *Hoods*" under construction in England, and Admiral Beatty looked shocked. He named the *Matsu,* peculiarly dear to Japan and nearly ready for sea duty, and the Japanese delegates were disconcerted. The minor delegations were not thrown off balance too greatly to show relief. The delegations were "still a little dazed" when, at a second plenary session three days later, Balfour and Kato for their governments accepted the American proposal in principle. What it should mean in practice became the main work of the conference.

This main work was not, however, the entire work for all of the conferees. There were side issues, to be treated as such by those concerned, in spite of their bearing on limitation and naval holiday. The reference to the mandated areas in the agenda meant Yap, upon which the United States and Japan had not yet come to agreement. The reference to China covered, among other matters, the return to China of the leasehold at Kiaochow which Japan had occupied when German power relaxed in 1914. The whole matter of the status of China among the nations was on the agenda for adjustment by the nine powers. Also, on the agenda, though not formally, was the Anglo-Japanese alliance, an obstacle to the smooth working of the assembled nations, and one which might wreck the whole negotiation. The leaders of the delegations were involved directly or indirectly in most of the parallel proceedings, some of which were handled so discreetly that the first public knowledge of them was the unanticipated announcement of accomplished facts.

But the naval ratio and the holiday came first, and the technical committees were set to work immediately upon the acceptance of the general principle. Since the United States was the only power with a huge naval program under way, it was called upon to make the greatest of the concessions when programs were to be abandoned. The public eagerness for economy as well as peace drove the administration, and lessened the bargaining power inherent in the existence of the American program of 1916. Only the *Maryland*, among the major units in that program of ten dreadnaughts, six battle cruisers, and ten light cruisers, had already been commissioned; but all were somewhere between the designing boards and sea duty, although two of the dreadnaught hulls, the *Washington* and the *Colorado,* were afloat and a third, the *West Virginia,* was to be launched before the conference was a fortnight old. The *Washington* was nearly ready for commission. For Great Britain and Japan the proposed ratio would mean the abandonment of a few ships or hopes apiece; for the United States, the abandonment of a whole new fleet.

It was not easy to equate unlike items and unfulfilled hopes. No two warships likely to be left in use under the ratio 5:5:3 were precisely alike in tonnage, speed, armament, or age. Within any period of the twenty years agreed upon as the age of approximate usefulness, the progress of naval designing and equipment made the older ships obsolete as against the newer. But somehow all must be fitted into the tables of gross tonnage to be allowed to each of the powers. Each nation had honest fear lest its surviving fleet might be left with too great a number of units nearly ready to be scrapped; each jockeyed to save the most modern of its capital ships. The American figures proved to be so precise that little headway was made in attacking their fairness; the arguments bore partly upon sentimental issues, partly upon the half-built vessels which should be allowed to be completed, and partly on the obsolete ships listed to be scrapped. There were arguments also on the fairness of the ratio, for it was hard for Britain to concede that the historic supremacy of its fleet should give way to parity with the United States; or for Japan to accept and sign an admitted naval inferiority at sixty per cent of the great powers. It was embarrassing for France and Italy, whose navies were at best only dreams of things to be, to register their weakness at 1.75.

While the navy labored over the adjustments within the ratio, Hughes and his co-workers plunged into the other business at hand. Day after day the delegates explained in full session their needs and their hopes. Night after night certain of them worked on compensations. It was rumored early in December that important news was imminent. Kato seems to have talked, making it necessary to hurry a plenary session in which it was announced on December 10, that a side agreement had been reached, outside the conference, among the United States, Great Britain, Japan, and France. They released that day the text of a treaty, signed three days later, whereby the high contracting powers agreed to consult among themselves respecting "their rights in relation to their insular possessions and insular dominions in the regions of the Pacific Ocean," and respecting threats against these rights made by "any other power." The core of the agreement was revealed in the fourth article, whereby upon its ratification the Anglo-Japanese alliance "which was concluded at London on July 13, 1911, shall terminate."

The agreement binding the great powers to confer was part of the price paid for Japan's consent to relinquish an alliance which had, in a way, marked the acceptance of that power on a status of equality with the great powers. The rest of the price was the inclusion in the treaty on the naval ratio of Article XIX which dealt with fortifications and naval bases in the region of their respective territories and possessions. After the limitation of Japanese naval strength to sixty per cent of that of Britain and the United States, Japan was concerned by the neighborhood of those powers. The American salient at Pearl Harbor was already in a way to become a major base, the possibilities of which had disturbed Japan when Hawaii was annexed in 1898. England possessed at Singapore a considerable base which was believed to control the strait between the Pacific and the Indian Ocean. In the intervening Pacific it was possible that policy might dictate heavy fortification of other British outposts such as Hong Kong, or American outposts such as Corregidor or Guam. The compensation included in Article XIX was the agreement by the United States to maintain the status quo west of the line of Alaska-Hawaii-Canal Zone, and agreement by Britain to maintain it east of 110 degrees, east longitude. In substance, Singapore and Pearl Harbor became the limits of British and American striking power in the waters adjacent to Japan.

The nine-power negotiation, proceeding as part of the business of the conference rather than as a side issue, failed to satisfy China, as the Versailles Treaty had failed to satisfy all the signatories. It failed to satisfy Japan, for it was reached after frank discussions in which it was made clear that the recent conduct of Japan in China and Siberia was gravely unsatisfactory to the other powers. The frank imperialism under which some of them had acquired their footing in eastern Asia was part of an era which was now under suspicion. Japan had begun its advance toward the leadership of Asia under old methods after the world had begun to change its rules. China, too weak to defend itself, had long been bullied by the Western powers, and was subject to humiliating limitations of its authority in matters of customs tariffs and legal jurisdiction. It had been under special coercion from Japan since 1914. The Nine-Power Treaty, which was signed on the last day of the conference, at least promised a new and happier day for China and a lessening of the disharmonies among the nations having a foothold on or near the China shore. The treaty pledged the signers to respect the independence of China, and its territorial and administrative integrity; to provide full opportunity for the development of an effective Chinese government; to maintain the principle of equal opportunity for the commerce of all nations within China; and, above all, to resume conference among themselves whenever a new situation should involve the application of the stipulations of the treaty.

Two other side negotiations necessary to remove causes of misunderstanding in the Pacific were carried on while the conference sat, and were recorded in agreements at the end. Japan and China came to terms with respect to the pledge on Shantung which Japan had given at Paris. Japan had there promised to withdraw from the leasehold at Kaiochow; and the conferees had refrained from putting a settlement of the Shantung question into the treaty. The agreement to withdraw occupation forces, and the adjustment of financial matters involved, were now recorded in a separate treaty, and in due time Japan left the peninsula. A similar evacuation of Siberia, where Japan and the United States had invaded eastern Russian possessions near the close of the war, was not reduced to treaty form. The United States, party to the invasion, had already pulled out its troops, but Japan still held on in areas adjacent to both Siberia and Manchuria, and to the Korean Peninsula. Late in January, 1922, Baron Shidehara announced to the Committee on the Pacific and the Far East that his country did not intend "to take advantage of the present helpless condition of Russia for prosecuting selfish designs," and that "it is the fixed and settled policy of Japan to respect the territorial integrity of Russia." A voluntary withdrawal of the Siberian forces came before the year was out.

The other separate arrangement, negotiated on the side, adjusted the American complaint arising from the Japanese mandate over Yap. The mandate system was largely of American origin, and was designed to avoid the return of the German colonies to Germany on the one hand and, on the other, to avoid the appearance of a division of the spoils of conquest among the victors. The inner group of the Peace Conference had made a preliminary assignment of colonial areas, to be confirmed by the League of Nations and to be exercised under its supervision. It had discussed the problem of the Pacific Islands which, split by the equator, went to British dominions and to Japan. The decision was recorded just as the Treaty was handed to Germany in May, 1919; but the record was less than complete. President Wilson believed that he had stated as final a reservation against the assignment of Yap to Japan, and declared categorically that he had never assented to it; but the reservation escaped the minutes of the meeting. When the importance of Yap as a cable station on the route to the Philippines was realized in the Department of State it became imperative that the reservation should be respected.

In December, 1920, the League of Nations approved the Japanese mandate in the sweeping and final terms in which Japan maintained that it had originally been assigned. The United States had already protested that its assent had not been given; and in later notes it maintained with both Japan and the League that the League had no right to complete the assignment without this consent. Japan clung to its claim, the League found no record to justify the American contention, the abstention of the United States from the League complicated the approach, and the Harding administration took up the protest where the Wilson administration had been forced to drop it. Failing to get action from the League, Hughes took the protest directly to the four major powers whose leaders had had a hand in the original assignment of the mandate. The delegations of the four were now in Washington, where Japan was sensitive and the United States was insistent. A compromise was reached. Japan retained the mandate over Yap, but the free use of the cable rights was accorded and guaranteed to the United States in a treaty signed just after the adjournment of the conference in Washington. Although the formal completion of the various side arrangements was generally deferred until the end of the conference, most of the basic agreements were reached before announcement of the Four-Power Treaty, and were part of the price paid for the acceptance of the navy ratio.

The Pacific adjustments were, however, only a part of the price to be paid for the naval holiday and ratio. England was gracefully released from the embarrassment of the Japanese alliance, Japan's face was saved when a bilateral alliance was replaced by a quadrilateral agreement, and the power of Japan's fleet at its sixty per cent strength was buttressed by the limitation of British and American striking power to the respective lines of Singapore and Pearl Harbor. But there was more to be paid. The Hughes proposal had covered the whole of naval strength, and the agenda had hinted at some arrangement for a general disarmament which would include land forces. Both of these horns had to be pulled in because of objections in which Japan and France were prime movers. In the end the naval ratio was whittled down until it embraced only capital ships which now received their first effective definition.

Every steel warship, from the time the earliest came into use, had been an experimental creation, each larger and more modern than its predecessor. The armed ships on every navy list ranged all the way from small units, unarmored and obsolete, to the latest creations of the builders' craft. A battleship was perhaps best thought of as an armored steel ship; but all armed ships were designed for battle at their several levels. The United States began to use the term formally when the keel was laid for its Number One, *Indiana*, which was commissioned in 1895. The successors of the *Indiana*, wherever or by whom built, were longer, broader, more heavily armed, more adequately armored; but the term "dreadnaught" came into use only in 1906 when an English battleship named *Dreadnought* went to sea. This vessel was so far ahead of every predecessor that it created a class of its own. It was so huge, indeed, that when Germany proceeded to imitate it, the locks of the Kiel Canal proved too narrow to permit the passage of such a vessel from the Baltic to the North Sea. The necessary enlargement of the Kiel Canal was not completed until 1914. The *Dreadnought* was so broad of beam as to raise questions about the capacity of the locks of the Panama Canal, and the ability of the United States to pass vessels of similar dimension from the Atlantic to the Pacific. One of the Hughes proposals stated a maximum tonnage of 35,000 for such capital ships as might be built for replacement purposes when the time should come for replacement after the naval holiday. For the first time the capital ship received an upper limit when this proposal was incorporated in the final treaty.

It was reasonably certain that when new ships should be laid down they would overcrowd this upper limit; but nothing in the Hughes proposal suggested a tonnage above which minor craft should take on the designation of capital ship. The lower limit was not needed if the limitation was to cover everything afloat. As the details of the ratio were worked out and as its coverage of the auxiliary craft was debated, Italy and France on one hand, and Japan on the other, made it impossible to spread the ratio over the whole of naval strength. Japan, with few remote needs and heavy neighborhood interests, and with limited means, insisted on free discretion at the cruiser level for whatever tonnage it might care to maintain. With the major powers of Britain and the United States barred from the western Pacific by the deadlines, Japan could meet most of its needs with cruisers and submarines. France and Italy supported the protest. They chafed under their admission of naval inferiority, demanded a free hand in their coastal and Mediterranean waters, and defended their dependence upon the submarine as the poor man's weapon.

There had been a hope that the use of the submarine would be severely curtailed; but the hope failed before an insistence of the weaker powers which threatened to wreck the negotiation. And when the "Treaty . . . Limiting Naval Armament" was signed at last on February 6, 1922, it left every nation's strength in auxiliary craft at whatever point the policy of the nation might dictate. However, it gave the lower limit to the battleship class and the top limit to what hereafter became the cruiser class. The agreement covered only warships of more than 10,000 tons, standard displacement, and carrying guns above eight-inch diameters. It made room for experiment with aircraft carriers, but room no larger than the still unsettled question of the usefulness of aircraft made reasonable.

The same matter of security which brought the weaker powers to the defense of their lighter ships and their submarines brought France to the defense of its right to whatever land force it needed. The security of France had never ceased to control the policy of the Quai d'Orsay. It was still vital, and the old threat of invasion from the Rhineland was at its heart. Distrusting Germany and, in lesser measure, Italy, and knowing from experience where a German blow would strike first, France declined to be a party to reduction of armament on land, and made its case. The most that could be accomplished beyond the ratio for capital ships was a separate treaty outlawing the use of gas in warfare, and restricting the use of submarines. No merchant ship was hereafter to be attacked by a submarine unless it should refuse to submit to visit and search after warning, or unless it should disobey the orders of the searching vessel.

The treaties signed at the closing session of the Washington Conference on February 6, and the incidental treaties signed within a few days, represented a settlement in anticipation of which each participant had come with hopes, and from which each salvaged something of what it wanted. All of the participating nations had been eager to accept the holiday and the ratio if only to be rid of the fear of the advent of the United States as the leading naval power. England could accept the principle of Anglo-American equality with complacency, fortified by a possibility that the emotions which drove Harding and Hughes to action might keep actual equality from becoming a fact. France and Italy were left free to work out their own national schemes of defense. Japan retained its dignity unimpaired, if not elevated to the level of its desire, and it could at least breathe freely with the western Pacific and eastern Asia no longer within easy cruising range from naval bases superior to its own. The American emotion was gratified, composed as it was of a desire for economy, of distaste for war, of a lack of driving fear, and of conviction that peace ought to be attainable by international legislation. Whether the cause of peace was advanced by the complicated settlement was a question for the future; but before the treaties became effective attention began to be directed to one clear consequence of the prices paid: the future of the western Pacific area was handed over to Japan.

Even the wisest of men, when by chance they get into high office, are undependable prophets. Even the noblest aspirations, when unmixed, are not certainly realizable; and when they are prodded by hopes of some advantage or by rebound from something else are less likely to be attained. But in 1922 there were few voices raised to challenge the compromises incidental to the settlement, and fewer to challenge the objective. Mark Sullivan, impressed until the end, believed that the greatest of the advantages was the prevention of a possible contest between Britain and the United States for the maritime supremacy of the world.

There was a note of supreme gratification in Harding's voice when on February 6 he brought the seventh plenary session and the Washington Conference to an end, "without surrender of sovereignty, without impaired nationality or affronted national pride." He hailed a "new and better epoch in human affairs," and congratulated the "Gentlemen of the Conference" upon having "halted folly and lifted burdens, and revealed to the world that the one sure way to recover from the sorrow and ruin and staggering obligations of a world war is to end the strife in preparation for more of it, and turn human energies to the constructiveness of peace." Whoever wrote the words he read, he spoke them with visible conviction. An experienced newspaperman, he was able to write easily; a seasoned politician, he spoke effectively; but he made no pretense of universal knowledge, and there was no effort made to check the growing rumor that his secretarial staff briefed him for his public utterances. He was as American as the Main Street on which he had lived his life, and as capable of confidence in the enterprise in hand. It was basically the enterprise of Hughes, but the support of the President came from within himself.

Harding took the treaties to the Senate, when the last of them was signed, and by the end of March the Senate had given its assent to all. There was no organized Democratic opposition similar to that which the thirteen Republican irreconcilables had directed against the Treaty of Versailles. There were individual opponents. Josephus Daniels, from his editorial sanctum, was to complain that the sea had been surrendered to Britain, the air to France, and the East to Japan; but only the Four-Power Treaty raised enough doubts in the Senate to compel the attachment of a reservation to its assent. To make assurance doubly sure the senators attached to it an understanding that there was in it "no commitment to armed force, no alliance, no obligation to join in any defense." Only one senator, France of Maryland, voted against the seventy-four who sustained the naval treaty; twenty-one failed to vote, and among these there were only three—Brandegee, Norris, and Reed—who had fought the former treaty to the bitter end. Borah, Johnson, and La Follette voted yea. The National Council for the Reduction of Armaments had already memorialized Congress to refrain from building up to the limit permitted by the ratio; and on the day that the Senate gave assent the House passed an army appropriation act for 1922–1923 limiting the land forces to 115,000 enlisted men. Disarmament was being tried.

It was eighteen months after the signing of the treaties before the exchange of ratifications made it necessary to begin actual reduction where the treaty called for it. France and Italy were slow to ratify; they were filled with new fears arising from trouble in the eastern Mediterranean which threatened them with another war. But at last, on August 17, 1923, official promulgation took place in Washington. The navy was ready for American compliance. Fifteen old battleships, a good riddance, were made ready for elimination; some were to be converted to other uses—the old *Kearsarge* (1900) was rebuilt as a crane ship, and was still on hand to lift heavy parts out of maimed ships when they came back from the Pacific for repairs a quarter of a century later. Some were to be used as targets until they sank—in 1923 the *Iowa* (1897) was battered to death by navy guns in Panama Bay. Some were to be sold and dismantled as scrap. Of the 1916 program, seven of the ten dreadnaughts were broken up; one of them, the *Washington* was allowed to be used as a test hull for the first systematic bombing of a modern naval unit, and went down off the Capes of the Chesapeake in technical controversy in 1924. Of the six authorized battle cruisers, four were scrapped, and the hulls of two were allowed to be converted into the carriers *Lexington* and *Saratoga*. The ten authorized cruisers, no one of which was yet in use, were outside the ratio, being under 10,000 tons. The first of their new class, the *Omaha,* was ready for commission early in 1923; the tenth in 1925.

The unanimity with which the demand for limitation had been pressed upon the administration had made compliance in negotiation and execution a nonpartisan obligation. The partisan intentions of the administration, first uncovered in March, 1921, were another story. These had been eclipsed by the upsurge of the new approach to peace, and were still indistinct. The Congress had come back from its midsummer recess of 1921 and, with an interval of only a fortnight between sessions, it had plunged into the regular long session of 1921–1922. So far from being unanimous on party matters, it faced internal revolt.

Chapter XV * Farm Bloc and Party

NDULGING ITSELF in a month's recess after August 24, 1921, the Sixty-seventh Congress had not yet fallen under the spell of a party program. What it had done in the approval of the Colombia treaty, the termination of the war, the restriction of immigration, the adoption of a budget system, and the consolidation of veterans' agencies, was generally nonpartisan as well as unavoidable. It and the administration were still under the pressure for disarmament, out of which the treaties of the next February were to emerge, and from which no administration was free for fifteen years. But in the field of domestic policy it had no more than reached the point at which the Republican majority realized the depth and difficulty of its doctrinal schism.

The difficulty was foreshadowed in the debates over the War Finance Corporation and the emergency tariff, and was showing itself in the discussions under way concerning the general tariff revision which Fordney had in hand. A few days before the recess, the same western Republican group which had forced the party leaders in tariff policy recorded a distinct victory in the enactment of a sweeping law for the regulation of the livestock industries. Before the end of the year the Boston *Transcript* was deploring the end of party government as rebellious Republicans and aggrieved Democrats joined to press for "a square deal for the farmers." "The comic-paper farmer is evidently extinct," it announced before the Washington treaties were signed; and it noted how the farmer statesmen "started in to raise hell and had over-production." Harding soon made use of a foreign word, relatively new to the American vocabulary, when he spoke sharply of the organization of "blocs" to advance some special purpose.

[251]

Gray Silver, who helped to organize the Farm Bureau Federation, and who had a rich history as strategist in farmer movements, mobilized his senatorial friends during the fight for the emergency tariff, and bound a group of them to a loose affiliation in his office on May 9, 1921. Nearly a hundred representatives were sympathetic with his effort to organize a pressure group, irrespective of party lines. In the House, where most of the members came from east and north, the elements of cohesion were weaker than in the Senate where two senators from one of the Dakotas had votes which counted as much as two from New York. Some twenty-two senators adopted a farmer program, and chose as their chairman Senator William S. Kenyon of Iowa. Their movement was not halted when Harding removed their leader by making him a federal judge in January, 1922. Arthur Capper, senator from Kansas, took Kenyon's place and at once recorded the genesis of the uprising in *The Agricultural Bloc* (1922). The antecedents of the farm bloc may be found among the western Progressives who turned on Taft, and in the Republican "silver senators" who held a balance of power in the party during most of the 'nineties. But no temporary grouping had hitherto had the aid of an organization reaching down to the dirt farmer in the counties, or marshaled by professionals comparable to the leaders of the Farm Bureau Federation and the other agricultural associations.

The senators from the prairie states and the farming areas were effective pleaders of the farmers' cause, and the support of farmers was so essential to the success of any party purpose that they could command a hearing. Farmers were used to bearing down upon the big business in whose interest the approaching tariff revision was being undertaken; and they welcomed oratorical fireworks in their behalf. Harrison of Mississippi, with the zest of a Democrat in the presence of Republican trouble, described the state of affairs:

Beggars at almost every door. Tramps riding the blind baggage on every railroad train. Five million persons out of employment . . . Hundreds of mills and factories closed . . . thousands of empty box cars lying idle . . . Our export trade is falling off, our ships are idle, the warehouses are filled . . . The present presents a dark and gloomy day to this once prosperous and contented people.

Clay, a hundred years before, was not more vivid when he sketched the landscape as the farmer saw it, and embraced the protective tariff as a means of bringing prosperity to the farm. But he had not had to argue down, as party leaders now must do, the antipathies of the farmer to the manufacturer who was the first and the chief beneficiary of the tariff.

Fordney's Committee on Ways and Means had been at work on the new tariff schedules since the opening of the special session. The Young emergency tariff had been a necessary concession to western unrest, not to be permitted to interfere with the revision which the manufacturing interests in the Republican party had in mind. The Senate leaders Lodge and Penrose, and McCumber and Smoot who were the seniors on the Committee on Finance, awaited the action of the House, where the measure had to start. They were well aware that the debate in the House would be brief and inconclusive. The House proposal was likely to be abandoned when the Committee on Finance should prepare its amendments for the Senate. They were aware, too, that while the House was engaged in the initial debate it would have little time for the consideration of other business. On July 5, Lodge as leader of the Senate suggested that a recess be taken for most of the following month. No new business would come out of the House because Fordney was preparing for the formal introduction of his tariff on July 6.

The Senate defeated the motion for a recess, by a thin vote in which most of the Democrats were willing to let the Republicans make the decision. Norris led the opposition, for he was promoting various measures for farmer relief, and wanted the attention of the Senate. Kenyon and La Follette supported him. The administration leaders found themselves opposed by a successful revolt against their control. The new coalition had in mind the passage of laws for the furtherance of exports, the regulation of trading on the grain exchanges, and, most of all, the regulation of the business of the meat packers. This last was no new topic, for the packers of the Middle West had been under fire for decades since the herds of steers, grazing their way up the long drive from Texas, had begun to be funneled by the railroads into the stockyards at Omaha, Kansas City, and Chicago, and thence through the packing houses where they had been processed for consumption.

The packers acquired a strangle hold on the industry, although a full half of American meat was processed and consumed in the neighborhood of its origin. Their hold was much like that which the refiners with their tank cars and pipe lines maintained over the oil industries. In many areas, being the chief buyer, they could fix the price. Their network of outlets made it possible to give sharp competition at the retail end of the process, and to venture beyond meat products into dealing in products commonly sold where meats were sold. The packers had from the beginning been attacked for unfair combination in restraint of trade, for extorting favors from the common carriers, for permitting too great a spread between the price of steers and the price of steak. In more recent years their control of buying agencies, refrigerator cars, and distributing networks had made it profitable for them to deal in perishable foods, and other foods and by-products, until it was possible for their enemies to denounce them as a food monopoly. A suspicious parallelism in the policies of the "big five"—Armour, Cudahy, Morris, Swift, Wilson—suggested that instead of competition there existed illicit conspiracy in their operations. The Federal Trade Commission of 1914 had repeatedly investigated them and Congress had held exhaustive hearings in which their aggrieved customers and competitors displayed grievances. The Department of Justice had proceeded against them; and the last fixed event in the war upon them had been an agreement on their part to desist from practices criticized by the Department of Justice as illegal. The "big five" denied illegality but accepted a "consent decree" which was recorded in the Supreme Court of the District of Columbia on February 27, 1920.

The decline in farm prices in 1920, and the knowledge that big business was proceeding to enrich itself by new high tariffs, helped to instigate a renewal of the attack on the packers until they became a symbol of the burdens on the farmer. After prolonged hearings the Senate had passed the Gronna bill in January, 1921— too late to get agreement with the House in that session. The House had ideas of its own, and was disposed to strengthen the hand of the Federal Trade Commission; whereas the Gronna approach was through a new agency in the Department of Agriculture which might restrict the powers of the commission as well as the activities of the packers.

The issue was carried to the new Congress, as much because it was a token as because it embodied a solution, with Haugen of Iowa pushing it in the House and Norris in the Senate; and with party leaders more ready to hamper the Federal Trade Commission than the packers. At any time in any debate eastern Republicans were likely to deplore the spread of government regulation of business which had occurred since the passage of the Interstate Commerce Act (1887), and to resent the inquisitorial powers of the Federal Trade Commission. Both had been launched under Democratic presidents. President Harding's prayer for "less government in business, more business in government," was repeatedly quoted with approval.

The House sent the Haugen bill to the Senate early in June; it was much the same bill which it had wanted to pass in the winter and which protected the Federal Trade Commission. In the Senate the Committee on Agriculture and Forestry (Norris, chairman) reported it for passage with an amendment; but the amendment affected the whole bill except the enacting clause, for it was really the Gronna bill with modifications: it concentrated authority in the Department of Agriculture, and increased the authority. The voting in the Senate, while Democrats watched with interest, revealed the associates of the new bloc to be at variance with their more regular party associates. Near the end of the debate, with Kenyon temporarily in the chair, Norris and Capper recited testimony to show that the leading agricultural organizations preferred the Norris proposal. The conservative Republicans held together to displace the Norris amendment and to restore the House proposal, and then voted in vain to stop the final passage. The bill went then to conference, where it lingered for more than forty days. When Norris and his allies defeated the Lodge motion for a recess in July, this was a piece of the business which they proposed to see completed, and the recess came only after it was done (August 24–September 21). The price which the bloc had to pay to get it out of conference was more than Norris liked, and he refrained from signing the conference report. The House conferees stood their ground, and Kenyon accepted the weakened bill rather than nothing. It was substantially the Haugen bill which became the "Packers and Stockyards Act, 1921" on August 15, 1921. The packers were divorced from ownership of the stockyards and from their retail outlets, and were directed to limit their activities to those which were primarily concerned with meat. The Interstate Commerce Commission was left with supervision of the transportation of cattle to the stockyards, the Federal Trade Commission was not deprived of its power to investigate. The Department of Agriculture was vested with large authority over the meat industry. The more flexible of the regular Republicans accepted the inevitable and voted to accept the conference report; but among the negative votes were those of Brandegee, Knox, Moses, Warren, and Watson. And Moses, ever to be depended on for an epithet, was soon grumbling about the "invisible empire of the Ken[yon]-Cap[per]-Klan."

Two other measures to which the bloc had thrown its weight were signed on August 24, as Congress recessed for its vacation. A future trading act was passed in the hope of restricting speculation in wheat on the grain exchanges, and the War Finance Corporation was given new powers. It had been revived over Wilson's veto early in the year, and now it was authorized to issue bonds to the extent of a billion dollars to assist in financing foreign sales of agricultural products.

The Ku Klux Klan, on whose name Moses based his pun, was much in evidence after Congress reassembled. The Invisible Empire showed signs of developing into a nativist movement similar to that of the A.P.A. of the early 'nineties, and the Know-Nothing party of the early 'fifties. It was no novelty, in moments when party bonds were relaxed, for antiforeign and anti-Catholic movements to gain driving force. These were now strengthened by an aggressive isolationism, by-product of the struggle over the League of Nations. Irritation over the race issue had led the South to attempt secession, to attempt to evade the Fifteenth Amendment by means of the "grandfather clause" and literacy qualifications for the suffrage, and to support prohibition as a means of race control. The South was basically Protestant in religion, and its preponderance of rural areas threw it into a natural opposition to the urban centers in which the foreign-born contributed heavily to the total population. The new movement carried a threat to existing party lines, and was a carrier of more than the patriotic Americanism which its leaders boasted.

In spite of all protestations to the contrary, its membership included militant groups whose antipathies to Negroes, Jews, aliens, and Catholics were building the picture of the Klan in the public mind. The ostentatious secrecy in which its doings were shrouded, and the equally ostentatious parade with which its members appeared in public in their robes and masks, made it more than another manifestation of the American "joining" habit.

The New York *World* had followed the trace as the Klan spread its organizers over the South, where the New Orleans *Times-Picayune* charged the Invisible Empire with circulating a bogus Knights of Columbus oath at Protestant church conventions. The Hearst papers fought the Klan, giving to its *Searchlight* a sort of light which the order disliked. Anti-Semitism was in the air, encouraged by Henry Ford's Dearborn *Independent,* in which the forged "Protocols of the Elders of Zion" had appeared, and in whose columns the "international Jewish bankers" were under repeated attacks.

The lower South was not large enough to hold the persistent salesmanship of Klan organizers. They disturbed New York when they announced their intention of invading the East. They set up Klans in the Far West in the summer of 1921. They found Indiana a fruitful field, where they became too powerful to be liked by politicians of either party, and too dangerous to be openly denounced. William Allen White thundered against the Klan in his Emporia *Gazette,* but it entered Kansas; and it was known in Wisconsin. It professed to receive as Klansmen only "native-born white American citizens, who believe in the tenets of the Christian religion and who owe no allegiance of any degree or nature to any foreign government or institution, religious or political." Officially, the organization denied all hates, but by its definition of membership it made appeal to citizens who cherished them. The menace of the Klan to party lines, and worse, came to a head in October when a House committee held public hearings on resolutions calling for a sweeping investigation of the order, and William Joseph Simmons, described as Imperial Wizard, took the witness stand.

The appearance of the Imperial Wizard before the Rules Committee on October 11 failed to produce the full-dress investigation which opponents of the Klan demanded. The Department of Justice had made inquiries of its own, but Congress avoided action.

Simmons denied responsibility for the floggings and violence
ascribed to his order, laid the attack to pure malice on the part of
the New York *World* and William Randolph Hearst, repudiated
the suggestion that the Klan was anti-anything, avowed a pure
pro-Americanism, and broke down spectacularly at the close of his
appearance. But congressmen who were doubtful about their districts and states were made more doubtful by the display of the
power of the movement, which had not yet reached its crest. It was
dangerous to befriend the Klan, dangerous to fight it

It was not only the Ku Klux Klan which in the autumn of 1921
revealed a wide awareness of an approaching congressional election. This was apparent through the prolonged debates in which
the leaders of the majority party were forced to come to terms with
the supporters of the farm bloc, lest these join with the opposition
to wreck what there was of party policy. The sounding board for
this political nervousness was provided by a revenue act of 1921,
in behalf of which Representative Fordney opened the debate before the recess, and which was finally accepted by both houses and
signed by the President only on the last day of the session, November 23.

The strategic position of the Senate gives it a tight rein on economic legislation. Its greater independence, as compared to the
House, based upon the long term of its members, makes it able
to withstand pressure from without. By the same token, its smaller
size makes it imperative for a majority party to continue to command the votes of its members, and enables a rather small dissenting
group in the dominant party to seize a balance of power whenever
the minority is in a mood to coöperate.

The new Republican tariff, which Fordney put through the
House easily and promptly, was to receive its heavy treatment and
its final shape in the Senate. This had been the case with every
tariff since the Civil War. The problems incidental to the Fordney
tariff were never far away from congressional thought from the
time debate was opened on it on July 7 until Harding signed it at
long last on September 21, 1922. "The Republican Party," said
Fordney when he presented its first draft, "takes it for granted that
the people of this country, with a vote cast in November, spoke out
loudly for protection." This was probably true, since the Demo-

cratic party no longer made heavy attack upon the principle of protection as such. Yet it gave no clue to the sort of tariff which would be acceptable to even the manufacturing interests, let alone the farmer interests which pervaded both parties; or to the minority whose position in opposition drove it to search for joker clauses and for undue favoritism for big business. The economic discussions in the Sixty-seventh Congress constituted one long debate, from which there emerged from time to time one measure or another. The revenue act, which came from Fordney's committee, played a large part in these discussions, and revealed the cross-purposes which affected a financial program.

The war revenue act of October 3, 1917, was no longer suited to the needs of the Treasury now that the peace was at hand. Its amending act of February 24, 1919 had left intact new principles of taxation which were widely unpopular. The new administration had pledged itself to economy in government, bringing forth the budget bill as evidence of sincerity; and to reduction of revenue to match the lowered costs of operation, to which the new revenue act was an earnest.

The old American habit of relying on the tariff as the chief source of revenue was in process of modification now that the income tax had revealed its power as a fiscal tool. The old tariff had been a social-economic agent, behind which manufacturing interests had organized to push for their protection. The new income tax had been urged upon the country as much for social possibilities as for Treasury receipts; its inevitable consequence was to breed resistance in the business which must either pay corporation taxes or excess profits taxes. And it bore heavily upon the huge private incomes with its surtaxes. These incomes became visible targets now that they emerged from old-time secrecy.

Fordney brought the new revenue bill into the open on August 17, 1921, and demanded that the House pass it with only four days' debate. John N. Garner, in his tenth term as representative from Texas, met it with an initial charge that the shift from customs-house revenue to income tax revenue had brought down upon Congress an organized pressure from the group whose incomes had been derived from the advantages of protection. He knew that there were other pressure groups, for the farm bloc had shown its hand anent the packers' act, signed two days before. "If I thought there was one-tenth the friction on this side of the House . . . that there is on that side of the House I would despair of ever seeing the Democratic Party in power again." And there were Republicans who feared that internal dissension might again bring back the Democrats—as in due time, it did.

The brief debate before the House which sent the revenue bill to the Senate on August 20 was long enough to display the cleavage between orthodox Republican philosophy and agrarian Republican dissent. It was Hawley of Oregon (who was one day to make a tariff of his own) who explained that the way to lessen unemployment was to remove the burden which hobbled business. But it was Nelson of Wisconsin who spoke for the western farmer, describing for his associates a cartoon of a cow, on which, against the background of a map of the United States, "an old good-natured country cow" was pictured. Its head was toward the West "where the people feed her the richest fodder"; its udder hung over Wall Street "where the captains of industry drained her daily"; and he inquired, with a note of warning, what would happen "when the old country cow comes to and starts to kick."

The House proposal, drafted in the spirit of Fordney and of Hawley, embraced some lowering of the revenue, the reduction of the surtaxes on large incomes, the repeal of the war tax on excess profits; and as each of these points was taken up in the Senate, it met opposition from Democrats and from the bloc. The Senate made 833 amendments to the text, and yielded only seven of them to House insistence in conference. One of the proposals to amend, which would have increased the measure's power to provoke, came from Senator Reed Smoot of Utah, whose ability, industry, and conservatism had enabled him to live down his high standing in the Mormon Church, and whose colleagues had made him chairman of the Republican Senatorial Campaign Committee. Smoot proposed to offset the loss of revenues through tax reduction by the imposition of a sales tax on retail business. No one could deny the convenience and the simplicity of a sales tax in the matter of collection. Its principle was old in the United States, for it was the basis of the internal revenue tax on tobacco and alcohol; and it was now demonstrating its fiscal power in the gasoline tax on which the states were beginning to rely for highway improvements. But in fiscal theory the sales tax was a direct contradiction of the principle that taxes should be levied in accordance with ability to pay. Any tax on retail sales must bear most heavily upon that social class whose incomes are insufficient to endure taxation. Its adoption, at a time when it appeared to be chiefly an escape tax for the sake of the rich, was impossible in 1921. But the Smoot amendment was not voted down until the very end of the long debate. It had been vigorously supported by the *Examiners* and the other papers of the Hearst chain, and after it was defeated Hearst took several dozen members of Congress on a special train to Canada, where he hoped they might admire the workings of a sales tax there in force.

Interrupted and delayed by the other business of the session—including the peace treaties with Germany and Austria-Hungary, and the preparation for the Washington Conference—the revenue debate was long drawn out. In this, and in other debates upon matters concerning the welfare of the farmer, the farm bloc was able to increase its weight through adhesions from the Democratic side; until at last Senator Lodge was constrained to meet with the farm bloc members outside the committee rooms. He sat with them, not to bludgeon them into line, for they were quite as tough as he was, but to find out how much the party organization would have to pay for the passage of the bill. La Follette was denouncing "the crime to untax wealth and . . . to make the poor bear the burdens of Government while wealth escapes." The *Wall Street Journal* was denouncing the party leaders for "pusillanimous surrender" to the bloc.

But the choice was surrender, or no bill, or a bill forced through by a bloc-Democratic coalition, and Lodge wanted both a bill and one which Republicans had passed. He had conceded much to the irreconcilables in connection with the strategy of the Treaty of Versailles, and he conceded once more. Most members of the bloc joined with the Democrats in the vote which excluded the sales tax from the list of Senate amendments. The surtaxes on large incomes were increased above those voted in the House, although Johnson of California (who had voted for the Smoot amendment and had been the attorney for William Randolph Hearst) complained of a law "which requires one army of experts to teach honest people how to pay . . . [and] another army of experts to teach the dishonest how to cheat." The Senate bill left to the "old-time leaders" on whom, as Garner chuckled, the bloc had "put one over," little more than the repeal of the tax on excess profits. Lodge and Penrose, practical and partisan, accepted what they could get, urged the passage of the bill and of the conference report, and the bill became a law.

With the passage of the revenue act a period of Republican leadership was near its end. Pennsylvania, long near the center of authority in financial legislation, lost both of its senators before the year was out. Philander C. Knox, signer of the round robin and an irreconcilable, and as able a member as the Senate had, died in October, 1921. Boies Penrose, for many months sick, but not too sick to control the course of the leaders on the revenue act, died on the last day of the year. The Pennsylvania hierarchy, descending from Simon Cameron through his son Donald to Quay, and from Quay to Penrose, was extinct. Penrose, pictured as the supreme boss, had twice survived the direct election of senators which had been supposed to terminate the dominance of bosses. The sudden deaths left his state in party chaos. The situation within the state gave unexpected hope to the persistent reformer, Gifford Pinchot. It brought to the chairmanship of the Committee on Finance in the next session Porter J. McCumber of North Dakota, upon whose shoulders was to fall the burden of the completion of the tariff.

Knox walked out of the Senate in apparent health on October 12, 1921, and died that night. He had just watched Borah, blandly declaring a lack of desire to embarrass the administration, throw an obstruction across the path of the impending Washington Conference. He had himself had a hand in preparing the issue over the Panama Canal tolls, for it was he as Secretary of State under Taft who received from James Bryce the early protest of England against the exemption of American coastwise ships from these tolls, voted in 1912. Knox had brushed the protest aside as premature, for no toll-free ship had yet passed through the canal. Wilson, convinced that the exemption was in violation of the pledge of the Hay-Pauncefote treaty that the canal should be "free and open to the vessels of all nations" without discrimination, had received the aid of Root and Lodge in driving a repeal of the exemption clause through Congress in 1914. Almost at the moment when the invitations for the Washington Conference were dispatched Borah, never forgiving the repeal, introduced a measure to restore the exemption. The debate, beginning early in October, made the undisciplined condition of the Senate manifest again. In spite of its inconvenient timing and its doubtful fairness, the Borah resolution passed the Senate on October 10. Penrose voted for it; Knox was paired for it. Lodge, who had voted against the exemption in 1912, and for its repeal in 1914, followed the wish of Harding as he voted against the revival. The measure commanded many Democratic votes, many western, and split nearly every group within the Senate. The House, under firmer administration control, quietly shelved it.

If Congress was undisciplined, so was labor, both within itself and with reference to the rest of society. Both commanded the attention of a President who wanted peace without quite knowing where to find it. The industrial turbulence of 1919 had quieted down after the steel and coal strikes of that year, although grievances had been established instead of peace. The American Federation of Labor, meeting in Toronto in 1920, had clung to its policy of keeping out of politics. Meeting in Denver, in June, 1921, it had internal troubles, for its Irish members pressed it to take sides for Ireland and join in a boycott of British goods. It had factionalism, when the reëlection of Samuel Gompers was opposed seriously for the first time since the 'nineties. John L. Lewis of the United Mine Workers presented himself as a rival of Gompers in a contest involving the old cleavage over craft unionism against the vertical or industrial union. Gompers won by a two to one vote, but there were more groups of workers ready for outlaw strikes, and union officers had less authority than in the past. The Federation was disturbed by wage cutting and employer interest in the open shop, by the continuance of unemployment, and by sporadic cases of grafting labor leaders who brought disrepute upon the movement. It was distressed by the use of troops on strike duty, and by the spread of a movement for the establishment of state police. The growth of this movement was ostensibly, and actually, an effort to reinforce peace officers whose activities were limited by their county lines;

but it was believed by labor to be a deliberate attempt to create a strike-control force better trained and more competent than the national guard.

The state constabulary made its appearance shortly after the anthracite strike of 1902. The need for it was emphasized by the ineptness of national guardsmen in the presence of disorder, by the shortcomings of local officers of the law who owed their position to politics and who knew that strikers were also voters, and by the disasters provoked by the use of private armed guards such as the Pinkerton operatives. Pennsylvania led off, after long experience with guardsmen, federal troops, and deputy sheriffs; and with the rough elements of society who seized upon a strike to show themselves. The first superintendent of the Pennsylvania state police was picked from Philadelphia's crack City Troop of cavalry. Captain Groom's mounted officers began to patrol state highways by 1906, and when the automobile came upon the roads there was new and greater need for such patrol. By 1920 such police existed in some eight states, and the patrolmen were speeding on motorcycles. In type, the constabularies had something of the character of the Canadian Northwest Mounted Police, something of the frontier Texas Rangers. Massachusetts, brooding over the police strike of Boston, adopted the system in the summer of 1921. Labor was disposed to speak of the constabulary as "cossacks," to denounce them as strike breakers in uniform,—and to respect their disciplined authority.

The West Virginia hills, some of the people of which still indulged in hang-overs from the days of private family feuds, provided an illustration of unsettled labor. On the western side of the state, between the Kanawha and the Big Sandy, the hills covered one of the greatest American soft coal fields in the midst of an agricultural community. There were wagon mines, operated by farmers in their spare time, and company mines which proved difficult to unionize. The region, like other coal fields, was suffering from overproduction and the shift of industry to electricity and oil. Here, in Boone County, and Logan, and Mingo on the Kentucky border, there was war. Union miners were bitter against exploitation by the companies—who were supposed to "own" local government—and quite as bitter against nonunion workers who were ready to take their jobs. They fought with company detectives as well as with the "scabs" who came into the field from the hills.

At the end of August Harding issued a proclamation directing the mobs to disband and ordered federal troops into West Virginia from Camp Sherman in Ohio. These did not arrive in time to prevent a pitched battle between miners and deputies, but they quickly established a military peace. The Logan County war provided a text for harsh debate, prolonged investigation, and inconclusive trials for murder. It intensified the issue for labor, and made one for the proponents of law and order.

An even larger issue, though it escaped violence, was brewing after the Railroad Labor Board handed down a ruling in June which sustained a cut of twelve and a half per cent in railroad wages. Labor had been bitter in its opposition to the creation of the board, and the brotherhoods prepared to strike rather than to submit. Warren S. Stone of the Locomotive Engineers charged the railroads with noncompliance with the Esch-Cummins act and with an attempt to organize company unions to replace the brotherhoods. The steadiest of all the American unions—those of the engineers, conductors, firemen, trainmen, and switchmen—voted to strike, and the Railroad Labor Board declared that such a strike would be against the law. Harding showed no disposition to invoke war powers such as those directed against the United Mine Workers in 1919. The railroads faced a tie-up of their services at a moment when the Farm Bureau Federation was calling for an immediate lowering of freight rates. Postmaster General Hays announced that mail would continue to move, strike or no strike. The farmer of the West and the brotherhoods were pulled closer than ever to that pooling of the interests of farmer and workman which had long been the objective of third-party statesmen; but the showdown was deferred. The steelworkers and the coal miners had been reluctant to fight the government in 1919. The railworkers were reluctant now. Three days before the deadline, which had been set for October 30, the brotherhoods called off the strike but left the controversy still ominous in politics.

The duty of orderly government to serve the valid interests of all its people without discrimination in favor of any of them, and to maintain the public interest without placing too much of the burden upon any single group or class, was manifest through this summer of clashing interests. Farmer pulled against labor, and with labor against wealth; and each of the three was ready to charge the others with treachery or greed. Each worked upon party and upon government, as it pressed to gain or to retain. There was no superman to define the public welfare in language in which each competing interest could see its affairs built fairly into the affairs of all. The postwar disintegration had increased the difficulty of finding a common platform upon which even to discuss the balance. The administration sought to find the answers, driven by political necessity if not by principle. In September Harding resorted to the method of unofficial conference, with unemployment as his theme. In January, 1922 he tried it again, this time in agriculture.

Herbert Hoover, Secretary of Commerce, was permitted to arrange the conference upon the basis of a means to better employment and upon the improvement of relations between labor and the employer. The announcement was made on the eve of the sending of the army into West Virginia. Harding addressed the consultants on September 26, and took time for a personal interview with one Urbain Ledoux who, as "Mr. Zero," had publicly offered himself for sale on Boston Common. There were unionists in the group and employers, bankers and economists. None could tell precisely how many were unemployed or how to define those who were without work. Gompers guessed at five millions—with no relief from Congress in sight. Others guessed either more or less.

The issue before the administration was to find more work, or to permit the Treasury to be drained for direct relief. The conferees worked through committees and sent to Congress reports indicating that they knew the general situation; but they found no general willingness to set up a dole, and little willingness on the part of any group to hamper itself for the advantage of another. The problem was passed from the hands of the Unemployment Conference to those of the statisticians and economists; the former to devise more accurate methods of measuring unemployment, the latter to pursue their studies of the incidence and consequences of crises. Owen D. Young was chairman of a committee which turned in a report on business cycles which did better for the pathology of the disease than for practical remedies. Hoover's conclusion contained no suggestion of a solution: "The greatest waste is periodic slackening of production and resultant unemployment." The Harding concept of normalcy, which had helped to elect him, was outmoded. The essential duties which government must learn to perform in the future were still to be defined, and the methods of fulfilling them were still to be discovered.

Before the year was out the date for the agricultural conference was set by Henry C. Wallace. Transportation, credit, and crop marketing were to be considered in relation to the necessities of the farmer; and here, as in the matter of unemployment, the old pattern of American thinking must be revised before solutions could be reached. When the conferees—more than three hundred of them —assembled on January 23, 1922, all of the groups interested in the perennial problem were represented, and there were new allies present to advance the farmer's cause. Western bankers and western manufacturers who served the farmer trade had been drawn in because of their concern for their own business as well as for the public interest. Hugh S. Johnson was there, with his driving energy, backed by intimate experience on the War Industries Board. George N. Peek, president of the Moline Plow Company, was with him. They had worked out plans with reference to the disposal of the surplus without disturbing the price of agricultural commodities in the American market. Price-fixing was at the basis of nearly every remedy to be suggested; and price-fixing was as contradictory to every past concept as remedy could be. The *New Republic* centered the problem upon the discrepancy between the price which the world could pay for American food and the price the farmer must pay for the clothing, housing, and implements which he must buy. The intangibles added to the difficulty, for the American farmer, resenting the word "peasant" even more keenly than he resented the fact of peasant status at the bottom of society, had caught more than a glimpse of a better status for himself. Like the workman, he could not be content with a society in which his place was frozen; and there was no prospect of relief unless gross income could be increased or other classes in society could be compelled to share their advantages. In solving these problems, said the *New Republic,* the tariff could be no help. There was not much help to be gained by a further smearing of Wall Street, but William J. Bryan was at the conference to continue the attack which he had maintained for thirty years.

The farm organizations were on hand, with representatives who revealed unity in determination and division in method of approach. But they could agree that farm financing was part of the problem, and that the banks of the Federal Reserve system were unable to extend the sort of credit needed by their clients. Commercial paper, with short maturities, could not serve the investment need for long-term mortgages. The Federal Land Bank system, created in 1916, to provide long-term credit, could not provide the financing for the requirements of the farmer's crop year. The need for a new system of intermediate banks was displayed, but the only way by which credit could be extended to any borrower who lacked collateral was one in which the government could be brought to guarantee the loans and itself assume the burden of the losses entailed by misfortune or default. The agricultural conference marked a new phase of an old debate, rather than a solution of the problem. Agriculture, declared the President on the opening day, "is truly a national interest and not entitled to be regarded as primarily the concern of either a class or a section." Here he paused, and then threw another obstacle into the deliberation as he added "—or a bloc."

Harding had struck a political blow at the farm bloc a few days before the conference met, when he elevated Kenyon to the federal bench, thereby fooling Elmer Davis who, writing over his own name though sometimes quoting "Godfrey Gloom," commented that "the farm bloc was dissolving under the skilful touch of President Harding like a traffic block handled by a veteran traffic cop." There was a party need that it should dissolve, for the primaries were approaching and the future control of Congress was at stake. The Washington Conference, completing its work on the treaties as the agricultural conference deliberated, added no party strength to the administration.

Chapter XVI ★ The Business of Politics

Under any form of government the business of staying in office tends to distract the attention of the official from his business as trustee for his people. The more seriously he takes himself and the party of his choice the more he is bound to consider his program in connection with the continuity of party power. And the more completely he may serve some special influence, the greater is his servitude to the demand of his backers for continuity of control. The presidents of the United States, so far as the record reveals the men who have held the office, have not failed to feel increasingly their public responsibility and to make a struggle against undue pressure, whether from party or from bloc. There is something in the office which tends to make a man want history to think well of him.

The degree of success attained by them has been partly limited by their own ability. The system whereby presidents have been nominated and elected has not been designed for the selection of the ablest or best. Success has been affected as greatly, perhaps, by the contradictory complexities of public policy as by such doctrinaire enthusiasm as candidates may have expressed while out of office. When a Chief Executive has seemed baffled by a situation, his background and his intelligence may have been to blame, or the stubbornness of the issues; but there is little evidence to suggest that any American President has knowingly sold his country short.

Luck, complexity, and a kindly disposition were against Warren Gamaliel Harding as the "honeymoon year" of his presidency approached its end. He had been unable to bring peace and program

[269]

into his party, and was in a position of less advantage than when he was inaugurated. The majority leader in the Senate, Lodge, had lost much of his prestige. The stubborn isolationist, Knox, and the master strategist, Penrose, were no more. Hays, the flexible conciliator who had helped bring the party into some unity of purpose, was about to surrender his position of Postmaster General in order to bring peace between the movies and the public. The very extent of the Harding majority in 1920 had brought embarrassment. The Republicans in the House, their majority increased from forty to one hundred and sixty, more or less, were nearly half of them new to Congress. The old leaders in both houses were largely those whose republicanism had survived the years of Democratic power. The ancient cleavage in the party had not been closed, and the new problems of society tended to widen it. While the Sixty-seventh Congress wound up the business of its special session and passed into the long session of 1921–1922, the depleted Democratic opposition was taking stock with reference to the next election, in November, 1922; and the party within the party was making plans.

The Democratic party based its hopes upon Republican dissent. When it organized its usual Congressional Campaign Committee there were some twenty-three states from which no Democrat sat in the House, and its problem was to retain the slim hold which it possessed. The Democratic National Committee chose Cordell Hull as successor to the chairman under whose leadership Governor Cox had been so signally defeated. This Tennessean had lost the district which he had controlled for fourteen years, when Harding encroached upon the solidity of the South to carry Tennessee; but he was on his way back to greater things. He was as yet hardly more than marshal for the Solid South, and could not know whether his "dry" compatriots there could be kept in alignment with the "wet" northern Democrats and Alfred Emanuel Smith, who like himself had suffered temporary eclipse in 1920. Yet he looked to Republicans to provide his ammunition, and encouraged his party members to widen the Republican breach wherever this was possible. If the majority party was ruled by men too set to a pattern to see the present, the Democrats were led by those who were old enough to know that they might hope. The very household of the President was attacked, and the first head fell on May 2, 1922.

Before this first head fell—it was that of Harry S. New who was defeated for renomination as senator from Indiana—the administration forces had gained their most costly victory. The Senate, on January 12, 1922, had by a vote of 46 to 41 sustained the right of Truman H. Newberry to hold the seat from Michigan to which he had been elected in 1918. Every voting Democrat had voted against him as well as nine Republican dissenters, among whom were the persistent leaders of the western revolt: Borah, Capper, Kenyon, Ladd, La Follette, and Norris. The victory came a few days before the elevation of Kenyon to the bench, and after the contest had been magnified into a national episode by trial, conviction, investigation, and partisanship.

The money spent in behalf of Newberry in the primary had been a scandal, as was admitted by the Senate resolution which seated him. The precise amount was not mentioned, but the resolution asserted it to have been "too large, much larger than ought to have been expended"; and moreover such expenditure was "contrary to sound public policy, harmful to the honor and dignity of the Senate, and dangerous to the perpetuity of a free government." The conviction of Newberry for violation of the federal corrupt practices law took place in March, 1920; and its overturn by the Supreme Court on constitutional grounds, in May, 1921. The Senate investigation which came next, adding heat to the party wrangles of the summer, turned the Newberry case into an issue of political virtue in which his defenders faced defeat until they included in the resolution to seat him a denunciation of the methods by which he had been nominated and elected. The opposition made much of his apparent election, and more of the vote which kept him in the Senate, until each senator who voted for him was justified in fearing that if he were up for reëlection in November this vote would be used against him. The "bucolic battalion in the Senate," as the New York *Times* called it, gained a new issue in the Newberry case, and it had a new leader when "Arthur Capper, the heart of bleeding Kansas" came to head the farm bloc. The choice of a successor to Kenyon was to give the "heart" of Iowa a better chance to bleed.

Harry S. New, candidate for a second term from Indiana, was by inheritance and conviction a stalwart Republican and was, more-

over, so close to the White House that an attack on him was an
attack on the President. He found himself confronted in the Indiana primary by a former senator who had been crowded out of
his seat in 1911, as too progressive for his party. Albert J. Beveridge, young and oratorical, had come into the Senate after the
Spanish war, had given support to the more progressive movements
which flourished during the first decade of the century, and had
given his energies to the candidacy of Roosevelt in 1912. As keynoter and chairman of the Progressive convention he had been a
leader in the revolt against Taft. Forced outside the politics of his
state, he had turned historian, with four monumental volumes on
John Marshall (1916–1919) as evidence of a sort of industry and
skill unusual among politicians. He seized upon the Newberry case
as the issue against New, but defended "the glory of Republican
statesmen [in] that they were guided by fundamental principle and
never by shallow expediency." He disavowed hostility to the President or the party, but fought the political family of Harding as he
had fought Taft and his lieutenants. It required elasticity on the
part of the other Indiana senator, James E. Watson, who had been
a strategist for Taft in 1912, to support Beveridge and Harding in
the same speech during the canvass which ensued, but Watson was
above all a party man. Beveridge disposed of New in the primary,
but was left with leisure to continue his historical studies on the
life of Lincoln when the voters in November preferred to send a
Democratic senator, Samuel N. Ralston, to Washington.

Before the political analysts had measured the significance of
the ousting of New, they were confronted with another upset of
well-laid party plans. The loss of the two dependable stalwart
senators from Pennsylvania, Knox and Penrose, deprived the Republican party of tested and relentless leadership in the state which
had become the very center of protective tariff forces. Ever since
Quay, as chairman, and John Wanamaker, as treasurer of the Republican National Committee had put campaign fund contributions on a sound financial basis in the campaign of 1888, the Pennsylvania manufacturers had realized the financial value of tariff
rates. They had contributed to campaign funds according to their
hopes, and had accepted the party leadership of Quay and his successor. They had been realists in recognizing the great political

ability of Penrose, even though rumors respecting his personal and political character did not match the high social standing of his family. In the Pennsylvania primary, called for May 16, it was necessary to nominate successors to both senators, as well as to select candidates for the post of governor. There was no Penrose to bring about party unity by coercion, if it could not be attained by persuasion.

Sectionalism, never well-concealed in Pennsylvania, where the metropolitan interests of Philadelphia and Pittsburgh have always been at variance, and where the farming and mountain areas between the two great cities have distrusted the urban regions, appeared in the party offerings. Distinguished city lawyers, George Wharton Pepper and David A. Reed, were brought forward, one from each end of the state. Neither was a political artisan or a national figure of the caliber of Knox and Penrose. Each was a compromise among the groups struggling for the succession to the power of Penrose. But both won nomination in May, and election in November.

The slate was threatened when Gifford Pinchot, commissioner of forestry, presented himself in the primary as candidate for the Republican nomination for governor. Pinchot's association with forestry was better established than his identity with the Republican party. In the former capacity he had brought the new science to the United States, and from his post in the young Forestry Service of the country he had made a close contact with Theodore Roosevelt. From Pinchot, and from like-minded scientists, Roosevelt had assembled the ideas of national interest which came to be expressed as conservation of natural resources. Pinchot was chairman of the White House conference on conservation in 1908. Yale man though he was, he led the attack on Taft in 1909; and Taft dismissed him from the Forestry Service on grounds of insubordination in 1910. His candidacy for the governorship caught the interest of the middle region of Pennsylvania, and of the women voters. He was strong with those who were out of sympathy with the city party organizations which had commonly shared the "plums" of office—it was Quay who had once promised to "shake the plum tree" for the benefit of supporters of the organization. The rebel proved to have supporters, as well, among some who were ordinarily party regulars, but who now had ambitions of their own respecting over-all party control. An eastern manufacturer, Joseph R. Grundy, whom the *Nation* was later to describe as "prince of tariff lobbyists," was sufficiently at outs with the Philadelphia machine to throw his influence to Pinchot. Nomination by the Republican party in Pennsylvania was nearly the same as election. Pinchot won both tests, providing another fragment of testimony to the breakdown of party regularity and the dissatisfaction of the voters.

With the internal revolt once started, each new rebuff to the friends of the Harding administration gave it more drive. The primary came to Iowa on June 5, where it was necessary to nominate a successor to Judge Kenyon. Newberry was again an issue, to be played up as evidence of corrupt politics in the party organization, and as indicating a determination on the part of wealth to control the government. Kenyon, who was to be replaced in Iowa, had indeed voted against seating Newberry, but his acceptance of a promotion from Harding was made to look like a desertion of the farmer interest; and there was no corner of the country in which the plight of the farmer was stated with greater passion than in Iowa. There were depressed regions in the wheat country, where farmers had rarely been prosperous, and in the South where subsistence agriculture was still typical for blacks and for many whites. But Iowa had known better things, and having farther to fall had fallen harder. Well-educated and potentially prosperous, with a greater percentage of its area suited for rich farming than was available in any other state, and close to large consuming areas, Iowa had risen high on the wave of war prosperity and had been sunk when farm values collapsed in 1920. It was the place and the time for an expounder of the cause to make a case. The expounder was found in the person of Smith W. Brookhart, a veteran of the Spanish war and a national guard colonel in the World War, something of a lawyer and much of a farmer, and an expert small-arms marksman in his leisure hours. Brookhart was able to express in the Granger country of the Upper Mississippi valley the sort of noisy democracy which sometimes appeared in the deep South. The New Orleans *Times-Picayune,* which was a good judge of political eloquence, described him as more radical than La Follette, less political than Hiram Johnson, and with less graceful oratory than

Borah. He had been a Progressive in 1912, had fought in vain for the seat of Cummins in 1920 on the issue of the railroad act, and was now the most audible of the six contestants for nomination to succeed Kenyon. He disdained a dress suit, as a badge of social arrogance, was unterrified by the austere elegance of Lodge, and called himself a "plain dirt farmer" who would avoid the "sinister" social lobby in Washington. He won the primary and was elected in November.

The days of June were less than fair for the party leaders upon whose continued sagacity and support Harding was compelled to rely. There was certainty that they had not delivered, and doubt whether they could deliver, any program which would be acceptable to the voters in November; yet it was equally certain that without them there could not be any party program at all. They were working in fear of being forced by a coalition of Democrats and restive Republicans, such as had undermined Taft in 1911 and wrecked the party in 1912. Some of them showed signs of being unwilling or unable to remain in their posts of responsibility. Mondell of Wyoming, whose long seniority had brought him to the position of majority leader in the House after the election of 1918, was through. He was ready to surrender his seat and to stake his future upon an attempt to gain a seat in the Senate. A Democratic cattleman, John B. Kendrick, was up for reëlection and for the right to continue to sit by the side of the stalwart Republican Francis E. Warren, who had been senator since the admission of the state. Mondell took the chance, and lost, and Kendrick continued for another term.

Fordney of Michigan, brought by seniority to the chairmanship of the Committee on Ways and Means, was ready to retire from Congress and made the announcement before the month was out and before the tariff bearing his name had passed the Senate. His voluntary retirement, however it may have been impelled by the weariness of twelve terms of service, came so close upon the Brookhart victory in Iowa as to suggest that he had read the signs. Kellogg of Minnesota, a dependable administration senator, managed to secure renomination in his primary on June 19, beating a former representative, Ernest Lundeen, who had voted against the war in 1917 and who boasted of having been once deported from a

Minnesota town because of his fight against the League of Nations. But there were three parties in the primary, one of them bearing the name Farmer-Labor and securing a place on the November ballot for Henrik Shipstead, a Minneapolis dentist, a candidate whom dissatisfied voters could support, and did. The most serious blow to administration prestige came at the very end of the month when the chairman of the Senate Committee on Finance, Porter J. McCumber, was defeated for renomination in the middle of his prolonged fight to get the tariff through the Senate.

McCumber, the one Republican senator who stood by the Treaty of Versailles and the Covenant of the League until the end, weakened his hold upon North Dakota by his independence. His management of the farmer's emergency tariff had not restored the hold. His state, admitted too late to have had a Granger past, was populated by the Granger kind. It had been a center of farmer unrest, teeming with demands for measures of relief and with distaste for railroads, grain elevators, and big business, ever since the Nonpartisans had appeared at the beginning of the World War. Much of the leadership and doctrine of the Nonpartisans was derived from the teachings of La Follette of Wisconsin, the home state of many of the citizens of North Dakota. They had installed a governor, Lynn J. Frazier, in 1916, and had reëlected him in 1918; and under his direction the state had embarked upon broad programs of direct activity in behalf of the farmer and against the corporations. In 1921 the errors in the programs and the defects in execution had enabled their opponents to institute recall proceedings against Frazier and to remove the governor from office; it was the first successful movement of the sort. There were those who rejoiced in the victory, asserting that "communism fails again"; but Frazier was thereby made into a martyr to the farmers' cause and entered the primary of June 28, 1922, contesting as a Republican with McCumber. The latter had added to his sins among his constituents by voting to seat Newberry. He remained at his post in Washington, announcing himself as a "straight, conservative Republican," while the radicals swept the state. The administration forces watched the primary canvass with extra concern because the rule of seniority in the Senate committees would normally bring Robert Marion La Follette nearer to the chairmanship, should McCumber be driven out of office. The nomination of Frazier, and his election in November, gave North Dakota two Nonpartisan senators. Edwin F. Ladd, a food chemist by profession and a college president, had attained the other seat in 1920.

By the end of June the Congress was in need of another such recess' as it had taken during the summer of 1921. The House, unoccupied while it awaited Senate action on the tariff, was able to take a vacation from June 30 until August 15, but there was no rest for the Senate. There was much besides hard labor and fatigue that seemed to make a recess desirable. All the representatives, and a third of the senators, were uneasy about the political temper of their constituents, and their own future service. Party lines were loosening, North and South, under the impact of local and class interests. With the farm bloc as their spearhead, farmers were gravely dissatisfied and politically unstable. Labor, like agriculture, was discovering new grounds for complaint. The complacency of labor had just been jolted by a unanimous decision of the Supreme Court, written by the new Chief Justice, whereby that exemption from prosecution for conspiracy in restraint of trade which had been won in the Clayton act of 1914 seemed to be materially curtailed.

William Howard Taft had been easily confirmed as Chief Justice early in the administration, but there was little enthusiasm for his appointment among the surviving radicals who had fought him while he was President. He had at once taken a firm grip upon the business of the court. Under the Constitution and the judicial oath, he and his associates had no option but to declare unconstitutional such acts of Congress as seemed to them to transcend the powers vested in Congress. Judicial review of the acts of legislative bodies had been an old practice before the Constitution was framed. Its exercise was invariably a cause of protest when the measure voided made an appeal to a widely held sentiment, but was inevitable under a written Constitution which asserted itself to be "the supreme Law of the Land."

When the American Federation of Labor met in Cincinnati on June 12, 1922, it was confronted by the decision, only a week old, in the case of The United Mine Workers of America vs. the Coronado Coal Company, in which the dictum of the court declared

that an unincorporated union and its funds were not exempt from
suits for damage done under the authority of the union. Professor
Felix Frankfurter thought that the unions had been strengthened
by the body of the decision which cleared the union of responsibility in the case in hand. But labor leaders saw in the dictum a
step in the direction of full legal responsibility of unions. Organized labor had taken heart from the line of the Clayton act declaring that "the labor of a human being is not a commodity or article
of commerce," and from the explicit exclusion of nonprofit unions
and agricultural organizations from treatment as "conspiracies in
restraint of trade" under the Sherman act. The Coronado decision
failed to uphold the coal company, and overruled the lower courts
on the ground that interstate commerce was not sufficiently involved to bring the action under the Constitution, and that the
evidence did not establish criminal compliance with directions
from either the United Mine Workers or the local union involved
in the labor dispute. But the opinion of the Chief Justice, unchallenged by dissent, seemed to revive the old notion of the financial
responsibility of unions and their members which had made the
case of the Danbury hatters famous in labor history.

Issues were accumulating which gave labor and agriculture a
mutual distrust if not a completely mutual interest. Farmers have
never gone into enthusiastic action in favor of the short working
day and the right to strike demanded by labor. Labor has never
given dependable support to the farmers' demand for a guaranteed
price for food. For each of these groups the administration, its supporters, and its appointees had now become an obstacle to the attainment of goals. Taft had written another opinion offensive to
labor half a year earlier, in which the right to picket during the
course of a strike was the target. This opinion was delivered in
the case of Truax *vs.* Corrigan, arising from a suit of an Arizona
restaurant keeper against the union whose picket line had wrecked
his business. The Arizona law deprived Truax of his remedy, for
it specifically forbade the injunction which he asked to have issued
against the union. As early as the party conventions of 1908, labor
had asked for a limitation of the power of courts to issue injunctions in strike cases, and Arizona had complied. The majority of
the Supreme Court held that the Arizona injunction law was a

denial of the due process guaranteed by the Fourteenth Amendment, and that the injured party had a right to an opportunity to seek redress. Those who were angered by the decision recalled the fact that Taft had postponed the admission of Arizona because of a constitutional provision for the judicial recall, and believed him to be as reactionary in his new post as in his earlier one. The fact that the court was divided five to four made it possible to denounce a single justice for trying to determine a national policy, and to denounce a system which permitted decision by a bare majority. Justice Oliver Wendell Holmes dissented, with Justices Brandeis, Clarke, and Pitney; and those who were disposed to look for the law in the dissenting minority rather than in the majority opinion of the court, believed that the Truax decision was bad law as well as an expression of conservatism or of class interest.

If labor was worried by the Truax and Coronado decisions, it was irritated by a unanimous decision, again written by the Chief Justice, in the case of Bailey *vs.* the Drexel Furniture Company. Frustration was coupled with irritation, and dissatisfaction went beyond group interest to embrace liberal thought in general, for the issue here was the question of child labor. The attempt to abolish commerce in the products of child labor had once before been blocked by a Supreme Court decision. It had been ruled that the commerce clause of the Constitution was not broad enough to cover the exclusion of the products of child labor from interstate commerce. Viewing the objective as beyond the power of Congress, the court had declined to admit the validity of the method. The same objective, written into the revenue act of 1919, was approached under the taxing clause and the income tax amendment. By these methods the attempt was made to abolish the commerce by means of a heavy surtax upon incomes derived from it. As in the earlier instance, the test case came from the new industrial region in the South, where state law lagged in the protection afforded to children in industry. The North Carolina case of Bailey *vs.* the Drexel Furniture Company revealed the Chief Justice perhaps as completely as it revealed the legal difficulties inherent in the American division of authority between state and nation. No one could doubt that child labor was repulsive to Justice Taft who, when President, brought the friends of the children into conference at the White House, and had not only signed the law creating the Children's Bureau but had entrusted the organization of the Bureau to Julia Lathrop, its eager proponent. The state of mind in 1922 was one in which liberals were unready to believe that in this decision Taft was driven by conscientious respect for the obligations of the Constitution. The Socialist in Congress, Meyer London, complained that in its Supreme Court the United States had an "unreformed house of lords as the supreme government."

The Chief Justice conceded in the Drexel case that all taxation had consequences upon society apart from those that were purely fiscal, and he tolerated such as were merely incidental to an intent to raise money; but, he said, "there comes a time in the extension of the penalizing features of a so-called tax when it . . . becomes a mere penalty." When the penalty became the purpose, and the tax was no more than the carrier of the penalty, and when the purpose was outside the grant of constitutional powers, it was time to call a halt. Here, he called it without dissent from his colleagues on the court. In his line of argument he was confronted by the dialectics of the southern critics of the protective tariff, for they had long maintained that protection was a policy outside the enumerated powers of the Constitution. Liberals criticized the decision, asking why, if a tax for protection was constitutional, a tax for social reform was invalid; and advocates of the reform swarmed into public debate to deny the right of any judges to defeat the public will. Senator La Follette went to the convention of the American Federation of Labor to urge the adoption of a constitutional amendment forbidding the Supreme Court to invalidate any act of Congress; others saw no remedy except through an amendment specifically extending the power of Congress over child labor.

If the mind of labor had been disturbed by nothing more than its suspicion of the Supreme Court as an agency of reaction, it would still have been happier than it was in the summer of 1922. Labor war had broken out in the soft coal fields of southern Illinois where the unions had discontinued work after April 1, on the lapse of a wage agreement without the negotiation of another. Here was a community dependent on the mines, and sharply divided between workers and operators, with little neutral population. After weeks of deadlock the company arranged with a strike-

breaking outfit to bring in nonunion workers, picking up the
unemployed around Chicago and calling them the Steam Shovelmen's Union. It protected the plant and the new crew with a stockade, guarded by private police. Local anger, sharpened by weeks
of unemployment, broke out after the receipt of a telegram from
John L. Lewis, of the United Mine Workers, in which the alleged
Steam Shovelmen were described as an "outlaw organization" and
no more than "common strike-breakers." A local mob of union
miners and sympathizers stormed the stockade on the afternoon of
June 21, and three men were killed. The nonunion men surrendered the next day. Marching from the stockade to Herrin, they
were attacked on the road, and nineteen died. There was confusion
at Springfield, and troops needed to keep order were never sent.
The local community was disposed to think it treated the "scabs"
as they deserved; and although the grand jury of Williamson
County, where the outrage took place, indicted scores of suspects,
the trial juries failed to convict. The prolonged investigations and
trials spread into the next year, to provide a text for both sides of
the labor controversy. There was much talk of suits for damage
against the United Mine Workers, under the doctrine of the Coronado decision.

The railroad shopmen disregarded the order of the Railroad
Labor Board, and went on strike on July 1, when an approved wage
cut became operative. They were less effectively organized than
the four senior railroad brotherhoods which had been dissuaded
from striking in 1921, and their component crafts were less exclusively of the railroad. Machinists, blacksmiths, electrical workers,
and the others, had a wider range of employment than did conductors and locomotive engineers. On the margin between these
craftsmen and the professional railway men, the maintenance-of-
way men wavered over the decision, and finally continued on the
job. But a tie-up in the shops meant tie-up over the whole railroad
net; and coming at the time of the soft coal strike it threatened a
curtailment of industry and widespread public inconvenience.
There was more behind it than mere wages, because of labor's conviction that coal operators were engaged in a deliberate conspiracy
to break the unions, and that the railroads were counting on their
company unions to weaken the power of the national organizations.

The White House backed up the Railroad Labor Board and the Esch-Cummins act from which its authority came, and announced that the trains would continue to run. Unions and employers were equally reluctant to accept government control of their activities.

Before the end of July the situation was critical, the Interstate Commerce Commission declared a national emergency, and Secretary Hoover was named chairman of a commission on coal distribution. President Harding explained in a public letter his obligation under the law, admitted the right of Americans to cease work, denied the right of the unions "to prevent the production of coal," and criticized sharply both unions and employers for their unwillingness to accept the orderly working of the law. By the end of August, conference and mediation proving futile, the Administration took to the courts. Attorney General Daugherty asked for an injunction against the striking shopmen, as Palmer had asked for one against the soft coal miners in 1919. The law was different, but the approach was the same; and to the defects of Daugherty, which were already accumulating, there was added that of being a strike-breaker. The federal court in Chicago made the injunction permanent in September, just before the members of Congress, who suspected the temper of their constituents, went home to test suspicion with reality.

Political dissatisfaction, uncovered as the spring primaries ran their course, continued to show itself as the labor issues came to the surface in the summer. On the borderland between labor and politics, the issue of communism again caught public attention and stiffened the fears of American conservatives, who regarded the violence of labor controversy as a forerunner of political revolt. The Communist party held what it planned as a secret convention in western Michigan on August 22, and was raided by deputy sheriffs who dragged into custody dozens of prisoners, including Charles E. Ruthenberg, the secretary of the party, and William Z. Foster, who had been a guiding spirit of the steel strike in 1919.

The prisoners were brought to trial at St. Joseph under a new Michigan syndicalism law, and the clash between freedom of speech and fear of subversive movements was kept alive for many months. Ruthenberg, too prominent an official of both party and convention to be ignored, was convicted in 1923. Foster, who was tried first, escaped conviction. The technical issues were the fact of membership, whether membership alone was enough to justify conviction, and whether the prosecution must prove that the defendant had explicitly urged violence for the purpose of overturning government. Anita Whitney, an admitted Communist and defendant in the California case, was still in the clutches of the law; the California Supreme Court having rejected her appeal two days after the riots at Herrin. Foster, not yet so much a Communist as he was to become, denied his membership in the party, thus forcing on the prosecution all the difficulties inherent in proving a case against a secret organization and in establishing a crime of opinion. He had the backing of the American Civil Liberties Union, and owed something to the skill of his counsel, Frank P. Walsh, who had served to offset Taft on the National War Labor Board. The Civil Liberties Union, busy in the defense even of Communists' rights, could not escape the attack of being in agreement with Communist opinions.

The autumn primaries brought no surcease to the worries of the administration. New radicals had won nomination in the spring; old critics were sustained in the fall; and firm friends were threatened with defeat in November, even though they secured Republican renomination. The Democratic opposition, disturbed in as many ways as were the Republican forces, was gaining hope from the Republican disorders.

Hiram Johnson entered the California primary in August, with a single term behind him, in which he had shown stubbornness of purpose as well as intractability in the party sense, and during which he had become a national figure more rapidly than was usual for a new senator. He had been maneuvered out of the presidential contest in 1920, and had removed himself from the vice-presidency which might have come to him; and he had ambitions for 1924. Meanwhile he must secure renomination in order to retain his standing. His national success had not been relished by his enemies at home, where his original election had been as a Progressive with Republican endorsement. The voters liked him better than the leaders did. Stalwarts were still against him, some of them the more firmly because of the support given him by the Hearst *Examiners* of San Francisco and Los Angeles. Many of his original supporters had deserted him because of his isolationism. But Johnson won the nomination over the San Francisco shipbuilder who was picked to run against him, and he was to run ahead of the party ticket, and to remain a thorn in the side of the administration.

For La Follette of Wisconsin it was a third reëlection, not a first. No state was more truly the seat of the progressive movement than was his, and he had retained at each election the lead established while he was the engineer of the "Wisconsin idea" as governor. In 1916 he had retained the nomination and seat although conservative Republicans kept a stalwart governor in the capitol. The war had disturbed the political lines in his state, but not early enough to defeat him in 1916, or recently enough to be remembered in 1922. He had worked himself back to the aggressive lead of those who were willing to follow him. By 1922 one of his lieutenants, John J. Blaine, was governor and was renominated in the same primary. The team swept the state.

The Newberry case was everywhere brought into the debates, as material with which to establish the bad reputation of the Republicans who had voted to seat him. Democrats and liberals alike made use of it, the former with an eye upon the election, the latter in the primaries; and there was a definite threat to bolt a stalwart nomination. A week after La Follette was sustained in Wisconsin, both Lodge of Massachusetts and Townsend of Michigan went into their own primaries, and emerged with renomination. Since Newberry was not up for renomination at this time, his unhappy colleague who had supported him was made the scapegoat for his sins and was attacked as though it was he who had been beneficiary of the election in 1918. The three other contestants for his seat divided the vote, permitting him to win by mere plurality; but to win only for September. Lodge was in control of his party in Massachusetts, but in doubt whether his party could carry the state. It was noted that a reëlection would leave him only leader emeritus, for the party and the country had changed since his first election to the Senate thirty years before, and since his earlier entry to public life as a "scholar in politics." The administration took what temporary comfort it could from these three primary victories, as well as from those of Poindexter in Washington and Frelinghuysen in New Jersey.

Democratic hopes fattened on Republican troubles, which were soon to be increased by others, of which the Democrats themselves had enough. The Klan was riding in the South and earning disrepute by its slogans, its intolerance, and the violence of its members and imitators. Simmons, Imperial Wizard, held the first Imperial Klonvocation in Atlanta in May, on the seventh anniversary of the rebirth of the order. In August the Klan received painful prominence in Louisiana. Two kidnapings, following the flogging of the victims by masked mobs at Mer Rouge, were laid to Klansmen; and when the bodies of the unfortunates were found the charge became murder. It was as impossible to find juries willing to believe that any specific defendant had done the murder in Louisiana as it had been to find juries willing to convict at Herrin. There was name-calling between the sections; for when voices in the North denounced lynchings in the South southern voices were raised to ask why the North did not prevent labor killings in its own home area. A Missouri representative, Leonidas C. Dyer, had put through the House a federal antilynching bill. Republican votes passed it, although the caucus would not make it a party measure. The southern senators announced their determination to filibuster endlessly against it. Whether it was constitutional or not was a matter of honest doubt, but it had the backing of the National Association for the Advancement of Colored People and was reported favorably by the Senate Committee on the Judiciary in July, 1922. Its passage was not pressed, and it was left to arouse filibusters in later sessions; but as a northern and Republican intrusion upon the South it was a provocation tending to break down some of the resistance which might otherwise have retarded the progress of the Klan.

The Klan appeared to be more important than the party in Texas when the opponents of Charles A. Culberson undertook to prevent his return to the Senate and fought him in the midsummer primaries. Culberson was completing his fourth term in the Senate, but had recently gained the hostility of Klansmen by an open disapproval of their objective and their method. He was, moreover, in the way of a former governor, James E. Ferguson, who had been impeached and removed from office in the autumn of 1917, on charges of misuse of public funds. Ferguson had declared that he would run again for vindication, and chose the seat of Culberson for his attempt. There were half a dozen Democrats who sought the seat which would be allotted at the primary, since in Texas Democratic nomination was as good as election.

One of the aspirants was Earle B. Mayfield. He did not admit association with the Klan, but received its open support; whereas Ferguson, like Culberson, opposed its influence. The issue was blurred by the fact that Ferguson was "wet" and Mayfield had the support of the Anti-Saloon League. The July primary was indecisive in that no candidate received half of the votes cast; but Culberson was eliminated and Ferguson and Mayfield were left for the run-off primary in August. Mayfield was nominated and elected, and was to hold his seat in spite of inquiry by the Senate. His disclaimer of the Klan was not widely credible. The disturbing power of the order upset the nerves of politicians in the South and in the border states.

The emotional disturbances of the summer brought disorder into Democratic plans without endangering Democratic victory in the South. In New York, where the landslide of 1920 had installed a Republican governor, Nathan L. Miller, in place of Alfred E. Smith, the efforts of Democrats to regain control of the state were impeded by the interminable struggle between Tammany and the up-state Democrats. And there was no peace within Tammany. Peace was the more important because Democrats who thought they read the signs of the times were looking ahead to 1924 and knew the necessity of controlling New York if they were to control the succession to the presidency.

It was somewhat hard to tell whether William Randolph Hearst was a citizen of California—where his mansion at San Simeon was becoming more impressive every year and where his journalistic influence was behind the career of Hiram Johnson—or a citizen of New York where the mayor of the city of New York, John F. Hylan, tried to boom him for governor in the spring of 1922. He was at least registered in New York. At the western end of that state William J. Connors of Buffalo, for partisan reasons of his own, took the Hearst campaign in hand, thought he was as good as nominated by June, and alarmed the opponents of Tammany influence, whether they were Republican or Democrat. A personal feud between Smith and Hearst embittered the contest. Hearst disavowed ambition, called Smith a "plaster and lath" Democrat, and politely advised Hylan himself to run. But Hearst was suspected of higher hopes, in a radical-agrarian fusion in 1924. He was extending his chain of papers in up-state New York in a manner which suggested an intention to seek public office. He acquired the *Evening Telegram* in Syracuse and the *Evening Journal* in Rochester, and he had the *Herald* as well as the *Times* in Washington before the end of 1922. Such extensive ownership of newspapers signified a desire for an empire in journalism or for a career in high-level politics as governor, or senator, or even president. But the suggestion of his name in New York was enough to inspire a search for a Democrat who might hope to command the whole vote of the party. The name of Franklin D. Roosevelt, now a convalescent from poliomyelitis, was mentioned; but in August Roosevelt wrote to "Dear Al," joining in the pressure upon Smith to return to politics. Tammany was not eager for the burden of the name of Hearst upon the ticket, and acquiesced; as did Smith who was named to contest the candidacy of Miller for reëlection. Hearst accepted the ticket, and after the November election the friends of Smith were able to raise the cry of "on to Washington."

The session of Congress came to an end before it was certain whom the Democrats of New York would urge for the governorship, and members of Congress were back in their homes to estimate their chances. At the very end Harding had attached his name to the tariff after a running debate which ran through two whole sessions. The tariff issue had been affected by nearly every measure of the period and had in turn affected nearly every measure. It involved the financial status of the Treasury, the relations of classes which were getting out of hand, the repayment of the war debts due the United States from the Allies, and the interests of organized veterans who were demanding adjusted compensation. What its completion would do to the voting in November could only be guessed when the session ended on September 22, 1922.

Chapter XVII ★ The Fundamental Policy

Every tax, as Chief Justice Taft conceded in the child labor case, affects more than the revenue of the Treasury. It affects the available income of the citizen, the prosperity of industry, the livelihood of regions, the accumulation of capital, and the attitudes of the individual. If there were enough wisdom to insure perfection in the rates and incidence of taxation the levies would still constitute a burden by lessening the control of the individual over his earnings, in order to place them at the disposal of the state. With the increasing determination of the voter that government should do for him what he was incapable of doing for himself, the weight of the unavoidable burden of the tax progressively increased. It was near the turn of the century that the demand for new types of service, whether by nation, state, or local government, fanned out over new fields. Until the first World War the tariff, aided modestly by the internal revenue, paid the bills. Protection of industry had been a consequence of every tariff, if only because the levy of an import duty influenced the price at which an imported commodity could be sold in the United States. In 1890 the McKinley tariff gave a new turn to legislation by the weight it gave to the nonfiscal objective of protection for industry; and in the three decades thereafter the competition for protective rates tended to overshadow the raising of revenue. Almost from the beginning the protective aspect had been fought as an unfair favoring of industry and as inherently unconstitutional; but at every period of revision new industries sought advantage from the rates, and more theoretical opponents were forced to choose between their theory and their local industries. With the McKinley

[288]

bill the intent to assist every American industry, existent or un-
born, became fundamental policy in years of Republican ascendency, whereas in Democratic years this intent was subordinated
rather than upset.

The unavoidable other effects of a tax were intensified by the
new policy. They would have been real and disturbing even if
there had been wisdom enough to adjust the protective rates to
the precise levels which might, according to the notion of the moment, produce equality in competition with foreign producers, or
assure to the American a closed market. They would have been
real if, among those who demanded protection, there had been
self-denial enough to prevent pressure for rates amounting to open
or concealed subsidies. Only in good times was it easy to persuade
the farmer, west or south, that the tariff policy was not based upon
the favoring of a class; in bad times he became mutinous. The Mc-
Kinley tariff, reinforced by the hard times which engendered Popu-
lism, contributed to the party reversal of 1890 and to the return of
Cleveland to the presidency in 1893.

The degree of statistical or technical wisdom necessary for tariff
making did not exist in any disinterested group within the United
States. The drafting of tariff schedules by ill-formed congressional committees, under pressure from favored interests, made it
possible to turn a public policy into private and unintended advantage. The rapid industrial progress of the United States, the
appearance of new commodities on the market, and the elimination
of others made tariffs inadequate within a few months after
passage; this meant, of course, continuous revision by Congress.
The McKinley bill, which aimed at covering all aspects of tariff
policy, stated the law in fifty-eight pages of the *Statutes at Large*.
By the time the revolt against the Payne-Aldrich tariff made the
Underwood-Simmons revision possible in 1913, the new bill, aiming at a revenue tariff and the elimination of favoritism, required
eighty-nine pages. The tariff law upon which Fordney began to
hold hearings on January 6, 1921, and to which Harding added
his signature on September 21, 1922, covered 132 pages. And every
item in the thousands which were enumerated and the additional
thousands which fell into the "basket clause" without enumeration meant something between injury and advantage to those

whose livelihood depended upon the commodity concerned. The possibility that tariff making would again swing western Republicans to the support of a Democratic ticket was in the mind of the engineers of the new law and of its opponents.

The substitution of a Republican tariff for the Underwood-Simmons bill was a foregone conclusion from the day of Harding's victory in 1920. A revision was called for because of the obsolescence of the existing law, even if the issue of protection had not been involved, and steps to bring it about were taken before Woodrow Wilson retired to private life. The Republican leaders, most of whom had been in Congress even before Wilson's administration, had fought the Underwood-Simmons bill on its original passage, and had helped in drafting the Payne-Aldrich bill of 1909. They now proposed to interpret their victory as they pleased and to take advantage of it. Their hand was forced by the upsurgence of farmer demand for adequate protection, as the last session of the Sixty-sixth Congress met in December, 1920. As soon as the holidays were over they yielded to the demand, helped pass the measure reviving the War Finance Corporation over Wilson's veto, and presented him at the end of the session with an emergency tariff drafted on the insistence of the farmer interests. When this was vetoed on the day before Harding was inaugurated it became a "must" matter for the special session which met in April—a price to pay for the votes required to pass a major revision.

The Committee on Ways and Means, most of whose members were to carry over into the Sixty-seventh Congress, opened the hearings for the new law immediately after the revival of the War Finance Corporation. After the hearings were concluded Fordney and his Republican associates retired into secret session to draft a bill. The minority members of the committee were allowed no share in the drafting, and cooled their heels in exclusion until the draft was presented to the new Congress. This was the usual course, and the excluded members, as usual, scolded because of the high-handed tactics of the majority. Republicans, when in the minority in 1888, had denounced the "star chamber" tactics of the Democrats when the latter made use of the method in connection with the Mills bill; but they followed the precedent when they had a chance. The introduction of the bill, as H. R. 7456, was delayed by priority business on legislation for the termination of the war and the erection of the federal budget, by the appropriation bills and the emergency agricultural tariff. At each step thereafter in the unfolding of the party policy new impediments to action made their appearance, and new side issues which must be met before the detailed rates could be written into final schedules. Instead of satisfying the uneasy West, the concessions granted gave rise to more demands, so that while the House was clearing the way for the tariff debate the farm bloc took shape in the Senate and seized something resembling a balance of power between the administration and the opposition.

It was not until the end of June that the time was ripe for the introduction of the new bill, and, from the day when Fordney presented it, the fight became three-cornered because the Democrats set up a partisan front—broken only when as individuals they had to protect their own industries—and the majority representatives were not in agreement. Frear of Wisconsin presented a minority report objecting in particular to the vigorous embargo on dyes and chemicals which had at first been grafted onto the farmers' bill. This restriction had the appearance of favoritism to a budding American monopoly. The followers of La Follette embraced among their settled convictions a deep distrust of the influence of big business upon Republican policy. This distrust was held in common by the Granger movement, the Populist party, and the Progressive party.

The bill as introduced carried a complete revision of titles and rates. As Schedule 11, the rates on wool and woolens proved to be as disruptive as they were when stated in Schedule K of the Payne-Aldrich bill. The situation respecting wool was typical in tariff construction. The sheep areas demanded high protection on wool, whereas the wool manufacturers demanded free wool and a high rate on woollens. When it was proposed to protect the manufacturers and to add to the protective rate a compensatory rate to cover the loss owing to the rate on raw wool, the sheep regions protested the favoritism to the manufacturer and the high cost of clothing.

Novelties in the Fordney draft, which had been discussed while the emergency tariff was pending, were the principle of American valuation as basis for the levy of *ad valorem* duties, and broad powers enabling the President to raise or lower rates when it seemed desirable to compensate for foreign discriminations upon American exports. The Democrats were allowed a few days to read and study the draft after it was introduced on June 29, meanwhile Republicans held a caucus upon procedure. Fordney called up the bill on July 7. The debate in the House was brief; made brief because of a special rule imposed by the majority, limiting amendments from the floor, and setting July 21 for the final vote. Democrats cried "gag," as those in opposition normally do, but the bill went through by a vote of 288 to 127. In spite of their internal schism Republican representatives held together on the vote.

Although protection was fundamental it was only a part of the business of the party. The tariff was expected to strengthen the Treasury, where its revenue items were of great concern. The administration was pledged to economy and to a balanced budget. Tariff taxes and internal revenue must together provide the income of the government, and expenditure must be controlled if the costs of government were not to run beyond receipts. At the very beginning of the debate in the House Harding appeared in the Senate on July 12 to demand postponement of the costly bonus bill. It had already been approved in the House as an adjusted compensation measure but no financial arrangements had been made to meet its costs. The Senate yielded for the moment, but the demand was only checked. There were too many veterans in every congressional district for either senators or representatives to remain indifferent on the eve of an election. The bonus threatened the budget if enacted, and party control if denied.

It was impracticable to fix the tariff rates until the probable returns from internal revenue—chiefly the income tax—had been determined. When, therefore, the Fordney bill went to the Senate it was agreed to defer action upon it until the revenue bill had been passed, and the debates on this were not finished until the end of the session on November 23. But the cleavages were much the same on both measures, and the clash of section, class, and party appeared in much the same language whichever bill was under discussion.

The Senate Committee on Finance considered the bill from July 21, 1921 until April 11, 1922, while Congress worked through its entanglements and public attention was diverted from the tariff by interest in the Conference on Limitation of Armaments. Penrose died and McCumber took his place as chairman, Smoot of Utah coming next in rank. Hearings were held on an elaborate scale, with the usual result that those who desired protective rates filled Washington with their lobbies and flooded the committee with their statistical tables, purporting to prove the dangers of competition from Europe and the need to keep Europe from excluding American-made goods. Every month of delay hardened the pressure, and increased the dissatisfaction of some groups over the demands of others. Watson of Indiana, however, doing yeoman work for the leaders, declared that "The Republican Party is either a protective tariff party or it is nothing," and the fruitless task of reconciling competing interests continued.

While the Senate considered the Fordney act, another fiscal matter intervened and was determined. On February 9, upon the very heels of the naval conference from which it was hoped amicable relations would ensue, the President signed a law depriving himself of discretionary power to negotiate with the Allied debtors respecting the war loans, creating a special commission for adjusting terms of payment, and substantially subjecting every agreement to the approval of Congress. The Republican members, out of hand in both houses, had agreed to protect the interest of the United States in the war debts as well as to pass the bonus bill which had been pigeonholed the preceding July.

When party procedure was mapped in the Republican caucuses in January, 1922, the tariff discussions had already dragged out for a full year, and the Senate Committee on Finance was still wrestling with the 2,082 amendments which were to be attached to the House bill when it was finally reported back to the Senate. The problem of the war debts was too pressing to be deferred until after the passage of the tariff, and the disposition to regard the loans to the Allies as an expendable part of the American reinforcement had evaporated since the conclusion of the Treaty of Versailles. Those who opposed this Treaty were predisposed to demand payment in full; some who had favored participation by the United

States in the League of Nations had been disillusioned by what seemed to be the absence of a will to peace in parts of Europe; some thought in terms of ten billion dollars and feared that the American taxpayer would have to raise that portion of the total which might be forgiven or evaded. Both Senate and House had had the matter under consideration in the summer of 1921, but public debate had been deliberately avoided while the disarmament conference was in session, lest unkind words might roil the waters of the conference.

The authorization for the loans, appearing in the loan acts of April and September, 1917, had run to ten billion dollars, most of which had been advanced before the Armistice; and most of it had been spent in the United States where the war prices had yielded a generous profit. When the accrued interest was added to the principal sums the total exceeded ten billions. There had been little discussion of repayment when the loans were authorized. The sagging power of the Allies needed to be bolstered by the economic reinforcement which was at the beginning expected to be the principal contribution of the United States to victory. The ambassadors did not hesitate, when they took their credits from the Treasury, to sign demand notes, payable in gold coin of the United States. The notes provided that the interest rate should not be less than the United States was paying to its own citizens.

Before the Democratic administration was ended the desirability of mutual forgiveness of loans had been suggested to the United States by borrowers. In succeeding months the Allies could not fail to connect repayments with the sums in reparation to which the Treaty had pledged the defeated enemy. It would have pleased all of them if the reparations could have been funded in German bonds, handed to the Allies, and used by them to adjust claims among themselves. The result would have been a lifting of the burden of the debt, but the United States would have received in payment only German reparation bonds, the value of which as a prudent investment was nearly nothing. The German mark was already on its downward course, and noisy agitators were already telling the Germans that they were not bound by the Treaty of Versailles. American opinion was rapidly losing confidence in the working of the Versailles arrangements, and accepting the idea that only the American reinforcement had saved the Allies from defeat, this idea hardened to an insistence that the borrowers must pay their debts regardless of their ability to collect from their own debtors.

There was a sharp contradiction between the tariff policy and the determination to collect the debts. This was noted in the debates, and was to launch the tariff war of the 'twenties, but it was not pressed with an insistence strong enough to deter Congress from following both policies at once. The purpose of the tariff was to prevent entry of competing European goods into the American market; yet the only conceivable way in which European countries could pay their debts and interest was through export to the United States of goods the sale of which would build up credits with which to meet the obligations. Payment in money was impracticable, even if the Allies had not had prior obligations to their own reconstruction far in advance of their financial resources.

The authorization acts had left the loans to the discretion of the President, and it was possible to argue convincingly that it was within his power to adjust the terms of repayment, or even to scale down the debts to the ability of the Allies to pay. The bill which Penrose presented to the Senate in the spring of 1921, phrased in this belief, had vested the negotiations in the Secretary of the Treasury subject to the approval of the President; but it met with objection in the Senate because of the growing fear that the terms might be too easy on debtors and too burdensome on American taxpayers. The House took up the matter in the autumn and determined to keep a congressional hand on the financial transactions, diplomatic though they were. Its bill proposed basic terms for funding agreements and demanded that they be negotiated by a commission created specially for this purpose. The growing public determination to treat the debts as debts convinced the administration that the Penrose plan was impossible and that a commission was inevitable. The House bill was taken up in the Senate before the Washington delegates had gone home, chiefly because the life of the conference was longer than had been anticipated.

Andrew W. Mellon was determined to keep his budget balanced. He had fought for greater relief to the large taxpayers than Congress would countenance in the revenue act, and he was aware that to protect his investment a creditor must keep his demands within the ability of the debtor to pay. He had asked the Senate committee for plenary powers in the matter of adjustment, though disavowing an intent to accept German bonds in lieu of direct payments from the debtors. He believed, as did the President, that this was a matter of foreign affairs within the constitutional jurisdiction of the President and one in which Congress had no right to intrude or to assert a power of control. The only limit to which the administration wished to be held was that of "the best interests of the United States of America," as it should determine them.

McCumber, in Penrose's place, opened the debate on the amended House bill on January 23. Simmons from the minority added to the difficulties by proposing a substitute in which the enactment of the bonus was undertaken and the debts were relied on for the necessary payments. More than ninety per cent of the debts and accrued interest which were to be funded were owed by the four principal Allies: Great Britain owing 4.6 billions, France 3.7, Italy 1.8, and Belgium 0.4; Britain and France were themselves heavy creditors of other Allies. Their assurance of being repaid was even less than that of the United States.

The debate on the funding bill ran through nine days, throwing into the *Congressional Record* words which increased the disharmonies between the United States and the Allies. It ended in the surrender of the administration to superior forces. A World War Foreign Debt Commission was created, to include the Secretary of the Treasury and four others—Harding picked them from Congress —to work under the President. But in the attempt to force repayment in national bonds of the debtors, bonds which the United States might sell in the open market, the commission was forbidden to extend the maturity of the bonds beyond June 15, 1947, or to accept an interest rate below four and one half per cent, or to permit the bonds of one country to be accepted in satisfaction of the debt of another. Simmons' substitute was tabled, but the promise had been given that the bonus in another shape would be put through Congress. Harding signed the law on February 9, 1922, the day before he delivered the Washington treaties to the Senate.

The restrictions written into the law were so rigid as to compel the agreements, when they were at last negotiated, to be submitted to Congress not merely for information but for specific enactment.

The debtors had refused to accept such onerous terms. England, most solvent of the Allies, was first to negotiate a funding agreement, and in February, 1923, Harding was forced to appear in Congress to ask its consent to the best which he and the commission could offer. The debt was to remain national and not to be thrown on the open market, it had sixty-two instead of fifteen years to run, and its interest rate was cut to three per cent until 1932, and to three and one half per cent thereafter. Even this much nearly wrenched apart the government of Bonar Law, who had succeeded Lloyd George; and led Balfour, of the earlier cabinet, to sound again a plea for cancellation in a circular to Britain's debtors, informing them that England would exact from them only what it must pay to the United States. Balfour jarred American ears when he described the complexity of these wartime financial relations as "one great transaction." Congress, too, yielded to necessity and ratified the contract. But no other debtor government could be induced to pay as much as England, driven by commercial pride, had promised.

It was still two months after the signing of the funding act before the Senate received the tariff from the committee. The treaties of Washington were ratified in the interval. The Permanent Court of International Justice came into being at The Hague without American participation. The European powers went into conference at Genoa upon their economic and political affairs, with their prime creditor absent, and were startled when the Soviet government and Germany signed a treaty at Rapallo to regulate their joint concerns. The appearance of the proletarian delegation at Genoa, dressed in the scrupulous costume of diplomacy including high silk hats, was as surprising as was their evident determination to do business on their own account. Meanwhile the Republican members of the Senate Committee on Finance, their public hearings concluded, continued to work on amendments to the Fordney bill and to see behind closed doors the representatives of such business interests as they cared to see. Each week brought changes in the world situation and in the American equilibrium which needed to be weighed in the formulation of the tariff schedules.

McCumber formally reported the results of his labors on April 11, deferring the opening of the debate until April 20 so that the minority members of his committee might have time to read it. He admitted that it was the worst possible time to have to make a tariff in the midst of world-wide economic confusion, yet this very fact made it the more important to bring the tariff up to date. The tariff was no longer merely a matter of adjusting foreign trade on the basis of relative costs. It was greatly affected by wide variations in national wealth, by manipulations of foreign exchange, by the loss of buying power among the customers of the United States and within the agricultural population at home. It was a long "legislative day" which began on the calendar day of April 20 when the debate was launched in committee of the whole. For 105 calendar days, through August 2, the Senate kept to the subject as of the legislative day of April 20, interrupting its sessions only by recesses, and resuming the next morning without the intervention of other business except by unanimous consent, and without inviting Divine blessing by the usual morning prayer. Before the death of a member brought about an adjournment instead of a mere recess, a southern senator had attributed the confusion and contradiction of purpose in the proceedings to the absence of the daily prayer.

The McCumber amendments made a new bill out of the Fordney draft. The emergency tariff had been extended twice, as the general tariff waited. Most of its schedules were now worked over and incorporated, and were, like the other schedules, framed in a spirit of rigorous protection. The desire of the House for American valuation of imports in the imposition of *ad valorem* duties was rejected by the Senate committee. The embargo schedules, arousing farmer ire when thrust into the emergency bill, had been abandoned in the House draft but were now back in place. But the House demand for a flexible tariff had been retained. Harding had insisted, in his message at the opening of the session on December 6, upon being allowed the right to raise or lower rates to meet "unusual and changing conditions," and the Senate committee had concurred. The trouble was that Europe was too poor to buy agricultural exports but it was unwilling to buy manufactured exports; and this situation had to be faced. Flexibility was designed to enable the President to bring pressure upon customer countries which discriminated directly or indirectly against American goods. The time had passed when the simple tariff aim was to raise revenue by means of duties on noncompeting imports, and to deter importation of competing goods. The promotion of American exports which a later government sought to attain by persuasion and bargaining for reciprocal advantage was now sought by punitive adjustment of the tariff rates.

The flexible clauses survived the long debate and were included in the tariff as finally written. The Tariff Commission was brought into the discussion, for it was upon information furnished by it that the President was empowered to take action when, in his judgment, the interests of the United States would be served thereby. Whether his judgment was good or bad, it was likely to be better than a compromise result worked out among the contradictory pressures upon the floor of Congress. He was at liberty to take articles off the free list and to impose a fifty per cent duty upon them. He might also look into the costs of production in countries of origin, and if they differed materially from those of the United States he might alter the duties fifty per cent up or down. He might use the same procedure to offset price cutting which worked a disadvantage to American producers. And he might look into such arrangements as imperial preference among the British commonwealths, and meet them with his flexible rates. This was, by and large, a new principle in tariff legislation, and an effort to use the control of imports as a measure for the extension of American exports into reluctant markets abroad.

The opponents of the tariff pointed out the inconsistency involved in the attempt to maintain at once a closed American market and a free world market. The contradiction between the Republican tariff policy and the congressional policy on war debts gave rise to scornful debate without deterring leaders who knew their mind. The fact that flexibility would operate, if it should operate, to the advantage of quantity producers in big business who could sell anywhere if discriminations were removed, turned some of the supporters of the farm bloc against it. A cleavage appeared among American manufacturers, splitting the interests of those for whom foreign competition was a menace from those of the great industries which were able to pay high American costs of manufacture and yet undersell the world. The international bankers and the international traders no longer saw eye to eye with the small producers, but in the final voting the party held together, for the only tariff they could get was the tariff they could pass. Little but jeers could be expected from Democratic senators, but hecklers from the minority emphasized the inconsistencies without changing votes.

The Democratic senators contributed the most words to the debate, until they were repeatedly charged with running a filibuster in order to keep the tariff in the public mind until the eve of the November elections. This they denied, asserting that the thousands of items on the schedules and the hundreds of amendments proposed by the Senate committee required examination and exposure. "The tariff bill," declared Fletcher of Florida, "could not be passed without the consent of Senators representing the classes it will rob." He was countered by McNary of Oregon, one of a "tariff bloc" headed by Gooding of Idaho, which accepted what it must for the sake of what it craved. The new bloc, said McNary, "is composed entirely of Republicans who are alone interested in the production of agricultural products."

Although the Democrats were belabored by equally insistent demands for protection of home industries, they kept up the running fire of their criticism. Few of them talked free trade as against the interests of their constituents. The onion growers of Texas complained bitterly of an invasion of the Spanish onion from across the Rio Grande. John Garner of Texas suffered from the jeers of Republicans when he had onion trouble. Sniping could not be put down. The argument began with acetic acid, at the head of Schedule 1, and after ten days of it McCumber complained that "we still have not passed the vinegar stage." The flexibility provision was attacked on the ground of unconstitutionality, being treated as a delegation of legislative authority to the President. The administrative history of the United States was reviewed to prove or disprove the right of Congress to set up a general rule and then leave to the executive the duty of deciding the facts upon which the rule should operate. Not all who liked the idea of flexibility liked as well this increased authority of the President, but the majority yielded to the argument that in these matters prompt action was of essence, and prompt action by the Congress was unattainable.

Prompt action, already long deferred in the tariff dispute, was further deferred by the proposals embodied in Schedule 1: Chemicals, Oils, and Paints. Acetic acid, removed from the free list and thrust forward as a challenge, was merely the first item to receive attack. It showed a power of survival which brought argument back to it long after the thirteen other schedules had been reached. No jury could have been worse prepared to do a fair job on the whole program than a legislative body each of whose members faced a pressure which might unseat him if defied. After acetic acid came the long lists representing a relatively new industry in the United States and including dyestuffs and the coal tar derivatives. The manufacture of these materials had been rudimentary before 1914 and, like that of explosives, had increased its value during the World War. German scientists had led in these fields of chemical industry, and the new Germany looked to the recovery of the fields with the war once ended. The recovery was opposed on two basic grounds, that of the future military needs of the United States, and that of the profitable use to which the industries could be put if once established in the United States. The House had objected in vain when what amounted to an embargo on dyes and chemicals had been inserted in the emergency tariff by the Senate. When similar restrictions were added to the Fordney bill, and this time on a permanent basis, they added to the difficulty of holding western and eastern Republican interests on a common course.

It was not new for a tariff to act as midwife to an industry. The McKinley bill had made provision for the birth of tinplate manufacture in the United States, and had endowed the anticipated infant industry with protective rates. This time, the chemical industries were to be the adopted child, abducted from the former enemy. The train of events began with the Trading with the Enemy act of 1917, whereby all enemy-owned property in the United States was put under the protective custody of the Alien Property Custodian, A. Mitchell Palmer. Included in the German holdings was the group of patents on chemical dye processes, taken out by the foreign owners under the American law, and protecting their exclusive rights to the processes. The Alien Property Custodian became trustee for these interests, to conserve the property on the one hand, and on the other to keep it from being used to the disadvantage of the United States during the war. He was to maintain the control until Congress should determine a policy after the peace.

There were doubts respecting the limits which might control this policy, since an ancient treaty with Prussia seemed to pledge the signers to freedom from confiscation of enemy property in time of war. On the other hand there was American-owned property in Germany, and there were large American claims for damages done at German instigation between 1914 and 1917, and for the costs of the American army of occupation. A commission for the registration of these claims, created in the summer of 1922, worked under handicap owing to the priority of the Allies respecting German payments, and to doubts of the ability or willingness of the German government to pay claims after they had been adjusted. Palmer sold some of the German-owned property if it was easily marketable or liable to wastage, turning it into trust funds in the name of the owners. Just before the Armistice the law was amended to permit the sale of other assets. By this time Palmer had risen to be Attorney General, and Francis P. Garvan had succeeded him as Custodian.

Under the amended law the German patents, of which there were more than 4,000, were to be sold. Some had to do with explosives, and there was concern lest these be left to the exclusive control of German owners. Others, concerning dyes or chemicals, had constituted a near-monopoly for Germany before the war; whereas the war had turned American activity to this field. Patriotism and profit were mingled. The Chemical Foundation was incorporated to bid for the patents when they were sold, and declared its purpose to license their use by American firms. It was formed with the coöperation of the Custodian, who took its presidency, while members of his staff were placed on the directorate. The price for which the patents were sold was far below reasonable value, but once the sale was consummated the German ownership was ended.

American ownership of the dye and chemical patents was not enough, for there was fear that by sheer skill and ingenuity the German firms might be able to recover the American market even without owning the patents. A demand for embargo clauses directed against the industries was gratified by appropriate clauses in the emergency tariff, as well as by the amendments attached to the Fordney bill by the Senate committee. Democratic critics denounced the sale as robbery of the German owners, and attacked the new setup as favoritism to the American licensees of the Chemical Foundation. There was sharp criticism from the Republican side, Moses scolding the greed and impatience of the American industries. He declared that "the dye and chemical industries are plainly the spoiled children of the Finance Committee," and that dyes were its "special darling." The western interests saw nothing but high prices, sheltered by the embargo and the patents, and more pampering of wealthy corporations. But the tariff bloc accepted much of what it disapproved for the sake of what it could get. Knox was quoted in the debate as having said that the sale of the patents was a fraud; many of his associates who were preparing to vote the agricultural schedules said that these too were in many cases a fraud.

The demand for American valuation, pressed in the House in connection with the emergency tariff, was pressed again into the Fordney bill. It seemed to the House easier to value imports for tariff purposes upon their arrival at the American customs house than to ascertain the value at the place of manufacture. In the countries of origin, and among competing countries, actual costs varied, for depreciated currencies and special prices for export goods confused the picture. It was unlikely that foreign countries would welcome American investigators examining the books of business to determine actual costs. The Senate fought off the demand for American valuation, though yielding it somewhat. By the plans permitted in the flexibility clauses it was made possible for the President to make use of American valuation if other methods of appraisal failed. The Senate managers emphasized the fact that many common imports had no precise American counterpart which could be used in the appraisal process, and also that many commodities had a wide range of prices within the United States. Freight charges alone caused a variation in price after the goods left a customs house. The tariff bloc was forced to be content with mitigation of the dye embargo and with the continuance of foreign valuation as the general basis of the law.

"Tomorrow," said the New York *Times* on August 18, 1922, "the vast ungainly conglomerate of gratuitous and reciprocal favors and logrolling will be sent to conference." The fight in the Senate had been the dominant feature through 122 days, bringing into the open nearly every industrial or sectional need or greed. It had been prolonged by partisanship and stubborn opposition. Enforced termination had failed when on July 7 Vice-President Coolidge laid before the Senate a cloture petition bearing the names of fifty-two signers. On the roll call vote the forty-five yeas were confronted by thirty-five nays and, as the necessary two-thirds was lacking, the debate rolled on for six weeks more. The members of the House took their recess, but upon learning how many Republican seats were in danger, they were back in session a few days before the Senate voted on the bill. It was passed on August 19, forty-eight to twenty-five, with Borah the single Republican senator to vote against it. La Follette, however, was paired against it, and Norris who was absent let it be known that he would have voted "no." The farm bloc voted with the party. "So the bill was passed," said the *Congressional Record,* adhering to its stereotyped formula; but it had only passed the Senate. There was yet another month before it was to receive the signature of President Harding, and in the meantime it went to conference, was reported back, recommitted and again reported before the obstructions within the dominant party were broken down. The dye embargo was sacrificed for party peace. And during this month the veterans' bonus, which had received parallel and intermittent attention since the beginning of the administration, was prepared to test Harding's courage and devotion to a balanced budget.

When Harding appeared before the Senate on July 12, 1921, to beg that body to refrain from passing the bill for adjusted compensation which was under debate, the bonus had already become a veteran on the docket, with proponents who claimed adjusted compensation as a right and decried the use of the word bonus as suggesting mere gratuity. An early version had passed the House in the preceding administration, shortly before the Congress adjourned in order to permit members to attend the national conventions, both of which adopted planks in support of some scheme of veterans' relief. The speeches of the presidential candidates could be interpreted as pledging themselves to the principle. Harding, in his intrusion upon the Senate to block the bill, accepted the idea of a national responsibility for the welfare of the veteran, but asked it to refrain from acting until the new budget should be established, and until means for meeting the costs should be provided. The Senate recommitted the measure and the committee shelved it, yet it could not be forgotten. The American Legion was pushing it for the benefit of the members; congressmen were favoring it to catch the soldier vote. And the citizens less concerned than these were impressed by the difference between the modest stipend of the soldier and either the wages of the man who stayed at home or the compensation of the civil servants, in whose interest Congress had voted a bonus in order to help meet war prices.

The bonus issue was one in which it was hard to oppose the grant without appearing to be indifferent to the services of the men who had borne arms, and it was easy for all to support it who sought to make political capital out of it. It was made safer to support because the administration could be relied on to retard action. The savings to be brought about by reduction of military expenses appealed to the Treasury as a means of bringing the budget into balance and of fulfilling the pledge of economy in government. No two sets of estimates of the probable cost of the bonus agreed, but simple arithmetic made it clear that cash distribution to more than four million eligibles would run the total into billions. A few, only a few, members of Congress denied the thesis of the bonus advocates and asserted that military service is one of the unescapable duties of the citizen, entitling those who are incapacitated in the performances of that duty, and their dependents, to considerate treatment, but not establishing a right to financial compensation after the safe performance of the duty. It was an issue ideally suited to be advanced by pressure politics for it possessed a direct financial aspect for every veteran. The Senate bill remained in committee through the summer of 1921, while the House revived the proposals in the regular session.

Attempts were made to find funds with which to meet Harding's demand that provision to pay for the bonus should accompany its enactment. The advocates of a sales tax, beaten in their attempt to include it in the revenue act, reverted to it in the winter of 1922, with the President's endorsement. The farm bloc wanted the bonus but would not accept the sales tax. Attention was turned to installments and interest upon the war debts, with Simmons bringing up his proposal to build the bonus into the debts bill. His proposal would have left the taxpayer to carry the war debts and it was tabled by the Senate, although the farm bloc liked it. Again in February Harding explained his position, trying to avoid what would look like indifference to the services of the veterans, but not yielding his determination to avoid "embarrassment to the Treasury." The service men, he wrote to Fordney, were as greatly concerned with "the return to abundant employment" as were other citizens. The wounded and the sick, "impaired by their war service," were a first obligation, and not all of these were as yet provided for.

The party conferences in both houses agreed, in spite of admonition, to pass a bonus bill during the session of 1922, and the House started to formulate it. It steered it in the direction of the President's wishes, hoping thereby to ensure his assent. On March 23 it sent a bill to the Senate.

The immediate financial commitment was limited to the payment in cash for amounts under fifty dollars. Sums larger than this were made the basis of compensation certificates payable in full in twenty years or upon death. The total allowed to each veteran, computed on length and place of service, was increased by twenty-five per cent, and further increased by compound interest at four and a half per cent until maturity; it held before the veteran the promise of substantial advantage in early middle life, yet postponed the date at which the Treasury must carry the load. To meet immediate needs without draining the Treasury at once, it was provided that the banks might lend the holders of the certificates up to half the value of the original sums, and that the government should guarantee payment; but fulfillment of this guarantee was to be deferred for three years. By this time, it was hoped, the Treasury would be free from its immediate refunding embarrassments, the payments from the Allies would be flowing in, and the government might face the financial obligations with greater equanimity than in 1922. It would also be a new administration which would have to face them. There were critics of the scheme, who sought to load it with things other than cash. They expected to vote for it yet asserted that its passage in 1921 was a bid for votes in November. Its passage of the House was nonpartisan, 333 to 70.

McCumber, one of those devoted to the measure, and whose primary in North Dakota was due in three weeks, reported the bill to the Senate on June 8, supporting it with two petitions of a million signers each. The tariff was under debate, as it had been since April 20, but he hoped that the Senate would lay it aside for a few days in order to enact the bonus. Scoffers declared that the administration did not intend it to come to vote until after the passage of the tariff, or perhaps during the session, although the Republican conference had as recently as April 18 declared again that it should be passed. Within the next few days the matter was taken to the White House, where the President was still adamant for the completion of the tariff; and on June 20 the Senate passed a motion of Watson pledging itself to bring up the bonus upon the passage of the Fordney-McCumber bill, unless it was disposed of earlier. Under the Senate rules it was impossible to keep speeches on the bonus out of the tariff debate, but a few minutes after the tariff was sent to the House on August 19, McCumber brought up the bonus and gave it right of way.

While the tariff was in conference the Senate passed the bonus. There was nothing new left to be said upon it. The returns from the country, brought back by Representatives after their recess, indicated that if anything could be done to prop the Republican chances in November it needed to be done now. If the party should be rebuked, they said, it would be the fault of bad advisers to the President. Passing the Senate at the end of August, and passing conference ten days later, the bill went to the White House on September 15. It was returned with a veto message on September 19. Harding held his ground, again admitting the obligation to the veterans, but holding that it was not sufficient to warrant unbalancing the budget or committing the country to the payment of large sums for whose raising no arrangement had been made. General Dawes, who had brought the budget into life, praised the veto, conceiving no worse use for public funds than the distributing of doles to young men "for merely performing the duties of civilization." The American Legion, speaking through Hanford Mac-

Nider, its commander, urged Congress to override the veto; and the House was willing, 258 to 54. The Senate upheld the President, though a shift of four votes would have turned the bill to law. When the bonus was at last enacted, it was done over the veto of Calvin Coolidge; when it was proposed to enlarge the borrowing possibilities of certificate holders in 1931, the veto of Herbert Hoover stopped it; when cash payment ahead of the date of maturity was voted in 1934, the veto of Franklin D. Roosevelt had to be overcome before the funds could be distributed in the name of relief.

On the day after the Senate upheld his veto of the bonus, Harding signed the Fordney-McCumber tariff bill. He and the party accepted this measure, with all its inconsistencies, as fundamental policy. Two days later Congress adjourned, to await the reaction of the country.

Chapter XVIII ★ "Lame Duck"

NEVER BEFORE had the "lame duck" limped in such a glare of publicity as in the weeks after the returns from the election of 1922 were tabulated. The term "lame duck" had long been in use. It applied to the member of Congress whose public service had been terminated by defeat, and who would limp back into private life upon the following fourth of March, to nurse his political wounds. Defeated politicians were familiar figures in every form of parliamentary government, but only in the United States did they retain power to direct the course of government for a considerable period after their defeat. The congressman whose career was halted—under American practice generally for good— had ahead of him another session of Congress through which he would sit and aid in the passage of new laws. His rival, who was elected, had normally to wait thirteen months before he would be in a position to carry out the desires of his constituents. The anomalous situation came about by chance, not by intent.

The selection of March 4, 1789, as the date upon which the new Constitution should become operative and the new Congress and President should begin the fixed periods of their service, was the work of the old Congress, preparing to bring its successor to life. The government began on that day in only a technical sense. Travel difficulties deferred the appearance of quorums in New York, quorum delay postponed the count of the electoral vote, and it was April 30 before Washington, duly notified, took the oath of office. Thereafter, March 4 continued to mark the beginning and end of the several terms of representative, senator, and president, and there could not be any shifting of the day except by amendment of the fundamental law. For more than half a century the condition of roads in winter made early spring elections so difficult, and access

[309]

to the capital so inconvenient, that the states chose their representatives and electors when they pleased, and through mere convenience drifted into the habit of autumn elections, after the harvest.
Not until the election of 1848 had Congress exercised its right to
set a day for the choice of presidential electors and given to the
Tuesday following the first Monday in November its standing as
election day. Even then some of the states followed their own preferences as to the time of choosing representatives, while their senators emerged from combat in the legislatures at irregular dates.

It thus resulted that the general preference for holding elections
in November brought about the choice of representatives four
months before their term in office began. The preference of Congress for winter sessions fixed the normal date for the beginning of
legislative labor on the first Monday in December, nine months
after the several terms began. Once elected, the members of Congress did not normally do much but answer their mail and draw
their pay for thirteen months unless the public business required
the president to assemble them in special session. And always the
outgoing Congress continued to pass laws for a short session after
its successor had been chosen.

A sharp turnover in the membership of Congress was anticipated
with growing nervousness as the Sixty-seventh Congress plodded
through its long session of 1922. Every party measure brought its
fight and left impeding scars. Measures which were enacted paid
the price of compromise within the majority. As the procession of
primaries eliminated administration Republicans, one after the
other, the Democratic leaders encouraged the Republican rebels
and talked of regaining control of the House in 1922, and of the
presidency itself in 1924. And among the rebellious Republicans
there were more than whispers of the possibility of a party split,
and a new fusion of farmer, labor, and progressive interests. Borah,
too independent himself to have much to do with it, prophesied
that a new party would sweep the country in 1924 unless the Republican party modified its economic policies. He gave the warning on the eve of the election of November 7. Robert M. La Follette swept Wisconsin for renomination to the Senate in September and stepped into first place among the leaders of the new insurgents. His friends had surveyed the prospect as early as February,

1922, when they launched a Conference for Progressive Political Action in Chicago. One of them declared "one party is a boil and the other is a carbuncle. Take your pick." They prepared to count their gains and resume the conference in Cleveland as soon as the returns were in.

The returns confirmed all but the worst of the administration fears. The nominal control of Congress was retained though heavily reduced, but the ability of the administration to control the members elected as Republicans was destroyed. The landslide upon which Republicans returned to full power in 1920 had more than come to rest. In the Senate eight seats were lost, reducing the party lead over Democrats from twenty-two to eight. Six of the lost seats went to the opposition, two to independents. In the House the Democrats captured seventy-five seats, leaving to the majority a lead of eighteen instead of 168. After March 4, 1923, it would be misleading to assert that the Republican party was in control of either house. With so slight a lead the control would have been threatened even if all Republicans always agreed.

The numerical change in the party balance was upsetting to any party course, and the number of new members—freshmen Representatives—was so large as to present a problem of mere assimilation. Seventy-five new Democrats, proud of their defeat of Republican incumbents, were to demand to be heard. There were some fifty more, quite as new, whose election had not shifted a party name but who gained their districts after primary fights in which more conservative members of their own party had been ousted. Nearly a third of the new Sixty-eighth Congress was to be new, noisy, and ambitious. The probability that they could not take their seats for thirteen months, and that they must postpone official advocacy of whatever reforms they had in mind, was hard to bear. Their complaints were reinforced by the complaints of the liberals already in the House and reëlected. Demanding action at once, they attacked the lame duck period in principle. It outraged them that the lame ducks whom so many of the victors had defeated should be able to keep the fresh representatives of the people from the promised work. The Sixty-seventh Congress was to go down in history as the lame duck Congress.

The personal change in Congress was as upsetting as was the numerical. The Republican floor leader of the House, Mondell of Wyoming, had not even attempted reëlection, preferring to try to get into the Senate; but in vain. The chairman of the Committee on Ways and Means, Fordney, had simply quit. New steersmen of debate must replace them. In the Senate the opposition had struck heavily at the political household of the President. New of Indiana had gone down in the May primary, and Beveridge who defeated him was unable to hold the party vote in November. Kenyon of Iowa, who was disturbing enough as chairman of the farm bloc, was replaced by Brookhart who was to be even more irritating. McCumber, chairman of the Committee on Finance, had gone down before Frazier of the Nonpartisan League in June. What the primaries began the election finished. Poindexter of Washington, a bitter opponent of the League of Nations, was replaced by a Democrat in a region where the League was disliked. Kellogg of Minnesota, surviving the primary, was defeated by the Farmer-Labor candidate, Shipstead. Townsend of Michigan, unhappy associate of Truman H. Newberry, lost his seat less on his record than because of his support of his colleague; and Newberry, accepting the verdict of the election as condemnation of himself, resigned his seat before Congress met again. Frelinghuysen of New Jersey was replaced by Governor Edward I. Edwards, an outspoken "wet."

The reason for the reaction could not be reduced to a simple formula. Obviously, party regularity was ceasing to be a dependable bond. Obviously, also, no one idea was dominant on election day, to be a binder for the votes. There was not even such a general craving for a change as prevailed in 1920. There was little evidence of desire to elect Democrats as Democrats, and the excuses for eliminating Republican candidates were nearly as numerous as the eliminations. Many of the contests were merely local. The League of Nations, as an issue, cut both ways. There was no reward for Lodge, who had managed the Treaty issue until he killed it, for his reëlection was by a vote humiliatingly low; McCumber, who had supported the Treaty until the end, went down. Newberryism played a large part in the shouting, perhaps a smaller part in the voting. "Stand-pat-ism" was violently attacked, but Republicans who, disliking the tariff, found something of advantage in it, rarely deserted the party candidate on its account. Prohibition played an uneven part. Daugherty was under fire for irregularity in enforcement, but Governor Edwards was sent to the Senate.

The dealers in alcoholic drinks were almost alone among the manufacturers for whom nothing had been done and there were few in high office who had even a word of comfort to offer. Their market was shut down. Wartime prohibition had closed it for the short run, and the Eighteenth Amendment had made the closure as tight as the constitutional structure of the United States permitted. Before the amendment went into force on January 16, 1920, movements for its repeal had been launched and some of them had been incorporated. It was quite as constitutional to agitate for the repeal of the amendment as it had been to urge its adoption. Out of the miscellaneous organizations in opposition the Association Against the Prohibition Amendment emerged as leader in a relentless war. The program was explicit: to bring about a repeal of the Volstead act, to leave the enforcement of the amendment to the several states, and at last to repeal the amendment. The association, and others like it, had few well-known names among their officers but they had money to spend. The industries for whom money spent in pressure represented prudent investment saw eye to eye in the desire for repeal, yet were rivals among themselves. The vintners and the brewers represented themselves as less dangerous than the distillers, and sought exemption for light wines and beer; but the distillers, try as they might, could not make hard liquor resemble a nonintoxicating drink. All of them saw the advantage of having their money spent under names other than their own.

It was harder to restrain the personal habits of the millions than to punish the illegal behavior of a few, as the Commissioner of Internal Revenue soon found out. The responsibility for enforcement was assigned to him, without the means and without control over other agencies of government associated in the task. There was not, and there never had been, machinery in the United States capable of restricting breweries and distilleries to nonbeverage alcohol manufacture, and capable of watching at the same time the illicit producer and the outlets through which his wares were passed to willing customers. The American distaste for inquisitorial government was intensified in the case of a law which struck at personal indulgence. The profits for those who engaged in the business rose as its unlawfulness drove from it all but the lawbreakers.

The Congress whose votes overrode the veto when it passed the Volstead act included many who "drank wet but voted dry." At the moment of enactment they voted as their constituents demanded. The myth was soon abroad, however, that the amendment had been passed in secrecy, taking unfair advantage of the absence of young men in the service of their country—a myth inconsistent with the local and state-wide majorities which had brought fruition to the movement during the war period. But the myth was good enough to be used as though it had been founded on fact. The restraint imposed upon personal liberty by the enforcement act and by the amendment was turned into a grievance and a provocation of crime. There were some who persuaded themselves, and hired first-rate lawyers to try to persuade the courts, that both were unconstitutional. Even Elihu Root took briefs to this effect. When the Supreme Court refused to take seriously the attack upon constitutionality, and admitted it to be the right of Congress to establish by law the point (one half of one per cent) at which a beverage should be regarded as intoxicating, there were left only two courses for the opponents of prohibition to pursue: to agitate for repeal or to employ a bootlegger.

Congress failed to provide adequate machinery for enforcement, as earlier Congresses had failed to make it possible to administer the public lands either efficiently or with respect for law. The army of inspectors necessary for enforcement would have been costly and the nature of the work had little appeal for those whom the salaries might have attracted. Unrelated bureaus, each with other business of prime importance, were called upon to coöperate. The coast guard was responsible for keeping illicit cargoes from American shores, the customs service had jurisdiction over the land approaches from Canada and Mexico, the internal revenue officers were charged with prevention of evasion within the United States as well as the collection of income taxes from those who were successful in evasion, and the federal attorneys prosecuted cases in the courts. There was no way of ensuring that citizens sitting on juries would have a disposition to convict, or that crowded courts would have time to hear the cases before the evidence evaporated, or that different courts would be uniform in handling similar cases. The amendment vested in Congress and in the several states the "con-, current power" to enforce prohibition, but there was no way to compel the states to act alike in this concurrent enforcement, or to act at all.

The governor of New Jersey, Edward I. Edwards, spoke the opinion of an industrial population with a heavy admixture of foreign born when he openly denounced prohibition as an infringement upon personal liberty; and he had some reason to hope that there might one day be room for a "wet" candidate for the presidency. Governor Alfred E. Smith, returned to Albany by the election of 1922, spoke the same language in the largest of metropolitan communities. He was willing, in the spring of 1923, to endanger a nomination that might have come to him on the basis of public service by approving an act of the New York legislature repealing a state enforcement act passed upon the adoption of the amendment. New York left this duty to federal law.

The large cities were generally wet in opinion and in fact, and many of their people were disposed to believe themselves victims of social restriction imposed by rural votes. Their law officers, bound just as completely by the Volstead act as though a concurrent state law were existent, lacked the moral support from public opinion without which social legislation can hardly be enforced. When they were diligent they invited defeat for reëlection; when lax they incurred moral reproach. Citizens experimented with home brew or bought their grapes in bulk to turn them into wine. Outside their homes the illicit business of the speakeasy added a zest to that which was offered by alcohol. Bootleggers built up lists of private customers and devised ways of delivering their wares by stealth.

The Canadian border crossings became channels for an alcoholic invasion of the United States, with trucks or boats clearing the Canadian customs and sneaking into Detroit or Plattsburg. The coast guard was aware of rumrunners safely offshore beyond the three-mile limit, and invited international episodes when it went to sea to break up the traffic. The list of internal revenue agents killed in the performance of duty was already long by 1923.

And the bootleggers themselves, defending their unlawful interests, were in increasing war with highjackers who raided their trucks and stole their liquor. Having no legal remedies, they met force with force. The by-products of enforcement included law breaking by citizens, graft in local politics, and bootleg fortunes. The most notable of the practicable convictions were based upon evasion of the income tax rather than upon the crime itself or the violence accompanying it.

American life was passing through a painful transition not only from war to peace but from old standards to new, and from one industrial era to another. The federal principle was receiving shocks the severity of which was increased by the tendency of opinion to be regional and by the desire of opinion to make action national. It was less easy than ever to maintain the sharp line between over-all rules necessary to the general welfare and local preferences within the reasonable realm of state autonomy. The price which must be paid for the acceptance of over-all rules is toleration of local differences, for such rules take on the appearance of intrusion when they are voted by one region to be enforced upon another. Prohibition, however desirable in itself, and there were already numerous entries on the credit side, imposed upon the urban states a rule of conduct acceptable to rural regions. The fight on child labor, supported largely in the North, seemed impertinent to much of the South, as the demand for the abolition of slavery had once seemed to be. The effort to define mob violence, make it a federal offense, and thus put a stop to lynching, seemed to the South to be sectional coercion, made worse by the indifference of its proponents to labor violence in the industrial North. Urban opinion blamed the troubles that attended prohibition upon rural coercion.

Confusion prevailed among the voters. The President of the United States, who was also a voter, felt it. "There was grief in the business of being Chief Executive," says Harding's biographer. It was grief because of the crosscurrents which had not yet developed main channels, because the landscape observed from the White House was different from the landscape seen from the office of the Marion *Star*, because of the behavior of intimate friends whom Harding had put in office, because his habits as a citizen were not always consistent with his duties as President.

His friend Forbes, in the Veterans Bureau, was under attack with charges ranging from inefficiency through misbehavior to graft. His mentor Daugherty was defying critics who sought his impeachment for impropriety and who whispered that he had pets on the wrong side of prohibition. His senatorial associate Fall, as Secretary of the Interior, had talked Denby into shifting to him the administration of the naval oil reserves, and hostile senators were probing into the conditions surrounding the transaction. The legend of personal unworthiness which was soon to be magnified by politics was not yet bringing Harding under fire, but his tolerance and his devotion to his friends were leading him into blind alleys from which there was no easy retreat. His personal habits and prohibition were in conflict. "Drinking a good deal," (as Allan Nevins states) he treated the private quarters of the White House as off-bounds from the official rooms of the Chief Executive. There his friends found liquor, and there his critics knew it had been found.

The critics, indicting American society for its evasion of prohibition, were indicting it on other counts. A southern revivalist, who called himself the "Texas Cyclone," invaded New York in the spring of 1922, seeking to reform the city. "Every great war has been traced to the depravity of women," he thundered, "and they never were so bad as they are today." Among the evidences cited as establishing the depravity, the smoking of cigarettes was one upon which New York was somewhat sensitive. It had been victim of a slip in the secretariat of the aldermen, whereby it was made to appear that an ordinance had been passed forbidding women to smoke in public. The police commissioner, taking it seriously, had added the duty of enforcement to the other burdens of his uniformed force. The ordinance had, in fact, been rejected; but it had indeed been presented to the board, and there were those who wished that it had been enacted. Official denial by the Board of Aldermen never caught up with the story, for it covered the country. There were other places where similar attempts at the control of manners by law had been debated and even tried. In Chicago, women smoked in the gallery and hooted while the aldermen voted down such a measure.

It was equally typical of the United States that those who disapproved of tobacco and who saw a menace to morals in women's

smoking should endeavor to restrain the habit by law, and that
those who saw no sin in smoke should resist and evade all efforts
to restrict their freedom to indulge. There was no doubt that the
cigarette had established itself in society in the generation since it,
and the monocle, and the dude, and general effeminacy had been
associated in one pattern. It was more popular at the end of the
World War than at the beginning. Women had learned to smoke,
and children were imitating them. The Commissioner of Internal
Revenue, reporting on the production of cigarettes in the United
States, provided a yardstick for measurement. From seventeen billion cigarettes on which revenue tax in 1915 had been paid, the
number had risen to forty-seven billion in 1920, and rose to eighty-
two billion in 1925. The manufacturers sensed the number of potential women customers, and pushed the trade. The millions of
profit which resulted were turned in part into the hydroelectric
development of the southern piedmont and in part wrought a
useful social by-product. Channeled into the little Trinity College
in the home town of "Bull Durham" tobacco they turned it into
a great university which took the name of Duke, in gratitude to
the owner of the tobacco millions. Carnegie millions had covered
the United States with libraries on profits derived from steel. Petroleum millions had created the University of Chicago and identified the name of Rockefeller with fundamental research. The
good, the bad, and the negligible were so imbedded in the American composite as to defy separation.

As each of the ingredients of American culture was in turn
brought into focus, it tended to force the other ingredients to the
margin of the screen, and rarely were all Americans contemplating
the same one at once. When any of them was made scapegoat for
society, virtue became as ingenious as vice in overstressing or ignoring facts. Youth of both sexes, in the reconstruction of manners,
became aggressive as it claimed its "rights," and attracted attention
when it exercised them.

Youth, like its elders, moved with more freedom, with motor cars
at hand. Its doings, like theirs, came into the open, for public play
was supplanting entertainment in the home. As apartment residence encroached upon the home, limiting its space, diversion was
sought outside. As shortage of servants drove householders into

hotel life, the latter came more and more to live in public. The movie theaters brought children and their parents upon the streets after dark, and main streets were brightened by new tricks in illumination. Dancing places drew children far from home in father's car, and those who had no access to a car set up more pressure to stimulate the motor industry. Freed from the limitations of wartime life and from the tight discipline of military life, Americans who could were taking full enjoyment on their rebound. The year 1922 was recognized and deprecated as the "flapper age"; but young girls in their defiance formed "flapper clubs" and claimed the right to smoke, to make up, to dance as they pleased, and to wear one-piece bathing suits. New York claimed to be infested with a "curious organizations of he and she flappers" known as "Shifters," which the *Times* described as a "flappers' Ku Klux."

There was no doubt that youth was more in evidence than it had ever been. Schools and colleges, functioning between parental bewilderment and youthful energy, had their troubles with the widening use of cigarettes. Should girls be expelled from school for smoking? And how about the teachers? Was a teacher disqualified if she bobbed her hair? In San Francisco a vigilance committee of women was formed to break up smoking among high school girls, and members of women's clubs brought the doings of daughters— other women's daughters—into debate throughout the country. The crusade to maintain the manners of an older time went farther. In Arkansas a school district expelled a school girl who would not pledge herself to refrain from the use of powder on her face; yet the use of rouge and lipstick was rising from beyond the margins of good society into respectability. The potential customers for cosmetics offered to the advertisers a field for exploitation as profitable as that for tobacco, and aids to beauty could be bought both at shiny shops and at the five-and-ten. What the well made up stars of the movies did for the beauty parlor business can only be guessed at. The problem was not confined to the American scene. A London court, faced with a night club case, had gravely to declare that knee-length gowns were not necessarily immodest.

The movies, purveying entertainment to the millions, were at the same time setting standards of behavior. The studios were full of stars, silent as yet while they stood before the cameras. But when they were off the set they were often so full of life that their behavior was an embarrassment to their employers and a source of scandal which gave concern to the public as well as to the industry. The new form of entertainment had passed out of its period of improvisation and was settling down to quantity production for a world market. It was easy to translate the captions into the language of any country where there was a potential audience and to export what appeared to be a picture of American life. Vacant stores were no longer sufficient for conversion into movie theaters, and palatial lobbies were beginning to house the queues of customers waiting for vacant seats. The producers, many of whom had survived in competition with the first experimenters, were grouping themselves in large and wealthy units. Their associations were discussing the problems of the trade, and they were following the sunlight into southern California where their new community on the western edge of Los Angeles was making the name of Hollywood known around the world.

The stars were likely to be young, and bewildered by sudden wealth. Not all of the actors of the theater could make the transition from speech to pantomime. There was only one Charlie Chaplin. But bright young faces were so marketable on the screen that their possessors became famous almost overnight. They lived for their public, their fan mail, and their pay; turning much of the last into luxurious estates, outside the gates of which the tourists gaped. In their private lives—if they could be called private—they set a standard of their own. Their escapades were always news and sometimes scandal.

It was a matter of public interest when in the spring of 1920 "America's Sweetheart," Mary Pickford, procured a Nevada divorce; rumor had it that she contemplated immediate remarriage. The interest was heightened when the state of Nevada instituted proceedings for annulment of the divorce on the ground of collusion between Miss Pickford and her former husband. Before the annulment suit was filed she had married Douglas Fairbanks, an equally popular and highly athletic star, and there was a period of uncertainty about the status of the new couple until the Nevada courts upheld the divorce. She had dodged Reno, already famous, for the more quiet court at Minden. The case gave rise to caustic comment, and was something of a blow to youth which preferred to have its idols stay fancy free.

It was not new for public opinion to be concerned with the private lives of public characters, but movie characters, built up by press agents for commercial reasons, were so important to the producers that reputation and receipts were closely joined. The industry could not afford injury to the standing of its stars. Great sections of the public were so disturbed by both the lives of the actors and the quality of the pictures that movements for reform threatened the business. State legislatures were listening to demands for boards of control and for official censorship, and were occasionally passing restrictive laws.

Calamity struck the industry when a wild party brought an end to the profitable career of Roscoe C. (Fatty) Arbuckle. This slapstick comedian was popular in all countries where films were shown, for his smile and his abundant figure were negotiable in any language. But he was host in his suite in a San Francisco hotel on Labor Day, 1921; and when a young actress died a few days later under suspicion of criminal attack, he was held on a charge of manslaughter. Doings and misdoings of the movie personnel were paraded through three trials, in which the state sought his conviction, making the Arbuckle case a theme for preachment and editorial comment everywhere. An early trial ended in a disagreement after the jury had been out for forty-four hours. A second trial, in January, 1922, ended in a second disagreement after key witnesses forgot their earlier testimony. On the third trial, Arbuckle was acquitted in April; but a few days later his films were ordered withdrawn from exhibition.

It was possible to withdraw the films, subject to possible future release, because the film industry had meanwhile submitted itself to discipline. Professional baseball had established a precedent when it set up Judge Kenesaw Mountain Landis as its moderator after the scandal of the World Series of 1919 had threatened both its integrity and its profits. On Saturday, March 4, 1922, the Postmaster General withdrew from the Cabinet in order, on the following Monday, to take up new duties in the employ of an association of motion-picture makers and distributors. Will H. Hays, an elder in the Presbyterian Church, thus entered upon a new career, and the films undertook to keep themselves and their people decent enough to evade the threat of a censor, yet bright enough to hold their business. Before Hays took office a film director named Taylor was found murdered in Los Angeles, with more scandal for actors and industry. It was to be a long fight, in which the "Hays Office" was tolerated only because the alternative to it was worse.

The problems of the "czar," as Hays was familiarly known, would have been easier of solution if the press had been less ready to exploit sensation and misbehavior, if audiences had more easily revolted, and if it had not been the duty of the press agent to keep his star before the public by whatever fact or fake he could get into print. The audiences were highly tolerant whatever critics thought. Only a few days after the Arbuckle party means were found to bring beauty to the gaze of the public and to serve trade at the same time. "Miss Washington" was crowned at Atlantic City after a beauty contest.

More than beauty was desired by the hotel business. The summer resort trade had a way of coming to a sharp end after Labor Day. To extend the season for a day or two, a new device was tried, and drew a crowd. Young girls, drawn from civil life rather than from the professionals who had put Mack Sennett's "Bathing Beauties" upon the margin of screen propriety, were invited to show themselves and to engage in an intercity competition. The sedate *Times* reported that in the midweek after Labor Day a thousand of them, in eight miles of rolling chairs, paraded on the Boardwalk. Howard Chandler Christy acted as judge of beauty (Jack Dempsey was to do it in a later year); Hiram Maxim, garbed as King Neptune, awarded the crown; and the camera men were enabled to flood the rotogravure sections with pictures of the contestants in what was regarded as daringly scanty garb—for the ban on bare knees had been lifted by the police for the occasion. The spectacle caught the attention of the public and of promoters at large. In 1922 the winner among the representatives of more than fifty cities, most of whom had been victoriously displayed at home, became the "Miss America" of her year.

It had become difficult, in the United States, to determine the boundaries within which propriety hemmed the lady, or what was permissible for youth of either sex. The fashion designers pushed the upper limit of what looked like youth into the thirties, and those who were living in their third decade read *Flaming Youth,* and liked it. The contradictions in behavior made the United States a problem for itself, and a source of bewilderment to the outsider. Emily Post began in 1922 to write, and to sell, her books on *Etiquette* for a market which had never before demanded so much advice on manners and correct behavior. Henry L. Mencken, literary editor of the *Smart Set,* whose audience was being diluted with so many trying to be "smart," was soon to launch his *American Mercury* as the self-elected champion of the revolt against convention.

Not all who offered themselves as champions were elected, but Andy Gump, chinless hero of a comic strip, picked this year to present himself as candidate for political office. He could not win, for he was only the figment of an imagination. He could not even claim residence in a congressional district, for he lived among the back pages of a chain of newspapers stretching from coast to coast. But readers everywhere admitted themselves in this uncertain year to be among his constituents, and some wrote in his name on the November ballots. Sidney Smith, his creator, provided the serial comic strip which had been built into that composite of news, opinion, and partisanship which was the Chicago *Tribune.* Andy was a national figure in whom many readers in many regions saw something of themselves—or of others. He saw no reason why he had not as good a right as any to offer himself as an independent candidate for Congress, "100 per cent for the people." "The people are getting tired of the old party promises," he told one of his strip neighbors; "they're looking for men with no political entanglements, men without fear or favor who don't jump at the crack of the bosses' whip—that's Andrew Gump." He competed for the affection of the people with Walt, who was courting the Widow Blossom in an adjoining strip; and with Maggie, who in a different chain was involved in the perennial complications of *Bringing up Father.*

Andy was modern in his campaigning. He was not modern enough to have discovered the possibilities of the microphone, but he was aware of the movie audiences to which the Four-Minute Men had made patriotic appeal. The cartoons showed his well-known face on the screen among the major offerings, while his canvass for votes followed the chronology of the election which was under way. And when the candidates who existed in the flesh learned how many of them had become lame ducks, Andy was counted out, took his contest to Washington, and was counted out again, after a goodhumored satire on the electoral process.

The lame ducks of 1922 had more service before them than had those of most elections, for there were still to be two more sessions of the Sixty-seventh Congress, making four in all. The special session of 1921, followed by the regular long session of 1921–1922, had uncovered the lack of pattern in public thought and the lack of teamwork in the majority party. In addition to the routine business of the appropriation bills there remained for consideration a modification of the network of federal banking institutions, largely in response to western pressure. There was, too, the antilynching bill, waiting for consideration in the Senate after coming from the House in January, 1922; and this was threatened with a stubborn filibuster if it should be taken up. The administration had another measure of its own. The merchant shipping bill of 1920 had been a mere temporary compromise which must be reconsidered if the United States was to avoid slipping back to unimportance as a carrier of ocean freights. The President had given his backing to a proposal to assist the merchant marine with a federal subsidy, and had tried in vain to push it into consideration. The long session having evaded compliance, he called Congress back into its third session a fortnight after the election, hoping it would pass his bill. A fourth session, meeting as usual in December, would bring the Sixty-seventh Congress to its end.

The demand that action be taken to end the lame duck interval, and to make the Congress more directly and immediately responsible to the electorate, was given impetus by the election. It was heightened by resentment at the determination of the administration to force a lame duck Congress to vote a permanent shipping policy. Harding had no sooner urged this action, after the session opened on November 20, than Caraway of Arkansas offered a resolution declaring it to be the sense of Congress that "it is unwise to place in the hands of rejected public servants the power to adopt fundamental legislation," and that "all Members defeated at the recent polls [should] abstain from voting on any but routine" matters. The resolution, only an opinion in a field in which Congress had no power to act, was referred to the Committee on Agriculture and Forestry, from which George W. Norris, the chairman, was sure to report it back. Here it was turned into a proposed amendment to the Constitution. Reported back in December, it had two days on the floor in February, and was sent to the House by a vote of sixty-three to six. It provided that the term of the president should thereafter begin on the third Monday in January following his election, that the terms of senators and representatives should begin on the first Monday in January (thereby allowing time for the count of the electoral vote), and that the Congress should meet at least once a year and ordinarily on the first Monday in January.

The lame duck interval would have been eliminated if passage had been completed and if ratification of the amendment had followed, but the proposed change had ten years more to wait, in spite of Norris' tireless efforts in advocating it. The House was not allowed even to take it up. Mondell, in the last days of his service there, gave it no help. Campbell, chairman of the Committee on Rules, and himself a lame duck, denied it right of way by special rule. Half the members of the Committees on Rules and on Election of President, Vice-President, and Representatives, were to be absent when the next Congress should convene. But not all of those whose seats were to be filled by others in the Sixty-eighth Congress were to be gone from the service of the United States. Harding took care of some of them. He brought New into his Cabinet, sent Poindexter to Peru as ambassador and Kellogg to England, and put Mondell on the directorate of the War Finance Corporation. The President had lost the power to control Congress, but retained his courage and remained devoted to his friends.

Chapter XIX ★ The New Federalism

CROSSCURRENTS of partisanship, contradiction of local interests, and uncertainty as to general objective, throw much of the business of democratic government into apparent confusion in times of national peace. This is normalcy. There was more than normal confusion in the postwar years because of rebound from distasteful regimentation, because of the destructive effect of war upon habit, and because of physical and social changes quickly following a released technology. But this confusion is only a part of the American picture. Extravagance in behavior and stagnation in politics did not bring about a stoppage in the continuous orderly unfolding of American life. At every crossroads of the country the people took part in some rebuilding of the physical plant of the nation; and when the realization of their desires appeared to be impeded by the complex interlocking of national, regional, and private interests they found ways of cutting through the obstructions.

The United States, by sheer compulsion of events, was becoming more of a nation and less of a federation than the founders had dreamed. Its machinery of operation had held it together in spite of civil war, and had been brought to bear in huge and successful impact upon world war; yet it called for continuous modification as new needs arose. The name of Herbert Hoover was attached to such a modification in November, 1922. By interstate compact a first step was taken in a field of which the founders could not have been aware.

Among the matters for the treatment of which there was no positive directive in the Constitution, or even in the English common law which most states had built into their legal systems, was the control of resources the ownership of which might be contested

[326]

between state and federal government. It is too much to have expected the founders to envisage situations and imperative needs which were nonexistent in the eighteenth century. They had no conception of what the power to "regulate Commerce . . . among the several States" would come to mean, when they wrote it into the Constitution; or what the word "Commerce" would one day embrace. The power over commerce became the charter for expansive action. Justified by the words, and reinforced by judicial approval, the federal government wrote the law for navigable rivers. Custom and precedent, however, left the nonnavigable streams where they had been in the common law, subject to the ownership of those who owned the land through which they flowed except as their action might impair the riparian rights of other owners, downstream.

The division worked well enough so long as running water was interesting chiefly to those with boats or those who owned adjacent banks. It was inadequate when shortage of water and growth of the practice of irrigation gave rise to controversy over an interstate stream, from which the upper state might draw the whole flow, leaving to the lower state only a dry channel except in times of destructive flood. The state of Kansas brought suit against the state of Colorado early in the century, protesting the diversion of the water of the Arkansas River, and Justice Brewer who wrote the Supreme Court decision in 1907 could find no fixed rule upon which to decide the case. The decision was simply practical: that the diversion did more good to Colorado than harm to Kansas, hence Kansas could have no redress. The legal basis was complicated by the preference of Colorado as a western state for a doctrine of prior appropriation which protected users in the order in which they had filed claims to a measured share of water, whereas Kansas accepted the doctrine of riparian rights based upon the ownership of adjacent banks.

While the Kansas-Colorado suit was in the court, the Colorado River went into flood just as the Gila River emptied a second flood into its lower reaches. The banks could not restrain it and the levees gave way, inundating much of the Imperial Valley in southern California and endangering the structures of the Southern Pacific railroad. This flood produced for E. H. Harriman one of the more bitter controversies with Theodore Roosevelt. There was no legal doctrine for assessing the costs of safe-guard work. The Colorado River became a problem. Few would have said that it was navigable and therefore a federal responsibility. The old port of entry at Yuma, dating back from gold-rush days and maintained when occasional steamers came up the river from the Gulf of California, was moribund, for the railroads had captured the traffic. The port itself was due to be discontinued in 1923. If the river was not navigable Congress had no rights except as owner of the adjacent lands, and the Supreme Court had said as much in brushing the government aside as intervener in the Kansas-Colorado suit. The rights of control were spread among the seven states of the basin and the United States as owner of public lands. None of the parties had the powers necessary to authorize works capable of protecting the land from flood or of impounding the water for beneficial use. Since every irrigation dam presented a possibility of electric power, the question of who should develop it and who should own its profits added another item of interest.

The Bureau of Reclamation, organized in 1902, kept to its work upon projects along federal streams and the adjoining lands which could be brought under ditch. The Colorado River continued to be a menace and an undeveloped opportunity. After the World War a local League of the Southwest took up the matter in the interest of the states of the basin; and with the appointment of Herbert Hoover as Secretary of Commerce there was an agent in the government who was well informed on the regional interests and the engineering problem.

A way out of the deadlock was sought in an inconspicuous clause of the Constitution, negative rather than positive: "No State shall without the Consent of Congress . . . enter into any Agreement or Compact with another State." The power here implied was as vague as the grant whereby "Treaties made . . . under the Authority of the United States, shall be the supreme Law of the Land." Only recently the elastic quality of this grant had been revealed in the case of migratory birds which Congress had sought to protect by public law. When it appeared probable that the Supreme Court would deny that this protection of wild game was a regulation of interstate commerce, President Wilson had negotiated with Canada a treaty pledging the signers to joint protection. Congress thereupon passed an unquestioned law to enforce the treaty obligation; and thus the United States had by its own action added a legal cubit to its stature. Such powers as lay within the reach of states entering into compacts with the approval of Congress were unrestricted in words and were without limit until the courts should call a halt.

The interstate compact had rarely been used before Congress, in 1919, gave its assent to an agreement for the building of the earliest vehicular tunnel under the Hudson River, after New York and New Jersey had asked for it. There had been only nine other compacts in a century and a quarter, all unimportant, and all relating to matters of boundary adjustment or rights in adjacent waters. In 1921 Harding signed an act authorizing the seven states of the Colorado basin to enter upon a compact respecting the waters of the Colorado River, a compact which should become operative upon subsequent approval of its terms by Congress. The Colorado Commission was set up under direction of Secretary Hoover for the drafting of the compact.

The water engineers of the several states commonly represented the governors in the deliberations over which Hoover presided in the ensuing year. Topography broke the basin into two parts, the upper, where winter snow pack provided most of the water, and the lower, below Lee's Ferry and the Grand Canyon, where the Gila River was the principal tributary. The problems to be settled concerned flood control, irrigation facilities, water supply for the growing community around Los Angeles, and the disposal of incidental electric power. On November 24, 1922, Hoover met with the commissioners of the seven states at Santa Fe, and signed the compact. A few days later Mondell introduced a bill which the House referred to the Committee on Irrigation of Arid Lands—a bill granting the assent of the United States when the states had approved it and the President had proclaimed it. The approval was long in coming, for Arizona was dissatisfied, but the first major step in a new direction had been taken.

Before the Colorado River Compact was signed the governors of New York and New Jersey had given their approval to a program for the joint development of the port of New York, pursuant to another interstate compact. The new federalism was being carried forward in a direction different from that of the southwest states. The Colorado compact merely cleared the way for procedure by the United States through the Reclamation Bureau; the Hudson compact created a quasi-autonomous authority with powers of its own apart from those of either state or nation. The sharp geographic limits of local governments were everywhere being modified within the states, where the division of authority among state, county, and city was unrealistic in the face of problems concerning them all and overlapping their boundary lines. The states were increasingly approaching these problems as units, disregarding normal jurisdictions. There were school and high school districts, sewage districts, fire protection districts, water supply districts, superimposed upon the political map. It was to this situation that Frederick J. Turner was referring when he wrote, in the autumn of 1922, that the United States was becoming a federation of sections rather than of states, and that the chief value of state sovereignty was as "a constitutional shield for the section." It was with recognition of this that the legislature of the state of Idaho revived an old longing for a boundary which made sense, and asked for the addition to itself of the Bitter Root Valley of western Montana, and the Spokane plains of eastern Washington. The boundaries of the states, unreasonable though many of them were, were too well set to be changed, but the new technique of the compact had come to hand.

There was clearly a twilight zone, within which no state could do business because of lack of jurisdiction, and into which the United States was prevented from entering because of the lack of specifically delegated power conveying the right. The doctrine of implied powers, the enunciation of which by Chief Justice John Marshall had made the case of McCulloch vs. Maryland a landmark in constitutional law, had done much to put off the time at which the twilight zone would interfere with the execution of expedient matters. "Let the end be legitimate," he had written, "and means which are appropriate . . . and which are not prohibited . . . are constitutional." He had put an end to the narrowest of constructions of the Constitution, and had provided the basis for a century of expansion of federal activities. But there still remained a twilight zone, filled with the new problems of an increasing population and a crowded land, beyond the reach of all of the states and beyond the means of some, and upon which Congress could not enter without a broader view than that of implied powers.

The Tenth Amendment, last of those of the Bill of Rights, seemed to set a limit beyond which even "implied" powers could not go: "The powers not delegated to the United States by the Constitution, nor prohibited by it to the States, are reserved to the States respectively, or to the people." As problems pressed for action, some legislators reluctantly took refuge in this amendment as an additional defense against new measures. The advocates of new measures, otherwise blocked, sought by argument to enlarge the scope of the word "implied," and, failing in this, tried to find some other justification in the Constitution. They were giving their attention to two words in the eighth section of article one. Now these two words were either a rhetorical flourish and therefore added nothing, or they were a delegation of powers making much of the rest of the Constitution unnecessary.

The two words were "general Welfare." The clause, otherwise conferring upon Congress the power to tax, states the general purpose of taxation: "to pay the Debts and provide for the common Defense and general Welfare of the United States." It is difficult to suppose that any Congress would pass laws for any other purposes. Since the very next clause permits Congress "To borrow Money on the Credit of the United States," it is improbable that the phrase "to pay the Debts" was intended to grant an additional power. Since providing "for the common Defense" is followed by specific authorizations to declare war and to maintain an army and a navy, it is likely that this clause, in this place, was no more than generally descriptive. And since there is nowhere a mention of "general Welfare" except as the objective of the whole Constitution, there is ground for convincing argument that no additional powers were conferred by the use of the words. Had the words conveyed any authorization they would have made Congress the judge of its own powers which would have been directly inconsistent with the doctrine of a government of delegated powers. But the argument for interpreting the "general Welfare" clause as a grant of power was so convenient for those who felt the need of pushing federal activity into the twilight zone that it was coming into frequent use, and was eventually to carry conviction even to the Supreme Court.

Some of the manifestations of the new federalism were based upon direct implication, as in the case of reclamation of arid lands, derived from the sweeping power to "make all needful Rules" respecting territory and other property of the United States. Others were less immediate in their derivation, but it had been learned that state resistance to federal encroachment, if it was encroachment, could be lessened by the conferring of resultant benefits; and there was no doubt of the heavy and increasing pressure of constituents upon Congress for getting local projects paid for from the federal treasury. It was unusual for a region to reject a share of federal aid on the grounds that such aid infringed upon the reserved rights of the states and of the people.

The dollar-for-dollar method of inaugurating new services and breaking down resistance was a decade old when President Harding signed a bill on November 23, 1921 for the "welfare and hygiene of maternity and infancy." The change in the theory of federal relations which it forecast had not been emphasized by powerful opposition until after precedents had been established. In a similar way, the earliest of the national highways, the Cumberland Road, was well advanced in construction before it was seriously argued that internal improvements at federal expense were unconstitutional. The Weeks act of 1911, chief precedent for the new procedure, provided for coöperation between the United States and the several states in the prevention of forest fires. The wedge slipped in easily, for the government had an interest in the preservation of the national forests, and even the wealthiest of the lumber companies saw much to be gained from a fire-prevention policy which would increase and conserve the value of their stands of timber. It slipped in during a conservative Republican regime, and before large taxpayers had become suspicious of reforms which were to be paid for by surtaxes on the higher incomes. The eastern centers of wealth had not yet come to feel that the sparsely settled West was fattening on their earnings. The Democratic administrations accepted the precedent and built upon it.

Agricultural education, to be promoted by the "conditional subsidies" of the fifty-fifty system, was the objective of the Smith-Lever act of 1914. The program went far beyond that of the Morrill acts for the encouragement of education in agriculture and the mechanic arts, and brought the government in Washington into direct participation in work which was to be done within the states. One of its consequences was the spread of agricultural agents into the counties and the resulting organization of farm bureaus. From the last of these there developed a powerful lobby to exert pressure upon Congress behind the leadership of the American Farm Bureau Federation. The farm bloc of 1921 was supported by this pressure. The states accepted the grants, covered them with their own contributions, and saw agricultural colleges, agricultural extension, and experiment stations flourish. The farmers' surplus, which was already holding down the prosperity of the farmers, was enlarged by the improved methods which resulted. The law brought to the farming country advantages which were beyond its own financial means to effect. If followed as a matter of course that the regions benefited gave their support to the Federal Highway Aid act of 1916. The more the government extended aid, the more aid it was invited to extend.

A Federal Board of Vocational Education set up in 1917, broadened this program of federal aid to the states. The purpose was now to train boys and girls for "useful employment" in agriculture, industry, commerce, and in the home; and forty-six states had complied with its terms before the end of the year. It was a simple matter to extend the jurisdiction of the board when the end of the war brought with it the problem of soldiers to be rehabilitated and when labor demanded that industrial rehabilitation be added. There were supporters for still further expansion of federal activities in education and for the elevation of the Bureau of Education into a department with a seat in the Cabinet. The issue of the privilege of the states to maintain and control their systems of education now arose. Fear of standardization and of federal dictation of aims and methods aroused enough opposition to block this movement for a federal department of education. But the wide variations in educational opportunity which prevailed in the United States kept the demand alive. The reluctance to enter upon new extensions of federal support for most of the proposals and to accept the control of policy which attended it, was only sporadic among the states. The reluctance was concentrated among the regions and interests whose influence was most powerful with the Harding administration. And in 1921 the decade of new fifty-fifty grants in aid came to an end. They were to be revived at a later date. But the grants already pledged kept increasing year by year.

The last of the series of new enterprises received the approval of the President while the Washington Conference was in session, on November 23, 1921. The drive for social legislation and for the improvement of the opportunities of the underprivileged had been a part of the Progressive movement. Even earlier than this, there had been a movement away from charity toward constructive aid; and the more the social workers saw of the conditions under which the less-privileged Americans existed, the greater became their earnestness in promoting remedial laws, whether local or federal. They had to fight ignorance, for the well-to-do in the towns did not know about the slums, and the prosperous states knew little of the life of the less prosperous. They had inertia to face, because of the American conviction that there was work for everyone who would work and that poverty was the penalty for indolence. Self-interest had to be fought, for the measures they proposed would cost money and increase taxes, and those whom the social workers sought to help were generally neither organized nor vocal, whereas their opposition had power of organization.

Jane Addams, Lillian D. Wald, and Julia C. Lathrop were among the leaders who demanded new social policies, stating the case for the children, for their mothers, and for the unfortunate. Parallel to their efforts were the movements for compulsory education laws, for lengthening the period of schooling, and for minimum wage laws. From much the same groups came the pressure for federal prohibition of child labor, to be blocked twice by the Supreme Court as unconstitutional.

Even though the court would not countenance federal activity to correct a situation, it was still possible for Congress to have it studied, and this Congress did. President Taft signed the bill creating the Children's Bureau, and named Julia C. Lathrop as its chief. Attached in the first instance to the Department of Commerce and Labor (the creation of which had itself marked a step in federal examination of over-all conditions), the bureau had been shifted to the Department of Labor when that department acquired separate existence in 1913. It became at once a persuasive agency, reporting upon conditions which distressed those who examined them, and describing the efforts of dissimilar local and state governments to remedy them. It developed the idea that bad conditions anywhere in the United States did damage everywhere, and that the need for action was real whether it was in harmony with constitutional federalism or not. The Children's Bureau was not very old before it called attention to the high death rate of infants and the urgent need for the practice of sound hygiene among women and children. It was Senator Morris Sheppard of Texas who brought before Congress the proposal for another extension of federal activity.

Before the end of the Wilson administration, the Senate passed what was to become the Sheppard-Towner bill, but the matter went over and was not brought up again until June, 1921, when it called for a new board which should direct a coöperative study of child hygiene and maternity welfare. Sheppard, renewing his fight for it, called attention to the high rate of infant mortality—a quarter of a million deaths a year—and to the fact that half the deaths were preventable. The opposition was insistent rather than powerful. From some of the states, those well-advanced in public hygiene, came protests against being taxed for the benefit of the indifferent states. Taxpayers objected to being taxed more—for any purpose. There was sectional opposition, since some of the regions receiving or about to receive federal aid might draw out of the Treasury actually more than they paid in. There was some religious objection to federal intrusion upon a field which some churches regarded as peculiarly their own. Reed of Missouri, most caustic of the opponents, jeered at a federal supervision of the number of babies a family should be encouraged to have; and some who believed that Soviet Russia had broken down the home regarded the measure as a step toward free love.

The defenders of the measure collected the statistics which the Children's Bureau had assembled, insisted that the aid would have to pass through the coöperating bureau of the state concerned, and denied that the home would be weakened or that Washington would stand *in loco parentis*. Kenyon, who supported the law in the House, asked why it was more constitutional to spend money to lessen the incidence of hog cholera than to bring similar benefits to the citizens of the next generation and their mothers. Reed, however, jeered until the last. When the Senate had passed the bill he moved to amend its title so as to describe it as a law "to authorize a board of spinsters to control maternity and teach the mothers . . . how to rear babies"; but his colleagues were unresponsive.

Pushed aside by other business through most of 1921, the Sheppard-Towner act reached the White House at the end of the session, and was signed at once. Heavy majorities in both houses had overridden opposition. The minor controversy over who should direct the new board was settled by having it composed of the chief of the Children's Bureau, the chief surgeon of the Public Health Service, and the Commissioner of Education, with actual administration under the Children's Bureau. The aid was pledged for a five-year period as an experiment, and hope was expressed that this would be the last of the coöperative ventures—as it proved for the time to be. Aid was extended later in the decade for three more years, but was allowed to lapse on June 30, 1929. The sectional doctrinal clash over the expenditure of public money for welfare projects brought about a temporary halt in the practice. Yet, through the decade, the fifty-fifty enterprises called for continually greater appropriations as the United States became increasingly aware of the magnitude of the task it had undertaken. The objection of the states to having the federal government take an active or controlling part in the internal affairs was less compelling than their readiness to profit by the grants.

Only a fortnight before Harding signed the Sheppard-Towner act he approved another of the coöperative measures which was in the long run to remake the internal map of the United States. There was little fundamental objection to the revision of the Federal Highway Aid act of 1916, which turned it into the Federal Highway act of November 9, 1921.

The first remaking of the internal map of the United States was the work of the railroad movement between 1830 and 1890, when the network of tracks spread across the continent and into every state. The year 1888 produced the largest new mileage of any year. By 1890 there were some 2,600 miles of railroad for each million users, and the main lines of trackage provided for the growing population as many miles of line per million as the country was ever likely to obtain. Thereafter, for some twenty years, new mileage merely kept pace with population growth; and after that the ratio declined. The railroad coverage was substantially complete, requiring for future operation only additional tracks, new terminals, and better rights of way. The system, improving with the years, came to carry more passengers and heavier freights but it needed little in the way of additional main lines. As the system developed the rights of way came first and the rolling stock was designed to flow over them. It was a monopoly system because of the corporate ownership of the tracks and the difficulty of finding profitable routes for new lines, or funds to construct them.

The automobile remade the map again, but it reversed the process. Its rolling stock came first, but the rights of way—the roads— had to be contrived after the cars were in existence and their owners were ready to roll. The problem was not that of better service over fixed and unalterable routes, but was one of constructing universal routes fit to carry cars and their users to their several destinations.

How the new mobility within the boundaries of the United States was to affect the character and habit of the coming generation of Americans was still to be observed. But the pressure for highways was based upon the demand of users, and was in this sense unlike the pressure of the railroads—service corporations which were already dangerously monopolistic. The reclamation of the arid lands, that brought about an extension of the federal power of the United States, might have been a different story had the users of water been themselves able to construct the necessary dams and ditches, or had they been willing to entrust the task to corporations working for private profits. Deprived of either of these approaches to satisfaction, the arid areas turned to federal aid as naturally as automobile users turned to it when they procured the first aid act in 1916. In five years the shortcomings and defects of this act, and the nature of the need, compelled revision.

The act of 1916 was only a first step. It promised five years of federal subsidies to a new frontier of improved highways which was to sweep across the map leaving every region, as it crossed it, mobile within itself and tied into a national terrain upon which the state lines were only annoyances. The earlier frontiers of the farms and of the railroads, had made transit across the continent without a plan and were driven more by individual initiative than by the incidental help from acts of Congress. The new network of all-weather, hard-surfaced highways was placed under the immediate supervision of a Bureau of Public Roads in the Department of Agriculture; but under a supervision not powerful enough at first to ensure a national system as the outcome. Backed by increasing public demand, it was, however, federal in its inception. During its five-year period the experiment uncovered the magnitude of the problem and the inadequacy of the first approach.

It was recognized from the start that not all of the states were financially able to pay their share for the coöperative construction of highways. Their areas to be served were out of proportion to their population and taxable property. The federal contribution was therefore adjusted on a three-way basis: one-third each on population, area, and miles of rural post roads. But the emphasis on the rural post roads proved to stand in the way of an effective improvement of main-traveled routes. The states proceeded to prepare their lists of projects, fragmentary in character, often for purely local advantage, often more concerned about roads from farm to market than about a national system. It was not unnatural that each county town hoped to find itself upon a route selected for construction or improvement; or that within the states there was sharp controversy over the routes to be followed by trunk highways. The authority of the Secretary of Agriculture to see that each aided stretch was related to what would upon completion become a system was left in doubt. The routes which were already carrying the heaviest automobile traffic were so likely to be close to the tracks of the railroad net that they could not qualify for aid under the rural post route clause. And so many of the states did not yet have a measured picture of their own needs that the recommendations of their new highway bureaus were undependable. By the close of the war, under the federal stimulus, the states were better prepared to deal with the engineering factors, and were ready to join with the automobile associations, the car manufacturers, and the industries concerned with road building in the demand for a revision of the original act.

They had, meanwhile, learned that their own tax systems would need to be revised if they were to raise the funds to match the federal contributions as well as to improve the highways which were too local to command federal attention. Bond issues were floated, east and west, as soon as the war controls over capital were loosened, and new sources of taxation were searched for. Gasoline proved to be the best measure for determining the advantage which the citizen enjoyed because of the improved roads. A sales tax collected at the pump placed the cost upon the shoulders of the users in proportion as they used the roads. The collection of the tax was easy and direct. The earliest of the gasoline taxes seems to have appeared in Oregon in 1919, but the method was adopted generally and proved to be so remunerative that the receipts enabled the states to build roads without their legislatures having to meet the costs from more general funds; and they increased with every car or truck which was brought into operation. It increased so rapidly, and so painlessly, that the sales tax as an all-purpose revenue builder gained adherents, and the states were tempted to divert parts of the gasoline fund to purposes other than the road improvements to which it was pledged. The bond issues played their part in the blanket of state and local debts with which the voters covered themselves for their immediate advantage.

The essence of the bill which Harding signed in November, 1919 was that projects approved for federal aid should be such "as will expedite the completion of an adequate and connected system of highways, interstate in character." The states were at once called upon to submit lists of seven per cent of their three million miles of roads, an amount believed to be large enough to include all principal routes, to reach all major city areas, and to bring most of the population within reach of modern communication. From the 200,000 miles of projects thus submitted, some 50,000 miles were checked off for consideration within the next few years, with priority given to the main trunk routes.

There were many hurdles to be crossed between the first selection of a route and the final ceremonial cutting of the barrier ribbon when the finished stretch was opened to public use. Even then there were hurdles, for only too often a stretch proved to be inadequate to the demands of traffic even before it was completed. Heavy vehicles created a real problem, for if the roads were not strong enough to carry them, they broke the roads. Additional lanes were required to accommodate the traffic. The increasing speed of cars called for the elimination of dangerous corners. And as experience accumulated the engineers straightened the routes, leveled the heavy grades, and struggled to keep abreast of the increasing requirements.

Federal interest and local hopes were often in disagreement. The states, glad to receive the cash, were often reluctant to accept the counsel and the specifications which came with it. The nature of the enterprise pushed federal authority into the local jurisdictions, and state officers fulminated against bureacracy while they clamored for larger subsidies. Nothing, however, could have prevented the new federalism from taking part in the expansion of the highway system.

The decision to continue highway aid on the fifty-fifty plan was delayed in Congress by debates on methods of control. If the states had had their choice in the matter the subsidies would have been handed directly to them, to be expended as they pleased. The other extreme was a demand for a federal department of highways which should itself plan and build the roads. The United States Chamber of Commerce favored the latter system. When Harding, at the opening of his special session in 1921, recommended action—prompt action—before the five-year act should expire on June 30, the type of control was still in controversy. Senator Townsend, manager of the bill, had a preference for a highway commission, but the Secretary of Agriculture, hitherto responsible for the road improvements accomplished, insisted that his Bureau of Public Roads was best equipped to protect the public interest, and had better knowledge of the needs of the regions to be served than any other agency of the government.

Army preference was for direct federal management, for the army was worrying about strategic needs after its experience with motor transport in France. Pershing's staff officers were preparing maps to show where roads should be built in order to permit free movement of troops and supplies, in the event of military necessity. Western congressmen, remembering the suggestion of the Zimmerman note that Japan might hope to occupy the United States west of the Colorado River, were urging military roads. One of these was to be a Pacific coast highway, a second was to pass along the north and south valleys just east of the coast range, a third was to lie farther east, along the edge of the Nevada desert, where it might operate in safety behind the bulwark of the Sierra Nevada. Officers of the army were telling such audiences as would listen that in the event of an invasion by Japan the whole of the United States west of the Rocky Mountains would have to become a military area—that of the Ninth Corps—and that the supply system for its defense would have to be in the vicinity of Salt Lake City, where Fort Douglas was already a name on the map. Secretary David F. Houston, in the Democratic administration, had defended the claim of the Bureau of Public Roads to administer the system. Secretary Henry C. Wallace continued the defense in the Harding Cabinet, and the law was written as he urged it.

Thomas H. MacDonald, new chief of the Bureau of Public Roads, had acquired experience as state highway engineer in Iowa. He was still in the bureau when it became the Public Roads Administration of the Federal Works Administration on the eve of Pearl Harbor, and when a Defense Highways act of November, 1941, put final touches upon a nearly completed system which was soon to carry the traffic of total war. As director of the Bureau of Public Roads he took charge of the administration of the highway act of 1921. His insistence, and the inherent nature of the business, put an end to the hodgepodge of named highways launched by booster organizations which had come to the fore after the Lincoln Highway Association had blazed the way. By 1923 his experts had put together a tentative map of arterial roads reaching every important American city, without too much defiance of the essential conditions of American topography.

Mountains had to be crossed, and their passes, followed by the trails and later by the railroads, continued to be the best places at which to penetrate them. Rivers cut across the routes, and Congress was diligent in authorizing bridges over those which were both obstructive and navigable. The names chosen by the promoters of highway schemes, sometimes as fantastic as the routes selected, sometimes patriotic, made up a long list from which MacDonald selected a score or more as he undertook to supplant them with a system. The Lincoln Highway had been followed by others bearing the names of Lee and Davis, Jefferson and Roosevelt, as well as those of lesser heroes; by "Old Spanish Trails," "Pike's Peak Ocean to Ocean," and "Broadway of America," a project from New York to San Diego. Harding himself was induced to dedicate a "Zero Milestone" on the Ellipse south of the White House for the Lee Highway in June, 1923. Some of the new federal-aided routes began to be constructed, lifted from the status of promoters' schemes to reality; but more than attractive names were needed for a system. It is not easy in a democracy to hold to a pattern of the public interest in the face of pressure and logrolling driven by the hope of local gains.

By 1925 the highway departments of the coöperating states had been forced to concentrate upon trunk lines, for left to themselves they would have been long in agreeing upon the points at which these should pass from state to state. They nominated, and the bureau selected and approved upon grounds of sound engineering rather than upon those of local scramble, and in the autumn of the year the fancy names were scrapped. The roads were given numbers as methodically as townships had been designated in the survey of the national domain. Even numbers were assigned to highways running east and west, odd numbers to those running north and south, with Federal Highway 1 skirting the Atlantic Coast and Federal Highway 101 skirting the Pacific. The markers of the new system soon bore the appropriate numbers upon a standard shield. A few of the fancy names lingered in local use, for parts of their routes were closely followed by the new construction. Along the shoulders of Highway 50 many of the Lincoln markers still appeared; the Victory project and Highway 40 had much in common; the name of the "Old Spanish Trails" lingered along the southern border route from Jacksonville through El Paso to the extreme southwest. The state highway departments competed with the gasoline companies and the automobile associations in providing dependable maps for the traveler. The margins of the new roads blossomed with filling stations, tourist camps, and "hot dog" stands as with every succeeding spring more Americans took to the highways.

The Federal Highway act of 1921 was fundamental in the transformation of the United States which the rediscovery of the roads was to bring about. Henry Ford had run his millionth Model-T off the assembly line before the act of 1916 was passed; his fifteen millionth took to the road before he closed his plant to retool it for a modern car in 1926. The unities which the federal system was to serve were well started before it was realized that busses and trucks were to force the railroads to struggle for survival.

State lines as well as railroads struggled. New desires, with votes behind them, and new needs which must be met by national action if they were to be met at all, threatened to destroy their significance. The oldest of the lines were no more than the consequence of an arbitrary partition of an open continent, when they were imbedded in the colonial charters. The drafting clerks who prepared the charters for the seals knew so little of the American terrain, even if they knew all that was then knowable, that hardly a line or a definition was so clear as to be accepted by the two colonial jurisdictions which it separated. Before independence, the king in council made repeated interpretations; after the adoption of the Constitution the Supreme Court listened to suit after suit by state against state. The newest of the state lines, made by Congress as the national domain was broken up into territories, and as these were further subdivided for the residence of new state governments, were even more arbitrary than those of the colonies. Astronomical lines, parallels, and meridians, were placed upon the map as though they had some reference to the resources upon which men must live. Congress had not been consistent even in this. Until 1850 it had been content to accept the meridians as numbered west from the Royal Observatory at Greenwich; in that year it yielded to patriotic assertiveness and thereafter, until all the states were defined, numbered the meridians from the United States Naval Observatory in Washington. It made trouble for map makers when it was discovered that the new base was just too far west of the seventy-seventh meridian west of Greenwich to fall upon it, yet not far enough west for the ordinary map to show the difference. But the best of the state lines, by whomever drawn, had little significance with reference to the highways of the nation, to the air above, or to the resources beneath the ground or the water.

The airmen, racing back and forth above the states, making new records for speed and altitude and endurance in the air, used the ground only to take off and to land, and demanded a system of control which was indifferent to political subdivisions on the ground. In 1919 they ran their military derby across the continent, a year later a mixed air and rail route was carrying the mail from New York to San Francisco, by 1924 a military plane had been flown around the world by Lieutenant Lowell H. Smith.

The air which carried the planes carried also the increasing calls from the radio transmitters, in spite of the interference owing to complete anarchy in the use of wave lengths. It was at the end of 1922 that Major General James S. Harbord left the army to direct the affairs of the Radio Corporation of America, and already there were close to a million radio receiving sets in use. A new form of commerce was at hand, for the plugs for advertisers were already being interjected between news items and amusement features. Secretary Hoover was eventually to take part in celebrating the first quarter-century of broadcasting, and to remind his hearers of his futile hope in 1922 that advertising could be excluded from the air. Whether the new commerce was interstate or not, since it passed above the states in an atmosphere over which no state had as yet established jurisdiction, was open to argument. But the waves, once launched, could not be repelled from any jurisdiction by any law; and no state could control even its own stations at both the sending and the receiving end. The control of interstate commerce had been forced upon the nation by the logic of events. This logic was now at work upon a new medium.

As Secretary of Commerce, Hoover brought together his first big conference on radio in 1922, seeking by voluntary agreement to bring about coöperation. The only law on the books had been passed in 1912 by a Congress which had no conception of what radio would mean within a decade, and the Attorney General was to rule in 1926 that under this law the Department of Commerce had no authority to be even a clearing house for registering voluntary policies. The conference urged control legislation upon Congress, and a second conference held in 1923 renewed the urge, the sending stations having increased tenfold. There was still no new law when in 1924 Hoover supported the recommendation of his third conference, nor was there one until a temporary Federal Radio Commission was created in 1927, when six and a half million receiving sets were in use in the United States. A new necessity for action by the United States as an entity had forced itself into American life.

Beneath the ground and the rivers and the territorial waters of the nation lay the mineral resources which had played a large part in the struggle for a conservation program. The laws determining their exploitation and the title to them, so far as they had been passed at all, had been enacted before oil entered into world economy and before hydroelectric power had started a scramble by the utilities companies. Only in 1920 had basic statutes undertaken to protect the national interest in running water and in oil, and these laws were limited in their application to the areas in which the nation as such could claim a right. England had no occasion to protect mineral rights as the property of the crown, for minerals were negligible in colonial economy. The United States, acquiring and enlarging the public domain, had not reserved the minerals to the nation except in special cases and had commonly permitted the ownership of resources beneath the ground to be attached to the ownership of the surface. Gold was where men found it, and a placer-mining law permitted citizens to acquire title to their claims even on the public domain.

As owner of the surface of such land as still remained in the public domain the United States had the rights of any other owner of the surface. In many of the land grants, enacted to encourage the agricultural occupation of the domain, the law had indeed reserved to the government such known minerals as might exist. It was possible legally to dispossess owners who, knowing of the existence of minerals, took title to the land as agricultural; and during the period of the fight over conservation the courts were called upon to cancel railroad holdings on the ground that they had been fraudulently classified as agricultural. The discovery and development of the great oil fields made available a new mineral resource, and one for which the laws governing the hard minerals were inadequate. It was possible for a single well to pump not only the oil beneath the surface claim, but that of a great pool underlying neighboring claims belonging to other surface owners, private or governmental.

When prospectors found the pool of oil beneath the Red River and parts of Texas and Oklahoma, the resulting litigation rose to the Supreme Court, because the location of the boundary line between the two states was still in doubt and the ownership of royalties of great value was at stake.

The boundary itself was not hard to fix. It was based on a treaty between the United States and Spain, signed in 1819, in which it was defined as running from the Sabine River at its intersection with the thirty-second parallel of North Latitude, due north to Red River, thence following the course of the river to the meridian of one hundred degrees west from London, and "then, crossing the said Red River" and running north along the said meridian. When Oklahoma claimed that the words "then crossing the said Red River" meant that Texas must stop at the southern bank of the stream, the Supreme Court agreed. Texas lost claim to the ownership of any part of the river bottom and to the underlying oil.

The case was not yet ended, for Oklahoma as a state was not conceded to own the river or the bottom. The United States intervened with the claim that since the Red River in this region was not navigable its bottom lands and their resources belonged to the owners of the bank as they could show title. The political area of Oklahoma extended to the Texas shore, but the riparian rights of Oklahoma or private owners of the shore could not extend beyond the middle of the stream. The whole of the southern half of the river bottom, which was not even in Texas, was claimed as part of the public domain. This was the doctrine of the English common law, effective over the colonial area and assumed by the United States. The Supreme Court upheld it in later suits, after delivering the basic decision on April 11, 1921. The determination of the federal claim brought frustration to the hope of Oklahoma. The suggestion that the state as a state had no property rights except as clear title could be shown to have been specifically given it, spread nervousness among the states. The states had everywhere assumed the existence of such rights, had filled in lake and river bottoms and changed shore lines, and they now saw that the United States might charge them with illegal appropriation of the public domain.

The new doctrine, expounded late because the occasion for expounding it came late, was capable of being extended to lands beneath salt water. Eastern states, with a colonial past, and Texas which retained its landed rights upon entry into the union, might claim the ocean bottom out to the conventional three-mile limit with whatever title to it England or Spain had had. The Pacific states, admitted to the union on soil to which the union had taken the basic title before admitting them, could not advance a claim to title by succession. Whatever their political limits, the only land they owned was that to which title had been transferred to them by the United States or as the result of purchase. Yet the oil pool beneath the Red River, which brought the issue to the front, was matched by another pool off the coast of California underneath the tidal waters of the Pacific, into which oil wells had been sunk and from which oil was being drawn.

Already, before the decision in the Oklahoma-Texas case was handed down, Congress had partly caught up with the oil prospectors by passing the law of 1920 to regulate drilling on the public domain and to take royalties from such wells as came into production. The period was passing in which easy and profitable exploitation of the public domain was the order of the day. An interest of the nation in the oil royalties from its domain was challenging the hopes of states and those of private exploiters. Only by means of interstate compact, eventually to be approved by Congress, was it possible to regulate the draft from pools which any well might tap. More immediately, the question of basic ownership became vital. Three months after the Supreme Court established the treaty boundary of Texas, the California legislature passed a law reserving to the state all minerals underlying lands of its ownership. It specified those which lay beneath "river beds, lake beds, overflowed, tide, and submerged lands."

On the last day of the Sixty-seventh Congress, March 4, 1923, Harding signed a law directing the Secretary of the Interior to determine valid claims of citizens and domestic corporations to rights in the oil bottoms south of the medial line of Red River, as they were when the oil law was passed on February 25, 1920; and to issue permits to drill and operate under royalty according to the terms of that law.

Chapter XX ★ The Last Chance

THE SIXTY-SEVENTH CONGRESS was a lame duck Congress after the election of 1922. The members, with the date of exit so clearly indicated for so many, were faced with the need to enact all that could be managed before the fourth of March. The unseatings had brought bitterness into the ranks of administration supporters. They had incited minority members to jeers and they angered the restive element among the majority because of the time which must elapse before the next Congress could take over the business of the nation.

Before the year 1923 should have run its course the preparations for another presidential election would have been begun, and the vote upon which that election must depend would be greatly affected by what might transpire during the winter of 1922–1923. The ability of the Republican organization to control the vote had been challenged; the ability of Harding even to secure renomination had been placed in doubt. Coolidge as Vice-President had not aroused enthusiasm, and strategists were talking of a western Vice-President to balance the ticket and make it more palatable to dissatisfied farmers. The administration and the party had need for results to which to point with pride, and it was certain that the Sixty-eighth Congress, when at last it should meet, would be less responsive to leadership by Harding than the Sixty-seventh had been. That meeting, however, need not come until December, 1923, unless the Congress that was still sitting should leave necessary work undone on March 4, 1923. Time was of the essence, as were results. Two days after the election, Harding called the members of the Sixty-seventh Congress back to Washington to take up on November 20, 1922, a piece of unfinished business: the passage of a subsidy for the protection of American merchant shipping.

[348]

At this time a new American precedent was being established. Before the House settled down to fight through the ship subsidy bill which was to be its chief business, and before the Senate plunged into a southern filibuster against consideration of the Dyer antilynching bill, Mrs. Rebecca Latimer Felton of Georgia was seated as the first woman senator. Her colleagues, from the Vice-President down, were uncertain about her title to a seat, but she was allowed to draw $287.67 in salary for a fraction of two days' work and $280 in mileage, and to enjoy a triumph which few desired to deny her. Senator Felton had spent many of her eighty-seven years in advocacy of prohibition and woman suffrage, and when Thomas E. Watson died shortly after Congress adjourned in September the governor of Georgia had an opportunity to pay a compliment to the women of the South. She was appointed to serve until a successor had been elected, and the successor, Walter F. George, was chosen on November 7. George was thus senator-elect when the third session of the Congress met a fortnight later, but he gallantly refrained from presenting his credentials until the lady had presented hers and had had her day in office. Sworn in on November 21, she was recognized on November 22 and spoke graciously of this new and romantic experience and of its historical significance; and she mentioned Nancy Langhorne Astor of Virginia, just elected as the first woman member of the House of Commons. Senator Felton bowed out gracefully as the credentials of Senator George were presented. The status of women was rising. A new act permitting American women who married foreigners to retain their citizenship had just come into effect.

Another senator whose bowing out was noted as widely as that of Mrs. Felton was Truman H. Newberry. Target of violent protest, he accepted the defeat of his colleague, Townsend of Michigan, as ending his own usefulness in the Senate. He went down fighting, feeling no sense of guilt, and filled with "eternal satisfaction" at "having by my vote aided in keeping the United States out of the League of Nations." Upon this mixture of chivalry and defiance the Sixty-seventh Congress resumed its deliberations.

David Lawrence, writing for the papers, said that were the United States like England President Harding, after the rebuke of November, would be out of office like David Lloyd George. The

English premier, having lost his grip on the coalition, resigned in October to make way for Bonar Law and a conservative government. The English election on November 15 reduced the war leader to minority status for the rest of his career. Harding, however, retained his office, faced his uncertain future, and took up an aggressive position before the members of Congress whose "resolute hostility"—perhaps never more manifest—he recognized.

The status of the merchant marine was unsatisfactory on every count when he addressed the houses on the second day of the session. For eight years it had suffered from delay, expansion, and then collapse. For nearly half a century before the World War, American shipping had been inadequate for the carriage of American freights. The maritime cargoes of the world had been largely carried under foreign flags. Every proposal to amend the situation had been mangled by opposition to the method advanced. There had been stern resistance to encroachment by government in the field of private business, jealous objection to favoritism to the shipping interests, and partisan opposition; and there was the underlying fact that in the field of an international competition American shipwrights could not keep their building costs down to the level of their foreign competitors. Cheap foreign labor kept the wage of seamen below that of Americans who worked ashore. In 1915, as an outcome of Andrew Furuseth's crusade for seamen's rights and La Follette's generalship, a new law added to the difficulties when it attempted to set a standard of wages and conditions to apply not only to American ships but to all ships trading in American ports. The World War found the United States unprepared to deliver wares to foreign buyers when belligerent and neutral shipping turned to other work or tied up in port.

From the beginning of the war President Wilson insisted that the government be given power to lead in the construction of an American merchant marine; but it was not until September, 1916, that resistance was overridden and the United States Shipping Board became a fact. It was not until the following April that the Emergency Fleet Corporation was set to work. The shipping program of the World War was a monument to American ingenuity and speed, but the allotted time was too short for the new ships to go to sea, so that the merchant fleet became a fact only after the

Armistice ended the imperative need for it, and by the summer of 1922 the Shipping Board owned or controlled 1,707 ships, aggregating eleven million tons. Many of the vessels were unfit for a trade which must show a profit, for the drive to build them had aimed at speed in construction rather than economy in original cost or cost of operation.

With the falling off of war cargoes, the inability of foreign countries to pay for what they needed, and the financial slump of 1920–1921, it came about that more than two-thirds of the new fleet was inactive and without hope of profitable business. The costs continued, and there was no way of avoiding the capital losses which must be charged against war necessity. The new law, enacted in June, 1920, brought no relief and failed to permit the government to liquidate the fleet and retire from business. Calling for a new board of seven members, Congress compelled Wilson to reconstruct the board; but the Senate failed to confirm the appointment of the persons whom he nominated. It was left to Harding to select the personnel, who were at last organized under Albert D. Lasker, a Chicago advertising man, in June, 1921. In the meantime the shipping program was substantially without a head.

Harding had demanded a new legislative policy in February, 1922, but had not been able to induce Congress to give it serious consideration during the long session. It was highly controversial, and the President's policy was certain to be fought by members whose votes would be needed for the passage of the tariff. Mellon pressed him for action, for the costs of a fleet which had no future were draining the Treasury. The floor leaders insisted on deferment, but agreed to attempt to pass a bill in a special session. The election served notice that the new Congress would be refractory.

When the President met the third session, to set the tune on November 22, he defended his proposal for a revision of the law of 1920 on the grounds of policy and economy. He had voted for that law while senator from Ohio, but as President he was burdened by its execution. "We entered the World War," he said, "almost wholly dependent on our Allies for transportation at sea . . . expended approximately three billions, feverishly, extravagantly, wastefully, and impractically . . . [and] acquired the vast merchant fleet which the Government owns today."

He proposed to extricate himself from the pains of ownership and operation. The government was to withdraw from the business, take the necessary loss, get rid of ships and land installations which could not be used with profit, and for a term of years assist private owners willing to take the risk on so much of the fleet as seemed to be usable. The assistance was to consist of a subsidy to cover the difference in costs of operations between these ships under American law and foreign ships. Liberal terms of purchase and a measure of tax exemption were to accompany the subsidy. The objective was to keep the American flag in competition on the high seas, to reduce overhead, and to prevent the rapid deterioration of the ships. Harding was worried by the use by the opposition of the unpopular word "subsidy"; and by the attack on "special privilege" by some of his listeners who were quite ready to demand it for large numbers of their constituents. He preferred to talk of "government aid,"—aid quite as proper as the provision of funds "to promote good roads for market highways," or grants in aid of railroads, or aid to industry by means of a tariff. The House at once adopted a special rule calling for a vote after a week of argument, and the debate began.

Democrats, almost to a man, clung to the principle of operation by the government, as it had been applied in the creation of the Shipping Board, and later revised, in a Democratic administration. The Republican majority, some 300 of the 435 representatives, could not be controlled, and split on lines different from those which had prolonged the debate over the tariff. The farmer organizations were not unanimous. Most of them were hostile, but Howard of the Farm Bureau Federation was quoted on both sides. Big business had been divided on the tariff, but now the American Chamber of Commerce and the National Association of Manufacturers were generally traveling with the administration. Gompers of the American Federation of Labor expressed the view of his executive council in opposition, and his belief that the votes recently counted were intended to express hostility to the subsidy. The railroad brotherhoods, already indignant because of the Esch-Cummins law, were prepared to be equally indignant if the shipping interests as well as the railroads should be favored with aid. Partisan tactics were amply displayed: by Bankhead of Alabama who, as leader of the debate for the opposition, made all the use he could of Republican dissenters like Frear and Nelson of Wisconsin; by Garrett of Tennessee when he described the Republican administration as running true to form "with the very death rattle in its throat"; and by the administration itself in playing up such support as was available from the agrarian camp.

The opponents of the bill made much of the charge that once contracts had been entered into with ship operators the country would be pledged to at least ten years of continuance of the subsidy policy, and that it was indecent for a lame duck Congress thus to bind its successors. The advantages to be gained by the greater privately-owned fleets (those of Standard Oil and American Fruit) received heavy attack. When the New York *Tribune* asserted that no believer in the tariff could oppose the subsidy, the words were taken by opponents as confirmation of their charges. It was asserted that Republicans had put off passage until elections from well-grounded fear, and that they had rushed thereafter to force adoption by lame duck votes. Certainly the lame ducks made passage possible when the votes were counted on November 29. There were only twenty-four more yeas than nays, but some sixty-nine lame duck Republicans voted with the Democrats against the bill.

While the House, under administration lash, was preparing its subsidy bill for the Senate, the latter was rendered inactive by its own rules. The Dyer antilynching bill was ready for consideration, as it had been since the House passed it in January, and northern and western votes seemed to be ready to accept it if only it could be brought under debate. There were some strict constitutionalists—Borah was one of them—whose desire for action was held in restraint by their belief that such a bill would be an invasion of the proper authority of the states. Other supporters, however, responded to the pressure of constituents which had been growing since the Klan began to ride and since the Association for the Advancement of Colored People took a lead in demanding protective legislation. These were willing to risk the constitutionality.

Public opinion south of the Potomac was so strongly against the Dyer bill that every attempt to bring it to the floor of the Senate had been countered by a threat to paralyze all action by means of a filibuster. The antilynching bill was one of those proposals for a national rule in which the support came largely from the states that were least likely to have to bear its burden. It attempted to give a legal definition to the word "mob," imposed heavy penalties upon persons convicted in lynching cases, and assessed damages upon communities in which lynchings occurred. In spite of all pressure for its passage, it offered such a threat to administration measures that the attempt to consider it in the Senate was put off through the spring and summer of 1922, and deferred until the special session. Full-page advertisements in its support greeted the Congress when it returned to duty after the election.

Underwood of Alabama took charge of the promised filibuster the purpose of which was to prevent the bill from even being taken up, let alone brought to a vote. Lodge, who favored the bill, was old enough in service to recall the filibuster against his force bill in 1891 which had deadlocked Congress until proponents yielded. The issue had then been the effort to reduce the representation of the states in the proportion in which they denied to citizens of the United States the right to vote guaranteed them by the Fourteenth Amendment. Underwood called the Dyer bill another force bill, defending his determination to defeat it on the ground of duty to his constituents and to the federal system; while at various oratorical levels from his own down to that of Heflin of Alabama his southern coadjutors kept the Dyer bill from being taken up. At the same time, they prevented the Senate from doing other important business. When again the Republicans were forced to yield, to give way to the regular December session, Underwood was speaking at length upon a dilatory motion to amend the *Journal* because the name of the reading clerk had been omitted. Lodge announced peace. The Republican caucus had agreed not to press the matter again during the present Congress.

While the southern senators were defending their version of states rights the forces which La Follette could command were completing an organization to advance the interests of agrarian Republicans and to protect them from the ship subsidy when that measure should come up in the regular session. That they had an eager eye upon the succession to Harding was obvious. The strategy of the western blocs in obstructing legislation and in procuring compromises gave them encouragement.

On the invitation of La Follette, and of the People's Legislative Service which his friends had been operating for several months, a secret conference was held in Washington on the Friday before the fourth session was to convene; and the results of the caucus were released at a round-table dinner on Saturday. It had been determined, as definitely as the future could be pledged, that no new party was in contemplation, but that the members of a new Progressive bloc would coöperate with all who agreed with them in Congress. Although there was much overlapping of membership there were differences in personnel between the thirty-two representatives and senators who had sat in the caucus and the farm bloc of Capper or the western tariff bloc of Gooding and McNary. But there was general willingness among them to challenge the administration in matters of direct and regional interest. George W. Norris of Nebraska had sat as chairman of the caucus; and it was only natural that the Progressive bloc should throw its support to his lame duck amendment as well as to his more extreme proposal to substitute for the electoral college a direct popular vote in the choice of president.

Although it was not itself a party, the Progressive bloc was close to groups which played with the idea of a new labor-farmer-liberal party. Even Borah foresaw a third-party sweep in 1924 unless the Republican party should alter its course. The Committee of Forty-Eight had not given up hope and found courage renewed by the election of 1922. The Conference for Progressive Political Action, the chairman of which was William H. Johnston, head of the machinists union, met for caucus in Cleveland early in December. The railroad brotherhoods, nursing their grievances against the Esch-Cummins act and the powers of the Railroad Labor Board which it had brought into existence, were ready to move into politics. They shared with the La Follette group the desire to curb the powers of the Supreme Court. Their friends in the House, inspired in part by the action of Attorney General Daugherty in using federal injunctions in the railroad strike, were searching earnestly for grounds upon which to base an impeachment action. The lame duck session with which the Sixty-seventh Congress would come to an end, was to be a battlefield for measures of reform and for political maneuver.

The special session, futile or forced, rounded out its last fortnight. It remained in debate until the very last, adjourning only
ten minutes before the noon hour on Monday, December 4, 1922,
when Calvin Coolidge, in the Senate, and Frederick H. Gillett, in
the House, called the bodies together for the terminal session. This
was Harding's last legislative opportunity and the presidential campaign of 1924 was started. Four days later the President in person
laid before the Congress a program in which he hoped to salvage
measures of his own and at the same time to combat the insurrection in his party.

"There is no acceptance of prewar conditions anywhere in the
world," he said as the applause of greeting—notably lacking support
from Robert Marion La Follette—died down. Everyone "craves
readjustment for everybody but himself." He made a plea for the
retention of what was good in the old order and, since out of the
old order war itself had come, for a new order which, "made secure, never will permit its recurrence." He plunged at once into
labor trouble and farm misfortune, deploring both, taking credit
for the prolongation of the work of the War Finance Corporation
and suggesting an expansion of the duties of the Farm Loan Bureau
into a new field of agricultural credit. His mind was full of the
problems of transportation and of the effect of the automobile upon
the railroads. "The motor car," he said, "long ago ran down Simple
Living, and never halted to inquire about the prostrate figure
which fell as its victim." He was concerned with the need of the
nation for uninterrupted operation of the transportation system,
and for proper rates; and for labor he suggested a modification of
the adjustment services at which the Labor Board had aimed. He
wished that the country might have escaped the coal and railway
strikes "which had no excuse for their beginning and less justification for their delayed settlement," and which impeded the return
to peace. And he was almost sharp in blaming labor for its insistence
"on holding to the war heights" which had been attained, and in
criticizing the "heedless forces of reaction" for seeking to return to
"the prewar levels." Both were wrong.

The address included kindly reference to a dozen proposals
worthy of being worked into the structure of the new order. But
there was not a word about the ship subsidy which the President

was determined to see enacted. This word was perhaps not needed, since on the following day Jones of Washington was to report favorably his revision of the House bill amending the merchant marine act, and on December 11 the Senate was to pass into committee of the whole for its consideration. A poll of the body revealed that there were already forty-four hostile votes should the bill ever come to a vote; and these were enough to defeat it by obstruction. It would take only five more to defeat it on a roll call.

The tactics of filibuster differed in the Dyer bill and in the ship subsidy. In the former, with the bill reported favorably to the Senate, the obstructionist debate which Senate rules permit was successful in preventing that body from even considering the bill. Not that it failed to receive discussion. Under the rules, what a senator shall say, once he is upon his feet, and how long he shall take to say it, depend upon his sense of public duty, save on the rare occasions when the formal cloture has been invoked by petition. Many senators, in all parties, have at times rationalized this sabotage of majority rule. It had taken the cloture to bring the Treaty of Versailles to a vote in 1919. Administration senators who in this fourth session resented the filibuster against their measures were forced to listen to recitals of their own behavior when they had been of the minority. The surrender on the Dyer bill was complete. That on the subsidy bill was to be as complete, though effected by different tactics.

The subsidy bill was taken up in committee of the whole on December 11, 1922. It was still there on Washington's birthday, when the Senate took time out for a rereading of the Farewell Address and when there were only ten days left in which to complete the business of the session. Those who fought it, and who justified their action to their own satisfaction, sought to keep it in committee of the whole until the latest possible date, confident that in the next Congress it could not even be revived. It could be reported out only by an affirmative vote which they hoped to block; should it be reported out, they hoped to hold the floor and prevent a final roll call until the session and the Congress should end on March 4. The filibuster did not prevent the performance of other business, for by unanimous consent the terminal legislation of Congress was in some instances allowed to pass, the holder of the floor yielding it temporarily for the purpose. As February advanced without action, the filibuster became intense, until business was in deadlock on Monday, February 19, and the White House had to be informed of the improbability of the subsidy bill's even coming to a vote, and the possibility of its being defeated if it did.

The Senate allowed itself to pass the lame duck amendment of Norris and to send it to the House. It allowed the agricultural credits bill to run its parliamentary course. But the all-day filibuster against the subsidy now took shape, threatening to break the records for continuous speech established by La Follette when he fought the Aldrich-Vreeland bill in 1908, and that of Jones, manager of the present bill, when he obstructed consideration of the bill to create the United States Shipping Board in 1915. The action raged for five days, until the administration forces abandoned hope of wearing down the opposition. Ladd of North Dakota, elected as a Republican because Nonpartisans endorsed him, had much to say about filled milk which his farmer constituents despised. Borah, more nearly a Republican than Ladd, coöperated with many words on Soviet Russia—words which prolonged the filibuster by inciting Lodge to reply. Brookhart, newly from Iowa, chose February 22 for an unscheduled oration on George Washington, with digressions on the sins of big business. On the Democratic side, Reed of Missouri found the foreign status of the West Indies provocative; Harrison of Mississippi made speeches on subsidy time but actually on the theme of rural credit; Williams of Mississippi and McKellar of Tennessee added to the history of the filibuster when they discussed Republican performance in the past; Sheppard of Texas recited the history and record of the League of Nations. By Friday night the administration was ready for a truce. Jones, who had flaunted a "very loud red necktie" through the fight, appeared on Saturday morning wearing a tie which Harrison noted with glee. It was "pure white, showing surrender." The bill was beaten without a vote. When a few days later Robinson of Arkansas moved to bury it decently by sending it back to the committee which had reported it, it was kept before the Senate by the bare minimum of forty-eight votes; but the administration strategists knew that not even this number could have been counted on to vote to pass the bill.

In the face of the filibuster, the dearest projects of the administration were defeated in the two sessions following the election of 1922, and the work of Congress was reduced to a minimum embracing only those measures for which unanimous consent to consider could be procured. The administration allowed the subsidy bill to die in the committee of the whole rather than accept defeat by vote. It coöperated with many of those who were resisting action in order to complete credit legislation for the farmers, which the opposition in both parties desired, and whose tendency was hoped to soften the clash within the Republican party. There were moments between Christmas and adjournment when subsidy and agricultural credit clashed for right of way, but the greatest obstacle to bringing action upon the latter was the number of proposals for relief, their varying approaches to it, and the critical attitude of the oppositions to the conduct of the existing credit agencies of the government.

Congress had approached the general question twice within the decade, and twice it had set up financial networks to aid business and to hobble what had been described by the Pujo committee in 1913 as the money trust. From the report of that committee, prepared for a Democratic House in the administration of President Taft, the proponents of a change in the laws had drawn much of their ammunition. The Federal Reserve act, emerging from the debate before Woodrow Wilson had been a year in office, was a milestone in the spread of federal authority over the institutions of American business life. Three years later, in 1916, its companion statute, the Federal Farm Loan act, had matched the network of Federal Reserve banks with another of Farm Loan banks. The former did business chiefly with the short-term paper of current commercial transactions; the latter dealt in those long-term obligations likely to be recorded in mortgage bonds. Neither went as far as advocates of easy and controlled credit urged, and both systems became objects of criticism based upon their methods and management. The public was slow to learn that whereas the benefits it hoped to gain might bring about adoption of procedures in a planned economy, the inherent virtues of that economy depended on the defense of the system's logical extension against abuse. There is perhaps no way in which creditors and borrowers can be kept in happy accord after a loan has been granted. The United States had seen many outbursts of indignation on the part of the latter when they had found it inconvenient to fulfill their contracts.

Whether the systems would have been adequate for the decade, had there been no World War, is uncertain. The consequence of that war, inflation of agriculture to abnormal distention, prepared the way for agricultural collapse upon the return of peace, and this in its turn provided the basis for the demands pressed upon Congress after 1919. Between the field in which the Federal Reserve banks functioned and that of the Farm Loan banks, between long-term and short-term accommodations, a neglected area had developed, in which agriculture suffered. The collapse of 1920 made any sort of farm loans dubious as prudent investment, apart from the fact that the farmer had need for a special type of loan unsuited for either system. He needed crop loans covering the period between planting and harvest, and loans to cover the holding of the crop until market and price should make its sale profitable. Partly as completion of the federal banking system, partly as direct aid to suffering farmers, another system of banks appeared to many to be indispensable.

Harding had much to say about the misfortune of the farmer in his address in December, 1922, and no one disagreed when he said of agriculture that its "ill fortune is national ill." He had reservations upon the matter, reservations not unreasonable in the presence of the inability of farmers to agree upon their needs. Agriculture, he conceded, "has the vicissitudes which no legislation can prevent, its hardships for which no law can provide escape"; but he believed that Congress could provide "financial facilities" for agriculture as it had provided them for other commercial and financial enterprises. There were those who claimed that when agriculture had no market, and when the price did not return the costs of production, the farmer had little collateral upon which to borrow; and there were extremists, whose day in Congress was still to come, who saw no possible relief except through a guaranteed price for farm products in the domestic market. But bill drafters were at work in both houses and the committees were crowded with their contradictory suggestions. The administration was as willing to have action taken as were the authors of the bills, though for different reasons. Mellon watched with critical eye lest an impossible burden be placed upon his budget.

Capper of Kansas, head of the farm bloc, as well as Lenroot of Wisconsin and Norris of Nebraska, had measures ready to be introduced when the regular session convened. Companion measures were presented to the House. The debate on the Capper bill, reported to the Senate from the Committee on Banking and Currency, began in the middle of January; and when at last a measure was ready to be presented to the President in the closing hours of the session it was this bill, with modifications and additions, which lay upon his desk. It was so nearly acceptable to all that it had lost all value as a measure of placation. Those who demanded it accepted it as something gained by extortion; those who yielded gained no advantage by their yielding. The House passed the conference report by a vote of 276 to 34; the Senate did not even bother with a roll call.

Describing itself as the Agricultural Credits Act of 1923, it was a series of amendments to the Federal Reserve and Farm Loan Board acts, liberalizing the former and adding to the administrative duties of the latter. The War Finance Corporation, whose life had been prolonged for the sake of the farmer, was to disappear when a new network of Federal Intermediate Credit banks was ready to function. One of these was to be attached to each of the dozen Farm Loan banks, with power to discount the paper of agricultural and live stock industries and coöperative marketing associations. Under supervision of the Farm Loan board they were empowered to lend money within the intermediate range and to borrow for the purpose on bonds of their own issue. Farmers themselves were given the right to set up National Agricultural Credit Corporations to insure a greater flexibility of credit. Short of lending public money unsecured by prudent collateral, the gap in the banking structure was for the time filled.

The session, last chance as it was to be for Warren G. Harding, was not without victories for the administration, in spite of the political feuds and cross-purposes which had destroyed the fundamental solidarity of American economic and political opinion. The basic appropriation bills had been worked through Congress, making it unnecessary to call a special session of the Sixty-eighth

Congress earlier than its normal December date. It had been a long pull for the people and for Congress which had been in almost continuous session for seven years. Indeed, prior to the long recess of 1915, Wilson had kept the Congress at almost continuous labor since his inauguration. After the recess of 1915 the sessions had been so protracted that they nearly filled each year, and special sessions closed the gaps. Only in 1920, when Congress was out of Washington between the June conventions and December, had there been a normal release from duty. The hope of the Republican insurgents that the President would be forced to call a special session shortly after March was not fulfilled, and Harding, believing that a political vacation would be good for the country, let it be known that he saw no need for an early calling of the new Congress. The divergences of opinion and demand, an aftermath of war, were beyond the power of Harding to command; perhaps beyond the power of any leader. Time, tranquillity, and satisfaction in a growing industrial prosperity, might be expected to work a political sanitation.

Harding had resisted the pressure of radicals—both within and without his party—and of conservatives as well, for the irreconcilables were strong around him. Fall and Mellon were in the Cabinet; but so were Hughes and Hoover. Fall, indeed, was on his way out, to direct the improvements on his ranch at Three Rivers, New Mexico—improvements the disastrous after effects of which were to be more than burdensome to him and to all who had been associated with him. When Hoover declined to shift from Commerce to Interior, as the Congress ended, Dr. Hubert Work was transferred thither from the Post Office where he had succeeded Hays in 1922. And a place as Postmaster General was found for New of Indiana, a lame duck since the primary of 1922. Hughes, meanwhile, received the President's support, in clear defiance of those to whom the League and all that accompanied it was anathema. Hughes had been a signer of the manifesto of the Republican advocates of the League in 1920. His elaborate argument in favor of adherence to the protocol establishing the Permanent Court of International Justice was sent to the Senate in the last moments of the session, with a recommendation for its approval. Watson of Indiana assured Harding that insistence would split the party on another plane, and the chairman of the Republican Congressional Campaign Committee thought it would be the last straw. But the President booked an engagement to address the Associated Press in New York where, though he repudiated the League, he urged adherence to the Court. Johnson of California hurried to New York to denounce the intention of the President. La Follette followed, to denounce the speech. A majority of the Republican members of the Senate Committee on Foreign Relations in the Sixty-seventh Congress had been hostile to the Court; and all of them were to continue to sit when the Sixty-eighth convened.

It was beyond the power of Harding to lead the Senate to an approval of the Permanent Court protocol, either as it was signed or with reservations protecting what the opposition senators took to be American interests. Large forces of public opinion backed them in their opposition. But it was equally beyond the power of the opposition to disentangle the United States from the affairs of Europe. The facts played into the hand of the President. On February 7 he interrupted a Senate debate on War Department appropriations and a House debate on a definition of what constituted a "crop failure" in order to present to Congress in person the text of an agreement on the British war debt which had been signed a few days earlier. It was a year, almost to the day, since Congress had sought to tie his hands, hoping to control the negotiation of financial settlements by means of a commission and mandatory legislation. The stipulations of the funding law were so unworkable that the Congress was given the option between no settlement at all and one which the British government would sign. The new Chancellor of the Exchequer, Stanley Baldwin, had come to Washington late in 1922, with Montague Norman of the Bank of England in his train. He proposed a direct negotiation, for his government was caught in a squeeze between its financial limitations and its desire for cordial relations with the good American customer. The cabinet of Bonar Law, with no means of cutting the loss arising from British loans to continental debtors, was eager to get "out of the mess," as George Harvey put it; but Harvey had also told a British audience that "England can't get out, and we shall probably have to get in. We can't get away from necessities.

We know it. We have no illusions about it." From one who had so bitterly opposed the League and its entanglements, this was an admission. And Congress, which was wrestling with Harding's demand that it backtrack and let him do the negotiating, had to yield. It gave approval to the compromise on the last day of February, in one of the intervals in the deadlock. It agreed to accept less than it demanded; but the President had extracted from England a better settlement than any other of the war debtors could be induced to sign.

The debts to the United States, and the other debts among the European Allies, were in the minds of the debtors inextricably connected with the reparations which Germany had been forced to promise, and which the German government had little ability and less intention to pay. No argument could weaken the conviction that the war against Germany had been a joint venture in which American money and European losses were free contributions to victory, not involving debts of honor. It was easy for the continental Allies to persuade themselves that, because of late entry upon the crusade, the United States was still morally in their debt and owed them further recompense on the ground of culpable delay.

The deep financial troubles of Europe were made more disastrous by the political confusion still prevailing. The invaded countries, owing huge domestic debts to their own citizens whose property had been under the feet of the armies, could not balance their budgets even if they disregarded the loans from their associates in the war. The enemy countries were still in chaos. The new countries, brought into existence along the western edge of Russia, were more conscious of their national aspirations than they were coöperative for peace. From the Baltic to the Near East, there was something closely resembling war.

In the Levant, the terms imposed upon Turkey by the Treaty of Sèvres brought about a nationalist uprising against the Sultanate. Kemal Pasha, with his nationalist troops, threw the Greek armies out of Smyrna in September, 1922, and his national assembly at Angora declared in November that it was the government of Turkey and that the Sultanate was abolished. Turkey declined to be pushed out of Europe, and found support among the Allies for its demand to retain Constantinople and the straits between the Black Sea and the Mediterranean. Before November was over a new conference at Lausanne was at work upon a revision of the Sèvres proposal. The successful "march on Rome" in October had brought Benito Mussolini to the head of the Italian government, in time for him to exchange his black shirt for the conventional garb of diplomacy and make appearance at Lausanne. The revolts against the governments which had either lost the war or gained too little at the peace spread into Germany, where a premature uprising of Bavarian Nazis was for the moment checked. The *hakenkreuz* movement, now two years old, was gaining followers, although American papers were not always sure whether the name of Adolph Hitler, its leader, was Wilhelm or Otto. Cecil Brown, in Germany for the *Times,* described the Nazis as both nationalistic and anti-Semitic.

The Baltic states—Esthonia, Latvia, and Lithuania—recognized indeed, were uncertain on their feet, while Poland had an urge for land despite the efforts of the Allies to stabilize the map of Europe. Troops of Poland, in the wars after 1919, took from Lithuania its ancient administrative center of Vilna, although Vilna had passed to Lithuania by treaty with Russia and by approval of the Allies; and the Allies ratified the seizure. Deprived of its capital, and lacking a suitable port on the Baltic, Lithuania turned to Memel, just outside of East Prussia on the east, where the Allies had put a French administrator in charge pending decision as to the assignment of the town. Lithuanian troops settled the matter by occupying Memel early in 1923, over the protest of the Council of Ambassadors, who nevertheless ratified the fact. Russia had been too weak to prevent Poland from determining the common boundary to its own taste in the Treaty of Riga. The Allies, differing too much among themselves to frame a policy, had lacked the power to enforce one even if it had been adopted.

The disputes among the Allies, and the limitations of the power of the League of Nations, contributed to the satisfaction of the American irreconcilables at the rejection of the Treaty of Versailles. The impotence of the Reparations Commission, on which the United States had only an observer, was marked. Throughout 1922 it was unable to hold Germany to its promised payments.

England was no longer in harmony with France, whereas Italy and
Belgium commonly supported the latter when the premiers met,
or the ambassadors counseled. France had not yet ratified the
Treaty of Washington to bring naval limitation into operation.
The new government of William Cuno as Chancellor of Germany
was threatened on one side by the Bavarian Nazis, and on the other
by the Allies who demanded payment and were able to list apparent defaults in justification of whatever pressure they might
want to exert. His government, like that of his predecessor Wirth,
was operating Germany on paper marks the value of which had
become microscopic as the end of 1922 approached. The premiers
were in session in London in December, with France demanding
the seizure of the industrial region of the Ruhr as a retaliation for
the default and a means of collecting the reparations at the source.
They adjourned in disagreement, to meet again in January; meanwhile France prepared an army of occupation. Outvoting England
three to one, the Allies declared Germany to be in default; and the
French army marched on January 11, 1923.

Even those Americans who most decried participation in the affairs of Europe could not fail to see the confusion and suggest remedies. Johnson was confirmed in his determination to keep out of
it. Borah, equally determined to avoid permanent commitments,
insisted that now was the time for another international conference,
to adjust the economic affairs of the world; yet he took the administration to task for doing nothing to protect the German people
from the military power of France. Harding was again caught between the fires, but he listened to Hughes.

The latter chose for his platform a meeting of the American
Historical Association in New Haven during Christmas week, and
there he walked the narrow line between advising action and assuming responsibility. He suggested that Germany's creditors
abandon their political approach to reparations, make a careful
examination of the ability of the bankrupt enemy to pay, and thereafter readjust their demands to what was possible. He assumed no
responsibility on the part of the United States, and no desire to act
as arbiter in the affairs of Europe. He had no wish that France
should lose a part of her just claims, no confidence in force as a
means of settlement, and was certain that there could not be eco-

nomic stability in Europe unless Germany, too, was stable econom-
ically. If the Allies should determine upon such a course as he suggested he had confidence that distinguished Americans could be
persuaded to serve on a commission of financial inquiry. He left
the matter there; but the Allies took it up, and to Charles G. Dawes
the thankless task was eventually assigned. Meanwhile the administration opposed the Borah movement for an economic conference, and Johnson gave the reasons why it would be unavailing.
How could the United States invite the powers to a conference on
debts and refuse to consider an adjustment of their debts to the
United States? How could it, as host, meet their request that it
contribute to economic welfare by lowering its tariff wall? How
could it meet the problem of displaced persons and unemployment
and yet maintain the barriers to immigration which its laws set up?

The public debates in the United States which paralleled the pre-
liminaries to the occupation of the Ruhr revealed in equal measure the American unwillingness to assume responsibility and the
extent of American interest in the solvency of Europe. It was impossible for the administration to formulate the clear foreign policy which critics demanded from both sides, for the policy was
fundamentally that of avoidance rather than of action. Neither
Congress nor the people was ready for concessions to relieve the
tension, or for force. As France made clear its determination to
occupy the Ruhr, the Senate hurried to passage a resolution advising the administration to withdraw American troops from their
bridgehead station at Coblenz. The military appropriation bills
for 1923–1924 had not yet been passed, they involved cuts rather
than increases, and the debates upon them provided occasion for a
running discussion of the relationship between the United States
and Europe. The administration, moreover, needed approval of
its proposal for the adjustment of the British debt. Major General
Henry T. Allen was ordered out of Germany on January 10, 1923,
the day before the French took over the Krupp plant at Essen. On
January 24 the flag of the United States was hauled down.

The final session of the only Congress whose deliberations Warren Gamaliel Harding was destined to guide or to review came to
an end at noon on March 4, 1923. It ended with as little program
for common action as the premiers had had, or the leaders of the

new countries of middle Europe. The latter continued in their use of force when negotiation failed. The members of Congress went their several ways, in peace at least, with nine months before them in which to study the temper of their constituents. The life of their country flowed on, without much reference to what they had done, or had failed to do, for enough of the people were so prosperous as to be without despair and those who were near to despair had still their hope.

More than the normal fraction of the members went home for good. A few of the lame ducks had new public work awaiting them, thanks to a chief whose popularity still lasted and whose loyalty to his friends pleased more than it discouraged. Almost none thought him either great or without loyalty to his conception of his baffling job.

Some of those who left Washington, not directly touched by the controversies of the recent past, had valedictories to speak or farewells to listen to as they passed out of the American political picture. Each of the houses paused at the end to make time for these. Each lost a member whose term of service connected the present with the prewar past, whose regard for the nation and the party was unchallenged, and whose departure emphasized the completeness with which the United States had slipped from one phase of its existence to another.

John Sharp Williams of Mississippi was "going home to rest," refusing even to write his memoirs for the papers. For thirty years he had served in House and Senate, and "no one ever slept when John Sharp Williams spoke." A southerner, but not a "professional southerner," he had "all the weapons of oratory from satire and sarcasm to eulogies of the purest English." A scholar and a partisan, "clean but careless" in his dress, he had an engaging way of seating himself almost under the feet of a senatorial opponent and listening "as though enraptured." Williams was going by his own choice back to his home in Yazoo City, "on a rural free delivery route."

Back to Danville, Illinois, Joseph Gurney Cannon was going after a service even longer than that of Williams. The latter had been chiefly of the opposition, accepting it as the duty of Democrats to heckle Republicans through long years when Republicans controlled the Senate. Cannon had been of the Republican Old Guard pushing measures through parliamentary hazards to completion. For fifty years, less two terms when the forces of adversity had been too strong for him, he had been a representative from Illinois. He had as few doubts about the Republican right to rule as Williams had in opposition to it, and as Speaker he had governed the House through four critical Congresses. The Quaker background which his biographers invariably stressed was in less than harmony with the rough masculinity in which cartoonists delighted for a generation. Something of the Lincoln tradition—on its unkempt side—found in him its continuator. "I suppose a reformer has his place," he had once told his associates; but he had never discovered it. For himself, he was part of the governing majority of the party whose majorities had ruled the United States for most of his years of service. He had become a legend long before he went back to Danville.

The conflict of organized interests, ever in struggle to control the policy of government, had carried the United States into a new era before Williams and Cannon retired. That conflict, and those interests, had brought about the tangle from which the proprietor of the Marion *Star* was left to extricate himself when the Sixty-seventh Congress adjourned.

Chapter XXI ★ "Two Hard Years Ahead"

The PIONEER, houseboat of the Edward B. McLeans, was made ready at Ormond Beach, Florida, as the session ended, for the Hardings were to use it as a home during a leisurely cruise down the east coast waterways to Miami. The McLeans, with the freedom coming from inherited money and a fondness for the company of the important, maintained a hospitality which made their Washington mansion a wonder place and their Palm Beach establishment a convenient annex. McLean, with the disposition of a playboy and such education as private tutors could instill, had found himself in possession of his industrious father's papers, the Cincinnati *Enquirer* and the Washington *Post*. Evelyn Walsh, his wife, had succeeded to bonanza millions extracted by her father from the Colorado mines of Leadville and Ouray. They entertained the procession of notables who marched through Washington with lavish food, abundant drink, and, on occasion, "hot" prizefight films which the law forbade to be transported in interstate commerce.

When the congressmen went upon their several ways the President welcomed the time for the first real vacation since his inauguration; while his wife, convalescing from a long illness, welcomed the sun. The burden of office had weighed upon Harding, who was not accustomed to the unavoidable and conflicting duties that piled up on his desk. He, too, welcomed the southern sun, golf with congenial companions, and the possibility that the fish would bite. Sawyer, the family doctor, now on duty at the White House as a reserve brigadier general, was of the party whose train rolled south on March 5. Dawes and McLean were to be of the usual foursome, as well as Lasker, once a vigorous supporter of the presidential hopes of Hiram Johnson, in whose hands now lay the administration of the unamended shipping act.

During the next fortnight, the reporters who commented upon the appearance of the President noted the disappearance from his face of lines of wear and tear. These had been a matter of concern as they increased in the long two-year pull since his inauguration. The back-breaking job of the presidency had been doing its work. He now acquired a healthy tan and jested about his golf score, without revealing it. He did, however, denounce as a canard the charge that his score was so bad that he had broken several clubs in anger. They moored the houseboat near the better courses, where the camera men were given a chance to catch the President in action. On the tenth day from Washington the party reached Miami, to pause until the end of the week before doubling back to St. Augustine, and going thence to Augusta, Georgia, for another stop.

What was in the mind of the President, with nine months and no Congress ahead of him, is a matter of conjecture. Such light as his papers may shed is screened by the memorial association, their custodian. But no president can approach the beginning of election year without concern for what it may mean to him; no supporters can approach it without concern for their own future; no opponents can fail to speculate on its possibilities. The evidence that Harding had wished to be nominated even once is incomplete; that he desired renomination and reëlection, or believed that his health could stand the strain, is even more in doubt.

It is likely enough that he had no confidence in his ability to secure a second term, in the face of the split in party counsels which had widened since the convention of 1920. Mere renomination was probable, because of the advantage of an incumbent president in controlling the machinery of nomination. But some of the lines in his face which yielded before the Florida sun may have been occasioned by inside knowledge that, with bad breaks in publicity, even renomination might be impossible. It is not certain, however, that he was aware of the bitter fate impending for Albert B. Fall who retired from the Department of the Interior on March 4, 1923.

Fall left the Cabinet with his associates thinking well of his capacity, not doubting his honesty, and disposed to rejoice that his private affairs were looking up. Certain of his official transactions were under scrutiny; but the scrutiny was chiefly by those from whom the administration expected nothing but attacks, and had concerned oil, which had a habit of causing perennial controversy. The leasing to private oil companies of drilling rights in the naval oil reserves had aroused criticism and set off investigation. Harding had specifically underwritten what had been done. He had signed an executive order in May, 1921, transferring the administration of the reserves from the Secretary of the Navy to the Secretary of the Interior; and the law permitted such leasing. The controversy thus far concerned the expediency of the action, and the policy has continued to be one upon which honest petroleum engineers have differed.

Fall, acting under the executive order, had proceeded in secrecy and without competitive bidding to lease drilling rights in the Elk Hills field in California to interests controlled by an associate of his early mining days, Edward L. Doheny; and those in the Teapot Dome field in Wyoming to the Mammoth Oil Company, represented by Harry F. Sinclair. The latter lease, coming to public attention in April, 1922, had led La Follette to demand an investigation and the Senate to entrust it to the Committee on Public Lands. Thomas F. Walsh, a Democratic senator from Montana, was appointed chairman of a subcommittee and given charge of the spadework preliminary to open hearings. It was still possible, as Harding contemplated the future in the South, to regard the oil inquiry as no more than normal congressional partisanship. If he had known what Walsh was to discover from witnesses, he would have been entitled to lines of worry. But Walsh was not yet ready to make announcement of progress, and until he began the open hearings in the following October he was not even aware of what his dragnet was to bring to the surface.

Whatever the merits of a leasing policy, the methods whereby the leases were executed could not stand the light of day. They led to the long series of suits, civil and criminal, which made the words Teapot Dome synonymous with scandal. The Supreme Court, annulling the Elk Hills lease, was to describe it as "conceived and executed in fraud and corruption" as well as in defiance of law. The criminal courts, releasing in the testimony much that could never be completely established, found it impossible to convict any individual for bribery of a Cabinet officer, yet managed to convict Fall for receiving bribes from those who had been acquitted of guilt in bribing him. Fall served his term in jail, the first to do so on account of malfeasance in the Cabinet. Far from the "grateful sense of satisfaction" which he uttered in a "soliloquy" as he left the Cabinet, he was to die a sick and broken man. Yet other words in his soliloquy were sharply applicable to the country which he mis-served, the Congress which wrote its laws, and the party which administered while normalcy was the order of the day. "If the community doesn't know pretty well what it wants," he said, "and especially if it is in a frame of mind to be dissatisfied with whatever it gets, it can be reasonably sure of not getting much."

There was grief in the heart of the President, if not foreboding, as he cruised the inlets. He had been obliged to dismiss a friend from public service. At the end of the session, Brigadier General Frank T. Hines had been given charge of the Veterans' Bureau in place of Charles R. Forbes. It was too much to have hoped that Colonel Forbes, breezy and plausible as he was, could have escaped attack during the early months in which the veterans' agencies were being brought into orderly arrangement under the act of 1921. The United States was as yet in no position to fulfill its obligations under the heads of hospitalization and rehabilitation; meanwhile veterans were both necessitous and insistent and the American Legion was exerting continuous pressure in their interest. Relief was slow in reaching its beneficiary, and natural irritation was aggravated by the refusal of the President to approve a bonus unless Congress provided funds with which to pay it. But charges of more than confusion and maladministration trickled in. There were rumors of politics, and of favoritism or worse, in the selection of hospital sites. In the late autumn of 1922 word reached the President of reckless or criminal sale of public property for which Forbes was responsible. It was hard for Harding to believe that a friend had let him down even when so close a friend as General Sawyer brought the bad news. The showdown with Forbes came in January, 1923, when the latter was permitted to go abroad, ostensibly for a vacation and recuperation, leaving his resignation behind him. He passed out of office at the end of February, and into a period of exposure, trial, and conviction of crime involving not only public funds but also the lives and health of the very men with whose safety he had been entrusted.

The President, hurt by betrayal, never knew the worst. Congressional investigation had still to bring out testimony to misbehavior other than financial. There was unsuspected irony in the inclusion of Colonel Thomas W. Miller among those who were considered for the position from which Forbes was dismissed. Miller had been appointed Alien Property Custodian by Harding, had sat with a committee to recommend a veterans' policy, and was on the executive committee of the American Legion. The courts were in due time to convict him of conspiracy in the handling of enemy property and to bring Attorney General Daugherty, under suspicion in the transaction, although the trial jury could not agree upon the guilt of the latter. Forbes was later discovered to have behind him a record of desertion from the Marine Corps in his younger days. Miller had had an honorable and decorated career in the war, rising from private to lieutenant colonel.

There was more grief awaiting Harding when he arrived in Miami on March 14, for one of his friends, who had bought the house he had owned while senator, was that morning found locked in his bathroom, an apparent suicide. Charles F. Cramer had been counsel for the Veterans' Bureau, had been the agent of Forbes in many of its transactions, and had left the service of the bureau when his chief retired. The possibility that conscious guilt or involvement had been a cause of his death had to be faced.

There were other worries for Harding, more personal than that of responsibility for the behavior of men whom he had appointed and about which he may not have been informed. He seems to have been in debt, although the facts in the matter were not made public. His sense of public propriety seems not to have kept him from speculation in the stock market; though with too little success to suggest that he was buying or selling on dependable inside information. Stories of heavy debts to his brokers were to follow him to his grave. Following him, as well, was the charge of an illegitimate daughter, said to have been born in 1919, of whom Nan Britton claimed to be the mother. The fact may have weighed upon his mind; the destructive power of such a charge could not have escaped him. Americans in high office are well aware of the damage which may be done by flagrant libel, and of the greater damage done when charges are sustained. Harding had already lived through a whispering campaign—the proof or disproof of which was lost among the thin records of a frontier past — and those who wished to accept it believed that there was a Negro among his ancestors. Whispering, from the other side of the party line, had attacked the moral character of Woodrow Wilson.

But it was only in another administration that exposures "made Harding's memory only a rag in the gutter," as Mark Sullivan had expressed it. What little was known of scandal while he lived was rarely mentioned. His popularity was never soured by suspicion. It is not possible to say how much of what exposure was later to attempt to establish was ever known to him, or how greatly he was disturbed by what he knew. He ended his outing with a kindly press. He was again in Washington, and with his Cabinet, by April 10; and a fortnight later he sat in the stand of the Yankee Stadium in New York while the Yankees beat the Senators and Babe Ruth delivered a home run on request. He was a week too late to be present at the opening of the Stadium, but was entirely willing to be photographed by the side of the "King of Swat." The duty which had brought him to New York was the furtherance of his desire to bring about American participation in the World Court without too greatly alienating those of his adherents to whom the World Court seemed to be as menacing as the League had been. Only the first half of his term in office had elapsed, and he had, as he had said at Palm Beach on March 18—it was all that he had said—"two hard years ahead."

Whatever the President was thinking about the next term he kept from the public, although he had no way of controlling what others might say about it. The slate makers were already at work. Simeon D. Fess, now senator from Ohio and formerly chairman of the Congressional Campaign Committee, had prophesied that the "renomination of President Harding is as certain as that the party will hold a convention." Hoover, commending from Palo Alto the "sanity and progressive character of his policies," had said as much.

Watson of Indiana, for whom the election had provided a Democratic colleague in the Senate, was sure of his renomination but apprehensive of a third party as a consequence. The *Nation*, caustic but not excited, for which the last session "might have been worse," foresaw that he would be renominated to be defeated. Coolidge, whose own future was uncertain, believed that the people would demand it because of "the great record of accomplishment under his leadership." But it was Daugherty, with whom the fame and future of Harding was an obsession, whose word carried most emphatically.

Daugherty had been sick, but not so sick as to abandon the southern trip on the special train, and had gone on to Miami instead of leaving the train for the houseboat at Ormond. Still using a wheelchair in Miami, he was visited there by the President on March 14, the day that Cramer was found dead. Three days later, although the President and his associates were carefully avoiding public mention of politics, Daugherty called in the newsmen and, speaking as though with authority, told them that Harding would run again.

Coming from Daugherty, the announcement was accepted as inspired, and Harding did not repudiate it. Within a few days, however, word got around that the Attorney General had spoken out of turn, thereby embarrassing the President whose mind was by no means made up. Daugherty was soon admitting that he had spoken only his own mind and expectation. It made little difference, for the question was in the air and it was already understood that the Hardings were contemplating a long summer trip to the West. The announcement was treated as an overture to a "virtual transcontinental campaign tour."

There had been talk of such a tour to be made during the summer of 1922, but neither the health of the presidential family nor the state of public business had permitted the talk to turn into reality. Presidents, while in office, had established many precedents for such visiting among the people, driven by varying mixtures of curiosity, kindliness, and politics. McKinley had reached the Pacific Coast, and Roosevelt and Taft and Wilson; and Congress had at long last made specific appropriation of travel funds so that people and president could meet each other, face to face. A new Far West had made its appearance since Grant, as ex-President had been driven, in state and black broadcloth, behind six sleek bays, from the ferry slip to the inner courtyard of the new Palace Hotel in San Francisco. Since 1879 the railroad net had brought the bonanza West within its meshes; a highway net was now tying it more closely to the Union. The bonanza past had become a cherished tradition, and the schoolboy whose future Grant may have prophesied had ripened into a senator whose power to disrupt his party was a fact in politics. Hiram Johnson was on vacation in Europe as Harding worked upon the itinerary of his trip.

The disastrous consequence for Hughes of his coastal trip in 1916 was a notice not to disregard the West. The sad ending of the Wilson tour in 1919 was the occasion of warning comment, lest undertaking too much the president might so commit himself as to break down under the strain of travel, incessant speaking, and the continuous pressure of curious crowds. Try as Harding did to create the impression that his purpose was recreation, and inspection of Alaska, and a better acquaintance with the people, he could not evade the common belief that his trip meant politics. Yet it is highly probable that the impression which he sought to spread was what was really in his mind, and that he was holding in abeyance the decision upon his own future course. He had spoken of the "two hard years ahead" just after Daugherty broke out the news. He knew his physical condition better than the public or the politicians could know it. He had come to the belief that prohibition included the president as well as the common citizen and was finding it hard to accommodate himself to it. He was said to have bought back his boyhood Ohio home for a residence, was engaged in the sale of his newspaper, and was ready to make a new will; and he may even have told his old friend Dr. Sawyer that he did not expect to live to return to Washington.

The open West and the uncertain future were before the Hardings as the country lived without Congress through the spring of 1923. Less and less the doings under the dome of the Capitol and in the offices of the White House were commanding the sustained attention of Americans. In the more than four years since the signing of the Armistice the effective interest in the world abroad had been replaced by new interests in the world at home. The open road was calling as never before, and within the frame of a new

prosperity there was little room for details of American maladjustment.

Americans, generally, were occupied with material concerns, and
whatever was news had exaggerated importance. It no longer staggered the imagination—as the *Nation* had been staggered in 1920—
to think of the miracle of air mail spanning the continent. It was
taken as a matter of course when preparations to broadcast the
speeches of the Harding tour were made public. The exhibit of new
models at the automobile shows aroused only the desire to acquire.
The building booms changed the city sky lines, and the change was
taken for granted. The new highways loosed city dwellers from
servitude to streetcar lines, and made them free to occupy suburban
homes; and domestic architecture built the shells of houses around
the new conveniences which were ready to be installed inside.
There must be space and connection for radio, vacuum cleaners,
oil-burning furnaces, automatic refrigeration, and bathroom
equipment of bewildering color; not to mention a garage, or perhaps two. There was money to be spent, and it was being spent as
the United States moved into a new chapter in the history of its
living habits. And every new device meant new factories, new jobs,
new buying power, and more new gadgets. Back of these it meant
new companies, new mergers, new networks of utilities, and new
issues of securities to compete with the gadgets for a share of the
capital which in the United States alone was piling up as though
there had not been a war. But there was more to it than material
things, and more for the social historian one day to appraise.

The great foundations were channeling many of the millions of
capital into the betterment of education and research, while every
year a larger fraction of Americans of college age were on some
campus. The normal doings of students gave to their athletic
stadia—which were larger and more numerous every autumn—more
prominence than their importance warranted. In the classrooms
the old activities flourished, and new adventures were undertaken.
Here, at least, there were increasing interests in the world and its
civilization, and attempts were in the making to open windows
through which the undergraduate could see it all. There were attempts as well to rebuild American loyalties upon knowledge of
American institutions. Constitution Day received formal celebra-

tion at the hand of patriotic societies on September 17, 1919; and thereafter many states tightened their laws respecting the teaching of American government at the various school levels. Some of them went so far as to bolster American tradition, lest a new international interest should result in reëxaminations of tradition. In Wisconsin a bill of 1923 set up a regular procedure for eliminating any school book which "falsifies the facts regarding the war of independence . . . defames our nation's founders . . . or misrepresents the ideals and cause for which they struggled." Other states discussed even more sweeping censorship, Washington was asked—in vain— to eliminate teachers who spoke "slightingly or contemptuously" of the Framers, the Constitution, or the preservers of the federal Union. New York made a rigorous loyalty oath mandatory upon all teachers, but stopped short of accepting a Higgins bill banning from the schools whatever book "ignores, omits, discounts, or in any manner belittles, ridicules, falsifies, distorts, questions, doubts, or denies" the events leading to the independence and the establishment of the United States. The expansion of classroom activities induced new building programs, new libraries, and new laboratories, while behind the doors of the seminars more students, and better, were working at the higher levels of study and research. American confidence in the usefulness of education showed no sign of waning and begot increased support from the tax rolls, and from those in a position to provide endowments, and those with young people to be educated.

Amusement took its toll from the swelling pay rolls. The movies, growing because of their own cheap attractiveness, were encroaching upon the legitimate stage. On the week end that Daugherty chose to give his statement, *The Covered Wagon* made its appearance in a Broadway theater, catering to the interest in the open road and the frontier past. But the theater was still the top attraction. Flo Ziegfield's *Follies,* romping through its eighteenth edition, crowded his theater, and made room for Will Rogers and his lasso although without lessening Ziegfeld's glorification of the American girl. Its younger rival, *The Passing Show,* offered everything that could be asked, "except perhaps delicacy," and still more girls with "hardly a stocking among them." But there were patrons at more than physiological levels. John Barrymore, with one hun-

dred and one consecutive performances of *Hamlet* to his credit
in New York, broke the record of the younger Booth in the winter
of 1922–1923; and three more Hamlets followed him in New York
before the year was out. Jane Cowl, with one hundred performances
of *Romeo and Juliet*, made another record in the early spring. A
National Theater was endowed and launched. John Drew celebrated his fiftieth year on the stage, and Sara Bernhardt died.
Americans fearful of dangerous Russian influences were yet not
afraid to patronize the popular *Chauve Souris* of Balieff.

It was a fair question whether the Americans or the English
owned Shakespeare; but on both sides of the Atlantic in this spring
the three hundredth anniversary of the publication of the first
folio edition of his plays was celebrated. Of the five hundred copies
which Isaac Jaggard printed in 1623 at a pound apiece, the ownership of some two hundred could still be traced. More of these were
passing into the hands of rich Americans after every sale at Southe-
by's. Dr. Rosenbach had recently paid eight thousand pounds for
one of them, which was later added to the huge collection of Henry
Clay Folger. Folger, with funds derived from Standard Oil, was
adding to his collection to be housed next to the Library of Congress as a national possession. Other collectors were gloating over
their shelves of precious imprints, and taking full advantage of
the estate taxes which compelled the English to dispose of family
libraries. Scholars' libraries, assembled on the Continent, were finding new homes on college shelves. Henry E. Huntington, magnate
in his own right, and husband of the widow of his more famous
uncle Collis P. Huntington, was packing into his home near Pasadena unique imprints which were to attract students of literature
to California. Charles Lang Freer of Detroit had completed his
work, presenting his art collection to the nation, and a museum in
which to house it. Mellon, Secretary of the Treasury, was to follow
his example; and the Fields of Chicago had already shifted their
great museum of natural history to a new home on the improved
front along Lake Michigan.

The minor indexes to the content of the American mind and interest during this spring of relief from contentious politics suggest
that the relief was welcome and the people had been public-minded
long enough. Emile Coué, "the latest magician," arrived in New

York, to set off a chanting of his phrase "Every day in every way, I am growing better and better." He came in January, to lecture to believers and scoffers about his new cult of "auto suggestion," and to launch an institute bearing his name. Sir Arthur Conan Doyle came also, enriched by the popularity of *Sherlock Holmes,* but now interested only in proving that he had established contact with the spirit world. The psychic phenomena, which professional magicians challenged noisily, had become more important to him than the dangers of Bolshevism or the intricacies of international politics. Doyle had lifted the detective story to the level of literature of escape, and his followers were harvesting the field he had cultivated. One of them, Mary Roberts Rinehart, had advanced from *The Circular Staircase* and *The Bat* to a business so profitable that she took a charter from the state of Delaware and became a corporation. Simon and Schuster were on the verge of sharpening American wits with the first of their crossword puzzle books, and thereby promoting a craze which, by 1925, had "conquered the world." The style book *Vogue* published its thirtieth anniversary number at the beginning of 1923, chronicling its transition from the "Age of Innocence" to the sophistication of "This Freedom"; and a handful of audacious writers chose the first of March as the auspicious moment to bring out a new kind of news weekly called *Time* in which they took liberties with the English language. Only a little slower were the editors whose *New Yorker* (1925) was to cater to sophisticates.

"Not nostrums but normalcy," the single contribution of Warren Gamaliel Harding to American phraseology, was directed to a generation wearied and annoyed by the inconveniences owing to war. The weariness was the greater because it came at the end of a long decade of argument on the fundamental structure and objective of American government. No good cause which all support is important in democratic politics. But any good cause, the attainment of which means frustration to an existing interest, to a region, or to a group, must be paid for by sacrifice and accomplished by majority coercion or by compromise. In the human balance, the accumulated resentments of overridden minorities may acquire a vigor sufficient to overcome the lethargy of satisfied majorities, yet may lack a pattern for procedure upon any common course. Harding

spoke as a candidate in 1920 against his background of conservative
Republicanism. His party had taken advantage of all the dissatis-
factions which were in the air. The normalcy of which the candidate had dreamed was an intangible, not to be reduced to a blue-
print. The real normalcy was the condition of democracy in time
of peace when neither driving fear nor inspiring hope exists to
force into the background for the moment the interest or the region or the group desire. A lumbering vehicle in comparison with
authoritarian government, democracy is at its worst in the periods
when all that may be hoped for is a compromise among the interests, not good enough to solve a problem or bad enough to stir up
resentments able to destroy the peace. Even at its worst, it pre-
serves for its people the power to control their machinery of government and to order their own lives. At its best, on the rare occasions when some emotion brings the mass of the people into united
action behind government leadership it can be made to deliver such
power as was released in 1917–1918.

It was the misfortune of Harding to preside over a period of letdown and fatigue, and to have won his place in a campaign in which
necessary party strategy was to avoid giving displeasure to any of
the voting groups which, for whatever reason, would welcome the
defeat of the party of Woodrow Wilson. His leadership as a candidate was as good as those who named him had a right to expect
from him; but it was evasive of realities, balancing approval of this
with avoidance of that. In his offices at Marion he had to listen to
extremists on both sides of nearly every theme in which the voter
had an interest. When he was advanced to the White House he
found himself in a sphere for which his past had not prepared him,
and in which with normalcy around him no leader could have
carried policy to fruition. He performed the duties of his office with
what strength he had, functioning not on the bayonets of armed
forces but on the spearheads of pressure groups competing for advantage through the democratic process.

As he worked upon the itinerary of his western trip, he picked
out many of the centers of uneasiness, to challenge in their own
home towns some of the party leaders who had harassed him, to
talk to their constituents and probe their minds. He need not tour
the North and East, where any candidate of his party was almost

certain to command support. He need not tour the South, where only a dreaming politician would interpret cordiality to a Republican visitor as having meaning on election day. It was futile to tour the granger West, where La Follette was the prophet, and where in Minnesota a special election was to be under way to send to the Senate a successor to Knute Nelson, whose death occurred while the itinerary was in the making.

Minnesota had sent Nelson to Washington five times, and there he had taken high rank among Republican regulars. Only in his fifth term did the newly militant Farmer-Labor movement turn his colleague Kellogg out as his associate, to replace him with a younger colleague, Henrik Shipstead. The junior senator-elect, like Nelson, was of Scandinavian ancestry; but by contrast he was a rebel against Republican party rule. "Wheat is possessed of a devil, an anti-Republican devil," said the New York *Times,* as agrarian liberals headed into Minnesota to campaign for a second Farmer-Labor Senator in the person of Magnus Johnson, and to help the voters bring the state into their party line. La Follette crossed the border from Wisconsin, Brookhart came up from Iowa, Frazier invaded from North Dakota. Burton K. Wheeler, Democrat though he was, came in from Montana to make trouble for Republicans. And as Harding reached the end of his trail, to drive a symbolic last spike in the new Alaska railroad to Fairbanks, he learned the bad news that Magnus Johnson was senator-elect.

Death struck again, close to the White House group, before it was time for the presidential special train to start west. This time it was a hanger-on of Daugherty who was found, an apparent suicide, in the latter's hotel apartment on the morning of Memorial Day. Jesse [Jess] W. Smith had been something of a mystery since he came to Washington with the Ohio group. He had no official position, yet managed to enjoy office space near his patron in the Department of Justice. He made use of government cars, circulated on the fringes of public life, and had money of unknown origin to spend. A reputed "fixer" serving those who sought to evade prohibition enforcement, his status was suspected before he died, and was made to become more suspect in later months when the affairs of Daugherty were trailed through the courts. Loose mouths in the Senate were to say that he had been murdered because he knew too much, and that he had been extorting campaign funds from bootleggers. His former wife believed him a suicide, driven to it because Daugherty had found him a burden and turned him off. Gaston B. Means, private detective, convicted conspirator, and admitted liar, was to smear charge and truth in a hopeless mixture when his "ghost writer" brought out his *Strange Death of President Harding* (1930). Whatever Jess Smith was, he had been accepted as an intimate by many who were responsible for the integrity of the administration; and what those whose intimacy he abused may have known about him was not to be revealed. On the night that he died in Daugherty's apartment, the owner of the residence was sleeping at the White House.

With two dozen correspondents and camera men in the press cars, the presidential train pulled out of the Union Station on the afternoon of June 20, 1923. The party was official rather than recreational. General Sawyer was included as friend and physician. Cabinet members joined and left as need and business dictated. Lesser officials, friendly or not, attached themselves for short distances for the glory to be derived from association; and Harding welcomed them, for he had no hates. In the manuscript of his first speech, to be delivered in St. Louis, he had explained his trip: "I shall not attempt to coerce the Senate of the United States. I shall make no demand upon the people. I shall not try to impose my will on any body or anybody. I shall not embark upon a crusade." The Syracuse *Post-Standard* sent him off with commendation, saying he "has grown as any Senator, sincere and honest, would grow when endowed with greater responsibilities and duties."

Many of the nineteen set speeches called for by the itinerary were already in type for transmission by mail, ahead of their delivery. Wilson had lost some of his needed publicity in 1919 because his speeches were not always available for the press in time for printing while they were still news. Harding, trained to easy composition by his years in journalism, was a fluent writer. The newsmen said he had prepared himself with the facts behind the speeches by long hours with books in the White House. His secretarial car carried the stenographers, and his personal assistant, Judson C. Welliver. Welliver had managed publicity at Marion during the campaign, had gone into the White House with his chief, and was suspected of writing many of the words that Harding spoke. It was not the first time that a president had assistance in the drafting of his public utterances, nor was it to be the last. But if Welliver arranged the words it was not because Harding was incapable of doing it for himself.

Some one, at least, had failed to do the historical spadework in connection with one of the minor addresses of the trip, a speech to be delivered in Oregon in celebration of the eightieth anniversary of the arrival there of the first train in the migration of the covered wagons. The printed text arrived in Portland well ahead of the special train, and those who read it discovered that its draftsman had failed to know what research had done to the legendary history of the state, and had incorporated heroic doings for Dr. Marcus Whitman which not even Oregonians accepted any longer as having been performed. Warnings were wired to the President, but in vain. When he took the platform on July 3 he drew out the unfortunate speech, admitted with engaging frankness that he had been told of its defects, and read it because it was the speech he had with him. It was a good speech, whoever wrote it, right or wrong.

The texts which Harding had prepared or had had prepared, however, were in substance his. They lacked the careful balancing for the sake of votes which characterized his campaign utterances— and, indeed, the speeches of Hughes in 1916. They reveal, instead, what the office had done to its incumbent in teaching him the problems ahead of the United States, and a program such as a well-intentioned man believed might steer its way through the conflict of interests, regions, and groups which made up normalcy. He avowed that he was not embarking upon a crusade, but he chose to urge American membership in the World Court in the very center of the opposition to it.

Twice he spoke formally in Missouri, where Republican leaders were openly against the World Court and where James A. Reed was bitter about it. The Court, separated from the League of Nations and made self-perpetuating, was Harding's theme in St. Louis. In Kansas City, where the railroad interests were in arms against a regional regrouping of the railway systems, he chose to defend the regrouping and at the same time to challenge the demand of railroad labor for government ownership.

Advancing westward into the grain country, he had selected
Hutchinson, Kansas, for a speech to farmers on the world causes
of agricultural depression and on what the tariff and the intermediate credit banks would do to relieve it. Capper of the farm
bloc was there, and the farmer audience on the state fair grounds
was courteous if not convinced. The President was already showing
traces of the strain of travel. A long drive around Kansas City in
the summer sun had blistered his lips so that it was hard to speak;
yet outside Hutchinson he took the controls on a farm tractor to
pull a harvester around a wheat field, and descended to help shock
the wheat. He spoke briefly from his rear platform on Sunday at
Colorado Springs, rested in Denver during the afternoon, and on
Monday told a Denver audience that the Eighteenth Amendment
would never be repealed and that prohibition must be enforced.
Those who listened to him, or read the speech, noted its challenge
without names directed at Governor Smith of New York, who had
recently signed the Curvillier bill repealing the prohibition act of
his state and leaving the government of the United States to do its
own enforcing. He had words to say on coal as he passed through
Cheyenne, and a repudiation of government operation of the
mines. At Salt Lake City, the next day, he spoke in the Tabernacle
on taxation and government costs, and could have pride, as the
fiscal year came to its end, in the fact that for the first time since
the war the Treasury was substantially out of the red.

Without words, he effectively touched western interest by taking
time to visit Zion National Park in Utah and to pass the next Sunday in the Yellowstone National Park. The reorganization of the
public playgrounds under the law of 1916 and the capable administration of Stephen T. Mather as director of the service, were working the casual monuments into a coherent system. A park-to-park
highway was on the maps, at least, as a guide to tourists.

Borah joined the train when it passed through Idaho, although
he had hurried to St. Louis ahead of the President to combat in
advance the World Court speech. He was almost ready to believe
that with the reservations stated by the President the Court would
be safe enough to join. The speech at Helena was for union labor
and against Bolshevism; and again for the Court. In Butte it was
on the revival of business. Before Harding reached Portland on

July 4 he had driven an electric locomotive down the Bitter Root grade, defended a policy of conservation through use at Spokane, and been made an honorary Cayuse Indian in connection with the pioneer celebration at Meacham, Oregon. He advocated restriction of immigration at Portland, announced at Tacoma that the steelmen had accepted his urging to do away with the twelve-hour day in their mills, and steamed into the Pacific on the navy transport *Henderson* for the Alaska leg of his trip. It was beyond his power, or that of any of his party, to tell with accuracy what he had accomplished. The audiences manifestly liked him, but, said the newsmen, they were not much interested in politics.

The Alaskan jaunt filled three weeks until the party, travel-worn and Mrs. Harding nearly exhausted, was back at Vancouver, B.C., for a reception on Canadian soil. Here peace and the undefended frontier was his theme; and here the papers brought news that Hiram Johnson, home from his vacation in Europe, had again opened fire on the World Court at a New York dinner given him by supporters of the old Bull Moose campaign. Harding had ahead of him only the three important addresses at Seattle, San Francisco, and Los Angeles, and a leisurely voyage through the Panama Canal. He settled down to the final revision of his addresses, for he was carrying his fight into the state of Johnson and the hall in San Francisco where Cox and Roosevelt had been nominated in 1920.

The President reviewed the Pacific fleet in Puget Sound, spoke at Seattle on the ultimate statehood of Alaska and on the need for a navy of first rank until such time as the world should be ready to disarm. On the night of July 27 he rejoined the special train, a sick man. From Grant's Pass on the next morning as the train rolled south, it was wired that he had a touch of ptomaine poisoning, attributed to "slightly tainted crab meat" served him on the *Henderson*. When they arrived in San Francisco on Sunday morning— the train was taken around the lower bay to avoid the crossing on the ferry—Harding was able to walk from his car to the automobile, but Sawyer put him to bed at once in the suite at the top of the Palace Hotel and called in the doctors. Ray L. Wilbur, distinguished in medicine before he became president of Stanford University, was among the consultants; Work, doctor as well as Secretary of the Interior, was with them; there was the navy doctor,

Boone, and also Cooper, called in as diagnostician. Their calm
bulletins were convincing that the condition of the invalid was not
serious, but that the rest of the trip must be canceled. After recuperation in San Francisco the President must return to the White
House. The World Court speech which he had prepared for July
31 was released to the press. And in the early evening of August 2
the President died. He died, without warning, as his wife was reading to him from the *Saturday Evening Post* an article on himself
by Samuel G. Blythe: "A Calm View of a Calm Man." A blood clot
had followed the pneumonia which had followed his collapse.

"Warren Gamaliel Harding—Gentleman," was the summary by
John Sharp Williams, and William Jennings Bryan was moved to
say that he "left a name that will never die." The words of the
party of the President and the estimates in the editorials upon his
death, are bewildering in their contrast to the picture of the man
and his administration of normalcy which gained currency during
the eight more years of Republican ascendancy and the dozen
Democratic years which followed. The "tragedy of the life of Warren Harding," as Hoover put it when in 1931 he dedicated the
Harding memorial at Marion, was more than the personal tragedy
of a man who was badly cast in the part he had to play. It was the
tragedy of all Americans and their political habits in the elevation
of leaders. It was the tragedy of the party system, for the death of
Harding made him a safe scapegoat for his party fellows and a safe
target for opponents. It was a tragedy because his years revealed
democracy in its least effective moment. He had arisen above himself before he died. His successors profited from his defects. His people, in their next chapter, were to work at the problems within the
frame which he had constructed on his "voyage of understanding."

Index

Abbott, Lyman, 162
Actor's Equity Association, 95
Adamson law, 93
Addams, Jane, 334
Agriculture: wartime gains, 101; technological changes, 101-102; farmer movements, 102, 103; education, 102; county agents, 103; National Farm Bureau Federation, 103; a business, 165; 1920 collapse, 189-190, 211-220, 360; emergency tariff, 189, 191, 219-220; Young proposal, 220-221; dumping, 221; Norris' efforts for relief, 253; Haugen bill, 255; agricultural conference, 267-268; farmer dissatisfaction, 277; Farm Loan banks, 359-360
Alcock, John, 81, 82
Aldrich, Nelson W., 190
Alien Property Custodian, 223, 301-302
Allen, Henry T., 6, 212, 367
American Defense Society, 26
American Federation of Labor, 25, 89, 94, 98-100 *passim*, 263, 277-278
American Legion, 91, 140, 182, 188, 288 ff., 305, 308; *Weekly*, 229
Anglo-Japanese alliance, 184, 233, 240, 242
Antilynching bill, Dyer, 285, 324, 349, 353-354, 357
Armistice, 1, 2, 6; "false," 2; signed, 9; continuation of, agreement, 14
Army: demobilized, 3-4, 6, 19, 22, 23, 139; camps, 7; Motor Transport Corps, 78-79; Air Service, 79; National Guard or federal reserve? 141-142; 1919–1920 appropriation, 141; reorganization act, 141
Arnold, Henry H. (Happy), 80
Austria: signs at St. Germain, 15; admitted to conference, 109; broken up, 109
Aviation, 79-84, 344; airmail, 83

Baker, Ray Stannard, 16, 17, 54
Baker, Newton D., 78, 84
Baldwin, Stanley, 363
Balfour, Arthur James: pledges English support to Palestine, 60; war debts, 212, 297; Washington Conference, 237, 240
Bankhead, William Brockman, 352-353
Barkley, Alben, 230
Baruch, Bernard, 24, 44-45, 88, 111
Benson, William S., 8
Berger, Victor L., 28, 90, 91, 106
Berkman, Alexander, 91
Berlin treaty, 9
Beveridge, Albert J., 36, 107, 272, 312
Bolshevism: revolution, 21; propaganda in southern Europe, 30; Third International, 30; Judiciary Committee to investigate, 30; political structures to ward off, 56; secret agreements exposed, 60; "red scare," 88
Bonus: Hearst papers campaign for, 92; insistence upon, 228-229; Senate bill, 229; Harding demands postponement, 229, 233, 292, 304-305; threat to budget, 229, 292, 305; House approves, 292, 304; support for, 304-305; bill to Senate, 306, to White House, 307; Harding vetoes, 307-308, 373; passes over Coolidge's veto, 308
Borah, William E.: declines Wilson's invitation, 41, 48; attacks Covenant, 43, 49; questions Hitchcock on Ireland, 48; demands draft of Covenant, 108; conference with Lodge on Treaty, 110-111; investigation of campaign funds, 154; proposes naval holiday, 185, 234, 235; votes against Taft Court appointment, 199; on Irish vote, 216; Nine-Power Treaty, 249; votes against Newberry,

Ugr
D
619
P42
1966
v.3

DATE DUE

T-groups: A survey of research

T-groups
A survey of research

Edited by

C. L. Cooper
Department of Psychology,
The University, Southampton

I. L. Mangham
Department of Management Studies,
The University, Leeds

WILEY–INTERSCIENCE
a division of John Wiley & Sons Ltd.
LONDON NEW YORK SYDNEY TORONTO

Library of Congress catalog card number 79-146549

ISBN 0 471 17122 5

Printed in Great Britain by Adlard & Son Ltd.
Bartholomew Press, Dorking, Surrey

Preface

What is a T-group?

The training or T-group is an approach to human relation training which, broadly speaking, provides participants with an opportunity to learn more about themselves and their impact on others and, in particular, to learn how to function more effectively in face-to-face situations. It attempts to facilitate this learning by bringing together a small group of people for the express purpose of studying their own behaviour as it occurs when they interact within a small group. There are certain features that distinguish this type of group from a conventional group discussion. Tannenbaum, Weschler and Massarik (1961) have outlined the main distinctions. First, the training is primarily 'process-oriented' rather than 'content-oriented'. That is, the primary stress is on the feeling level of communications rather than on the informational or conceptual level. This emphasis is accomplished by focusing on the here-and-now behaviour and themes in the group. Second, the training is not structured in a conventional manner. Opportunities are provided for the individuals to decide what they want to talk about, what kinds of problems they wish to deal with, and what means they want to use in reaching their goals. No one tells them what they ought to talk about. As they concern themselves with the problems caused by this lack of direction, they begin to act in characteristic ways: some people remain silent, some are aggressive, some tend consistently to initiate discussions, and some attempt to structure the proceedings. With the aid of the staff member, these approaches or developments become the focal points for discussion and analysis. The staff member, or trainer, draws attention to events and behaviour in the group by occasional interventions in the form of tentative interpretations which he considers will provide useful data for study. Third, the heart of a T-group laboratory is found in small groups, allowing a high level of participation, involvement and free communication. Intense involvement with the group is an essential feature of T-group programmes, in contrast to other methods. On the face of it this involvement should be of advantage in producing lasting changes in the attitudes and behaviour of participants. It is certainly true that most studies report few attitudinal changes for participants who show *low* involvement in training activities.

It is exceedingly difficult to arrive at an exact figure, but it is probably no exaggeration to claim that thousands of managers, administrators, social workers, teachers and university students in North America, Western Europe, and the Far East now have direct experience of T-group training. As this technique of human relations training grows in popularity so it tends to attract more and more suspicion and some outright hostility. One significant factor is that the detractors rarely include ex-participants; indeed some of the ex-participants become, in Massarik's (1965) phrase, the 'overly zealous proponents' of the method. As Greening (1964) has pointed out, it is inevitable and appropriate that people should have emotions and values about this kind of training, but these feelings—for or against—are not in themselves an adequate basis for an evaluation of the method. Whilst not denying the importance of the long-overdue consideration of the ethical aspects (Lakin, 1969) of this type of training, this book proceeds from the position that human relations laboratory training exists, that managers volunteer or are sent on such courses, and that the experience has measurable consequences. It is this aspect, and not the propriety of T-groups, that we wish to review and evaluate.

C. L. COOPER
I. L. MANGHAM

References

Greening, T. C. (1964) 'Sensitivity training: cult or contribution.' *Personnel*, **41** (3), 18–25.

Lakin, M. (1969) 'Some ethical issues in sensitivity training.' *American Psychologist*, **24**, 923–928.

Massarik, F. (1965) 'Some first (and second) thoughts on the evaluation of sensitivity training: A sensitivity training impact model.' Washington, D.C.: National Training Laboratory.

Tannenbaum, R., I. R. Weschler and R. Massarik (1961) *Leadership and Organization*. New York: McGraw-Hill.

Acknowledgements

The value of this book was greatly enhanced by the advice and comments of Dorothy Stock Whitaker, Peter B. Smith, Fred Massarik, Stephen Fink, Vernon L. Allen and Galfrid Congreve.

We would also like to thank our indexer, Diana Marshallsay, and our secretary and typist, Margaret Freeman.

Acknowledgements are also due to the following authors and publishers for permission to reprint articles in this book:

Culbert, S. A. (1968) 'Trainer Self-Disclosure and Member Growth in Two T-groups'. *Journal of Applied Behavioral Science*, 4, 47–73.

Friedlander, F. (1967) 'The Impact of Organisational Training Laboratories upon the Effectiveness and Interaction of Ongoing Work Groups'. *Personnel Psychology*, 20, 289–309.

Friedlander, F. 'The Primary of Trust as a Facilitator of Further Group Accomplishment'. To appear in the *Journal of Applied Behavioral Science*.

Gassner, S., J. Gold and A. M. Snadowsky (1964) 'Changes in the Phenomenal Field as a Result of Human Relations Training'. *Journal of Psychology*, 58, 33–41.

Harrison, R. and B. Lubin (1965) 'Personal Style, Group Composition and Learning'. *Journal of Applied Behavioral Science*, 1, 286–301.

Lubin, B. and M. Zuckerman (1967) 'Affective and Perceptual Cognitive Patterns in Sensitivity Training Groups'. *Psychological Reports*, 21, 365–376.

Lubin, B. and M. Zuckerman (1969) 'Level of Emotional Arousal in Laboratory Training'. *Journal of Applied Behavioral Science*, 5, 483–490.

Mann, R. D. (1968) 'The Development of the Member-Trainer Relationship in Self-analytic Groups'. *Human Relations*, 19, 84–117.

Rubin, I. (1967) 'The Reduction of Prejudice through Laboratory Training'. *Journal of Applied Behavioral Science*, 3, 29–50.

Smith, P. B. (1964) 'Attitude Changes Associated with Training in Human Relations'. *British Journal of Social and Clinical Psychology*, 3, 104–113.

Steele, F. I. (1968) 'Personality and the "Laboratory Style"'. *Journal of Applied Behavioral Science*, 4, 25–46.

Valiquet, M. I. (1968) 'Individual Change in a Management Development Programme'. *Journal of Applied Behavioral Science*, 4, 313–325.

The authors would also like to extend their appreciation to the editors and publishers of the *Journal of Management Studies* and the *Training and Development Journal* for providing them with permission to reprint articles previously published in their journals.

Contents

Introduction

The problems of research

Questions asked about the consequences of T-group training have been numerous and few have been answered clearly and unequivocally. They range from the philosophical and ethical—is it right to interfere with people's psyches (essentially incapable of an empiric response)—to the pragmatic but highly important, is training transferable. There are also the questions about the dynamics of the process itself. How does the group develop? What relationships are critical to this development? How important are factors such as trainer behaviour, length of training, composition of the group, trust, feedback?

The questions, other than the ethical ones, can be placed in two categories (Lakin, 1969); those concerned with basic or pure research and those concerned with applied research. This distinction, we submit, applies not so much to the *manner* of the research as to its *purpose* (Suchman, 1967). There can be little doubt as the following chapters will testify, that the more one can satisfy the rules of scientific method in designing and carrying out a piece of applied or evaluative research, the more confidence that can be placed on the objectivity of the findings. The manner, therefore, is, hopefully, similar but the desired outcomes are often different. The primary objective of basic research, in answering a question such as 'what is the nature of sub-group formation in sensitivity training groups', is the discovery of knowledge, the proof or disproof of a hypothesis. It is essentially hypothesis-oriented, no action *need* follow. Therefore, the major criterion of the 'success' of research into questions at the basic end of the research continuum is, as Campbell and Dunnette (1968) suggest, whether or not the findings are *scientifically* valid.

Where they are on less sure ground is when they argue that the research into questions at the applied end of the continuum should reach the disarmingly simple standards 'necessary for scientifically evaluating training'. The primary objective of research into applied questions—does the training transfer, what are the outcomes—is to determine the effectiveness of certain procedures. Here the 'success' of the research is judged by its usefulness to the trainer in improving his techniques or to the manager in implementing his organizational development programme. No doubt in these circumstances scientific criteria will still determine the degree of confidence one may place in the findings of a piece of research, but administrative considerations—will the research affect the training programme, can we arrange control groups, do we have the time and facilities for pre and post-measures—will play a very large role in the way the study is conducted.

Obviously, the distinction is not one of black and white. Much research is a mixture of basic and applied types but it is a distinction which can be useful in looking at research in T-group training since it does help to illuminate some of the difficulties encountered by researchers.

Basic research, for example, in order to satisfy scientific procedures may make excessive demands on participants and trainers and, in so far as it makes these demands, can be detrimental to the overall impact of the training. Occasionally basic researchers adopt a manipulative, exploitative approach which runs counter to the philosophy of T-group training. Frequently the design of the basic research requires that information be withheld from the training staff and the participants to prevent 'contamination of the results'. This approach is unlikely to receive much support or encouragement. Basic research also can be seen as adopting a neutral, high-distance stance *vis-à-vis* the 'subject' and this too runs counter to the values intrinsic to T-group training.

Ideally, as we have mentioned earlier, the manner of research into T-groups should meet the conditions necessary for the establishment of scientific confidence. Depending upon the specific nature of the investigation this would mean: (1) measures taken before, during and after the training; (2) measures and observations to include not only attitudes and perceptions but also *behaviour* of subjects; (3) matching of experimental with control groups and (4) control of the interactional effects of measures and behaviour (Campbell and Dunnette, 1968).

The ideal flow chart for a piece of research into T-groups would be similar to that appropriate for any experimental design. Since at this stage the problems of basic and applied research are similar we can illustrate by reference to the latter alone. The flow chart for evaluating a T-group training programme would look as below.*

Such a flow chart would illustrate optimum principles and sequences to be followed in conducting a valid experimental design to evaluate a training programme.

In T-groups the ideal has rarely been achieved. Virtually each and every step outlined in the flow diagram brings problems. Let us walk a piece of research through in order to understand the problems better.

* Adapted with permission from Greenberg, B. G. and B. F. Mattison (1965) The Ways and Wherefores of Programme Evaluation, *Canadian Journal of Public Health* **46**, p. 298.

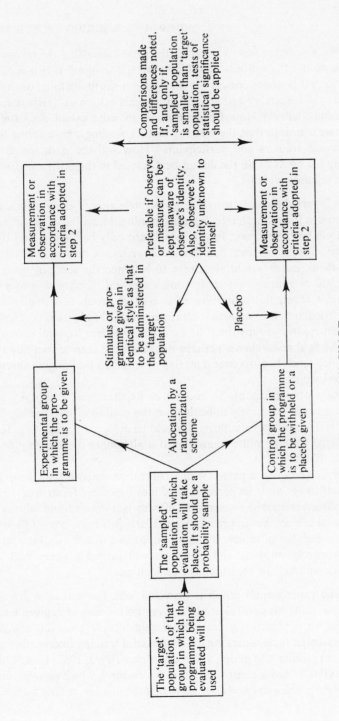

FLOW CHART

The 'target' population of that group in which the programme being evaluated will be used

The 'sampled' population in which evaluation will take place. It should be a probability sample

Allocation by a randomization scheme

Experimental group in which the pro- gramme is to be given

Control group in which the programme is to be withheld or a placebo given

Stimulus or pro- gramme given in identical style as that to be administered in the 'target' population

Placebo

Preferable if observer or measurer can be kept unaware of observee's identity. Also, observee's identity unknown to himself

Measurement or observation in accordance with criteria adopted in step 2

Measurement or observation in accordance with criteria adopted in step 2

Comparisons made and differences noted. If, and only if, 'sampled' population is smaller than 'target' population, tests of statistical significance should be applied

Step 1: The researcher has to persuade the practitioner that the research is (a) worth doing, (b) will not 'interfere' with the training. If it is basic or pure research this step is critical—is the research worth anything to anyone other than the researcher and the rather abstract notion of 'furtherance of scientific knowledge'? How frequently and to what extent does the researcher want to interrupt the training to take readings, have forms filled out, interview trainers and participants? How will the participants feel about being subjects? Can the design be disclosed to them without jeopardizing its scientific validity?

Step 2: It is very difficult to provide rigorous selection of experimental and control groups for research into T-group training. Matching of participants and controls on the relevant factors would not only be difficult and time-consuming, assuming that one knew the relevant factors and could measure them, but it would also serve to heighten the sense of being an experimental or control subject. In some cases, e.g., the training of a top management team, the possibility of a control group is virtually non-existent. Friedlander, in an article reprinted in this book, used *comparison* rather than *control* groups since, as he notes, the term 'control group' as used by the field researcher is perhaps nothing more than 'a soothing misnomer which tends to gloss over a myriad of variables that might otherwise be quite relevant'.

Allocation of participants to control or experimental groups by randomization is also extremely difficult since the essence of the training may be that it is undertaken voluntarily. It could be achieved if some were to be given delayed training rather than denied it altogether or given a placebo (Massarik, 1965).

Further, the fact that a person is in a control or experimental group can bias his self-image and the perception of him by others (Harrison, 1967). Ideally, observers should be unaware of who is a control and who is an experimental subject, but in practice particularly in a back-home follow-up study such elegance of design is almost impossible to achieve. Interaction between controls, subjects and observers will probably occur and will certainly compound the measurement difficulties.

Step 3: The experimental group is provided with the particular training programme whilst the control group is given no training or is given a substitute. The use of placebos is clearly extremely difficult; since it is not clear what the essential factors making for a successful training intervention are. Thus it is very difficult to design a non-experience (Byrd, 1967; Fink, 1969). Dunnette (1969) used a control group in his research which *merely played games, solved puzzles and problems, discussed the weather or local and world*

affairs, and 'diligently' avoided any discussion related to interpersonal factors.
In terms of basic research no doubt such a design was practicable, in terms
of applied or evaluative research the payoff may not be worth the costs of
enforced estrangement over a period of days.

Step 4: The measurement or observation stages also give rise to problems.
If participants are asked to respond to questions about their behaviour in
groups, they may be alerted to work towards the 'correct answers' and to
complete the later measures not on the basis of actual changes but on the
basis of what they perceive to be desirable changes. To combat this the
researcher seeks to reduce response set, to phase out normative questions,
and, possibly, to be obscure about his intentions. Both researcher and
participant can end up playing mutually inauthentic roles and, in so far as
this happens, the 'scientific' results are sceptical. Research in other fields
(i.e. experimental psychology), whereby the subjects seek to guess and then
to satisfy the intuitions of the researcher, are not uncommon.

The way around such a problem is to be authentic in the researcher-
subject relationship and to explain intentions and research design. Such
directness, of course, raises the spectre of 'contamination of results' and one
is back to square one: what is the purpose of the research and for whom is it
intended? If it is to further scientific knowledge and essentially for the consumption of fellow-researchers, then our measures must be stringent and
rigorous and must not influence the training outcomes. If it is to help design
better programmes and is for general consumption then we might even
design the instruments so that they can influence the training even whilst
we are evaluating it. In fact, this may be the only course open to researchers
in T-groups since there is a potential conflict in using measures that can be
perceived as mechanistic in a situation which is designed to provide an
organic and spontaneous experience.

Measures taken well after the experience create further problems. In
following-up transfer of training, for example, we cannot realistically link
training and outcomes in a simple causal chain. Administrative changes,
promotion, salary overhead, new responsibilities, delegation, may have
brought about much greater changes even on such factors as 'use of
conflict', 'relational facility', 'listening' than has T-group training
(Mangham and Cooper, 1969).

Purpose and organization of the book

The research presented in the following chapters is both basic and
applied. Wherever possible we have sought to include work which has
adopted a scientific manner even where it has not been primarily under-

taken for a scientific purpose. Much of the work presented falls into the grey area between basic and applied research; we hope, however, that it will not be summarily dismissed as unsound and unscientific. We had two purposes in mind in writing this book; (1) to provide the practitioner with a compendium of the empirical literature into the effects and dynamics of T-groups in order that he may be in possession of information necessary in making practical decisions associated with organizing and the conduct of T-group training; and (2) to provide the researcher with an up-to-date account of T-group research, which we hope will clarify the present state of such research and enable him to decide on what should constitute the research focus in the future. This latter objective stems from the fact that there are so many instruments, criteria, and approaches used in T-group research (of all kinds) that it appears that there must be a lack of agreement about what constitutes the research focus.

In an effort to meet these objectives the book has been organized in the following manner. First, in terms of format, each chapter contains a brief review of all the empirical literature in a particular area and is then followed by one or two research articles printed in their entirety. The articles have been selected, wherever possible, on the basis of the following criteria: the use of adequate control groups; when assessing change, measures taken before and after training; minimum variability in the training experience between groups; adequate sample size—all in all, research judged by the authors and fellow-colleagues to be a major contribution to the development of a particular area of T-group research. By including the research article in full, we hope to provide the researcher with the latest and most methodologically sound models of research design in each of the mainline areas of T-group research as well as providing the practitioner a 'look-in' at the kind of methodology employed in these areas.

Second, in terms of chronology, we start by reviewing the literature, in Chapters 1 to 3, which evaluate the effectiveness of the T-group. For if, as Bunker (1965) has pointed out, lasting and effective attitude and behaviour change cannot be demonstrated, the remaining issues such as the impact of the trainer or the effect of different group compositions on learning, would be superfluous. Then, in Chapters 4 to 6, we attempt to review the studies concerned with the *process* or dynamics of the group, concentrating on the trainer behaviour, group composition, and intra-group dynamics (i.e. trust, feedback, etc.). In Chapter 7, we attempt to follow the fate of the group by reviewing the studies concerned with assessing the course of development of the T-group.

References

Bunker, D. R. (1965) 'Individual applications of laboratory training.' *Journal of Applied Behavioral Science*, 1, 131–148.

Byrd, R. E. (1967) 'Training in a non-group.' *Journal of Humanistic Psychology*, 7, 18–27.

Dunnette, M. D. (1969) 'People feeling: joy, more joy, and the "slough of despond".' *Journal of Applied Behavioral Science*, 5, 25–44.

Campbell, J. P. and M. D. Dunnette (1968) 'Effectiveness of T-group experiences in managerial training and development.' *Psychological Bulletin*, 70, 73–104.

Fink, S. (1969) 'The non-design of a laboratory.' *Human Relations Training News*, 13.

Harrison, R. (1967) 'Problems in the design and interpretation of research on human relations training.' In *Explorations in Human Relations Training and Research*. National Training Laboratories, Number 1.

Lakin, M. (1969) 'Some ethical issues in sensitivity training.' *American Psychologist*, 24, 923–928.

Mangham, I. L. and C. L. Cooper (1969) 'The impact of T-groups on managerial behaviour.' *Journal of Management Studies*, 6, 53–72.

Massarik, F. (1965) 'Some first (and second) thoughts on the evaluation of sensitivity training: A sensitivity training impact model.' Washington, D.C.: National Training Laboratory.

Stock, D. (1964) 'A survey of research on T-groups.' In L. P., Bradford, J. R. Gibb, and K. D. Benne, (Eds), *T-Group Theory and Laboratory Method*. New York: John Wiley.

Suchman, E. A. (1967) *Evaluative Research Principles and Practice in Public Service and Social Action Programmes*. Russell Sage Foundation.

CHAPTER 1

The Effectiveness of T-groups in Producing On-the-Job Change*

The crucial problem in assessing the after-effects of T-group training is in the selection of the measures of change. The kinds of behavioural change that the method is designed to produce—increased job effectiveness, inter-personal competence—are not simple, unidimensional changes, and there are no easy criteria for their measurement. The investigator is usually forced to rely on evaluations made by observers—the trainee himself, his work associates or someone brought in specifically for the purpose. Since each of the categories of observers is open to bias, many of the better studies have used procedures for checking the amount of agreement between different observers (Smith, 1969).

The earliest follow-up study was conducted by Miles (1965) and involved 34 American elementary school principals who had participated in a two-week T-group laboratory in 1958. He used two control groups of untrained principals for comparison, one randomly chosen and the other nominated by the trained principals. All were asked to describe, via an open-ended change-description questionnaire, the ways in which they had changed their job-centered behaviour over an eight to ten month period following the T-group. These self-reports were compared with similar descriptions completed by 6 to 8 of their work associates. 73 per cent of the T-group trained participants, in comparison to 29 and 17 per cent of the nominated and random control groups respectively, were reported to have changed ($p < 0.01$). Most of the changes reported referred to increases in sensitivity to others, egalitarian attitudes, skills of communication and leadership, and group task and maintenance skills. Miles' data show not only a statistically significant difference in change between the trained and the control groups,

* A condensed and revised version of a paper which was published by the authors in the *Journal of Management Studies*, **6**, 1969, 53–72.

1

which might be expected, but also a consistency in the kind and direction of change reported by work associates of the trained group.

In addition to the open-ended instrument which revealed the changes enumerated above, Miles employed two other measures; the Ohio State Leader Description Questionnaire (Stogdill and Coons, 1957) and the Group Participation Scale (Pepinsky, Siegal and Van Alta, 1952). In the case of these measures no significant behavioural changes which could be attributed to the laboratory experience were found. Miles notes in retrospect that the O.S.L.D. questionnaire in particular seems unsuitable for use as a change-measuring instrument, since each participant's score is derived by summating a number of his associates scores thus potentially distorting the total score through averaging effects. Nonetheless, the O.S.L.D. questionnaire has been demonstrated to be useful in measuring change in non T-group training situations (Fleishman, Harris and Burtt, 1955).

Miles also considered the organizational factors that could influence on-the-job changes. He collected organizational measures in the following areas:

(1) Security—as measured by length of tenure in present job.

(2) Power—as measured by the number of teachers in the participant's school.

(3) Autonomy—as measured by the length of time between required reports to immediate superiors.

(4) Perceived Adequacy of the Organization's Functioning—as measured by a Likert-type rating scale.

The results of these measures indicate that the majority of high changers during training who have high or moderate power and security at work also derive the most lasting benefit from the experience. Those who are seen to change little during the training and also are seen to have little power and little security derive less benefit on their return to work. The middle group— high short-run changers with low organizational power and security and low short-run changers with high power and security—show about a 50 per cent chance of net change on the job.

To further test the generality of Miles' findings, Bunker (1965) studied a sample of participants from six different training laboratories conducted by the National Training Laboratories during 1960 and 1961. His basic methodology followed Miles in that a matched-pair control group was obtained by participant nomination and open-ended behaviour-change descriptions were obtained from 6 to 8 coworkers and 'self' for each subject. Bunker used a total of 346 subjects, trained and controls. In addition, he developed and utilized an objective coding system, which was designed 'to increase scoring reliability in assessing the descriptive statements returned by the various raters and which also sought to provide an assessment of the components in each subject's total change score'.

Bunker found that 66·7 per cent of the T-group trained participants as compared with 33·3 per cent of the matched-pair control group were reported by their work associates to have changed. As with the Miles' study, non-trained subjects were also perceived to have changed, in Bunker's case one-third of them were so reported. This is possibly attributable (1) to real change occasioned by events other than T-groups, which have no monopoly of the change market, or (2) to the fact that when respondents are asked to accommodate a researcher by providing change descriptions they hate to disappoint him and so tend to look for something to put down. As Bunker notes, vague and global descriptions occur with about equal frequency for both experimental and control describers and such 'please-the-researcher' responses are likely to be an important component of the base rate of change. Nonetheless, the agreements in the detailed descriptions of behaviour changes for the experimental subjects are significantly higher than for the control subjects and make it more credible that training effects are in fact being measured. The changes which were reported more often for the experimental subjects as compared with the matched controls were:

Receiving Communications: more effort to understand, attentive listening.

Relational Facility: cooperative, easier to deal with.

Awareness of Human Behaviour: more analytic of other's actions, clearer perception of people.

Sensitivity to Group Behaviour: more conscious of feelings of others, more sensitive to the reactions of others.

Sensitivity to Other's Feelings: sensitivity to the needs and feelings of others.

Acceptance of Other People: more tolerant, considerate, patient.

Tolerant of New Information: willing to accept suggestions, less dogmatic.

In addition, he found that 74 per cent of those in the upper-third of the distribution of total change scores were in the upper-third of the distribution of laboratory learning scores. Bunker concludes from this that back-home application of laboratory learning appears to be much less probable for those who do not become actively involved in the training process.

The only British study (Moscow, 1969) to use the verified change procedure, has shown that T-group participants drawn from management show changes very similar in type and frequency to those reported by Bunker.

Schutz and Allen (1966) report the results of a study of 71 participants in the 1959 Western Training Laboratory in Human Relations. The participants completed the FIRO-B questionnaire before and after the two-week laboratory and six months later. This questionnaire is composed of six Guttman scales of nine items each, which purports to measure an individual's 'expressed' behaviour and behaviour 'wanted from others' in the interpersonal areas of inclusion, control and affection. These participants also completed a series of open-ended questions asking for their perception of both positive and negative effects of the laboratory. FIRO-B was also given to a group of 30 college students at approximately equal intervals to serve as a control group for the effects of passage of time and the normal test re-test fluctuations. Schutz and Allen's hypothesis that the laboratory experience would change people selectively, depending upon their initial personality was supported. For example, they claimed that the overly dominant would become less dominant; the overly submissive would become more assertive; the overly affectionate tend to become more discriminating; and the reserved become more friendly. They note that if this ideal were to be achieved it would mean, quantitatively, that before and after scores would differ in an *unsystematic* fashion. Therefore, correlations between before and after scores for the laboratory participants and between after and follow-up scores should be significantly lower than corresponding correlations for control group subjects. This turned out to be the case, the overall correlations between administrations for all scales combined were much lower for the experimental group than for the control.

The qualitative material (gathered by the open-ended questionnaire), was subjected to an extensive content analysis using a technique of dichotomous decisions, developed by Schutz (1952). Overall, 83 per cent of all responses indicated favourable effects of the laboratory experience; 4 per cent indicated an unfavourable change and 13 per cent indicated no change at all. The primary effects are reported by the participants as follows (1) increased intellectual understanding of interpersonal, individual and group behaviour; and (2) increased personal effectiveness and competence as a person. A great many of the respondents felt that their insight and awareness about people had increased and many found specific applications to their back-home jobs. Participants also reported a decrease in personal feelings of tension, an increase in flexibility, honesty, confidence and acceptance in their relations with other people. Some reported no change and still others reported worsening of relations with others. However, the latter, in almost every case reported, felt the overall effect was positive even though the initial results were not rewarding.

Schutz and Allen note that the effects of the laboratory took time—some two to four months—to be evidenced. They also note that the majority of positive effects remain constant or increased with time though one-fifth of the effects faded. Participants attributed the changes primarily to the T-group itself. Virtually not one mentioned activities which they considered peripheral to the T-group, such as films and seminars of on-the-job application.

It is to be noted that this study is based entirely on self-report methods and that the control group which only numbered 30 was in no sense a matched-pair group. Participants were obviously older and differed occupationally from the control subjects and the initial FIRO-B scores differed between the groups, which may indicate the inappropriateness of a student control group. That the participants in the WTL laboratory apparently did not consider the seminars of on-the-job applications to be important is a strange finding and one which is not supported by the work of Bunker and Knowles (1967) who have made a comparison of behavioural changes resulting from laboratories of different lengths and containing different emphases.

They report a comparative study of enduring behaviour changes following human relations training laboratories of three weeks and two weeks duration. A behaviour change description questionnaire, similar to that described in the previous paragraph was used to elicit descriptions of a subject's post-laboratory behaviour changes as seen by the subject himself and seven of his coworkers. (This follows on the work of Lippitt (1949).) A matched control sample was obtained and assessed in the same manner.

Two inter-related measures of change were derived from the questionnaires: the 'total change score' composed of the total number of different changes mentioned by a subject and his coworkers; and the 'verified change score' composed of those behaviour changes which are mentioned by two or more persons in a set of descriptions. A set of seventeen inductively derived content categories were also used to make a qualitative analysis of the changes. The results show that while both laboratory trained samples differed from the control sample on both measures, they also differed significantly from each other. Both the perceived change score and the verified change score reveal more changes made by the three-week sample. The content analysis suggests that the three-week laboratory participants made more overt behavioural changes as opposed to the more passive attitudinal changes made by the two-week sample. Bunker and Knowles note however, that duration of training was not the only independent variable involved. From an analysis of the training activities they note that the three-week laboratory spent some twelve hours of programme time dealing with the application of training to the on-the-job situation, often with direct attention to an individual's specific problems whilst the two-week laboratory entirely excluded this activity. Therefore, the two-week programme was qualitatively different including a greatly reduced emphasis on the application of laboratory learnings to the participants ongoing organizational situations. The specific programme activities, therefore, concerned with the transfer of training appear to have fulfilled a particularly important training function, since the three-week trained participants not only showed more changes but also more active changes. The data presented in this study suggests that participation in specific back-home planning activities may help the trainees to cope with the organizational requisites for behaviour consistency. Bunker and Knowles conclude that if learning is to be transferred and integrated into the participants organizational relationships, a programme activity separate from the T-group and aimed directly at facilitating the application of learning to the on-the-job situation should be included in the overall design of the laboratory.

Valiquet (1968) randomly selected some sixty participants from T-group type programmes run within a company. Final results were available for 34 participants and 15 matched-pair control group subjects, each subject, control and experimental, nominating some five observers. Using Bunker's categories Valiquet discovered statistically significant differences between experimentals and controls on the total number of changes, both those reported by more than two independent observers and those reported by the subjects themselves. Furthermore Valiquet's study adds to Bunker's in that 'risk-taking' and 'function flexibility'—the ability to be an effective group member and to accept change—were shown to be higher for ex T-group participants. Valiquet concludes that these differences occurred because the programme reaped the rewards of in-company training, higher risk but greater pay-off in terms of on-the-job application.

The studies of Miles, Bunker and Schutz provides substantive evidence that changes do take place in perceived and rated behaviour on the job as a result of sensitivity training, but they provide no evidence of the difference between this kind of training and other training programmes. Boyd and Ellis (1962) have made an important contribution in this area by comparing the effects of T-group training with the effects of a more conventional programme of human relations training built around case discussion and lectures. Both forms of training lasted for two weeks and were part of an in-company training programme for a Canadian Utility company. There were 42 subjects, in three different groups, participating in the T-group training programme; 10 subjects in the lecture/case discussion programme (matched in terms of age, length of service, education and kind of position as nearly as possible to the participants in the T-group programme), and

12 untrained matched-control group subjects. The evaluation was made six weeks and six months after the completion of the courses and was assessed by interviews with the subject's supervisor, 2 peers and 2 subordinates. Observed behavioural changes were obtained for each participant attending either training programme and also for the non-trained matched-control group, assessed in terms of the number of observers reporting change in subjects.

The observers of the non-trained managers reported least positive change —some 36 per cent; observers of the participants in the lecture/case discussion programme were in the middle—some 52 per cent observed change; and 70 per cent of observers of the T-group trained personnel reported a change. The difference between the various groups is statistically significant; differences in the number of observed positive changes on the part of the laboratory trained group, as compared with the non-trained group and the lecture/case group, were significant beyond the 5 per cent level. It is also notable that the T-group participants were observed to have made *undesirable* changes more often than members of either the non-trained group or the lecture/case discussion group.

In analysing what the participants said they had learned from each programme, Boyd and Ellis report: 'Learning about group behaviour was distinctive of the Laboratories. This included such things as the loss of contributions to the group through failure to listen, the effect of pressure in creating resistance, and how unstated purposes often impede group work. Learning about other people occurred in both groups . . . . However, the laboratory resulted in more direct learning by experience as against conventional training which tends to a more intellectual learning about a subject.' It is noteworthy that not only do observers report more positive changes for the T-group subjects but also a greater variety of change. Boyd and Ellis summarize this as follows: 'One of the most frequently reported changes in behaviour for the laboratory group was an increase in listening which accounts for about 12 per cent of the reports. By listening is meant paying more attention to what other people are saying, being easier to communicate views to and so on. Equally frequent is better understanding and better contribution in group situations such as meetings. Third, but still accounting for 10 per cent of the comments was an increase in tolerance and flexibility. To a lesser extent the laboratory participants were said to have more self-confidence and to express themselves more effectively.'

Chris Argyris (1965) also reports an evaluation of the relative effectiveness of lecture *versus* laboratory education in the subject areas of interpersonal relationships and group dynamics. Using a very complicated design and applying a set of categories previously discussed, he concludes that the processes generated in the lecture approach are very similar to those which create difficulties in back-home groups. The lecture groups did not increase in interpersonal competence whereas the experimental groups in nearly every case showed significant overall changes in the direction of increasing interpersonal competence. He concludes that a relatively 'poor' laboratory produced more behavioural change than the lecture approach.

On the negative side

Unfortunately, the critics of the T-group approach do not appear to base their criticisms on very thorough research (McNair, 1957). Nonetheless, there are one or two studies other than the impressionistic which document the less effective groups. Harrison (1962), conducting an evaluation of a programme instigated by Argyris, found that participants in a T-group activity showed significant changes in concept usage when describing other participants. However, when describing associates who had not participated in the training the findings of change were equivocal. What is more these participants reported great difficulty and some frustration in responding to others who did not or who had not participated in the training with them. In effect, Harrison's findings reveal that few positive effects of T-group training were carried beyond the training situation itself except in situations where ex-participants interacted with other ex-participants.

Harrison (1966) followed up these findings by a further study investigating conceptual change which used a larger number of subjects, a longer period of training, and a design which measured change at more than one point in the post-training period. Harrison's major point was that participants in training would become more oriented to interpersonal process. They were expected to change in their description of others towards the use of more concepts dealing with feelings, attitudes, emotions and perceptions. His second hypothesis was that changes in concept usage would be related to ratings of participants' behaviour in the laboratory. The data support the hypotheses in most respects. There is a significant change in concept usage following the training experience, and this change appears to be progressive shortly after the experience, reaching significant proportions when measured three or four months later. The second hypothesis is also supported: those who are seen as seeking, facilitating, and using the feedback of other's feelings and perceptions towards themselves tend to change towards the use of more expressive concepts. In short, he claims that interpersonal concept systems are amenable to change through group experiences and these changes appear to be associated with the extent to which the individual participates in the training process itself, a point which we had stressed earlier.

Somewhat less encouraging, Wolfe (1965) reports a study of the use of T-group type exercise in an in-service development programme designed specifically for school administrators and supervisors. He notes that an analysis of time utilization failed to reveal significant changes in patterns of behaviour. Likewise he claims that there was no significant change perceived in the behaviour of participants by those with whom they worked closely.

Argyris (1964) reports a study of twenty top executives in a large corporate division where he found a significant shift on the part of an experimental group towards a set of values that encouraged the executives to handle feelings and emotions, to deal with problems of group maintenance, and to develop greater feelings of responsibility on the part of their subordinates for the overall effectiveness of the organization. His study shows, however, that the impact of laboratory education only continued at a high level for just over six months. During the tenth month there was a fade out of training. A further study was undertaken and data was obtained to suggest that the executives had not in fact lost their capacity to behave in a more open manner, but they had had to suppress some of this because of organizational factors which were not conducive to openness. Again one cannot help but notice the effect of the organization upon the trainee.

Conclusion

We can conclude with some general points about the quality of the research to date. Nearly all of it suffers from methodological weakness of some form or other: in most of the studies where participants and controls are rated by peers, subordinates and superiors it is the participants who nominate the raters. This could give rise to distortion in that raters obviously are aware that the subject has or has not been on a T-group, and, if they are reasonably close to the subject, they are likely to have discussed its intended effects with him. The experience of the authors has been that on more than one occasion when research forms have been sent out prior to the T-group programme, the respondent has discussed the items with his colleagues or boss. It is conceivable that the immediate feedback given in such a pre-laboratory experience may be far more effective than the T-group itself. There is, therefore, some danger of contamination of findings by the method of participant nomination of raters and rater knowledge of T-groups and their aims. A further problem is that most of the studies available to date have not used pre and post-measures but have relied heavily on post-only questions such as 'in what ways if any has X changed his behaviour in the past year?'. One of the difficulties of a pre–post measurement design, however, is that one has to decide before the training what effect is expected. If one does this one cannot be certain, as Smith (1969) suggests, of having measured the requisite variable before training.

Still another drawback is contained in the very nature of the question asked above. X may have changed his behaviour, but this does not necessarily make him more effective at his job, as Underwood's (1965) findings, though based on small numbers, indicate. There is little evidence to support or discount the notion that greater openness, better listening, toleration, etc., contribute to effective company performance, though Willits (1967) provides some evidence that the degree to which managers communicate 'openly' with their company presidents is found to correlate significantly with overall company performance.

With these reservations, it is reasonable to conclude that there is moderately strong evidence of lasting and effective change in individuals participating in T-group training. In particular the studies we have cited provide confirmation that:

(1) Significantly more changes are reported for T-group trained participants than either matched-pair control group subjects or participants of other training programmes comparable in length and in objectives.

(2) There is a high agreement among observers in the kind and direction of change reported: improved skills in diagnosing individual and group behaviour, clearer communication, greater tolerance and consideration, and greater action skill and flexibility. (The latter is less well demonstrated than any of the former.)

(3) Finally, the changes noted in these studies were found to last for some time after training, though there are conflicting reports of fade-out after 10–12 months.

References

Argyris, C. (1964) 'T-groups for organizational effectiveness.' *Harvard Business Review*, **42**, 71.

Argyris, C. (1965) 'Explorations in interpersonal competence—I.' *Journal of Applied Behavioral Science*, **1** (1), 58–84.

Boyd, J. B. and J. D. Ellis (1962) *Findings of Research into Senior Management Seminars*, Toronto: The Hydro-Electric Power Commission of Ontario.

Bunker, D. R. (1965) 'Individual applications of laboratory training.' *Journal of Applied Behavioral Science*, **1**, 131–148.

Bunker, D. R. and E. S. Knowles (1967) 'Comparison of behavioural changes resulting from human relations training laboratories of different lengths.' *Journal of Applied Behavioral Science*, **3** (4), 505–523.

Fleishman, E. A., E. F. Harris and H. Burtt (1965) *Leadership and Supervision in Industry*. Columbus: Personnel Research Board, Ohio State University.

Harrison, R. (1962) 'Impact of the laboratory on perception of others by the experimental group.' In Argyris, C., *Interpersonal Competence and Organizational Behavior*. Homewood, Illinois: Richard D. Urwin, 261–271.

Harrison, R. (1966) 'Cognitive change in participation in a Sensitivity Training laboratory.' *Journal of Consulting Psychology*, 3 (6), 517–520.

Lippitt, R. (1949) *Training in Community Relations; Research Exploration Towards New Groups*. New York: Harper.

McNair, M. P. (1957) 'Thinking ahead: What price human relations.' *Harvard Business Review*, 15–39.

Moscow, D. (1969) 'The influence of interpersonal variables on the transfer of learning from T-groups to the job situation.' *Proceedings of International Congress of Applied Psychology*. Amsterdam, 380–386.

Miles, M. B. (1965) 'Changes during and following laboratory training: A clinical–experimental study.' *Journal of Applied Behavioral Science*, 1 (3), 215–243.

Pepinsky, H. B., L. Siegel and E. L. Van Alta (1952) 'The criterion in counselling a group participation scale.' *Journal of Abnormal and Social Psychology*, 47, 415–419.

Schutz, W. C. (1952) 'Reliability, ambiguity and content analysis.' *Psychological Review*, 59 (2), 119–129.

Schutz, W. C. and V. L. Allen (1966) 'The effects of a T-group laboratory on interpersonal behaviour.' *Journal of Applied Behavioral Science*, 1 (3), 265–286.

Smith, P. B. (1969) *Improving Skills in Working with People: the T-group*. London: Department of Employment and Productivity.

Stogdill, R. M. and A. E. Coons (1957) *Leader Behavior: Its Description and Measurement*. Ohio: Bureau of Business Research.

Underwood, W. J. (1965) 'Evaluation of a laboratory method of training.' *Journal of the American Society of Training Directors*, 14, 34–40.

Valiquet, M. I. (1968) 'Individual change in a management development program.' *Journal of Applied Behavioral Science*, 4, 313–325.

Willits, R. D. (1967) 'Company performance and interpersonal relations.' *Industrial Management Review*, 91–109.

Wolfe, W. W. (1965) 'A study of a laboratory approach to in-service development programmes for school administrators and supervisors.' Unpublished Ph.D. Dissertation, University of Texas.

Individual Change in a Management Development Program*

Michael I. Valiquet

Development Associates Ltd, Ottawa, Canada

Research into laboratory processes and outcomes has suffered from a lack of precise methods and continuity of effort essential to the construction of empirically grounded theoretical models of learning and behavior change. Data are presented here from a study of perceived behavior changes in employees of a large industrial concern one year after their participation in training. Participants are seen by co-workers as increasing significantly more than controls in effective initiation and assertiveness, in capacity for collaboration and operational skill in interpersonal relations, and in diagnostic awareness of self and the ability to fulfill perceived needs.

Further systematic inquiry into the determinants of laboratory education is needed to complete the spectrum of alternative designs and outcomes.

The primary purpose of this study was to assess one aspect of an organizational development program conducted on an experimental basis by a large industrial concern in several of its operating units. This facet was the degree in which the stated values underlying the program had been translated by participants into actual changed behavior and attitudes on the job. Since the basic hypothesis of training is that of 'transfer' (the transmissibility of what is learned in the training situation to the customary work situation), verification of the direction and extent of such transfer becomes an important link to any overall program evaluation.

As understood by the evaluator, the primary goal of the program was to achieve increased utilization of the unit's human resources and improved collaboration in working toward common goals. To this end, the participants were assisted in analyzing the consequences of their own actions and encouraged to consider and experiment with alternative managerial assumptions, attitudes, and behavioral patterns.

Operationally, the program comprised three phases: identification of the basic causes of ineffectiveness; the determination of the changes necessary

* Published in *Journal of Applied Behavioral Science*, **4**, 1968, 313–325. The author is greatly indebted to Warren Bennis for his enduring interest and encouragement throughout the research, and to Roger Harrison for his many helpful suggestions in the writing of this paper.

13

to correct this ineffectiveness and development of the requisite competencies to make the changes; and, finally, the actual implementation of the changes on a controlled schedule for specific positions and teams in such a way as to build employee understanding, commitment, and collaboration in the changes.*

Given this conceptual framework, the evaluator chose to develop a research design and methodology which would provide valid data for assisting the impact of the program on the attitudes and behavior of participants in terms of the stated training objectives. In brief, this aim involved the selection of criteria which were at once measurable and operationally meaningful, the development of adequate measuring devices, and, finally, the application of these instruments to data gathered with respect to the individual's on-the-job behaviour and attitudes.

A secondary purpose of this study—but of no less significance to the applied behavioral scientist than the evaluation itself might be to the organizational practitioner—concerns the area of methodology. Evaluative research on the application of laboratory training has tended to suffer from a lack of precise methods and a lack of replication. This tendency is probably part of the syndrome of any new science, reminiscent of the Gilbreths' quest for the 'one best way', and representing both cause and effect of the paucity of normative data. Researchers have somehow avoided building upon the methods and instruments of others. The painstaking work necessary for improvement and refinement has not been done, and instrumentation has therefore remained crude.

Research design and methods

The present study, on the other hand, uses an instrument which has been developed through two previous studies (Miles, 1960; Bunker, 1965). The intention here was twofold: first, to further test the reliability of the instrument used by Miles and Bunker; and second, to add to their work in providing the beginning of a body of normative data on differential learning outcomes of laboratory training. As Bunker (1965) remarks, 'There is strong evidence that groups, individuals, and entire training programs have differential learning outcomes' (p. 147). Miles' research treated of a single occupational group; Bunker's work increased the generality of the findings by dealing with a large heterogeneous population of strangers. The

* One facet of the strategy for change which distinguished this program from similar efforts was the use of change agents drawn from within the company, well-versed in the technical skills and organizational milieus in which they were to operate and uniformly trained in behavioral science theory and methodology.

present study, for its part, examines managers in an in-company training setting.

A random sample of 60 experimental subjects was chosen from lists of participants in the program at four different company locations. These departments were chosen because in each of them the training had begun at least a year previously, giving the participants an opportunity to test and internalize the new values, attitudes, and behavioral skills in their working environment, and allowing the researcher to tap whatever residual effects had survived the state of early posttraining euphoria and erosive constraints in the working environment.

A 'matched-pair' control group was obtained by asking each experimental subject to nominate another manager who held an identical or almost similar functional role to that of the participant but who had not participated in the training. This method of choosing controls permitted the researcher to negate the effects of large discrepancies in ability or opportunity on the potential for change.

The primary data source was an 'open-ended perceived change' questionnaire completed by five 'describers' for each subject. These describers were chosen at random from a listing submitted by each subject of seven to ten names of persons with whom he had worked closely for at least a year. Subjects were asked to select a variety of peers, superiors, and subordinates deemed qualified to assess the subject's on-the-job behavior and any perceived change in that behavior 'over the last year'.

The open-ended question to describers was posed thus: 'Over a period of time people may change in the ways they work with one another. Do you believe that the person you are describing has changed his/her behavior in working with people over the last year as compared with the previous year in any specific ways?' A similar question was put to the subjects themselves to elicit descriptions of their own behavior.

The major strategy then was one of classifying the types of changes comprising each subject's 'total-change score' (the total change perceived by the describers) and of determining whether any significant difference existed between the experimental and control groups. The method of assessing the change and arriving at a 'total-change score' is described below.

Criterion selection. The large volume of verbal material contained in the responses to the open-ended question required an objective method for classifying and counting the responses to permit statistical comparison. The content categories chosen for classifying the data involved 21 constructs which had been inductively derived by Bunker and which had been found to be both organizationally relevant and personally meaningful to a large number of respondents from diverse organizational settings.* These constructs or variables seemed intuitively to encompass the attitudinal and behavioral change-goals of the program—openness, consensus, management of conflict, self-control, distribution of influence, and so on. Moreover, since these constructs had been inductively derived and tested over a sufficiently long period in a broad spectrum of organizational cultures, it was felt that they could be confidently imposed on the cultural mix very likely to be represented in our sample of four widely decentralized divisions.

The scoring task thus involved assigning each mention of a specific change to one of the 21 content categories. The latter fall into three comprehensive sets: overt changes in behavior (A), inferred changes in insight and attitude (B), and global or nonspecific changes (C). The descriptions scored in the 'A' categories tend to refer to overt operational changes—the subject is seen as doing more or less of something or acts more often in a particular way. Set 'B', on the other hand, includes responses based on first-order inferences by the describer as to the internal state of the subject based on behavioral cues (e.g., attributions of insight or sensitivity to group processes). The 'C' category set is used as an empirical dustbin for the many nonspecific and marginally scorable descriptions of vague behavioral changes and gross changes in character which may be received from describers. In addition, it is likely that these global descriptions incorporate a large part of the 'normal' or base rate of change and growth evident in most people.

It should be noted that while precise category fit, according to the scoring conventions to be described below, was demanded for category sets 'A' and 'B', less rigid requirements were imposed on set 'C', on the grounds that it comprised changes which were either doubtful or irrelevant to the research task. With this lone qualification, the scoring in each category depended upon an explicit statement of qualitative or quantitative difference in the subject's on-the-job behavior or attitudes. Changes could be positive or negative, reflecting increases or decreases in quantity and greater or lesser utility.

Scoring. For each describer response a score of one was assigned for each category in which there was one (or more) mention. The total-change score for each subject was then obtained by adding up the individual scores on each of the five describers' responses. Next, by combining all cell values

---

* The author is indebted to Professor Bunker for permission to use the scoring system that he and his colleagues at the National Training Laboratories developed and tested. To save space, his inductively derived categories for content analysis have not been repeated here. (See Bunker, 1965, p. 139.)

(0 or 1) in the matrix of categories and describers for all subjects, a variety of change scores can be obtained: the total-change score for experimental subjects *vis-à-vis* controls, separate scores for category sets 'A', 'B', and 'C'; for self-ratings as opposed to describer ratings; for different experimental groups by location; and a 'verified' change score developed by counting the number of observations on a particular subject where two or more describers concur.

The completed questionnaires were stripped of group identification to ensure a blind-process and were independently recorded to check drift in the use of the categories.

Results and conclusions

While the rate of return on mailed questionnaires is notoriously low, and the resultant problem of subject 'self-selection' can be extremely destructive to otherwise well-conceived research strategies, the simplicity of this questionnaire and the accompanying explanatory letter combined to give decent response statistics. Of the random sample of 60 experimental subjects originally canvassed, 39, or 65 per cent, replied; and of the 31 control subjects provided by these, 18, or 58 per cent, returned questionnaires. After others were eliminated because of recent transfers or lack of describer response, 49, or 54 per cent of both the original experiment and control group, were included in the study. Of approximately 450 describers who received questionnaires, over 50 per cent returned usable responses.

The initial comparison of experimental and control subjects is made on the basis of total-change scores. This analysis, presented in Table 1, with the distribution of the total research population divided into thirds,* indicates that a significantly greater proportion of participants than nonparticipants were in the middle and top thirds of the distribution of change scores.

The probability of obtaining a value of chi-square as large as 11·37 if the two groups were not different is less than 0·001. While the value of chi-square is substantially smaller than that obtained by Bunker, the results are comparable at his stated level of significance.

When this same type of analysis is executed solely on the basis of the changes recorded by describers in category set 'A', the results are (coincidentally) identical (see Table 2), indicating that participants in the training

* This procedure has been followed for the purposes of comparison with Professor Bunker's experiment. Cell values have been combined to permit use of the chi-square test. To provide a more stringent check of such a small research population (N = 49) and cell values, the 'exact' procedure for calculating chi-square was employed where necessary and found not to reverse any decisions concerning the null hypothesis. (See Croxton and Cowden, 1955, p. 686.)

Table 1—*The distribution of total-change score*

Total-change score	Experimental subjects	Control subjects	Total
Upper two-thirds (Scores of 4 to 17)	28	5	33
Lower one-third (Scores of −1 to 3)	6	10	16
N	34	15	49

$\chi^2 = 11.37$
(d.f. = 1)
$p(\chi^2 = 11.37) < 0.001$

Table 2—*Distribution of experimental and control subjects with respect to change scores in category 'A'*

	Experimental subjects	Control subjects	Total
Upper two-thirds (Scores of 2 to 10)	28	5	33
Lower one-third (Scores of 0 and 1)	6	10	16
N	34	15	49

$\chi^2 = 11.37$
(d.f. = 1)
$p(\chi^2 = 11.37) < 0.001$

program (experimental subjects) demonstrated significantly greater behavioral change toward program goals than did nonparticipants (control subjects).

Repeating the same procedure independently for the attitudinal category set 'B' (see Table 3), a similar pattern occurs, although this time only to the 0·01 level of significance. A somewhat *post hoc* interpretation of this result is that the participants, while not necessarily embracing the managerial alternatives advanced during their training sessions, nevertheless felt free to experiment with the new modes of behavior. This would account for the higher frequency of actional as opposed to attitudinal change, and such a supposition would be supported by the significantly higher level of 'Risk Taking' observed in experimental subjects (see Table 5). Whatever the symbolic effects of the training may have been, a professed goal of the program was 'freedom of choice' of individual managerial behavior, a goal which, from the indications outlined above, appears to have been largely met. Only when the experimental control comparison is extended to the

Table 3—*Distribution of experimental and control subjects with respect to change scores in category 'B'*

	Experimentals	Controls	Total
Upper two-thirds	22	4	26
Lower one-third	12	11	23
N	34	15	49

$\chi^2 = 7.07$
$(d.f. = 1)$
$p(\chi^2 = 7.07) < 0.01$

'global' change data (i.e., category set 'C') does no significant difference between the two groups occur.*

This empirical result lends credence to the hypothesis advanced earlier that the 'C' category changes constitute an important component of the 'normal' or 'base' rate of change observable in nearly all human beings, and emphasizes the discriminating power of the other change categories.

Lest the indications at this juncture of the analysis be deemed more artifactual than substantive, the raw data are now subjected to a more demanding test. Table 4 presents the difference between experimental and control groups on the basis of 'verified' change scores, i.e., where a subject had one or more specific observations of change confirmed by concurrence among the responses of two or more describers.

The questions well might arise as to whether describer bias induced by awareness of the subject's participation or nonparticipation in the program

Table 4—*The number of subjects with one or more verified changes*

	Experimentals	Controls	Total
One or more changes verified by describer concurrence	25 (73%)	2 (20%)	27
No verification	9 (27%)	13 (80%)	22
N	34	15	49

$\chi^2 = 15.22$
$(d.f. = 1)$
$p(\chi^2 = 15.22) < 0.001$

* Of the total research population, five experimental and nine control subjects were described as having changed along these lines. The two-cell table yields a nonsignificant chi-square value of 1·14.

would affect the results, whether the describers could easily contrive a set of situationally relevant behavioral changes, and whether indeed they would be motivated to do so. The high number of 'no change' as well as positive change responses received from describers, the random process of describer selection, the discriminating power of the many change categories, as well as the Table 4 results, make such an occurrence seem highly unlikely. More than two-thirds of the experimentals, as compared with fewer than one-third of the controls, had one or more specific changes confirmed by the reports of two or more describers. This difference in the proportion of verifications adds substance to the interpretations made of Tables 1, 2 and 3, and compares closely with the findings of Bunker.

Finally, Table 5 presents an analysis by scoring category of the differences in proportions of subjects reported as changed in each of the two groups. Some notable similarities and differences with respect to Professor Bunker's results are brought to light. First, we must concur with his findings that laboratory training outcomes tend to be individual and varied, even where the program is conducted in a single industrial organization. In only one of the scoring categories does the proportion of subjects reported as having changed exceed 50 per cent.

Table 5—*Differences between experimental and control groups proportion of subjects reported to have changed*

	Scoring category	Proportion perceived to have changed		Differences
		Experimentals	Controls	
A–1	Sending	0·29	0·07	0·23[a]
A–1	Receiving	0·18	0·07	0·11
A–2	Relational Facility	0·35	0·13	0·22[a]
A–3	Risk Taking	0·32	0·07	0·26[b]
A–4	Increased Interdependence	0·56	0·13	0·43[b]
A–5	Functional Flexibility	0·35	0·07	0·29[b]
A–6	Self-Control	0·35	0·13	0·22[a]
B–1	Awareness of Behavior	0·18	0·07	0·11
B–2	Sensitivity to Group Process	0·12	0·07	0·05
B–3	Sensitivity to Others' Feelings	0·32	0·13	0·19
B–4	Acceptance of Others	0·32	0·07	0·26[a]
B–5	Tolerance of New Information	0·32	0·13	0·19
B–6	Confidence	0·12	0·07	0·05
B–7	Comfort	0·21	0·07	0·14
B–8	Insight into Self and Role	0·44	0·13	0·31[b]

[a] $p < 0.05$.
[b] $p < 0.01$.

However, whereas Bunker found that 11 of the 15 categories discriminated between experimental and control subjects beyond the 0·05 level of significance, here only 8 of the 15 so discriminate.

The simplest explanation of this result would appear to lie in the differences between the two programs studied, particularly in terms of the stated goals of each and the environments in which the programs took place. Bunker studied heterogeneous groups of strangers who after training dispersed to a wide variety of occupational roles in a broad range of organizational types and sizes. The goals of the NTL program he studied are probably best described in terms of *all* of the criterion variables used in this research. The present study, on the other hand, while not treating of a single occupational group, is concerned with a relatively lesser number of occupational roles in a particular organization. Moreover, the operational goals of this program were couched strongly, and specifically, in terms of *adapting the changes with which students were experimenting to the organizational setting*. What is implied here is that the participants of this program tended to focus on the *application* of a narrower range of program values.

This line of reasoning is reinforced by a further difference between the two studies. Bunker found that seven of the eight categories in set 'B' discriminated at the 0·05 level or better while only four of the seven categories in set 'A' had comparable power. In the present study the situation is somewhat reversed, with some interesting qualitative differences. Six of the eight behavioral categories discriminate at the 0·05 level or better, while only two attitudinal categories demonstrate similar power. The reasoning advanced earlier seems relevant here. Participants perhaps felt free to experiment with new modes of behavior on the job while not necessarily fully convinced of their effectiveness. As some behavioralists argue, attitude change may not be a necessary antecedent to behavioral change. A further divergence between the two studies which supports this argument is that where Bunker found no significant difference in his experimental and control groups with respect to 'Risk Taking' (A-3), it is here found to be significant at the 0·01 level. This, perhaps, may be explained by the fact that Bunker's experimental group was exposed to a stimulus situation of shorter duration and remote from its operational environment, whereas the subject program was relatively continuous and carried out for the most part within the operational environment. What is implied here is that gradual and protracted training within a generally supportive atmosphere may better lend itself to experimentation and the exposing of one's self and one's ideas, than returning from a 'cultural island' to the perhaps erosive effects of an environment which has not necessarily been conditioned to change. Additionally, there is the fact that the training here was accompanied by other forms of change—organizational, structural, et cetera—which may have reinforced a spirit of experimentation.

Another significant divergence from Bunker's results lies in the discriminating power of Category A-5, 'Functional Flexibility'. Whereas Bunker discovered this factor also to be relatively nonsignificant, here it is found to be of major importance. Reasoning similar to that advanced for the high incidence of 'Risk Taking' appears relevant. Given that a score for 'Functional Flexibility' requires evidence of *both* diagnosis and the ability to act to fulfill perceived needs, it seems reasonable to expect higher incidence of the second criterion in an organizational climate which has been carefully nurtured at all management levels to accept the reality of change and the necessity of adapting to it.

The findings with respect to 'Increased Interdependence' (A-4) and 'Insight into Self and Role' (B-8) are also somewhat dissimilar to those of Bunker. Here they are found to be of greater significance, which, in the case of 'Increased Interdependence', may merely reflect the relevance of the variable to this particular program and organization. It is interesting to note, however, that the same common theme of increased operational skill in interpersonal relations, together with increased capacity for collaboration observed by Bunker, also exists here, albeit with different emphasis.

The increase in diagnostic awareness of self and role observed here distinguished program participants from controls at a higher level of significance than in the case of a heterogeneous group of NTL participants. It may be that an improved perception of one's own attributes and limitations, particularly with respect to the job, is more readily acquired through social interaction with one's actual 'family' group, rather than in the comparative psychological safety of a 'stranger' group.

One further qualitative difference between the two programs lies in the cluster of categories which Bunker describes as 'increased and more effective initiation and assertiveness' (A-5, A-3, B-6). While the NTL programs seem not to have had their major impact in this area, the two actional variables are found here to be quite significant. 'Confidence' (B-6) is not; but perhaps the significant increase in 'Self-Control' (A-6) as a sort of tempering or 'braking' effect, together with improved 'Functional Flexibility' (A-5), may reflect the participants' diagnosis that their major needs did not lie in this direction.

Implications for laboratory education

When the results are compared with Bunker's study of a large, heterogeneous population of strangers, his general findings are supported, but with some interesting qualitative differences. In particular, the greater number of significant changes observed in this study occurred in the overt, operational categories rather than in the inferred, attitudinal categories, as was more often the case in Bunker's study. A variety of factors may have been at play in producing this differential result, the most important of which appear to have been the composition of the groups (family *versus* strangers), the apparent program goals, and the environment of change in each case.

Tentatively, it is suggested that actional, as opposed to attitudinal, change may be better supported in a program specifically designed for such a purpose and buttressed by concomitant changes of other kinds in the organization. The program studied here seems to have been able to thwart the psychological resistances—particularly the waning of the training 'honeymoon'—which have plagued so much development effort in the past. This is not to say that *all* participants learned to accelerate their adaptive processes and to obtain better control over them. To hope for so much would be quixotic. The data do indicate, however, that a majority of the laboratory participants were able to integrate their newly acquired attitudes and behavioral skills into their personalities and ongoing work relationships.

But as Bunker and others have stressed, now that improved criterion measures of long-range behavioral change are available, there is an urgent requirement for further systematic investigation and comparative analysis of alternative training designs, processes, and outcomes to enrich the soil of substantive knowledge concerning laboratory education and to enhance the range and validity of alternative programs. Until this is done, the processes of choice remain slightly more scientific than augury.

References

Bunker, D. R. (1965) 'Individual applications of laboratory training. *J. appl. Behav. Sci.*, **1** (2), 131–148.

Croxton,F. E. and D. J. Cowden (1955) *Applied General Statistics*. 2nd ed. New York: Prentice-Hall.

Miles, M. B. (1960) 'Human relations training: Processes and outcomes. *J. counsel. Psychol.*, **7** (4), 301–306.

CHAPTER 2

Before and After the T-group*

In this chapter we shall review the evidence that has accumulated around what Martin (1957) terms *internal criteria*. Internal criteria are measures linked directly to the content and processes of the training programme but which do not necessarily have implications for behaviour away from the programme. External criteria are those linked directly with job behaviour, and research studies bearing on this area are reviewed below. The areas we shall be considering are: studies concerned with attitude change, perceptual change, personality change, and growth in diagnostic ability.

Attitude Change

In designing evaluation research to assess the impact of T-group training during the training period a number of approaches are possible. One may design measures related to the outcomes one expects, such as measures of self-awareness or attitude flexibility or diagnostic ability. Or one may design a wide variety of measures for the purpose of detecting whatever changes do in fact occur, expected or not. Most of these studies initially undertaken used the second strategy, since there were few measures available for assessing the kinds of social skill attributes associated with T-group training (Smith, 1969). As a result of these studies and the development of more sophisticated techniques of attitude and behaviour measurement, more measures of the first type have been devised. It is with studies utilizing the more sophisticated techniques that we shall be concerned.

It is common in a T-group for the participants to analyse the staff member's behaviour and to discuss their feelings and beliefs about authority, power and leadership. A large number of the attitude change studies have in one form or another examined participants' attitudes toward authority. Kernan (1964) attempted to see if attitudes toward authority as measured

* A slightly modified version of a paper published by the authors in the *Journal of Management Studies*, **7** (1970), 224–239.

by Adorno's F-scale were affected by T-group training. 40 T-group participants and 20 control subjects were tested before and after a three-day T-group for engineering supervisors. He found no significant change in participants' F-scale score as a result of the training. In addition, he found no changes in responses to measures of attitudes toward the use of different leadership types, or changes in Thematic Apperception Tests of 'tolerance, toughness, friendliness, interpersonal problems, dominance or nurturance'. The pre and post-tests, however, were carried out under different conditions (some participants completed the questionnaires under actual job conditions while others off the job), which makes the results less satisfying.

Carron (1964) used Adorno's F-scale and the Leadership Opinion Questionnaire in evaluating T-group training in terms of changed attitudes (with a group of Research and Development Managers). He obtained attitude measurements on both T-group participants and control group subjects at four different points in time: before training, immediately after training, six months later, and at a follow-up 17 months after the end of the training. The LOQ is concerned with two kinds of leader behaviour, consideration and initiating structure. The consideration dimension measures the degree to which a leader shows concern for the well being of his subordinates, helps the groups, uses participative decision-making and is generally supportive of his subordinates. The initiating structure dimension measures the degree to which the leader plans, organizes and controls, defines procedures and responsibilities and generally the degree to which he establishes a structure to guide his subordinates in their work. Carron found, analysing the data across groups, that the training programme did change authoritarian and leadership attitudes but that they were not permanent (not noted some 17 months later). He felt, however, that the 'across group analysis' was not an adequate method of analysing attitude change since it measured only magnitude and not direction of change and 'statistical averages for a group simply do not tell what is happening to the individual members'. The changes measured by the F-scale and the LOQ became clearer when he employed a vector analysis of the data showing both magnitude and direction. He found that the training had the effect of decreasing authoritarian attitudes and of causing participants to place higher value on consideration and less value on structure, which he interprets as desirable change. This opinion is contrary to substantial evidence (Fleishman and Harris, 1962; Halpin, 1957) to suggest that attitudes and behaviour characterized by high consideration *and* high structure are associated with effective and successful leadership for widely different organizations (House, 1967). In other words, the study indicates that the participants believed more in the need for one kind of desirable leader behaviour, namely consideration, and less in a second, namely structure.

Asquith and Hedlund (1967) administered the LOQ and the SI (Supervisory Index) to evaluate the changes in attitude toward supervisory practices during a management development training programme involving a one-week T-group. No change in participants' attitudes on either of these instruments was found. The T-group, however, was only one part of the training programme and it could be that the management lectures which made up the bulk of the programme may have interfered with the results of the T-group. In addition, no attempt was made to use a control group as a basis of comparison.

Nonetheless, results of studies utilizing the LOQ yield far from satisfactory evidence that the T-group has lasting effects on attitudes.

A different measure of attitude has been used in a number of studies on participant attitude change, the FIRO-B (Schutz, 1958). This questionnaire assesses the respondents' attitudes toward two salient areas in the behaviour of any T-group, control or power and affection or close personal relations. It is composed of six Guttman scales of nine items each. The scales measure an individual's *expressed* behaviour and the behaviour *wanted from others* in the interpersonal areas of inclusion,* control, and affection. Smith (1964) used the FIRO to compare 108 T-group participants with 44 control group subjects on other management training courses. Subjects completed the FIRO questionnaire near the beginning and again near the end of their course. Before an assessment was made of participant change, measures were obtained during the T-groups which indicated that the FIRO scales were indeed correlated with participant behaviour in the group. Smith argued that changes to be expected in this questionnaire would not be increases or decreases but movements toward the median position on the scale, since extreme scores, as Schutz (1958) points out, are consistent with a more rigid, inflexible attitudinal style. It was found that T-group-trained participants showed a marked tendency for their scores on the control and affection scales to move toward the median. It may be, however, that this movement is a function of initial score bias such that the high initial scorers moved downward and the low initial scorers moved upward, and in addition, that there may be more high and low initial scorers among the T-group trained than the control group subjects.

Controlling for initial scores, Cureton (1968) replicated Smith's study in a group of students in a college of education. 50 students participated in a T-group and 48 in a more conventional course on human relations. Pre and

---

* The inclusion scales have been frequently omitted since they were found by Smith (1964) to be highly correlated with the affection scales.

post-training FIRO scores were obtained and the T-group trained participants showed a movement toward the median on the FIRO sub-scales
while the 48 controls showed significantly less movement.

Changes in the FIRO scores were also obtained by Schutz and Allen
(1966) for 71 participants in the Western Training Laboratory in Human
Relations. The participants completed the questionnaire before and after
the two-week laboratory and six months later. FIRO was also given to a
group of 30 college students at approximately equal intervals to serve as a
control. Overall correlations between administrations were much lower for
the T-group trained participants than for the control group. That is, the
former showed significantly more change on the FIRO sub-scales than the
latter. Directionality was not considered. They also found that the T-group
changed people selectively on the basis of their initial personality attributes
such that overly dominant became less dominant while overly affectionate
more discriminating.

Changes on the FIRO were not found by Meigniez (1961) using a French
translation of FIRO in 3 French T-groups (no control group). The lack of
any significant change in this case may be attributed to cultural differences
in attitudes toward control and affection.

Baumgartel and Goldstein (1967) used the FIRO and the Allport–
Vernon 'Study of Values' to test the prediction that participants would
become more like the highly valued members of the group in their attitudes
over the course of the group. The participants' ranked their fellow-students
to determine which were the 'most-valued' members of the T-group. The
various scores for each of the sub-scales of the FIRO and the Study of
Values questionnaires, administered at the start of the course, were correlated with the sociometric ranking of the most-valued members obtained
at the end of the course. There were two significant correlations with sociometric position: highly-valued members had high expressed control scores
on the FIRO and lower religious value scores on the Study of Values. The
FIRO and the Study of Values were re-administered at the end of the
course to test the above hypothesis. Only the reduction in religious value is
supported by the data, there was no significant change in the expressed
control scores. However, two other FIRO scores did show significant
changes: participants increased in their wanted control scores and decreased
in their wanted affection scores. The conclusion is drawn that some support
for the expectation was found that the 'uses of internal criterion of poor
ratings would seem to be promising for assessing effects of training'. Very
little supporting evidence was found, however, to justify such a claim. In
addition, one must question the assumption made that 'if we can learn the
characteristics or attributes of those persons who are esteemed as group

members in the natural course of events, presumably people with high interpersonal competence, then we can use a measure of the *amount of change toward the characteristics* as an indicator of a positive training outcome'.

Several attitude change studies have been conducted which utilize questionnaires directly relevant to the group being studied. Elliott (1958) for instance, compared 16 employees of an engineering company who participated in T-group training with 15 employees (matched for age, intelligence, and organization function) who were not trained. Two measures of change were used; the Supervisory Attitude Scale developed by Castle (1952), and a second one, developed by the investigator, entitled 'How Groups Work'. On both scales changes toward a greater emphasis on human relations in supervision were found for the trained employees which was significantly greater than for the untrained men. While the sample is small the results are interesting in view of the fact that the Castle scale has not been shown to change in response to other human relations training courses.

Bowers and Soar (1961) conducted a study into the effects on teacher's attitude and behaviour of a T-group training programme. They used an untrained control group of teachers, similar to the trained ones. A comparison of pre and post-training results indicated that T-group trained teachers showed significant positive change in their attitudes toward pupils and democratic leadership, but the control group also showed a change so that the difference between them was not significant. Further analysis of the data shows that teachers who were well-adjusted, as measured by the personality inventory, and those who emphasized verbal presentation in their classroom behaviour, were more likely to change their attitudes toward student participation than the equivalent group of teachers without training. The authors conclude, therefore, that the effect of the training was to help teachers realize their potential, that is, to increase the degree of difference between greater and lesser skill.

The studies reviewed in this section examined change in the attitudes toward social behaviour of those trained, behaviour which is regarded as the most important in the case of non-directive training groups. The main attitudes considered were those toward power or leadership and affection behaviour. Overall the studies seem to indicate that changes in these attitudes did occur as a result of training, and in some cases, that they moved in the direction of a more flexible position. One must take note, however, of the ambiguity of the findings. Like so many areas of T-group research, there remains a great deal to be done, both in terms of replication and original research which seeks to link attitude changes, if any, with specific dynamics of the groups.

Perceptual change

One of the questions often asked of the T-group is whether this type of training will in some way affect the personality of the participants involved. One aspect of this question is whether the group members increase the 'clarity and accuracy of their perception of their own behaviour'. Most of the measures used in studies of this sort have focused on the change in the discrepancies between a person's description of 'actual self', 'ideal self', and 'average-other perceptions of self'.

An early study designed to assess the discrepancy between 'actual self' and 'ideal self' was carried out by Bennis, Burke, Cutter, Harrington and Hoffman (1957) with 12 students who participated in a semester-long T-group. They assessed changes in perception of actual and ideal self using a 34-item inventory of possible role behaviours (for example, 'tries to understand the contributions of others'). The students rated each of the possible role behaviours on a 7-point scale on the basis of how descriptive the items were of them and how descriptive they were of ideal role behaviour. No significant increase in similarity between actual and ideal was found.

In a study with a larger sample, Burke and Bennis (1961) obtained ratings of 'actual self', 'ideal self', and 'self as rated by others' from 84 participants of six different NTL* groups. They used a Group Semantic Differential questionnaire of 19 bipolar, adjectival rating scales with instructions to participants to respond in three ways: (1) 'The way I actually am in this T-group', (2) 'The way I would like to be in this T-group', and (3) 'Each of the other people in this group'. The ratings of others were averaged to provide a pooled or average description of each participant on each of the 19 scales. They found that the discrepancy between actual self and ideal self was much less at the end of the training than at the beginning. They also found that the participants showed more change in actual self than in perceived ideal self, which they suggest is the result of an emphasis in the T-group of here-and-now behaviour in the group rather than of the ideal group member. In addition, a participant's perceived actual self and the perception of him by others in his T-group were more similar at the end of the training than at the beginning. But in this case the group members changed much more in the ways in which they perceived other individuals in the group than these individuals changed in their perception of self, which, they suggest, indicates an increase in the consensual validation of behaviour by members of a T-group. Since no control group was used it is difficult to assess whether the changes are a function of the T-group or simply the passage of time or some other extraneous factor.

* NTL—National Training Laboratory, currently the central focus of T-group training in the United States.

Grater (1959) used the Bills' Index of Adjustment and Values to obtain descriptions of 'actual self', 'ideal self', and 'others' before and after an 11-week leadership training course for 30 university students. The course was not entirely a T-group in that it focused mainly on leadership problems experienced by the participants and minimized interpersonal behaviour and feedback in the group situation. Even though the training course lacked some of the elements of a T-group, results similar to those of Burke and Bennis were obtained. The discrepancies between 'actual self' and 'ideal self' were significantly reduced over the course of training (once again due mainly to changes in perception of actual self); and the expected decrease in the discrepancy between descriptions of actual self and the average group member was found, but not at a statistically significant level.

Carson and Lakin (1963) replicated the Burke and Bennis study with only two groups of subjects but improved upon the original design by providing a control condition. Participants filled out a 16-item rating scale questionnaire in respect to themselves and every other participant in their group two-weeks before and two-weeks after training. One group was used as its own control by completing the questionnaire six weeks prior to training. The results were less than satisfactory, one group supported most of the results in the original study while the other showed little change following training (incidentally, this was the group which acted as its own control).

Unlike the aforementioned studies, Gassner, Gold and Snadowsky (1964) conducted a comprehensive, well-controlled study of phenomenal-self changes. In the first part of the study they administered Bills' Index to 46 students one day prior to and two days after the completion of the T-group. 21 students who submitted applications for a forthcoming T-group were used as a control, responding to the above questionnaire over an equivalent time interval. They found a significant decrease in the discrepancy between perceptions of actual self and ideal self in both the T-group trained and control group subjects. In addition, both groups showed a significant decrease in discrepancy between perceptions of actual self and average-other perceptions. This aspect of the results was similar to the Grater and the Burke and Bennis findings. However, when the degree of change between the T-group and the control group on both of the above discrepancy measures was examined, it was found that the T-group changes did not differ significantly from the control group.

In the second part of the study, 45 T-group trained students were compared with 27 students enrolled in psychology courses at the same university. In this study a modified form of the Burke and Bennis graphic-rating scale series was administered to the participants at the introductory session of the T-group. Control group subjects completed the rating scales over a comparable time interval. In this study they found no significant decrease in discrepancy between perceptions of actual self and ideal self in either the T-group or the control group subjects. They did find, however, a significant decrease in the discrepancy between the perceptions of actual self and average-other perceptions. However, when the groups were compared the difference between them was not statistically significant. The two control conditions in this study add an important dimension to this line of research since it provides us with a basis of comparison. A better control group, however, might have been one in which the subjects were participating in a more conventional course of instruction in human relations, such as a lecture or group seminar, and one covering the same time interval as the T-group.

While all of the above studies have assessed in one form or another training induced changes in clarity of self-perceptions, none of them has forged the link between the changes and the means employed to produce them. Research of this sort has only recently been undertaken. The best example of this is a study conducted by French, Sherwood and Bradford (1966) to test whether changes in self-identity are influenced by the amount of personal feedback received. Data was collected from two two-week T-groups (ten members each) at a number of points in time: beginning of the first week, end of the first week, end of the second week, and ten months after the T-group (to test whether changes in self-identity were permanent or whether there was regression to the pre T-group level). Each subject filled out a questionnaire containing 19 bipolar scales measuring different dimensions of self-identity. The amount of personal feedback was experimentally manipulated: on the one extreme, high feedback condition, the participant was rated on one of the bipolar scales by the nine other T-group members in terms of his present behaviour, those ratings were fed back to him in written form, and his behaviour on this scale was discussed in detail with two members of his T-group. On the other extreme, low feedback condition, he was not rated by the other members of the group, no information was fed back to him, and there was no scheduled discussions.

Five conditions with different amounts of feedback were produced and it was expected that changes in self-identity would be greater for the condition with the greatest amount of feedback. They found no consistent change in self-identity during the first week of training, most change during the second week, and less change (though still statistically significant) for the follow-up period. With respect to the systematic amount of feedback on different amounts of change in self-identity they found that Condition E, which contained no feedback, showed less change than the other conditions (all of whom contained some personal feedback) for the total time period. However, they found little statistical difference between A, B and C conditions of feedback, although they contend that there was no measure to determine how much feedback was actually produced in each condition. In addition, they tested two other hypotheses: (1) the greater the importance or centrality of a dimension of self-perception to the participant, the greater the change in his self-identity, and (2) the lower a person's self-evaluation or the higher his dissatisfaction on a dimension of self-perception, the greater the change on his self-identity. Some support for the second hypothesis was found, while there was no support for the first hypothesis. They conclude by saying that their 'results give some support to the proposition that a person's self-identity is influenced by the opinions that others have of him which they communicate to him and that the more that is communicated the more change there is in self-identity'.

There are, of course, pitfalls in this research: (1) the number of subjects used in the study was small, (2) no control was employed, and more importantly (3) there is no evidence that experimental manipulation was successful. This should not, however, detract from the importance of the study, which is the first of its kind to assess phenomenal self changes in terms of the means employed to produce them.

In summary, while it may be reasonable to expect changes in the way in which an individual sees himself as a result of T-group training, the only well-controlled study (Gassner and coworkers, 1964) to assess this leads to the suggestion that the T-group does not produce these changes any more than the simple passage of time or the mere act of re-taking a self-description questionnaire after a period of thinking about one's previous responses. This seems to suggest either that the self-perception questionnaires are empirically inadequate and thus interfere with attempts to measure self-percept change or that T-group training does not have a measurable effect on the self-concept of the participant.

Personality change

Turning to another criterion measure during the training period, we were surprised to find less than a handful of studies relating T-group experiences to personality change itself. It may be that interest in this area is slight because changes in such fundamental personality traits may be just too much to expect in such a short-lived experience.

Most of the criterion measures used in these studies are obtained by means of standardized personality questionnaires or projective tests. In an early study, Zimet and Fine (1955) assessed the consequences of a T-group on 15 New York chief school administrators in the public schools. In order to evaluate the personality changes a picture story technique was used. This Picture Story Test (PST) consisted of 18 pictures; 6 from the TAT, 6 from the School Apperception Test, and 6 from a previous research study. Each subject was asked to make up a story to fit each of the pictures. The PST was administered during the initial and final sessions of the 16-weekly sessions in the laboratory. The pre and post-test protocols were recorded, transcribed and coded. The stories were then analysed for attitudes expressed by each subject and were represented by scores on each of a number of scales. There were 6 scales in each of 3 major areas of attitudes toward self, attitudes toward other adults, and attitudes toward children. In addition, the Combs Desires list which is made up of 36 items was used to measure change in motivation.

On balance, the school administrators' conception of self, others, and children as recorded in the PST indicated movement in the direction of *increased* adequacy, liking, acceptance and equality. When the Combs Desires' items were analysed for pre and post-tests differences, a change in a positive direction was found on a number of items. Increases were found in their 'desire to believe best about another'; 'desire to help, aid, assist someone of a group in a social or humanitarian sense'; 'desire not to hurt, punish, or kill, not to attack, destroy, avenge, inflict pain to self or society'. As the authors suggest, 'on the whole the changes that were recorded in this instrument indicate movement in the "democratic" direction'.

While these results are in the direction one might expect in terms of T-group goals, the danger of making inferences from studies without adequate control groups has been demonstrated innumerable times (for example, Gassner and coworkers, 1964).

Using a larger sample but again lacking a control group, Massarik and Carlson (Dunnette, 1962) designed a study to assess changes in personality variables similar to the previous study. Based on a before and after administration of the California Personality Inventory, they found that 48 hours of T-group interaction among 70 students brought about only minor changes in the expected direction of increased spontaneity and slightly lowered overall control.

In addition to the variables of adequacy and spontaneity, David Reisman's theory of social character based on the concepts of inner and other-directedness has been linked to the goals of the T-group. As Kassarjian (1965) suggests:

'Sensitivity training as it is offered in many training laboratories through the country has often been labeled as being an ideal training experience for organization men, for teaching the techniques of other-direction. On the other hand, some supporters of sensitivity training claim quite the opposite, that sensitivity training opens the communication channels within the person . . .. Hence it is training for inner-direction.'

With this difference of opinion in mind Kassarjian (1965) sought to investigate whether there was a shift toward inner or other-direction after an extensive T-group experience. He undertook this investigation into four student and six adult T-groups, using control groups of similar composition. The T-group subjects were administered the I–O Social Preference Scale (Kassarjian, 1962), a measure of inner and other-direction, at the beginning and end of the training period. Control group subjects were given the instrument during the same week, at the beginning and the end of the week. The I–O Social Preference Scale consists of 36 forced-choice items, which yielded predicted relationships with other variables in previous research, notably with the Strong Vocational Interest Blank and Allport–Vernon–Lindzey Scale of Values.

The t tests tabulated between the means of the control and the experimental groups for the student and adult groups yielded no significant differences in shifts. Thus, the short-term effects of the T-group do not seem to be related to a shift toward either inner or other-direction. Since previous research has had predictable success with the I–O scale it is unlikely that the scale does not measure inner and other-direction. It is more likely, as Kassarjian suggests, that 'to expect that a single training experience over a 10 to 15-week period would create a measurable change in the basic underlying social character of a person that has taken 20 to 40 years to instill, may well be too much to expect . . .'.

It has frequently been suggested (Miles, 1965; Smith, 1964) that T-groups should increase one's sensitivity to the needs of others and insight into one's own motives and behaviour as it affects others. Rubin (1967) has set out to test this prediction. He has hypothesized that as a result of T-group training: (1) an individual's level of self-acceptance should increase; (2) an individual's level of acceptance of others should increase; and (3) those who increase in self-acceptance should increase more in acceptance of others than those who do not change or decrease in self-acceptance. The Dorris, Levinson, Hanfmann Sentence Completion Test (SCT) (1954) was used to measure the effect of T-groups upon an individual's level of self-acceptance. The SCT includes 50 sentence stems. Half of the stems use first-person pronouns, and half, a third-person pronoun or pronoun or proper name. The first and third-person items are matched in context, for example, when he gets angry he . . .; when I get angry I . . .. The individual stem completions were coded in such a way that the more willing a person was to admit 'ego-threatening' material the greater his level of self-acceptance. In addition to self-acceptance a 15-item scale was developed to measure human-heartedness (HH) or acceptance of others.

Fifty participants who were involved in a two-week residential T-group programme were used in the study. The subjects were randomly split into two groups of unequal size. The smaller group ($N = 14$) was tested via mailed questionnaire two weeks prior to their participation, which provided subjects to serve as their own control. The entire group was then tested upon their arrival but before the first group session. The final measures were obtained the morning of the next-to-last day of the laboratory.

Analysis of the data by partial correlation found substantial support for the hypotheses. The first two hypotheses were upheld but the one suggesting that those who increase in self-acceptance will increase more in HH than those who decrease or do not change in self-acceptance was too broad. As Rubin states 'it appears instead that some minimum increases in self-acceptance (20 per cent in this study) is necessary in order for any significant change in HH to be immediately observable.' While these results are encouraging, there is still the strong possibility that any one of a number of other human relations training methods would produce similar results. Further research using comparison groups, that is, groups trained by some other method, should be encouraged to discount the above possibility.

In conclusion, it seems that personality change, as measured by standardized personality questionnaires and projective techniques, has not been demonstrated. While some of the studies are encouraging, a number of problems remain. First, the multiplicity of research instruments and criteria used makes any comparison or integration of the findings impossible. This state of affairs reflects the lack of agreement and clarity about the T-group goals relevant to personality change and, consequently, about the research focus in this area. Second, few control or comparison groups are used. And lastly, as Campbell and Dunnette (1968) emphasize 'changes in such basic personality variables may be just too much to expect from such a relatively short experience, even if the T-group is a good one'.

Diagnostic ability

This section covers changes in the ability to diagnose interpersonal phenomena and the related field of changes in the use of interpersonal concepts.

One of the earliest studies in this area was conducted by Bass (1962) in which he assessed the effects of T-groups on sensitivity to interpersonal behaviour. He showed parts of the film *Twelve Angry Men* to 34 managers before and after a two-week T-group. To measure sensitivity, he queried each participant about the film by use of an incomplete sentence test. Each participant was asked to respond to such questions as: 'The reason that the architect (Henry Fonda) went to the drinking fountain was that . . .' or 'The old man changed his vote because . . .'. From the results, Bass concluded that the T-group resulted in participants becoming more sensitive to the interpersonal relationships in the film.

It could be argued, however, that merely taking the test or seeing the film twice enhances scores. Under the circumstances control groups, both of trained (by some other method) and untrained subjects, should have been used to discount the above possibilities. Bass did, however, show the film to two other groups of trainees after training only, in order to assess possible effects of seeing the film twice. Since all the groups responded similarly on the post-test questionnaire, it was suggested that the increased sensitivity must be due to the training and not to seeing the film on two occasions.

In addition, he found that the sensitivity scores obtained by the sentence completion technique matched opinions of peers and staff psychologists', which he concludes '. . . the inference being that management training laboratories do increase participant's sensitivity'. It must be pointed out, however, that this ability to understand interpersonal relationships though demonstrated in response to the film *Twelve Angry Men* was not assessed in this study in relation to the T-group or the participants within it.

Harrison (1966) built upon the work of a number of cognitive theorists in attempting to measure changes in concept preference in interpersonal perception. His major hypothesis was that T-group trained participants should become more oriented to intrapersonal process, that is, they should change in their descriptions of others toward the use of more concepts dealing with feelings, attitudes, emotions, and perceptions. In addition, they should use more descriptions oriented to interpersonal process: the dominant or submissive relationships a person establishes, his warmth or coldness, his comfort or discomfort with others. Further, Harrison argued that if conceptual changes are caused by the training, then the extent of the change should be related to effective participation in the training activities.

115 participants took a modified form of Kelly's Role Repertory Test before, three weeks after, and three months after training. The results were processed by a coding scheme developed by Harrison (1962) and, in addition, each participant was rated by his group in terms of how he responded to feedback on his own behaviour.

As predicted, there was a change toward the use of more inferential-expressive concepts but this only became significant during the 12th to 24th week following the laboratory. In addition, Harrison found that the feedback ratings were correlated with inferential-expressive change scores.

Harrison notes, somewhat cautiously, that in studies of this kind it is often impractical to obtain an adequate control group. He argues that experimental manipulation lessens the possibility of the results being simply an artifact of the measurement process and the relationships found in his study between ratings of active learning and changes in concept usage provide strength to his argument.

Argyris (1965) used a set of categories designed by himself to measure interpersonal competence as a basis to evaluate the relative effectiveness of lecture *versus* T-group training in the areas of interpersonal relationships and group dynamics. Though this is primarily an evaluation study Argyris does succeed in demonstrating that T-group trained participants do change behaviourally in the way they tackle case studies. They tend, on the whole, to be much more trusting and open in discussing and diagnosing case studies than do control groups of lecture trained course members.

Finally, Oshry and Harrison (1966) report a study in which data was collected from 46 participants in a two-week T-group for middle managers. They used the Problem Analysis Questionnaire, which is designed to measure diagnostic style in individual patterns of analysing interpersonal work problems. They hypothesized that participants with regard to the 'focus of work-related problems' should (1) increase in perceived importance of self as a cause, (2) decrease in perceived importance of others as cause(s) and (3) decrease in perceived importance of environmental factors as causes. As predicted there were statistically significant increases in the perceived importance of self as a cause of work-related problems and statistically significant decreases in the perceived importance of other(s) and environmental factors.

The authors also found that although the T-group tends to orient participants away from the back-home environment, the diagnostic orientations learned about self in relation to the T-group appears to generalize to learnings about self in relation to work. Specifically, the analysis of the questionnaire suggested that at the end of the T-group but before re-entering his work environment the participant perceives:

(1) His work would seem to him to be more human and less impersonal.

(2) He sees clearer connections between how well interpersonal needs are met and how well the work gets done.

(3) He sees himself clearly as the most significant part of his work problems.

(4) He sees no clear connection between his new perceptions and how he translates these into action.

The authors themselves are well aware of the serious limitations of a single research design without controls but they believe that the results from a pilot project are of sufficient interest to warrant publication.

Conclusion

In concluding this chapter we can only point to the essentially mixed results. Very few of the studies reviewed yield unequivocal results, possibly because of inadequate measures or poor research design. Perhaps it is unwise to expect basic perceptual or personality changes to be manifested; perhaps critical changes do occur, but these are not measured by the available instruments. For example, a participant may learn how to manage his feelings of hostility better, to use his aggression more appropriately and a relatively crude measure will not necessarily pick this up. It is noticeable that none of the measures utilized take into account the nature of the eliciting situation—hostility or aggression in one set of circumstances may be critically different from its use in another. For example, a participant could score highly on hostility in an early session and highly in a late session but his hostility may be functional and appropriate in the later session. Unless we take into account the nature of the eliciting situation, we simply record no change in hostility.

In view of the measurement difficulties, therefore, it would be less than fair to conclude that T-group training has no lasting effect on perceptual or personality variables.

References

Argyris, C. (1965) 'Explorations in interpersonal competence—II.' *Journal of Applied Behavioral Science*, **1**, 255–269.

Asquith, R. H. and D. E. Hedlund (1967) 'Laboratory training and supervisory attitudes.' *Psychological Reports*, **20**, 618.

Bass, B. M. (1962) 'Reactions to "12 Angry Men" as a measure of sensitivity training.' *Journal of Applied Psychology*, **46**, 120–124.

Baumgartel, H. and J. W. Goldstein (1967) 'Need and value shifts in college training groups.' *Journal of Applied Behavioral Science*, **3**, 87–101.

Bennis, W., R. Burke, H. Cutter, H. Harrington and J. Hoffman (1957) 'A note on some problems of measurement and prediction in a training group.' *Group Psychotherapy*, **10**, 328–341.

Bowers, N. D. and R. S. Soar (1961) 'Evaluation of laboratory human relations training for classroom teachers.' Unpublished manuscript, University of South Carolina.

Burke, H. L. and W. G. Bennis (1961) 'Changes in perception of self and others during human relations training.' *Human Relations*, **14**, 165–182.

Campbell, J. P. and M. D. Dunnette (1968) 'Effectiveness of T-group experiences in managerial training and development.' *Psychological Bulletin*, **70**, 73–104.

Carron, T. J. (1964) 'Human relations training and attitude change: a vector analysis.' *Personnel Psychology*, **17**, 403–424.

Carson, R. C. and M. Lakin (1963) 'Some effects of group sensitivity experience.' Paper read at Southeastern Psychological Association meeting, Miami Beach, Florida, April 1963.

Castle, P. F. C. (1952) 'The evaluation of human relations training for supervisors.' *Occupational Psychology*, **25**, 191–205.

Cureton, L. (1968) Unpublished M.Ed. thesis, University of Sussex.

Dorris, R. J., D. Levinson and E. Hanfmann (1954) 'Authoritarian personality studied by a new variation of the sentence completion technique.' *Journal of Abnormal and Social Psychology*, **49**, 99–108.

Dunnette, M. D. (1962) 'Personnel management.' *Annual Review of Psychology*, **13**, 285–314.

Elliott, A. G. P. (1958) 'An experiment in group dynamics.' Unpublished manuscript. Simon Engineering Ltd.

Fleishman, E. A. and E. F. Harris (1962) 'Patterns of leadership behavior related to employee grievances and turnover.' *Personnel Psychology*, **15**, 43–56.

French, J. R. P., J. J. Sherwood and D. L. Bradford (1966) 'Change in self-identity in a management training conference.' *Journal of Applied Behavioral Science*, **2**, 210–218.

Gassner, S., J. Gold and A. M. Snadowsky (1964) 'Changes in the phenomenal field as a result of human relations training.' *Journal of Psychology*, **58**, 33–41.

Grater, M. (1959) 'Changes in self and other attitudes in a leadership training group.' *Personnel and Guidance Journal*, **37**, 493–496.

Halpin, A. W. (1957) 'The leader behavior and effectiveness of aircraft commanders.' In Stogdill, R. M. and Coons, A. E. (Eds.), *Leader Behaviour: Its Description and Measurement*. Ohio: Ohio State University, 65–68.

Harrison, R. (1962) 'The impact of the laboratory on perceptions of others by the experimental group.' In C. Argyris (Ed.), *Interpersonal Competence and Organizational Effectiveness*. Homewood, Ill.: Irwin-Dorsey.

Harrison, R. (1966) 'Cognitive change and participation in a sensitivity training laboratory.' *Journal of Consulting Psychology*, **30**, 517–520.

House, R. J. (1967) 'T-group education and leadership effectiveness: a review of the empiric literature and a critical evaluation.' *Personnel Psychology*, **20**, 1–32.

Kassarjian, W. M. (1962) 'A study of Riesman's theory of social character.' *Sociometry*, **25**, 213–230.

Kassarjian, H. H. (1965) 'Social character and sensitivity training.' *Journal of Applied Behavioral Science*, **1**, 433–440.

Kernan, J. P. (1964) 'Laboratory human relations training: its effect on the "personality" of supervisory engineers.' *Dissertation Abstracts*, **25**, 665–666.

Martin, H. O. (1957) 'The assessment of training.' *Personnel Management*, **39**, 88–93.

Meigniez, R. (1961) 'Evaluation des resultats de la formation.' L'Association Francaise pour l'Accroissement de la Productivite, Paris.

Miles, M. B. (1965) 'Changes during and following laboratory training: a clinical-experimental study.' *Journal of Applied Behavioral Science*, **1**, 215–242.

Oshry, B. I. and R. Harrison (1966) 'Transfer from here-and-now to there-and-then: Changes in organizational problem diagnosis stemming from T-group training.' *Journal of Applied Behavioral Science*, **2**, 185–198.

Rubin, I. (1967) 'The reduction of prejudice through laboratory training.' *Journal of Applied Behavioral Science*, **3**, 29–50.

Schutz, W. C. (1958) *FIRO: A Three-Dimensional Theory of Interpersonal Behavior*. New York: Holt, Rinehart & Winston.

Schutz, W. C. and V. L. Allen (1966) 'The effects of a T-group laboratory on interpersonal behavior.' *Journal of Applied Behavioral Science*, **2**, 265–286.

Smith, P. B. (1964) 'Attitude changes associated with training in human relations.' *British Journal of Social and Clinical Psychology*, **3**, 104–113.

Zimet, C. N. and H. J. Fine (1955) 'Personality changes with a group therapeutic experience in a human relations seminar.' *Journal of Abnormal and Social Psychology*, **51**, 68–73.

Attitude Changes Associated with Training in Human Relations*

Peter B. Smith

School of Social Studies, University of Sussex

Members of training groups in human relations change their attitudes toward social behaviour in a way that members of other groups do not. Those trained showed a convergence toward median scores on scales measuring their attitudes toward power and close personal relationships. These attitudes were found to be related to perceptions of their actual behaviour by other group members. Perceptions of the behaviour of those scoring median on the attitude scales were generally consonant with current descriptions of 'effective' behaviour.

Introduction

Training in human relations by non-directive methods has now been under way in the United States for more than 15 years. Despite the pioneering work of Bion (1961) more than 20 years ago in London, only in the last 5 years have such methods been widely used in Britain. The phrase 'training in human relations by non-directive methods' is used here to mean any method which relies primarily on the trainee achieving insights into the nature of social behaviour by discovery rather than by formal instruction. The intentions of those developing non-directive training have been to set up conditions which facilitate such learning by discovery. This has normally meant bringing together a group of people for the purpose of studying the behaviour of their own group, with the aid of a staff member, often known as the trainer. The trainer's task is to indicate by occasional interventions, in the form of questions or tentative interpretations, the areas of behaviour which he regards as providing useful data for study. Such trainer interventions often do not focus directly on the tasks which the groups may set themselves, but on the processes by which the goals of the group are achieved. The development of these methods in Britain has been surveyed by Crichton (1962).

The assessment of the insights which are achieved by those undergoing training poses methodological problems which few studies have yet over-

* Published in the *British Journal of Social and Clinical Psychology*, 1964, 3, 104–112.

come. Miles (1959, 1960) has provided a concise summary of contemporary training aims in terms of increases in:

'*Sensitivity:* the ability to perceive what is actually going on in a social situation (including both behavioural events and inferred feelings of other persons).

Diagnostic ability: the skill of assessing on-going social situations in a way that enables effective action; the employment of appropriate explanatory categories to understand reasons for presented interaction.

Action skill: the ability to intervene effectively in on-going situations in such a way as to maximize personal and group effectiveness and satisfaction . . .'.

The most direct test of increases in these three variables would be a study of the job behaviour of those trained, since a crucial component of training must be that the insights achieved are transferable by the individual into his normal life-situation. Miles (1960) showed that the job behaviour of 34 schoolteachers was perceived to change after training, both by the teachers themselves and by their associates. The teachers perceived themselves in ways which Miles classified as 'more sensitive to the needs of others' and 'showing greater action skill', while the associates most often saw the teachers as showing improved leadership skills and communicating more openly. These changes were not found among the controls. In a study by Harrison, reported in Argyris (1962), changes were examined in the ways in which those who had been trained perceived associates who had not. It was found that descriptions by at least some managers of their untrained associates showed an increased use of 'interpersonal–emotional' terms. The controls described their associates uniformly in terms of 'rational–intellective' concepts. The trained managers were thus utilizing data about their associates which the controls were discarding as unimportant. This change would be most closely related to increases in Miles' variable sensitivity. These and other studies of training outcomes are discussed more fully in Smith (1962b).

The present study examines changes in the attitudes toward social behaviour of those trained; such changes may *imply* increases in Miles' three variables. The attitudes considered were those toward control behaviour, which is concerned with power, and affection behaviour, which is concerned with close personal relationships. Control and affection behaviours are among the most important in the interaction of non-directive training groups. Issues relating to control behaviour often focus on the role of the trainer who, by refusing to lead in the expected manner, sets the group a leadership problem which it must solve. Likewise, issues relating to affection behaviour usually arise as concerns about how much each individual shall reveal of his personal feelings. The training group is a situation which arouses mild anxiety in many people. Faced with ambiguity, each person soon shows his characteristic patterns of origination of control and affection behaviours.

Attitudes toward control and affection behaviours were measured on four Guttman scales derived from Schutz's (1958) FIRO. For each behaviour one scale (the 'expected' scale) measures how often the respondent expects to show the behaviour himself, and the second scale ('wanted' scale) measures how often he wants others to show the behaviour. If the simple postulate is established that we seek to repeat those patterns of behaviour that we find rewarding, both scales can be considered as yielding data as to what the respondent finds more rather than less rewarding. A respondent with a high 'expected' score and a low 'wanted' score will be most highly rewarded when his behaviour is more active than that of others in his group. Conversely, a respondent with a low 'expected' score and a high 'wanted' score will be most highly rewarded when he can behave more passively than most members of his group. In this paper the difference between a man's 'expected' and 'wanted' scores will be referred to as his reward score. The use of the reward score will be to predict whether an individual prefers control behaviour to affection behaviour. As such it clearly measures only the *relative* rewards derivable by the individual from these two behaviours; there is not usually any reason to expect reward scores to relate to an individual's *overall* reward levels, for example whether he is satisfied or dissatisfied with his membership of a group. This distinction is a familiar one in economics, and has been discussed at length in Homans (1961) and Thibaut and Kelly (1959). Reward scores were divided as nearly as possible into equal thirds described as positive, zero and negative. A positive reward score is one for which the 'expected' score exceeds the 'wanted' score.

Schutz suggests that those with positive or negative reward scores tend to respond to anxiety-provoking situations in a fixed way, whereas those with zero reward scores are less anxious and therefore more able to respond to any situation adaptively. For example, in the case of control behaviour, the negative reward scorer tends to avoid or withdraw from situations in which he must exercise control, so as to minimize his anxieties about controlling people; the positive reward scorer exercises compulsive control wherever he can, in order to reassure anxieties that he is basically incapable of controlling others; but the zero reward scorer is able both to control and to be controlled, as the situation demands, without undue anxiety.

The changes resulting from non-directive training will vary with the personality of each individual. Those with positive reward scores may be expected to learn of some of the unintended effects of their behaviour, and to become more skilled in regulating their patterns of interventions in accord with the needs of the situation. Those with negative reward scores may learn of the greater rewards to be derived from active intervention. A convergence toward the median may therefore be predicted. This expectation may be compared with Berlew's (1960) findings relating sensitivity to motive strength. Using projective tests, he found that ability to predict other people's perceptions of their own behaviour was greatest among those who scored median on tests of need-power and need-affiliation. If projective measures of need-power and need-affiliation can be considered as equivalent to Guttman scale measures of attitudes toward control and affection, Berlew's findings indicate maximum sensitivity among median scorers.

The mechanism whereby such convergence toward the median might occur can be readily envisaged. One of the processes encouraged by trainers is the 'giving and receiving of feedback'. This is a process whereby group members tell each other what impact their behaviour has had on them. Training group members thus obtain a much fuller picture of the effects of their behaviour on others than they do in everyday life. The permissive atmosphere of a training group provides the member with an opportunity to try out and learn new roles or methods of responding to familiar situations.

The prediction of appreciable changes in attitudes after training poses the question of whether the attitudes are related to actual behaviour. Since the FIRO scales used take the form of action-oriented statements (e.g. 'I let other people decide what to do'), a positive relationship may be foreseen. Borg (1960), Sapolsky (1960) and Smith (1962a) have reported significant relationships between FIRO scores and independent measures of actual behaviour, such as amount of verbal participation.

Method

All subjects were either managers on training courses or undergraduates studying management at various universities. All but two were men. The managers were predominantly graduates of between 30 and 40. The 108 experimental subjects were members of eleven non-directive training groups, four of undergraduates and seven of managers. The 44 control subjects were members of six discussion groups, one of undergraduates and five of managers. These discussions were led by a staff member, acting in a more or less directive role, and considered aspects of social psychology relevant to management problems. Manager groups mostly met intensively for a few weeks while undergraduate groups lasted through the academic year.

The attitude measure used was Schutz's (1958) FIRO questionnaire, which consisted originally of six Guttman scales describing the respondent's perception of how often he performs certain behaviours and how often he likes others to do so. The four scales used in this study were slightly revised for British usage, and were those describing attitudes toward control and affection behaviours.

Subjects completed the FIRO questionnaire near the beginning and again near the end of their course. At the same time all but three groups made checklist nominations of the behaviours which they had perceived in other members of their group. These nominations were used to test the validity of the FIRO reward scores. The checklist comprised six control behaviours, six affection behaviours and three behaviours which were not classifiable as control or affection behaviours:

Control behaviours

> Striving for individual recognition
> Discussing usefulness of meetings
> Dividing up the task
> Making rules or laying down procedures
> Attempting to dominate or to control
> Rebelling or obstructing the group

Affection behaviours

> Laughing and showing happiness
> Attempting to preserve group unity
> Reconciling antagonisms
> Attempting to draw people in
> Showing close friendship
> Discussing close personal details

Other behaviours

> Withdrawing from group activity
> Disliking or rejecting others
> Submitting to others' wishes

Results

The coefficients of reproducibility of the four Guttman scales of FIRO are shown in Table 1. Highly significant test–retest reliability was found for both control and affection reward scores. When positive, zero and negative scores were compared, using the scores obtained early and late during each group's duration, chi-square for control was 53·3, and for affection 39·4

3

Table 1—*Coefficients of reproducibility of*
FIRO scales

FIRO scale	Coefficient
Expressed control	0·91
Wanted control	0·93
Expressed affection	0·96
Wanted affection	0·94

(Smith, 1962a). Both these values of chi-square are significant for 4 degrees of freedom at $p < 0.001$.

While the reward scores are therefore reliable within gross limits, this does not necessarily mean that no changes occurred in the attitudes of those trained. The predicted changes are:

(i) a fall in positive reward scores, and
(ii) a rise in negative reward scores.

Table 2 compares the changes in non-directive training groups and the control discussion groups.

Table 2—*Number of subjects showing rise or fall in reward scores*

	Initial reward scores								
	Positive			Zero			Negative		
Subjects	+	=	−	+	=	−	+	=	−
Experimentals									
Controls	5	6	29	11	5	11	20	6	15
Affection	4	7	12	11	5	12	30	9	8
Controls									
Controls	8	3	11	2	2	5	7	3	3
Affection	3	2	8	5	2	6	8	2	6

In the experimental groups, 91 scores changed in the predicted direction and 32 in the reverse direction. This is highly significant ($p < 0.001$: 1-tailed binomial test).

In the control groups, 36 scores changed in the direction predicted for the experimental groups and 24 in the reverse direction. This change is not significant. When the change found in the experimental group is compared with that in the control group, the difference is again significant ($p < 0.001$). The most marked changes in the experimental groups were the fall in positive control reward scores and the rise in negative affection reward scores. The method of analysis adopted can give no indication of the magnitude of the changes found, but it does show that they occurred frequently.

The division of control and affection reward scores into equal thirds means that the subjects can be subdivided into nine separate types. However it is not expected that the behaviour of each of the nine types will be differentially perceived by others. For example, subjects with negative reward scores will be predominantly inactive, making it difficult for others to perceive control or affection behaviours: it is predicted that they will be perceived as showing 'neither control nor affection' behaviours. The nine types have been combined into the five classes for which different predictions may be made. These are:

1. Control reward score positive and affection reward score negative.
2. Affection reward score positive and control reward score negative.
3. Both reward scores positive, or one positive and the other zero.
4. Both reward scores zero.
5. Both reward scores negative, or one negative and the other zero.

The general predictions were made that positive reward scores would be associated with frequently occurring perceptions of control and affection behaviours, while zero reward scores would be associated with a chance occurrence of perceptions of the behaviours, and negative reward scores with a significant lack of perceptions of the behaviours. The specific predictions derivable for each class are shown in Table 3.

The occurrence of each of the 15 behaviours on the checklist was analysed separately. The degree to which each of the five classes was characterized by the various behaviours was established by consideration of the occurrence of checklist nominations in the class, relative to their occurrence in the total sample. Ratios were computed for each behaviour and every class, as follows:

$$\text{Ratio} = \frac{\text{Actual no. of nominations in class}}{\text{Expected no. of nominations in class}}$$

where

expected nominations = total nominations for all classes × the
proportion of total subjects in the class.

Table 3 tests whether the most and least characteristic behaviours of members of each class were those that had been predicted from FIRO reward scores. The ratios were rank ordered and the predictions tested by the Mann–Whitney U-test.

The predictions are significantly upheld for Classes 1, 3 and 4, and

Table 3—*Relationship between behaviour predicted from FIRO reward scores and behaviour assessments by other group members*

Class	Prediction	p
1	C will predominate	$< 0 \cdot 02$
2	A will predominate	$< 0 \cdot 10$
3	C and A will predominate	$< 0 \cdot 01$
4	No predominant behaviour	$C < N$, A n.s.
		$A < C$, N n.s.
		$N < C$, A n.s.
5	N will predominate	n.s.

Key: C—Control behaviour
　　　A—Affection behaviour
　　　N—Behaviours which are neither control nor affection
　　　The classes are defined above.

approach significance for Class 2. Class 5 contains those group members whose behaviour is least easily perceived, so that the failure of the prediction is not unexpected.

This paper has outlined some of the stated aims of those active in non-directive training. It has also given evidence as to the changes actually found in some training groups. If the training is successful, there should be a close correspondence between training aims and actual changes. The ratios calculated show which of the behaviours on the checklist were perceived as most characteristic of group members of the various personality types derived from the FIRO reward scores. Since those trained tend toward zero reward scores, those who already have zero reward scores should come closest to exemplifying Miles' three training aims—'sensitivity', 'diagnostic ability' and 'action skill', while those with positive or negative scores should be less well placed.

Table 4 shows the distribution between the five classes of the behaviours on the checklist. For each behaviour a value of chi-square was computed to test the randomness of the occurrence of the behaviours. The table includes only those behaviours which were perceived differentially among members of the different classes ($p < 0 \cdot 05$). The table shows marked differences between the behaviours characterizing the different classes, and also in the degree to which the classes were characterized by distinct behaviours. Members of Class 1 were characterized by self-oriented high activity control behaviours and a mimumum of affection behaviour. Members of Class 2 were characterized by the absence of control behaviours rather than a high incidence of affection behaviours. Members of Class 3 showed predominantly high activity behaviours, both control and affection, many of which

Table 4—*Behaviour of the different classes of training group members*

	Class					Chi-square
Behaviours	1	2	3	4	5	
Control						
Striving for individual recognition	1·68	0·73	1·28	0·51	0·64	36·86
Discussing usefulness of meetings	1·12	0·74	1·17	1·24	0·85	12·94
Dividing up the task	0·89	0·52	1·06	2·25	0·95	11·27
Attempting to dominate or to control	1·57	0·56	1·49	0·36	0·58	38·00
Affection						
Laughing and showing happiness	1·02	0·79	1·25	0·98	0·83	14·36
Reconciling antagonisms	0·40	1·10	1·14	1·86	0·94	10·27
Showing close friendship	0·37	0·96	1·58	0·64	0·78	17·68
Neither						
Withdrawing from group activity	0·82	0·86	0·61	0·98	1·42	22·30

The classes are defined on p. 49. Ratios are obtained by dividing actual numbers of checklist nominations by the number to be expected on the basis of nominations in the total population. The table includes only those behaviours whose distribution between the classes differed from randomness at $p < 0.05$. The values of chi-square are shown on the right.

were self-oriented. Conversely, Class 5 showed a lack of high activity control behaviours and typically withdrew from group activity. The most frequent behaviours in Classes 1, 2, 3 and 5 were thus high activity self-oriented behaviours or else withdrawal from group activity.

However, it is the behaviour of Class 4 members which is of particular interest because the class is made up of zero reward scorers, towards which other members of training groups have been shown to change their attitudes. Members of Class 4 were the most clearly characterized of any class, obtaining both the highest and lowest values of the ratio. The characteristic behaviours were those that take into account not only the needs of the individual but also those of the group. In contrast to the infrequent self-oriented behaviours, the Class 4 member was often perceived as 'dividing up the task', 'reconciling antagonisms' and 'discussing usefulness of meetings'.

Discussion

The training group in human relations is a potent agent for change of attitudes about social behaviour. The effects of the individual's learning about the ways in which others perceive his behaviours may include marked changes in his habitual behaviours and in the way others come to perceive these behaviours. The evidence cited in support of these statements in this paper gives only general indications of their probable truth. Human relations training is currently conducted with many different emphases and no evidence is yet forthcoming as to whether these different emphases affect the training outcomes. The two Leeds training groups were conducted as 'sensitivity training', which usually means that the trainer indicates a greater preference for discussing participants' feelings rather than the development of group roles. On the other hand the six Simon (Engineering) training groups had trainers who behaved in more varied ways and the groups participated also in more formal lectures and exercises in social psychology. The three Cambridge training groups showed an intermediate emphasis.

Burke and Bennis (1961) reported increases in similarity of perceptions of individuals by self and others in training groups. Such a study gives no evidence as to increases in *sensitivity*, since perceptions late in the life of a training group are based on much greater information than earlier perceptions. The present study, in contrast, shows that attitudes changed toward the median, and that median scorers were perceived in ways that have been described; but early perceptions were not separated from late ones. Thus the changes found could not be artifacts derived from the possibility that training group members may come to know each other much better than the control group members.

Early writers in the field of human relations often stressed the need to reduce or eliminate social conflict. Their critics (e.g. Whyte (1956), McNair (1957)) tended to feel that this emphasis represented an attack on individuality, a too-ready advocacy of submission to group pressures in the interests of smooth social working. Recent writers on human relations training have laid much more emphasis on the need to recognize and bring into the open substantive conflicts (e.g. Argyris, 1962). Effective group behaviour is seen as that which is based on a realistic knowledge of differences of viewpoint as well as of similarities. Parallel thinking is implicit in Miles' definition of 'action skill' cited earlier, where he states that interventions should maximize both personal and group satisfactions. Where these are not reconciled there will be conflict. This conception of effective behaviour is well illustrated by the present findings. The zero reward scorer is perceived as showing close friendship as infrequently as the self-oriented control behaviours. Indeed there is a tendency for him also to be perceived as 'rebelling or obstructing the group', but chi-square for this behaviour does not quite achieve the required significance level.

The changes in attitudes found can be seen as a response to a situation in which customary behaviours proved to be inappropriate. Whether the changes persist will depend primarily on the reactions of the trained man's associates in the weeks after his return from the course, and on the degree of continuing support which he receives from others who participated in the training.

References

Argyris, C. (1962) *Interpersonal Competence and Organizational Effectiveness.* London: Tavistock.

Berlew, D. E. (1961) 'Interpersonal sensitivity and motive strength.' *J. abnorm. soc. Psychol.*, **63**, 390–394.

Bion, W. R. (1961) *Experiences in Groups.* London: Tavistock.

Borg, W. R. (1960) 'The prediction of role behaviour in small groups from personality variables.' *J. abnorm. soc. Psychol.*, **60**, 112–117.

Burke, R. L. and W. G. Bennis (1961) 'Changes in perceptions of self and others during human relations training.' *Hum. Relat.*, **14**, 165–182.

Crichton, Anne (1962) 'Personnel Management and Working Groups.' *Institute of Personnel Management, Occasional Papers*, **18**.

Homans, G. C. (1961) *Social Behaviour: Its Elementary Forms.* New York: Harcourt–Brace.

McNair, M. (1957) 'What price human relations?' *Harvard Bus. Rev.* **35**.

Miles, M. B. (1959) *Learning to Work in Groups.* New York: Teachers' College, Bureau of Publications.

Miles, M. B. (1960) 'Human relations training: processes and outcomes.' *J. couns. Psychol.*, **7**, 301–306.

Sapolsky, A. (1960) 'Effect of interpersonal relationships upon verbal conditioning.' *J. abnorm. soc. Psychol.*, **40**, 241–246.

Schutz, W. C. (1958) *FIRO: A Three-Dimensional Theory of Interpersonal Behaviour.* New York: Rinehart.

Smith, P. B. (1962a) 'Role differentiation in small social groups.' Cambridge: Unpublished Ph.D. thesis.

Smith, P. B. (1962b) 'A survey of research into attitude and behaviour changes resulting from "human relations" training.' *Working Papers in Industrial Management*, I. Industrial Management Division, University of Leeds.

Thibaut, J. W. and H. H. Kelley (1959) *The Social Psychology of Groups.* New York: Wiley.

Whyte, W. H. (1956) *The Organisation Man.* New York: Simon & Schuster.

Changes in the Phenomenal Field as a Result of Human Relations Training*

Suzanne M. Gassner
Jerome Gold
Alvin M. Snadowsky

Department of Student Life,
The City College of the City University of New York

A. Introduction

Fundamental to the phenomenological approach to the understanding of human personality is the differentiation between the phenomenal self (including the self-concept) and the general phenomenal field (7). A relatively high degree of congruence between an individual's self-concept and his ideal self is considered to be an indication of good adjustment (6, pp. 55–75; 8; 13). Moreover, it has been found that an individual's acceptance of himself is positively and significantly correlated with his acceptance of others (2, 11, 12, 14).

Recently, a number of experiments reported that human-relations training leads to changes in the phenomenal self. Burke and Bennis (5), using an adaptation of Osgood's Semantic Differential to test the changes brought about by a three-week human-relations training program, reported a significant reduction in the discrepancy between the participants' self-image and ideal image. Grater (9) arrived at similar results using the Bills' Index of Adjustment and Values to test the effectiveness of an 11-week leadership training program for 30 college students. However, the hypothesized decrease in the discrepancy between the average other person and the ideal self was not found to be significant, though results were in the predicted direction.

The City College of New York conducts a three-day human-relations training program (HRP) based on the design pioneered by Bradford, Lippitt and Gibb (4). The aims of the program are to help the participants gain an understanding of behavior (both their own and that of others) and to provide an atmosphere conducive to change. Initial evaluation of the HRP was

* Published as a separate and in *The Journal of Psychology*, 1964, **58**, 33–41. We wish to thank the City College Fund for the grant-in-aid which supported the publication of this research.

based on the participants' responses to a postmeeting reaction form. Reactions to the program were overwhelmingly enthusiastic, with 99 per cent of the students reporting that they had gained new skills and insights. Staff trainers have also reported that program participants became progressively more effective group members during the course of the HRP.

Based on these preliminary observations, it appears that The City College human-relations program, though considerably shorter in duration than those programs mentioned above, might nevertheless produce similar fundamental changes in the phenomenal self. It is therefore hypothesized that participation in the HRP causes an increase in the similarity between (a) an individual's self-concept and ideal-self concept and (b) an individual's self-concept and image of the average other.

The possibility that changes occur in areas of the participant's phenomenal field other than in his phenomenal self also seemed worth investigating. Bass (1) studied the kinds of changes that occur in the general phenomenal field as a result of the training programs. He found that human-relations training leads to an increase in participants' sensitivity and understanding of interpersonal relations. Other kinds of attitude changes may be produced as a result of such programs. An integral part of the HRP is the demonstration and practice of skills required for effective democratic leadership. It is therefore expected that a significant increase in an individual's understanding of democratic leadership functions, and changes in his attitudes concerning such functions, occur as a result of participation in the HRP.

The first two experiments of this investigation, which parallel those reported in the literature, used a modified form of the Bills' Index of Adjustment and Values and a graphic rating scale to measure the changes that occurred in the divergence between the self-concept, the ideal-self concept and the image of the other, for participants in the HRP. In the third experiment, attitudes toward democratic leadership functions, and understanding of them, were measured. However, unlike several of the research efforts referred to above, the instruments used were also administered to a control group.

B. Experiment 1

1. Method

(a) Subjects. Ss were 67 City College undergraduates. Forty-six were student trainees who attended the sixth semiannual HRP, the Experimental (EI) group. Twenty-one were students who submitted applications for the forthcoming program, the Control (C1) group.

(b) *Procedure.* One day prior to the onset of the HRP and two days after the completion of the Workshop, a modified form of the Bills' Index of Adjustment and Values (3) was administered individually to each subject. Ss were told that they were participating in a study to obtain information about the beliefs and attitudes that C.C.N.Y. students have about themselves and other people. Using a series of 50 adjectives, Ss rated themselves on the following statements: (a) 'This is characteristic of me', (b) 'I would like this to be characteristic of me', and (c) 'Most C.C.N.Y. students my age would like this to be characteristic of them'. Each statement headed a separate page followed by the series of adjectives.

(c) *Scoring.* The absolute discrepancies between the various statements on each of the adjective ratings were calculated for each S. The geometric mean was computed to provide a D score for each S for both administrations. Nonparametric statistics were used in the analysis of the data, because the distribution of the D values is not known.

2. Results

Results of the Wilcoxon matched-pairs signed-ranks test (Table 1) show that there was a significant increase in similarity between self-perceptions and ideal-self perceptions in both the E1 and C1 groups. In addition, both groups showed a significant increase in similarity between self-perceptions and average-other perceptions.

Table 1—*Increase in similarity between self-ideal and self-other perceptions sixth HRP—modified Bills' Index of adjustment and values* (*Wilcoxon matched-pairs signed-ranks test with z score transformations*)

Population	T	N	z	p
Self-ideal				
Experimental	242·5	46	3·26	0·0006[a]
Control	18·0	21	3·40	0·0006[b]
Self-other				
Experimental	87·0	46	4·96	<0·0001[a]
Control	15·0	21	3·48	0·0004[b]

[a] one-tailed test
[b] two-tailed test

However, when the changes in self-ideal D scores (from the first to the second administration of the test) were examined, it was found that E1 group changes did not differ significantly from C1 group changes. Similarly, self-other D scores did not change in a significantly different fashion for the two groups (Table 2).

Table 2—*Tests of the differences between D scores for the experimental and control groups*

Test	Experiment 1 (N=67)		Experiment 2 (N=72)	
	Self-ideal	Self-other	Self-ideal	Self-other
Rank test (z)	0·04	1·57	0·44	1·59
Sign test (χ^2)	0·06	0·57	0·06	3·60

C. Experiment 2

1. *Method*

(a) *Subjects*. Ss were 72 City College undergraduates. Forty-five were student trainees who attended the seventh HRP (E2 group) and 27 were students enrolled in psychology courses at the college (C2 group).

(b) *Procedure*. In the E2 group, a modified form of the Burke and Bennis graphic-rating-scale series was administered to the trainees at both the introductory session and the closing session of the HRP.

Ss were told that they were participating in a study of word meanings and that 'the object of the study is to find out how you like to describe yourself and others'.

Three concepts were rated against a uniform series of bipolar traits that were selected for their relevance to the attitudes being measured. The concepts were (a) the way I actually am in a City College group, (b) the way I would like to be in a City College group, and (c) the way other City College students generally act in a group. Each concept headed a separate page and was followed by the series of 18 scales.

The instructions given for the second administration were 'to take into account your experiences during the past three days. You may feel free to change your original responses or to respond as you did initially. In any case your answers should be an accurate description of yourself and other people as you see them.'

Control group Ss completed the graphic rating scale twice, with a three-day time interval, during regularly scheduled classroom sessions. The instructions were identical to those used for the E2 group.

(c) *Scoring*. D scores were computed using the procedure described in Experiment 1.

2. *Results*

The results of the Wilcoxon matched-pair signed-ranks test (Table 3), indicate that in the E2 and C2 groups there was a significant increase in similarity between self-perceptions and average-other perceptions. However, unlike the findings of Experiment 1, there was no significant increase in similarity between the self-concept and the ideal-self concept in either the E2 or C2 groups.

Table 3—*Increase in similarity between self-ideal and self-other perceptions seventh HRP—graphic rating scale (Wilcoxon matched-pair signed-ranks test with z score transformations)*

Population	T	N	z	p
Self-ideal				
Experimental	405·5	45	1·26	0·10[a]
Control	156·0	27	0·79	0·43[b]
Self-other				
Experimental	232·0	45	3·21	0·0007[a]
Control	105·0	27	2·02	0·041[b]

[a] one-tailed test
[b] two-tailed test

Using both the rank test for two independent samples and the sign test (Table 2) it was found that when the changes in the E2 and C2 groups were compared, the differences were not statistically significant.

D. Experiment 3

1. *Method*

(a) *Subjects.* Ss were 122 City College undergraduates. Ninety-four were student trainees who attended the seventh and eighth HRPs (E3 groups) and 28 were students enrolled in psychology courses at the City College (C3 group).

(b) *Procedure.* At the introductory sessions of the seventh and eighth HRPs, a 'Democratic Leadership Attitude Scale' was administered to a group of 43 and 51 trainees respectively. The 23 items of the scale were selected from the Ideology Questionnaire* by a panel of judges (staff trainers). Only

* Adapted from an Ideology Questionnaire developed by David Jenkins and others at Bethel National Training Laboratories in Group Development.

questions that measured attitudes toward and understanding of democratic leadership were chosen. Ss were asked to rate the statements on a five-point scale (from strongly disagree to strongly agree). They were told that the statements referred to opinions regarding a number of leadership issues about which some people agreed and others disagreed. The second administration was conducted during the final evaluation session. Ss were instructed to 'feel free to change your original responses or respond as you did initially'.

Control group Ss completed the first administration of the Democratic Leadership Attitude Scale during a regularly scheduled classroom session. Two days later Ss were again asked to complete the forms.

(c) *Scoring*. Using the judges' responses as a criterion, each of the 23 items was assigned a correct answer that was either 'agree' or 'disagree'. Subjects received points as follows: (a) If the correct answer was 'agree' an answer of 'agree or strongly agree' received $+1$; an answer of 'disagree or strongly disagree' received -1; and an answer of 'undecided' equalled zero. (b) If the correct answer was 'disagree', the scoring was in reverse to the above. The maximum score was 23; the minimum, -23.

2. *Results*

Whereas both E3 and C3 groups were initially equal in their attitudes toward and understanding of democratic leadership concepts, the difference between the groups after the HRP was statistically significant (Table 4). This difference was caused by the increase in understanding of democratic leadership concepts that occurred in the experimental group.

Table 4—*Tests of the differences between means on the democratic leadership attitude test*

Group	N	Pre-test	Post-test	t
Seventh HRP				
Experimental	43	12·7	16·4	5·32[b]
Control	28	12·6	12·3	0·52
t	—	0·098	3·94[b]	—
Eighth HRP				
Experimental	51	12·5	15·8	6·75[b]
Control	28	12·6	12·3	0·52
t	—	0·096	3·27[a]	—

[a] Significant at 0·01 level
[b] Significant at 0·001 level

E. Discussion

HRP trainees shifted their perceptions of themselves and others in the predicted directions. This aspect of the results is similar to the findings that Grater, and Burke and Bennis report. However, unlike the experiments they report, when a control group was used, it was found that similar changes in the phenomenal-self attitudes could be demonstrated, and the extent of change between E and C groups was shown to be statistically insignificant. The control group adds an important dimension to this research because the information it provides forces a rejection of the initial conclusion that HRP participation causes change in the phenomenal self. If a control group had been used in previous research, the conclusions may have been modified or reversed and personality structure may have been found to be more stable than the earlier experiments have indicated.

Another possible interpretation of the results of earlier studies is that methodological inadequacies of self-rating scales counteracted attempts to measure changes in the phenomenal self. Wylie (16) suggests that a subject may try to present himself as having attitudes other than those that are actually true of himself, and that he may not be willing to reveal certain information about himself. A further consideration is the effect of familiarity on future responses to scale words. Taylor (15) found a marked increase in the similarity between the self-image and the ideal-self image on repeated tests conducted over a short time interval. Finally, Jourard and Lasakow (10) have pointed out that subjects will describe their attitudes and opinions much more openly than they otherwise will, when the things described do not relate directly to the subjects' own perception of their personality; such studies do not cause as much defensiveness on the part of the participants and thus contribute less to distortions in their responses. These interpretations suggest that conclusions pertaining to changes in the phenomenal self that occur over a short period of time should be re-examined.

Human-relations training seems to stimulate growth and understanding in areas not directly related to the phenomenal self. Because highly significant changes in the participants' understanding of an attitudes toward democratic leadership were found to occur during the training experience, while no such changes occurred for members of the control group, it was concluded that the HRP is effective in teaching certain leadership principles and in developing particular attitudes toward democratic methods. This study and the one conducted by Bass (1) point to other dimensions of the phenomenal field which have been demonstrated to change over a short time period. It might be worthwhile, therefore, to investigate further the kinds of changes in concepts, other than those pertaining to the phenomenal self, that may be the outcome of human-relations training.

F. Summary

Recently research claims to demonstrate that changes in the phenomenal self occur as a result of human-relations training. Participants in a three-day human-relations program were tested on an adjective checklist and a graphic rating scale, which were used as indices of change in the phenomenal self. In general, predictions that a reduction in the trainees' discrepancy scores between the self-concept and both the ideal self and the image of the other were confirmed. Similar changes were observed to occur in the control group, but the differences between the results for the experimental and the control groups were not significant. However, when a measure of attitudes toward and understanding of democratic leadership functions was administered to both training participants and a control group, a highly significant change was found to occur for the experimental group, while no such change was observed in the control group. This information suggests that (a) personality structure may be more stable than the reports of recent experiments indicate, (b) methodological inadequacies of self-rating scales may interfere with attempts to measure changes in the phenomenal self, and (c) the measurement of attitudes other than those relating to the self is a fruitful area for further investigation in human-relations programs.

References

1. Bass, B. (1962) 'Reactions to Twelve Angry Men as a measure of sensitivity training.' *J. Appl. Psychol.*, **46**, 120–124.
2. Berger, E. M. (1952) 'The relation between expressed acceptance of self and expressed acceptance of others.' *J. Abn. & Soc. Psychol.*, **47**, 778–782.
3. Bills, R. E. (1958) 'Manual for the Index of Adjustment and Values.' Auburn: Alabama Polytechnic Inst.
4. Bradford, L. P., G. L. Lippitt and J. R. Gibb. (1956) 'Human relations training in three days.' *Adult Leadership*, **4** (10), 11–26.
5. Burke, R. L. and W. G. Bennis (1961) 'Changes in perception of self and others during human relations training.' *Hum. Relat.*, **14**, 165–182.
6. Butler, J. M. and G. V. Haigh (1954) 'Changes in the relation between self-concepts and ideal concepts consequent upon client-centered counselling.' In C. Rogers, and R. Dymond, (Eds.), *Psychotherapy and Personality Change*. Chicago, Ill.: Univ. Chicago Press.
7. Combs, A. W. and D. Snygg (1959) *Individual Behaviour. A Perceptual Approach to Behavior.* (2nd ed.) New York: Harper.
8. Cowan, E. L., F. Heitzler and H. S. Axelrod (1955) 'Self-concept conflict indicators and learning.' *J. Abn. & Soc. Psychol.*, **51**, 242–245.
9. Grater, M. (1959) 'Changes in self and other attitudes in a leadership training group.' *Person. & Guid. J.*, **37**, 493–496.
10. Jourard, S. M. and P. Lasakow (1958) 'Some factors in self-disclosure.' *J. Abn. & Soc. Psychol.*, **56**, 91–98.

11. McIntyre, C. J. (1952) 'Acceptance by others and its relation to acceptance of self and others.' *J. Abn. & Soc. Psychol.*, **47**, 624–625.
12. Omwake, K. (1954) 'The relation between acceptance of self and acceptance of others shown by three personality inventories.' *J. Consult. Psychol.*, **18**, 443–446.
13. Rogers, C. R. (1951) *Client-Centered Therapy*. Boston: Houghton Mifflin.
14. Sheerer, E. T. (1949) 'An analysis of the relationship between acceptance of and respect for self and acceptance of and respect for others in ten counselling cases.' *J. Consult. Psychol.*, **13**, 169–175.
15. Taylor, D. M. (1955) 'Changes in the self concept without psychotherapy.' *J. Consult. Psychol.*, **19**, 205–209.
16. Wylie, R. C. (1960) *The Self Concept: Critical Survey of Pertinent Research Literature*. Lincoln, Nebr.: Univ. Nebraska Press.

The Reduction of Prejudice through Laboratory Training*

Irwin Rubin

Alfred P. Sloan School of Management,
Massachusetts Institute of Technology

An experiment was conducted to test the hypothesis that increases in self-acceptance, resulting from sensitivity training, have the theoretically predictable but indirect effect of reducing an individual's level of ethnic prejudice. The role of an individual's level of psychological anomy,† hypothesized to condition the influences of sensitivity training, was also examined. The results suggest that sensitivity training may well be a powerful technique in the reduction of ethnic prejudice, particularly among those who are low in psychological anomy.

Introduction

Robert Kahn has stated (1963, p. 14), 'The theory of T Groups implies that reduction in prejudice should be one of the results of a general increase in sensitivity to the needs of others and insight into one's own motives and behavior as it affects others. No research is available, however, to test this prediction'.

Prior research (Bunker, 1963, 1965; Gordon, 1950) has shown that one of the effects of sensitivity training is an increased level of self-acceptance among the participants. In addition, it has been demonstrated that the way a person feels about himself is positively related to the way he feels about others (e.g., Stock, 1949; Sheerer, 1949). These two factors when combined, suggest the following question: Does raising a person's level of self-acceptance have the theoretically predictable but indirect effect of raising his level of acceptance-of-others?

The crux of this experiment is not that sensitivity training *per se* can be demonstrated to increase acceptance-of-others. The salient point to be tested is that demonstrated changes in a theoretically related variable (self-acceptance) produce this effect.

* Published in *Journal of Applied Behavioral Science*, **3**, 1967, 29–50. The author is grateful to Professors Edgar Schein, and William McKelvey and to David Meredith, all of M.I.T., for their many helpful comments on various drafts of this paper.
† For the definition of this term, see p. 70.

A second area of interest concerns the factors that might condition the kinds of learning an individual experiences as a result of sensitivity training. Certain personality types may be more susceptible than others to the influences of sensitivity training (Miles, 1960; Steele, 1965). The personality variable chosen for investigation in this study was psychological anomy. The rationale for this choice will be discussed in detail later.

Hypotheses

The following specific hypotheses were tested:

1. As a result of sensitivity training, an individual's level of self-acceptance will increase.

  (a) An individual's focus during the T-group sessions (as determined by trainer ratings), leaning toward more personal areas, will be associated with increased self-acceptance.

2. As a result of sensitivity training, an individual's level of acceptance-of-others will increase.

3. Those low in anomy will increase more in self-acceptance and acceptance-of-others than those high in anomy.

  (a) An individual's level of anomy will be unaffected by sensitivity training.

4. Those who increase in self-acceptance will increase more in acceptance-of-others than those who do not change or decrease in self-acceptance.

5. Changes in self-acceptance *will lead* to changes in acceptance-of-others.

Definition of variables

Sensitivity training

The major independent variable in this study is what has come to be known as sensitivity training or laboratory training.* In a broad sense, it can be defined as . . .

an educational strategy which is based primarily on the experiences generated in various social encounters by the learners themselves and aims to influence attitudes and develop competencies toward learning about human interactions (Schein and Bennis, 1965, p. 4).

Many phenomena occur within the T-group, and it is not within the scope of this study to examine the differential impact of each of these upon the variables of 'self-acceptance' and 'acceptance-of-others'. An attempt,

* For a complete discussion of all that is involved in a sensitivity training experience, see Schein and Bennis (1965).

however, was made to control for the effect of two specific aspects of all that occurred within the T-group. The trainers involved were asked to provide *for each individual*—at the end of the laboratory—the following information: (1) To what extent did the person explicitly discuss the topic of race relations (on a scale from 'not at all' to 'very much', i.e., 50 per cent of the time)? (2) What was the nature of the individual's focus during the T-group (on a 7-point scale from Group Process = 1 to Personal Development = 7)?

Self-acceptance

The term 'self-acceptance', as it is used in this paper, involves a willingness to confront ego-alien as well as ego-syntonic aspects of the self and to accept rather than deny their existence. Implicitly, it connotes some sense of rationality or 'realistic acceptance' as opposed to, for example a person's claim, 'I am superman, I accept myself as superman. Therefore all of you are underlings!'

The Dorris, Levinson, Hanfmann Sentence Completion Test (S.C.T.) (Dorris, R. J., Levinson, D. and Hanfmann, E., 1954) was used to measure the effect of sensitivity training upon an individual's level of self-acceptance. The S.C.T. includes 50 sentence stems. Half the stems use first-person pronouns and half, a third-person pronoun or proper name.* The first- and third-person items are matched in content;† e.g.,

When he gets angry he
_____
When I get angry I

The measure of self-acceptance used in this study was derived in the following manner: Individual stem completions were coded‡ for ego-threatening content.§ The term, 'ego-threatening', was defined as follows:

* First- and third-person items randomly distributed rather than appearing sequentially.
† The person instructed to complete each of the stems as quickly as he can using more than one word. After finishing all the items, he is asked to go back, reread his responses, and place a (+) sign next to those sentences that he feels refer to some personal experience or that reflect the way he might feel or act under the specified circumstances. If a sentence has no personal relevance, a (−) sign is used. In introducing the self-reference technique, the authors assumed that the denial of self-reference may be indicative of the subject's lack of awareness of the personal tendency expressed in the completion.
‡ Each pair of items was copied on separate pieces of paper. The respondent's identification number was placed on the *reverse side*. This procedure made it impossible for the coders to know whether the response was 'pre' or 'post'. It also eliminated the halo effect that might have been created by reading an individual's total record.
§ The correlation coefficient between two independently coded samples was $0 \cdot 89$. (See Johnson, 1949, p. 97, for the formula used to compute this coefficient.) The author gratefully acknowledges the assistance provided by his colleague, Tim Hall in this phase of the study.

'Any item which states or strongly implies any attitude, feelings, or action, which if accepted by* ——————— as *applying to oneself*, would involve confronting at least a mild degree of psychological pain'. For example, expression of fears, socially unacceptable responses, admission of inferiority or incompetence, extreme hostility or aggression, and so on were coded as threatening.

The assumption was then made that the more willing a person is to admit the personal relevance of ego-threatening material, the greater his level of self-acceptance. Therefore, the number of ego-threatening responses next to which the respondent placed a (+), divided by the total number of ego-threatening responses (# ET), yields the measure of self-acceptance (ETA)† used in this study.

It is important to note that, by this definition, self acceptance (ETA) can increase because the numerator increases or the denominator decreases. To clarify this point, it is hypothesized that the absolute number of statements coded as being ego-threatening will *not* change as a result of sensitivity training. The rationale here is that sensitivity training will not rid a person of his basic conflicts and anxieties nor does it attempt to help him make light of his times of crises. Instead, in some ideal sense, sensitivity training may help a person to find in himself the natural tools that enable him to effectively cope with these things. This will result, for example, from positive, nonevaluative feedback, the opportunity to test ideas and beliefs (increased 'reality testing' about oneself), and a high level of trust and openness resulting in greater authenticity. An environment is created within which there should be a reduction of an individual's need to use projective defense mechanisms which act to distort his perception of himself and others.

Acceptance-of-others

Harding and Schuman (1961) conceptualize prejudice as the departure from or failure to adhere to three ideal norms of behavior: the norm of rationality, the norm of justice, and the norm of human-heartedness. In this experiment it was decided to focus upon the norm of human-hearted-

---

* For the females, the phrase, 'the majority of women associated with the nursing profession', was inserted because virtually all the females in the experimental population fell into that category. For the males, who were more heterogeneous, the phrase, 'the average male in our culture', was inserted. Two forms of the scale—male and female— were used for this research.

† Throughout the remainder of this paper, the following symbols will be used:
1. Et means ego-threatening.
2. # ET means absolute number of sentences scored as ego-threatening.
3. ETA means self-acceptance as defined above.

ness (HH)* which enjoins a person's emotional *acceptance-of-others* in terms of their common humanity, no matter how different they may seem from oneself. The major dependent variable in this study, in other words, is not prejudice *per se* but only the effective component of the individual's attitude.

The scale is made up of 15 items† of the following type:

> The white school board in a community builds two new schools and fixes the school lines so that almost all the Negro children go to one new school and all the white children to the other new school. How do you suppose most of the Negroes in the community would react to this?
>
> ——— a. While there are some exceptions, many Negroes are mainly concerned with getting money for food, rent, and other things, and so do not have too much interest in the matter of schools one way or the other.
>
> ——— b. Every community is different, and it is almost impossible for someone not living in it to know enough about the situation to judge.
>
> ——— c. The average Negro parent would not like what the school board has done about drawing school lines.
>
> ——— d. The average Negro parent would simply be pleased to have a new school for his children, especially if it were equal to the white school in every way.

The measure of human-heartedness used in this study was derived in this manner: The respondent was asked to rank each of the four choices following an item from 1 ('most likely reaction') to 4 ('least likely reaction'). Each respondent's series of ranks was then compared with a theoretically ideal set of ranks‡ and the absolute difference between ranks was computed. The sum of these differences across the 15 experimental items yielded the respondent's human-heartedness score (HH). This score could range from 0–120 (i.e., 15 items times a maximum difference of 8 points for any item).

* Throughout the remainder of this paper, the symbol HH is used to represent an index of a person's level of acceptance-of-others.

† In addition, four control items are included to check on the extent to which response set is operating.

‡ Howard Schuman and the writer *independently* ranked all items as to how the 'most human-hearted person' would assign his ranks. We agreed on 100 per cent of the first and second ranks and 88 per cent of the third and fourth ranks, yielding an overall per cent agreement of 94 per cent.

Psychological anomy

The personality variable chosen for investigation in this research was psychological anomy,* defined as a sense of normlessness, 'the feeling that the world and oneself are adrift, wandering, lacking in clear rules and stable moorings . . . a feeling of moral emptiness' (McClosky and Schaar, 1965, p. 14). This definition is analogous to Seemans's second major usage of the alienation concept—*meaninglessness* wherein 'the individual is unclear as to what he ought to believe—when the individual's minimal standards for clarity in decision making are not met' (Coser and Rosenberg, 1964, p. 530).

McClosky and Schaar (1965) present evidence to suggest that anomic responses are powerfully governed by cognitive and personality factors independent of or in combination with social influences. They conclude that anomy 'results from impediments to interaction, communication, and learning, and is a sign of impaired socialization'. In other words, given that anomic feelings result from a lack of learning, 'whatever interferes with one's ability to learn a community's norms, or weakens one's socialization into its central patterns of belief, must be considered among the determinants of anomy' (p. 20).

In a real sense, the T-group represents for its members a new community or society with a set of norms unlike those to which the members have become accustomed. The individual participant, if he is to benefit from sensitivity training, must be able to see and understand the norms of this new culture. Only then will he be able to decide rationally† whether they are personally relevant and functional and if so, to truly internalize these new learnings.

The high anomic person might experience difficulty in understanding and internalizing the dominant norms of the T-group. Furthermore, due to the relatively short duration (two weeks) of the experiment and the here-and-now focus of the T-group, no change was expected in a person's level of anomy.

The study

Subjects

The laboratory population studied in this research were the participants

---

* The scale used to measure this variable is a nine-item Guttman scale developed by McClosky and Schaar (1965). The items are of the following form:

(a) People were better off in the old days when everyone knew just how he was expected to act.

(b) It seems to me that other people find it easier to decide what is right than I do.

† W. G. Bennis, E. H. Schein, D. E. Berlew and F. I. Steele, (1964) discuss this point in terms of a possible meta-goal of sensitivity training—'expanded consciousness and sense of choice'.

in the Osgood Hill* 1965 summer program in sensitivity training. The program was two weeks in length (June 25–July 7), and the participants 'lived in' in the sense that they slept on the premises and ate virtually all their meals together.

There were 50 participants—30 females and 20 males. They ranged in age from 23 to 59, with a mean age of 33 years. The majority had at least a B.S. degree and a few had advanced degrees. The majority came from the New England area, but several came from Miami, Cleveland, and Chicago. There were eight Negroes in the population, and the trainers made certain that each of the five T-groups† that were formed had at least one Negro and an even proportion of males and females.

Occupationally, the males were a relatively heterogeneous group that included several businessmen, teachers, policemen, clerics, graduate students, government employees, a male nurse, and dentist. The females were much more homogeneous, the majority of them being associated with the nursing profession (students, teachers, practising nurses, and nursing supervisors).

Experimental design and procedure

One of the problems facing the researcher interested in evaluating the effects of sensitivity training is that of finding a relevant control group. The participants in a laboratory are, in one sense, a self-selected group—a circumstance which negates the relevance, for control purposes, of just any group of warm bodies.

Thus the experimental design utilized in this study was one in which the subjects served as their own controls. Herbert Hyman (H. Hyman, C. R. Wright and T. K. Hopkins, 1962, p. 42) utilized this approach in his evaluation of the effects of citizenship camps, as did Carl Rogers in his attempts to evaluate the effects of psychotherapy. As Hyman points out:

> With such a procedure, matching of experimental subjects and controls presents no difficulty, for the same persons constitute both groups. By determining how much instability there is in the group's attitudes, opinions, or other character-istics *during a normal period of time* we could then estimate how much of the change manifested during the experimental period exceeds the normal change resulting from other factors.

Within this design, the total available experimental group (N = 50) was randomly split into two groups of unequal size. The smaller group (N = 14)

* Osgood Hill is in Andover, Massachusetts. It is owned and operated by Boston University. The author wishes to acknowledge the cooperation and assistance provided by the entire staff group of Osgood Hill in the successful completion of this study.

† Two of the trainers were females—one of whom was a Negro—and the remaining four were males. (One group had two trainers.)

was tested (O_{1C}) via mail questionnaires two weeks prior to their arrival at Osgood Hill. The entire group was then tested (for controls: O_{2C} and for experimentals: O_{1E}) upon their arrival, but before the first T-group session. The final 'after' measures (for controls: O_{3C} and for experimentals: O_{2E}) were obtained the morning of the next to last day of the laboratory.* This timing was necessary in order to provide a feedback session to all participants prior to their departure at the end of the laboratory.

This design can be depicted in the following manner:†

June 11	*June 25*	*July 5*
$O_{1C} \dfrac{\text{controls}}{\text{2 weeks}}$ (N = 11)	$O_{2C} \dfrac{\text{controls}}{\text{T-group}}$	O_{3C}
	$O_{1E} \dfrac{\text{experimentals}}{\text{T-group}}$ (N = 30)	O_{2E}

Results

Control group

Table 1 presents the test-retest scores for the control group (O_{1C}, O_{2C}) and the initial test scores for the experimental group (O_{1E}). A series of *t* tests were performed that compared scores for O_{1E} versus O_{1C} and O_{2C} in order to determine empirically the degree of similarity between experimentals and controls. None of the resulting *t*'s reached statistical significance, with *p*'s being greater than 0·50. On the basis of these results, it is assumed that the members of the control group represent a population comparable with the experimentals on the major variables.

It can also be seen from Table 1 that among the members of the control group $\overline{\text{Ap}}$ increased slightly, $\overline{\# \text{ET}}$ increased slightly, and $\overline{\text{ETA}}$ and $\overline{\text{HH}}$ both decreased slightly. In using a *t* test for dependent samples (Blalock, 1960), it was observed that none of the resulting *t*'s reached the 0·60 level of significance. On the basis of these results, it is assumed that the controls do not change significantly from O_{1C} to O_{2C} on any of the major variables. It is assumed, therefore, that any changes found among experimentals cannot be attributable to the main effects of instrument instability and/or practice.

---

* All administrations, other than O_{1C}, were conducted by the author on a group basis.

† Of the available control group of 14, two persons never arrived and one returned an unusable questionnaire, leaving a final control group of 11. Of the available experimental group of 36, one missed the pretest and five returned unusable questionnaires, leaving 30 for the final experimental group.

Experimental group

It was hypothesized that $\overline{Ap}$ and $\overline{\# ET}$ would not change as a result of sensitivity training. Examination of Table 2 reveals that $\overline{Ap}$ and $\# ET$ decreased slightly over this two-week period. Using a t test for dependent samples, it was found that for ΔAp (change in $\overline{Ap}$), $t = 0.84$ with an associated $p < 0.40$ two-tail (N = 30); and for $\Delta \# ET$ (change in $\# ET$),

Table 1—*Before–af terscores for control group* (O_{1C}, O_{2C}) *and before scores for experimental group* (O_{1E})

(N=11)		
O_{1C}	$O_{2C}{}^a$	$O_{1E}{}^a$ (N=30)
(a)		
$\overline{Ap} = 5.5$	$\overline{Ap} = 5.8$	$\overline{Ap} = 6.5$
(b)		
$\overline{\# ET} = 11.0$	$\overline{\# ET} = 12.0$	$\overline{\# ET} = 13.5$
(c)		
$\overline{ETA} = 66.0$	$\overline{ETA} = 65.0$	$\overline{ETA} = 55.0$
(d)		
$\overline{HH} = 46.5$	$\overline{HH} = 47.5$	$\overline{HH} = 46.2$

(a) $\overline{Ap}$ represents mean level of anomy. Scores ranged from 1·10, with a low score representing a low level of anomy.

(b) $\# ET$ represents the mean absolute number of statements scored as being ego-threatening, with the range from 5 to 23.

(c) $\overline{ETA}$ represents mean level of self-acceptance, i.e., the number of ego-threatening statements accepted divided by absolute number of ego-threatening statements. Scores ranged from 0 to 100 per cent, with a low score indicating a low level of self-acceptance.

(d) $\overline{HH}$ represents mean level of human heartedness. Scores ranged from a low of 18 to a high of 80. The lower the score, the closer the respondent's set of ranks was to the theoretically perfect set of ranks and, therefore, the higher his level of human-heartedness.

[a] $O_{2C} + O_{1E}$ were gathered at the same point in time, just prior to the first T-group session.

$t = 0.70$ with an associated $p < 0.45$ two-tail (N = 30). We are unable to reject the null hypothesis of no difference and can therefore assume that sensitivity training had no appreciable effect upon an individual's level of anomy (Ap) or upon the absolute number of ego-threatening statements generated by an individual on our sentence completion test.

The next major hypothesis concerns Δ ETA* (change in self-acceptance).

* ΔETA refers to change in self-acceptance score—ETA score after the laboratory minus ETA score before the laboratory.

The prediction here was that self-acceptance would increase as a result of sensitivity training. Examination of Table 2 reveals that ETA went from a mean of 55·0 per cent to a mean of 67·0 per cent. The differences between these means (*t* test for dependent samples) is significant at the 0·01 level one-tail (N = 30, $t = 2.58$, $p < 0.01$). It is therefore concluded that as a result of sensitivity training, an individual exhibits a greater willingness to accept the personal relevance of ego-threatening material; i.e., his ETA increases.

With respect to ΔHH* (change in human-heartedness), it was predicted that an individual's level of human heartedness would increase. Operationally, this means that his 'after' HH score would be lower than his 'before' HH score. Table 2 reveals that HH decreased from 47·2 to 42·0. The difference between these means (*t* test for dependent samples) is significant at the 0·01 level one-tail (N = 30, $t = 2.54$, $p < 0.01$). In other words, the rankings an individual assigned after the laboratory corresponded more closely with expert rankings than those he assigned before the laboratory— he was found to be more human-hearted.†

Table 2—*Before–after scores for experimental group* (N = 30)

T-group (2 weeks)	
O_{1E}	O_{2E}
$\overline{Ap} = 6.5$	$\overline{Ap} = 5.9$
$\overline{\#ET} = 13.5$	$\overline{\#ET} = 13.2$
$\overline{ETA} = 55.0$	$\overline{ETA} = 67.0$
$\overline{HH} = 47.2$	$\overline{HH} = 42.0$

Conditioning influence of anomy

We turn now to an examination of the conditioning influence of anomy with respect to the observed changes in ETA and HH. It was predicted that those E's low in anomy (Ap) would change more on ETA and HH than

* ΔHH refers to change in human-heartedness score—HH score after the laboratory minus HH score before the laboratory.

† The critical test here is whether ΔETA and ΔHH among the experimentals differ from ΔETA and ΔHH among the controls. A Mann-Whitney U-Test (Siegel, 1956, pp. 116–127) was therefore performed on the difference between the changes. This analysis yielded a $Z = 1.76$ for the ΔETA's ($N_1 = 11$, $N_2 = 30$, $p = 0.05$ one-tail) and a $Z = 1.76$ for the ΔHH's ($N_1 = 11$, $N_2 = 30$, $p = 0.04$ one-tail). In other words, *not only* do the experimentals change while the controls do not, but the *experimentals also change significantly more* than the controls.

those high in anomy (Ap). The skewed nature of the distribution of Ap scores (the majority of respondents scored either 1 or 8, 9, 10, with virtually no scores in the middle) suggested that the most relevant test of these hypotheses would be to split the group at the median Ap score and to compare the magnitude and direction of ETA and HH differences among groups. Utilizing the Mann-Whitney U-test, it is observed that those below the median in Ap increased significantly more on ETA than those above the median in Ap ($N_1 = 19$, $N_2 = 19$,* $Z = 1 \cdot 77$, $p < 0 \cdot 04$ one-tail). A similar trend was found with respect to HH scores ($N_1 = 19$, $N_2 = 19$, $Z = 1 \cdot 56$, $p < 0 \cdot 06$ one-tail). In absolute terms, those low in Ap increased seventeen per cent on the average. With respect to HH, those low in Ap decreased six points on the average, while the high Ap's decreased only two points. In summary, strong support is provided for the hypothesized conditioning influence of Ap on changes in self-acceptance (ETA), and marginal support is provided with respect to changes in human-heartedness (HH).

Central hypotheses

In the light of the results of these preliminary analyses, we are now in a position to examine the central hypotheses of this study:

1. Those who increase in self-acceptance will increase more in human-heartedness than those who either do not change or decrease in self-acceptance.†

2. Changes in self-acceptance will lead to change in human-heartedness.

With respect to the first, of the 38 members of the total experimental group, 23 increased on ETA, six did not change, and nine decreased in ETA. The sample was therefore split into $+ \Delta$ETA (positive changers in self-acceptance, $N = 23$) and 0ΔETA (zero or negative changers in self-acceptance, $N = 15$). On the average, the $+ \Delta$ETA group decreased five points in HH, a result which is statistically significant at the $p < 0 \cdot 01$ level one-tail ($N = 23$, $t = 2 \cdot 80$). The 0ΔETA group also decreased in HH an average of three points, but this change does not reach significance ($N = 15$, $t = 1 \cdot 03$, $p < 0 \cdot 20$ one-tail). However, the difference between these changes is *not* significant (Mann-Whitney U-Test, $N_1 = 15$, $N_2 = 23$, $Z = 1 \cdot 0$,

---

* For the purposes of this and the following analyses, the eight of 11 control group members who returned usable responses after the laboratory (O_{3C}) were added to the 30 experimentals. These eight persons changed as much (percentagewise) in ETA and HH after the laboratory as did the experimentals. In addition like the experimentals, they did not change in Ap or # ET. This raises our available population from $N = 30$ to $N = 38$.

† The *initial* correlation between ETA *versus* HH was $R = - 0 \cdot 32$ ($N = 41$, $p < 0 \cdot 05$ one-tail). The minus sign is explained by the fact that a high level of HH is represented by a low score.

$p < 0.16$ one-tail). The hypothesis in its present form cannot be un-equivocally supported.

In order to shed some light on the reasons for this result, individual change scores on ETA were examined more closely. There appeared to be a sharp discontinuity in the distribution of scores. Several persons increased a moderate amount in ETA (8 to 14 per cent), but then the next highest change was 21 per cent. There were 13 persons who increased 21 per cent or more in self-acceptance. When we examined this group of high $+ \Delta$ETA's *versus* the remainder of the sample, the following results emerged: The high $+ \Delta$ETA group decreased an average of 8·0 points on HH (N = 13, $t = 3·0, p < 0·01$ one-tail), while the remainder of the sample decreased an average of 2·0 points on HH (N = 25, $t = 1·3$, $p < 0·12$ one-tail). A Mann-Whitney U-Test on the difference between these differences yielded a Z = 1·76 ($N_1 = 13$, $N_2 = 25$, $p < 0·04$ one-tail). In other words, those who increase a great deal in self-acceptance (ΔETA > 21 per cent) will increase significantly more in human-heartedness than those who decrease in self-acceptance or increase only a moderate amount.

One way to test the hypothesis that changes in self-acceptance lead to changes in human-heartedness is to utilize the method of partial correla-tion.* The three-variable† model to be tested can be depicted in the follow-ing manner:

Within the framework of this research, we should like to know the direc-tion of the causal arrow in the relationship between ΔETA and ΔHH. In order to infer that ΔETA is causing ΔHH, the following mathematical condition must be satisfied‡ (Simon, 1954; Blalock, 1960):

---

* The utilization of partial correlations to infer causality rests upon several assump-tions. In addition, all other possible models must be eliminated. A complete discussion of these assumptions and the methods for eliminating irrelevant models can be found in Simon (1954) and Blalock (1960).

† Anomy (AP) was chosen as the third variable because, as discussed earlier, it was unaffected by the training experience but was related both to changes in self-acceptance and changes in human-heartedness. Other ways exist to prove causality but, for these, different experimental designs are required.

‡ Numerical subscripts are used for simplicity: 1 = Ap; 2 = ΔETA; 3 = ΔHH.

The correlation of Ap *versus* ΔHH with the effect of ΔETA removed should be less than the zero order correlation of Ap *versus* ΔHH; i.e., $R_{13 \cdot 2} < R_{13}$.

Table 3 presents the data from which the required zero order correlations are computed. The dichotomous nature of the Ap scores suggested that a tetrachoric correlation method would be most appropriate. Under appropriate conditions (Guilford, 1956), this method 'gives a coefficient that is numerically equivalent to a Pearson r and may be regarded as an approximation to it'. In every case, the high *versus* low split was based upon those above and below the median.*

Substitution of the zero order correlations into the partial correlation of formula (Blalock, 1960) yields an $R_{13 \cdot 2} = + 0 \cdot 09$ and the mathematical condition stated above is therefore satisfied.† It is important to note that this analysis does not enable one to rule out a direct effect of sensitivity training on HH. Nor does it eliminate the possibility that sensitivity training influences another variable which may be termed 'feelings-orientation' which, in turn, influences ETA and HH. All it suggests is that some change in HH does result from a change in ETA.‡

Trainer ratings

Trainers were asked, at the end of the laboratory, to characterize the nature of each individual's participation during the T-group session on a scale from 1 (Group Process Orientation) to 7 (Personal Development). In addition, the trainers rated for each individual, the 'Salience of the Topic of Race Relations' (i.e., per cent of time spent discussing the Topic).

It was hypothesized that changes in self-acceptance (ΔETA) would be associated with an 'individual orientation' leaning toward Personal Development. Again this hypothesis is supported only when we compare the high + ΔETA group with the remainder of the sample. The average trainer rating for the high + ΔETA's was $5 \cdot 2$ (i.e. leaning toward Personal Development), as compared with $3 \cdot 8$ (i.e., leaning toward Group Process)

* Median AP $= 5 \cdot 0$.
Median ETA $= + 8$; i.e., 8 per cent increase in self-acceptance.
Median HH $= 2 \cdot 0$, i.e., 2-point decrease in HH score.

† A more conservative approach here is to split the total sample at the median ΔETA score and compute the tetrachoric correlation between Ap *versus* ΔHH within each subsample. The split was made, and the results are almost identical with those obtained when the partial correlation formula was used.

‡ A Kruskall–Wallis one-way analysis of variance (Siegel, 1956, pp. 184–193) among the five T-groups on all major variables was performed, and none of the resulting HH's reached the $0 \cdot 50$ level of significance two-tail. From this result, it can be assumed that there was no significant trainer effect, nor can the observed changes be attributed to some other factor unique to any one of the T-groups.

for the remainder of the sample. This difference is significant ($N^* = 30$, $t = 2.16$, $p < 0.02$ one-tail).

No directional hypotheses were made concerning the effect of 'Salience of the Topic' on an individual's change in human-heartedness. The 20 persons for whom these ratings were available were split into two groups— high (20 to 50 per cent of time) *versus* low (0 to 20 per cent) salience, and

Table 3—*Contingency tables necessary to compute tetrachoric correlations between Ap, ΔHH and ΔETA*

A	Low Ap	High Ap
High ΔHH	13	10
Low ΔHH	6	9

$$^R Ap, \Delta HH = -0.255 \ (R_{13})$$

B	Low Ap	High Ap
High ΔETA	13	6
Low ΔETA	6	13

$$^R Ap, \Delta ETA = -0.550 \ (R_{12})$$

C	High Ap	Low Ap
High ΔHH	15	8
Low ΔHH	4	11

$$^R \Delta ETA, \Delta HH = 0.575 \ (R_{23})$$

changes in HH within the two groups were examined. The low-salience group decreases an average of eight points in HH, while the high-salience group decreases an average of only one point in HH ($N_1 = 10$, $N_2 = 10$, $Z = 1.65$, $p < 0.10$ two-tail, Mann–Whitney U-Test). In other words, there appears to be somewhat of a negative relationship between the amount of time spent discussing the topic of race relations and the change in human-heartedness.†

Discussion

Generalizability of results

One question which comes up immediately is the extent to which the findings of this study are generalizable. It was pointed out earlier that the members of the experimental population all shared a certain level of 'motivation to attend a laboratory'. It is not yet known what personality

* The sample is reduced here because one set of trainer-rating forms was never returned to the researcher.

† The correlation between 'Salience of Topic' and initial HH score was zero, as was the correlation between 'Individual Orientation' and the initial ETA score.

variables, for example, differentiate those who are 'motivated to attend' from those who are not. Even if knowledge of these parameters did exist, it would then have to be demonstrated that they have relevance in terms of differential learnings resulting from training. This broad issue is beyond the scope of this study. However, several related sub-issues are manageable.

Concerning the distribution of initial self-acceptance scores, a reasonably normal distribution of scores with a mean value close to 50 per cent was observed. Unfortunately, no norms exist to indicate what the expected average score might be. Two comparison samples, however, are available: the average ETA score among the college sophomore group studied by Dorris *et al.* (1954) was 53 per cent, and among a pretest group of 30 Sloan Fellows at M.I.T. (with a simplified index of self-acceptance being used), the mean score was 50 per cent. In addition, the results of the present study suggest that even some of those who were initially very low in self-acceptance could be 'reached' by sensitivity training.

Concerning human-heartedness scores, Schuman and Harding (1963) found in their main standardization sample that the average HH score (with a simplified measure being used) leaned toward the 'unhuman-hearted' end of the scale. The distribution of initial scores observed in this study was skewed in the other direction—toward the human-hearted end of the scale. The atypical* educational level of the Osgood Hill sample, with the majority having at least a bachelor's degree, helps to explain this difference. It may be that a certain level of education is a necessary prerequisite to learning via sensitivity training. This proposition is as yet untested empirically.

What kind of sensitivity training

Another question of importance deals with the impact of different emphases in sensitivity training.† The results of this study highlight the importance of a 'personal development' as opposed to a 'group process' orientation. The greatest increasers in self-acceptance and, consequently, in human-heartedness were those whose predominant focus during the T-group sessions was in more personal areas.

From a pragmatic viewpoint, if one wishes to use sensitivity training as a means to reduce ethnic prejudice, then, within the Schein and Bennis (1965) framework, the individual should be viewed as the client, and learning about self and others should be stressed at the levels of awareness and changes

* The terms 'typical' and 'atypical' used in this section, have as their frame of reference a random sample of adults drawn from the general population'.

† Schein and Bennis (1965) present a three-dimensional schema for classifying the goals of a laboratory in these terms: What is the learning about? Who is the ultimate client? What is the level of learning?

4

attitudes.* Furthermore, given the specific goal of prejudice reduction and a personal focus, a shorter laboratory might be feasible. Much research is needed to determine the optimal mix of group process *versus* personal development orientation, the relative impacts of various kinds of supplementary cognitive inputs, and the effect of laboratory duration on the amount of change observed.

One of the most interesting findings in this study involved the strong conditioning influence of anomy with respect to changes in self-acceptance. The success of sensitivity training as an educational strategy rests upon an individual's ability to see and understand the dominant norms of self-exposure, openness, and feedback which develop within the T-group. What remains to be demonstrated by future research is the role of anomy as a conditioning variable for learning criteria other than increased self-acceptance.

The roles played by discussion of the topic of race relations and the presence of Negroes in the T-group are still unclear. Pure discussion does not help those who are doing the talking. This situation does not mean that the observed changes in human-heartedness could have occurred without any such discussion. The nontalkers† may have benefited immensely from listening to the more vocal members of the group. On the other hand, the talkers may have been 'intellectualizing'—a technique commonly employed in T-groups to keep the discussion on a less threatening level. This negative effect of participation has been observed by other researchers,‡ and further research is necessary to better understand the dynamics of the relationship between participation (amount and content) and change.

Concerning the effect of racially mixed groups, it may be that for a majority of the white participants the T-group experience was the first opportunity they ever had to meaningfully interact with a Negro. During the T-group discussions, many insights may have occurred that served to highlight a feeling of 'oneness' or common humanity. For example, 'He (a Negro) has feelings and emotions just the same as I!' Research is needed to examine in greater detail the specific patterns of interaction (e.g., Negro to white) and discussion content within a mixed T-group and their effects on the attitudes people have toward one another, as well as the effects of an all-white group.

* For an excellent description of this form of sensitivity training, see Irving R. Weschler, Fred Massarik and Robert Tannenbaum. The self in process: A sensitivity training emphasis, in *Issues in human relations training*, No. 5 in NTL's Selected Reading Series. Washington, D.C.: National Training Laboratories 1962. Pp. 33–46.

† 'Nontalker' does not mean 'silent member', but refers instead only to the substance or content of an individual's discussion. The most vocal member, in terms of total participation, may never have mentioned the topic of race relations.

‡ Personal communication from David Kolb of M.I.T. concerning some research he is conducting an individual change within T-groups. 1965.

Change in self-acceptance versus *change in human-heartedness*

One of the central hypotheses in this study was that those who increase in self-acceptance will increase more in human-heartedness than those who decrease or do not change in self-acceptance. The data suggest that this hypothesis, in its original form, was too broad. It appears instead that some minimum increase in self-acceptance (20 per cent in this study) is necessary in order for any significant change in human-heartedness to be immediately observable.* Perhaps, where sensitivity training really 'took' (in the sense of great increase in self-acceptance), those involved may have been better able to immediately make the mental transfer from self-acceptance to human-heartedness. The others may have needed some period of incubation in order for this transfer to occur.

Support for this interpretation is provided by Katz (D. Katz, I. Sarnoff and C. M. McClintock, 1956, 1957) who found that as a result of a self-insight manipulation no changes in prejudice were observed immediately after the experimental induction, but that highly significant shifts occurred several weeks afterwards. In other words, a 'sleeper effect' appeared to be operating. The written case study utilized by Katz *et al.* (1956) to increase self-insight is certainly less intensive than a two-week sensitivity training laboratory and may well be less powerful. It is possible, therefore, that changes in human-heartedness will persist after the laboratory and, in fact, may become more marked among the group who experienced only moderate increases in self-acceptance.† This hypothesis could not be tested because it was necessary to provide a full feedback session‡ for the laboratory participants prior to their departure.

Finally, the reader has undoubtedly noticed that by changing a few words, e.g., 'T-group' to 'therapy group' and 'trainer' to 'therapist', this study could have been concerned with the effect of client-centered psychotherapy upon prejudiced attitudes. Both the T-group and the therapy group provide the elements of psychological safety, support, and opportunities for reality testing assumed necessary to effect an increase in an individual's level of self-acceptance and consequently, by our model, to decrease one's level

* The risk of maximizing change variations by examining a small subgroup of the total population is reduced considerably by the findings concerning individual focus during the T-group sessions. The great changers in self-acceptance were also those whose focus during the T-group was in more personal areas.

† The Bunker studies (1963, 1965) discussed earlier suggest that many of the learnings derived from sensitivity training *do* remain with an individual over a long period of time.

‡ The reason for this was only partially based upon ethical considerations. Of equal importance was the fact that the data which were fed back to the participants became topics for discussion in the few remaining T-group sessions and therefore, hopefully enhanced the learning value of their training experience.

of ethnic prejudice. To the extent that future research and practical experience substantiate the conclusions drawn from the present study, a step has been taken toward solving a problem posed by Adorno (T. W. Adorno, E. Frenkel-Brunswick, D. J. Levinson and R. N. Sanford, 1950, p. 976) some 17 years ago.

Although it cannot be claimed that psychological insight (self-insight) is any guarantee of insight into society, there is ample evidence that people who have the greatest difficulty in facing themselves are the least able to see the way the world is made. Resistance to self-insights and resistance to social facts are contrived, most essentially, of the same stuff. It is here that psychology may play its most important role. Techniques for overcoming resistance, developed mainly in the field of individual psychotherapy, can be improved and adapted for use with groups and even for use on a mass scale.

References

Adorno, T. W., E. Frenkel-Brunswick, D. J. Levinson and R. N. Sanford (1950) *The authoritarian personality*. New York: Harper and Row.

Bennis, W. G., E. H. Schein, D. E. Berlew and F. I. Steele (1964) *Interpersonal dynamics*. Chicago: Dorsey.

Blalock, H. M. (1960) *Social statistics*. New York: McGraw-Hill.

Bunker, D. (1963) 'The effect of laboratory education upon individual behaviour.' *Proc. of the 16th Annual Meeting*, Industrial Relat. Res. Ass., December, pp. 1–13.

Bunker, D. (1965) 'Individual applications of laboratory training.' *J. appl. Behav. Sci.*, **1** (2), 131–148.

Coser, L. A. and B. Rosenberg (Eds.) (1964) *Sociological theory—A book of readings*. New York: Macmillan.

Dorris, R. J., D. Levinson and E. Hanfmann (1954) 'Authoritarian personality studied by a new variation of the sentence completion technique.' *J. abnorm. soc. Psychol.*, **49**, 99–108.

Gordon, T. (1950) 'What is gained by group participation?' *Educ. Leadership*, (January), 220–226.

Guilford, J. P. (1956) *Fundamental statistics in psychology and education*. New York: McGraw-Hill.

Harding, J. and H. Schuman (1961) 'An approach to the definition and measurement of prejudice.' Unpublished manuscript, Harvard University.

Hyman, H., C. R. Wright and T. K. Hopkins (1962) *Application of methods of evaluation*. Los Angeles: Univ. of California Press.

Johnson, P. C. (1949) *Statistical methods in research*. New York: Prentice-Hall.

Kahn, R. (1963) 'Aspiration and fulfillment: Themes for studies of group relations.' Unpublished manuscript, Univ. of Michigan.

Katz, D., I. Sarnoff and C. M. McClintock (1956) 'Ego defense and attitude change.' *Human Relat.*, **9**, 27–45.

Katz, D., I. Sarnoff and C. M. McClintock (1957) 'The measurement of ego defense as related to attitude changes.' *J. Pers.*, **25**, 465–474.

McClosky, H. and J. H. Schaar (1965) 'Psychological dimensions of anomy.' *Amer. soc. Rev.*, **30** (1), 14–40.

Miles, M. B. (1960) 'Human relations training: Processes and outcomes.' *J. Counsel. Psychol.*, **7** (4), 301–306.

Schein, E. H. and W. G. Bennis (1965) *Personal and organizational change through group methods: The laboratory approach.* New York: Wiley.

Schuman, H. and J. Harding (1963) 'Sympathetic identification with the underdog.' *Pub. Opin. Quart.*, 230–241.

Sheerer, E. T. (1949) 'The relationship between acceptance of self and acceptance of others.' *J. Consult Psychol.*, **13**, 169–175.

Siegel, S. (1956) *Nonparametric statistics for the behavioral sciences.* New York: McGraw-Hill.

Simon, H. A. (1954) 'Spurious correlation: A causal interpretation.' *J. Amer. Stat. Ass.*, **49**, 467–479.

Steele, F. I. (1965) 'The relationships of personality to changes in interpersonal values effected by laboratory training.' Unpublished doctoral dissertation, Massachusetts Institute of Technology.

Stock, D. (1949) 'An investigation into the interrelations between the self-concept and feelings directed toward other persons and groups.' *J. consult. Psychol.*, **13**, 149.

CHAPTER 3

The T-group as a Vehicle of Organizational Change

For a large number of participants T-group training means a one- or two-week residential experience with a group of managers or administrators from a wide variety of organizations. They are taken out of their organizational environment and role and put through an isolated experience that is likely to change their attitudes and behaviour and, consequently, their conception of their job. Over the last few years many people have questioned this approach because, they argue, changing only one aspect of the organizational system, namely the manager, attempts to affect the social environment of the organization on 'too narrow a front'. Pugh (1965) extends this argument, 'it is not the individual but his network of social relationships which is basic, and attempts to alter it through the individual must remain only marginally effective. Indeed there is the suspicion that if a really major change were brought about . . . this could result in *increased* tension and conflict in the "back-home" situation.'

In short, the problems of re-entry can be great and, in at least one third of the cases (Miles, 1965; Bunker, 1965), this is not achieved with success. It has been suggested by some (Miles, 1965; Bamforth, 1965; Smith and Moscow, 1966) that a more effective way of increasing and insuring the transfer of T-group learnings is to encourage organizations involved in this type of training to establish 'custom-built' training programmes. As Bamforth (1965) suggests after an in-company T-group programme lasting seven years; 'it became clear as time went on that the use of group training in a work situation was more effective and appropriate . . . than the heterogeneous groups (groups composed of strangers from a wide variety of organizations), which led to "classroom encapsulation"'. He went on to say that the work groups made it possible to explore 'reality relationships' such as those between boss, subordinates and colleagues.

We wish to turn at this stage, therefore, to a consideration of organizational change through the laboratory methods. A number of studies of the effects of these programmes have been undertaken, which provide additional information for evaluation, although few of them are as methodologically sound as some of the foregoing studies of individual learning and follow-up change.

Argyris (1965) has developed a set of categories to measure what he terms interpersonal competence for use in evaluating the impact of the T-group on group and organizational behaviour. These categories are dichotomized into positive and negative aspects of group/organizational functioning. Within the former he lists at the *individual and interpersonal level*: owning up to, openness, and risk-taking; within the latter; not owning up to, not being open and rejecting risk-taking. On the *group norms* level the positive categories are individuality, concern and trust; on the negative side, conformity, antagonism and mistrust. These categories, which are further refined into feeling and ideational levels, have been used with respectable reliability in a number of studies of T-group and discussion/case study groups.

Argyris (1964) has used them to evaluate the effects of five T-group type meetings on the behaviour of a board of directors. Scores on the first three sessions were compared with scores during the training activity and scores derived from board meetings conducted during the twelve months following the T-groups. Antagonism scores were seen to have decreased throughout the period and there were significant positive changes in 'concern for others', 'feelings and ideas', 'openness' and 'helping others'. Argyris concludes, with reservations, that a comparison between scores for board meetings immediately before the change session with meetings conducted 8 and 12 months after the intervention, indicates a significant and desirable growth in interpersonal competence. One of the interesting things about this study is that Argyris is not simply relying on paper and pencil tests of perceived behaviour as do many of the other studies. His focus is clearly upon a specific organizational group, its training experience and its subsequent performance as rated by two independent observers working from tape recordings. Unfortunately, as no control was used, one cannot rule out change resulting from system development, the presence of the experimenter (rather than the nature of the experiment), or other situational factors. It is worth noting, however, that the direction of change is in line with change facilitated by other T-group experiences in other situations.

Morse and Reimer (1956) were responsible for a field experiment which used a trained matched-control group for comparison with T-group trained subjects. The clerical staff from four comparable divisions of a firm were assessed and all the supervisory staff in these four divisions received training; two groups in laboratory methods, which emphasized the importance of participative decision-making, while the other two were given a lecture and discussion course on the need to coordinate and centralize the decision-making within the organization. The authors found a marked increase in productivity in all four divisions of the company with a marginally greater increase for the divisions trained to centralize decision-making. However, an assessment of labour turnover figures revealed a sharp increase in turnover in the division trained to centralize decision-making, but no change in the T-group trained divisions. Thus, in the former divisions, as Smith and Moscow (1966) have interpreted in a recent article, 'a high increase in productivity was linked to a marked decrease in morale' while in the latter 'a slightly lower increase in productivity was achieved with no less morale'. The evidence, however, is more useful for a consideration of the consequences of different managerial styles than for a real evaluation of laboratory training, since there is no evidence that similar results would not have been arrived at had the T-group trained supervisors acquired their participative style through lecture/case discussion methods.

Underwood (1965) also reports a field experiment in which the effects of T-group training were measured, in this case with engineering and manufacturing staff in an electronics company. The training programme consisted of one two-hour session per week of T-group training for 15 supervisors drawn from several departments and organizational levels over a 15-week period. A 15 subject matched-control group (by department, supervisory level, age and sex) was selected for comparison. Positive and negative changes were measured by reports from the trainees' work associates, who were not informed about the research design or the training programme. The observers or work associates were asked to report anonymously to the author any changes in the subjects' characteristic behaviour during the 15 weeks of the training programme and the 15-week period following the programme. He found that nine of the T-group trained subjects as compared with seven of the control group subjects were observed to show change one or more times. Although this was not a large difference—no statistical treatment was performed on the data—he did find a large difference in the frequency of incidents reported between the two groups. Observers of the participants of the T-group programme reported 25 changes in the 30 week period whereas the observers of the control group reported only 11 changes in the same 30 week period; a T-group training to control group change ratio of 2·3 : 1. The observers then codified the changes as either more or less effective supervision. In the T-group trained group 15 of the 25 observers were said to increase leadership and

supervisor effectiveness of the subjects, 7 to decrease effectiveness and 3 had
no bearing on leadership. The control group showed eight increases, two
decreases and one no influence. One interesting feature of the research
design is that the *observers* are asked to classify the new behaviour and not
the researchers as in the previous studies; for the first time in a study of this
kind associates not only report changes but, in effect, say what they think
of them in terms of effectiveness. This really highlights the potentiality of
bias in measures of *perceived* change; in other studies the associates report,
and the researchers classify new behaviour according to *their* frame of
reference. The difficulty is that the researchers' values can sometimes be out
of line with the values of the organization. Underwood's study attempts to
avoid this difficulty. As he himself writes:

'The experimental subjects were reported to show decreased effectiveness in the
personal category in a substantial number of reports. An analysis of these changes
reveals a heavy emotional loading in the nature of the change. It is speculated that
these subjects were venting emotion to a greater degree than usual and to the
ovservers, *operating in a culture which devalues such expression* this behaviour
yielded a negative evaluation.'

By implication one could say that whilst openness, acceptance, expression of feelings, and a generally more democratic approach may be valuable
from the point of view of the T-group trainer it is not necessarily seen as
such by the organization. As with some of the other studies, the organizational climate or culture seems to be a critical factor in the transfer of
training. While the size of the sample population used by Underwood is
relatively small and the results far from conclusive, this study certainly
appears to highlight the importance of the situation in which the laboratory
trained person is required to operate.

A further study involving the use of laboratory training within an organization development programme was conducted by Buchanan and
Brunstetter (1959). In one department of a large aircraft company 224
supervisors and higher management participated in a series of T-groups.
A matched control group was provided by a second similar department of
the company. Sometime after the training programme the trained and the
non-trained control supervisors were asked to rate which of a list of
organizational functions (45 in all) were being performed more or less
effectively than a year previously. They found that the trained supervisors
reported significantly greater improvement in their department than did the
control group subjects. In addition, the improvement reported from the list
of organization functions were on items closely related to the training programme such as 'improved effectiveness of meetings', 'better use of delegation', and so on. These results should be treated with caution since they are

self-report measures only and it is possible that participants who believe in a training programme and who have assimilated its peculiar language will tend to give higher ratings after than before in order to confirm their own beliefs.

Friedlander (1967) reports the results of an evaluation of what he terms organizational training laboratories. The nature of this training in general refers to laboratory sessions where all members of a particular work group attend, the purposes being: (1) to identify problems facing the work-group system and the reasons for their existence; (2) to invent possible solutions to the problems in the form of needed system changes; and (3) to plan implementation of these solutions through regular and newly-constructed channels. Within this context, Friedlander notes, the group explores numerous inadequacies in interpersonal and intergroup processes which directly or indirectly influence the total work system.

Over a two-year period 12 groups of civilians employed in a services' research and development station were studied. These 12 groups composed of from five to fifteen members and represented four levels in the organizational hierarchy. They met regularly, usually weekly, and were essentially task-oriented work groups. Four of the groups eventually participated in organizational training laboratories; the others did not, thus providing the project with four training groups and eight comparison groups (Friedlander does not consider them as controls since he considers the term 'a soothing misnomer which tends to gloss over a myriad of variables that might otherwise be quite relevant').

Proceeding inductively from interviews and discussions, together with a scanning of the professional literature, Friedlander used a factor analysis to arrive at underlying dimensions of group phenomena. These dimensions were tapped by a specifically devised instrument the Group Behaviour Inventory (Friedlander, 1966). The G.B.I. was administered twice to each of the 12 groups. For the four training groups the second administration followed the training by six months. For the eight comparison groups, the second administration followed the first administration by six months.

Two separate analyses of covariance were performed on each of the six group dimensions. In the first set, the four trained groups were compared with the eight comparison groups. In the second set, the groupings were ignored and changes in the mean of 31 individuals who participated in training were compared with the changes in the mean of the 60 individuals who did not participate. The results of the two analyses were similar. On the group level significant changes occurred involving team effectiveness in problem solving (Factor I), mutual influence among group members (III), and members sense of personal involvement and participation in group meetings (IV). Dimensions where no significant improvement occurred included feelings of approachability toward the chairman (II), intergroup trust and confidence (V), and the general evaluation of group meetings (VI).

Friedlander concludes that significant improvements in effectiveness and the interaction process in work groups do occur as a result of participation in organizational training laboratories, and that these improvements take place in areas which are of direct personal and organizational relevance to members of the on-going work groups. In addition, they endure for a period of at least six months beyond the training experience. Friedlander's findings, however, are somewhat baffling in at least three respects: (1) significant increases in mutual influence and participation were not paralleled by gains in trust; (2) greater team effectiveness was achieved without concomitant increases in the evaluation of group meetings; and (3) there was a heightened sense of involvement and participation with no significant improvement in members' rapport with their leader.

Finally, Wilson, Mullen and Morton (1968) report the results of a comparison between what they term organization training laboratories and sensitivity or T-group training. As Morton puts it 'the Organization Training Laboratory attempts to change not only the individual but the organization climate in which the individual must continue to live'. In the organization training laboratory apparently the face-to-face feedback process focuses on 'managerial styles' rather than on 'personal behaviour' type characteristics which may or may not be related to management (Morton and Bass, 1964). As Wilson and coworkers conceive it organization training emphasizes team decision-making and problem-solving. It is concerned expressly with how effectively a team uses its material and human resources. It does not avoid individual learning but this is acquired in a work-oriented context that encourages transfer or learning back to the world of work. The authors argue that team training experience may have more impact on individual behaviour on the job, where the impact of T-group training may have a broader and more intense impact on the individual and all of his interpersonal relationships. Using a questionnaire designed to determine managers' perception of the value of training experience to themselves as individuals and to themselves as managers, Wilson and coworkers sought to compare the impact of traditional laboratory training as compared with organization training laboratories. The results as presented in Table 1 suggest that these courses were approximately of equal value to the managers as individuals. However, when the focus shifted to the individual as a manager or as one responsible for building team effort the results clearly favour the organization training method. Differences are statistically significant, with the exception of the cases of managers quoting

Table 1—*The proportion of managers who considered their training experience of considerable value after attending a sensitivity training programme or an organization training laboratory*

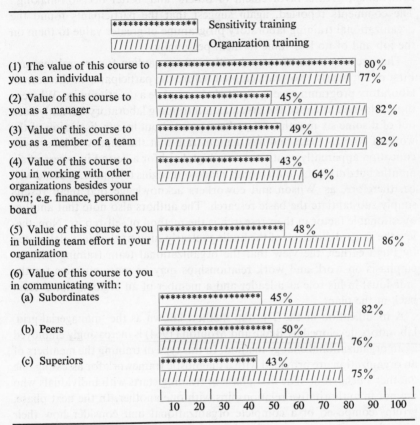

working with other organizations besides his own, for example finance, personnel. The questionnaire requested reports on activities initiated or discounted since the laboratory training. The twenty-eight persons from the normal laboratories reported thirty-nine activities; twenty-one persons from the organization training laboratory reported ninety-three activities.

Wilson and coworkers note that those from the normal laboratory, who made comments, reported primary changes in the areas of better listening, sensitivity to self, better understanding of self and others, and being more considerate. Only in the category of sensitivity itself did the persons from the normal laboratories give more reports than the persons from the organizational training laboratory. In addition, a proportionally larger number from the organizational training laboratory reported 'being less controlling', 'greater involvement of others' and 'better decision-making'. The comments reported, again suggest that the participants found the organizational training laboratory programme of greater value to them on the job and of no less value to them personally.

These results must be treated with extreme caution for several reasons. First of all, nearly two years elapsed before the participants in the normal laboratory programme were required to complete a questionnaire. Whereas those who had attended the organization training laboratory had only been out of it some six months. As we have pointed out in our discussion of the work of Argyris these findings demonstrate that the impact of laboratory education apparently continues on a high level for a period in excess of six months but during the tenth month a fade-out begins to appear. It could well be, therefore, as Wilson and coworkers acknowledge that these results simply substantiate the basic research. The authors also note that another questionable factor in their research is the method of self-report. Nonetheless the general direction of the findings clearly support the ideas elaborated by Pugh earlier, the view that the organizational team training with its emphasis on work and work relationships may be more effective for the individual in his role as a leader and a member of an organizational team back at the plant.

A modification of the T-group method known as the 'managerial-grid' laboratory developed by Blake and Mouton (1964) is increasingly employed as an organizational change method. In this type of training the members of an organization are provided with a diagnostic framework for assessing one another's behaviour. The first phase of training starts with individuals who are not in authoritative relationships with one another. In the next phase, groups composed of a complete organizational unit consider how their phase 1 experience (groups of initial strangers) affects the way in which *they* work together. Barnes and Greiner (Blake, Mouton, Barnes and Greiner, 1964; Greiner, 1967a, 1967b) undertook an evaluation of the managerial-grid in a large American petrochemical company of 800 managers. They reported a number of major changes in the company's performance, which included increased profits, reduction of controllable costs, and more positive managerial attitudes. There was, however, no control data for untrained companies or companies trained by some other method in the same market situation. In addition, many substantive changes within the organization were occurring at the same time, such as 600 men being declared redundant (which obviously affected wages saved and may have had other side effects). These changes also resulted in collaboration with a management consultant, which may have been as important as the actual training in contributing to change.

Smith and Honour (1969) improved upon the above study in at least one respect by establishing control conditions. They examined changes within a British factory after managerial-grid training and compared these with concurrent changes at a second untrained factory within the same organization. There were 49 trainees in the first factory and 51 untrained controls in the second, matched for age and seniority. Questionnaires were completed before and four months after training. The trainees were also interviewed at various intervals after training. Just over one-half of the trainees reported improvement in their relationship to their subordinates, whereas the subordinates who we might expect to be more objective saw the changes in only one-third of the instances. Changes were particularly noted in group meetings and committees within the company. The untrained managers showed much lower change rates. Overall the study confirmed that the predicted changes did occur, but only among a minority of those trained. No attempt was made in this study to assess the change in profitability or cost-control as a result of grid training. Both the Barnes and Greiner and Smith and Honour studies used for the most part a recall method, whereby trainees were asked to recall after training what their situation was like before training. We must consider the possibility of the findings being biased as a result of this methodological approach. The possibility exists that a 'halo' of favourable response to the training may have led the trainees 'to paint the pre-training situation blacker than it really was'. With grid-training the research evidence remains scattered and only partially conclusive.

Conclusion

The studies of the use of T-groups as tools of organization change are much less complete and more difficult to compare than those evaluating individual change. This stems not only from the lack of willingness by companies to conduct experiments and controlled evaluation in organization change, but also from the inherent difficulty in measuring and comparing the effectiveness of different organizations who tend to use different criteria for effectiveness. The findings cited above are no more than encouraging, more complete and organized data is needed in this area. Buchanan (1965) has pointed out 'what is needed is more attention to strategies of organization development and to adapting laboratory training theory and methodology to fulfil the strategy, and to devising ways of assessing the impact of such programmes.'

References

Argyris, C. (1964) 'T-groups for organization effectiveness.' *Harvard Business Review*, **42**, 71.

Argyris, C. (1965) 'Explorations in interpersonal competence—II.' *Journal of Applied Behavioral Science*, **1** (3), 255–269.

Bamforth, K. (1965) 'T-group method within a company.' In G. Whitaker (Ed.), *T-group Training: Group Dynamics in Management Education*. Oxford: Blackwell, 69–77.

Blake, R. R. and J. S. Mouton (1964) *The Managerial Grid*. Houston, Texas: Gulf Publishing Co.

Blake, R. R., J. S. Mouton, L. B. Barnes and L. E. Greiner (1964) 'Breakthrough in organisation development.' *Harvard Business Review*, **42**, 133–155.

Buchanan, P. C. and P. H. Brunstetter (1959) 'A research approach to management development—Part II.' *Journal of the American Society of Training Directors*, **12**, 18–27.

Buchanan, P. C. (1965) *Evaluating the Effectiveness of Laboratory Training in Industry*. Washington, D.C.: National Education Association.

Bunker, D. R. (1965) 'Individual applications of laboratory training.' *Journal of Applied Behavioral Science*, **1** (2), 131–148.

Friedlander, F. (1966) 'Performance and interactional dimensions of organizational work groups.' *Journal of Applied Psychology*, **50**, 257–265.

Friedlander, F. (1967) 'The impact of organizational training laboratories upon the effectiveness and interaction of on-going work groups.' *Personnel Psychology*, **20** (3), 289–309.

Greiner, L. E. (1967a) 'Antecedents of planned organizational change.' *Journal of Applied Behavioral Science*, **3**, 51–86.

Greiner, L. E. (1967b) 'Patterns of successful organization change.' *Harvard Business Review*.

Miles, M. B. (1965) 'Changes during and following laboratory training: A clinical-experimental study.' *Journal of Applied Behavioral Science*, **1** (3), 215–243.

Morse, N. and E. Reimer (1956) 'The experimental change of major organizational variable.' *Journal of Abnormal and Social Psychology*, **52**, 120–129.

Morton, R. B. and B. M. Bass (1964) 'The organizational training laboratory.' *Training Directors Journal* (October).

Pugh, D. (1965) 'T-group training from the point of view of organization theory.' In G. Whitaker (Ed.), *T-Group Training: Group Dynamics in Management Education*. Oxford: Blackwell, 44–50.

Smith, P. B. and T. F. Honour (1969) 'The impact of phase 1 managerial grid training.' *Journal of Management Studies*, 6.

Smith, P. B. and D. Moscow (1966) 'After the T-group is over . . . .' *New Society* (December).

Underwood, W. J. (1965) 'Evaluation of a laboratory method of training.' *Journal of the American Society of Training Directors*, **14**, 34–40.

Wilson, J. E., D. P. Mullen and R. B. Morton (1968) 'Sensitivity training for individual growth—routine training for organization development.' *Training and Development Journal*, **22** (1), 47–54.

The Impact of Organizational Training Laboratories upon the Effectiveness and Interaction of Ongoing Work Groups*

Frank Friedlander

School of Management,
Case Western Reserve University

Introduction

Action taken to resolve problems which hinder the effectiveness of work groups is a topic touched upon only occasionally in the research literature. For the most part innovations in group training efforts, such as group problem-solving and sensitivity training, have fallen apparently outside the boundaries of industrial psychology, despite the fact that much of this training currently occurs in industrial settings. On the other hand, a number of studies have been reported in such journals as *Human Relations* and the *Journal of Applied Behavioural Research*. In part, this may be because group training programs deal with the social and environmental factors, and not merely with individual differences in characteristics. It may also be because group training involves efforts toward change, and not merely acceptance and measurement of a *status quo* situation. In an article relevant to these issues, Sanford (1965) strongly advocates programs and studies aimed toward understanding the conditions and processes of developmental change, the social settings in which these changes occur and, in particular, the settings that have been designed to modify people in some way.

This article is concerned with an evaluation of the impact of change programs which will be called here *organizational training laboratories*. The nature of this training quite naturally varies among groups in some ways. In general, however, the laboratory sessions last approximately four to five days and are attended by *all* members of a particular work group. The purposes of the sessions generally are (a) to identify problems facing the work-group system and the reasons for their existence, (b) to invent possible solutions to the problems in the form of needed system changes, and

* Originally published in *Personnel Psychology*, 1967, **20**, 289–309.

(c) to plan implementation of these solutions through regular and newly-constructed channels. Within this problem-solving context, the group explores numerous inadequacies in interpersonal and intergroup processes which directly or indirectly influence the total work system.

It is important to note that these training sessions deal with the intact work group as an integrated system into which is introduced procedural and interpersonal change, rather than with a collection of strangers representing different organizations—or unrelated components of the same organization. This difference is relevant to the expected training impact and, therefore, to the research design and criteria.

Much of the previous emphasis in training seems to have been upon evoking changes in the *individual* primarily in the isolated island of his training context. The organizational training laboratory is directed at helping the individual bridge the hazardous, yet critical transition from his trainee role to the 'real life' role of his back-home environment, and at preventing dissipation of the training effects. Since much of the discussion centers upon the relevant work problems which the group actually faces, and since the members of the training group are also the members of the organizational work group, ideally there is a perfect consolidation of the training and organizational membership roles. The back-home and the here-and-now are one and the same.

To the researcher, this shift in emphasis implies not only a criterion of more enduring change, but perhaps a qualitatively different one. Research emphasis is not only upon behavioural change in the individual, but also upon change of the individual within his organizational context, and changes in the organizational context or organic system of which the individual is one interacting part.

Although back-home criterion for evaluating laboratory training is frequently an implicit assumption made by both the consultant and the researcher, it is seldom made explicit in the design of the training or in the design of the research. 'Change process', as Mann (1962) points out, 'needs to be concerned with altering both the forces within an individual and the forces in the organizational situation surrounding the individual.' This point is dramatically emphasized by Bennis, Benne and Chin (1962) in their discussion of programs and technologies of planned change:

Isolating the individual from his organizational context, his normative structure which rewards him and represents a significant reference group, makes no sense. In fact, if it sets up countervailing norms and expectations, it may be deleterious to both the organization and to the individual.

It is usually assumed that changes in individual behaviour 'will lead to increased effectiveness in the back-home situation; and this, rather than change *per se*, is the "raison d'etre" for the training group' (Stock and Thelan, 1958).

Those who have concerned themselves with back-home impact have reported mixed results. Trainees attending as a team have been found to change more than trainees attending as individuals (Lippitt, 1949). Similarly, Riecken (1952) found that those who attended work camp, and who had continuing contact with others from developmental experiences, were most likely to retain attitude changes. On the other hand, Bennis (1963) uses the term 'fade-out' to describe lack of durability of training results when participants return to their company. Shepard (1960) reports that the impact of laboratory experience was greater on personal and inter-personal learning than in changing the organization. Harrison (1962) reports that trainees increased their use of emotional and interpersonal descriptions of each other, but did not increase such descriptions of their fellow employees back home. The thorough and extensive study by Fleish-man *et al.* (1955) lends further disturbing evidence—that although training resulted in immediate changes in self-perception, this impact soon gave way to the leadership style of the trainee's supervisor once the trainee returned to his organizational context. Mann (1962) summarizes these disappointing results as follows: 'At best, these studies suggest that this type of training has little or no general effect . . . . Training which does not take the trainee's regular social environment into account will probably have little chance of modifying behaviour. It may very well be that human relations training— as a procedure for initiating social change—is most successful when it is designed to *remold the whole system of role relationships . . . .*'

In a parallel manner research, which ignores the impact of training upon the organization or the ongoing work groups of which it is composed, may be utilizing a criterion of low and temporary relevance. The appropriate research criteria for training that deals with the work groups within an organization is *group* change within the organizational context.

In the light of the above assumptions, the purposes of this research project were to study the impact of several organizational training labora-tories upon problems that were of most relevance and utility to the group members of intact organizational work groups who had participated as a group in training laboratories. The data which evolved from this study are also utilized to shed further light on several additional issues concerning potential changes in organizational work groups.

Background

The organizational context in which this project was embedded consists of one of the armed services' largest research and development stations, employing approximately 6,000 personnel. Eighty per cent of the employees are civilians, including about 1,200 scientists and engineers. The organization's mission covers the complete research and development spectrum from basic research through applied research: design, development, test, engineering, evaluation, and limited production. Its products are in all fields of ordnance: rockets, guided missiles, underwater ordnance, propellants, explosives, and aircraft fire-control systems.

In early 1962, a series of individual interviews was held with the members of the Policy Board, the highest level group in the organization. The proposed topic did not concern the Board or its meetings as such. However, it soon became evident that the members were not content merely to discuss the 'planned' topic; instead they dwelled rather consistently and concertedly upon the Board membership and leadership, and the interactions and effectiveness of the Board meetings.

The series of interviews resulted in two decisions—one action-oriented and one research-oriented. In view of the perceived inadequacies that members expressed of the group and its meetings, and in view of the willingness on the part of both group members and the internal consulting staff to do something about these inadequacies, a decision was made to bring in an outside trainer-consultant to work with the group. The second, and parallel decision, was to initiate a research study which might provide an evaluation and an increased understanding of the entire training phenomenon as it would occur in its organizational context.

It became apparent to the initial stage of the research study that at least one group which did *not* participate in the training experience (a comparison group) would be needed with which to compare any changes that might occur in the Policy Board. Over a two-year period the participation of 11 additional organizational work groups was obtained, making a total of 12 groups involved in the study. These 12 groups, described in more detail elsewhere (Friedlander, 1966), represent four levels in the organizational hierarchy. The groups are composed of from five to 15 members, who meet (usually weekly or bi-weekly) and work together regularly for a variety of purposes, including problem discussion and resolution, general co-ordination, information dissemination, decision-making, policy formulation, future planning, etc. As such, the 12 groups represent traditional task-oriented work groups which use typical lateral and hierarchical interaction patterns toward their task accomplishment. Four of the groups eventually participated in organizational training laboratories; the others did not, thus providing the project with four training groups and eight comparison groups.*

* The term 'comparison group', rather than the experimental psychologist's term

Research design

The previously-mentioned series of interviews with members of various work groups resulted in the collection of an extensive amount of material dealing with the problems and the issues which members perceived as important in their work groups. The content of the material concerned such issues as co-operation, competition, openness, initiative, self-awareness, participation, spontaneity, creativity, intimacy, effectiveness, conflict, communication, divergency of ideas, procedural adequacy, authority relations, exploitation, mutual influence, and consensus. Detailed notes were taken during the interviews and the verbatim comments made by group members were re-phrased into questions to form the main body of a questionnaire. Additional group-descriptive variables were obtained through discussions with members of several different groups. Relevant group-descriptive dimensions, issues, and hypotheses recurrent in the professional literature provided a third source of information. In addition to evaluations of adequacy and effectiveness of the group and its meetings, the variables encompassed perceptions of the actual network of feelings—both in terms of the perceptions of one's own position in the network as a member, and of the perceptions by members of relationships existing between other members of the group.

Directly quantifiable data were also collected for each individual concerning the number of meetings he had previously attended, the number of topics he had submitted for the agenda, the number of problems he felt needed discussion at the next meeting, the percentage of time he had talked, and his estimate of the percentage of time the chairman had talked. A nine-adjective semantic differential of the concept 'X Department Staff Meetings' were also included.

In an effort to reduce these items to a comprehensive set of dimensions, a factor analysis was performed from which six underlying dimensions of group phenomena evolved. A detailed account of the construction, development, and factor analysis of the items is described elsewhere (Friedlander, 1966). However, since these six dimensions were utilized as principle variables in the current research, a brief description of each is provided:

I. *Group Effectiveness*: This dimension describes group effectiveness in

---

'control group' is used throughout this paper since there is virtually nothing controlled in these eight groups. While it is true that they did not participate in a planned training experience, it is also likely that many events occurred in the eight groups during this period which had a positive or negative impact upon characteristics relevant to this study. Perhaps the term 'control group', as used by the field researcher, is a soothing misnomer which tends to gloss over a myriad of variables that might otherwise be quite relevant.

solving problems and in formulating policy through a creative, realistic team effort.

II. *Approach to* vs. *Withdrawal from Leader:* At the positive pole of this dimension are groups in which members can establish an unconstrained and comfortable relationship with their leader—the leader is approachable.

III. *Mutual Influence:* This dimension describes groups in which members see themselves and others as having influence with other group members and the leader.

IV. *Personal Involvement and Participation:* Individuals who want, expect, and achieve active participation in group meetings are described by this dimension.

V. *Intragroup Trust* vs. *Intragroup Competitiveness:* At the positive pole, this dimension depicts a group in which the members hold trust and confidence in each other.

VI. *General Evaluation of Meetings:* This dimension is a measure of a generalized feeling about the meetings of one's group as good, valuable, strong, pleasant, or as bad, worthless, weak, unpleasant.

The questionnaire from which this data was obtained is described here as the Group Behaviour Inventory (GBI). Group members were introduced to the study at one of their regular meetings. After a discussion period where questions were answered, a copy of the GBI was distributed to each member of the group to be completed at his leisure in the privacy of his own office. Each member was asked to affix an identification code number of his own choice to the GBI so results of a planned second administration of the questionnaire might be compared to the first one. The GBI was administered twice to each of the 12 groups. For the four training groups, the second administration followed the training by six months. For the eight comparison groups, the second administration followed the first administration by six months.

Inquiries, methods and results

The remainder of this paper will incorporate selected issues which the research project attempted to explore, the methodologies used to explore each issue, the results of the analyses, and a brief discussion of the possible relevance of the results.

Issue 1—General impact of organizational training laboratories

What changes took place within the four work groups which participated in organizational laboratory training relative to any changes that took place

within the eight work groups which did not participate in organizational training laboratories—for each of the six group dimensions?

In order to shed light on this question, analyses of covariance (ANCOVA) were performed. In a statistical sense, the procedure tests whether, after training, differences between training groups and non-training groups remain after a statistical adjustment has been made for differences before training. In a sense, the ANCOVA attempts to approximate a situation in which each of the 12 groups is equated before training has occurred (Winer, 1962).

Two separate ANCOVA's were performed on each of the six group dimensions. In the first set, the four training groups were compared with the eight comparison groups. In the second set, the groupings were ignored and changes in the mean of the 31 individuals who participated in training were compared with the changes in the mean of the 60 individuals who did not participate. The results of the two analyses were similar. The extent and direction of change in the four training groups *vs.* the eight comparison groups are depicted in Figure 1.

It is immediately apparent from Table 1 that group dimensions in which a significant change occurred involved team effectiveness in problem solving (I), mutual influence among group members (III), and member's sense of personal involvement and participation in group meetings (IV). Dimensions where no significant improvement occurred included feelings of approachability toward the chairman (II), intragroup trust and confidence (V), and the general evaluation of group meetings (VI). Thus, a random group which had participated in laboratory training might phrase its perceptions as (1) we now expect and achieve greater participation in group meetings, (2) we now have a greater influence with each other, and (3) we now are a more effective team in solving problems; but (4) our chairman is no more approachable than he was, (5) we are just as much a collection of competitive individuals as we were, and (6) our group meetings are no more worthwhile than they were.

This pattern of change represents some interesting interdimensional relationships. Group effectiveness (I) and evaluation of meetings (VI) might well be considered syntality dimensions in that they are measures of the group acting as a whole. Yet, in only group effectiveness (I) did members of training groups perceive significant change. This might be considered as a change in effective synergy (Cattell, Saunders and Stice, 1953), which is that portion of group energy devoted to attaining group goals. The change also represents perceived improvement in productive performance. As a function of laboratory training, greater team effectiveness was evidently achieved without concomitant increases in evaluation of group meetings

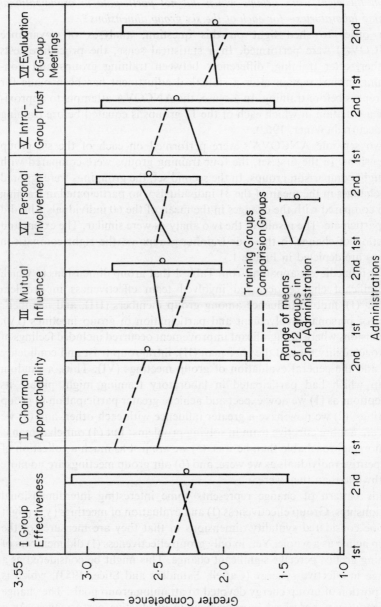

Fig. 1. First and Second Administration Scores on Six Group Dimensions.

Table 1—*Comparisons of relative gains for training members* (*T*) vs. *comparison members* (*C*) *in each of six group dimensions by analysis of covariance*

Group dimension	Relative gain[a]		Difference in gain (T–C)	F-level[b]	
	Trainees	Comparisons		Individuals	Groups[c]
I. Group effectiveness	2·40	2·14	0·26	5·01*	3·98*
II. Leader approachability	2·51	2·47	0·04	0·14	0·21
III. Mutual influence	2·55	2·32	0·23	6·53*	4·94*
IV. Personal involvement	2·64	2·44	0·20	7·15**	6·76**
V. Intragroup trust	2·36	2·34	0·02	0·03	0·00
VI. Evaluation of meetings	2·09	1·93	0·16	1·15	0·79

[a] Relative gains are represented by the adjusted means in the ANCOVA. All signs are necessarily positive as a result of the computational method rather than indicating that no decrement occurred.

[b] The F-levels for the column marked 'Individuals' indicate the significance of the ANCOVA in which the 31 trainees were compared to the 60 comparison members as *individuals*. The column marked 'Groups' indicates the significance of the ANCOVA in which the four training groups were compared to the eight comparison groups. In the latter method, all groups received the same weight regardless of differences in size of membership.

[c] Relative gains for the four training groups and the eight comparison groups are not shown. These were highly similar to relative gains by individuals.
* $p < 0.05$.
** $p < 0.01$, d.f. = 1·88.

(VI). Furthermore, these increases in effective synergy were not supported by similar increases in the maintenance synergy of increased trust and reduced competition (V).

In accordance with the literature in the area of group change and group dynamics, changes in all six of the group dimensions might have been hypothesized. For example, durable modifications in group ideology and social practice are frequently considered in terms of increased mutual influence (III), heightened involvement and participation (IV), and increased trust (or decreased competition) (V) among group members (Lewin, 1947, pp. 330–344; Coch and French, 1948). While the laboratory experience did result in significant increases in mutual influence and participation, no parallel gains in trust were found. The implication that increased trust is correlated with gains in effectiveness, mutual influence, and participation is not upheld in this study. Similarly, in this study it was found that laboratory training can result in a heightened sense of involvement and participation (IV) despite no significant improvement in members' rapport with their leader (II). Among groups which have participated in training laboratories, the coaction of heightened involvement, participation, and expectations (IV) on the one hand, and reduced leader approachability (II) on the other hand, may lead to the eventual frustration of group members and a declination in their involvement.

The combination of increased mutual influence (III) and greater member involvement (IV) after training participation implies that there is far more nteraction among members in the group setting. But this interaction without concurrent improvement in intragroup trust (V) suggests that members are tackling group problems more as a collection of competitive individuals —each utilizing his own skills, rather than an interaction of the unified group, typified by intragroup trust and confidence—drawing upon the total-group competence.

These results, in general, point to the complexity of the training impact upon group members. Concomitant changes in all dimensions do not seem to occur. In particular, group members who have participated in training laboratories perceive themselves as a more effective problem-solving team despite the finding that certain hypothesized changes in the inter-personal processes do not appear to be significantly modified.

Issue 2—Diversity of impact of training upon individuals on each of the six group dimensions

What is the impact of training in terms of changes in the ranking of individuals on each of the six group dimensions?

The previous analysis (Issue I) indicated that laboratory experience resulted in significant improvements in group effectiveness (I), mutual influence (III) and personal involvement (IV). That analysis was concerned primarily with changes in *average group* competence in training and control members. However, it is also possible that the impact of laboratory experience has diverse impacts across *individuals* who participate. Hypothetically, if this diversity is such that gains and decrements in group competence (as perceived by each individual) cancel out each other, no *average* change across trainees will have occurred. Yet, it is possible that every individual has changed his perception of his group; i.e. half in a positive direction and half in a negative direction. In order to test this possibility, correlations between pre and post-scores on each of the six dimensions were computed separately for those who participated in laboratory experience and those who did not.

Correlation coefficients for training members and comparison members, as well as the differences in coefficients for each dimension, are listed in Table 2. The magnitude of the correlation is indicative of the consistency of the rank order of individuals before training as compared to after training.

Table 2—*Pre and post-correlation coefficients for trainee members and comparison members*

Group dimension	Comparisons	Trainees	Difference in correlation $(C-T)^a$
I. Group effectiveness	0·80	0·55	0·25*
II. Leader approachability	0·81	0·50	0·31*
III. Mutual influence	0·71	0·54	0·17
IV. Personal involvement	0·80	0·43	0·37**
V. Intragroup trust	0·68	0·57	0·11
VI. Evaluation of meetings	0·64	0·42	0·22

^{a} Tests of significance were computed after r to z transformations of all correlation coefficients.
* $p < 0.05$.
** $p < 0.01$; Comparisons, $N = 60$; Trainees, $N = 31$.

The correlations for control members, in effect, are a measure of the (test–retest) reliabilities of the six dimensions.* It is immediately apparent from Table 2 that group members who participated in organizational training laboratories during the six-month period experienced a diversity of impacts, whereas group members who did not participate in such training maintained an unusually stable ranking on the six dimensions. This difference in stability (or change) among individual rankings was significant in the case of group effectiveness (I), leader approachability (II), and personal involvement (IV). Trainees changed significantly more in relative perception of their group on these dimensions than did the comparison members. This diversity is understandable in that laboratory experience can be expected to affect different individuals in different ways; in part as a function of each person's specific needs, and also in his mode of interaction in the training experience. The impact of laboratory experience upon perceptions of mutual influence (III), intragroup trust (V), and evaluation of meetings (VI) was somewhat more consistent when compared to that of comparison members; but no significant differences between trainee and comparison members were found on these dimensions. This seems to be due to less consistency on these dimensions among comparison members rather than to significantly greater consistency among training participants.

In dimensions of group effectiveness (I) mutual influence (III), and personal involvement (IV), it will be remembered that the analysis of

* Of the first six factors, the test–retest reliabilities of scales V and VI are somewhat low. However, since the six-month interval is longer than usual for test–retest reliabilities and since the internal consistency reliability of these scales is relatively high, the reliabilities are viewed as acceptable.

Issue I indicated a significant training impact. The results of this section can now be incorporated with the previous analysis to indicate that, although the impacts of training in group effectiveness and mutual influence are diverse across individuals, they are definitely positive in direction. The impact upon mutual influence (III) was significantly positive and consistent.

Finally, in perception of leader approachability (II), no significant changes occurred in the *average* competence of trainees as a result of laboratory experience, but the training impact was significantly diverse to have resulted in a larger number of both positive and negative changes. The 0·81 correlation for comparison members in perception of leader approachability and the significant decrement in this dimension for comparison members (Figure 1) imply a *deterioration* which is disturbingly consistent across group members who did not participate in laboratory experience.

Issue 3—Possible Biases in the Selection of Training and Control Groups

Prior to training, did the competence of training groups differ from that of comparison groups?

In a field study of this kind, the researcher obviously has little prerogative in selecting matched groups for training and control purposes. He must generally abide by the decisions of the organizational groups with which he deals. The question then arises as to the similarity of the training and comparison groups prior to training.

To explore this question, analyses of variance were performed which indicated that the comparison groups had significantly greater competence than the pre-training groups on three of the six group dimensions: group effectiveness (I), approachability of the chairman (II), and intragroup trust (V). These data are indicated in the first three columns of Table 3. Statistical (covariance) methods were used to compensate for these initial differences. However, such methods are not equivalent to experimental methods in which all groups are matched on each dimension prior to training.

Perhaps the more relevant question concerns the reasons for greater competence in the comparison groups (and less competence in the pre-training groups) before training. Note the words 'before training', rather than 'before the research project'; the administration of the GBI to the comparison groups actually was part of the research project. Obviously it is impossible to measure group adequacy before measuring group adequacy —it would have been neat to have done so, for then some light would have been cast upon the effect of the administration of the GBI.

If the assumption can be made that comparison groups were, in fact, more competent than pre-training groups, then a bias in selection of groups did exist. Such a bias might well be attributed to a selection process in

Table 3—*Mean raw scores in six group dimensions before and after research project for four training groups and eight comparison groups*

Group dimension	Before research project			After research project			Changes	
	Trainees	Comparisons	T–C	Trainees	Comparisons	T–C	Trainees	Comparisons
I. Group effectiveness	2·08	2·35	−0·27*	2·31	2·28	0·03	0·23*	−0·07
II. Leader approachability	2·46	2·78	−0·32*	2·37	2·62	−0·25*	−0·09	−0·16**
III. Mutual influence	2·44	2·40	0·04	2·61	2·37	0·24*	0·17*	−0·03
IV. Personal involvement	2·53	2·57	−0·04	2·68	2·51	0·17	0·15*	−0·06
V. Intragroup trust	2·13	2·58	−0·45**	2·25	2·45	−0·20	0·12	−0·13
VI. Evaluation of meetings	2·04	2·13	−0·09	2·08	2·02	0·06	0·04	−0·11

* $p < 0.05$.
** $p < 0.01$; Comparisons, N = 60; Trainees, N = 31.

which groups that perceive themselves as less effective gravitate toward training as a mechanism to alleviate procedural and interpersonal inadequacies. If this is the case, then the questionnaire is merely validly reflecting these inadequacies.

An alternative explanation, which incorporates and builds upon the above concepts, suggests that differences between comparison and training groups are artifactual and are due to researcher–participant interactions. It is quite possible that the process of reading, considering, and responding to items in a questionnaire serves as important stimuli upon each group member, and that the nature of these stimuli differs for pre-training members as opposed to comparison members. For example, in this study pre-trainees (1) had already planned to participate in a training laboratory when they completed the GBI, (2) had therefore considered at least some of the issues raised by the items in the GBI, (3) had hopes that something was going to be done about these issues, and (4) had perhaps reacted with greater acceptance and realism, and with less defensiveness, to the GBI items. Comparison members on the other hand (1) had probably not considered the issues raised by the questionnaire, (2) were informed that they were participating as a comparison group (although the word comparison was not used), (3) had reacted to the lack of previous confrontation and to their label of 'comparison group' with a desire and a need to demonstrate the competence of their group to themselves and to the researcher. Furthermore, since no training was planned—nor was any likely to be planned—increased dissonance of the comparison groups would have resulted from their admission to the researcher and to themselves of any inadequacies with no corresponding remedy (laboratory training).

Issue 4—Possible artifacts in measuring the relative changes of the training groups *vs.* the comparison groups

What changes occurred in the comparison groups when considered separately from the training groups? Did these changes affect measurement of the training impact?

A casual glance at Figure 1 will show that the mean competence for the comparison groups declined on all six dimensions.

Did the significant relative improvements that were found in Issue I occur within the training groups only because of this 'unfair' comparison with comparison group decrements?

Separate analysis indicates that the apparent decrements of the comparison groups did not differ significantly from a zero change for five of the six dimensions, but a significant decline did occur on the chairman approachability dimension (II) ($p < 0.01$). For the training groups, gains in dimensions I, III and IV do differ significantly from zero and thus are of consequence whether compared to the decrement in comparison groups or compared to a zero change.

As mentioned, during the course of a six-month period, the comparison groups declined significantly in the extent to which they perceived their chairman as approachable. This decline presumably occurred as a result of events which took place during the six-month interval. Similar findings of an increase in competence for training groups and a corresponding *decrease* for comparison groups is not uncommon. Miner (1960) reports that supervisors attending a course in psychology showed significant gains in attitude toward the human relations aspects of their jobs, while a control (comparison) group from the same department *evidenced a significant decline*. The author reasons that 'the training acted in such a way as to ward off or minimize those factors operating to produce an increase in negative attitudes . . .'. In other words, he suggests that *all groups would have declined* in attitude had not training occurred for some groups. This explanation would seem to assume that some negative event had transpired within the context in which *both* training and comparison groups operated, and yet no such event is noted. It is also difficult to explain the decline in chairman approachability (II) in the current study as one which might also occur if divorced from the research project itself. To do so would imply that groups in their natural organizational settings undergo continual deterioration on at least one dimension; that of chairman approachability. Rather, this decline might be viewed as a function of participation by comparison groups in a research project—without their concurrent participation in the corresponding laboratory experience.

In Issue 3 of this report, the suggestion was offered that the tendency for comparison groups to describe themselves as more adequate in the first administration of the GBI was a function of researcher–participant interactions and the realization that no laboratory training would be forthcoming. But what happened to these auspicious descriptions as the comparison groups reassembled continuously over a six-month period and were confronted recurrently with whatever inadequacies they gradually perceived? Our hypothesis is that the opportunity to express their reactions (concerning the group and its meetings) to the feelings that had been aroused over a six-month period materialized *in the form of the second administration of the GBI*. Prior to the research study, members had an unclear perception of the role of the group leader, or of their expectations of this role as it affected them in terms of chairman approachability. The first administration of the GBI queried comparison group members with blunt questions as sensitive issues which they were unprepared to confront at that time. But after six months of observing those inadequacies which did occur, expectations and standards of the leadership role became clearer. Since current leadership practice did not conform to these expectations, comparison group members now perceived significantly greater inadequacies in the rapport and approachability of their chairman.

Discussion

This study has indicated that significant improvements in effectiveness and interaction processes of work groups do occur as a result of participation in organizational training laboratories. These improvements take place in areas which are of direct personal and organizational relevance to members of the ongoing work groups and endure for a period of at least six months beyond the training experience. The specific problem areas in which significant positive changes occurred were group effectiveness, mutual influence among members, and personal involvement and participation. Those areas which showed no significant changes were leader approachability, intragroup trust, and the evaluation of group meetings. In general, these findings point to the complexity of the impact of organizational training laboratories upon ongoing work groups.

A further analysis has indicated that training participation not only has an impact upon the work group as a unit, but also upon individuals (relative to each other) within the group. Changes in perceptions of those individuals who participated in training laboratories were more diverse over the six-month period than were the changes of perceptions of those who did not participate. Although the diversity in change was apparent on all six dimensions, it was statistically significant in group effectiveness, leader approachability, and personal involvement.

Several questions were raised as a result of some of the unforeseen findings of this study. It was noted that groups which did not participate in training were significantly more competent than training groups on several dimensions *prior to the training*. This difference may be attributed to the training selection process in which groups that perceive themselves as less competent gravitate toward training. An alternative hypothesis is that pre-training differences were due to researcher–subject interactions. It was suggested that comparison group members were not playing the role assigned to them by the researcher (Back, Hood and Brehm, 1964). Rather, they reacted to the first administration of the GBI with a need to demonstrate the competence of their group to themselves and to the researcher. Comparison and training groups differed in this respect in that the former experienced no previous confrontation of the issues raised in the GBI, nor could they expect any remedy for an admission to work group problems.

References

Back, K. W., T. C. Hood and Mary L. Brehm (1964) *The Subject Role in Small Group Experiments*. Durham, N.C.: Duke University.

Bennis, W. G. (1963) 'A new role for the behavioural sciences: effecting organizational change.' *Administrative Science Quarterly*, **8**, 125–165.

Bennis, W. G., K. D. Benne and R. Chin (Eds.) (1962) *The Planning of Change*. New York: Holt, Rinehart and Winston.

Cattell, R. B., B. R. Saunders and G. F. Stice (1953) 'The dimensions of syntality in small groups.' *Human Relations*, **6**, 331–356.

Coch, L. and J. R. P. French (1948) 'Overcoming resistance to change.' *Human Relations*, **1**, 512–532.

Fleishman, E. A., E. F. Harris and H. E. Burtt (1955) *Leadership and Supervision in Industry*. Columbus: Bureau of Educational Research, Ohio State University.

Friedlander, F. (1966) 'Performance and interactional dimensions of organizational work groups.' *Journal of Applied Psychology*, **50**, 257–265.

Harrison, R. (1962) 'Evaluations and conclusions.' In C. Argyris, *Interpersonal Competence and Organizational Effectiveness*. Homewood, Ill.: Richard D. Irwin, Inc.

Lewin, K. (1947) 'Group decision and social change.' In T. Newcomb and E. Hartley (Eds.), *Readings in Social Psychology*. New York: Henry Holt.

Lippitt, R. (1949) *Training in Community Relations*. New York: Harper & Brothers.

Mann, F. C. (1962) 'Study and creating change.' In W. G. Bennis, K. D. Benne and R. Chin (Eds.), *The Planning of Change*. New York: Holt, Rinehart and Winston.

Miner, J. B. (1960) 'The effect of a course in psychology on the attitudes of research and development supervisors.' *Journal of Applied Psychology*, **44**, 224–232.

Riecken, H. (1952) *The Volunteer Work Camp: A Psychological Evaluation*. Cambridge, Mass.: Addison-Wesley Publishing Co.

Sanford, N. (1965) 'Will psychologists study human problems?' *American Psychologist*, **20**, 192–202.

Shepard, H. (1960) 'An action research model.' In Esso Standard Oil Company, *An Action Research Program for Organizational Improvement*. Ann Arbor, Mich: Esso Standard Oil Company, Foundation for Research on Human Behaviour.

Stock, Dorothy and H. Thelen (1958) *Emotional Dynamics and Group Culture*. Washington, D.C.: National Training Laboratories.

Winer, B. J. (1962) *Statistical Principles in Experimental Design*. New York: McGraw-Hill.

5

CHAPTER 4

The T-group Trainer*

In a book concerned with T-group training, *T-Group Theory and the Laboratory Method*, Blake (1964) states that the primary task of the trainer in a T-group is one of 'creating the most productive climate in which the participant can accept responsibility for his own development and can develop valid communications with others'. Tannenbaum, Weschler and Massarik (1961) suggest that to facilitate this the trainer performs several broad functions in the group. First, he provides numerous focal points for discussion and exploration. For example, he may focus attention on his role of authority figure or use research instruments in structuring particular situations for potentially useful insights. Second, he establishes a model of behaviour in the group. He may encourage and accept criticism, express his own feelings, or direct feedback to other people. And finally, he facilitates the flow of communication by initiating, clarifying and encouraging the discussion of essential issues: issues of leadership, group avoidance, interpersonal conflict and intimacy.

The empirical studies of the trainer are of four sorts. The first provide an assessment of the relationship between trainer personality and trainer style; the second, indicate participant perceptual change in reference to the trainer; the third, the trainer's impact on group development; and the fourth, the processes of trainer influence as it relates to participant change.

Relationship between trainer personality and trainer style

There are two studies that evaluate the trainers personality and his style. Deutsch, Pepitone and Zander (1948) looked at a leader of a basic skill training group (the forerunner to a T-group). The study was designed to show the interrelationship between the personality needs of the trainer and his resultant behaviour in the group. His personality was measured by TAT, Rorschach, Sentence Completion, Ideology Interview and Questionnaire, and a self-administered life history questionnaire.

His behaviour in the group was assessed by the Workshop Faculty (staff members of the T-group), without prior knowledge of the clinical results. The clinical examination indicated:

'Superior intellectual ability, turned creative imagination to immediate and practical aspects of work, sufficiently socially adaptable but has internal turmoil. Basically sensitive to others, affilitative and non-aggressive. Skilled in communication, tactfulness and social responsiveness; combined with this ideology should make for an effective democratic group leader.'

A content analysis of his behaviour in the T-group revealed the following:

'Warm and friendly, gets ideas across easily, never interrupts a group member, sensitive and careful not to hurt anyone's feelings, no strong emotional displays such as from moroseness to manicness, extremely unassertive, rarely undertakes critical analysis, and spontaneous.'

This study illustrates the way in which the trainer's predilections based on personality characteristics may influence his training philosophy and behaviour.

Reisel (1959) performed a similar clinical study on two well-established trainers. A research clinical psychologist carried out the study by observing each of the subjects as they worked with student T-groups. He attended all the sessions for both the groups and after each session met individually with each of the trainers for a clinical interview lasting between 30–45 minutes (the interviews were taped). In effect, the study attempted to show the continuous interrelationship between trainer personality and trainer behaviour in the group. The following excerpts represent the picture drawn of these relationships:

Trainer I:

'The first trainer's main characteristic was his self-effacing attitude toward himself and toward his work. He tended to play a warm and benevolent role of father figure for his group. These characteristic traits, the clinician interpreted, served to hide a large portion of underlying anxiety over the expression of hostility. His role of trainer was thusly carried out without the awareness that it was a means by which he could attract attention and gain vocal vision for purposes of satisfying his strong needs for affection.'

Trainer II:

'He was characterized by the clinician as having a powerful need to produce. This trainer was seen as highly ambivalent in his behaviour because of his insatiable need to be successful. He attempted to behave in a way that would achieve outward success, as an authoritarian, and at the same time tried to avoid being authoritarian. Consequently he denied the existence of his power in the group but stuck to it unawares.'

The effectiveness of the trainer, it would seem, depends not only on his training, the type of group being trained, or other sociocultural determinants, but also on certain of his personality characteristics. The findings of these two studies are highly tentative, being based on only three cases, but as far as they go, they illustrate that the trainer's personality has an effect on his training style in the group.

Participant perceptual change and the trainer

A second set of studies have attempted to look at T-group members' perceptual change in relation to the trainer. Lohmann, Zenger and Weschler (1959) performed a study to determine whether changes occur in students' self-perceptions and their perceptions of trainers during a T-group. The subjects were male and female college students in three T-groups. They used the Gordon Personal Profile which yields measures of ascendancy, responsibility, emotional stability, sociability, and a total self-evaluation score (a summated score of the previous four measures). Scores were obtained for students' self-perception, students' perception of the trainer, and for the trainer's self-perception. They found that trainers were seen by the students as significantly more adequate at the beginning than at the end of the group. However, the test of another hypothesis indicated a tendency for the students to see their trainer as more adequate than themselves, despite diminished idolization. And lastly, a trend was noted in the direction of the convergence of the students' perception of the trainer and the trainer's self-perception by the end of the group. These findings provide some evidence of the trainer's pre-eminence in the group, especially during the initial stages, and, in fact, although there is a diminished idolization of him, the tendency is to continue to see him as more adequate than themselves.

Vansina (1961) was also interested in the participants' perception of the trainer. He hypothesized that the T-group has an influence on its members' attitudes and opinions, and, since the experience is related to the problem of leadership, these should move closer to those of the trainer. He used two groups of social work students on a four-day residential course. After the introductory session every member of the group, as well as the trainer, described, by means of an item-sort, his image of his actual-self and of his attempted-self (image of ideal leader). This was repeated in the penultimate session when the participants made a new sorting. He found that the participants' attempted-self image became significantly more similar to that of the trainer at the later sorting.

There can be little doubt that the trainer's intervention in the group effects participant change to some degree and in one form or another. This change may take many forms: for example, the trainer may force compliance, serve as a model, or offer help and information. Lohmann and co-workers and Vansina have assessed participant change regarding the trainer, but they did not provide direct information about the meaning of the change and thus the reader has to make inferences from the data. To make such inferences meaningful, a consistent theoretical framework which accounts for the mechanisms and dynamics of the change is needed. This is particularly apparent when one attempts to make predictions about subsequent perceptions or behaviour.

Trainer's impact on group development

In recent years, there has been considerable emphasis on group development *vis-à-vis* the trainer. Stock and Hill (1958) suggested that the trainer's location within the sub-group structure of the group could partially explain why groups develop in given ways. Two groups were observed and a Behavioural Rating System was developed to examine a sample of meetings in terms of quality of work and emotionality. Each of the groups was found to be different in its level of work and expressed emotionality, over the period of group life. Each member was asked to describe his own group-related behaviours and feelings (a series of descriptive statements based on 'most like' and 'least like' himself). These were factor analysed and number of each group's self-perception subtypes were found (for example, Group A was identified as 'interested in maintaining work-oriented, non-personal relationships with others, they are withdrawn, exhibit considerable confusion and anxiety'). Thus, the group's development could be understood in terms of the kind of subtypes that emerge and the amount of consensus within them. It was suggested that the location of the trainer in terms of various emotional and work subgroups (for example, 'if in one or two mutually incompatible and warring subtypes he was blocked in conflict resolution'), the nature of the consensus of these subgroups, and its compatibility with other groups of varying levels of consensus could provide information on group development.

Stermerding (1961) performed a study which reflected the influence of the trainer on group development. He used two Dutch T-groups composed of management consultants and trainers in industry. A tape-recording was made of the groups throughout the experience. The participants were asked daily to fill in forms that required them to state in which of three possible areas they were learning from the group; about themselves, about groups, or about their daily work. They were also given a case study of a decision-making group, at the beginning and at the end of the experience, and asked to describe the kinds of things that were happening in the case. Their replies to the case study were then content analysed into five categories; general normative approach, personality, stereotyping, role functioning, and process-analysis. The trainer behaviour was examined via an analysis of the tape recordings of his interventions. And finally, a trainer assessment form was used by each trainer in evaluating, at the end of the group, their respective groups in terms of movement toward task, maintenance, sensitivity, and over-all effectiveness. A content analysis of the trainer interventions revealed that Trainer A showed a group-oriented approach, while Trainer B directed most of his interventions toward individual group members. Corresponding to this, Group A significantly differed from Group B on a number of process variables: Group A was seen to accentuate the 'group' aspect of learning while Group B emphasized equally the learnings about themselves and their daily work; Group A described the second case study in more process-analytic terms (in their observations of the actual interaction process of the case study) while Group B described it more in terms of role functioning (the relations of an individual in the social context); and finally, Group A was seen by its trainer as moving toward maintenance, sensitivity and overall effectiveness while Group B was seen as moving toward task only. The author draws the conclusion that trainer behaviour and group development are inextricable related. Once again we have some indication of the impact of the trainer in the T-group system, and yet, the link between the trainer and individual learning or group development is still unclear, that is, *how* or by what process does he influence these outcomes?

Psathas and Hardert (1966) investigated the effects of the trainer interventions on the pattern of group behaviour, specifically its normative behaviour. They hypothesized that the trainer interventions 'contain implicit norm-messages indicating to members what norms should be established in the group'. Seven two-week T-groups were studied each containing 12 members. A tape recording was made of the first three and last three sessions for each group and a verbatim record was kept of trainer interventions. At the close of each session the participants and the trainer were asked to write down the most significant trainer intervention. An inventory of norms was established by surveying the T-group literature. A list was then compiled, which grouped the normative items into *ought* and *should* statements, and a list of norm-categories was then established. The results indicate that 'trainer interventions can be reliably classified into these categories' (potentially biased since the authors did the sorting), and thus, 'implicit in trainer interventions, then, is a message concerning what members should or ought to do, and his view of what constitutes appropriate T-group member behaviour'. In addition they found that trainer interventions were consistently judged to fit into four normative categories more than any others; analysing group interaction or process, feelings, feedback and acceptance concern. These categories were consistently high from one time period to another, which the authors suggest reflects the persistent trainer problem of establishing these norms. It is notable, however, that analysing group interaction or process is highest in the early time period whereas acceptance concern is highest in the late time period, which they imply, offers evidence of some pattern in group development.

Although not specifically structured to investigate the trainer *vis-à-vis* group development, Psathas and Hardert's study is highly relevant to this issue. One is forced, however, to question the assumption that a reliable classification of trainer interventions into norm-categories is evidence that the trainer is actually communicating to the members what should or ought to be done. The validity of the assumption can be more directly tested by examining, perhaps, the complete intervention episode (i.e., the trainer's intervention and the subsequent member response).

Another study (Mann, 1966), examines the member-to-trainer relationship in the development of the group. Two self-analytic groups were used for the study. They were composed of university students who met five times a week for 50 minutes each session, for a total of 32 sessions, and were heterogeneous in terms of age, sex and background. Verbatim records and tape recordings were used throughout the groups. A scoring-system was designed to measure 'each act initiated by a group member for the state of his feelings toward the trainer'. The scoring system included 16 categories broken down into three major headings: Impulse area ('member's aggressive and libidinal ties with the trainer'), Authority Relations area ('power and dependency issues'), and an Ego State area ('member's feelings toward himself in the context of the relationship with the trainer'). A scheme was then developed to provide a theory of the development of member–trainer relations, in assessing the similarities and differences on the above variables between the two groups. The five stages of this development are as follows:

Stage 1: *Appraisal:* 'The trainer is the focus for much of the anxiety aroused in members by the new situation; they tend to perceive and use him as an ally in reducing their anxiety and controlling their impulses; they tend to project their ego-ideal onto the trainer, partly as a means of allaying anxiety, but also as a means of setting a satisfying relationship; and he is a source of frustration.'

Stage 2: *Confrontation:* 'Expression of hostile or counter-dependent feelings serves both to challenge the authority of the trainer, and to express the member's exasperation with the trainer's failure to reciprocate affection and esteem. Or, he is at this point serving the purpose of "naming the devil", of crystallizing the vaguely apprehended dangers and uncertainties inherent in a new group.'

Stage 3: *Re-evaluation:* 'The stage is one in which the previous images of the trainer are tested for their continuing usefulness, and an important means of re-evaluation of the image occurs when the members compare the ego state appropriate to the image with how they feel at the moment.'

Stage 4: *Internalization:* 'A shift of the members toward the trainer as internal object. There are two phases in this stage, identification and work. What constitutes success or productive effort? What is work in this group? And how do we go about it?'

Stage 5: *Separation:* 'Anticipation as the group comes to a close, loss and sadness at the losing of the relationship with the trainer.'

He found a number of similarities and differences between the two groups with regard to the above scheme. The primary differences, he suggests, were a result of the way in which each group dealt with the trainer in the confrontation period. Group 2 expressed a great deal of hostility toward the trainer and avoided the issue of appraising him. Group 1, however, confronted the dependency and authority position of the trainer. As a result Group 1 entered the re-evaluation stage and engaged in reparative work, 'to undo and control the aggression of the previous period', whereas Group 2 showed signs of distress and were frightened about the expression of hostility and concerned about its containment. In consequence, Group 2 never entered the internalization stage to any great extent and was left with the need to deal with unresolved issues of anxiety and depression arising out of the confrontation stage. Group 1's reparative work and consequent decrease in anxiety provided it with a period of internalization, although within this stage some anxiety and hostility reappeared.

Mann's study provides a valuable contribution in understanding the importance of the trainer in the T-group. It increases our knowledge of the possible consequences of dealing with authority-based issues and provides an overall schema of group development that encourages a focus on the participant's experience of the learning relationship.

Trainer influence and participant change

A number of points have been made about the variables which need to be considered in describing the trainer's impact in a T-group. No study, however, can escape the obligation to be clear about the conditions necessary to establish a connection between the trainer and the results of his influence on change. The studies discussed in the last three sections, in one form or another, indicate the effect of the trainer in the T-group environment, but none of them state in what form this influence exists and how this relates to participant learning. 'Hopefully, we shall soon have instruments which will permit us to assess trainer style as an independent variable and relate it to kind and extent of outcome' (Harrison, 1966).

Some research of this kind has recently been undertaken. Peters (1966) examined the relationship between trainer identification and personal change. He found that participants who identified with the trainer, assessed by direct, indirect, and projective measures, showed personal learning within the T-group. In respect to trainer identification the participants' self-percept (measured by a semantic differential) converged with their perception of the trainer and the trainer's self-percept. This convergence was noted for most participants in six two-week T-groups. In addition, it was discovered that the more similarities (i.e. same-sex and occupational similarities) between the trainer and the member, the stronger the relationship between convergence and personal change. Peters' interpretation to account for the sex-matching and occupational similarity was that for 'identification to lead to personal change in the T-group may require a model whose attitudes, values and behaviour are relevant, functional and realistically attainable for the person'. That is, that the trainer is a more realistic reference-other or *role-model*.

The study, whilst interesting, has several shortcomings. It assesses personal change by reference to trainer ratings and peer ratings at the end of the group. This has two disadvantages: first, they are post-only measures; and second, neither of these measures of 'change' had been validated unequivocable (Miles, 1959; Bunker, 1965). The control group, as acknowledged by Peters, is more properly what Friedlander (1967) would call a 'comparison group'. Certainly in Peters' case the so-called control group differs markedly from the trained group. The former consisted of graduate students in their early twenties, while the latter consisted on the whole of high status middle-aged administrators (business, school, nursing, government and public administration officials). It would have been better, therefore, to have used a matched control group for comparison.

It is also worth noting that the convergence was clearly significant on only the indirect measurement scale; on the other scales, increases were only of borderline significance.

Nonetheless this study is interesting in that it attempts to link participant change directly to the trainer and to indicate that identification is a relevant learning mechanism in T-groups.

Culbert (1968) investigated the effects of self-disclosing trainer behaviour upon members of two student T-groups. The same trainers participated in both groups. They were provided with 'job descriptions' which set forth guide-lines for their behaviour in each group. These descriptions called for the trainers to behave similarly in both groups, that is, to differ only on the experimental condition of being more self-disclosing (mSD condition) in one group and less self-disclosing (lSD condition) in the other. The first part of the study substantiates that the experimental manipulation was successful. The trainers were judged as more self-disclosing in the mSD condition than in the lSD condition by each of three separate measures.

The data generated by this study showed that the members of the lSD group more often perceived their two-person relationships with the trainers and their specified dyad partners as therapeutic, and the mSD participants more frequently viewed their relationships with *non-critical* others as therapeutic.

As Culbert points out, interpretation as to the desirability of this difference is not clear. It could be argued that the members of the mSD group have learned to create better relationships free from dependence on the trainer. Relationships, that is, that have 'extra-group transferability'. Alternatively, it could be argued, that the lSD participants, in being centrally involved with critical members, may be participating in qualitatively richer relationships than members of the mSD group. Culbert speculates that a very high degree of self-reference behaviour in the mSD group may have been a factor in the lack of two-person therapeutic relationships.

The self-awareness data showed the mSD group as having a significantly higher degree of self-awareness than the lSD group, a difference which narrowed with time. Culbert concludes from this that the results are consistent with *modelling theory*. The subjects of the mSD group appear to have modelled their participation after their self-disclosing trainers. This explanation, Culbert notes, is given further support from clinical impressions reported by the two trainers and the group observer.

In his conclusion, Culbert argues strongly that there is an optimum level of self-awareness for T-group participation and that early attainment of this level is to the group's advantage. It follows from this that self-disclosing trainer participation is called for at least during the early meetings. Upon attainment of this self-awareness level the trainer could productively 'pull in' and be less self-disclosing. It is to be noted, however, that much of this conclusion is speculative in view of the small sample size and in the absence of unambiguous data.

Bolman (1969) added to Culbert's approach in investigating the relationship among certain dimensions of trainer behaviour (similar to self-disclosure) and member learning. He found that one trainer variable was crucial in the learning process, the variable represented by the factor labelled congruence-empathy. It was found that trainer congruence-empathy was positively related to participant learning (as measured by self-rated learning, others' learning, and peer-rated learning). While the data in this study was limited in that it was based only on the perceptions of the group members, it does support the evidence in other social influence situations (Rogers, 1957; Barrett-Lennard, 1962) that change agents who are seen as congruent or honest provide opportunities for individual learning.

Cooper (1969) investigated Kelman's (1961) theory of social influence in respect to the trainer in T-groups. He focused in on two processes of social influence; identification and internalization. It was proposed that the participants' perception of trainer characteristics will determine which process of social influence is likely to result and, consequently, the way in which participants will change. He found that in an identification-based trainer influence process, that is, when the trainer was seen to be attractive: (1) the participant became more like the trainer in his attitudes (as measured by Schutz's (1958) FIRO-B) and behaviour (as measured by tape analysis); (2) changes in the participants' self-concept did not occur; and (3) the participants' work associates did not report them as having significantly changed six to nine months after the T-group (on a measure based on the Bunker (1965) categories). In an internalization-based trainer influence process, that is, when the trainer was seen to be congruent: (1) changes occurred in the participants' self-concept (change toward an increased match between self-percept and ideal-percept, self-percept and other participants' perception of him, and self-percept and actual behaviour); (2) changes in the direction of the trainers' attitudes and behaviour did not occur; and (3) the participants' work associates reported them as having changed six to nine months after the T-group.

Although the data collected by Cooper support the Kelman social influence model, it is important to note some of the assumptions implicit in this study. First, it was assumed that attractiveness and congruence are mutually exclusive dimensions, this, on the surface at least, may not be the case. Second, it was assumed that it is the participants' perception of the trainer's behaviour and not the trainer's actual behaviour that is the primary basis of influence in the relationship.

More fundamentally, an assumption throughout this chapter has been that the trainer is the principal source of influence. At the same time, we must consider whether factors other than the trainer—such as group composition, group format, intragroup dynamics—may be determinants of participant change. In future research we must examine each of these factors by introducing them into the analysis and investigating how the relationship between trainer behaviour and participant change is affected by them.

It cannot be claimed that any of the above studies have exhausted all aspects of trainer influence. They all, however, are provocative of further research.

Conclusion

Much of the trainer research reviewed in this chapter is replete with difficulties which limits the generalizability of the findings in respect to the practical considerations in the organization and conduct of T-group training. There are a number of problems posed by all such studies:

(1) The findings are based, on the whole, on small samples.

(2) Most of the studies rely for their measurements on participant perception of behaviour and not on direct observation of changes in behaviour by unbiased observers.

(3) There is a lack of agreement and clarity about what constitutes the research focus, which is reflected in the widely varying instruments and criteria used.

(4) Little attempt was made to establish a causal relation between observed group or individual changes and the trainer behaviour employed to produce them.

(5) Our survey revealed only one study specifically designed to investigate the effects of the trainer on follow-up change.

References

Barrett-Lennard, G. T. (1962) 'Dimensions of therapist response as causal factors in therapeutic change.' *Psychological Monographs*, **74**, 42.

Blake, R. R. (1964) 'Studying group action.' In L. P. Bradford, J. R. Gibb and K. D. Benne (Eds.), *T-Group Theory and Laboratory Method*. New York: John Wiley & Sons.

Bolman, L. G. (1969) 'Effects of the trainer on his T-group.' Unpublished manuscript, Carnegie-Mellon University.

Bunker, D. R. (1965) 'Individual applications of laboratory training.' *Journal of Applied Behavioral Science*, **1**, 131–148.

Cooper, C. L. (1969) 'The influence of the trainer on participant change in T-groups.' *Human Relations*, **22**, 515–530.

Culbert, S. A. (1968) 'Trainer self-disclosure and member growth in two T-groups.' *Journal of Applied Behavioral Science*, **4**, 47–74.

Deutsch, M., A. Pepitone and A. Zander (1948) 'Leadership in the small group.' *Journal of Social Issues*, **4**, 31–40.

Friedlander, F. (1967) 'The impact of organizational training laboratories upon the effectiveness and interaction of on-going work groups.' *Personnel Psychology*, **20**, 289–307.

Harrison, R. (1966) 'A conceptual framework for laboratory training.' National Training Laboratory working draft.

Kelman, H. C. (1961) 'Processes of opinion change.' *Public Opinion Quarterly*, **25**, 57–78.

Lohmann, K., J. H. Zenger and I. R. Weschler (1959) 'Some perceptual changes during sensitivity training.' *Journal of Educational Research*, **53**, 28–31.

Mann, R. D. (1966) 'The development of the member-trainer relations in self-analytic groups.' *Human Relations*, **19**, 84–117.

Miles, M. B. (1959) *Learning to Work in Groups.* New York: Teachers College, Columbia University.

Peters, D. R. (1966) 'Identification and personal change in laboratory training groups.' Unpublished Ph.D. thesis, Alfred P. Sloan School of Management, M.I.T.

Psathas, G. and R. Hardert (1966) 'Trainer interventions and normative patterns in the T-groups.' *Journal of Applied Behavioral Science*, **2**, 149–170.

Reisel, J. (1959) 'The trainer role in human relations training.' Paper read at the Western Psychological Association meeting, April, 1959.

Rogers, C. R. (1957) 'The necessary and sufficient conditions of therapeutic personality change.' *Journal of Consulting Psychology*, **21**, 95–103.

Schutz, W. C. (1958) FIRO: A Theory of Interpersonal Relations. New York: Rinehart.

Stermerding, A. H. (1961) 'Evaluation research in the field of sensitivity training.' Unpublished manuscript, Leiden: Netherlands Institute of Preventive Medicine.

Stock, D. and W. F. Hill (1958) 'Inter subgroup dynamics as a factor in group growth.' In D. Stock and H. Thelen, *Emotional Dynamics and Group Culture.* New York: New York University Press.

Tannenbaum, R., I. R. Weschler and F. Massarik (1961) *Leadership and Organization.* New York: McGraw-Hill.

Vansina, L. (1961) 'Research concerning the influence of the T-group method on the formation of the participants' social values and opinions.' In *Evaluation of Supervisory and Management Training Methods.* Paris: Organization for Economic Cooperation and Development.

Trainer Self-Disclosure and Member Growth in Two T-groups[*]

Samuel A. Culbert

Behavioural Science Department,
University of California, Los Angeles

This study compares the effects that 'more' or 'less' self-disclosing trainer behavior had upon members of two T-groups. Part I of the data analysis substantiates that the experimental manipulation took place as intended. Part II shows that while an equivalent number of 2-person 'perceived therapeutic relationships' were formed in each group, Ss in the group with less self-disclosing trainers (*lSD*) more often entered them with their dyad partners and trainers; Ss with more self-disclosing trainers (*mSD*) entered relationships more often with other members. Part III shows that although both groups eventually attained the same level of self-awareness, the *mSD* group did so earlier. A revised prescription for trainer behavior is advanced, suggesting that the trainer might optimally begin his participation with a high rate of self-disclosure and become more selective with time.

Noticeably missing from the literature on T-groups is research on trainer behavior. This gap exists despite widespread acceptance of the T-group trainer as a key factor in group process. The absence of trainer research is no oversight; it bespeaks the complexity of this research topic. Such complexity centers around the need for a methodological strategy that takes account of the particular training orientation being studied. That is, trainer behavior should not be researched without specifically considering both the training goals and the processes the trainer adopts in implementing them.

The orientation of the trainers in the present study is that of Clark (1963). Very briefly, it specifies that shifting 2-person encounters among group participants, encounters of the kind endorsed by Rogers (1961), is the most effective process for bringing about personal growth. Accordingly, the aspect of trainer behavior being investigated here, *trainer self-disclosure*, is evaluated relative to its ability to produce this type of inter-personal encounter, termed 'perceived therapeutic relationships' (PTRs), and the goal that these relationships are hypothesized to bring about in the member,

* Published in the *Journal of Applied Behavioral Science*, **4**, 1968, 47–73. The researcher extends deepest thanks to James V. Clark, Tommy M. Tomlinson and H. Kenneth Bobele, all of whom contributed greatly to the completion of this project.

'increased self-awareness'. It is noted that data have already been collected to support the connection between the number of PTRs formed reciprocally, or 'mutually', between pairs of T-group participants and individual increases in self-awareness (Clark and Culbert, 1965).

Also involved in the methodology of this study was a decision on data collection. A strategy needed to be formulated on how much data would be required to measure effectively trainer self-disclosure and the hypothesized dependent variables of PTRs and member self-awareness. Data relevant to each of these variables are generated in voluminous amounts within even a single T-group. Moreover, the exacting methodology used in this study is considered to have a good amount of generalizability. Thus it was decided to extract data from but two T-groups, each corresponding to different degrees of trainer self-disclosure.

Purpose

This study is an attempt to assess the differential effects along two measures of personal learning—one interpersonal and one intrapersonal—between the members of two T-groups where their identical co-trainers, acting consonantly, have been more and less personally self-disclosing. More specifically, the following hypotheses are formulated:

1. Members of a T-group where the co-trainers are 'more personally self-disclosing'* will enter into a greater number of 'mutually perceived therapeutic relationships' than members of a T-group whose trainers are 'less personally self-disclosing'.

   a. Similarly, the members of the group with the more self-disclosing co-trainers will perceive their dyad partner, with whom they have met regularly over the span of the group life, as being more 'therapeutic', in their 2-person relationships, than will members of the T-group where the trainers are less self-disclosing.

   b. Likewise, members of the T-groups with the more self-disclosing co-trainers will perceive these trainers as being more 'therapeutic', in their 2-person relationships, than will members of the other T-group with whom these trainers have been less self-disclosing.

2. Members of the T-group where the co-trainers are more self-disclosing will experience a greater positive change in 'self-awareness', early to late, than the members of the T-group where the trainers are less self-disclosing.

---

* Quotes are used to designate terms which will be operationalized and subjected to measurement in this study.

Procedure

Subjects

The Ss were 20 upper-division and graduate students participating in two T-groups as course work for academic credit. Each group was composed of six females and four males, none of whom had previous T-group experience. Assignment to the groups was made as follows: each student was given the Jourard Self-Disclosure Questionnaire and paired with another S of the same sex who scored similarly on this premeasure. A matched-pair assignment was made subject to one alteration, that of placing previously acquainted Ss within the same T-group. This was an attempt to minimize intergroup communication, as none of the subjects were to know the 'condition' of their group.

The Ss met twice a week for 2-hour sessions over a semester's span of 14 weeks. One of these weekly sessions was spent in a T-group with the two co-trainers and the other in a dyad pairing with another group member, not a trainer. The same, randomly assigned, dyad pairings were held for the semester's duration. The times and meeting places for these group and dyad meetings were staggered to discourage intergroup communication.

Trainers

The same two male co-trainers participated in both T-groups. Their participation evened out each group into six females and six males. One of these trainers* was quite experienced both in T-group theory and practice, and the other trainer (this researcher) was a relative newcomer to T-group training at the time of the study. Both trainers ascribed to similar philosophies of member learning, following the guide-lines established by Clark (1963).

Conditions

The trainers were provided with 'job descriptions' which set forth guide-lines for their behavior in the group. These descriptions called for the trainers to follow parallel lines of personal conduct in both groups, that is, to differ only on the two experimental conditions of being more self-disclosing (mSD condition) in one group and less self-disclosing (lSD condition) in the other. In both instances, however, the trainers were to do their best to promote member self-disclosure. Once a week, and more often when needed, the two trainers discussed with an observer the problems they were experiencing in holding to these conditions.

* James V. Clark.

Measures

The measures used in this research were of two types, one requiring the Ss cooperation in filling out questionnaires and the other made without S's knowledge, using data collected from tape recordings of the T-group sessions. An overview of these measures and their purposes in this study is contained in Table 1.

Self-disclosure questionnaire. The questionnaire was a 40-item revised edition by Jourard of the Self-disclosure Questionnaire developed by Jourard and Lasakow (1958). It was administered in two forms. The first was the conventional one ('Who Knows You?'), where the respondent

Table 1—*Overview of measures used in self-disclosure study*

Experimental variable	Measure	Purpose	Rater
I. Conformation of experimental conditions	A. Self-disclosure questionnaire (inverted form)	Measure of how well Ss believe they know the two trainers	All 20 Ss
	B. Content categorization	Objective breakdown of self-statements made by trainers by per cent and type	Two specially trained judges (graduate students familiar with group process)
	C. Ratings of five-minute transcripts	Impressions of trainers' in-the-group process	Two clinicians experienced in group process
II. Hypothesis 1: Mutually and one-way perceived therapeutic relationships	A. Relationship inventory	Ratings of degree in which each S views every other S in his group as exhibiting therapeutic behavior toward him	All 20 Ss plus the 2 trainers
	B. Self-disclosure questionnaire (standard form)	S's ratings of degree to which he is known by dyad partner	Ten dyad pairings using all 20 Ss
III. Hypothesis 2: Member self-awareness	A. Process scale speech ratings	Evaluation of changes in member self-awareness from early to late meetings	Three specially trained judges (undergraduate students)

checks off, with respect to specified target persons, what of his own self (personal information) is known by these others. Two administrations of this form were given; one was made prior to the start of the T-groups with the target persons being the S's closest male and female acquaintances, and the second administration came just before the final group meeting with the same two target persons plus the S's dyad partner. Nongroup targets were used to provide a frame of reference for interpreting the scores of the dyad partners. The second form ('Whom Do You Know?'), was a variant of the first one. Each of the questions from 'Who Knows You?' was inverted so that the respondent was checking off what personal information he, as a receiver, had about the target person. This form was administered but once, just prior to the final group meeting and specified as target persons the two co-trainers plus the S's dyad as target partner.

Relationship inventory (RI). The present version of the RI is a 1964 modification of the one Barrett-Lennard (1962) developed two years before. It is a 64-item questionnaire yielding numerical scores on the extent to which one person perceives another as having positive regard, empathy, congruence, and unconditionality of regard toward him. Adding the scores for these four variables yields a fifth RI score, the sum of the other four. A more detailed description of these variables is contained in the Clark and Culbert (1965, p. 185) article as well as in Barrett-Lennard's (1962) monograph.

In this study the RI was used to measure each S's perception of the extent to which he sees himself as receiving the therapeutic qualities of positive regard, empathy, congruence and unconditional regard from a given other within the context of their interpersonal relationship. The RI was filled out by each S *vis-à-vis* every other S, plus the two trainers. These data were collected but once, just prior to the final group meeting. A one-way, 'perceived therapeutic relationship' (PTR), on a given dimension, was defined as an S rating another S above the median on the rating he assigned to all S's for that dimension. A 'mutually perceived therapeutic relationship' (MPTR) was similarly defined; only in this case both members of a 2-person relationship rated each other as being above the medians of the ratings they assigned to others. In order to include the trainers in the calculation of MPTRs, it was also necessary for them to fill out RIs on their individual perceptions of each of the S's in the two experimental groups.

Problem expression scale (PES). This scale was used to operationalize changes in the qualitative variable of 'self-awareness'. It is a seven-point rating scale which was originally designed to measure process changes occurring in individual psychotherapy (van der Veen and Tomlinson, 1962).

The PES has subsequently been used in research on group therapy (Truax, 1961) and for research in sensitivity training (Clark and Culbert, 1965).

The previous methodology is identical with that previously used in the just-mentioned T-group research. Thirty speech segments were selected for each S on a random basis from tape recordings of the T-group sessions, 15 early and 15 late. Inasmuch as each S did not participate equally in every session, and sometimes not at all, segments were selected from four early sessions (Sessions 1–4) and four late ones (Sessions 11–14). Segments from sessions 5 and 10 were used for Ss who did not produce a large enough participation sample in the selected sessions.

The 720 speech segments (from two groups of ten Ss plus two trainers with 30 segments each) were coded and typed on index cards. These cards were randomized and submitted in staggered order to three judges who had been trained along the lines prescribed in a manual developed for PES raters (Bobele, 1965). Each judge worked independently, assigning numerical ratings to each segment. The particular rating for a given segment corresponded to that one of seven stages of the PES scale which, in the judge's opinion, best described the entire speech segment. Segments which appeared to be mostly at a given stage, but showed some of the next higher stage, received a rating of 0·5 higher than the given stage.

Content analysis of trainer speech segments. A content categorization of a random sample of speech segments spoken by the two co-trainers was made in order to determine the extent to which the experimental manipulation was carried out. This particular analysis was adapted from the originally developed by Bugental (1948), fully operationalized by Weschler and Reisel (1959), and described in a manual by Reisel (1959). Two phases of the system are relevant to this study. First there is the determination of *thought units*. A thought unit is defined as a series of words expressing a single idea or thought; basically it is equivalent to a simple grammatical sentence. Second is the assignment of thought units to *content categories*. There are three types of categories having to do with self-references which, for these purposes, imply self-disclosure. The first type of self-reference refers to a trainer talking exclusively about himself. In this case he is either the subject or the subject and object of the thought unit being categorized. Such thought units are assigned to the content category 'S'. The second type of self-reference refers to the trainer discussing the way some group member or group incident affects him. Such thought units are collected under the symbol '→ S'. The third type of self-reference refers to the trainer discussing the effect his participation is having either on the group or on some subset of group members. These thought units are collected under the symbol 'S →'.

As mentioned above, this content analysis was applied to the random sample of speech segments made by the two co-trainers. In all, 120 speech segments were analysed, 15 early and 15 late for each trainer in each of the two experimental conditions. Two judges were selected on the basis of having clinical or sensitivity training backgrounds. As with the judging of PES ratings, these judges underwent a mutual training period but made their ratings independently.

Ratings of five-minute transcripts. This measure was used to collect data bearing on the impressionistic meaning the experimental manipulation held for two experienced clinicians heretofore not involved in this experiment.* Utilizing a table of random numbers, five-minute segments of unedited group process were transcribed. A total of 30 segments were selected, 15 from each experimental group. Within each group, five segments were selected from the first three, the middle three, and the last three meetings. At least one segment was selected from each meeting, and an equal number of segments were selected from early, middle, and late thirds of the meetings. Random numbers completely determined this selection, subject to the frequency requirement that a minimum of three trainer speech statements be contained within each five-minute block.

A list of 21 bipolar adjectives of the seven-point semantic differential variety was constructed (see Table 6). The 21 items were selected for their relevance either to the trainer job descriptions governing the experimental conditions or for their relevance to the Rogerian conceptualization (Rogers, 1959) regarding the process of a 'helping' relationship.

The five-minute segments (coded for group, meeting, and speaker) were then submitted to the two clinicians, who independently rated each segment along the adjectives of the bipolar check list. The instructions for making these ratings were identical with those typically used in Semantic Differential research (Osgood, Suci and Tannenbaum, 1957). The raters were requested to focus on the combined effect of the trainers' behavior, making a single rating based on their impressions of the two trainers acting in consort.

Results

The results of this study can be most clearly presented in three parts. The first part contains data relevant to discerning the extent to which the experimental manipulation was carried out as intended. The second and third parts contain data bearing on the two member variables, 'perceived

* Gerard V. Haigh and Karl Pottharst.

therapeutic relationships' and 'self-awareness', hypothesized to be affected by the manipulation. The overview contained in Table 1 should be helpful in assisting the reader to follow this presentation.

Part I: Confirmation of experimental conditions

Self-disclosure questionnaire. This questionnaire was used, in the inverted form, to provide a measure of how much personal information the Ss (of both conditions) believed they knew about their trainers. The total ratings for each experimental group are illustrated in the first two columns of Table 2. The third column contains the total number of points assigned to dyad partners on this questionnaire and provides a reference point for interpreting the meaning of these data. Although the number of points

Table 2—*'Whom do you know?': total number of points assigned by members of each experimental group (N = 10)*

	Trainer 1	Trainer 2	Dyad partner
mSD	68	55	285
lSD	16	19	256

Notes: James V. Clark was trainer 1 and the researcher was trainer 2.

assigned to the trainers of the *mSD* group is greater than the number assigned to the trainers of the *lSD* group, these ratings are far below the number of points assigned to dyad partners, and in both cases indicate a relatively low knowledge of the trainers. A Mann–Whitney U (Siegel, 1956) was computed, comparing the two experimental groups on the combined ratings each S made of the two trainers. The U of 86·5 was significant at the 0·01 level (2-tailed test) and supported the experimental intent that the trainers would be viewed as more self-disclosing by the Ss of the *mSD* condition.

Content categorization. 'Early' and 'late' trainer speech statements were content-analysed to provide an objective breakdown both of the percentage and the variety of self-statements made by the co-trainers in each of the experimental groups. Since two judges were used in making these categorizations, percentages of interjudge agreement were calculated. Both the separation of speech segments into thought units and the content categorization of thought units were performed with high levels of agreement—88 per cent and 79 per cent, respectively. Moreover, no systematic differences were detected when agreement as to content categorization was broken down by experimental condition, trainer, or time: each subpercentage was above 77 per cent.

The between-groups comparison of thought unit categorization is presented in Table 3. Percentage-wise, the combined trainer effort was as desired, producing almost twice the percentage of thought units categorized as self-references in the *mSD* condition than in the *lSD* condition. A two-by-two chi-square made by dichotomizing thought units into self- and non-self-references for each of the two experimental groups was highly significant ($\chi^2 = 35 \cdot 87$, $p < 0 \cdot 001$), statistically supporting the aforementioned inspection of Table 3.

Table 3—*Breakdown of content categorization of trainer speech segments: Experimental group × trainer × time*

| | mSD | | lSD | | lSD (corrected[a]) |
	Self-references	Non-self-references	Self-references	Non-self-references	self-references
Trainer 1					
Early	43 (0·402)	64	19 (0·380)	31	23·43
Late	79 (0·494)	81	42 (0·334)	84	69·64
Trainer 2					
Early	67 (0·670)	33	7 (0·117)	53	8·62
Late	59 (0·444) $\chi^2 = 8\cdot07$*	74	20 (0·220) $\chi^2 = 0\cdot69$	71	33·16
Total for both trainers	248 (0·496) $\chi^2 = 35\cdot87$**	252	88 (0·261)	249	134·85

Note: The numbers in parentheses are percentages of the total number of thought units represented by the number above.
[a] Corrected for differential frequency of trainer intervention.
* $p < 0\cdot005$.
** $p < 0\cdot001$.

The above categorization is best considered as a measure of the intensity of self-references and differs from the absolute quantity of trainer self-references made in the two experimental groups. This point is illustrated by the fact that while the trainers intervened more frequently in the *lSD* group than in the *mSD* group (the ratio between their combined frequencies was on the order of 3 : 2), they spoke longer in the *mSD* group: an average of 8·33 thought units per ratable intervention to an average of 5·61 thought units per ratable intervention in the *lSD* group. A 'corrected' trainer self-reference count was calculated for the *lSD* group so that quantity of these references might be compared (see last column in Table 3). Comparison of this estimate with the quantity of self-references in the *mSD* group is again consistent with the experimental intent to vary trainer self-disclosure. (The figures in each row of column 5 are lower than those in the same row in column 1).

Table 4—*Percentage[a] of self-reference in content categorization: trainer ×*
experimental group × time

	Trainer 1			Trainer 2		
	S	→S	S→	S	→S	S→
mSD Early	0·187	0·177	0·037	0·240	0·330	0·100
mSD Late	0·313	0·157	0·025	0·098	0·142	0·203
lSD Early	0·180	0·160	0·040	0·033	0·067	0·017
lSD Late	0·119	0·159	0·056	0·044	0·088	0·088

[a] Percentages are based on samples from the trainers' total participation.

Examination of the intragroup self-references (see Table 3) made by the two trainers shows statistically significant opposing trends between trainers in the *mSD* condition ($\chi^2 = 8\cdot07$, $p < 0\cdot005$), and similar trainer trends within the *lSD* condition, where χ^2 is nonsignificant. Overall, trainer 2 did the better job of holding the experimental conditions although his percentage of self-references decreased over time in the *mSD* group and increased in the *lSD* group. Trainer 1 began with comparable frequency in both experimental groups, making about four self-references for every ten thought units. However, with time, he participated with greater differentiation, making fewer self-references in the *lSD* group and more in the *mSD* group.

A breakdown of the specific types of self-references made by these trainers is contained in Table 4. The three types of self-references include the trainer talking exclusively about himself (S), the trainer discussing the way some group member or group incident affects him (→ S), and the trainer discussing the effect his participation is having either on the group or on some subset of group members (S →). The data for trainer 1 show that he uniformly avoided self-references of the S → variety in the *mSD* group and that he increased his combined percentage of self-references in this group. His increase in self-references was primarily accounted for by an increase in the S type reference. Trainer 2's percentage of self-references remained relatively constant in the *lSD* condition, while his percentage decreased considerably, over time, in the *mSD* condition. This decrease is noticeably accounted for by a shift from the S and → S types of thought units to the S → variety. However, when the data for the two trainers are combined, as in Table 5, these individual trainer differences cancel out, with the combined distribution of self-references remaining relatively constant within each group from early to late meetings.

Table 5—*Percentage of thought units content-categorized as self-references: experimental group × time*

	mSD				*lSD*			
	S	→S	S→	Total	S	→S	S→	Total
Early	0·213	0·251	0·068	0·536	0·100	0·109	0·027	0·236
Late	0·215	0·153	0·105	0·471	0·089	0·129	0·069	0·286
Total	0·214	0·192	0·088	0·494	0·092	0·122	0·055	0·266

Five-minute transcripts. Two experienced clinicians gave their impressions of the way the co-trainers performed in each of the experimental groups. Four sets of medians were compiled, one from each judge's ratings for each experimental group. The selection of median ratings was made on the rationale that the rating distributions would not necessarily be symmetrical. While the two judges' median ratings were not correlated ($r = 0.012$, $SD_1 = 0.650$, $SD_2 = 0.809$), they were in agreement. The percentage of agreement, using an agreement interval of 1·00, was 71 per cent. Those ratings not within this interval were split; i.e., the medians of each judge's ratings were higher than those of the others about half of the time.

The judges' median ratings were next combined to obtain an average median rating for each of the bipolar scales, on each of the experimental groups. These averages are presented in Table 6. The differences between groups on average median ratings for 15 of the 21 bipolar pairs were less than 0·5 apart. The trainers' behavior on these dimensions, then, is likely to have been similar in each experimental group. Three adjective pairs have a between-groups difference between 0·5 and 1·0. The inference from these data is that the trainers are likely to have performed differently on these dimensions in each of the two groups and were thus viewed by the judges as more 'genuine', more 'involved', and more 'personal' in the *mSD* group. Three adjective pairs have quite large between-groups differences, greater than 1·0. Thus, it is highly probable that the trainers were viewed as more 'vulnerable', as showing more 'feelings', and as being more 'self-disclosing' in the *mSD* group than in *lSD* group. Five of these six afore-mentioned differences are highly consistent with the experimental intent to have the trainers behave comparably in the two groups, except on the dimension of self-disclosure. The exception is on the dimension of 'genuine–artificial' where a 'less self-disclosing' trainer should be able to be viewed as equally

Table 6—*Average of median ratings assigned by judges after reading five-minute transcripts of trainer behavior[a, b]*

Dipolar adjective[c]	mSD	lSD	Differences		
			0·5	→ 1·0	> 1·0
*Direct–indirect	6·02	5·60			
*Genuine–artificial	5·13	4·44	X		
Attentive–inattentive	5·09	5·13			
*Vulnerable–invulnerable	5·03	3·75			X
Important–unimportant	4·94	4·76			
Expresses warmth–coolness	4·46	4·04			
*Effective–ineffective	5·07	5·19			
Likable–not likable	4·32	4·14			
*Understanding–not understanding	5·07	5·19			
Aware–unaware	5·34	5·43			
*Interpretive–noninterpretive	4·86	4·88			
Here-and-now–there-and-then	5·27	5·57			
Analyzes–does not analyze	4·55	4·98			
Shows feelings–hides feelings	5·31	3·96			X
Directive–nondirective	4·64	4·80			
Involved–uninvolved	5·68	5·13	X		
Strong–weak	5·17	4·87			
Self-disclosing–self-concealing	5·44	3·65			
Accepting–rejecting	4·75	4·58			X
*Facilitating–hindering	5·16	5·35			
*Personal–impersonal	5·13	4·30	X		
N=30					

[a] Ratings were made on a 7-point scale, range 1·0 to 7·0 with midpoint (neutral) at 4·0. However, the average of the median ratings has a range of 0·5 to 6·5 and a midpoint of 3·5.
[b] Values of 3·5 or greater are in the direction of the first adjective presented in the bipolar pair.
[c] Those adjective pairs preceded by an asterisk were reversed in order of presentation on the rating sheets used by the judges.

genuine to a 'more self-disclosing' trainer. The lack of between-groups differences of 0·5 or more seems consistent with the experimental intent for at least 14 of the 15 adjective pairs. The one possible exception is on the dimension 'expresses warmth–expresses coolness'. It seems probably that a 'more self-disclosing' trainer should be able to avail himself of more opportunities to express warmth than a 'less self-disclosing' trainer.

Part II: Hypothesis 1: *Mutually and one-way perceived therapeutic relationships*

The Relationship Inventory was used to measure how each group participant viewed every other group member on exhibiting therapeutic behavior in their relationship. Hypothesis 1 predicted that the members of the *mSD* group would form a greater number of MPTRs than the members of the *lSD* group. Comparison of the two 'total' rows in Table 7 shows that this was not the case. These two rows are quite similar. The limiting number of such relationships was 60 (six MPTRs for each of ten group members); about one-third of this limit was attained on each dimension in each group. The remaining entries in Table 7 do not show so much similarity as the

Table 7—*Number of mutually perceived therapeutic relationships formed among group members*

		Positive regard	Impathy	Con-gruence	Uncond. regard	Total
mSD	Dyad partners	2	0	1	1	2
	With trainers	7	7	7	6	7
	All others	12	11	10	12	13
	Total	21	18	18	19	22
lSD	Dyad partners	3	2	2	4	3
	With trainers	6	10	9	8	10
	All others	12	9	10	6	8
	Total	21	21	21	18	21

totals, although none of their differences is statistically significant. This lack of significance may be more a function of a small N than a reflection of a homogeneous population. The maximum possible number of MPTRs for members with trainers was 10. Table 7 shows that the members of the *lSD* group formed more MPTRs with their dyad partners and trainers while the participants in the *mSD* group formed more MPTRs with other group members who were not so central to the experimental design.

Hypothesis 1a predicted that the members of the *mSD* group would perceive their dyad partner as being more 'therapeutic' in their 2-person relationships than would the participants in the *lSD* group. The data in Table 8 do not support this hypothesis. Again, because of the small N, statistical inference is not possible. The limiting number here is also 10.

Hypothesis 1b predicted that the members of the *mSD* group would perceive their T-group trainers as being more 'therapeutic' in their 2-person relationships than would the participants in the *lSD* group. The data in Table 8 not only fail to support this hypothesis but indicate that the converse

Table 8—*Number of one-way perceived therapeutic relationships formed among dyad partners and by members with trainers*

		mSD	lSD	χ^2
Positive regard	Dyad partner	6	7	
	With trainers	12	9	0·40
Empathy	Dyad partner	5	6	
	With trainers	12	20	7·65**
Congruence	Dyad partner	5	6	
	With trainers	13	17	1·20
Uncond. regard	Dyad partner	6	8	
	With trainers	13	14	0·11
Total	Dyad partner	5	7	
	With trainers	12	19	5·16*

* $p < 0.02$ (two-tailed).
** $p < 0.005$ (two-tailed).

better describes what took place. An χ^2 test was applied to the dichotomized distribution of the frequency with which the trainers were perceived as 'therapeutic' and the frequency with which they were not so perceived. The limiting number for each group was 20 (ten members, each rating two trainers). Two of these χ^2s were significant: the one for empathy and the one for overall total. Thus it seems that the Ss in the lSD group viewed their 2-person relationships with the trainers as therapeutic, taken as a total, and empathic, as a specific component, significantly more often than did the Ss in the mSD group.

The source of the between-groups differences in 'therapeutic' relationships formed by the members with their trainers is given clarification by Table 9. The breaking down of data into relationships formed with each individual trainer makes it apparent that the 'with trainer' differences noted

Table 9—*Breakdown of relationships members formed with group trainers*

		Positive regard	Empathy	Con-gruence	Uncond. regard	Total
mSD One-way perceived	Trainer 1	8	9	10	8	9
as therapeutic	Trainer 2	4	3	3	5	3
Mutually perceived	Trainer 1	5	5	5	4	5
as therapeutic	Trainer 2	2	2	2	2	2
lSD One-way perceived	Trainer 1	7	10	10	8	10
as therapeutic	Trainer 2	2	10	7	6	9
Mutually perceived	Trainer 1	4	5	5	4	5
as therapeutic	Trainer 2	2	5	4	3	5

in Table 9 are due primarily to the relationships members formed with trainer 2. Inspection shows that trainer 2 was more often perceived as 'therapeutic' in the *lSD* condition than in the *mSD* condition, while trainer 1 was perceived rather uniformly in the two groups. Dichotomized χ^2s, with Yates' correction for small numbers (Walker and Lev, 1953) applied only to the 'one-way' data of trainer 2, are significant both for 'empathy' and 'total': $\chi^2 = 7.91$, d.f. $= 1$, $p < 0.01$, and $\chi^2 = 5.21$, d.f. $= 1$, $p < 0.05$, respectively. This finding parallels the significant χ^2s presented in Table 8.

Part III: Hypothesis 2: Member self-awareness

Member self-awareness was measured by the Problem Expression Scale (PES). The correlations among the three judges for their ratings of 720

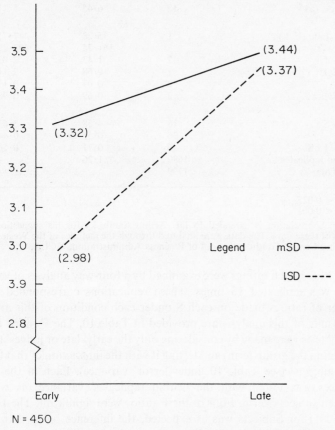

N = 450

Fig. 1. Mean PES Ratings, Early and Late, for Experimental Groups.

speech segments were within the range typically obtained for such ratings: for judges 1 and 2, r = 0·66; for judges 1 and 3, r = 0·62; and for judges 2 and 3 r = 0·59.

Figure 1 is a graph of the overall mean PES ratings for the two experimental groups. While initially the mean for the mSD group was significantly greater than the mean for the lSD group (U = 8968·5, z = 3·258, 2-tailed $p < 0·0014$), the means for these two groups converged with time.

Table 10—*Four-way analysis of variance for PES ratings (Ss only): experimental group × early–late × judges × subjects*

Source	d.f.	MS	F
Between			
Groups (G)	1	16·25	2·52
Subjects (S)	18	6·45	5·11**
Within			
Early–Late (E–L)	1	35·28	7·71*
Judges (J)	2	161·75	292·29**
E–L×J	2	1·43	2·03
G×E–L	1	9·68	2·11
G×J	2	0·07	0·13
G×E–L×J	2	0·69	0·98
Error			
E–L×S	18	4·58	3·63**
J×S	36	0·55	0·44
E–L×J×S	36	0·71	0·56
Within replicates	1680	1·26	
Total	1799		

* $p < 0·025$.
** $p < 0·001$.

Note: Appreciation is extended to Dr. Arthur Sandusky for his suggestion as to analysis of these data. The data were analyzed through the facilities of the Western Data Processing Center, Graduate School of Business Administration, UCLA.

The PES speech ratings were examined by a four-way analysis of variance which was replicated 15 times. These replications corresponded to the number of ratings made on each S under each condition of this analysis. The results of this analysis are provided in Table 10. The F ratios for the 'within' tests were made by considering only the early–late or judges' term(s) (neglecting the group term) and testing it with the interaction of that term(s) with 'subjects' (see Table 10 under 'error' variance). Each of the 'error' variances was tested with the 'within replicates' variance, as was the 'between subjects' term. Four of the F ratios were significant. The F (5·11, $p < 0·001$) for Subjects was as expected, the inference being that the Ss were significantly different in the ratings assigned to their verbal output.

The F for Early–Late was 7·71, $p < 0.025$, the inference being that PES changes take place within Ss as a result of the T-group experience, regardless of experimental condition. The F for Early–Late × subjects was 3·63, $p < 0.001$, the inference being that individual Ss change differently over time. The F for Judges was quite large, 292·29. This ratio is significant at a very high level of confidence, the 'inference' being that the three judges rated differently. However, while these judges rated differently they did so consistently as is borne out in their significantly high correlations with one another. The nonsignificant Fs for the two-way and three-way interactions with judges is also consistent with this interpretation.

The F for Between Groups was not significant. This result, however, is somewhat secondary in that the U testing of the early between-groups difference, noted previously and illustrated in Figure 1, was significant. Similarly the nonsignificant F for Group × Early–Late is of no central importance inasmuch as an early between-groups difference has already been identified.

The 'between-subjects' changes in PES ratings are displayed in Table 11. The larger early–late difference experienced by the *lSD* group is reflected in the data showing positive PES changes for all but one of this group's participants, S-10, whose performance remained just about constant. In the *mSD* group, which did not show a very large early–late group effect, Ss varied more widely in their PES changes than the Ss in the *lSD* group. Over both groups, only four Ss (two male and two female) had significantly positive PES changes. In each of these cases the S's early performance was at or below his group's 'early' mean. Only one S had a significant decrease in PES ratings. This was S-10 in the *mSD* group, who began her participation at the highest PES level obtained by a participant of either group, early or late, but over time lowered her PES 'style' until it more closely approached the *mSD* group mean.

Discussion

Part I of the results presents data which are wholly consistent with the experimental intent to vary trainer self-disclosure. The trainers were judged as more self-disclosing in the *mSD* group than in the *lSD* group by each of three perspectives from which their behavior was measured. In the *mSD* condition the participants claimed to know more personal information about the trainers than the participants in the *lSD* group claimed to know; two judges more often assigned randomly selected coded trainer statements from the *mSD* group to content categories labeled 'self-referents' than they assigned such statements taken from *lSD* group; and a pair of experienced clinicians, in rating their impressions of trainer behavior as

Table 11—*Early–late between-subjects changes in PES ratings*

	Subject	Early	Late	Change	U
mSD	1	3·51	2·93	−0·58	76
	2	2·52	3·33	0·81	56*
	3	2·74	3·54	0·80	83·5
	4	3·28	3·56	0·28	94
	5	3·37	3·13	−0·24	91·5
	6	3·41	3·98	0·57	72
	7	3·52	3·54	0·02	108
	8	3·16	3·02	−0·14	101
	9	3·31	3·74	0·43	90
	10	4·34	3·64	−0·70	54·5*
	T-1	2·90	2·94	0·04	106·5
	T-2	2·95	2·91	−0·04	110·5
lSD	1	2·97	3·18	0·22	96
	2	2·97	4·00	1·03	54·5*
	3	2·90	3·29	0·39	83
	4	2·81	3·39	0·58	75
	5	3·21	3·38	0·17	109
	6	2·94	3·72	0·78	53·5*
	7	2·80	3·71	0·91	56·5*
	8	2·77	3·06	0·30	87
	9	2·85	3·12	0·27	95·5
	10	3·53	3·47	−0·06	110
	T-1	2·61	2·67	0·06	111·5
	T-2	2·12	2·34	0·22	105

N = 15 Statements × 3 Judges = 45

* $p < 0.05$ (2-tailed).

Note: T-1 and T-2 are trainers 1 and 2. These ratings were influenced by the experimental instruction guiding their performance. The lack of any change is interpreted as evidence of their performance consistency.

contained in five-minute transcriptions of group process, differentially and similarly perceived the trainers' participation to be consistent with the 'more' and 'less' self-disclosing job descriptions the trainers had been instructed to follow. Thus, not only was the experimental manipulation successful, but the data further suggest that trainers have stylistic options in the way they choose to conduct their T-groups.

The Part II relationship data (RIs) show each group forming about one-third of the statistically possible MPTRs on each of the four dimensions of positive regard, empathy, congruence, and unconditional regard, plus the sum of these four. Following from the reasoning of Clark (1963), this indicates that an equivalent amount of therapeutic potential was developed in both experimental conditions. However, between-groups differences did appear when the relationship data were examined with respect to 'critical' others.* The members of the *lSD* group more often perceived their 2-person relationships with the trainers and their dyad partners as therapeutic, and the *mSD* participants more frequently viewed their relationships with non-critical others as therapeutic.

Interpretation as to the desirability of this difference is not clear. On one hand, the members of the *mSD* group, in being centrally involved with non-critical others, seem to have learned to form MPTRs independently of the major structure of this laboratory design. This suggests that they have learned to create therapeutic relationships on their own, with implications of extra-group transferability. On the other hand, the *lSD* participants, in being centrally involved with critical members, may be participating in qualitatively richer relationships than the ones possible with noncritical group members. A possible lead in understanding these RI data comes from comparing the between-trainers differences in PTRs and their styles of self-disclosing as tabulated in content categorization. While both trainers were viewed with a high frequency as therapeutic by the members of the *lSD* group, definite differences were noted in the *mSD* condition. Here trainer 2 was viewed as therapeutic both less often than was trainer 1 and less often than how he was viewed by the *lSD* group. Table 3 presents data which are parallel to this effect and lead to the speculation that trainer 2's very high early percentage of self-references in the *mSD* group may have been a factor in his lack of 2-person therapeutic relationships there. That his percentage of self-references declined considerably with time suggests that trainer 2 was, at some level of awareness, responding to group pressures aimed at getting him to disclose less.†

Alternative explanations exist; one plausible explanation has to do with the types of disclosures made by trainer 2. Table 4 shows trainer 2 making many more 'interaction' self-references and fewer 'self-only' references in the *mSD* condition than trainer 1. Thus it is not possible to determine whether it was trainer 2's high frequency of self-disclosure or high frequency of interactional disclosures, in the *mSD* group, which kept him from taking part in more of these relationships.

Likewise, one may speculate as to the cause of dyad partners' being perceived as therapeutic less often in the *mSD* group than in the *lSD* group.

---

* It is reasoned that the two trainers and the dyad partner comprised three 'critical' relationships for each group participant. The relationships with the trainers are considered critical because of the trainers' professional training and leadership positions in the group, and the relationships with the dyad partners are considered critical because of the captive way in which these pairings were structured.

† This corresponds with the impressions reported by both trainers. They claimed to experience *mSD* participants as attempting to get them to disclose less and *lSD* participants as attempting to get them to disclose more.

If the members of the mSD group either disclosed more or disclosed with a greater number of interaction references than members of the lSD group, then the lesser number of therapeutic relationships formed within the mSD dyad pairings would be consistent with the above line of explanation. Unfortunately limited amounts of data were collected measuring self-disclosure by group members. The Self-Disclosure Questionnaire was used but did not yield between-groups differences in disclosure to dyad partners. Without data which specifically tap the amount and the type of member self-disclosure that took place, no conclusions can be formed about the specific way in which trainer self-disclosure influences the participation styles of group members or the group's overall effectiveness. However, it is quite possible that self-disclosure enhances a trainer's overall effectiveness at the cost of his taking part in 2-person therapeutic relationships. In fact, as will be discussed below, this is exactly what appears to have taken place in the mSD group taking part in this experiment.

The Part III self-awareness data (PES ratings) showed the mSD group as having a significantly higher *early* PES mean than the lSD group, a difference which dissipated with time. Supplementary analysis* indicates that the elevated early mean is probably not the result of differences in group composition; more likely it reflects a greater amount of emotionality and spontaneity among members of the mSD group. This suggests that the early difference is a reflection of an accelerated PES mean for early meetings of the mSD group rather than a depression of this mean in the lSD group. While no conclusive causal determinant can be deduced from this analysis, the data are consistent with a 'modeling' theory. That is, based on their greater variability and higher peaks in PES performance, the Ss of the mSD group appear to have modeled their participation after their self-disclosing trainers. This explanation is given further support from clinical impressions reported by the two trainers and the group observer.†

A desirability interpretation for the self-awareness data hinges on whether there is any advantage to having high early PES ratings in addition to high late PES ratings. Evaluation of this issue (and the issue of 'critical' or 'noncritical' relationships) would be most meaningfully accomplished were

* Estimates of the mean PES ratings for the two groups were compared on a meeting-by-meeting basis. They indicated that the effect of the more self-disclosing trainers was almost immediate. In meeting 1, the mean rating for the mSD group begins higher than the mean rating for the lSD group, but comparable with the overall mean for early meetings of the lSD group. Almost immediately the mean ratings for the mSD group increase and show a far greater variability than is present in the sample of mean ratings from the lSD group. This differential variability persisted throughout late meetings. Further analysis-comparing log transformations of the PES variances for individual members—failed to turn up member between-groups differences.

† These impressions are reported in greater detail in Culbert (1966).

we to use longitudinal criteria. But no longitudinal data were generated, and one can only speculate as to whether the PES data produced by the *mSD* or by the *lSD* condition best favor an extension of member learning and growth to extra-group situations and relationships.

The type of self-awareness measured by PES ratings specifically entails an individual's first accepting the idea that he is centrally involved in his problems and then progressing through stages where he views his reactions to his problems and his contribution in effecting them. At higher levels he comes to understand the specific inputs of his own personality dynamics and finally comes to see his best personal alternative for dealing with a given problem. Thus one might speculate that speech statements earning higher PES ratings indicate that the speaker is gaining more preparation and practice for understanding involvements which extend beyond the T-group laboratory. The position advanced here interprets the total amount of self-awareness that takes place in a T-group to be an index of member gains and group productivity. One way to estimate this quantity is to measure the area under the trapezoid constructed by dropping two perpendicular lines from the gradient which connects the early and late mean PES ratings and anchoring them to the abscissa of the graph. According to this criterion, Figure 1 (which graphs the early-late PES means obtained in the present study) clearly predicts that the group receiving the more self-disclosing trainer participation will have the greater extra-laboratory gains.

Given the results of this study, a revision is suggested for the originally stated hypotheses which took a monolithic position with respect to trainer self-disclosure. The finding that the mean PES ratings produced by the *lSD* group eventually caught up with the mean ratings produced by the *mSD* group is believed to be due to a ceiling effect which places an upper limit on PES ratings. Such an effect has been noted by two other researchers who have used the PES scale to measure self-awareness.* However, even if a ceiling effect has operated to limit the upward rise of the early–late gradient for the *mSD* group, it still is not clear whether this ceiling represents an artifact of the PES rating scale or indicates that there is an upper level of self-awareness—about which individuals vary—that makes for the most profitable examination of problems, or both. If, as this researcher believes, there is some mean PES rating which characterizes the optimum level of self-awareness for T-group participation, the present data indicate that it can be achieved with or without high amounts of trainer self-disclosure. Since, as argued, the early attainment of this level is to the group's advantage, it seems that self-disclosing trainer participation is called for at least during early meetings. Such trainer participation might optimally stress

* Tommy M. Tomlinson and James V. Clark.

'interactional' types of disclosures. The data from the *ISD* condition suggest that upon attainment of this self-awareness level the trainer could just as productively 'pull-in' and be less self-disclosing. Gradual curtailment of trainer disclosures would give members the option of developing therapeutic relationships with 'critical' as well as 'noncritical' members. Hence, this revised prescription favors high early and selective late trainer self-disclosure. The trainer then would initially be providing an active model for self-disclosing participation. His gradual pulling back would free members to concentrate on their involvements with one another as well as with the trainers, as they see fit. Ideally this would provide them the independent experiences which would best transfer beyond the boundaries of the T-group laboratory.

In summary, three main effects of more self-disclosing trainer participation have been pointed to by the data generated in this study. First, this type of trainer participation resulted in group members' forming therapeutic relationships outside the three 'critical' ones promoted by the laboratory structure and favored by the *ISD* members. Second, either too much self-disclosure or too much of one or both types of 'interactional' self-disclosure by trainer 2 (especially during early meetings) may have keyed off resistances prompting some group members to avoid 2-person therapeutic involvement with that trainer. And third, more self-disclosing trainer participation apparently accelerates ratings of self-awareness and stimulates the members to approach more quickly their upper potential on the PES scale.

References

Barrett-Lennard, G. T. (1962) 'Dimensions of therapist response as causal factors in therapeutic change.' *Psychol. Monogr.*, **76**, No. 43 (whole no. 562).

Bobele, H. K. (1965) 'A rater's guide to the problem expression scale.' Unpub. mimeo. manuscript, Grad. School of Bus. Administ., UCLA.

Bugental, J. F. T. (1948) 'An investigation of the relationship of the conceptual matrix to the self-concept.' Unpub. doctoral dissertation, Ohio State University.

Clark, J. V. (1963) 'Authentic interaction and personal growth in sensitivity training groups.' *J. humanist. Psychol.*, Spring, 1–13.

Clark, J. V. and S. A. Culbert (1965) 'Mutually therapeutic perception and self-awareness in a T-group.' *J. appl. Behav. Sci.*, **1** (2), 180–194.

Culbert, S. A. (1966) 'Trainer self-disclosure and member growth in a T-group.' Unpub. doctoral dissertation, UCLA.

Jourard, S. M. and P. Lasakow (1958) 'Some factors in self-disclosure.' *J. abnorm. soc., Psychol.*, **56**, 91–98.

Osgood, C. E., G. J. Suci and P. H. Tannenbaum (1957) *The Measurement of Meaning*. Urbana: University of Illinois Press.

Reisel, J. (1959) 'A search for behavior patterns in sensitivity training groups.' Unpub. doctoral dissertation, UCLA.

Rogers, C. R. (1959) 'A theory of therapy, personality and interpersonal relationships, as developed in the client-centered framework.' In S. Koch (Ed.), *Psychology: A Study of a Science*, Vol. III. New York: McGraw-Hill.

Rogers, C. R. (1961) *On Becoming a Person*. Boston: Houghton Mifflin.

Siegel, S. (1956) *Nonparametric Statistics*. New York: McGraw-Hill.

Truax, C. B. (1961) 'The process of group psychotherapy.' *Psychol. Monogr.*, **75**, No. 14 (Whole No. 511).

van der Veen, F. and T. M. Tomlinson (1962) 'Problem expression scale.' Unpub. manuscript, Wisconsin Psychiat. Inst., Univer. of Wisconsin.

Walder, Helen M. and J. Lev (1953) *Statistical Inference*. New York: Holt.

Weschler, I. R. and J. Reisel (1959) *Inside a Sensitivity Training Group*. Instit. of Industrial Relations Monogr., UCLA.

CHAPTER 5

T-group Composition

Are T-groups more effective when composed of people who are similar or dissimilar to one another? This is the question that researchers in the area of group composition are trying to answer. Bennis and Shepard (1956), Schutz (1958), Harrison and Lubin (1965) and Harrison (1965) claim that heterogeneous groups present multiple learning opportunities for participants since they can model their behaviour on a range of styles present in their immediate group. In addition, it has been suggested that these groups are likely to induce change that is more generalizable since it is argued that heterogeneous groups more accurately reflect the variability and diversity of society at large. Stock (1964) in her review of research argues, on the other hand, that similarity of member orientation can facilitate communication and empathy and thus lead to a better climate for learning.

Harrison (1965), Harrison and Lubin (1965) and Pollack (1967) have provided us with the most systematic research in this area in recent years. Since their work relies partly upon the seminal findings of Lieberman (1958) and Schutz (1961) we shall briefly review their work before examining in some detail the work of Harrison and Pollack.

Lieberman (1958) utilized the RGST (Reaction to Group Situation Test) to compose two T-groups and to assess the magnitude of participant change. One group contained individuals who showed a marked preference for each of the five modalities of fight, pairing, dependency, counter-dependency and flight. The second group was similar to the first in all respects except that it excluded individuals high on the pairing dimension. Focusing on the participants high on counter-dependency, he found that they changed *least* in the group which excluded pairers. Further, he found that in this group authority issues remained the group preoccupation throughout its life. A climate obtained of continuous counter-dependent struggle. In the other group, the 'pairers' appeared to provide an acceptable

149

model such that the counter-dependents could experiment with a more co-operative style. This study sought to demonstrate that a group composed heterogeneously would constitute a learning environment in which a wider range of behaviours could be made available for members to explore.

Schutz (1961) composed groups homogeneously with respect to the members' 'expressed behaviour' and the 'behaviour they wanted from others' in the interpersonal areas of inclusion, control and affection (as measured by the FIRO-B—an attitude questionnaire devised by Schutz (1958)). He predicted that such compositions would lead to a high degree of recognition of within-group behavioural styles. On balance, he found that homogeneous groups could identify characteristics of their own group significantly better than chance. An interesting finding, though impression-istic, was that there were marked behavioural differences between groups. Each seemed to settle on a particular topic and each went into the topic to a greater depth than is usual in groups of this type. He concludes 'the pos-sibility thus emerges of composing groups with certain characteristics for a given purpose. For example, a training group to be introduced to a variety of group phenomena might better be made heterogeneous on the FIRO-B scales while the therapy or other type of grouping in which it is desirable to explore a single area in some detail could be composed homogeneously'.

Harrison and Lubin (1965) composed two different kinds of homogeneous groups based upon the individual's preferences for utilizing particular types of concepts in describing himself and others (Person Description Instrument—Harrison (1964)). The usefulness of the instrument was con-sequent upon their findings that individuals could be differentiated along two basic dimensions: an interpersonal or an impersonal/task orientation. The groups were homogeneously composed, one group consisting entirely of individuals high on interpersonal orientation and the other consisting of individuals high on the impersonal/task dimension. Rating was done by staff members who scored the expression of feelings, the perceived degree of intimacy obtaining in the groups, and the extent of learning achieved. Harrison and Lubin's basic hypotheses were: that the person-oriented group members would learn more than the impersonal-oriented members; that they would develop better personal relations; be more cohesive and be better able to understand and to cope with interpersonal issues. Two of the hypotheses were confirmed, the person-oriented group was more expressive and was more intimate, but there was no confirmation of the third hypo-theses. Indeed the results almost reached significance in the opposite direction—the impersonal group was rated as *learning* more. Harrison and Lubin reason that the 'personal' group did not have sufficient confrontation with alternatives. The 'personal' group members if anything, they suggest, were too comfortable in the T-group. The authors further argue that the impersonal-oriented members probably felt severe cultural shock in the T-group setting and were thus forced to reconsider their basic approach. The T-group experience itself was the necessary and sufficient confrontation for them and consequently lead to their learning more than their relatively unconfronted colleagues in the personal-oriented group. An important variable expressly considered by the authors, could have been the behaviour of the trainers in the respective groups. The impersonal-oriented group would possibly represent a greater challenge to trainer skill and, thus, would elicit greater if different efforts to facilitate learning. The personal-oriented group, on the other hand, would be likely to be more trainer-seductive: warm, intimate and expressive.

In another study Harrison (1965) re-analysed some data originally collected by Stock and Luft at Bethel. Midway through the experience individuals were removed from their regular T-groups to new groups which met for five sessions. Individuals were identified by staff members as being high, moderate or low in their preference for structure. The groups were then composed as follows: A homogeneous group consisting of individuals all high in preference for structure; a homogeneous group with everyone low in preference for structure; a homogeneous group with everyone moderate in preference for structure; and a heterogeneous group composed of half of the members being high in preference for structure and half being low in preference for structure.

Harrison found that members of the heterogeneous groups increased significantly more in terms of understanding themselves and others than did members of the homogeneous groups, when participant ratings were used as a measure. There was a tendency, though not statistically significant, for the members of the heterogeneous groups to be rated as being more effective in helping the group along than being able to express themselves more openly. The heterogeneous group did have more instances of conflict, but this apparently produced a confrontation with alternatives *sufficient* to enable participants in this group to learn more. The homogeneous groups, on the other hand, tended to create atmospheres which tended to confirm rather than confront the individuals' basic orientations.

Harrison (1965) reports a further study conducted by N.T.L. in 1964. Personal styles of members were identified by observation in an early phase of the laboratory, and 'controlled climate' learning groups were composed for the benefit of two types of problem members—the passive, low affect members were grouped with active, negative affect members in an attempt to provoke the former into an expression of anger and irritation. And passive, high affect members were placed with active, positive affect members to provide a protected atmosphere in which they could explore the possibility that expressed emotionality need not be destructive.

Each learning group was divided into homogeneous sub-groups which met by themselves during some parts of the programme to explore common problems. The passive, high affect members were able to be more active and apparently to make more progress than they usually do in more heterogeneous groups. The mixture of passive, low affect members with those high in preference of fight and counter-dependency met with only moderate success from a learning point of view, though the induction of group climate generally occurred as designed. These members were some-times passively led by the most counter-dependent ones, with the result that the hoped for increases in the activity level of the former did not take place. Where a group climate was not *too* high in fight and counter-dependency, on the other hand, the more passive members often did use the chance to explore alternatives. Harrison concludes that the staff agreed that it was feasible to plan the emotional climate of learning groups through group composition based on simple observational procedures and that the opportunities for learning may thereby be improved for relatively passive members.

The only large scale study that has directly focused upon the homo-geneity–heterogeneity issue in T-groups is that done by Pollack (1967). Using a subject population of 150 students, 77 males and 73 females, Pollack composed 16 groups such that four were homogeneous and 12 heterogeneous on Schutz's FIRO-B (1958).

The composition was based upon the expressed and wanted control behaviours of the FIRO-B. The control dimension was chosen as the critical compositional variable because it is a variable mentioned often in the literature as being critical to the development of groups, notably in Tuckman's review of group development (1965). Not only was the control dimension selected as the compositional variable it was also chosen as the primary index of change, though the Adjective Check List was also utilized as a correlate.

Pollack composed four different types of homogeneous groups:

(1) High expressed–high wanted;
(2) High expressed–low wanted;
(3) Low expressed–high wanted;
(4) Low expressed–low wanted.

The twelve heterogeneous groups were composed of individuals who manifested high, moderate and low scores on expressed and wanted control. As Pollack notes it would have been preferable to have more homogeneous groups, but this was not possible because the subjects, psychology students for the most part, did not score frequently at the extremes of the relevant dimensions.

It was predicted that members of heterogeneous groups would show more positive changes than members of homogeneous groups on the FIRO-B insofar as the difference between expressed and wanted behaviour of the three interpersonal needs of inclusion, control and affection would be reduced. When all three need areas were taken together this prediction was upheld, though when considered individually, none of the differences in each of the need areas attained significance in inter-group comparisons.

A further hypothesis was tested which predicted that members of heterogeneous groups would manifest more changes on the scales most concerned with interpersonal functioning as measured by the Adjective Check List: affiliation, nurturance, self-confidence, succourance and defence. The results show that none of the comparisons undertaken reached significance. No differences were found in the changes shown by either the homogeneous versus the heterogeneous groups, or in the entire sample as a whole.

A final prediction was that while members of homogeneous groups might feel at the beginning of their groups that their groups were more cohesive, attractive and effective than members of heterogeneous groups, this difference would dissipate and not be statistically significant at the conclusion of the T-group experience. A related prediction was that members of heterogeneous groups would show significantly greater increases in their ratings than members of homogeneous groups. As the T-group neared its conclusion, members of heterogeneous groups would manifest significant increases on items of the T-group rating scale, devised by Blake, Mouton and Frutcher (1962). These predictions were upheld.

The basis for Pollack's study is an attempt to relate the composition of groups to Harrison and Lubin's (1965) confrontation–support model of change. While the findings are consistent with the theory, they cannot be seen as offering support for the theory, since the number and kinds of confrontations occurring in the groups were not directly studied. Nonetheless Pollack claims that there were some subjective indications that heterogeneity did lead to more confrontation.

In view of the somewhat mixed findings it could be argued that as composition increases through a range from minimum to maximum heterogeneity there will be a corresponding increase in participants learning. Up to a certain point, however, further increases in heterogeneity will be associated with decreasing success. At some unspecified point a psychological law of diminishing returns begins to operate. If this line of argument is followed, and it has theoretical and empirical support in the related field of psychotherapy (Carson and Heine, 1962), group composition becomes not an either/or issue, rather it is the degree of heterogeneity which becomes critical.

Personality variables, composition factors and outcomes

Several other researchers have focused on issues relevant to composition, but not necessarily pertinent to the homogeneity/heterogeneity dichotomy. Swanson (1951), for example, investigated the relation between personality and group interaction using projective tests and interaction records. Watson (1950, 1953) has been similarly involved in attempting to use psychoanalytic theory to predict group behaviour, but as yet has produced little in the way of detailed support for her ideas.

Bennis and Peabody (1962) provide support for their ideas concerned with the impact of personality variables upon sub-group formation. They hypothesized that dependents would join up with dependents, counter-dependents with counter-dependents and personals—people who have a high need to be intimate—with other personals. In a relatively simple design, trainers were asked to rate their T-group members in the three dimensions indicated and each member was asked to indicate those three members with whom he got along least well. The authors conclusion, that there is a tendency for members to choose like-minded people and to reject unlikes, is supported significantly in the cases of counter-dependents and personals, less so in the case of dependents.

Other writers, notably Miles (1960) and Steele (1968) have tried to relate personality variables, composition inputs, to change in performance outcomes. In a very thorough study involving many factors, Miles concludes that the three personality factors he utilizes, namely ego strength, flexibility and the need for affiliation, have no direct relation to change. How these variables interact with other variables—commitment, involvement, feedback, trainer behaviour—is critical.

Steele (1968) in a paper reprinted here, investigated the possibility that learning from immediate experience requires a scientific posture toward the world and that this posture may be much more difficult for some personality types than for others.

Conclusion

There would appear to be fairly strong evidence that composition can critically influence the course of development in the T-group. Less strongly supported is the notion that composition influences the outcomes though all the evidence is directional. It would seem that though we can safely predict the climate given a rather crude manipulation of composition (Lieberman, 1958; Schutz, 1961; Harrison and Lubin, 1965; Greening and Coffey, 1966), we are not yet in a position to determine who will change and in what direction.

References

Bennis, W. G. and H. A. Shepard (1956) 'A theory of group development.' *Human Relations*, **4**, 415–437.

Bennis, W. and D. R. Peabody (1962) 'The conceptualization of two personality orientations and sociometric choice.' *Journal of Social Psychology*, **57**, 203–215.

Blake, R. R., J. S. Mouton and B. Frutcher (1962) 'A factor analysis of training group behaviour.' *Journal of Social Psychology*, **58**, 121–130.

Carson, R. C. and R. W. Heine (1962) 'Similarity and success in therapeutic dyads.' *Journal of Consulting Psychology*, **26**, 38–43.

Greening, T. C. and H. S. Coffey (1961) 'Working with an "impersonal" T-group.' *Journal of Applied Behavioral Science*, **2**, 401–411.

Harrison, R. (1965) 'Group composition models for laboratory designs.' *Journal of Applied Behavioral Science*, 1.

Harrison, R. (1964) Unpublished.

Harrison, R. and B. Lubin (1965) 'Personality style, group composition, and learning.' *Journal of Applied Behavioral Science*, **1**, 286–301.

Lieberman, M. (1958) 'The influence of group composition on changes in affective approach.' In Stock and Thelen (Eds.), *Emotional Dynamics and Group Culture*. Washington, D.C.: NTL-N.E.A.

Mathis, A. G. (1958) ' "Trainability" as a function of individual valency pattern.' In D. Stock and H. A. Thelen (Eds.), *Emotional Dynamics and Group Culture*. Washington, D.C.: National Training Laboratories, N.E.A.

Miles, M. B. (1960) 'Human relations training: processes and outcomes.' *Journal of Counseling Psychology*, **7**, 301–306.

Miles, M. B. (1965) 'Learning processes and outcomes in human relations training.' In E. Schein and W. G. Bennis, *Personal and Organizational Change Through Group Methods*. London: John Wiley.

Pollack, H. (1967) Unpublished Ph.D. thesis. University of California.

Schutz, W. C. (1958) FIRO: *A Theory of Interpersonal Relations*. New York: Rinehart.

Schutz, W. C. (1961) 'On group composition.' *Journal of Abnormal and Social Psychology*, **62**, 275–281.

Steele, F. I. (1968) 'Personality and the "laboratory style".' *Journal of Applied Behavioral Science*, **4**, 25–45.

Stock, D. (1964) 'A survey of research on T-groups.' In L. P. Bradford and co-workers, *T-group Theory and Laboratory Method*. London: John Wiley.

Tuckman, B. (1965) 'Development sequence in small groups.' *Psychological Bulletin*, **63**.

Watson, J. (1950) Unpublished. University of Michigan.
Watson, J. (1953) 'The application of psychoanalytic measures of personality to the study of social behaviour.' Paper read at the American Psychological Association Meeting.

Personal Style, Group Composition, and Learning*

Roger Harrison

Department of Industrial Administration, Yale University

Bernard Lubin

Indiana State Department of Mental Health

Part I

This is an investigation of differences in interpersonal behaviour and learning in a sensitivity training laboratory between highly person-oriented and highly work-oriented participants (identified through the Person Description Instrument III). Second, it is a study of the effects of a training design that involves both heterogeneous and homogeneous training groups.

It was expected, and confirmed at satisfactory levels of significance, that the person-oriented members would be seen as behaving more expressively and warmly and that they would be more comfortable and would feel stronger interpersonal ties within their homogeneous group than would the work-oriented members. It was expected, but with results approaching significance in the opposite direction, that person-oriented members would be seen as learning more than would the work-oriented members.

It is hypothesized that the person-oriented group found the laboratory a kind of psychic home without much challenge, whereas the work-oriented members experienced 'culture shock', and that this in fact pushed them toward change.

Part II

To test the learning model, data were examined from a laboratory in which each participant was assigned to a heterogeneous training group and to an experimental group composed in terms of preference for high, low, or moderate structure. The statistical and impressionistic data collected through member ratings of one another and through interviews with staff

* This study was carried out under Grant M-6466(A) of the National Institute of Mental Health. It was published in *Journal of Applied Behavioral Science*, 1965, 1, 286–301. A more detailed technical report of this study is available from the author(s).

and participants strongly suggest that homogeneous groups do not provide the confrontation needed for optimum learning. The superiority of the mixed high- and low-structure (and more stressful) groups in terms of member learning suggests that feelings of completion, cohesion, and emotional satisfaction may not be the appropriate criteria for evaluating the impact of a training group experience.

Part I

This is a study of the relationship between personal styles in interpersonal perception, and behaviour in unstructured training groups. It also explores some effects of homogeneous and heterogeneous grouping on behaviour and learning of the participants.

The theory on which this study was based has been presented and explored in previous publications (Harrison, 1962, 1964*, 1965). The theory postulates a close relationship between cognitive structure and interpersonal behaviour. By assessing a person's preference for certain kinds of concepts to describe himself and others, we discover those aspects of the interpersonal world to which he is ready to respond. Those concepts which he neglects or avoids in describing self or others are held to represent areas of indifference or aversion, aspects of the interpersonal world with which the person is less inclined to deal actively.

People notice in a situation those phenomena with which they are used to dealing; working with those aspects of the situation, they can bring to bear their own particular skills. By passing over and not attending to those aspects of the situation for which they do not have adequate concepts or behaviour skills, they reduce the complexity of the world to something more manageable. They focus on those areas where they have most competence.

Previous studies (Harrison, 1962, 1964†) have produced the Person Description Instrument III, which may be scored for preference for person-oriented versus work-oriented concepts. The individual describes three persons: himself and two close associates, using 27 semantic differential scales. He then goes back and picks out nine of the 27 scales which he feels best describe the person. Scales dealing with such personal characteristics as warmth and sympathy, openness and genuineness, control relations, and comfort in interaction with others contribute to the person-oriented score. Scales dealing with competence and ability, responsibility and dependability, energy and initiative are scored as work-oriented.

---

* The structure and measurement of interpersonal perception. The work is the subject of a forthcoming report.

† Ibid.

Objectives

We desired to investigate the differences in interpersonal behaviour and learning in a sensitivity training laboratory between highly person-oriented and highly work-oriented participants. We reasoned that persons with a strong preference for person-oriented concepts would exhibit relatively high comfort and effectiveness in the training situation. Those with a high preference for task-oriented constructs would find it difficult to understand and to react appropriately to much of the emotional and feeling-based behaviour which it is the task of the training group to expose and understand. We expected that the person-oriented members would relate more effectively to others, that they would more easily express their own feelings, and would find it easier to develop close, intimate relationships with others. Because of these initial advantages in adapting to the learning situation, we expected that the person-oriented members would learn more in the training laboratory.

A second objective of this study was to evaluate a sensitivity training design involving both heterogeneous and homogeneous training groups. It was hoped that homogeneous groups would give their members a unique opportunity to explore the consequences of the styles of perception and interpersonal behaviour which they held in common. We felt that we could learn more about the consequences of extremely personal or work-oriented styles of person perception by observing the operations of groups of people who shared an extreme style.

The study

The 69 persons (49 men and 20 women) in the 1962 Western Training Laboratories at Lake Arrowhead, California, were assigned to six heterogeneous groups for the morning sessions and reassigned to homogeneous groups for equal periods in the afternoon. The members with whom we are concerned belonged to two homogeneous groups composed on the basis of the Person Description Instrument III. One contained the ten members scoring highest on person orientation; the other contained the ten scoring highest on task orientation. For the morning sessions, these members were distributed evenly throughout the six heterogeneous morning groups.

To assess interpersonal behaviour and learning, sociometric questions were administered toward the end of the laboratory. Staff members also made ratings on each participant.

The ratings of interest to our study were along three dimensions:

1. The extent to which the individual openly expressed his feelings.

2. The extent to which others saw the individual as a person with whom they could establish close, warm relationships.
3. The extent to which the individual was seen as having learned in the training laboratory.

For each person, ratings on these dimensions are available both from those who saw him in the heterogeneous morning group and those who saw him in the homogeneous afternoon group. The following hypotheses were tested:

1. Members of the person-oriented group would be more expressive of feelings than members of the task-oriented group.
2. Members of the person-oriented group would establish closer, warmer relations with others than would members of the task-oriented group.
3. Members of the person-oriented group would be seen as learning more than members of the task-oriented group.
4. Members of the person-oriented group would experience more comfortable and more intimate relationships in their homogeneous afternoon group than would members of the task-oriented group.

The most rigorous test of the first three hypotheses is one making use only of the data obtained from persons who saw the participants in the heterogeneous morning groups. These data from participants and staff members were tested by the Mann–Whitney Test.

Results

Hypotheses 1 and 2 were confirmed at satisfactory levels of significance for the ratings from participants. The differences in trainer ratings were in the same direction, but reached only the 0·10 level of significance. It was concluded that the person-oriented members were indeed more emotionally expressive and more warm toward others in the training laboratory than were the work-oriented members. (The ratings from the homogeneous afternoon groups were overwhelmingly in the same direction.)

The results for Hypothesis 3, that person-oriented members would be seen as learning more than work-oriented members, were opposite to the predicted direction. They approached but did not quite reach the 0·10 level of significance (2-tailed test). This almost significant reversal of our hypothesis signaled the likelihood that our theory was inadequate. This finding is further discussed below.

The results for Hypothesis 4 were confirmed at high levels of significance. When choosing persons in the laboratory whom they saw as particularly expressive and with whom they felt they could be particularly close, person-oriented members were much more likely to choose members of their own homogeneous group than were the task-oriented members. The person-oriented members made about 60 per cent of their choices from within their homogeneous group on both questions, while the work-oriented members chose only 15 per cent of their own members on the expressiveness question, and 30 per cent on the intimacy rating.

The quantitative findings thus clearly indicated that the person-oriented members were seen by others as behaving more expressively and warmly, and that they were more comfortable and felt stronger interpersonal ties toward the members of their homogeneous group than did the work-oriented members. These findings were further confirmed by the descriptions obtained from staff members working with the homogeneous afternoon groups. The person-oriented group was described by its staff as made up of members who valued and sought close personal relationships with others. They experienced the group as a place in which they could be much more themselves than they could in other settings, and for some the homogeneous afternoon group became the major laboratory learning experience. The group was described by the staff member as reaching a depth and degree of intimacy which he had rarely experienced, although he had seen groups in which there was more movement and change for individuals.*

In contrast, the work-oriented group members were described as 'hard-working, overcontrolled achievers'; they had a 'strong need for control' and showed considerable 'constriction of emotionality'. They tended to be threatened by the expression of feelings by others, and they found it hard to experience and express their own emotional reactions. However, although the group experienced great difficulty in dealing with interpersonal relationships and feelings, it did move gradually toward greater freedom and expressiveness (Greening and Coffey, 1964).

The observations of the staff thus strongly confirmed the indications of the rating data. Our results support the hypothesis of a close relationship between concept preference in interpersonal perception and the actual behaviour that a person exhibits in his relations with others. This finding is of significance for both theory and practice.

Implications

In theory, our findings support those cognitive models of personality (Kelly, 1955; Harvey, Hunt and Schroder, 1961; Witkin, Dyk, Paterson,

---

* The staff member in this group was Harrington Ingham.

Goodenough and Karp, 1962; Harrison, 1965) which take the view that a person's relationships with the world are structured by a framework of 'constructs' or dimensions along which he orders salient properties of people and things. According to these theories, a person's ability to respond to phenomena is determined and limited by the constructs he has available for ordering and making sense of the phenomena. If a person does not have constructs which are adequate to particular kinds of phenomena, he cannot respond to events of those kinds in an organized fashion. In our study, the person and work-oriented members did indeed tend to respond to others along the dimensions or 'channels' which were provided for them by the constructs which they used in describing others and themselves. In the case of the work-oriented group, members were uncomfortable, cautious, and relatively less competent in responding to others along dimensions which were not so salient for them in their perceptions of others. (Since this training laboratory did not expose members to task demands, we have no way of knowing whether the person-oriented members would have been equally cautious and inept when it came to getting work done.)

For the practitioner, our findings suggest the possibility of selecting members who will respond in different ways in training groups and other interpersonal situations, and thus create different kinds of emotional climates and learning situations for one another.

In this connection, we should examine more carefully the unexpected differences in learning between the two experimental groups. Homogeneous training groups have been experimented with and defended on the grounds that they provide an increased learning opportunity for their members by confronting them with a group composed of others who 'mirror' their own style. In our study, however, the person-oriented group was lower than (but resembled in their ratings of learning) a mixed group of members who did not attain high scores in either direction on the Person Description Instrument III. The work-oriented members, on the other hand, received higher scores on learning than either the person-oriented or mixed groups, and the difference was nearly significant in the direction opposite to our prediction. This suggests that if the homogeneous grouping had any effect on the learning of the person-oriented members, it was probably a negative one.

The descriptions by the training staff of the two groups would support the interpretation that the person-oriented group was considerably less challenged by their learning experience than were the task-oriented members. From their workaday worlds they entered a protected situation in which their personal styles and preferences were confirmed, first, by the methods and values of the laboratory and of the training staff, and even more strongly by the confirmation they received from other members of their homogeneous group. It is probably not an exaggeration to say that for them the laboratory was a kind of psychic home, a place where they could relax and be themselves. This is not to imply that these members did not work hard or that they did not learn. It is likely, however, that the learning was more an elaboration of previous personal styles than it was a questioning of basic orientations or a real 'shaking up' and confrontation, as training experiences frequently are.

The work-oriented participants, on the other hand, were seen by the staff as 'out of step' with the values and norms of the laboratory. Their characteristic styles of relationship and of interpersonal perception were disconfirmed and proved inadequate by their experiences.

The work-oriented participants thus appear to have been more strongly confronted, challenged, and pushed toward change by their training experience. They experienced not only the pressures to conformity which are exerted by other members in a culture which values emotional expressiveness and personal closeness, but also the discomfiture involved in finding themselves ill-equipped to cope with the phenomena around them. In other words, we may hypothesize that the work-oriented members underwent a kind of 'culture shock' in their laboratory experience. At the same time, their homogeneous group experience may have provided them with the knowledge that they were not alone in their confusion and ineptitude, and it may have provided a respite from confrontations which was needed to maintain their anxiety at an optimum level for learning. This is suggested by Greening and Coffey's (1964) description of their training styles as staff members in this work-oriented group. The members' discomfort with emotionality was strongly communicated to the staff, and the latter responded by being gentle, permissive, and supportive. This support in going slowly may be badly needed by members who, unlike the person-oriented group, are daily having their values and interpersonal competence thrown into question not only by events in the laboratory but also by the expressed goals, methods, and values of the training staff and by the removal of accustomed structural and emotional supports due to the design of the laboratory.

A model for learning

This is indeed reasoning after the fact; it is detailed here because it gives rise to the central learning model which is explored in this paper and the paper which will follow.

According to this model, two processes are central in laboratory learning (and perhaps in any learning): confrontation with opposites, and support for one's current personal style. By confrontation we mean that, whatever a person's current orientation, he is faced with evidence that its opposite is viable and effective and that the opposite is held by other persons with whom he must come to terms in some way. This condition was met for the work-oriented participants in our study, but it was not met for the person-oriented members, who found both the laboratory and their homogeneous group especially supportive of their customary styles and orientations.

By support for one's current orientation, we mean the assurance that others, whom one can respect, hold views and ways of operating similar to one's own. In this way, a continuous tension between poles is maintained. The person neither 'loses himself' nor can he fail to take account of opposing orientations.

This model will be further elaborated and tested in Part II.

Part II* (Roger Harrison)

Part II investigates the effects on change and learning of polar confrontation with contrasting persons. The data were collected during Stock and Luft's (1960) study of the T-E-T Design but were not analyzed or reported in that paper. In this study, participants were identified after the third training group meeting by staff ratings as preferring 'high structure', 'low structure', or 'moderate structure'.

Designs and data collection

The design of the three-week laboratory was to have a relatively long period of group activity (11 sessions), followed by recomposition into E-groups for six sessions, and a return to T-groups for four sessions. Data were collected from the T-groups after the third, tenth, and fourteenth T-group meetings. These special E (for 'Experimental') Groups were composed as follows:

1. Homogeneous in preference for high structure.
2. Homogeneous in preference for low structure.
3. Half high and half low structure.
4. Homogeneous in preference for moderate structure (three groups).

Repeated participant ratings of one another's behaviour were collected throughout this laboratory. The mean ratings for each participant were

* Appreciation is due to the staff members of Session I, 13th Annual Summer Laboratories in Human Relations Training, National Training Laboratories. This group designed the laboratory and collected the data which are analyzed and re-examined in this report: Howard Baumgartel, F. Kenneth Berrien, Hubert S. Coffey, Joseph Luft, Dorothy Stock and Thomas H. Van Loon.

distributed to staff members in the laboratory by Baumgartel (1961). These data, which provided the only record of which the author is aware of the differential progress of participants with differing orientations throughout a laboratory, were reanalyzed to see whether they were consistent with the hypothesis of learning through confrontation of opposites.

Hypotheses

We tested two specific hypotheses:

1. The high-structure group would be seen as learning more in the laboratory than the low-structure group.
2. The mixed high- and low-structure E-group would have a greater effect on the learning of its members than any of the homogeneous E-groups, whether high- or low-structure, or homogeneously moderate in composition.

The high- and low-structure groups in Part II are similar to the work-oriented and person-oriented groups respectively in Part I. Stock and Luft (1960) describe the dominant characteristics of high- and low-structure members as follows:

'High structure'...refers to a constellation of characteristics including preference for clarity and order; ...less interest in personal feelings; ...a readiness to accept self and others as is; ...and a tendency to defer to persons perceived as power or authority figures.
'Low structure'...refers to a constellation of characteristics including...a readiness to explore the emotional atmosphere of the group, to recognize positive and negative feelings, and to examine interpersonal relationships...

We see the low-structure members as entering a sympathetic culture, while the high-structure members are entering an alien and confronting culture. High-structure participants are more deviant when compared with the norms and standards of a training laboratory, and so they may be expected to experience more dissonance and disagreement with others about group and interpersonal issues. Because of this confrontation, we would expect them to change more toward laboratory norms than the low-structure participants, whose behaviour is initially closer to the norm (Hypothesis 1).

When members enter a homogeneous E-group, we should expect them to build a climate which institutionalizes norms with which they are mutually comfortable. We should expect them to have no need for confrontation in those areas on which the group is homogeneous. For the high-structure group, these norms would include the avoidance of the expression of emotionality and the avoidance of close examination of interpersonal processes in the group, along with a norm for 'getting things done'.

For the low-structure participants, shared orientations would include the valuing of close, friendly interpersonal relationships, along with a good deal of free discussion of feeling.

The mixed high- and low-structure group, on the other hand, should be characterized by a good deal of tension between opposing camps. We should expect a good deal of 'fight' in such a group, along with rapid changes in group climate, as first one faction and then the other obtains the upper hand. In this group, alone of all the E-groups, confrontation should be expected to be at a maximum. While each member would have support from a subgroup for his own orientation, he would also be under attack from those in the opposing group. Thus, each member's personal style would be both confirmed and challenged by the experience. While the lack of more moderate members might make a true resolution of differences difficult, we would expect the conditions in this group to be more favourable for personal learning and change than in any of the homogeneous groups.

The data were obtained from ratings of each member by each other T-group member on the following six-point scales:

1. How well does this person understand himself in his relation to this group?
2. How effective do you think this person is in helping the group along?
3. In your opinion, how able is this person to express himself freely and comfortably in the group?
4. To what extent do you think this person really understands your ideas and feelings?

The specific predictions corresponding to the two hypotheses in this re-analysis of the data were:

1. Even before the E-group experience (T3 to T10), high-structure members would be rated as changing more on all questions than low-structure members.
2. Members of the mixed high- and low-structure E-group would be rated as changing more after the E-group experience than members of homogeneous E-groups (T10 to T14).

Results

Although the data from all four questions are in the predicted direction, the results are statistically significant only on the first and fourth questions:

understanding self in relationship to the group, and understanding others. The changes on these two questions are shown in Figure 1.

Stock and Luft (1960) interviewed participants and staff members in the E-groups. Their results confirm that the groups did indeed create climates and norms which tended to confirm rather than confront the basic orientations and personal styles on which the members were selected. The high-structure members felt themselves to be highly compatible; they engaged in a lively but somewhat shallow discussion; and they tended to avoid examination of their interrelationships and feelings about one another. The low-structure group, on the other hand, were preoccupied with self-analysis; they spent so much time examining their interrelationships that the group tended to stagnate for lack of action; and they consistently avoided conflict and the expression of irritation and anger.

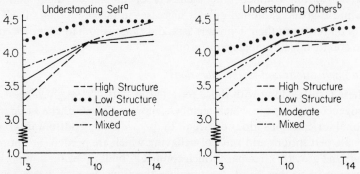

[a] Note: Difference, high vs. low structure, T_{10}–T_3, significant $p < 0.05$. Difference, mixed groups vs. other groups, T_{14}–T_{10}, significant $p < 0.02$.

[b] Note: Difference, high vs. low structure, T_{10}–T_3, significant $p < 0.01$. Difference, mixed group vs. other groups, T_{14}–T_{10}, significant $p < 0.03$.

Fig. 1. Mean Participant Ratings of E-group Members by Their Heterogeneous T-groups.

In striking contrast, the mixed high- and low-structure E-group was seen as having 'little tolerance for conflict; no one took a stand that persisted for more than a few comments at most, and the group seemed unable to deal with their feelings. The group was process-centered, but there was much fight, and they had a hard time getting down to anything' (Stock and Luft, 1960).

Thus the statistical findings and the impressionistic reports were both consistent with the predictions and with our learning model. Work- and structure-oriented participants find their personal styles greatly in conflict with the demands of the T-group and the laboratory, and hence they experience more pressure to adapt by changing their behaviour. Low-structure participants, on the other hand, find themselves more 'in tune' with the norms of laboratory training, and consequently they are less radically challenged by the experience.

When high- and low-structure participants were mixed, the group tended to polarize. Each member experienced the behaviour of the other sub-group as confrontation with an opposite orientation. At the same time, he received support for his values from his own homogeneous subgroup. Thus, members remained in tension between competing and irreconcilable ideas as to how the group should operate. It is important to note that neither staff nor participants felt that these issues were resolved. On the other hand, the evidence suggests that members did not give up, but continued to fight it out during the six sessions the E-group met. Far from suffering from their unresolved conflicts, the members of the mixed high- and low-structure E-group exhibited greater increases in understanding of self and others on return to their T-groups than did those who had experienced the more comfortable homogeneous groups.

Some implications and further questions

These results, along with those reported in Part I, strongly suggest that homogeneous groups in which members support one another's basic inter-personal orientations do not seem to provide the confrontation with alternate perceptions and ways of behaving which are needed for optimum change and growth. Groups in which conflict is 'built-in' by the composition appear, on the other hand, to stimulate their members to work toward more effective ways of dealing with people different from themselves. The optimum amount of confrontation is by no means clear. It may be that greater amounts can be tolerated for short periods of time than in a longer experience. A highly polarized E-group in this study might have produced discouragement on the part of the members if it had been the only learning group for them, instead of being a stimulating interlude. The optimum conflict is probably also a function of the psychological integration or ego strength of the participants.

Furthermore, while our data do not support the use of homogeneous groups to facilitate change, it still seems reasonable that under some circum-stances such groups are useful for providing support. This could be particu-larly true for members whose orientations are deviant from laboratory-supported values (e.g., the work-oriented group in the Harrison and Lubin study). Such persons, if not supported in their group, sometimes receive so much pressure from others that they are forced into withdrawal or other defensive maneuvers which inhibit learning.

The practically significant finding in this study is that of the superiority of the mixed high- and low-structure E-group for the learning of its members. This finding casts doubt upon the standards used by participants and often by staff to evaluate the success of T-group experiences. Ordinarily, we regard a T-group in which 'everything comes out all right in the end' as more 'successful' than one in which polarized subgroups of members continue to slug it out until the final gong, with no significant resolution of the initial differences. The results from this study are of course based upon a comparison of groups in only one training laboratory. If these findings may be trusted, however, they suggest that we should place an evaluation upon unresolved conflict which is diametrically opposite from our usual view. It may be that the groups which leave the most lasting impact are those which seem to drag on in conflict, never quite giving up, but never quite resolving basic disagreements among the members. It may be that the unresolved issues, the confrontations with differing outlooks and views, the feelings of outrage and dismay, puzzlement and challenge, last longer and are more of a force for learning than the warmth and comradeship and the feeling of completion and closure of a more 'successful' T-group experience. Such questions will, of course, have to be settled by further research and experience. It seems reasonable at least to suggest that the appropriate criteria for evaluating the learning impact of a T-group experience may *not* be the experience by staff and participants of feelings of completion, cohesion, and emotional satisfaction.

References

Baumgartel, H. (1961) 'Report on research: Human relations laboratory, session I, Bethel, Maine, summer 1960.' Unpublished manuscript. Washington, D.C.: National Training Laboratories.

Greening, T. C. and H. S. Coffey (1964) 'Working with an "impersonal" T-group.' Prepublication draft.

Harrison, R. (1962) 'The impact of the laboratory on perceptions of others by the experimental group.' Chapter II in C. Argyris, *Interpersonal Competence and Organisational Effectiveness*. Homewood, Ill.: Irwin-Dorsey.

Harrison, R. (1965) 'Cognitive models for interpersonal and group behaviour: A theoretical framework for research.' Explorations in Human Relations Training and Research (Whole No. 2). Washington, D.C.: National Training Laboratories.

Harvey, O. J., D. E. Hunt and H. M. Schroder (1961) *Conceptual Systems and Personality Organisation*. New York: John Wiley.

Kelly, G. A. (1955) *The Psychology of Personal Constructs*. New York: Norton.

Stock, Dorothy (Whitaker, D. S.) and J. Luft (1960) 'The t-e-t design.' Unpublished manuscript. Washington, D.C.: National Training Laboratories.

Witkin, H. A., R. B. Dyk, H. F. Paterson, D. R. Goodenough and S. A. Karp (1962) *Psychological Differentiation*. New York: John Wiley.

Personality and the 'Laboratory Style'

*Fred I. Steele**

Much laboratory training activity assumes that all individuals have adequate skills for learning from immediate experience. The following study is based on the alternate premise that this type of learning requires a scientific posture toward one's world, and that this posture may be much more difficult for some personality types than for others. The author investigated this premise using the Sensation–Intuition scale of the Myers–Briggs Type Indicator (1962), and assuming that the Intuitive (N) mode of perception would be more facilitative of operation in the 'Laboratory style' than the Sensation (S) mode. Using three laboratory populations, it was found that the S–N scale does predict tendencies toward laboratory interpersonal value orientations (as measured by the Managerial Behaviour Questionnaire) and ratings of effectiveness in a T-group. The scale was found less effective in predicting actual change. Several implications for laboratory selection and design are suggested.

Introduction

In recent years, there has been a steady growth in the use of the laboratory method for effecting organizational and individual change (Argyris, 1962; Bennis, 1962; Blake and Mouton, 1964; Bradford, Gibb and Benne, 1964; Buchanan, 1964; Schein and Bennis, 1965; Weschler and Schein, 1962). Accompanying this growth in use has been an increase in the amount of theoretical and research effort aimed at the development of a better understanding of the dynamics of laboratory training as a change process and as a social force. This report represents one facet of this continuing effort at better understanding.

For the purpose of this paper I shall define 'laboratory training' as any one of a number of change induction processes growing out of the explorations of the National Training Laboratories (Benne, 1964) that focus primarily on behavioural data internal to the change programme itself. The emphasis in these programmes is on using the actual experiences of the

* Fred I. Steele is assistant professor, Department of Industrial Administration, Yale University. The author acknowledges the financial support of the Richard D. Irwin Foundation for this research; the author thanks Edgar Schein, Warren Bennis, John Thomas, William McKelvey, Louis Barnes, Chris Argyris, Roger Harrison, and the NTL Institute for Applied Behavioural Science for all the other kinds of support so essential to the completion of this study. Published in the *Journal of Applied Behavioural Science*, 1968, **4** (1), 25–46.

participants themselves as the main inputs to learning. A major component in this process has usually been the T-group, or Training Group. Members of a T-group are encouraged to use their experiences with one another as examples of interaction and reaction, from which they can learn more about various phenomena including themselves, their impact on others, the impact of others on them, group functioning, leadership and its dynamics, and organization for a task.

Those who have worked as staff members at laboratory training sessions have at one time or another perceived some participants as learning from and/or functioning well at a given laboratory, while others have a relatively negative experience in terms of change or ability to understand what is happening. It was precisely this kind of perception on my own part which led me to the view that there is some real question as to what a laboratory training experience can be expected to accomplish for certain types of people.

The basic proposition that served as the foundation for the research reported here was very simple: It was the assumption that individuals who have certain relatively stable personality traits would tend to be more responsive than other types of individuals to the laboratory training process and also would tend to be more comfortable with the laboratory approach to organizational interpersonal relationships. Accordingly, the studies described in this paper attempted to determine whether scores on dimensions of 'laboratory interpersonal values' before and after a laboratory and also behaviour in a T-group could be predicted from prelaboratory scores on the Sensation–Intuition scale of the Myers–Briggs Type Indicator. This scale was chosen because it seemed particularly relevant to a major cognitive demand of the laboratory process, i.e., learning from the data of one's actual immediate experiences at the laboratory.

Background

From several previous research findings there was conclusive evidence that the basic assumption about the effects of personality on training outcomes was worth testing. In his study on the differential effects of personality on preference for participation in decision making on the job, Vroom (1960) found that, in the work groups he studied, participation was generally satisfying for those having a high need for independence and low authoritarianism scores; the reverse was true for those with scores low on need for independence and high on authoritarianism. Since one of the values assumed to be associated with the laboratory process is a sharing of control or influence, this finding would suggest that there may indeed be some limitations on the laboratory's effectiveness due to personality differences.*

In another type of study, Stern, Stein and Bloom (1956) found that personality types (stereopaths, preferring depersonalized and modified social relationships, rigid orderliness, and exhibiting pervasive acceptance of authority and denial of impulses) who were deviant in relation to the values of the college they were attending (which encouraged intellectual curiosity and exploration) did less well on tests, had lower grades, and a higher first-year dropout rate than nonstereopaths (Ch. 10). This finding highlights the possibility of mixed effects when different types' of people are placed in a culture which is oriented toward change in a specific direction.

Several studies have dealt with personality in relation to laboratory training; but I shall cite here only the two most relevant to the present discussion, since a more thorough review has already been provided by Stock (1964). Mathis (1955) found that laboratory participants characterized by intrapersonal conflict and tendencies toward free expression of fight and pairing were rated higher on changes in sensitivity, sophistication, and productivity than were those characterized by tendencies toward dependency, flight and immobilization.

The training study that is probably most important for our present purpose is one carried out by Miles (1960). He related three personality variables to change in performance on the job—which he took as one important measure of learning at the laboratory. 'Perhaps the most interesting finding was that none of our three personality variables (with the possible exception of flexibility) was directly related to gain at the end of the lab . . .. Rather, ego strength, flexibility, and need for affiliation played a clear role in the person's interaction with the lab, permitting him to unfreeze, become involved, and receive feedback. These process factors, in turn, were the major determinants of learning' (p. 306).

Several implications may be drawn from the studies discussed above. The Vroom and the Stern, Stein, and Bloom data would indicate that personality may indeed be an important factor limiting the effects of attempted changes toward more individual participation, be it in job decision making or in the learning process itself. Those who are most stereotyped, rigid, authoritarian, and so on appear to have a higher probability of becoming dissatisfied with and/or of dropping out of the programme.

From the studies of laboratory training itself, it appears that such

* Examined in another light, the present study may be considered as an attempt to go a step beyond Vroom's findings; that is, as an examination of the extent to which the limitations he found will still be in evidence for a more intensive change process aimed at specifically reducing the kinds of effects which he found.

characteristics as free expression, flexibility, and some sort of conflict or other motivation may be related to greater learning in the laboratory setting. Dorothy Stock (1964), in summarizing her review of the research on laboratory training, stated 'These findings converge on the idea that personality factors having to do with receptivity, involvement, lack of defensiveness, and a certain kind of energy or openness may be important facilitators of learning' (pp. 434–435).

Demands of laboratory process and its relationship to personality

Yet the results to date are not clear enough or complete enough to allow us to state with confidence either which personality variables, if any, relate to changes effected by a laboratory programme or how close we should expect this relationship to be. It was for this reason that I undertook further research on personality variables and the outcomes of laboratory training. From the mixed results obtained with the personality variables described above, from Stock's summary of possible 'facilitators of learning', and from my own observations of the training process and its complexity, I decided to reexamine a fundamental assumption of the laboratory training process; people learn best about behavioural concepts when they learn from their own immediate experience. This assumption seems to me to imply that all individuals tend to have an adequate ability to learn from the immediate data in the world around them, and I seriously question it. To me, the process of 'learning from the data' requires a number of skills: to think thematically; to deal with the reality of multiple causation of behaviour; to use analogies to clarify a process; to make connections and to see correspondences which may be quite appropriate but not one-to-one in their relationship to one another; and (tied in with the others) an ability to generate hypotheses and to understand the context in which the data occur.

It is the last of the skills on this list which are most important for our purposes. Basically, one cannot get useful, change-inducing information about the world and himself without being somewhat selective at certain times; and to be selective means to generate some set of rules or guidelines indicating what data are important for testing an idea as well as for generating the idea itself. In a T-group, we are asking people to become scientists in their day-to-day exchange with their environment. From the conduct of science we can, therefore, apply the principle that only by gathering selected data can the T-group process result in real learning; otherwise, the data can prove almost anything the actor wants them to prove, since they are usually determined by a number of conditions.

For example, when a T-group fails to make a decision within a time limit during an intergroup exercise, the literal-minded member may then say, 'My conclusion is that groups cannot reach decisions; that should be left to individuals. My experience has just proved this to me'. Others in the group may go farther, considering the possibilities that their poor performance was related to the lack of trust in the group, to the fact that they did not really want to make a decision then, or to the fact that they become so anxious about the time limit that they let their anxieties control them and block exploration. Going on to these kinds of alternatives instead of stopping at the first, most literal exploration of the data (which happens in many cases to fit preconceived notions of why things happen) requires a mode of thinking which can generate alternative explanations for the occurrence of a given set of events. Accordingly, I decided that a scale which attempts to measure exactly this dimension would be likely to differentiate those more and less responsive to and comfortable with the laboratory training process. This is the Sensation–Intuition (S–N)* scale of the Myers–Briggs Type Indicator (Myers, 1962). Conceived as a measure of preference for basic modes of perceiving or becoming aware of the world, the two ends which define the scale may be briefly described† as follows:

Sensation (S): This is the process of becoming aware of things directly through one of the five senses. The focus here is on factual stimuli in the environment. The type of individual who prefers this process focuses on facts, attention to detail, realism, practicality, and thoroughness.

Intuition (N): This is, by contrast, the process of indirect holistic perception, where the perceive adds to whatever is given (in the stimulus situation itself) through ideas and associations generated from within. The individual who prefers intuition cares as much about the multiple possibilities that occur to him as he does about the actualities. This type of person is characterized by insight, originality, ingenuity, grasp of the complicated, comfort with abstract thought, and a bent for experimentation.

Preference for one mode of perception (S or N) does not generally mean exclusion of the other. It merely means that one mode was more central during an individual's development and that he uses that mode when given a chance. 'Preference-type', then, represents the individual's habitual, purposeful ways of perceiving the world, chosen because he has found them to be good, interesting, and above all, trustworthy.

From this brief description of the S–N scale, we can make some fairly straightforward connections. For one, the Intuition end of the scale appears to be related to abstractness in Harvey, Hunt and Schroder's (1961) concrete–abstract dimension of cognitive complexity. Similarly, there

* Note that the symbol for Intuition is N, not I.

† The descriptions are a synthesis of Myers (1962), Ross (1962), and Saunders (1960).

7

would appear to be greater flexibility and tolerance for ambiguity associated with the Intuitive mode of perception. These are merely further
indications that the S–N scale could be quite central to the laboratory
process described earlier. Thus an Intuitive perceiver would appear much
more likely than a Senser to be able to operate in the 'scientific' manner that
the laboratory is trying to promote. He would be able to generate hypotheses, select among the data, and generalize across situations that are not
one-to-one in correspondence. This view is supported by the test developers'
findings that 93 per cent of a sample of 'creative men' (the majority were
scientists and architects) scored as Intuitives (Myers, 1962).

Accordingly, the general hypothesis was developed that those individuals
who scored higher (toward the Intuitive end) on the S–N scale would tend
to deal with their worlds in a more laboratory-oriented manner and would
be more effective in this setting and would learn more from a training
laboratory than would those individuals who scored lower (toward the
Senser end of the scale). The remainder of this paper describes the procedure and results of two studies designed to obtain information concerning
the validity of this hypothesis. Since somewhat different procedures were
used in each, the two projects are described separately.

Study A

In this study, two laboratory populations were used as subjects: participants in a two-week human relations summer laboratory sponsored by the
National Training laboratories, of whom 72 out of 84 provided usable data;
and 58 'middle managers' who went through a two-week 'Grid' laboratory
(Blake and Mouton, 1964) as part of a full academic year they were spending
at a graduate school of business administration, from whom 39 usable
responses were obtained.* The human relations participants were from a
wide variety of organizations and occupations, while the middle managers
were predominantly from business and industry.

Procedure

Which dependent variables to use as criteria of laboratory 'directions'
posed a familiar dilemma (Bergin, 1962; Miles, 1960). For both the human
relations and middle-manager laboratories it was decided that an appropriate criterion of change would be expressed 'organizational interpersonal
values'. These values are defined as personally held conceptions of how

---

* The fairly low response return in the middle-manager laboratory led to a check on
the distributions on the S–N scale (which was returned by 55 out of 58) for those who did
and did not provide complete data. There was no difference on the S–N dimension.

people should deal with others in organizational interpersonal situations. This criteria was chosen with the view that specific values, operating as standards of what is good or desirable in interpersonal work situations, are a focal force influencing behaviour in these situations; and further, that changes in values are an important outcome of laboratory training efforts.

These values are seen as solutions to basic problems (Kluckhohn and Strodtbeck, 1961) related to organizational interpersonal situations, and they may be characterized by what Buhler (1960) terms 'constructive intent'; that is, they are beliefs about what relationships should be like in an organization in order that it be effective or accomplish something.

An investigation of the literature on interpersonal and group behaviour (Argyris, 1962; Bales, 1950; Bennis, 1962; Benuis and Peabody, 1962; Fleishman, 1953; Leary, 1957; Lorr and McNair, 1963; Schutz, 1958) led to the formulation of four 'problems' which defined interpersonal value dimensions for this study. These dimensions were then simplified and assigned a 'laboratory' and 'nonlaboratory' end, as follows:

1. Control (C): How should control, power, influence, and so on be distributed in work relationships? The laboratory (high) end of the dimension was defined as 'Shared Control' and the nonlaboratory (low) end as 'Unshared Control'.

2. Trust (T): To what extent should parties to a work relationship strive to enhance their trust of one another? The laboratory end is 'High Trust', and the non-laboratory end is 'Low Trust'.

3. Feelings (F): To what extent are personal feelings relevant as elements of information to be shared and dealt with in a work relationship? The laboratory end is 'Feelings Relevant', and the nonlaboratory end is 'Feelings Irrelevant'.

4. Receptivity (R): To what extent should people in work relationships be open to receiving new information, points of view, or possibilities from others? The laboratory end is 'Openness', and the nonlaboratory end is 'Closedness'.*

5. Total: A fifth score—a 'total laboratory values' measure—was defined simply as the sum of the scores on the other four dimensions.

A new instrument, the Managerial Behaviour Questionnaire (MBQ), was developed to measure these four interpersonal values dimensions. The MBQ presents seven open-ended items, each in the form of a one-paragraph description of a conflict situation, the subject is asked to write two responses:

* This orientation would not, of course, be called 'closedness' in the individual's own words, but rather something like 'stability', 'perseverance', and so on. For an elaborate analysis of the dynamics of open and closed orientations to the world, see Rokeach (1960).

(A) what he feels he should do in the given situation, and (B) why he feels he should do this—what the personal guidelines are that are helpful to him in making his decision in each conflict situation. He is also asked to indicate on a 7-point scale how strongly or how 'sure' he feels about each answer.* Scores obtained empirically range from 65 (extreme nonlaboratory score) to about 140 (extreme laboratory score) on the individual dimensions, and from 320 to 550 on the 'Total' laboratory scores.

Each laboratory population received an orientation to the research project on the first afternoon of their respective sessions. The human relations participants and staff completed the Myers–Briggs Type Indicator (which contained the S–N scale) and the Managerial Behaviour Questionnaire in their T-group rooms. The middle managers took the same instruments home and returned them at one of the following meetings. At the close of each laboratory, both samples again completed the MBQ. Human relations participants filled it out on the Thursday afternoon before the Friday closing of their session, and the middle managers completed and returned the MBQ within six days after their last class period. In addition, the human relations subjects were given the S–N scale a second time, at the close of their laboratory session.

All of the MBQs were coded blind by the author, except for a random sample of 30 questionnaires that were also coded by an associate in order to check the reliability of the scoring system.†

Hypotheses

From the conceptualization outlined earlier, several specific hypotheses were formulated on the assumptions that (a) values before the laboratory would reflect individual differences plus the effects of the culture back home, and (b) values at the laboratory would reflect both of these factors plus the impact of the laboratory culture. Specifically—

I. Before the laboratory, there would be a positive correlation between preference for Intuition (N) on the S–N scale and the laboratory ends of the interpersonal values (MBQ) dimensions.

II. After the laboratory, there would be a positive correlation between Intuition and the laboratory interpersonal values.

* See F. I. Steele (1965) for the text of the MBQ, a more complete description of its rationale, instructions for coding, and data on reliability and validity. The criteria used for developing the MBQ appear to be quite similar to the recommendations made by Smith (1963) for a values measure; it is specific, it presents actual choice situations, it obtains statements in the respondent's own words, and so on.

† Correlations (Pearson r) between individuals' scores for the two coders were: Control: 0·821; Trust: 0·827; Feelings: 0·868; Receptivity: 0·643; Total: 0·935.

III. The positive correlations described in I and II would be larger after the laboratory than before it.

Results

One preliminary indicator that our hypotheses were at least plausible is the way the staff members at the human relations laboratory scored on the S–N scale. All six scored as Intuitive types (above 100 on the scale), and as a group they had a mean score of 135, a score which indicates a strong preference for Intuition. These very limited data do not validly prove, but they do suggest at least that a preference for Intuition is likely to be associated with the activities required by staff work in laboratories. This tendency can be seen more clearly if we contrast the staff scores with those for the participant samples: human relations (n = 72) had a mean score of 117·6, and the middle managers (n = 39) had 98·7 as their mean score.

Another preliminary question concerned the Sensation–Intuition scale and its use as a relatively stable measure of preference for cognitive functioning. This was checked by comparing the human relations scores from the before-laboratory and after-laboratory administrations. This after-laboratory mean was 116·1, a difference of only −1·5 points from the before-laboratory mean, and this difference was not significant. The correlation between before- and after-scores was 0·864. These data suggest that the S–N scale is quite adequate as a measure of stable personality differences, at least in the situation being studied.

Advancing to a direct test of our hypotheses, we shall now consider the associations between the S–N scale and the laboratory interpersonal values dimensions. Tables 1 and 2 present correlations before and after the laboratories for each sample. An analysis of variance showed that it was reasonable to consider each laboratory (as opposed to each individual T-group) as a single treatment situation; however, since the results for the two laboratories were somewhat different, they have been reported separately rather than pooled as a sample of 111 subjects.

The first hypothesis stated that Intuition would be positively correlated with high laboratory values scores before the laboratory sessions. For the human relations group, this hypothesis was supported on the Trust, Feelings, and Total dimensions. For the middle managers, however, this prediction was not upheld; in fact, the correlations tend to be in a negative direction.

Hypothesis II predicted a positive correlation between Intuition and laboratory values after the laboratory session. This prediction was clearly upheld for all values dimensions in the human relations sample. In the

Table 1—*Product–moment correlations[a] between laboratory values and the sensation–intuition scale (Human Relations Laboratory, N = 72)*

	MBQ values dimension				
	Control	Trust	Feelings	Receptivity	Total
Before laboratory	0·162	0·311**	0·321**	0·108	0·292**
After laboratory	0·321**	0·251*	0·301**	0·292**	0·398**
Critical ration for change in correlation from before to after	1·289[b]	n.s.	n.s.	1·661*	n.s.

[a] A positive correlation indicates an association between Intuition and the Laboratory Interpersonal Value on each dimension.
[b] Trend significance, $p < 0.10$.
* $p < 0.05$.
** $p < 0.01$.
*** $p < 0.001$; all tests one-tailed.

Table 2—*Product–moment correlations between laboratory values and the sensation–intuition scale (Middle-Managers Laboratory, N = 39)*

	MBQ values dimension				
	Control	Trust	Feelings	Receptivity	Total
Before laboratory	−0·210	−0·276	−0·015	0·061	−0·170
After laboratory	0·058	−0·111	0·335*	0·059	0·135
Critical ration for change in correlation from before to after	1·574[a]	n.s.	2·612**	n.s.	2·107*

[a] Trend significance, $p < 0.07$.
* $p < 0.05$.
** $p < 0.01$; all tests one-tailed.

middle-manager data, it was upheld only on the Feelings dimension; however, only one negative correlation remained.

Hypothesis III stated that the after-laboratory correlations would be larger than those before the laboratory. For the human relations sample, this hypothesis was found true for the Control, Receptivity, and Total dimensions, although only Control and Receptivity showed statistically significant changes. For the middle managers, there were positive increases for Control, Trust, Feelings, and Total, with all but Trust reaching significance.

Thus Hypotheses I and II relating Intuition to laboratory values before and after the laboratory were generally upheld for the human relations sample but not for the middle managers. This difference in results may be explained in part by the different characteristics of the two samples. As indicated earlier, the human relations participants came from a variety of occupations and types of organizations and included a good number of people in the helping professions. Middle managers were a much more homogeneous group, since almost all were employed in business or industrial organizations—just those kinds of organizations that have been described by Argyris (1962) as placing a high value on the traditional, formal values of hierarchical authority, rationality, and nonemotionality. With this latter population, then, the effects of the participants' back-home cultures may have been particularly strong and—with relative uniformity— directed away from the laboratory interpersonal values under consideration.

The process would go something like this: The Intuitives, according to the preference-type theory behind this study, would be more likely than the Sensers to have tried to deal with phenomena in the 'laboratory' manner early in their organizational life (i.e., to deal with feelings, to keep questions open for more data, to establish collaborative rather than hierarchical relationships, and so on). To the extent that this style was felt by those already well integrated into the organization to be inappropriate, the Intuitives were also more likely to have had negative sanction applied to them for that behaviour. Therefore, we might expect them to draw back somewhat after having been 'burned'. This sequence, although only speculation, is supported by the before-laboratory negative correlations for the middle-manager group, and by the generally positive shift in these correlations as the laboratory experience served to 'loosen them up'.

Finally, on the overall results there seems to be a higher positive correlation on the Control, Feelings, and Total dimensions than for Trust and Receptivity. Data from other work with the MBQ (Steele, 1965) indicate that these results may in part be due to the MBQ's greater effectiveness at measuring values related to sharing Control and Dealing with Feelings. Another factor may be related to a greater disparity between the laboratory orientation and a traditional organizational orientation on these two dimensions, at least in terms of expressed values.

Study B

The subjects for this study were undergraduate and graduate students who were participants in four T-groups held as courses during the regular academic terms. Each group met for $1\frac{1}{2}$ to 2 hours twice a week for approximately 16 weeks. In two of the groups the author served as trainer; in the other two groups the trainer was a fellow faculty member engaged in numerous training activities.

Procedure

At the first meeting of each T-group, the members completed the
Sensation–Intuition scale as part of the Myers–Briggs Type Indicator. No
other measurements were taken until the end of the term. During the last
session, the participants rated the members of their own T-group (excluding
themselves) on ten dimensions related to effective behaviour and change in
the group. These dimensions are shown in Table 3. In addition, the trainer

Table 3—*Pearson product–moment correlations between peer ratings of T-group
behaviour and the S–N scale (Four Student Groups, N = 45)*

Peer rating questions	Correlation with intuition
1. Worked hard to influence others toward his point of view	0·480***
2. Has usually been willing to go along with what others want to do	−0·150
3. Has been willing to disagree with or criticize others' ideas or actions	0·394**
4. Warm and supportive toward other group members	0·210
5. Seemed interested and involved in the group's activities	0·438**
6. Tried out new ways of doing things	0·406**
7. Helped clarify and make more understandable to others the events and processes in the group	0·491***
8. His overall effectiveness as a member contributed significantly to the group's progress	0·491***
9. He seemed to understand and learn from the reactions of others to his ideas and actions in the group	0·236
10. His overall effectiveness as a group member has increased	0·212

** $p < 0·01$.
*** $p < 0·001$; one-tailed tests.

for one group rated (on a 5-point scale) the members of his group on the
dimensions of Overall Effectiveness in Group, Change, and the four laboratory interpersonal values areas described earlier (see Table 4). These ratings
were obtained at a point when the trainers had no knowledge of either the
individuals' S–N scores or of their ratings by their peers in the T-groups.*

Hypothesis

The general working hypothesis for both peer and trainer ratings was
that a preference for Intuition would tend to be associated with higher

* The possibility that the author was contaminating the results by guessing at the
members' strengths of preference for Intuition was checked by comparing the data for his
two groups with the data for the other trainer, who had almost no familiarity with the
S–N scale and very little knowledge about the hypotheses being tested by the author. The
results were very similar for each pair of groups.

ratings on understanding, activity, experimentation, and so on in the groups and with perceived change, as well as with higher ratings on the laboratory values, at the end of the laboratory.

Results

The correlations between the S–N scale (with Intuition as the positive end) and the ratings by peers and trainers are shown in Tables 3 and 4. In the ratings by peers, there is a significant tendency to describe Intuitives as active, willing to own up to their ideas, involved experimenting, clarifying and making events understandable for others, and as contributing to the group's progress. The correlations on warmth, learning, and increase in effectiveness are also in the predicted direction but are not significant.

Table 4—*Pearson product–moment correlations between trainer ratings of T-group members' behaviour and values and the S–N scale (four student groups, N = 45)*

Trainer rating	Correlation with Intuition
Overall effectiveness in group	0·384**
Change in the T-group	0·262*
Values shared control	0·378**
Values high trust	0·298
Values sharing relevant feelings	0·410**
Values receptivity to new information	0·320*

* $p < 0.05$.
** $p < 0.01$; one-tailed tests.

In Table 4 we see that all of the correlations are positive and statistically significant, with Overall Effectiveness, Values Sharing Relevant Feelings ranking highest. As with the peer ratings, Change has one of the lowest correlations.

These data provide fairly solid support for the premise that a preference for Intuition as a mode of perception tends to make an individual comfortable and effective in laboratory training situations; by extrapolation they also suggest that the Intuitive would be more effective than the Senser at operating in the 'laboratory' manner in other settings (e.g., work or family). The findings are much less impressive on the question of the association between Intuition and change at the laboratory. Although the trainer ratings were significant on this dimension, in general these data do not indicate much predictive power as to who learns or changes from participation in a laboratory. Rather, the peer data can be seen as indicating a possible association between Intuition and a rather general factor of 'effectiveness' in operating in a 'laboratory' style. Add to this the trainers' general ratings (by definition) as well as their ratings on laboratory interpersonal values— these ratings which were made largely on the basis of behaviour in the group. The pattern is quite similar to the results of Miles (1960) which were described earlier.

Discussion and action implications

Our original prediction that a preference for Intuition as a perceptual mode would be a major factor in specifically determining who changes at a laboratory did not receive much support in these studies, although the trend is clearly in the right direction. The positive result for trainer ratings of change can be explained by a general 'effectiveness' factor on which the trainers were rating and by Miles's (1960) factors of involvement and reception of feedback. Similarly, the shift on Feelings from no correlation to a positive one of 0·335 in the middle-manager laboratory could be explained as a loosening-up following an overreaction pattern, as discussed earlier. Several factors could have contributed to the generally low results on Change. For one, regression toward the mean would be working against our change hypothesis. For another, using personality-types to predict who changes may be expecting too long a chain of variables to fall into place. (Again see Miles, 1960). Finally, it seems quite likely that specific changes effected in the laboratory setting are influenced by many other factors, in addition to individual cognitive preferences: the composition of the group (Harrison, 1965), the style of the trainer, or the establishment of particular kinds of relationships within the group (Clark, 1963).

Relative to the positive association between Intuition tendencies toward the 'laboratory style' of operation, most of the data do confirm the general hypotheses, both in terms of rated behaviour in the T-group (student laboratory) and in terms of the expressed or rated interpersonal values after the laboratory (human relations laboratory, student laboratory). The hypothesis did not hold up for the middle managers, probably for two reasons. One mentioned earlier is that they were a homogeneous sample, they were lower on the S–N scale, and came from more traditionally bureaucratic settings with stronger sets to behave in nonlaboratory ways. Another reason may be the nature of the Grid laboratory in which the middle managers participated. It is, by design, a much more highly structured and more specific type of laboratory: one of its major goals is the learning of a relatively concrete, specific system for diagnosing leadership behaviour. As a result, we probably should not have expected the same results from the Grid sample, since the original hypotheses were based on a view of laboratory training which included demands on the individual to generalize from complex data to even more complex situations, to make rough analogies, and to generate hypotheses from within which can be tested in the laboratory situation. These demands are not totally absent in the Grid laboratory setting, but they are not nearly so central to the process as in the human relations and student laboratories used as samples.

Overall, the data point to a connection between stable preferences for Intuition and a rather general factor which we may call the 'laboratory style' of behaviour; this 'style' includes high activity, individuality, and collaboration; and a preference for helping, experimenting, dealing with feelings, becoming involved, and understanding processes and relating them to other situations. Many of these behaviours represent what I described at the beginning as a 'scientific' posture toward the world; we therefore have here some evidence that not all people are likely to be able or will choose to operate in this scientific manner. From this study also has come more knowledge about at least one dimension, the Sensation–Intuition dimension, which appears to relate to this 'scientific' (or laboratory) style.

Of the many possible action-implications deriving from these findings, only a representative few will be mentioned here. First, one expressed in negative terms: It may not be realistic to try to change all persons toward a single laboratory style of behaviour, and, therefore, subjects such as those who are strongly Sensation-oriented should be screened out in advance of a laboratory. A second is less pessimistic: We should design specific learning experiences in which the context of the data is clear, in which the key variables are highlighted through design of the experience, and in which Sensation-oriented individuals are specifically helped to generalize to situations that on the surface appear very different from the one in which they are immediately located. We might also generate a relatively concrete list of goals for laboratory training for Sensers (or similar types)—a list which would differ in some essentials from the more complex 'scientific-mode' goals which we now tend to establish for all laboratory participants.

A third suggestion is even more interesting. We might question whether the preference for Sensation or Intuition is really as stable as the data from the human relations group indicate. The lack of change in their case may have been due to the fact that the laboratory was not specifically designed to change people in this area. We might therefore design laboratory programmes which are specifically aimed at helping Sensation-oriented individuals to appreciate, develop, and use the Intuitive mode to a greater degree. This might be a very useful preliminary step toward the development of a more laboratory-oriented 'style'.

In the main, this study has shown that 'learning from the data' is just too simple a way of conceptualizing both what happens in laboratory training and the kind of day-to-day process which that training is trying to foster. The problem for the laboratory participant is to learn from the data and to learn things which are appropriate for the context in which the data are imbedded. This learning process makes some fairly specific demands on individual participants, including the ability to generate alternative hypotheses as to why an event occurred; to make connections on the basis of 'hunches', which are then tested with new data; and to draw analogies between situations which do not completely overlap or fit perfectly. The studies reported in this paper indicate that an individual's relatively stable preference for different modes of becoming aware of the world (as measured by the Sensation–Intuition scale of the Myers–Briggs Type Indicator) may be one useful dimension for predicting whether given individuals will be able to meet the demands of the 'laboratory style'. In addition, the results indicate that the basic conceptualization of the Sensation–Intuition dimensions may be utilized to suggest a wider range of training experience better suited to different types of individual participants.

References

Argyris, C. (1962) *Interpersonal Competence and Organisational Effectivness.* Homewood, Ill.: Irwin Dorsey.

Bales, R. F. (1950) *Interaction Process Analysis: A Method for the Study of Small Groups.* Cambridge, Mass.: Addison-Wesley.

Benne, K. D. (1964) 'History of the T-group in the laboratory setting.' In L. P. Bradford, J. R. Gibb and K. D. Benne (Eds.), *T-group Theory and Laboratory Method: Innovation in Re-education.* New York: John Wiley.

Bennis, W. G. (1962) 'Goals and meta-goals of laboratory training.' *Human Relat. Train. News,* **6** (5), 1–4.

Bennis, W. G. and D. Peabody (1962) 'The conceptualization of two personality orientations and sociometric choice.' *J. soc. Psychol.,* **57,** 203–215.

Bergin, A. E. (1962) 'The effects of psychotherapy: Frontiers in the analysis of outcome.' Paper presented at Symp. on the Empirical Status and Future of Psychotherapy. *Amer. Psychol. Ass. Conv., St. Louis.*

Blake, R. R. and Jane S. Mouton (1964) *The Managerial Grid.* Houston: Gulf.

Bradford, L. P., J. R. Gibb and K. D. Benne (Eds.) (1964) *T-group Theory and Laboratory Method: Innovation in Re-Education..* New York: John Wiley.

Buchanan, P. (1964) 'Evaluating the effectiveness of laboratory training in industry.' Paper read at A.M.A. Seminar, New York, Feb. 24–26.

Buhler, C. (1962) *Values in Psychotherapy.* Glencoe, Ill.: Free Press.

Clark, J. V. and S. A. Culbert (1965) 'Mutually therapeutic perception and self-awareness in a T-group.' *J. appl. Behav. Sci.,* **1** (2), 180–194.

Fleishman, E. E. (1953) 'Leadership climate, human relations training, and supervisory behaviour.' *Personnel Psychol.,* **6,** 205–222.

Harrison, R. (1965) 'Group composition models for laboratory design.' *J. appl. Behav. Sci.*, **1** (4), 409–432.

Harvey, O. J., D. E. Hunt and H. N. Schroder (1961) *Conceptual Systems and Personality Organisation*. New York: John Wiley.

Kluckhohn, F. and F. L. Strodtbeck (1961) *Variations in Value-orientations*. Evanston, Ill.: Row, Peterson.

Leary, T. (1957) *The Interpersonal Diagnosis of Personality*. New York: Ronald Press.

Lorr, M. and D. McNair (1963) 'An interpersonal behaviour circle.' *J. abnorm. Soc. Psychol.*, **67** (1), 68–75.

Mathis, A. G. (1955) 'Development and validation of a trainability index for laboratory training groups.' Unpublished doctoral dissertation, Univer. of Chicago.

Miles, M. B. (1960) 'Human relations training: Processes and outcomes.' *J. counsel. Psychol.*, **7**, 301–306.

Myers, J. B. (1962) 'Manual for the Myers–Briggs type indicator.' Princeton, N.J.: Educational Testing Service.

Rokeach, M. (1960) *The Open and Closed Mind*. New York: Basic Books.

Ross, J. (1962) 'Faster analysis and levels of measurement in psychology.' In S. Messick and J. Ross (Eds.), *Measurement in Personality and Cognition*. New York: John Wiley. Pp. 69–81.

Saunders, D. R. (1960) 'Evidence bearing on the existence of a rational correspondence between the personality typologies of Spranger and Jung.' Research Bulletin Rb-60-6. Princeton, N.J.: Educational Testing Service.

Schein, E. H. and W. G. Bennis (1965) *Personal and Organisational Change Through Group Methods: The Laboratory Approach*. New York: John Wiley.

Schutz, W. C. (1958) *FIRO: A Three-dimensional Theory of Interpersonal Behaviour*. New York: Holt, Rinehart & Winston.

Smith, M. B. (1963) 'Personal values in the study of lives.' In R. W. White (Ed.), *The Study of Lives*. New York: Prentice-Hall. Pp. 324–347.

Steele, F. I. (1965) 'The relationship of personality to changes in interpersonal values effected by laboratory training.' Unpublished doctoral dissertation, M.I.T.

Stern, G. G., M. I. Stein and B. Bloom (1956) *Methods in Personality Assessment*. Glencoe, Ill.: Free Press.

Stock, D. (1964) 'A survey of research on T-groups.' In L. P. Bradford, J. R. Gibb and K. D. Benne (Eds.), *T-group Theory and Laboratory Method: Innovation in Re-education*. New York: John Wiley. Pp. 395–441.

Vroom, V. (1960) *Some Personality Determinants of the Effects of Participation*. Englewood Cliffs, N.J.: Prentice-Hall.

Weschler, I. R. and E. H. Schein (1962) *Issues in Human Relations Training*. No. 5 in Selected Readings Series. Washington, D.C.: National Training Laboratories.

CHAPTER 6

Intra-Group Dynamics

Gibb (1964a) makes the point that much of the early T-group research was generated to test some of the issues of academic interest in social psychology. This is particularly true of sociometric theory, which was the preoccupation of many early researchers (Stock, 1964). Increasingly research is being conducted on issues prompted by essentially T-group concerns, but in order for this to happen at all, descriptive and speculative work had to be generated. There is, obviously, still a very great need for 'sound theory', but there is an even greater need for refinement of theories in such a way as to clarify the experimental manipulations necessary to make a test of them. The writers included in this section have very little to build on other than the insights and descriptions of trainers, yet their research is arguably amongst the most important for the development of the training method itself.

In a short paper, Lubin and Zuckerman (1970) focus on the level of emotion generated in T-groups. Whilst this would appear to be the only paper on this subject, it does seem unfortunate that the comparison is made between T-group training and 'sensory deprivation' studies. It is to be doubted that even the T-groups most adamant critics would readily accuse it of being more stress provoking than the enforced restriction of visual, auditory and tactile sensations. As the authors themselves point out stress is used in a relative rather than an absolute sense; the T-group is *less* stressful than sensory isolation, but perhaps more important questions remain. Is it more or less stressful than other training methods? How functional or dysfunctional is the stress, if there is any, for the individual and for the group? Is there an optimum level of stress for growth? The questions remain, though Lubin and Zuckerman have produced the experimental manipulation which is so necessary to further movement from theory to research in this area.

Another area of potential and acknowledged importance is that of the development of trust. Most theorists see the establishment of trust as a critical issue in group development. McGregor (1968), for example, writes, 'The effective performance of a managerial team is in a basic fundamental sense a function of open communications and mutual trust between all the members, including the leader'. Probably the most active theorist and researcher in this field or sub-field is Gibb (1964b) and it is from his theories and researches that Friedlander, whose work is reproduced here, has derived his experimental manipulation.

Friedlander's conclusion that greater emphasis needs to be placed upon the formation of trust within a team, not only supports Gibb's theoretical model, it also neatly confirms McGregor's analysis of the dimension. Nevertheless, it produced one puzzling finding, that trust does not increase as the result of T-group training (Friedlander, 1967). According to Gibb's theory, the T-group provides the opportunity for the person to participate with others in creating a trusting climate, to become aware of the process of such creation and to learn how to generalize these learnings to other dyadic and group situations. Accordingly Friedlander's data on trust is very important, but he finds it to be a *prerequisite* of effective training not part of the training itself. It should be remembered, however, that Friedlander's groups were all ongoing organizational work groups and that the emphasis of the training was on problem-solving in a work-related context. It could be that the issues Gibb sees as critical are less likely to occur in non-stranger task groups such as the ones used by Friedlander.

Closely related to issues of trust are the studies currently being carried out by Clark and his associates at the Graduate School of Business Administration at the University of California, Los Angeles. Whilst not focusing directly upon trust, the emphasis in these studies is on what the authors term *mutually therapeutic perceptions* and it is interesting to note that the participants who shared the most 'awareness of self and other' behaviour were the ones who entered into interpersonal relationships in which the members perceive each other as 'high in level of regard, empathy, congruence and unconditionality of regard'. (See also Culbert (1968) in trainer behaviour chapter.)

Using a different theoretical model, one derived from Kelman's work on social influence, Smith and Pollack (1968) have also focused on the actual dynamics of the T-group.

Kelman's (1958) model of social influence, which, the authors argue, is readily applicable to learning in the T-group, distinguishes between influence based on compliance, identification, and internalization. Compliance occurs when an individual accepts influence because the influencer has the potential to reward or punish him. Identification occurs when an individual accepts influence from an agent because of the latter's attractiveness. Internalization occurs when influence is accepted because there is value-congruence between the agent and the individual being influenced. Smith and Pollack used measures of Kelman influence styles as predictor variables in a well-designed study covering two separate laboratories. Their general prediction was that those changes which persist after training will relate positively to internalization but not to identification or compliance. The prediction was upheld.

If it could finally be established that the nature of relationships established within the T-group are critical to the learning process, it would still be necessary to investigate what aspect of the relationship were important. One variable of theoretical importance here is the concept of 'feedback', and, as Gibb (1964) notes, a number of studies have been conducted in this area though most remain unpublished.

The work of Gibb (1952) himself is particularly interesting. Gibb's work tends either to be related to task-groups or to combine variations in role-playing as well as feedback, but nonetheless, it provides some useful data. In one study Gibb investigated the effect of role playing with and without feedback on self-insight, the capacity to conceptualize a new role, and the capacity to put a new role into practice (role flexibility). In the first area, self-insight, Gibb found that there was a significant difference between a group having a T-group experience and one without such training. The group which had role playing training as well as the T-group experience, however, showed 'a significant improvement' over all other groups.

Miles (1958) went further than Gibb and his associates by trying to identify the factors which influence the effectiveness of feedback. He argued that negative feedback would be more effective in inducing change than positive or mutual feedback. Obviously there is nothing startling about this idea since positive and neutral feedback may only confirm the subjects' presentations. Miles, however, was more interested in discerning the dynamics of change. Under what conditions is feedback accepted and acted upon? His study revealed, as predicted, that strong negative feedback was most effective in inducing change, but in some cases only when it was congruent with the subjects' motivational state. Strong negative feedback in the area of warm interpersonal relations to a person who regarded this area of behaviour as unimportant had little or no effect. A further finding was that the more threat-oriented an individual the less receptive he was to interpersonal feedback. Feedback about task accomplishment, however, was accepted much more readily even when motivation and orientation were not congruent with the direction of the feedback. It would appear to be more legitimate and easier to accept task-oriented feedback than to give and accept more person-centered feedback.

Conclusion

This section has focused on issues which are critical to the learning process. Again, we have been forced to conclude that the research results are more provocative than conclusive. There does, however, seem to be at least some support for (Clark and Culbert, 1965; Smith and Pollack, 1968) the notion that relationships established within the T-group are extremely important in predicting and understanding outcomes.

References

Clark, J. V. and S. A. Culbert (1965) 'Mutually therapeutic perception and self-awareness in a T-group.' *Journal of Applied Behavioural Science*, **1**, 180–194.

Culbert, S. A. (1968) 'Trainer self-disclosure and member growth in two T-groups.' *Journal of Applied Behavioral Science*, **4**, 47–74.

Friedlander, F. (1967) 'The impact of organizational training laboratories upon the effectiveness and interaction of on-going work groups.' *Personnel Psychology*, **20**, 289–307.

Gibb, J. (1952) 'Effects of role playing upon (a) role flexibility and upon (b) ability to conceptualize a new role.' *American Psychologist*, **7**.

Gibb, J. (1964a) 'The present status of T-group theory.' In L. P. Bradford and coworkers, *T-group Theory and Laboratory Method*. London: John Wiley.

Gibb, J. (1964b) 'Climate for trust formation.' In L. P. Bradford and coworkers, *T-group Theory and Laboratory Method*. New York: John Wiley.

Kelman, H. C. (1961) 'Processes of opinion change.' *Public Opinion Quarterly*, **25**, 57–78.

Lubin, B. and M. Zuckerman (1970) 'Level of emotional arousal in laboratory training.' *Journal of Applied Behavioral Science*, in press.

McGregor, D. (1968) *The Professional Manager*. London: McGraw-Hill.

Miles, M. B. (1958) 'Factors influencing response to feedback in human relations training.' Unpublished manuscript, Teachers College, Columbia University.

Smith, P. B. and H. Pollack (1968) 'The participant's learning style as a correlate of T-group learning.' Paper delivered to International Congress of Applied Psychology, Amsterdam.

Stock, D. (1964) 'A survey of research on T-groups.' In L. P. Bradford and co-workers (Eds.), *T-group Theory and Laboratory Method*. New York: John Wiley.

The Primacy of Trust as a Facilitator of Further Group Accomplishment*

Frank Friedlander

Division of Organizational Sciences,
Case Institute of Technology,
Cleveland, Ohio

Organizational and laboratory training programmes are frequently difficult areas in which to explore and test the validity of a specific theory. Most research on such programmes tends to be empirical, evaluative of a specific programme, and thus less relevant to a broadly applicable theory of change. The study reported in this article focuses directly upon Jack Gibb's model in which the formation of trust is theorized to facilitate (and in part be a prerequisite to) further group accomplishment. In this longitudinal study, we explored the impact upon later group accomplishment of early high and low trust, in groups which participated and did not participate in organizational training laboratories. Results indicate the pre-laboratory trust is a key predictor of eventual group accomplishment, although trust itself did not increase as a result of training. Furthermore, the trainee's concept and meaning of trust merged with his concept of an effective group and an effective group meeting as a function of training.

The concept of trust is one which is interwoven throughout much of the philosophical and analytical literature on group dynamics and organizational change. The degree of trust can be a useful concept in describing the climate of *intergroup* relations, such as that between two groups which are competing or cooperating (Shepard, 1964). Trust is also highly relevant to the climate *within* any one group, particularly if the formation of trust is a prerequisite to the group moving forward as a unit toward further accomplishment.

Foremost among theories which are concerned with trust as a facilitator to subsequent group development is that suggested by Gibb (1964). In this article, we shall describe a study which bears directly upon Gibb's theory of group development as contingent upon trust formation.

The theory

The formation of trust and acceptance of self and others, the reduction of fear, and the consequent growth of confidence, are seen by Gibb as con-

* A draft of a paper Published in *Journal of Applied Behavioral Science*, **6**(4), (1970).

cerns which facilitate subsequent individual and group development. Since the person learns to grow through his increasing acceptance of himself and others, he must learn to create defence-reductive climates that will reduce his own fears and distrusts. He then makes change possible for himself in other dimensions. Gibb views the critical function of T-groups as one of augmenting this process of personal learning.

Gibb suggests a contingency hierarchy in which the development of each factor facilitates subsequent development in other factors. Subsequent to acceptance and trust formation are sequentially, the flow of feelings, goal formation, and the implementation control mechanisms and organization. Although growth occurs as a concurrent and interdependent development on each of these four dimensions, it is optimal when the sequential order is maintained. Thus growth in each dimension is contingent upon growth in each of the dimensions preceding it in the hierarchy (Gibb, 1964).

Purpose

The purpose of the current study was to explore a core segment of Gibb's theory, specifically the extent to which intragroup trust is a necessary prerequisite to further group accomplishment. Adequate research of this issue demands a longitudinal study of group trust and group accomplishment. This was achieved by studying groups, which, over a period of time, interacted in their usual organizational environment and groups which, in addition, participated in laboratory training. By comparing these two sets of groups at different points in time, we were able to focus on the differing impacts on later group accomplishment of groups high and low in trust, and also note the impact of laboratory training upon the relationship between group trust and other dimensions.

A previous study (Friedlander, 1967) indicated that groups participating in laboratory training did *not* increase significantly in the degree to which members trusted one another. In the current study, we are not interested pursuing the issue of increased trust as a result of training. Rather, we intend to explore the degree to which initial group trust is predictive of other kinds of accomplishment at a later point in time. Does a group which has higher trust at one point in time accomplish more at a later point in time than a group with lower initial trust? If so, is the facilitative role of high trust augmented in laboratory training groups as compared to groups not participating in training?

The groups

In their regular back-home work setting, the twelve work groups in this study were coherent units composed of from five to fifteen members. Each met (usually weekly or biweekly) and worked together regularly for a variety of purposes, including problem discussion and resolution, general coordination, information dissemination, decision making, policy formulation, future planning, etc. As such, the twelve groups represented task-oriented work units which use typical lateral and hierarchical interaction patterns toward their task accomplishment. Four of these groups eventually participated in organizational training laboratories and the eight others did not, thus providing the project with four training groups and eight comparison groups.

The training

Since each of the training laboratories was lead by a different trainer, the nature of the training quite naturally varied among the four groups. In general, however, the sessions were conducted away from the organizational location, and were attended by all members of the particular work group. The purposes of the sessions were generally to identify problems facing the work group system and the reasons for their existence; to invent possible solutions to the problems in the form of needed system changes, and to plan implementation of these solutions through regular and newly constructed channels. Within this problem-solving context, numerous interpersonal and intragroup processes were explored which directly influenced the total work system.

Development of criteria

Frequently, in studies dealing with the impact of laboratory training, criteria (what is 'supposed' to change) are specified by the researchers, as an outcome of his own personal or theoretical interests. In this study, we attempted to derive criteria which were of direct concern and relevance to group members. The method employed utilized open-end interviews, followed by questionnaires developed from the interviews, followed by statistical analysis of the questionnaire responses into a smaller number of factors.

A series of interviews with group members prior to training resulted in the collection of an extensive amount of material dealing with the problems and issues which members perceived in their work groups. These interview comments were rephrased into questions to form the main body of a questionnaire. Relevant group-descriptive dimensions, issues, and hypotheses recurrent in the professional literature provided an additional source of information. In addition to evaluation of the adequacy and effectiveness of the group and its meetings, the variables encompassed perceptions of the actual network of feelings, both in terms of the perceptions of one's own position in the network as a member and of the perceptions by members of relationships existing between other members of the group.

In an effort to reduce these items to a more comprehensive set of dimensions, a factor analysis was performed from which six underlying dimensions of group process and interaction evolved. Details of the factor analysis and of the factor definitions may be found in an earlier study (Friedlander, 1966).

Definition and measurement of trust

Although we did not purposely devise a specific measure of trust, it is interesting to note that this construct nevertheless did evolve from the (factor) analysis. The nature and number of factors derived from a factor analysis generally cannot be predetermined.

One of the six factors which evolved was concerned almost entirely with perceptions of trust *versus* competitiveness within one's work group. The five items in this factor and the direction in which they were scored were:

There is a destructive competitiveness among members of the group (−).
Others in the group are reluctant to sacrifice ideas so that the group may agree (−).
There are too many personal opinions raised at meetings, as opposed to the broader point of view (−).
There is trust and confidence in each other among members of the group (+).
Conflict within the group is submerged, rather than used constructively (−).

It should be clear that the factor represents a bipolar dimension, running from intragroup trust to intragroup competitiveness. A group high on this dimension is one in which the members hold trust and confidence in each other. A group scoring low can be characterized more as a collection of individuals who are reluctant to sacrifice their individual personal opinions and ideas for the sake of a working consensus. This reluctance occurs in an environment of destructive competition and one in which conflict is submerged.

Definition and measurement of other group dimensions

The remaining five factors which evolved from the factor analysis, and which were considered as additional measures of accomplishment were:

Group effectiveness in solving problems and in formulating policy through a creative, realistic team effort. Groups high on this dimension arrive at creative team solutions, sharing responsibilities and problems openly.

Leader approachability describes groups in which members feel that the leader is approachable and that they can establish a comfortable relationship with him. Groups low on this dimension withdraw from the leader, do not push their ideas, do not behave according to their feelings, and seem intent on catering to the leader at the possible sacrifice of group output.

Mutual influence describes groups in which members mutually influence each other and the leader, and assume responsibility for setting group goals.

Personal involvement and participation is descriptive of groups in which members, want, expect, and achieve active participation in group meetings. The combination of high expectations and actual participation implies a fulfilment which is reflected in the desire to continue group meetings.

Worth of group meetings is a generalized measure of the feelings about the meeting of one's group—as either good, valuable, strong, pleasant, etc., or as bad, worthless, weak, unpleasant, etc.

The questionnaire from which these data were obtained, the *Group Behaviour Inventory*, was administered twice to each of the twelve groups. For the four training groups, the second administration followed the training by six months. For the eight comparison groups, the second administration followed the first administration by six months.

Analytical method

Two methods were utilized to explore the extent to which a high degree of trust is a prerequisite to further group accomplishment. In the first of these, we explored the extent to which eventual (post-study) group accomplishment could be predicted from an earlier knowledge of the degree of trust within a group. In the second analysis, we were interested in the degree to which the trust dimensions converged or diverged from other dimensions of group accomplishment. In both analyses, group accomplishment was defined (from the factor analysis) as greater Group Effectiveness, Leader Approachability, Mutual Influence, Personal Involvement, and Worth of Meetings. And in both analyses, we took into account the fact that some of the groups had participated in laboratory training while others had not.

The primacy of trust

In exploring the degree to which early trust is a predictor of later group accomplishment, it was necessary to deal with two related questions: (1) is early trust a better predictor of specific group accomplishment than any other early measure among training groups, and (2) is early trust a better predictor of later group accomplishment if training has occurred in the intervening period than if not?

The data indicate a positive answer to our first query. Entering Table 1 from the left (pre-study) margin, and viewing only the correlations for training groups (in italics), early trust predicts eventual Group Effectiveness better (r = 0·60) than does any other dimension; it is even a better predictor of eventual Group Effectiveness than early Group Effectiveness (r = 0·55). Similarly, early Group Trust is the best predictor of eventual Worth of Meetings (r = 0·54)—even better than predicted by the measure of Worth of Meetings (r = 0·42).

It should be noted that for training groups, better predictions *in general* can be made from a knowledge of early competence in that *same* dimension rather than from any other dimension (the coefficients in the diagonal cells are higher than any other coefficients in that same column or row). Thus, *Trust is the only group characteristic* that enables us to predict eventual Group Effectiveness and Worth of Meetings better than an early knowledge of these same two group dimensions.

We now return to our second query concerning the impact of laboratory training upon the importance of trust as a prerequisite to group accomplishment. Note in Table 1 that greater predictability from one dimension to another is generally possible for comparison groups than for training groups (coefficients not in italics are generally higher than those in italics). There are two major exceptions to this general finding. Again entering Table 1 at the left margin for the Trust dimension, we find that from a knowledge of early Group Trust, eventual Group Effectiveness can be predicted better for trainees (r = 0·60) than for comparison groups (r = 0·51). Similarly, among trainees early Trust is a far better predictor of eventual Worth of Meetings (r = 0·52) than among comparison members (r = 0·53).

Unlike any of the other variables measured in this study, Group Trust, prior to any training, seems to be a significant factor in the eventual accomplishment which groups reach. Groups high in Trust prior to training tend to be those which, after training, are effective and have worthwhile meetings. Correspondingly, groups in which members are competitive with one another prior to training, are those which, after training, are less effective and have less worthwhile meetings.

In a previous section, we mentioned some relevant findings from an earlier analysis of the same groups and the same training. Of the six dimensions of group accomplishment measured in this study, only three

Table 1—*Before–after correlations between group trust and five other dimensions of group accomplishment*[a, b, c]

Earlier (Pre-study) Measure of	Later (Post-study) Measure of					
	Group Trust	Group Effectiveness	Leader Approachability	Mutual Influence	Personal Involvement	Worth of Meetings
Group Trust	*0·57* 0·68	*0·60* 0·51	*0·23* 0·42	*−0·11* 0·05	*0·06* 0·34	*0·54* 0·33
Group Effectiveness	*0·32* 0·52	*0·55* 0·80	*0·01* 0·50	*0·09* 0·13	*0·22* 0·56	*0·37* 0·57
Leader Approachability	*0·29* 0·57	*0·30* 0·49	*0·50* 0·81	*0·06* 0·33	*0·34* 0·46	*0·31* 0·24
Mutual Influence	*−0·02* 0·31	*0·25* 0·25	*0·19* 0·33	*0·54* 0·71	*0·36* 0·45	*0·18* 0·27
Personal Involvement	*−0·08* 0·34	*0·11* 0·53	*0·11* 0·37	*0·28* 0·37	*0·43* 0·80	*0·05* 0·43
Worth of Meetings	*0·23* 0·31	*0·58* 0·58	*−0·08* 0·40	*0·13* 0·23	*0·22* 0·46	*0·42* 0·64

[a] Before–after correlations for trainees are in italics and for comparison members in regular print.
[b] For predictive purposes the table should be entered from the left (pre-study) margin, and then across that row to the appropriate post-study dimension. For example, the correlation between early group trust and later worth of meetings is 0·54 for trainees and 0·33 for comparison members.
[c] N = 31 trainees, N = 60 comparison members.

improved significantly as a result of laboratory training (Friedlander, 1967). Group Trust was one of those which did *not* improve. Thus, although trust itself did not increase as a result of training, it did act as a catalyst in augmenting the impact of laboratory training upon two other kanor dimensions of group accomplishment.

The convergence of trust with other dimensions

Whereas the previous section was concerned with the degree to which high trust prior to laboratory experience is linked with group accomplishment after training, this section deals with the degree to which the trust dimension converges with or diverges from other dimensions as a function of training. We are concerned here with the relationship between trust and other dimensions prior to training compared with the relationship between trust and other dimensions after training. Differences between these two sets of relationships will be indicative of the changing meaning and conception of trust as a function of training and non-training experience.

Within each cell in Table 2, the coefficient in the 'pre' column indicates the correlation between two dimensions prior to the training period, while the coefficient in the 'post' column indicates the correlation after the training. The relationship, for example, between Group Effectiveness and Worth of Meetings decreased 0·11 (from 0·70 to 0·59) for trainees, but increased 0·16 (from 0·60 to 0·76) for comparison groups. This difference of 0·27 (which is significant beyond the 0·05 level after an r to z transformation) indicates that the concepts of Group Effectiveness and Worthwhile Meetings *moved further apart* as a function of training. Apparently, prior to training, perceptions of Group Effectiveness and Worthwhile Meetings overlap to a large degree. Laboratory experience, however, serves in such a way as to allow members to differentiate between these two concepts (or sets of feelings). An effective group now is less necessarily one which has good, pleasant, and valued meetings.

The remaining interdimensional changes which are significant all indicate a *convergence* in dimensional concepts as a result of training, and *all are concerned with the dimensions of Group Trust*. The most pronounced of these is the increase in relationship between Group Trust and Worthwhile Meetings from 0·28 prior to training to 0·78 after training, a difference which is significant beyond the 0·01 level when compared to comparison members. Evidently, after laboratory training there is a strong tendency for worthwhile meetings to be characteristic of groups in which members hold trust and confidence in each other rather than groups which act more as a collection of competitive individuals. Prior to training, no such (significant) relationship existed between worthwhile meetings and intragroup trust.

Table 2—Correlations among six group dimensions prior to training and after training for training and comparison groups[a, b, c]

	Group Effectiveness		Leader Approachability		Mutual Influence		Personal Involvement		Worth of Meetings	
	Pre	Post	Pre	Post	Pre	Post	Pre	Post	Pre	Post
Group Trust	*0·41*	*0·60*	*0·28*	*0·38*	*0·05*	*0·00*	*0·29*	*0·20*	*0·28*	*0·78*
	0·66	0·54	0·67	0·41	0·22	0·17	0·48	0·23	0·36	0·43
Group Effectiveness			*0·52*	*0·44*	*0·28*	*0·19*	*0·32*	*0·24*	*0·70*	*0·59*
			0·57	0·55	0·27	0·30	0·68	0·51	0·60	0·76
Leader Approachability					*0·31*	*0·09*	*0·28*	*0·40*	*0·38*	*0·37*
					0·31	0·35	0·44	0·46	0·34	0·47
Mutual Influence							*0·49*	*0·65*	*0·30*	*0·19*
							0·42	0·43	0·27	0·38
Personal Involvement									*0·28*	*0·43*
									0·55	0·49

[a] Interdimensional correlations for trainees are in italics and for comparison members in regular print.
[b] Cells bounded by a heavy-lined box are those in which the change in correlation between two dimensions for trainees differs from the change in correlation for comparison members beyond the 0·05 level of significance. Tests of significance were computed after an r to z transformation.
[c] N = 31 trainees, N = 60 comparison members.

A second example of dimensional convergence occurs between the concept of intragroup trust and perceptions of Group Effectiveness in solving problems through team effort. After training, an effective group is seen as one in which members have trust and confidence in each other, whereas prior to training these sets of feelings are only moderately related.

A third example of convergence took place between Group Trust and Leader Approachability. Perceptions of groups in which members can establish an unconstrained and comfortable relationship with their leader are only moderately related to intragroup trust prior to training. Six months after laboratory experience, however, leader approachability within a group and trust within that group are seen as closely related.

It is important to note that all three instances in which concepts of dimensions *converged* as a function of laboratory experience involved the trust and confidence dimension. Prior to training, group effectiveness, leader approachability, and worthwhile meetings were relatively unassociated with feelings of trust and confidence among members. Subsequent to training, however, the concept of trust became significantly more associated with these three dimensions of group accomplishment. Thus, it can be said that subsequent to training, but not prior to it, as trust and confidence vary so do group effectiveness, leader approachability, and worthwhile group meetings.

Summary

1. Work groups in which members have high trust in one another *prior* to laboratory training reach greater degrees of group effectiveness and have more worthwhile meetings *after* laboratory training; conversely, groups in which members feel competitive with each other prior to training are less effective and have less worthwhile meetings after training.

2. The degree to which eventual (post-study) group effectiveness and worth of meetings is contingent upon already established feelings of trust is significantly greater in training groups than in comparison groups. Thus, trust acts as a catalyst in combination with laboratory training to foster group competence, but does not act in this way in groups which have not participated in training.

3. Although high trust seems to augment the impact of training, it does not seem to have increased significantly itself as a function of training.

4. Trust (prior to training) is the group characteristic which best predicts or accounts for post-training effectiveness and worthwhile meetings.

5. When the relationships among the several group characteristics before training are compared to those relationships six months after

laboratory training, the only significant convergent movements are those between group trust and group effectiveness, between group trust and leader approachability, and between group trust and worth of meetings. Thus, feelings of trust vary far more directly with group effectiveness, leader approachability, and worth of meetings subsequent to laboratory training than they do prior to training or without training. No other convergent movements were noted among the six dimensions.

Discussion

This study yields direct empirical data concerning Gibb's theory of the primacy of trust formation. It suggests that far more emphasis needs to be placed upon the formation of trust within a work group if that group is to go forward toward further accomplishment through laboratory methods. Greater efforts should be focused upon building this trust *prior* to laboratory training or at least very early in the training if durable increases in the group's effectiveness are to be gained.

Acceptance, confidence, and trust in each other may be a particularly relevant issue for members of an ongoing organizational work group which is striving to become an effective task-team through laboratory training. The natural history of such groups, *prior* to training, may have been one in which the responsibility for problem solving and group maintenance was vested in the formal leader rather than shared by the membership, in which formal rules rather than informality and intimate social action was the accepted norm, in which interaction was kept on an impersonal basis for fear that 'familiarity breeds contempt', in which procedural specifications rather than spontaneous self-initiated patterns were the mode of attempted progress, and in which persuasion, influence, and control were exerted under the assumption that members cannot be trusted to make decisions for themselves. These patterns, based upon fear and distrust, may have become an integral and accepted process by which the group 'knows' it can operate. The ongoing work group must learn, either prior to or early in the laboratory experience, that alternative modes of group operation based upon acceptance and trust of individual members and of the total group are equally feasible and potentially more effective.

Corollary to the effect of the group's natural history prior to the laboratory are members' realizations that the group will be returning to an organizational environment in which pressures will be exerted toward prior modes of operation. A relevant question in the minds of members might then be: 'Can I trust group members, the leader, myself, and my laboratory experience sufficiently so that I can experiment and innovate in my own behaviour patterns *during* the laboratory without the fear of negative repercussions *when I return to my back-home organizational environment?*' Groups attempting to move forward toward increased learning and accomplishment will be hindered to the extent that these fears and distrusts remain unexplored and unresolved. The major issue then becomes how to create a climate in which these fears and distrusts can be displaced by feelings of confidence and acceptance of oneself and of group members.

References

Friedlander, F. (1966) 'Performance and interactional dimensions of organisational work groups'. *Journal of Applied Psychology*, **50**, 257–265.

Friedlander, F. (1967) 'The impact of organisational training laboratories upon the effectiveness and interaction of ongoing work groups.' *Personnel Psychology*, **20** (in press).

Gibb, J. R. (1964) 'Climate for trust formation.' In L. P. Bradford, J. R. Gibb and K. D. Benne (Eds.), *T-group Theory and Laboratory Method*. New York: John Wiley. Pp. 279–309.

Shepard, H. A. (1964) 'Responses to situations of competition and conflict.' In R. L. Kahn and E. Boulding (Eds.), *Power and Conflict in Organisations*. New York: Basic Books. Pp. 127–135.

Level of Emotional Arousal in Laboratory Training

Bernard Lubin

Mental Health Centre at Kansas City, Kansas City, Mo.

*Marvin Zuckerman**

Albert Einstein School of Medicine, Philadelphia, Pa.

In order to study the level of emotional arousal produced by laboratory training, data from the highest level of a four T-group laboratory were tested against the following stress conditions from perceptual isolation investigations: six hours, eight hours, and 24 hours. Data were collected on a self-administering adjective check list which provided scores on anxiety, depression, and hostility. Analyses of covariance were conducted using pre-stress scores as covariates to provide statistical control in the absence of experimental matching of subjects.

Laboratory training mean scores on anxiety, depression, and hostility for the four T-groups at the highest level (stress condition) were significantly lower than the mean scores from the stress condition of three perceptual isolation studies. Comparison of the post-stress frequency distributions for the four samples indicates that no scores occur for laboratory training at or beyond the point traditionally accepted as deviant (T score of 70 on the standardization sample for the instrument), whereas the stress condition of each of the three perceptual isolation studies produced scores at or beyond this point.

The use of laboratory training (sensitivity training, group process training, T-group training) as an educational method has continued to increase since its development 20 years ago (Bradford, L. P., Gibb, J. R. and Benne, K. D., 1964). Argyris (*Business Week*, 1963) estimated that in the first 16 years of its use approximately 10,000 persons had participated in laboratory training conducted by the National Training Laboratories (now 'the Institute for Applied Behavioural Science'), the organization principally concerned with developing laboratory training as an educational method. During the past

* We wish to express our thanks to Harry Brittain and Alice W. Lubin for their assistance, and our special gratitude to James A. Norton. Partial support for this investigation was provided by Public Health Research Grant FR 00162-02. Originally published in the *Journal of Applied Behavioral Science*, 1969, **5**, 483-490.

five years, several thousand additional people have participated in training laboratories.

Two recent reports criticize laboratory training because of the alleged high level of stress to which participants are subjected (*Business Week*, 1963, Gottschack, 1966). The critical statements assert that the level of emotional arousal induced by laboratory training is extraordinarily high and is likely to be psychologically damaging to participants. In these critical statements, however, no objective evidence has been presented.

Whether laboratory training produces exceptionally high levels of stress should not be left for polemics; it is a question to be answered with empirical methods. The purpose of this paper is to provide some exploratory findings in regard to the question.

Method

This report involves a comparison of the combined mean scores from four T-groups on a measure of anxiety, depression, and hostility taken at the peak session (session six) of a one week laboratory training conference against mean scores on the same instrument from the stress condition of three situations in which known stress producing procedures were employed.

Forty-three male, managerial level Ss who were divided into four T-groups completed the Multiple Affect Adjective Check List (MAACL) (Zuckerman, M. and Lubin, B., 1965) just before the laboratory training conference began and at the end of each of the eight T-group sessions. (The MAACL consists of three experimentally validated scales: anxiety, depression and hostility.) Analyses of variance showed significant session differences on the three scales over the nine testing occasions. Means on the three scales increased steadily over the sessions, peaked at session six, and declined in the last two sessions. The highest scores on anxiety, depression and hostility scales occurred for all four T-groups session six (peak session). Therefore, session six, just after the midpoint of the conference, was the session in which the highest level of stress occurred.

Comparison data were collected in three independent studies. The MAACL was administered to normal male Ss in three perceptual isolation experiments (total N = 61).

In the perceptual isolation studies, measurements were made prior to the beginning of the experiments, and at the following post confinement points: six hours, eight hours, and 24 hours.

Results

Analyses of variance of anxiety, depression and hostility mean scores under pre-stress conditions for the laboratory training conference and the three perceptual isolation groups revealed significant differences, with laboratory training producing the lowest mean scores. In order to control for initial differences among groups, analyses of covariance were conducted, using pre-stress mean scores as covariates. (Analysis of covariance is a well known and accepted method of adjusting experimental data for initial differences on the same or closely related measures.)

The analyses of covariance resulted in significant F ratios for the three scales (anxiety, depression, and hostility). The significance levels were: anxiety $= 0.001$, $p < 0.005$, depression $= p < 0.025$, and hostility $= p < 0.0005$.

Table 1—*Stress session means*

Group	N	Anxiety		Depression		Hostility	
		Un-adjusted	Adjusted	Un-adjusted	Adjusted	Un-adjusted	Adjusted
Laboratory training (session 6)	43	7·93	8·21	15·77	15·97	8·19	9·20
Perceptual isolation (6 hours)	19	10·63	10·55	19·84	20·01	14·47	14·15
Perceptual isolation (8 hours)	29	10·52	10·41	18·79	18·72	13·93	13·26
Perceptual isolation (24 hours)	13	10·85	10·30	19·77	19·02	14·31	12·92

Table 1 presents both unadjusted means and means adjusted for pre-stress scores on anxiety, depression and hostility for the four groups.

The results of the *t* tests among the adjusted means are shown in Table 2.

As we are only interested in testing the hypothesis that the laboratory training combined means for session six are significantly *lower* than the post-stress means from each of the perceptual isolation studies on all three variables, the *t* tests are one-tailed tests.

Table 2—*t tests among adjusted means ($d.f. = 99$)*

Comparisons	Anxiety	Depression	Hostility
Perceptual isolation (6 hours) *vs.* laboratory training (session 6)	2·48*	2·65**	4·67**
Perceptual isolation (8 hours) *vs.* laboratory training (session 6)	2·64**	2·07*	4·17**
Perceptual isolation (24 hours) *vs.* laboratory training (session 6)	1·86*	1·71*	2·85**

* $= p < 0.05$.
** $= p < 0.01$.

8

All *t* values are significant and in every instance the combined mean (the four T-groups) for laboratory training at session six is lower.

In order to compare the frequency distributions of the three variables from the four studies, 5 × 4 tables were constructed for each variable. Raw scores were converted to their corresponding *t* scores (M. Zuckerman and B. Lubin, 1965, p. 7). Chi square tests for the three variables indicated a significant relationship between experimental condition and distribution of scores on the anxiety and hostility measures for both pre-stress and stress conditions. No relationship was found for the depression variables (Pre-stress: anxiety $= 0.01 > p > 0.001$;   depression $= 0.70 > p > 0.80$;

Table 3—*Frequency distribution of anxiety scores from stress conditions (frequencies converted to percentages)*

Group	N			*t* score			
		0–39	40–49	50–59	60–69	70 and +	Total
Laboratory training (session 6)	43	00	21	74	05	00	100
Perceptual isolation (6 hours)	19	00	11	36	21	32	100
Perceptual isolation (8 hours)	29	03	07	49	17	24	100
Perceptual isolation (24 hours)	13	00	08	38	23	31	100
		03	47	197	66	87	400/400

Table 4—*Frequency distribution of anxiety scores from stress conditions (frequencies converted to percentages)*

Group	N			*t* score			
		0–39	40–49	50–59	60–69	70 and +	Total
Laboratory training (session 6)	49	05	19	72	04	00	100
Perceptual isolation (6 hours)	19	05	05	47	37	06	100
Perceptual isolation (8 hours)	29	00	14	52	24	10	100
Perceptual isolation (24 hours)	13	00	08	61	23	08	100
		10	46	232	88	24	400/400

Table 5—*Frequency distribution of anxiety scores from stress conditions (frequencies converted to percentages)*

Group	N	0–39	40–49	50–59	60–69	70 and +	Total
				t score			
Laboratory training (Session 6)	43	19	16	51	14	00	100
Perceptual isolation (6 hours)	19	00	05	05	53	37	100
Perceptual isolation (8 hours)	29	00	10	24	28	38	100
Perceptual isolation (24 hours)	13	00	00	08	62	30	100
		19	31	88	157	105	400/400

hostility $= p < 0.001$. Post-stress: anxiety $= 0.01 > p > 0.001$; depression $= 0.10 > p > 0.05$; hostility $= p < 0.001$).

Tables 3, 4 and 5 present a summary of the frequency distributions for the four groups on the three variables under stress conditions. For ease of viewing, frequencies were converted to percentages.

A *t* score of 70 is generally accepted as the point beyond which scores on a psychometric instrument are considered to be unusually high, as that point represents a score that is higher than that achieved by 98 per cent of the standardization sample. Inspection of Tables 3, 4 and 5 reveals that under the highest stress level produced by laboratory training, *no* scores occur at or above the level of $t = 70$, whereas the stress condition of each of the perceptual isolation studies produced scores above this point.

Discussion

There is no generally agreed upon criterion of stress (E. E. Levitt, 1967), therefore, we have used a relative rather than an absolute definition, i.e., peak session scores in the laboratory training conference (session six) tested against scores on the same instrument from known stress producing situations.

Perceptual isolation experiments consist of confining the subject and restricting his visual, auditory and tactile sensations during this period. Previous studies utilizing the MAACL show a statistically significant increase over control conditions on anxiety and depression scores after six or more hours of perceptual isolation (M. Zuckerman and B. Lubin, 1965, p. 8).

We found that laboratory training at its most stressful point produces significantly lower mean scores on anxiety, depression and hostility than the stress conditions of three perceptual isolation studies. In addition, for laboratory training, no scores on the three variables (anxiety, depression or hostility, occurred at or above the point conventionally accepted as deviant for the standardization sample of the measuring instrument, whereas each of the stress conditions of the three perceptual isolation studies produced scores beyond the deviant point.

The findings may be generalized to other human relations laboratory training conferences which employ designs including, for example, T-groups, theory sessions, special interest seminars, and skill training exercises.

Laboratory training consists of experience-based learning and emphasizes, among other things, the analysis of current interpersonal transactions and group level phenomena in order to unfreeze behavioral–attitudinal–emotional patterns. From the outset, the identification, sharing and exploration of feelings is legitimized and encouraged. A wide range of feelings are evoked and shared: warmth, support, concern, affection, and helpfulness in addition to those feelings, such as anxiety and anger, which arise from a state of tension. The latter feelings are the ones emphasized by the small number of critics, some of whom have participated in laboratory training and some of whom have not.

As indicated by the title of this report, this study was conducted for the purpose of providing some objective data regarding the question of stress during laboratory training. Ideally, the design of this study should have been based upon the employment of the same subjects in all conditions in an appropriate crossover design.

Additional investigations might be oriented toward the selection process of participants for laboratory training. Other investigations could compare peak session data from laboratory training with a broad range of stress producing situations, and might contrast affective data from laboratories differing in design and focus such as: personal growth, community development, inter-group relations, conflict management, and organizational development.

References

Bradford, L. P., J. R. Gibb and K. D. Benne (1964) *T-group Theory and Laboratory Method.* New York: John Wiley.
Burke, H. L. and W. G. Bennis (1961) 'Changes in perception of self and others during human relations training.' *Hum. Rel.*, **14**, 165–182.
Business Week (1963) 'Yourself as others see you.' March 16, 160.
Gottschalk, L. A. (1966) 'Psychoanalytic notes on T-groups at the Human Relations Laboratory, Bethel, Maine.' *Compr. Psychiatry*, **7**, 472–487.

Levitt, E. E. (1967) *The Psychology of Anxiety.* Indianapolis: Bobbs Merrill.
Lubin, B. and M. Zuckerman (1967) 'Affective and perceptual-cognitive patterns in sensitivity training groups.' *Psychol. Rep.,* **21**, 365–376.
Zuckerman, M. and B. Lubin (1965) *Multiple Affect Adjective Check Lists: Manual.* San Diego, California: Educational and Industrial Testing Service.

CHAPTER 7

Course of Development in the T-group

It is not surprising that one of the central areas of T-group research is concerned with the identification of predictable phases or sequences within and across groups, since the identification of such developmental trends is of importance to the establishment of theory, research, and sound training design.

Tuckman (1965) has suggested that most of the theories can be synthesized to fit one model, the four developmental stages which he labels forming, storming, norming, and performing. Some theories, notably those of Bion (1961), Schutz (1958), and Hampden-Turner (1966) do not fit easily into this successive phase model, indeed they emphasize the recurrent cycle model which holds that the group will never fully resolve issues.

Not only are there conflicting theories of development, but also conflicting evidence. Lubin and Zuckerman (1967) introduce a distinction between *group development* which they note has sometimes been used to refer to significant differences among sessions in a single group and to refer to significant differences among phases in a single session, and *developmental trends* which is used to refer to events which appear at similar points in time in various groups. 'Group development' is used, hereafter, when we are referring to a single group over a period of time, and 'developmental trends' when we are referring to similarities over time and across groups. While there is little conflicting evidence with regard to group development, there is a great deal with regard to developmental trends.

There are a number of studies of group development and while many are anecdotal some notably those of Barron and Krules (1948), Stock and Ben-Zeev (1958), Hill (1955), and Mills (1964) employ highly reliable observational and rating techniques. Since the studies by Barron and Krulee, Hill and Stock and Ben-Zeev have been more than adequately summarized by Stock (1964), we shall only look briefly at Mills' findings before covering in

213

more detail the more recent studies expressly concerned with developmental trends.

Mills devised a rating system—Sign Process Analysis—to study the interaction of one human relations training course over the period of an academic year, some 68 sessions in all. He identified five principal periods: (1) the encounter; (2) testing boundaries and modelling roles; (3) negotiating an indigenous normative system; (4) production, and (5) separation. For each phase he identified the central issues, the predominant activity and the group properties which emerge. For example, the fourth stage, that of production, is marked by concern shown over whether or not the group can create something of lasting value, while for the member the issues are: can I communicate ideas that are both relevant and in such a form that they can be tested against reality? In the realm of activities the members apply what they know about the processes of observation, emotional expression, interpretation, formulation and testing. The emergent properties are marked by task redefinition, lowering of the level of group aspiration, and relaxation of norms governing what should or should not be expressed.

Mills adds to Tuckman's classification with his fifth stage, though his other stages could be forced, if somewhat inappropriately, into Tuckman's forming, storming, norming, and performing categories. Accounts of the terminal phase of the group are relatively rare and Mills' analysis which lays emphasis on the group as striving to convince itself that it has produced something of enduring value, serves to highlight the re-entry problem familiar to many T-group trainers.

It would seem that the evidence to support the notion of group development is clear, if largely subjective and anecdotal, whereas the evidence with regard to developmental trends is conflicting and ambiguous though for the most part largely empiric and non-anecdotal. Studies by Reisel (1959), Lakin and Carson (1964), and Lubin and Zuckerman (1967) do not unequivocally confirm the hypothesis of developmental trends, yet those by Mann (1967) and Dunphy (1968) do.

Reisel's work is interesting since not only does it span the two emphases in dealing as it does with both group development and developmental trends, but it also presents evidence which both supports and denies ideas about the latter. For Reisel the initial problem was that of finding if regularities existed in T-groups progressing through time and to describe the similarities that might be found. In order to do this he isolated three dimensions for describing phases in T-group behaviour; involvement, degree of emotionality, and satisfaction. Working from diaries kept by members of three groups over a thirty session period, Reisel rated participants on these three dimensions. Initially he pooled the data for all three groups and was able to conclude: (1) the general impact of training produces systematic patterns of reaction in its participants; (2) the greater the trainee involvement, the greater the emotional reaction (somewhat less firmly); (3) there is a strong suggestion that the greater the emotional reaction, the more the trainees experience dissatisfaction.

Moving from the macroscopic level, Reisel focused on reaction to training within groups. His major findings here were that: (1) group 1 showed cyclical behaviour on all dimensions; (2) group 2 had well-defined patterns (non-random sequences) including one cyclical pattern; (3) group 3 revealed the greatest diversity of behaviour, having sequences along the involvement and emotionality dimensions, but demonstrating a random flow of satisfaction. All Reisel could conclude is that 'each group develops an individualized personality, patterning or identity, coupled with generally meaningful regularities of development'.

Finally it was asked 'Along what, if any, of the patterned dimensions do the groups show similarity?' Early results suggested that when all individual members are studied as a unit ($N = 69$) convincing similarities emerged. However, when the groups were studied as separate entities considerable variation was noted. Reisel sought to understand this by making a comparison among all and between parts of groups in a search for possible similarities or differences. All groups seem to maintain the pattern of involvement, though only group 1 showed this significantly; to a lesser degree, satisfaction patterns tend to be the same, relatively high at the outset, swinging downwards as training progressed, and showing similar fluctuations for all groups. The major area of difference lay in the sphere of emotionality, no relationship across groups was revealed in this area.

Reisel concluded that if the study is taken in its entirety, the results provide empirical support for the theoretical views which hold that the T-group develops in a systematic rather than a haphazard fashion. Unfortunately, parts of his study indicate almost the opposite or, at very best, they can be seen as supporting the unique character of each group's emotional patterning.

Lakin and Carson (1964) also touch upon issues relevant to developmental trends in small groups. The authors investigated the extent to which participants in a sensitivity training group perceived changes in the group process. They collected data from participants in four T-groups at a two-week residential training laboratory conducted by a state mental health agency. The participants were required to provide ratings of the intensity of group concern for each of 11 variables for each of their 16 T-group meetings. Lakin and Carson discovered that there were significant variations in the ratings across the 16 meetings and that the four groups varied considerably in regard to the point at which particular variables gained and lost ascendency in the pattern of meetings. The groups differed maximally on the 'group atmosphere' variable; some groups emphasized this earlier than others by several meetings. 'Competitiveness' declined and 'cooperation' showed an increase, but none of the other variables showed a discernible trend. Like Reisel, the authors are forced to conclude that each T-group experience is more unique than it is standard.

The study by Lubin and Zuckerman (reprinted here) concludes similarly that there is low consistency of trends from one group to another, although their data supports the hypothesis of some similarity of group trends over sessions. On the other hand, both Mann (1966, 1967) and Dunphy provide studies which more firmly support hypotheses of developmental trends. Mann's (1966) study has already been reviewed in an earlier chapter, so we shall conclude this section with an examination of Dunphy's (1968) work.

His investigation was concerned specifically with two sections of a Harvard undergraduate course, 'Social Relations 120: Analysis of Interpersonal Behaviour' (these classes must be the most researched in the world: Bales, Slater, Mills, Mann, Dunphy). The primary focus of the investigation was changes as reflected in the content of weekly reports written by individual group members. Dunphy lists the advantages of this approach as being (1) reduction of verbal data to be processed, (2) enforced contribution from all, (3) study must focus on aspects of the group which members themselves regard as important. He appears to be unconcerned that these 'strengths' could also be regarded as weaknesses. In order to test for the existence, extent and nature of common phases movements, the entire text of the written reports was subjected to a computer system of content analysis called the General Inquirer (Dunphy, Stone and Smith, 1965). Dunphy predicted that:

(1) The content of the written reports from the two self-analytic groups will show similar quantitative and qualitative changes over time, i.e. common 'phase movements'.

(2) These phase movements will explain more variance in the data than will differences between the two groups.

(3) The characteristics of consecutive phase movements will reflect an emerging group unity and an increasing emotional involvement on the part of the group members.

Dunphy concludes the first part of his report by claiming developmental trends which support his hypotheses. He distinguishes an early period (phases 1–3) where relationships are largely negative and counterpersonal.

The first phase being an attempt to import external normative standards, the second and third characterized more by rivalry and aggression. The fourth phase is essentially negative but realizes a new concern for absenteeism and communications. The last two phases, on the other hand, are qualitatively different, with emotional concerns well to the fore.

Like Mann (1967) who uses sub-group formation as his explanatory device, Dunphy attempts to explain the generation and dissolution of his phases, though he uses the notion of 'role differentiation' to unlock the mystery. He concludes that groups have common role specialists and that these people serve as important reference points for members as group culture develops.

As Dunphy acknowledges we have no way of knowing how representative these two groups are: composition, for example, was not controlled; at its most basic level, age and sex could also influence developmental trends.

Nonetheless, the Mann and Dunphy studies represent a step in the right direction in that they not only seek to discover trends, but also to account for them in terms of the role behaviour of individuals or sub-groups.

Conclusion

The identification of predictable phases or sequences may be of importance to trainers but the very individual measures utilized often make it difficult to generalize from the findings. A great deal more work needs to be done in this area before results can be fully utilized in designing or monitoring training activities.

References

Barron, M. and G. K. Krulee (1948) 'Case study of a basic skill training group.' *Journal of Social Issues*, 4.

Bion, W. R. (1961) *Experiences in Groups*. London: Tavistock.

Dunphy, D. (1968) 'Phases, roles and myths in self-analytic groups.' *Journal of Applied Behavioral Science*, 4, 195–225.

Dunphy, D., P. Stone, M. Smith and D. Ogilvie (1965) *The General Inquirer: A Computer Approach to Content Analysis*. M.I.T. Press.

Hampden-Turner, C. M. (1966) 'An existential "learning theory" and the integration of T-group research.' *Journal of Applied Behavioral Science*, 2, 367–386.

Hill, W. F. (1955) 'The influence of subgroups on participation in human relations training groups.' Unpublished Ph.D. thesis, University of Chicago.

Lakin, M. and R. C. Carson (1964) 'Participant perception of group process group sensitivity training.' *International Journal of Group Psychotherapy*, 14, 116–122.

Lubin, B. and M. Zuckerman (1967) 'Affective and perceptual cognitive patterns in sensitivity training groups.' *Psychological Reports*, 21, 365–376.

Mann, R. D. (1966) 'The development of the member-trainer relations in self-analytic groups.' *Human Relations*, 19, 84–117.

Mann, R. D. (1967) *Interpersonal Styles and Group Development*. New York: John Wiley.

Mills, T. M. (1964) *Group Transformation*. Englewood Cliffs, New Jersey: Prentice Hall.

Reisel, J. (1959) 'A search for behavioral patterns in sensitivity training groups.' Unpublished Ph.D. thesis, University of California, Los Angeles.

Schutz, W. C. (1958) *FIRO: A Theory of Interpersonal Relations*. New York: Rinehart.

Stock, D. (1964) 'A survey of research on T-groups.' In L. P. Bradford and co-workers, *T-group Theory and Laboratory Method*. New York: John Wiley.

Stock, D. and Ben-Zeev (1958) 'Changes in work and emotionality during group growth.' In D. Stock and H. Thelen (Eds.), *Emotional Dynamics and Group Culture*. Washington, D.C.: NTL-N.E.A.

Tuckman, B. (1965) 'Development sequence in small groups.' *Psychological Bulletin*, 63.

Affective and Perceptual Cognitive Patterns in Sensitivity Training Groups*

Bernard Lubin

Indiana Department of Mental Health

Marvin Zuckerman

Albert Einstein Medical Centre

The identification of predictable phases or sequences in small groups is important for the development of theory, research, and training methodology. For the trainer, the establishment of reliable knowledge concerning group development would permit the design of more efficient training procedures and would permit him to devote more of his attention to novel group developments.

Conflicting evidence has appeared, however, concerning the occurrence of developmental trends in small groups. The work of Bales and Strodtbeck (1951) and Philip and Dunphy (1959) tends to confirm the hypothesis of developmental trends, while studies by Reisel (1959) and Lakin and Carson (1964) yielded negative evidence.

The phrase 'group development' has sometimes been used to refer to significant differences among sessions in a single group (Hill, 1955; Stock and Ben-Zeev, 1958) and significant differences among segments of a single session (Bales and Strodtbeck, 1951). For the sake of clarity, we wish to indicate that we are using the phrase 'developmental trends' to refer to predictable sequences of events which appear at similar points in time in

* Originally Published in *Psychological Reports*, 1967, 21, 365–376. © Southern University Press 1967.

We wish to express our thanks to Harry Brittain, Alice W. Lubin, and Morton Lieberman for their assistance, and our special gratitude to James A. Norton. Partial support for this investigation was provided by The Association For The Advancement of Mental Health Research and Education, Inc. and Public Health Research Grant FR 00162-02.

The training staff consisted of William Dyer, Daniel Hopson, Bernard Lubin, Alexander C. Rosen and Charles N. Seashore. Special appreciation is extended to Charles N. Seashore who facilitated the collection of data, and we are indebted to the other members of the staff for their cooperation.

various groups. In this definition, the emphasis is upon consistency or similarity of trends across groups.

This investigation attempts to extend the inquiry concerning developmental trends in small groups and to determine some of the affective and perceptual-cognitive patterns during a 1-wk. sensitivity group conference. The approach is from the perspective of the participants.

Method

Forty-five administrative level Ss participated in the conference.* They ranged in age from 32 yr. to 67 yr. (M = 47·3, SD = 7·9). The minimum educational attainment for any of the participants was 2 yr. of college work, and the mean was 3·4 yr. of college work. They were divided into four approximately equal groups in such a way as to maximize heterogeneity within each group in terms of geographical location, size of site of residence, age, and education.

The Multiple Affect Adjective Check List (MAACL) was administered to Ss 1 hr. prior to the beginning of the conference and at the end of each of eight training group (T-group) sessions. The development and validation of the MAACL is described elsewhere (Zuckerman and Lubin, 1965). It is an experimentally validated self-administering adjective check list consisting of 132 items from which three scores are derived: Anxiety, Depression, and Hostility.

At the end of each of eight T-group sessions, in addition to the MAACL, participants completed the following nine-point scale-questions. (Only the extreme cues are presented.)

		1	9
Q1.	I felt that this session was	Not worthwhile	Very worthwhile
Q2.	In regard to my participation in this session I was	Very inactive	Very active
Q3.	In this session, there was	Very little open sharing of feelings	Much open sharing of feelings
Q4.	The level of conflict in this session was	Very low	Very high
Q5.	In this session, the discussions	Had very little relevance to issues within the group	Were very relevant to issues within the group

* The data for this study were collected in an Institute of the National Council of Juvenile Court Judges. Analyses are based upon 43 of the 45 Ss for whom complete data were available.

Results and discussion

Representatives of sample

Thirty-nine of the Ss were individually matched for age, education, and sex with counterparts from the normative sample of the MAACL (Zuckerman and Lubin, 1965). The t tests between pre-conference Anxiety and Depression scores and those of matched normals were not significant, indicating that participants in this conference can be considered to have been drawn from the general population in reference to these two variables. The t test for Hostility was significantly lower than that for the normative sample ($t = 2 \cdot 4$, $p < 0 \cdot 05$). The non-significant t tests for Anxiety and Depression and the significant t test for Hostility, with a higher mean in the normative sample, support the hypothesis that conference participants were not more 'emotional' than the general population.

Emotional involvement in the conference

Each S's pre-conference scores were contrasted with the mean of his scores for eight sessions on Anxiety, Depression, and Hostility. The paired-observation t tests were significant at the $0 \cdot 01$ level for Anxiety, Depression, and Hostility, with conference means higher than pre-conference scores on the three variables, thus demonstrating 'emotional involvement' in the conference.

Analyses of group, session, and interaction effects

Although an attempt was made to maximize the heterogeneity of Ss when groups were initially composed, the analyses of variance indicated that the four groups differed significantly on the three affect variables at the pre-conference testing. Therefore, analysis of covariance was used in order to test for between-group differences during training sessions with difference in pre-conference of first-session scores partialled out. For the five-scale questions, first-session scores were employed as the covariate, with the sum of scores of the remaining seven sessions used as the dependent variables. For the three affect variables (Anxiety, Depression, and Hostility), pre-conference scores were used as the covariate, with the sum of scores for the remaining eight sessions as the dependent variables. No covariance adjustment was necessary, however, in the tests for session differences and group by session interactions since these are both 'within-subjects' effects (Winer, 1962, p. 607).

Group differences

The results of the analyses of covariance for between-group differences averaged over sessions are presented in Table 1. It is obvious that group differences are significant for four of the eight variables even after the initial group differences were controlled. Thus, we can say that groups differed significantly in their experience of Anxiety, Hostility, feeling that sessions were worthwhile (Q1), and perception of the level of activity (Q2). Groups did not differ significantly in terms of the perceived degree of openness and sharing of feelings (Q3), perceived level of conflict within the group (Q4), relevance of discussions to issues within the group (Q5), and Depression.

Session differences

Table 2 presents the summary of the analyses of variance for session differences for the four groups on the eight variables. Session differences were significant for all eight variables.

Analyses of trends

Table 2 also reveals that session by group interactions were significant for six of the eight variables. These interactions can be seen in Fig. 1 which presents the session by session changes for the four groups on the eight variables. In the case of the three affect variables, pre-conference means are included. In each case, the session by group interaction tests whether the trends over sessions for the four groups depart significantly from parallelism with one another. It is this level of analysis which tests for similarity of developmental trends among groups.

*Q*1. (*Worthwhileness of session*)—The session by group interaction is significant. Inspection of the figure shows that this is probably due to group 3's having a large drop at Session 3 and Group 1 remaining high at Sessions 7 and 8 while the other three groups drop.

*Q*2. (*Degree of activity during session*)—The session by group interaction is not significant at the 0·05 level. This is interpreted to mean that the four trends do not depart significantly from parallel with one another. However, Group 1 rises from Session 6 to Sessions 7 and 8 while the other three groups fall, as in the case of Q1.

*Q*3. (*Degree of open sharing of feelings*)—The interaction is significant at the 0·05 level. It appears largely due to the changes from Sessions 4 to 5 to 6 of Groups 1 and 4 as contrasted with Groups 2 and 3. Again, the curve of Group 1 rises after Session 6 while the other three groups fall. This is a consistent pattern for Group 1 on Q1, Q2, and Q3.

Table 1—*Tests of adjusted between group differences averaged over sessions: analyses of covariance*

Variable		Groups	Ss within groups
Q1	d.f.	3	38
	MS[a]	298·7424	45·3005
	F	6·5947	
	p	$0·001 < p < 0·005$	
Q2	d.f.	3	38
	MS	165·7421	40·7146
	F	4·0708	
	p	$0·01 < p < 0·025$	
Q3	d.f.	3	38
	MS	139·5003	54·0234
	F	2·5822	
	p	$0·05 < p < 0·10$	
Q4	d.f.	3	38
	MS	223·0556	84·8387
	F	2·6292	
	p	$0·05 < p < 0·10$	
Q5	d.f.	3	38
	MS	63·5849	64·1351
	F	0·9914	
	p	$0·25 < p < 0·50$	
Anxiety	d.f.	3	38
	MS	472·8767	142·4472
	F	3·3197	
	p	$0·025 < p < 0·05$	
Depression	d.f.	3	38
	MS	863·0939	346·2423
	F	2·4927	
	p	$0·05 < p < 0·10$	
Hostility	d.f.	3	38
	MS	1686·1319	183·3310
	F	9·1972	
	p	$< 0·0005$	

[a] All Mean Squares shown are adjusted for the appropriate covariate in each case. Please see text.

Q4. (Level of conflict)—The interaction is significant. This appears to be primarily due to the contrast between the changes of Groups 1 and 3 from Sessions 3 to 4 and the change of Group 3 as contrasted with all other groups from Sessions 7 to 8.

Q5. (Relevance of discussion to issues within the group)—The interaction is significant and the trend comparison resemble those for Q1.

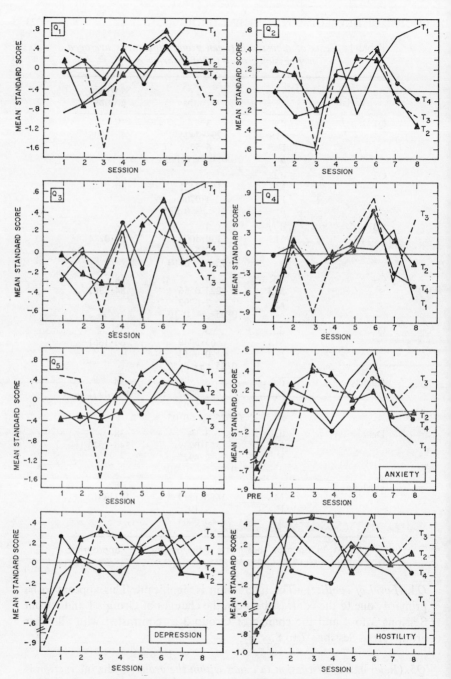

Fig. 1. Session-by-session changes on the eight dependent variables for each of the four T-groups. Please see text for definition of the variables. Points plotted are means of standard scores, with **SD** obtained from the pooled estimate of variance of all sessions.

Anxiety—The interaction is significant at the 0·05 level. Groups 2 and 3 appear to show similar trends and so do Groups 1 and 4 but the latter two differ markedly from the first two, especially at Sessions 3 and 4.

Depression—The interaction is not significant.

Hostility—The interaction is significant, and trend comparisons are very similar to those for Anxiety, except that Group 1 does not show the peak at Session 6.

Table 2—*Analyses of variance for session differences*

Variable		Sessions	Session × group	Session × subjects within groups
Q1	d.f.	7	21	273
	MS	22·497	9·204	2·155
	F	10·439	4·271	
	p	$<0·0005$	$<0·0005$	
Q2	d.f.	7	21	273
	MS	8·159	3·789	2·481
	F	3·289	1·527	
	p	$0·001<p<0·005$	$0·05<p<0·10$	
Q3	d.f.	7	21	273
	MS	7·056	4·002	2·209
	F	3·194	1·812	
	p	$0·001<p<0·005$	$0·01<p<0·025$	
Q4	d.f.	7	21	273
	MS	23·171	8·059	2·871
	F	8·071	2·807	
	p	$<0·0005$	$<0·0005$	
Q5	d.f.	7	21	273
	MS	18·983	7·939	2·351
	F	8·074	3·377	
	p	$<0·0005$	$<0·0005$	
Anxiety	d.f.	8	24	312
	MS	25·689	4·474	2·863
	F	8·973	1·563	
	p	$<0·0005$	$0·025<p<0·05$	
Depression	d.f.	8	24	312
	MS	101·200	11·072	8·476
	F	11·940	1·306	
	p	$<0·0005$	$0·10<p<0·25$	
Hostility	d.f.	8	24	312
	MS	45·285	10·526	3·860
	F	11·732	2·727	
	p	$<0·0005$	$<0·0005$	

Recapitulation

Groups differed significantly on four of the eight variables, significant session effects were found on all eight variables, and significant interactions were found on six of the eight variables. For the two variables for which the interaction was not significant, in the case of Q2 the F ratio fell between the 5 and 10 per cent significance levels and the pattern in Fig. 1 appears similar to those of Q1, Q3, and Q5. In the case of Depression the F ratio falls between the 10 and 25 per cent levels of significance and the

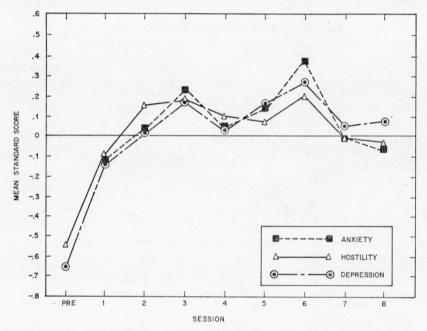

Fig. 2. Session-by-session on the three affect variables. Composite of the three T-groups. Points plotted are means of standard scores, with standard variation pooled over all sessions.

pattern appears similar to that on Anxiety. Thus the evidence indicates significant differences among sessions, implying some degree of similarity of group trends over sessions, but no consistent trends common to all groups. These findings confirm those of Reisel (1959) and Lakin and Carson (1964).

Despite the findings that groups differ significantly on four of the eight dependent variables, it seems to be instructive to present the composite trends for the four groups on all eight variables. These are presented in Figs. 2 and 3. Peaking seems to occur definitely at Session 6 for all variables.

No generalizable significance is attributed to Session 6 as such, as there is considerable variation in the number.

To the extent that participants feel that sessions are worthwhile, they report less anxiety, depression, and hostility. The relationship is certainly more complex than this statement alone would indicate. In this connection, the following additional findings should be considered.

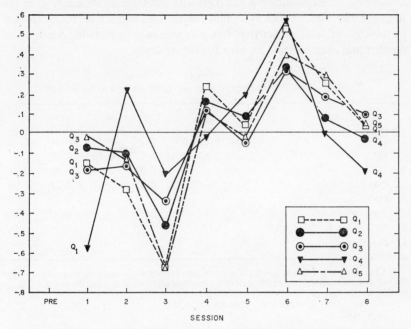

Fig. 3. Session-by-session changes on the five perceptual cognitive variables: composite of the four T-groups. Points plotted are means of standard scores, with standard deviation obtained from the pooled estimate of variance over all sessions.

There is a significant negative relationship between the effect variables and the degree to which feelings are openly shared in the group. As feelings are shared more openly, participants report experiencing less anxiety, depression, and hostility. These findings support a basic tenet of small group training philosophy that the open sharing of feelings tends to have a releasing effect upon group process and the behaviour of individual Ss.

By means of theory sessions, written materials, and the modelling behaviour of trainers, sensitivity training conferences stress the importance of keeping discussions focused upon interactions and processes that occur within the group. It is interesting to find that there is a significant negative relationship between Q5 (Relevance of discussions to issues within the group) and the affect variables. Overall, as discussions focus more upon issues within the group, Ss report experiencing less disturbing affect.

Although it is hazardous to rest any interpretation on non-significant correlations, it is worth noting that the correlations between level of activity (Q2) and level of conflict (Q4) with the three affect scales go in the negative direction, though to a small degree. This might have been expected in the case of level of activity, but it is somewhat surprising for level of conflict and may indicate an area for future study.

Table 3—*Intercorrelations among the eight dependent variables[a]*

Variable[b]	1	2	3	4	5	6	7	8
1. Q1		$0·58^c$	$0·85^c$	$0·42^c$	$0·76^c$	$-0·46^c$	$-0·44^c$	$-0·41^c$
2. Q2			$0·65^c$	$0·48^c$	$0·67^c$	$-0·12$	$-0·06$	$-0·11$
3. Q3				$0·47^c$	$0·82^c$	$-0·45$	$-0·40$	$-0·44^c$
4. Q4					$0·41^c$	$-0·21$	$-0·22$	$-0·08$
5. Q5						$-0·43^c$	$-0·41^c$	$-0·39^c$
6. Anxiety							$0·92^c$	$0·86^c$
7. Depression								$0·81^c$
8. Hostility								

[a] Correlations are based upon the sum of scores over eight sessions in the case of the five-scale-questions and upon the sum of scores over eight sessions plus the pre-conference testing in the case of the three effect variables.
[b] For definition of variables, please see page 220.
[c] $p = 0·01$.

A more parsimonious interpretation of the correlation matrix results if we observe that the correlations cluster into two groups: (1) the affect variables (Anxiety, Depression, and Hostility) and (2) the perceptual–cognitive variables (Q1, 2, 3, 4 and 5). Of the latter, the three that seem most directly related to satisfaction with group sessions (Q1, 3 and 5) have a relationship to the affect cluster.

The high intercorrelations among the affect variables (Anxiety, Depression, and Hostility) and among the perceptual–cognitive variables, respectively, reflect the common variance within each of these sets of measures. The intercorrelations among the scales of the MAACL are reported in Zuckerman and Lubin (1965), and the common variance among scale-questions of the type employed in this investigation has been reported by Blake, Mouton and Fruchter (in press).

Overview and implications

The statements by Bennis and Shepard (1956) and Bion (1961) which discussed the phasic development of small groups were heuristic in nature and were intended to stimulate research and further theory development. Such statements necessarily present the case in broad terms and under ideal conditions, and they usually leave unspecified such crucial variables as trainer behaviour, group composition, intercurrent events in the group, specific elements of the training design, etc.

In order to understand the empirical evidence concerning developmental trends in small groups, it is necessary to consider the nature of the groups employed in the investigations and the methods by which observations have been made.

In both the studies by Bales and Strodtbeck (1951) and Philip and Dunphy (1959) in which confirmatory evidence for developmental trends were found, the parameters of authority and group goal were clearly defined. Authority was represented by the experimenter who selected as, assigned them to groups, and specified the nature of the task. In addition, time pressure for group decision was imposed. Non-participant observers coded behavioural acts according to a classification scheme devised for problem-solving groups. Observed behaviour was recorded as it occurred during the group sessions.

In this investigation and in the ones by Lakin and Carson (1964) and by Reisel (1959), T-groups rather than problem-solving groups were employed. In T-groups, authority is a complex concept and the trainer's role usually remains ambiguous well into the life of the group. Although the training conference has definite objectives, e.g., learning about oneself in interaction with others, learning about the functioning of groups and organizations, no goal or specific task under time pressure is assigned to the group. The problem for the group in each session is to discover, out of the many interests and needs of participants, those which are salient in each session and to devise the most effective means for moving towards these goals. In the report by Lakin and Carson (1964) and in this investigation, rating scales and checklists were completed by participants at the end of each session concerning their perceptions and feelings about group process. Participants in Reisel's study (1959) noted their impressions in diaries from which quantitative indices were later derived by means of content analyses.

Due to the important differences between this study and the ones by Bales and Strodtbeck (1951) and Philip and Dunphy (1959), the present investigation should not be considered to be a test of Bales hypotheses.

Another potentially meaningful area for research, which was touched upon in this investigation, concerns the phenomenology of the participant in small group training (Lakin and Carson, 1964; Weschler and Reisel, 1959). We found that participants experience less negative affect in those sessions: which they feel worthwhile, wherein there is more open sharing of feelings and wherein discussions are more relevant to issues within the group. There is some suggestion also that participants experience less negative affect in those sessions in which they have been more active and in which there has been conflict within the group. The last statement refers to the possibility that confrontation and conflict, within the levels occurring in training groups, may be experienced by participants as stimulating rather than disturbing. Indirect support for this finding is provided by Harrison (1965), who reports more learning in groups composed so that heterogeneity of member characteristics is maximized. If it is assumed that heterogeneity may increase the probability of conflict, then heterogeneity seems to be associated with less negative effect.

The key role played by emotional factors in the process of attitudinal and behavioural change has been recognized (Bull, 1951; Rosenberg et al., 1960) and the vividness of the emotional component of the T-group experience is indicated by the many informal staff and participant references to the subject. However, there are only a few references in the training literature to the subject of affect, mood, or emotion.

Further investigations of developmental trends in training groups should include both observations made by non-participant observers and systematic reports of perceptions and feelings by participants about group process. The former should be derived from appropriate theory about small group training and the latter should involve comparable variables. Discrepancies between objective and subjective observations then might open additional areas for research. In such studies, trainer behaviour and group composition should be controlled, as these factors are important determiners of group process (Stock, 1964; Harrison and Lubin, 1965).

References

Bales, R. F. and F. L. Strodtbeck (1951) 'Phases in group problem solving.' *J. Abnorm. soc. Psychol.*, **46**, 485–495.

Bennis, W. G. and H. A. Shepard (1956) 'A theory of group development.' *Hum. Rel.*, **9**, 415–457.

Bion, W. E. (1961) *Experiences in Groups*. New York: Basic Books.

Blake, B. R., J. S. Mouton and B. Frutcher (1970) A factor analysis of training group behaviour. *J. soc. Psychol.*, in press.

Bull, N. (1951) 'The attitude theory of emotion.' New York: Coolidge Foundation (*Nerv. ment. Dis. Monogr.*, No. 81).

Harrison, R. L. (1965) 'Group composition models for laboratory design.' *J. appl. behav. Sci.*, **1**, 409–432.

Harrison, R. L. and B. Lubin (1965) 'Personal style, group composition, and learning.' *J. Appl. behav. Sci.*, **1**, 286–301.

Hill, W. G. (1955) 'The influence of subgroups on participation in human relations training groups.' Unpublished doctoral dissertation, Univ. of Chicago.

Laking, M. and R. C. Carson (1964) 'Participant perception of group process in group sensitivity training.' *Int. J. Gp. Psychother.*, **14**, 116–122.

Philip, H. and D. Dunphy (1959) 'Developmental trends in small groups.' *Sociometry*, **22**, 162–174.

Reisel, J. (1959a) 'A search for behaviour patterns in sensitivity training groups.' Unpublished dissertation, Univer. of California, Los Angeles.

Reisel, J. (1959b) 'The trainer role in human relations training.' Paper presented at meetings of the Western Psychological Association, San Diego, Calif., April.

Rosenberg, M. J., C. I. Hovland, W. J. McGuire, R. P. Abelson and J. W. Brehm (1960) 'Attitude organisation and change: an analysis of consistency among attitude components.' Yale studies in attitude and communication. Vol. III. New Haven, Conn.: Yale Univer. Press.

Stock, D. (1964) 'A survey of research on T-groups.' In L. P. Bradford, J. R. Gibb and K. D. Benne (Eds.), *T-group Theory and Laboratory Method: Innovation in Re-education*. New York: John Wiley. Pp. 395–441.

Stock, D. and S. Ben-Zeev (1958) 'Changes in work and emotionality during group growth.' In D. Stock and H. A. Theler (Eds.), *Emotional Dynamics and Group Culture*. New York: New York Univer. Press. Pp. 192–206.

Weschler, I. R. and J. Reisel (1959) 'Inside a sensitivity training group.' Los Angeles: Institute of Industrial Relations, Univer. of Calif. (Indus. Relat. Monogr. No. 4.)

Winer, B. J. (1962) *Statistical Principles in Experimental Design*. New York: McGraw-Hill.

Zuckerman, M. and B. Lubin (1965) 'Multiple affect adjective checklists manual.' San Diego: Educational and Industrial Testing Service.

The Development of the Member–Trainer Relationship in Self-Analytic Groups*

Richard D. Mann

Harvard University

The goal of this paper is to bring together and build upon two traditions in the study of small groups: (1) the clinical study of long-term, self-analytic groups, such as therapy, training, and class room discussion groups; and (2) the systematic observation of group interaction by means of act-by-act scoring of individual behaviour. The nature and development of the relationship between the members of self-analytic groups and the group's therapist, trainer, or instructor constitute the particular focus of this study.

The primary impetus for this work was a dilemma often expressed by those students of group phenomena, the present author included, who function both as researchers and as clinicians, as scholars and as trainers. We may sense a painful discrepancy between what we are equipped to study with acceptable precision as researchers and what we find either in the clinical work of such men as Bion (1961), Bach (1954), and Frank *et al.* (1952) or in our own experiences in training groups. The clinical and theoretical literature abounds with insights, subtleties, and depth which are seldom mirrored in our research operations. Thus, one side of the dilemma is that the researcher yearns to pursue the intricate but suggestive propositions found in a body of literature developed largely outside the traditional modes of research in social science.

The other side of the dilemmas derives from the experience of the clinician or trainer, often the same person as the researcher, but operating

* This work has been supported by grants from the National Institute of Mental Health and the Social Science Research Council. The I.B.M. costs were defrayed in part by a grant to the Harvard Computing Center by the National Science Foundation, and the programming was skilfully executed by William Jonghin. My colleagues and fellow trainers have offered many useful suggestions in the course of this study, and I wish to express my appreciation to Robert F. Bales, Maxine Bernstein, Dexter Dunphy, Theodore Mills, David Shapiro, Philip Slater, Charles Whitlock, and Norman Zinberg.

Originally published in *Human Relations*, 1966, **19**, pp. 84–117; this article is an abbreviated form of what can be found in Mann's book *Interpersonal Styles and Group Development*, John Wiley, 1967.

in another domain of his life. Somehow, in that domain things may not seem as clear. The vivid details of a particular group obscure one's view of the enduring truths. Events stream by, memory fails us, and we may imagine that the researcher could assist us in capturing or codifying the experience. Perhaps even more acute may be the sense that our residual impressions derive from only the most dramatic moments or unforgettable group members. Even beyond the kind of documentation that researchers can provide, the clinician may search for additional means of developing and testing explanatory propositions which will make the concrete experiences more sensible to himself and to others. The present study represents one response to this dilemma.

A number of writers (Bach, 1954; Bennis and Shepard, 1956; Coffey *et al.*, 1950; Kaplan and Roman, 1964; Mann, 1953; Mills, 1964; Psathas, 1960; Thelen and Dickerman, 1949) have attempted to outline the development of self-analytic groups by describing the group processes and members' feelings active at various points in time. They suggest several regularities in group development across a variety of groups. There is wide agreement that the issue of dependency upon the trainer is particularly important at the beginning of the group, and some authors also note an initial anxiety and/or resistance aroused by the new situation. Some of the developmental models imply that a crisis point in the member–trainer relationship is likely to be activated by a mounting frustration experienced by group members (Thelen, 1950) and by a wave of hostile and counter-dependent feelings (Bach, 1954; Bennis and Shepard, 1956; Mills, 1964). The period following this crisis is variously described, but many authors point to a work phase, in which the earlier preoccupation with member-trainer relationship is eclipsed by 'group-centered' activity and the ascendant issues of intimacy among members. Whereas some authors' descriptions seem to imply that the group ends during the phase of work, integration, or mutual synthesis, Mills (1964) extends his group development scheme to include a stage of separation. One issue to be raised in the present study is whether the member–trainer relationship, often described as salient for the group only in the early stages, develops meaningfully over the entire life of the group.

In recent years there have been a number of attempts to reduce much, if not all, social interaction to a limited set of underlying factors or dimensions. Schutz's (1958) postulation of three basic needs, which he labels inclusion, control, and affection, is reflected both in Bennis's (1957) scheme of oral, anal, and phallic stages in group life and in Kaplan and Roman's (1963) examination of dependency, power, and intimacy themes. Several factor-analytic studies of individual differences in group behaviour (Borgatta *et al.*, 1958; Carter, 1954; Couch, 1960; Mann, 1961) have isolated factors whose content is highly congruent with Schutz's three-dimensional model. The inclusion, control, and affection issues and their effect upon the member–trainer relationship serve as useful points of departure in this study.

Throughout the discussions in the literature (Bach, 1954; Bennis and Shepard, 1956; Bion, 1961; Coffey *et al.*, 1950; Ezriel, 1952; Foulkes and Anthony, 1957), the content and intensity of a group member's feelings toward the trainer are often seen as being at least partially determined by the transference of old relations and modes of relating to authority figures onto the new situation. As a result, many clinical interpretations of the member–trainer relationship have been cast in the rich and evocative imagery of the family scene.

Not only do a member's earlier experiences influence the member–trainer relationship, but this relationship, endowed as it may be with a number of over-determined or parataxic qualities, contributes to the quality of the ties between a group member and all other aspects of group life. The writings of Bion (1961) and Ezriel (1952) emphasize the ways in which a group member may both express and disguise his feelings toward the trainer through his dealings with other group members or through his comments on events and persons external to the group. These processes, including the mechanisms of displacement and projection, are demonstrated well in the studies of Bennis (1961), Mills (1964), Slater (1961a), and Thelen (1950).

One deficiency in the work on member–trainer relations to date is the absence of adequate interweaving between the clinical observations and theoretical formulations, on the one hand, and a set of observation techniques and results on the other. One approach might be to rely on retrospective reports and ratings by group members, as in the work of Stock and Thelen (1958) or Wechsler and Reisel (1959). A second approach, the analysis of transcripts and tape recordings, offers several advantages since the behaviour under study is closer in time to the arousal situation, more likely to be unguarded, spontaneous, and even inconsistent in revealing ways. More importantly, the member's overt behaviour in the group can be expressive in so many indirect and disguised ways that the observer has more opportunity to recognize the complexity of a member's feelings.

The observation schemes that have been applied to the study of self-analytic groups, Bales's (1950) interaction process analysis and Mills's (1964) sign process analysis, seem quite removed from the dynamic processes and feelings which clinicians tend to describe or perceive. The empirical studies of Mills (1964), Psathas (1960), and Talland (1955) suggest both the potential gains and the inherent limitations of these scoring systems. Interaction process analysis, with its partial emphasis on task categories such as giving opinion and giving orientation, was not designed to assess individual motives or feelings, but to record the effects of behaviour on the small group as a social system. Sign process analysis examines the application of culturally, or subculturally, shared standards of valuation to a set of objects, within and beyond the interacting group. Although Mills's use of his data to illuminate the developmental process in a self-analytic group is highly relevant to this study, his technique is asking questions of quite a different nature than those embedded in the present inquiry. In short, these more sociological observation systems should be supplemented by a scoring system more congruent with the psychological study of individual dynamics.

In contrast to previous work, this study attempts: (1) to examine the member–trainer relationship throughout the entire development of the group; and (2) to carry out this examination by means of act-by-act observations of members' feelings, using concepts which have been employed profitably in the clinical and theoretical literature. The remaining sections of this paper present the scoring system developed for this purpose, the data for two self-analytic groups, a developmental scheme for analyzing the member–trainer relationship, and a discussion of the two groups under study.

The member-to-trainer scoring system

The member-to-trainer scoring system is designed to assess and record the implications of each act initiated by a group member for the state of his feelings toward the trainer. Although any act may also have meaning for the member's relations with other group members or express his feelings toward objects outside the group, in this scheme only those meanings of the act which are relevant for the member–trainer relationship are scored. Essentially, the question asked is: 'If this act is expressive of, or, more conservatively, congruent with, the member's feelings toward the trainer, what is the best estimate of what those feelings might be?'

The problem of inference

The kinds of data from which the scorer infers that an act is relevant to the trainer vary considerably, from the most direct and deliberate expressions of feelings toward the trainer to indirect, disguised, or inadvertent expressions of feelings. For this reason, a member's act is examined first to determine the kind of inferences which are needed to connect it with a feeling relevant to the trainer. Each act is examined with respect to a series of possibilities:

1. Does the act express the member's feelings toward, or in relation to the trainer $(-T)$? If no such expression is inferred, the act is not scored.

2. If the act is expressive of the member's feelings toward the trainer $(-T)$, are these feelings expressed directly to the trainer or with explicit reference to him $(-T)$, or are they expressed indirectly, symbolically, or inadvertently $(-T')$?

3. If the feelings are expressed indirectly or symbolically $(-T')$, are they expressed toward some object (e.g. person, fictional character, or institution) which symbolizes the trainer for the member because of the similarity between that object and the trainer $(-T')$, or are they expressed toward some object which, for the member, is different from the trainer in some way, enabling the member to express his feelings toward the trainer by way of contrast and comparison $(-\overline{T}')$?

4. If the feelings are expressed indirectly or symbolically $(-T'$ or $-\overline{T}')$, are they expressed toward an object inside the group, such as the group as a whole or some other group member $(-T_i'$ or $-\overline{T}_i')$, or are they expressed toward an object outside the group, such as the Church, a political figure, or the Mona Lisa $(-T_o'$ or $\overline{T}_o')$?

5. If the act is expressive of the member's feelings toward the trainer $(-T$ or $-T')$, does the member identify himself as the possessor of these feelings $(M-T, M-T')$, or does he express his own feelings by attributing those feelings to someone else, such as another group member or a person outside the group $(M'-T$ or $M'-T')$?

6. If the member does not explicitly identify himself as the agent who is expressing or possessing the feelings $(M'-T$ or $M'-T')$, are the feelings expressed his own, as in the case of projected hostility or anxiety $(M'-T$ or $M'-T')$, or are the feelings different from his own and is the member attempting to differentiate himself from the other agent who is expressing the feelings $(\overline{M}'-T$ or $\overline{M}'-T')$?

This series of questions generates a set of fifteen types of scorable act, where each type represents a different kind of inference from the observed act to the inferred feelings. For our purpose in scoring, the fifteen types were collapsed into a set of four levels:

Level One: Acts which make direct reference to the trainer and in which the member either expresses the feelings as his own or attempts to differentiate himself from some other agent $(M-T$ and $\overline{M}'-T)$.

Level Two: Acts which express feelings toward objects inside the group and in which the member either expresses the feelings as his own or attempts to differentiate himself from some other agent ($M-T_i'$, $M-\overline{T}_i'$, $M'-\overline{T}_i'$, $\overline{M}'-T_i'$, and $\overline{M}'-\overline{T}_i'$).

Level Three: Acts which express feelings toward objects outside the group and in which the member either expresses the feelings as his own or attempts to differentiate himself from some other agent ($M-T_o'$, $M-\overline{T}_o'$, $M'-\overline{T}_o'$, $\overline{M}'-T_o'$, and $\overline{M}'-\overline{T}_o'$).

Level Four: Acts which express feelings toward the trainer or some symbolic equivalent for the trainer by attributing similar feelings to another agent ($M'-T$, $M'-T_i'$, and $M'-T_o'$).

The first task, then, in scoring an act is to determine what, if any, links exist (a) between the member and the agent to whom the feelings are attributed and (b) between the trainer and the object toward which or in relation to which the feelings are expressed. The process of setting up such equations, except in the case of direct $M-T$ acts, is a complex one. Certainly key phrases or modifying adjectives may indicate that the member has made a symbolic equation between an object and the trainer, the surrounding context may illuminate the meaning of a displaced feeling, or the tone of voice may indicate whether the member is identifying with or differentiating himself from the agent to whom the feelings are attributed. For example, if member A attacks member B for being too secretive, it may be that member A resents the trainer for withholding his feelings from the group, but not necessarily. In its context, the attack may represent an attempt, by contrast, to reward the trainer for a recent expression of feelings, or it may be an attempt by member A to bid for the trainer's approval by demonstrating that he is open and frank even if member B is not. In the ordinary flow of human interaction the set of equations which connect the manifest content of an act with its meanings and implications for the set of here-and-now relationships is seldom fully explicit. The scorer's task is to reconstruct a plausible and predictive set of such equations. It sometimes happens in training groups that the member reveals what he feels his equations are or have been, and sometimes the trainer or other members seek to clarify what the member has meant. But most of the time the scorer is left to figure it out on the basis of fragmentary evidence.

The problem of categorizing

Once the issue of whether an act is expressive of a member's feelings toward the trainer is settled, and the inferences necessary to make the connection are determined, the next problem is how best to conceptualize, describe, and record the feeling expressed. The member-to-trainer scoring system examines three main areas of a member's feelings: impulse, authority relations, and ego state. Within the impulse area, which is subdivided into hostility and affection, are eight categories which describe the state of the member's aggressive and libidinal ties with the trainer at the moment of the act being scored. Within the authority-relations area are three categories which describe those feelings relevant to the power and dependency issues between a member and the trainer. Within the ego-state area are five categories describing the member's feelings toward himself in the context of the relationship with the trainer. The three areas are not mutually exclusive, and they may be viewed as three separate scoring systems applied to a single act.

The particular set of sixteen categories chosen owes much to the prior work of Bales (1950), especially for distinctions made within the impulse area, to Bennis and Shepard (1956), for distinctions drawn within the authority-relations area, and to Bibring (1953), for his differentiation of the various ego states. In addition, Melanie Klein's (1957) concept of reparation was helpful in untangling the important modes of expressing affection. A description of each category is presented below, with a set of the most frequent examples and its theoretical rationale.

Member-to-trainer categories

Impulse area

Hostility

1. Moving Against—expressing dislike, mistrust, or anger; attacking, rejecting, ridiculing, insulting. The focus in this category is the expression of hostile feelings against the trainer as a person rather than against the trainer's contributions or surface behaviour. The target of hostility tends to be the trainer's motives, personality, or general competence.

2. Resisting—disagreeing, arguing, blocking or parrying the trainer's suggestions or interpretations. The hostility falling in this category is responsive or reactive, either to an actual initiation by the trainer or to the implicit pressures of the whole training situation. The target of this relatively impersonal hostility tends to be the role performance of the trainer or 'the whole system' which the trainer is seen as representing.

3. Withdrawing—ignoring the trainer, leaving the room or engaging in 'out-of-field' behaviour; expressing boredom, lack of involvement, or indifference. The hostility expressed through withdrawing is more passive and indirect than in the other three hostility categories. In this category are

9

found the various ways in which the member–trainer relationship is broken, or its importance denied.

4. Guilt-inducing—blaming, complaining, accusing, feelings misunderstood or abused, shaming. The crucial element that differentiates this category from the preceding three is the addition of a moral context for the hostility. By invoking a presumably shared value and comparing the trainer's behaviour unfavourably to it, the member is expressing a kind of moral indignation through which he allies himself with a set of superordinate values against the trainer.

Affection

5. Making Reparation—forgiving, apologizing, denying hostility, blaming self rather than trainer, 'making up' for prior hostility of self or other. This category attempts to capture those expressions of affection which depend on their proximity to hostility for their full meaning. Making Reparation may precede a hostile remark, as if to neutralize the hostility before the fact, or it may follow hostility, of any kind, as if to undo and atone for the damage.

6. Identifying—playing the trainer's role in relation to another group member, copying the trainer, incorporating the trainer's ideas as one's own, expressing a wish to be like the trainer. A member's positive feelings toward the trainer, or the degree to which he accepts what the trainer has said, may be expressed through the member's dealings with other group members. The inference made from the manifest content of such acts is that the member is attempting to differentiate himself from some other group member who, he implies, is not sufficiently identified with or accepting of the trainer.

7. Accepting—agreeing, yielding, conforming, expressing satisfaction with the trainer's role performance. The relatively impersonal affection recorded in this category is responsive or reactive to the trainer's role performance.

8. Moving Toward—expressing liking, trust or warmth; caring, admiring, praising. This category focuses on the expression of affection in personal terms, with a clear implication that the relationship is important and meaningful to the member.

Authority-relations area

9. Showing Dependency—expressing a need for approval, direction, structure, or control; attempting to please the trainer. The expression of dependency needs in the member–trainer relationship tends to imply: (a) that the member feels less sure of what to do, less able to carry out what he

wishes to do, or less confident that what he is doing or has done is satisfactory than he would like to feel; and (b) that the member expects or hopes that the trainer can provide the necessary direction, assistance, or approval. This expectation is often based on the member's belief in an enduring power structure within which the trainer's role is to provide support and control when needed. While this conception of the trainer's role may facilitate the expression of dependency, acts may be scored in this category which rest on far more limited notions of the trainer's power and responsibility.

10. Showing Independence—relating to the trainer as a peer, stating one's own standards and/or judging one's own behaviour by them, emphasizing the mutuality of giving and receiving in the member–trainer relationship, deciding on action on one's own grounds. Bennis and Shepard (1956) stress the importance of unconflicted or non-compulsive orientation toward the trainer in independent group members. In the act-by-act analysis of feelings, such a conception is mirrored best by evidence that the member feels able to accept or reject the trainer and his contributions without reference to an implicit power structure which must be created, maintained, or destroyed. In addition, acts of independence express a member's capacity to act and/or reflect on his own behaviour using his own set of standards without making sure that they are the same as, or different from, the trainer's standards.

11. Showing Counter-dependence—asserting a lack of need for direction, assistance, or support from the trainer; opposing trainer's power, rebelling against rules or norms, ridiculing dependency in others. This category is scored only when opposition to the trainer appears to be based on an assumption that the trainer is or intends to be more powerful than the group members. It represents a response from within an authority structure and can be understood best as an aversion to being in a weak, needy, or constricted position.

Ego-state area

Anxiety (*categories 12 and 13*)

12. Expressing Anxiety—showing embarrassment, tension, or uncertainty; feeling criticized, judged, or threatened; fearing angry or punitive response from trainer. The member's feeling of being in danger, threatened, or vulnerable may be expressed by an attempt to assess and describe either (a) in what way the trainer seems threatening or (b) the inner consequences of the threat for him.

13. Denying Anxiety—denying feeling tense, worried, or concerned about trainer; joking about what others see as threatening in trainer's

behaviour or status, covering up tension by giddy or silly behaviour, re-assuring self or others regarding trainer's intentions or evaluations. Demonstrating the simultaneous activation of both anxiety and defences against it is not a simple matter. It rests on evidence that an important component in the act is an attempt at self-reassurance through disparaging the potential danger, insisting that one is calm and not upset, or professing invulnerability in the face of apparent danger.

14. Showing Self-esteem—feeling satisfied with self, capable of being open and honest, proud, at ease, 'headed in the right direction'. Many of the acts scored in this category could, in other contexts, be seen as denials of either anxiety or depression. The crucial differentiating features are that acts of self-esteem are not primarily reactions to increasingly uncomfortable ego states, but rather are primarily expressive of what Bibring (1953) calls 'the secure and self-assured ego'.

Depression

15. Expressing Depression—feeling guilty, sad, helpless, powerless; expressing a sense of being worthless or a sense of 'sliding downhill'. Acts scored in this category reflect the member's state of lowered self-esteem and lowered sense of potency in the context of the member–trainer relationship.

16. Denying Depression—resisting an implied criticism, bragging and asserting own potency, showing elation following another member's expression of sadness, refusing to see any power differentiation between members and trainer, blaming trainer rather than self, showing manic denial of implied guilt or responsibility for having harmed others. Not all excitement or exhilaration is scored as denying depression: the fundamental question involves the antecedents and context of the act. This category focuses upon the attempt to restore self-esteem and decrease depression through the mechanisms of denial, suppression, and reaction formation.

Several scoring conventions might be mentioned here. The scoring unit, or act, is defined as an uninterrupted set of phrases or sentences within which one scoring is possible. If the feelings expressed change within one speech, a new act is scored; if the member is interrupted by another member or the trainer, his next initiation is scored as a new act, even if it is scored identically with his previous act. An act may be multiple-scored, except that only one category may be scored within any sub-area (i.e. hostility, affection, authority relations, anxiety, and depression).

The trainer's contributions to the group are scored in terms of the feelings he attributes, explicitly or implicitly, to a group member or to the group as a whole. Either by interpreting and reflecting certain feelings or by responding *as if* the members had certain feelings toward him, the trainer conveys his assessment of the member–trainer relationship. This assessment is scored into the same sixteen content categories used for the members. In addition, the scorer notes whether the trainer (i) disapproves or is critical of the feeling he perceives in the member; (ii) merely notices and calls attention to the feeling; or (iii) approves of or rewards the feeling. Though the results of this scoring of trainer behaviour will be used to compare trainers, the trainers' acts are not pooled with the members' acts under study in this paper.

Two case studies

Description of the groups

Two self-analytic groups in an academic setting were chosen for intensive study, and, while they contain many unique features, they satisfy at least the minimal criteria of generating high personal involvement and extensive examination of the group's own process.

The two groups were composed of persons enrolled in a course entitled 'Case Analysis: The Interpretation of Interpersonal Behaviour', during the 1961 and 1962 sessions of the Harvard Summer School. The groups met for sessions of fifty minutes, five times a week, for a total of thirty-two sessions.

Discussions were concerned primarily with the process and structure of the group and with the analysis of individual differences in behaviour and feelings. The groups were given human relations cases for discussion and were assigned relevant readings in individual and group psychology. Approximately two-thirds of the group discussions were focused inside the group. Grades were based on term papers due in the fourth and fifth weeks and on final examination which tested the student's ability to integrate the group experiences, the case material, and the readings.

Two or three times the number of people who could be admitted applied to each group. The twenty-five persons selected for each group were chosen partly because their application showed evidence of interest and partly because they permitted a heterogeneous distribution of age, sex, and background. Each group was approximately half males and half females. The ages ranged from eighteen to forty-five, with the median age around twenty-three. The 1961 group (hereafter referred to as S1) contained fewer persons who were already employed than did the 1962 group (hereafter referred to as S2). Some of the group members were taking one other course, or more rarely, two others, in summer school, but many were enrolled only in this course.

Group S2 had three non-participating observers present throughout: one male observer, one female observer (who later scored the member–trainer interaction), and one male teaching fellow who assisted in the grading of papers and examinations. The other major structural difference between the groups was that S2 regularly began with a summary of the previous session by a member assigned the task for that day.

More difficult to summarize objectively and succinctly are the differences and similarities between the two trainers. The trainer for S1 was in his late twenties and was less experienced in the trainer role than the one in S2, who was in his late thirties. Both were psychologists with research interests in small groups. Both trainers tended to be non-directive, especially at first. They tended to focus their later comments on processes in the group and to offer interpretations and raise questions for the group regarding the group situation and the feelings aroused by it.

By referring to the scoring of the trainers' interventions it is possible to compare the two trainers on their tendency to interpret or reflect members' feelings in idiosyncratic ways. The trainer in S1 initiated 7 per cent of the total number of acts for members and trainer combined, as compared with 6 per cent for the trainer in S2, a slight but statistically significant difference. No differences of substance were found in comparing the trainers' tendencies to criticize or reward members for their expressions of feelings. Roughly 70 per cent of each trainer' interventions were neutral or non-evaluative. Certain differences between the trainers were evident from the transcripts and tapes. The trainer in S1 was somewhat more volatile and likely to express impatience or irritation. The trainer in S2 was more distant in his dealings with group members. His interventions were often in the form of questions to the group as a whole, and a number of direct requests addressed to him were turned back to the group for discussion.

The trainers were quite similar in terms of the kinds of feeling they tended to notice and call attention to. The statistically significant differences are that the S1 trainer interpreted and mirrored to the group more Withdrawing, the S2 trainer more Accepting, Showing Dependency, and Denying Anxiety. All four of these differences are in line with actual differences between the groups, but there is no way of assessing from these data the circular relationship between members' feelings and the trainer's interventions, and the extent to which the trainer reflects those feelings he wishes to encourage remains an unanswered but tantalizing question.

In summary, the two groups were quite similar in setting, size, and composition. Certain routines, such as the report on the previous session, were different, but the cases, assigned reading, and general orientation of the groups were much the same. The trainers differed less in their conceptions of the trainer role than in their personal styles within the role. The range of personal feelings expressed by the S1 trainer was greater, and the psychological distance between him and the group was correspondingly less than for the S2 trainer.

Scoring procedures

Group S1 was scored from verbatim transcripts over a year after the group was run; group S2 was scored from the tape recordings as it went along, and the scoring was completed within a month of the final session. Unfortunately, the tape recordings of two sessions in each group were unusable because of failures in the recording apparatus. The first session of each group, a brief orientation meeting, was not scored. This left a total of twenty-nine scored sessions for each group.

The scorer's for group S1 were the group's trainer and a graduate research assistant who had been a member of S1 and who also served as observer and scorer for group S2 the following summer. The proportion of all acts examined by the scorers which were scored as relevant to the member–trainer relationship varied from 50 per cent in some sessions to 98 per cent in other sessions. Two studies were made of the reliability of the scoring, one comparing the results for two scorers and another comparing the results for a single scorer across a time interval of six months. In both studies there was over 85 per cent agreement on the definition of a scorable act, and agreement on the distribution of acts into the sixteen categories of the scoring system was significantly different from chance at the 0·001 level. The difference between the total number of acts for group S1 and the total number for group S2 is accounted for largely by (i) a decision not to score the often lengthy report on the previous session in S2 and (ii) the greater ease in scoring S1 from a verbatim transcript.

Results

One technique for analysing the development of the group over time is to disregard the absolute level of a category and to examine the changes within each category, noting those sessions in which the category is high or low relative to its own average level over all sessions. In this study the definition of a run was broadened to include the possibility of disregarding one session which was discrepant from the preceding and subsequent session.

Session-by-session trends

The results of this run analysis are presented in *Figs. 1* and *2*. In order to assemble the data in this form: (i) the raw frequency distribution across the sixteen categories for each session was converted into percentage form, using the total number of acts in the session as the base; (ii) the percentages in each category, over all levels, for the twenty-nine sessions scored were split at the median; and (iii) runs of high sessions or runs of low sessions were determined by noting those sets of at least three (or five out of six) consecutive sessions which were (a) at or above the median or (b) below the median. The runs of high or low sessions are indicated in the figures; the blank spaces for a category, then, indicate sessions in which the oscillation around the median was so rapid that no sustained burst of that particular feeling was evident in the group.

Within group S1, several trends emerge in this analysis. There were two major surges of hostility which occurred near the middle and end of the group. After the first few sessions, affection was high; it decreased during the first surge of hostility and then increased again until the second surge of hostility. In the authority-relations area, an initial period in which Dependency and Counter-dependency were high was followed by a period, coinciding with the first wave of hostility, in which Counter-dependency was high, and in the last half of the group Independence reached its maximum. Anxiety was high in the early sessions, and again toward the end of the group; Self-esteem was high in the middle sessions, and Depression was high in the later session.

The development of group S2 proceeded in a somewhat different fashion. Hostility was high, as in S1, toward the middle and at the end. Most of the affection, however, was concentrated in the early sessions, with the notable exception of Making Reparation which was high only at the end. The early sessions were high in all three authority-relations categories, and, as in S1, there were subsequent bursts of Counter-dependency and then Independence. Showing Dependency returned to a high level toward the end of the group. In the ego-state area, the development was from a period in which Self-esteem was at its maximum, to a period of high Anxiety, and finally to one in which Depression was high.

Analysis by phases

It is evident from the two figures describing the group development that each group moved through phases or sets of sessions within which much the same patterns of feelings were observed. As a means of estimating the boundaries of these phases, tetrachoric correlations between adjacent sessions were computed, using the data described above, i.e. the median splits on each category. The result of these computations was, for each group, a string of correlations, describing the resemblance of neighbouring

Category	Session																												
	02	03	04	05	06	07	08	09	10	11	12	13	14	16	17	19	20	21	22	23	24	25	26	27	28	29	30	31	32
Hostility																													
Moving Against	+	+	+	−	−	−	−	−	−	−	+	+	+	+	−	−	−	−	+	+	+	+	+	+	+	−	−	−	−
Resisting	−	−	−	−	−	−	−	+	−	+	+	+	+	+	+	+	+	+	+	+	+	+	+	+	+	+	+	+	+
Withdrawing				−	−	−	+	+	+	+	+	+	−	−	−	−	−	−	+	+								+	+
Guilt-inducing									+	+	+	−	−	−									+	+	+	+	+	+	+
Affection																													
Reparation			−	−	−	−	−	−	+	+	+	+	+	+		−	+	+	+	+	+	+	+		−	−	−	−	−
Identifying																	+	+	+	+	+	+	+	+	+	+	+	+	+
Accepting	−	−	+	+	+	+	−	−	+	+	−	−	−			−	+	−	−	−	−	−	−	−	−	−	−	−	−
Moving Toward			+	+	+	+	+	+	+					−	+	+	+		−										
Authority Relations																													
Dependency	+	+	+	+	+	+									+						+	+	+	+	+	+	+	+	+
Independence						−	−																		−	−	−	−	−
Counter-dependency	+	+	+						+	+	+	+	+	+															
Ego State																													
Expressing Anxiety	+	+	+	+	+	+	+	+	+	+	−	−	−	−	−	−	−	−	−	+	+	+	+	+	+	+	−	−	−
Denying Anxiety						−	−	+	+	+	+	+	+	+	+	+	+	+	−	−	−	−	−	−	−	−	−	−	−
Self-esteem						+	+	+	−	−	−	−	−	−	−	−	+	+					+	+	+	+	+	+	+
Expressing Depression									−	−	−	−	−							+	+	+	+	+	+	+	+	+	+
Denying Depression							−	−	−	−	−	−	−							+									

+ Burst of high sessions where burst = at least 3/3 or 5/6 above or below median.
− Burst of low sessions.

Fig. 1. Trend analysis by category for group S1

	Session																												
Category	02	04	05	07	08	09	10	11	12	13	14	15	16	17	18	19	20	21	22	23	24	25	26	27	28	29	30	31	32
Hostility																													
Moving Against					−	−	+	+	+	+	+	+	+	+											+	+	+	+	+
Resisting			−	−	−	+	+	+	+	+	+	+	+	−											+	+	+	+	+
Withdrawing				+	+	+	+	+	+		+	+	+	+	+	+	+	+	−	−	−	−	−	−	−	−	−	−	−
Guilt-inducing		+	+	+	+	+	+	+		+	+	−	−	+	−	+	−	−	−	−	−	−	−	+	+	+	+	+	+
Affection																													
Reparation			+	+	+	+	+	+								+	+	+		−	−	+	+	+	+	+	+	+	+
Identifying	+	+	+	+	+	+	+	+	−	−	−	−	−	−	−	−	−	−	−	−	−	−	−	−	−	−	−	−	
Accepting			+	+	+	+	+	+	+	+	+								−	−		+	+	+	+	+			
Moving Toward						+	+	+	+	+																			
Authority Relations																													
Dependency	+	+	+	+	+	+	+					−	−	−	−	−	−	−	−	−	+	−	−	−	−	+	+	+	+
Independence							+								+	+	+	+	+	+									
Counter-dependency																									−				
Ego State																													
Expressing Anxiety	−	−	−	−	−	−	+	+	+	+	+		+	+	+	+	+	+	+	+	+	+	+	+	+	−	−	−	−
Denying Anxiety	−	−	−	−	−	+	−	−	−	−	−	+	+	+	+	+	+	−	+	+	+	+	−	−	−	−	−		
Self-esteem	+	+	+	+	+	−	−	−	−	−	+	+	+	+	+	+	+	+	+	+	+	+	+	+	+	+	+	+	+
Expressing Depression	−	−	−	−	−	−	−	−	−	+	+	+	+	+	+	−	+	+	+	+	+	+	+	+	+	+	+		+
Denying Depression	−	−	−	−	−	−	−	−	+	+	+	−	+	−	−	+	+	+	+	+	+	+	+	+	+	+	+	+	+

+ Burst of high sessions where burst = at least 3/3 or 5/6 above or below median.
− Burst of low sessions.

Fig. 2. Trend analysis by category for group S2

pairs of sessions. Long runs of essentially similar activity within a group would result in positive correlations between the adjacent sessions; any substantial shift in the group's activity would produce a negative correlation at the turning-point. The boundaries of the phases to be discussed in some detail are defined by the presence of a negative correlation between the last session in one phase and the first session of the next phase. Where the phases are long and one session-to-session correlation within the phase is positive but quite low, the phases are divided into sub-phases for more careful analysis.

The percentage profiles for each phase or sub-phase in the two groups are presented in *Tables 1* and *2*. The statistical tests referred to in the tables compare with the percentage in a category for each phase with the percentage in that category for all other phases combined. The significance of the difference between percentages in adjacent phases was also assessed, and these results will be discussed in the text.

In the presentation of each phase or sub-phase, comments on the category rates as shown in the tables are supplemented by a brief descriptive account of the developing member–trainer relationships. The analyses presented in the tables are based on data for all scoring levels combined. However, where it seems useful to mention the degree to which the inferred feelings were expressed directly, the separate scoring levels will be discussed.

Group S1. For group S1, the first phase was the only one in which the majority of acts on the manifest level were expressions of feeling toward figures in the assigned cases, as reflected in a high proportion of acts scored on level three. However, the categories which were significantly high in these phases, Showing Dependency, Showing Counter-dependency, and Denying Anxiety, were high for all other levels as well. Identifying and Accepting were low in this phase. The major themes in the discussion were the proper behaviour for a new member of a group, weak males, the tendency of parents to make things worse by insensitive meddling, and various modes of handling parents. The two most salient issues for the group at this juncture appear to have been (i) whether members should express, or attempt to counter, dependency feelings toward the rather ambiguous trainer and (ii) how to assess the potential danger inherent in this new situation.

The acts in the second phase were scored mainly on level two, i.e. acts directed within the group but not explicitly toward the trainer. The sessions revolved around the issues of how much personal exposure was appropriate in this situation, what perils might follow from removing one's social mask, and how to achieve 'intimate interpersonal relations' with friends and, more

Table 1—Percentage profiles of member–trainer categories for group S1 by phase

Category	Phases and Sessions									Total
	1 2-4	2 5-7	3A 8-11	3B 12-13	4 14-17	5 19-21	6 21-26	7A 27-29	7B 30-32	
Hostility										
Moving Against	6·6	4·7	6·3	8·8**	4·5	3·9	6·9*	4·5	2·3**	5·5
Resisting	7·5	8·4	10·8*	6·9	10·0	11·1*	9·7	6·2*	7·5	9·0
Withdrawing	6·2	7·4	5·2	9·0*	4·5*	5·5	6·1	6·9	8·7**	6·4
Guilt-inducing	6·0	4·1*	8·0**	7·9	4·9	5·0	4·8	8·5**	4·5	6·0
Affection										
Making Reparation	5·7	4·2**	7·7	8·8*	10·5**	5·0	6·2	5·1	3·2**	6·4
Identifying	5·7**	7·8*	7·4**	6·5*	9·0	17·4**	11·4	11·4	13·4**	9·9
Accepting	5·1	9·1*	8·2	4·8*	6·3	7·2	6·2	5·7	7·9	6·9
Moving Toward	6·6	9·3**	5·2	5·4	5·4	6·0	4·4*	6·2	6·3	5·9
Authority Relations										
Showing Dependency	12·5**	7·6	8·7	9·6	6·8	5·8**	5·8**	8·0	7·9	7·9
Showing Independence	3·2	3·1	3·2	3·8	7·1**	4·9	2·4**	3·9	6·5**	4·1
Counter-dependency	6·0**	4·1	2·9	2·9	3·5	2·4	3·4	0·5**	1·7*	3·1
Ego State										
Expressing Anxiety	7·3	12·6**	7·8	7·3	7·7	6·8	9·8	10·5*	5·1**	8·4
Denying Anxiety	4·4*	4·3	3·8	1·5*	2·4	4·2	4·0	1·2**	0·8**	3·2
Self-esteem	2·1	2·0	1·9	2·7	4·0**	3·1*	1·0**	0·6	1·7	2·0
Expressing Depression	7·5	6·2*	7·8	7·5	5·3**	5·7*	9·2	12·7**	13·3**	8·3
Denying Depression	6·9	5·1*	5·1**	6·7	7·9	6·0	8·8*	8·2	9·2**	7·1
Base Numbers	722	740	1182	522	819	637	1216	648	709	7195

Note: Significance tests applied to the difference between each phase and all other phases combined.
* Significant at 0·05 level.
** Significant at 0·01 level.

importantly, with one's mother. There was a significant decrease in Showing Dependency, whereas Accepting, Moving Toward, and Expressing Anxiety were high in this phase. Perhaps the best summary of the phase would be that the group was concerned with the intimacy issues *vis-à-vis* the trainer. The group appears to have been polarized between those who expressed trusting and accepting feelings toward the trainer and those whose major feelings were ones of anxiety and apprehension.

From the second to the third phase the tone of the members' feelings shifted from positive to negative, with first Guilt-inducing and Resisting being high and then Moving Against and Withdrawing. The proportion of acts on level one, referring directly to the trainer, reached its highest level thus far in the group. In the first part of the phase the major focus of the hostility was on 'shoulds' laid down by authority and on the trainer's role and his expectations of the group. In contrast, the second part of the phase contained a more personal attack on the trainer both for 'betraying' the group, i.e. intervening via interpretations rather than leaving the group alone, and for exposing the group to a potentially damaging situation. In addition, one central group member who had alternated between a 'cool' rebellious stance and a position as the trainer's lieutenant and ally was bitterly attacked for being crude, insensitive, and unresponsive.

The group came as close is it ever would come to rejecting or expelling the trainer in the assertion to him, midway in the third phase, that 'You're all washed up', to which no members took exception. The attack on the trainer, and on the group member most identified with him in the minds of the group members, reflected a fusion of many issues. There was anger at the ambiguity in the trainer's role, which sometimes seemed permissive and even abdicating, but at other times controlling, critical, and generally unfair. In addition, the anger seemed to derive from a frustration of needs not for control, but for affection and sensitivity, both of which some members felt were in very short supply.

The fourth phase represented quite an abrupt shift in the group's relationship with the trainer. Three categories were higher in this phase than in any previous or subsequent phase: Making Reparation, Showing Independence, and Expressing Self-esteem. While Resisting increased, the other three hostility categories showed significant decreases from phase three to phase four. The most important development in the group during this phase was a debate over whether a rather impulsive act by the trainer implied that he was a 'schemer' or 'human', the issue being resolved, for most members, by a decision that he was human. The particular kind of human being the group had in mind was indicated by one suggestion that he was like the Mona Lisa. The preponderance of hostility in the previous phase was replaced by a preponderance of affection, especially Making Reparation. It appears that the dual issues of authority and intimacy, as they related to the trainer, were resolved by a compromise. The earlier equation of the trainer with the traditional male authority, suggesting power and threat derived from rules, judgments, and the capacity to punish, was modified by the inclusion of images more appropriate to one form of female authority, a distant but benevolent figure whose power and threat derive from the manipulation of love and attention. Both images remained with the group, some members preferring one, some the other, but the increases in Showing Independence and in Expressing Self-esteem suggest that this new resolution of member–trainer relations had a salutary effect on at least many of the group members.

The fifth phase was characterized by high levels of Resisting, Identifying, and Self-esteem. The major activity of the phase was a sequence of two splits within the group, where most of the group attempted to interpret the behaviour or modify the feelings of first one and then another group member who were particularly high on Resisting. Very little of the activity was directed toward the trainer explicitly, but there was considerable evidence that the trainer's views or approach had been heard and assimilated. This was the phase with the greatest preponderance of positive over negative feelings, but the reparation characteristic of the preceding phase was replaced by expressions of affection through the more indirect mode of identification with the trainer.

One new theme and several old ones dominated the sixth phase. The new issue was the end of the group, and in this phase both Expressing Depression and Denying Depression showed significant increases over the previous phase. The old issues were the question of the trainer's evaluations of group members, now made salient by the required papers and examinations, and the question of the trainer's insensitivity and capacity to hurt. Moving Against and Expressing Anxiety were significantly higher, and Identifying and Showing Independence were significantly lower than in the previous phase. This sixth phase was characterized by a mixture of sadness over the impending death of the group and apprehensive, resentful concern with the trainer's demands.

In the seventh and last phase, the discussions dealt mainly with evaluating the group and its effect on individual members, with death and immortality, and with the increasingly depressed tone of the group. The anxiety expressed in the sixth phase remained high for the first half of the seventh phase, but then declined sharply. The mode of expressing hostility shifted from the Moving Against of the sixth phase to Guilt-inducing and then to Withdrawing. Showing Independence increased at the end of the group. However, by far the most salient characteristic of the seventh phase was the high level of depression, a heavy, mourning quality which was broken by several wild interludes fantasying the rebirth and immortality of the group. The proportion of acts on level one was at its highest point in the final sub-phase, and the content referring to the trainer continued to be a mixture of such images as judge, doctor, and exploiter, with quite different images relating to bisexuality, feeding, and hunger.

Group S2. The development of the member–trainer relationship in group S2 began with the only phase for the group in which affection predominated over hostility. Identifying and Accepting were high throughout the first phase, with Moving Toward significantly high in the second half of the phase. An initially high level of Showing Counter-dependence was replaced in the second part of the phase by high levels of Showing Dependence and Showing Independence. In addition, Anxiety and Depression were low in the first phase.

A number of features characterized the discussion in the first part of phase one: (i) the older members, many of whom were teachers by profession, very quickly adopted the 'teacher role'; (ii) the younger members expressed their complaints about various overbearing or insensitive authority figures; and (iii) though some members seemed uncertain about whether the trainer's silence implied weakness, most members appeared to feel that the trainer and the course stood for worthwhile human values. The generally positive tone of the second half of phase one was fostered by the group's decision to have a party and by various attempts, particularly by the females, to obtain both the trainer's approval for the party and his promise to attend it. The other major issues of this sub-phase, which were connected directly with the decision to have a party, were: (i) whether group therapy was the appropriate model for the group, which involved the issues of how personal people should be; and (ii) how one can be spontaneous while under observation by oneself and by others.

Phase two began with the session following the party, which neither the trainer nor any of the observers attended. The phase was characterized by significantly high levels of Guilt-inducing, Expressing Anxiety, and Denying Anxiety. In addition, there were significant increases over phase one in Moving Against and Expressing Depression. All five categories which had been significantly high in the previous sub-phase (Identifying, Accepting, Moving Toward, Showing Dependency, and Showing Independence) decreased considerably.

In the session following the party, one group member arrived before the trainer and sat in the trainer's usual place. After the trainer had

Table 2—Percentage profiles of member–trainer categories for group S1 by phase

Category	Phases and Sessions									Total
	1A 2–5	1B 7–9	2 10–12	3 13–15	4 16–17	5 18–21	6 22–25	7A 26–29	7B 30–32	
Hostility										
Moving Against	9·8	4·0**	10·4	8·1	18·5**	6·7	5·5**	9·2	10·1	8·5
Resisting	9·4	9·4	8·8	9·4	7·2	4·6*	8·9	5·8*	7·9	8·0
Withdrawing	2·2	3·4	3·7	2·6	4·0	3·8	1·7	2·0	2·2	2·8
Guilt-inducing	7·3*	3·7	8·0**	4·9	2·8	3·8	3·8	5·0	5·7	5·1
Affection										
Making Reparation	3·9	2·9*	4·7	2·6	6·4	3·1	3·6	6·6*	8·1**	4·5
Identifying	13·4**	7·1**	2·2**	2·3*	2·4	3·3	3·4	2·4**	2·2*	4·7
Accepting	10·0*	12·1**	7·8	6·5	6·4	4·6*	8·0	4·8**	6·6	7·8
Moving Toward	3·5	6·0**	1·0*	2·9	0·8*	2·3	1·1*	2·2	2·9	2·7
Authority Relations										
Showing Dependency	14·1	17·3**	10·4	10·4	8·0*	10·0	11·2	12·4	16·2*	12·7
Showing Independence	3·1	5·3**	1·8	1·6	3·6	1·5	3·2	0·0**	2·2	2·6
Counter-dependency	5·9**	3·2	2·4	4·2	1·6	3·8	3·4	2·0	1·5*	3·2
Ego State										
Expressing Anxiety	4·5**	9·0	13·3**	9·7	13·3	16·2**	11·2	14·1**	5·4*	10·6
Denying Anxiety	2·9**	6·6	10·6**	7·1	14·5**	9·7	9·7*	5·0	5·4	7·6
Self-esteem	1·2	1·1	0·2	0·0	0·4	0·0	1·7	0·4	0·5	0·7
Expressing Depression	5·9**	5·0**	9·6**	19·2**	6·8**	18·5	16·0	20·3*	16·0	12·7
Denying Depression	3·1**	3·9*	5·1	8·4	3·2*	7·9	7·4	8·0*	7·1	6·0
Base Numbers	491	620	490	308	249	390	526	502	407	3983

Note: Significance tests applied to the difference between each phase and all other phases combined.
* Significant at 0·05 level.
** Significant at 0·01 level.

successfully reclaimed his seat, the group spent much of the session either in accusing the trainer of deserting the group or in discussing the theme of guilt. Prohibitions against being too personal in the group gained strength in this phase, and concern was widely expressed regarding the role of women and the silent group members. The immediate effect of the party was to raise two possibilities regarding the trainer, both of which the group had trouble in accepting or rejecting. One possibility was that the party amounted to an attack, of unknown impact, on the trainer, as a result of which the trainer was either wounded or silently furious. The other possibility was that the trainer's failure to attend the party proved his lack of feeling for the group and general untrustworthiness.

Phase three was quite similar in content to phase two, with one major exception. The predominant ego-state category shifted from Expressing Anxiety in phase two to Expressing Depression. The imagery surrounding the trainer shifted correspondingly, from an emphasis on the trainer as an untrustworthy and threatening object to the trainer as a powerful leader, potentially all good or all evil, who could control or toy with the group at will. In addition, many of the feelings toward the trainer were being displaced onto one group member whose championing of Freud and therapy had aroused much debate in the group.

In phase four, Moving Against and Denying Anxiety, on both direct and symbolic levels, reached their maximum point. Expressions of Depression declined abruptly from their high level in the previous phase. One group member and, indirectly, the trainer were attacked one day for being authoritarian and 'crude', i.e. seeing 'the sexual side of things', and then, the next day, another group member and, more directly, the trainer were attacked for having a bad influence, for misleading the group and inciting it to be aggressive. It is interesting to note that, in phase two, one technique used by the group members in their attempt to make the trainer feel guilty for not having attended the party was to claim, jokingly, that they had lost control during the party, and that there had been much drinking and sexual promiscuity. In phase four, the trainer and one member strongly linked with the trainer were accused of being too preoccupied with sexual matters. All of this suggests that phase four was a brief, if temporary, respite from the group's depressed reaction after the party. The sexual and aggressive feelings which were both a reason for and a consequence of the party were, in this phase, projected onto the trainer, creating an image of a malignant seducer.

In phase five, Expressing Anxiety and Expressing Depression were high. The discussion centered on guilt, responsibility, and fears of being either 'swallowed up' by overprotective mothers or unattended by people who are

10

detached and unresponsive. Both in relation to the trainer and in relation
a number of group members, especially the silent ones, a dilemma ha
arisen: strong desires on the part of many members to atone for some u.
specified guilt and to involve the trainer and the silent members in a clos
trusting relationship were counterbalanced by fears that if they *were* le:
detached, they would be either unbearably critical or overwhelming. The
fears were made more intense by the fact that, in addition to desires f(
closeness, there were feelings of anger and rejection toward the trainer, whic
made the situation appear all the more hopeless.

In the first session of phase six, the presence of unexpected guests in th
room precipitated a new development. The debate over guests and th
eventual decision not to expel them were followed by a series of discu
sions, the major theme of which was responsibility for one's fate. A
emphasis on free will and the originality of youth was accompanied by
modification in the image of the trainer. He was seen as somehow older an
wiser, the possessor of knowledge which all members wanted but some sti
feared and resisted. The more impersonal tone of the member–traine
relationship was mirrored in the fact that Moving Against and Movin
Toward were significantly low, while Resisting and Accepting increase(
significantly over the previous phase. Expressing Anxiety was lower an
Expressing Self-esteem was higher than in the previous phase, and Denyin
Anxiety was significantly high.

The seventh and final phase is divided into two sub-phases. Only Makin
Reparation, which was high, and Identifying, which was low, were sustaine(
across both sub-phases. The impersonal tone characteristic of the previou
phase was not maintained. Moving Against increased, while Resisting an(
Accepting decreased from phase six to phase seven. Expressing Anxiety
Expressing Depression, and Denying Depression were high only in the firs
part of phase seven, and Showing Independence was particularly low. In th
second part of the phase seven Expressing Anxiety decreased sharply an(
was significantly low. Showing Counter-dependency reached its lowes
point in the group, and Showing Dependence was high.

The discussion in the first half of phase seven was concerned primaril
with an individual's responsibility. There was general consensus that th(
burden of guilt for the destruction caused by Hitler, atom bombs, an(
capital punishment fell on everyone. The covert meanings of these discus
sions seemed to be delicately balanced between (1) making reparation b
relieving the trainer of full responsibility for the group's development an(
(2) expressing resentment that the trainer had failed to control the member
of the group. Both the attempt at reparation and the resentment were mor(
explicit in the final few sessions, as were the feelings of dependency. In a

,/ay, some group members seemed to be trying to start the group all over .gain. They were prepared to take responsibility and to forgive the trainer or what they had seen as his failures in the area of control, if not for failures n the area of affection. Notably absent from the discussion were the issues •f intimacy. In the final session, one member invited the group to a party .nd was refused in sepulchral tones.

:omparison of S1 and S2

Before comparing the development of groups S1 and S2, a comparison of he percentage profiles over all sessions might set the developmental dif-erences in a useful perspective. The analysis of high and low categories in uns of sessions and the phase analysis emphasized the within-group changes in each category, relative to the total over all sessions for that ;roup, but the groups did not have the same over-all amounts of the various :ategories.

Table 3 presents the percentage profiles, by group, for all sessions com-bined. Although there were several exceptions worth noting, S1 was higher n the impulse-area categories and lower in the authority-relations and ego-state areas. Furthermore, the percentage of all impulse-area acts scored in the affection sub-area for group S1 was 52·0 per cent as compared with 44·7 in S2.

When these overall differences are integrated with the developmental sequences in each group a fuller picture of the two groups emerges. For example, despite the fact that S2 was significantly higher, over all sessions, on Moving Against, the changes over time within each group were quite similar with one burst of direct hostility just before the midpoint and another near the end of the group. In addition, there was a tendency in both groups for the first wave of direct hostility to be preceded by an increase in Guilt-inducing. Whereas Withdrawing was high in group S1 during the first attack and toward the end, the rate was quite constant throughout S2, and all phases in S2 were lower than the lowest phase in S1.

In the affection area, the contrast in developmental sequences was mirrored by contrasts in overall levels. For the group S2 the early sessions were the highest on Identifying, Accepting, and Moving Toward. Not only was there a relative decline in Identifying and Moving Toward, but the group as a whole was considerably lower on these categories than S1. In contrast to S2, Identifying in group S1 was low in the beginning and high in the middle end of the group. Making Reparation emerged in the middle of S1, shortly after the first wave of hostility, and before the rise in Identify-ing, whereas the phases high in Reparation for group S2 were at the very end of the group.

Changes in Showing Dependency for the two groups were fairly similar, with high early phases being followed by low phases in the middle. However, S2 was characterized by a terminal increase of dependency, and the level of Showing Dependency throughout the group was much higher than in S1. Showing Independence was high in the early and middle sessions of S2 and high in the middle and final sessions of S1, and, over all sessions, S1 was higher on Showing Independence than S2. The overall percentages of Showing Counter-dependence were nearly the same in the two groups. For both groups, the highest sessions were the earliest ones, and there were moderately high sessions toward the middle of both groups' development.

Table 3—Percentage profiles over all sessions for groups S1 and S2

| | Group | | |
Category	S1	S2	p
Hostility			
Moving Against	5·5	8·5	0·01
Resisting	9·0	8·0	n.s.
Withdrawing	6·4	2·8	0·01
Guilt-inducing	6·0	5·1	0·05
Affection			
Making Reparation	6·4	4·5	0·01
Identifying	9·9	4·7	0·01
Accepting	6·9	7·8	n.s.
Moving Toward	5·9	2·7	0·01
Authority Relations			
Showing Dependency	7·9	12·7	0·01
Showing Independence	4·1	2·6	0·01
Counter Dependence	3·1	3·2	n.s.
Ego State			
Expressing Anxiety	8·4	10·6	0·01
Denying Anxiety	3·2	7·6	0·01
Self-esteem	2·0	0·7	0·01
Expressing Depression	8·3	12·7	0·01
Denying Depression	7·1	6·0	0·05
Total	7195	3983	

The amount of anxiety, both expressed and denied, was higher for group S2. While expressions of anxiety emerged in the early sessions and returned toward the end of S1, they emerged somewhat later in S2 and were high throughout most of the middle and late phases, declining only in the last three sessions. Expressing Self-esteem, which was high over all sessions for group S1, tended to reach its high point in one of the middle phases for both groups. Group S2 was higher on Expressing Depression; Group S1 was higher on Denying Depression. In both groups depression was higher in the late sessions, but the period of little depression for S1 was in the middle and for S2 was at the beginning of the group. In both groups there was some tendency for Denying Anxiety to be high just before Expressing Anxiety was high, and a similar tendency for Denying Depression to be high just before Expressing Depression was high.

The development of the member–trainer relationship

A useful schematic outline of the stages of development in member–trainer relations should be capable of handling the similarities and differences between the two groups under study. It should also be congruent, it is hoped, with prior and future observations.

The major focus of the scheme to be presented here is on the trainer as a psychological object for group members, an object which is apprehended at times as primarily external to the members and at times as primarily internal to the members. The developmental sequence contains five steps: Appraisal, Confrontation, Re-evaluation, Internalization, and Separation. The presentation of the scheme in serial order is not intended to imply some inexorable progression from one to the next without the possibility of recycling through a stage more than once. Rather, the scheme suggests a set of analytically distinguishable moments in the total member–trainer relationship. After presenting the total scheme, the histories of the member–trainer relationship in the two groups will be recast in terms of this paradigm.

Stage one: Appraisal

In the early session of a group, feelings toward the trainer derive from four main processes active in the group:

1. The trainer is the focus for much of the anxiety aroused in members by the new situation. By virtue of having, or appearing to have, the greatest familiarity with groups of this kind, the trainer is held responsible for the tension experienced by the members.

2. Members tend to perceive and use the trainer as an ally both in reducing their anxiety and in controlling their impulses. In many ways, a member's feelings toward the trainer are an externalization of his characteristic internal mode of relating to superego demands and prohibitions. The projection of superego functions onto the trainer may produce acquiescence and dependency, it may arouse rebellion and counter-

dependency, or it may result only in heightened anxiety and fear of censure.

3. Members tend to project their ego-ideal onto the trainer, partly as a means of allaying anxiety, but also as a means of setting up a relationship that will be satisfying. As a result, the early sessions of a group may have the quality of a 'honeymoon period' in which most of the inferences about the trainer's motives of personality are expressions of how members wish he would be.

4. The trainer's behaviour is a source of frustration for group members. Dependency needs go unmet; rebellion is not curbed through counter-measures; affection is not reciprocated; withdrawal and indifference are challenged by the rather personal tone of the interventions; and the anxiety remains high.

All in all, the early sessions contain quite a range of feelings, but one common denominator of them is that the trainer is external to the member, that he is an object to be reckoned with in whatever habitual ways the member brings to the group. The first stage is one in which the accumulated set of expectations derived from parents, teachers, and others is tried out for size, perhaps as much in hope that it will not fit as in hope that it will.

Stage two: Confrontation

At some point early in the group's development there tends to be an abrupt shift in the member–trainer relationship. Though one of the more prominent features of the stage tends to be the eruption of hostility, the issues involved are more complex than can be expressed by such terms as revolt or attack. Some of the major functions of the confrontation seem to be the following:

1. The expression of hostile or counter-dependent feelings serves both to challenge the authority of the trainer and to test the limits of his permissiveness. It is not uncommon for the accusation that the trainer is too controlling to be fused, as if there were no contradiction, with other accusations that he is not controlling enough. The sum total of all the complaints and insistencies that the trainer adjust his behaviour usually reflects both sides of members' simultaneous wishes for autonomy and security.

2. The increased hostility characteristic of the confrontation stage has its roots not only in the issue of control but in the issues of affection and intimacy. The content of the hostility in the two groups under study reveals the members' exasperation with the trainer's failure to reciprocate affection and esteem. Feelings of being abused, ignored, or rejected, feelings barely

stifled in the early sessions, find expression in this stage. In part the hostility contains an accusation that the trainer is unfair, and in part the hostility is the members' revenge and retaliation for the trainer's indifference. However, if ambivalence characterizes the members' feelings about the issue of control, it characterizes their feelings in the intimacy area as well. The confrontation includes not only the most direct hostility but some of the most direct appeals to the trainer to move closer to the group. While some voices are raised to suggest that the trainer leave, others tend to suggest that on his return he move his seat and be one of the group, that he get on a first-name basis with the group, or that he be more human. The seductiveness beneath the hostility suggests that the full meaning of the confrontation must take account of the persistent phantasies of closeness with the trainer as well as the desire to punish and reject him for his failure to gratify those wishes.

3. An important function of the hostility generated in this stage is to test the durability of the trainer, to assess his capacity to absorb an attack without either collapsing or retaliating in kind.

4. Finally, the confrontation serves the purpose of 'naming the devil' of crystallizing in the trainer the various vaguely apprehended dangers and uncertainties inherent in a new group. The ambiguous, half-in and half-out position of the trainer increases the likelihood that for most members the trainer is the most salient deviant, in the sense used by Stock, Whitman and Lieberman (1958). Not all members will agree that his deviance consists in being too personal, too reserved, too involved, or too independent, but many feel his deviance is a threat to the group. The confrontation is an attempt, in part, to control the trainer's deviant behaviour by appropriate punitive action.

Stage three: Re-evaluation

Following the confrontation, or, more properly, following each successive confrontation, the group has at its disposal a vast amount of new and relevant data to sift out and interpret. Various feelings have been expressed for the first time, to which the trainer has made some response, even if the response was silence. The hostility, and the particular forms it took, have aroused a number of internal responses in each member, and these must be sorted out for their meaning. The re-evaluation stage is one in which the previous images of the trainer are tested for their continuing usefulness, and one important means of re-evaluating an image occurs when the members compare the ego state appropriate to the image with how they feel at the moment. Several important processes which are likely to occur at this point may be outlined:

1. The members test out the appropriateness of their initial anxiety level and the accuracy of certain images of the trainer which expressed their anxiety. The fear of retaliation or punishment which arises after the confrontation stage is tested against the reality of the trainer's response. The confrontation stands as an admittedly severe provocation to the trainer, and much depends on his reaction to it, or at least on how the members interpret his reaction. The members are gathering crucial data on the trainer's self-control and his underlying malignance, both of which are highly relevant to their anxiety level.

2. At the same time, a rather new issue arises in the group, stemming from the confrontation, namely the issue of depression. The dual questions of the impact of the hostility on the trainer and the implication of the attack for the members' capacity to control their own aggression are raised. The increase in guilt and shame over being openly hostile interacts with the perceived effect of the hostility on the trainer. If the effect has been too great, the trainer too hurt, the guilt becomes a serious factor in the group. On the other hand, if the effect seems to have been negligible, and the trainer seems completely unmoved by the hostility, the members tend to experience his lack of response as rejection by an indifferent figure, and mistrust and anxiety will probably increase. Within some unspecifiable limits, however, the members may take the trainer's response to indicate both his durability and his continuing involvement, all of which bears on the members' fears of being uncontrollably dangerous and destructive. The second process that stems from the rise in guilt is the attempt to make reparation. In part the reparation is an attempt to deny the full implication of the anger expressed, but in part it reveals the other side of the ambivalent feelings aroused by the trainer. Reparation serves to maintain a desired relationship and to reassure the member that his capacity for hostility is counterbalanced and partially controlled by his capacity for affection.

3. The confrontation exposes, for all to see, how intensely involved with the trainer the members actually were, how vulnerable and dependent they had been. One aspect of the re-evaluation, then, tends to be a series of attempts to clarify the members' own standards and private sources of self-esteem. Although this process serves members' own needs of the moment, it has an interesting relevance to the trainer beyond the need to develop some independence from him. In the usual training group, it turns out that the most effective gift to the trainer, the one most likely to be received in silence, but gratefully, *is* the gift of a member's independent, self-accepting clarification of his own needs and values. Thus, while much of the re-evaluation is done without explicit reference to the trainer, it may often

have relevance to the process of reparation simply by virtue of being carried out in the presence of the trainer.

Stage four: Internalization

In this stage the relations with the trainer shift for some members, if not all, to relations with the trainer as an internal object. Much depends upon the particular history of the group up to this point, and the two major characteristics of this stage, identification and 'work', will take quite different forms as a function of earlier resolutions of the member–trainer relationship. In some groups this phase may be by far the longest; in others it may be ephemeral and recurrent for only brief periods.

1. The process of identification is an intricate matter in most training groups. Though it is convenient to refer to identification as a coherent and single process, in reality quite different mechanisms underlie the various kinds of identification observed in groups. Slater's (1961b) distinction between personal and positional identification is useful here. Personal identification, in the self-analytic group, would refer to a member's internalization of the trainer's perceptions, values, or style because the member feels affection or respect for the trainer as a person. It is this process that characterizes the internalization stage, rather than positional identification in which the member's envy and fear of the trainer's power impel him to destroy and supplant him. One might expect that positional identification would be reflected by a combination of identification with anxiety and/or hostility, whereas personal identification would be reflected by a combination of identification and affection.

Drawing upon the nature of earlier stages, it appears that internalization is mediated by a set of facilitating pre-conditions, probably not all of which are essential: (a) that the negative feelings toward the trainer and desires for autonomy be expressed by the members and absorbed by the trainer (Arsenian, Semrad and Shapiro, 1962); (b) that the feelings of anxiety and mistrust be reduced by realistic re-evaluation of the trainer's behaviour; (c) that the sense of guilt over expressing hostility be assuaged by realistic appraisal that the trainer remains intact and involved; and (d) that reparation in the form of positive feelings expressed and independent clarification of members' needs and values be accomplished.

From this set of notions it follows that a number of factors may conspire to block or disrupt the identification process. Particularly if the image of the trainer remains too malignant and threatening, or if the consequences of hostile feelings are thought to be too devastating, personal identification will tend to be difficult, shallow, or fragile.

Increases in anxiety reflect growing doubts about the trustworthiness and benevolence of the trainer, which lead to a growing unwillingness to permit the trainer to serve as an internalized adjunct to the member's more enduring personality structure. On the other hand, increases in depression reflect the member's sense of helplessness to maintain a positive relationship with the trainer, either because the member feels unable to control his hostility or because he disparages his capacity to work independently or well, as a form of continuing reparation to the trainer. As either anxiety or depression mounts beyond a certain point, internalization decreases, and the trainer tends to be seen again as an external object with whom the members must contend.

2. The capacity to work, to perform the expressive and analytic tasks of a training group, is put to a continuous and demanding test in this stage. The trainer's relevance is primarily as one source of internal standards of judgment, but not the only one, and as one model for performance, but not the only one. Many of the members' concerns expressed in the work phase revolve around other group members or the group's formal task, if any. Members may find that they have internalized different aspects of the trainer, and these aspects may or may not be mutually compatible. Some may identify with the value of openness he professes, others with the role of observer he seems to fill. And there is, throughout this stage, the continual need and tendency to determine what parts of the trainer's views or skills are relevant to either the members or the work at hand.

Even more central to this work phase is the challenge of developing satisfactory answers to a set of questions that plague the group: (a) What is work in this group, and what are laziness and avoidance of the task? (b) What constitutes success or productive effort? (c) How much of the group's time must be spent in productive effort, or even in attempting to work? The extent to which the trainer is directly relevant to this process derives from his having already provided, however, subtly, his views on work and failure by his interventions all during the group's development. In this stage it is not uncommon for a trainer's views to be expressed by a member as his own, not that their eventual acceptance by the group is a necessary consequence of this internalization. However, one of the most frequent outbursts in the group at this stage is the expression of irritation at the trainer for having deviously planted his views in the group, leaving no possible room for the members to make independent innovations.

Stage five: Separation

As the group comes to a close, several changes in the member–trainer relationship become evident. Some of the most important processes associated with the issue of separation may be suggested briefly:

1. To the extent that important bonds of affection and involvement with the trainer have developed, the end of the group arouses a genuine anticipation of loss and sadness. In addition to expressions of depression and anticipatory mourning, various attempts may be made to deny the full impact of the separation. The euphoric tone, the insistence that the group cannot really end because each person will carry the group away inside him, the promises to have a reunion, all these developments serve to emphasize the meaningfulness of the internalization process which has already taken place. But they serve also to conceal the unfinished business, the residue of negative or unpleasant feelings which could not be resolved.

2. Some of the stifled feelings of frustration, insecurity, or anger may emerge shortly before the end of the group. Part of this phenomenon can be attributed to a final broadside from the members whose negative feelings had gone unexpressed or unheeded throughout the group's history. But another part of the phenomenon derives from a more general attempt to undo the internalization process prior to separation, to reconstitute the trainer as an altogether external object. In this light, much, but not all, of the resurgent anxiety and hostility serves as a distancing device preparatory to separation.

3. The themes of failure become important in the final stage of the group, as reflected in the chagrin that all the hopes aroused in the group have a dwindling chance of being realized. It is not uncommon for one of these hopes, the phantasied relationship of intimacy with the trainer, to be acted on with some vigor. The pressure for the trainer to affirm the extraordinary quality of the group and to give it his benediction is but one of the many ways in which the trainer is asked to make a final break with his role in the group. It is as if the members were saying that only the most heartless and inhuman of creatures could deny the group its final request for total absolution and love. Pleas that the trainer should now, at last, reveal all his secrets are of the same general order.

Discussion of the case studies

To return to groups S1 and S2, some of the major similarities and differences in the nature of the member–trainer relationships can be highlighted and interpreted with reference to the developmental model. On the one hand, there were some general similarities between the groups, particularly in the initial stage of appraisal and the final stage of separation. On the other hand, the substantial differences between the groups in the nature and extent of the internalization process may be traced to equally divergent processes in the re-evaluation stage which followed the confrontation.

One facet of the re-evaluation stage is that members review and possibly modify the operative images which express their feelings toward the trainer. In group S1 the earlier images suggesting a controlling, insensitive, and dangerous object were joined, if not replaced, by more benign images, such as the reference to the Mona Lisa. The re-evaluation stage in group S1 was further characterized by active attempts to undo and control the aggression of the previous period. Reparative processes, which had actually increased before the hostility had fully subsided, were sustained over a number of sessions, and signs of distress in the ego-state area were relatively infrequent.

The period after the confrontation in group S2 was filled with signs of distress. The attack on the trainer seems to heighten the sense of danger, while arousing new concerns about members' incapacity to control their hostility. In a very real sense, most of the sessions following the confrontation were spent working on the dilemmas crystallized in the re-evaluation stage, and no sustained period of internalization followed the re-evaluation stage. Particularly striking was the delay in reparative processes until the terminal phase, when rather successful attempts were made to undo the attack on the trainer for perceived failures in the control area. However, review of the later phases of the groups will be deferred until after an examination of the possible antecedents of the differences between the two stages of re-evaluation.

The confrontation stages in the two groups were quite similar in many respects, but two differences stand out as possibly relevant to the divergent consequences of the hostility. First, the hostility expressed toward the trainer in S2 was more directly connected to the issue of intimacy than in S1, although both control and intimacy issues were salient in each group. The first wave of negative feelings in S2 followed the party and the trainer's failure to attend it. The disappointment and anger were expressed initially through members' attempts to make the trainer feel guilty for abandoning the group, then through attempts to transfer the responsibility for sexual and aggressive motives from group members to the trainer. Thus, one difference between the two groups arises from the fact that in S2 the expressions of hostility, stemming in part from frustrations in the affection area, intensified, rather than relieved, the members' feelings of mistrust, their sense of being rejected, and their feelings of helplessness.

A second difference between the confrontation stages of the two groups lies in the control area. While both groups contained a number of members whose initial response was to adopt either dependent or counter-dependent orientations to the trainer, group S2 contained a sizeable minority who worked hard to bypass the issue of appraising the trainer. These older members, most of whom were teachers themselves, demonstrated their conception of the group and their appropriate role in it by propelling the group into a highly task-oriented mood in the first few sessions. The relevance of this difference between the groups may rest in the fact that the confrontation in S2 represented, for the older members particularly, the collapse of a rather premature attempt at positional identification and work. The anger, the salience of the affection issue, even the focus on the trainer, all ran counter to the hopes of those who attempted to avoid any direct personal involvement with the trainer. In some ways, then, the source of S2's development was affected by the fact that the most independent members were active before, rather than after, the confrontation. They remained relatively inactive until the final phases, during which they were instrumental in suggesting some ways out of the dependent position that was characteristic of this group throughout its development.

Turning now to the consequences of the re-evaluation stage for the two groups, it appears that for S1 the immediate consequence of a decrease in anxiety and an increase in reparative processes was a period of internalization. The period was short-lived, however. Increases in anxiety and direct hostility signalled a disruption of the work phase, although the rate of identifying remained higher than before the first evaluation period. For group S2 it is difficult to isolate any period of sustained internalization, although phase six was characterized by the kind of image modification which often precedes identification. Much of the group's discussion following the confrontation period consisted of attempts to manage the unresolved issues of anxiety and depression which surrounded both the control and affection areas. In both groups, then, it is clear that feelings of being threatened and feelings of mistrust, on the one hand, and the sense of failure and ineffectiveness, on the other, operated to block or disrupt the process of internalization. Recurrent waves of hostility, continuing until the end of both groups, suggest a much-needed antidote to any simple notions of orderly progression through stages of development. Residual frustrations and changes in the nature of the trainer as a stimulus object combined to provoke further confrontations and further re-evaluations.

From the evidence gathered on these two groups at least, the process of separation appears to be a combination of two rather dissimilar dynamics. In one sense, there was a recapitulation of the groups' prior history, prompted by an intensification of unresolved issues. In another sense, the separation process involved attempts to deny any and all failures, as if the members and trainer as well were struggling to make the experience 'suitable for framing'.

For group S1, the unresolved issues that returned with some force were those of mistrust, now crystallized around grades and examinations, and the related issue of accomplishment. Much of the depression that dominated the final sessions was an expression of the members' feeling that it was useless to attempt any more work, or that the total experience had not been very productive. There were voices raised, some euphoric and others more dispassionate, to suggest that the sense of failure ignored the revised definition of work and success arrived at in the group. For group S2, the unresolved issues were the question of dependency, now intensified by the impending grades, and the chronic problems of apprehension and guilt. The authority and control area was reviewed, and rather direct and effective reparative processes were begun. The affection area was barely touched although the continuing ramifications of frustration in that area were evident in the particular form taken by the terminal depression.

The major techniques by which group members in S1 attempted to seal off and terminate the group experience, including their involvements with the trainer, were withdrawal, mourning, and manic denial. These efforts at reaching closure were mixed with continuing evidence of identification, but the separation process was increasingly predominant over the internaliza tion process. Although much of the discussion toward the end of S2 was directed toward re-evaluating the control issue, the final session was devoted to separation in a particularly interesting manner. Each member announced, in turn, and without comment from other members, what benefits he had derived from the group, his gratitude, and his final appraisal of the group. This mechanism expressed neatly the members' need to separate themselves from the trainer and other group members, permitting a smooth transition from the status of group member to the status of soli tary alumnus.

Conclusion

This study isolates the member–trainer relationship in self-analytic groups from what is obviously a far more complex set of relationships and processes. The assumption that group members may be expressing their feelings toward the trainer when they discuss events or individuals inside and outside the group is fundamental to this assessment of the member-trainer relationship. However, one could assume with equal profit that the reverse is true, that feelings toward the trainer reflect the state of the member-to-member relationships or a member's relationship with some-one outside the group. This study neglects, rather than disparages, the importance of other aspects of group development.

The effort to assess the member–trainer relationship, on the basis of not only direct references but indirect and symbolic acts, seems to have yielded meaningful results. Though much is overlooked in the member-to-trainer scoring system, especially the non-verbal behaviour, this method provides a fairly reliable and appropriate description of the members' feelings. The haunting problem of incomparable descriptions of two groups, or of two sessions within a group, may be partially solved by using this or some similar scoring system.

The developmental model constructed to analyse the member–trainer relationship outlines five stages: appraisal, confrontation, re-evaluation, internalization, and separation. It is clear from the two cases examined that the model is not a statement of the inevitable course of the member–trainer relationship. What it did provide for future research, is a framework against which the particular developments in a group may be examined. It suggests a series of interpersonal processes whose outcome will influence the members' future relationships with the trainer.

Where this study diverges from some previous discussion of group development is in casting what most authors conceive of as one goal of such groups, the process of group-centered work, in terms of the member–trainer relationship. Not only is the work phase closely related to the process of identification with the trainer, but it is both produced by and threatened by changes in the member–trainer relationship.

The periods of work which are characterized by independent efforts to perform the expressive and analytic tasks of the group may reflect the quite different processes of positional and personal identification. Where positional identification implies an effort to elbow the trainer out of his threatening or frustrating position, personal identification implies the trust and affection that underlie the internalization stage.

The influence of the member–trainer relationship on the members' capacity to work is further suggested by attending to which processes facilitate and which processes disrupt or block the members' efforts to internalize the trainer. Reality-testing, reparation, and various mechanisms of defense operate to control the disruptive consequences of hostility, anxiety, and depression. However, the two case studies suggest how difficult it is to attain or sustain this control in the face of intense feelings on the part of the members and continuing or increased pressure from the trainer.

The developmental model implies that the members of a self-analytic group are likely to experience the same feelings toward the trainer at the same time. This is only partially true. Nearly unanimous expressions of one feeling or another do occur, and Bion's (1961) notion of unconscious collusion fits some of the data. More often, however, any summary statistic for all members reflects one or more polarities within the group. Sometimes both polar positions can be subsumed within a stage of the developmental model, as when the expression and denial of anxiety are simultaneously high in the appraisal stage. At other times, however, the stage is named after the dominant mood or feeling, such as when a set of sessions is called the internalization stage despite evidence that resistance was high for a number of members. In calling attention to the feelings that are common to most of the members, the model fails to make explicit the obvious fact that some members may be expressing quite divergent feelings.

It remains to be seen what modifications of these methods and concepts will follow from the study of additional groups. Variations in what the members bring to the group by way of expectations, personal conflicts, or characteristic behavioural styles can be assumed to affect the outcome of the group, as can variations in the trainer's conception of the group and his personal style. What this study may offer is a way to investigate such problems and the beginning of a conceptual framework for their analysis.

References

Arsenian, J., E. V. Semrad and D. Shapiro (1962) 'An analysis of integral functions in small groups.' *Int. J. Group Psychother.*, **12**, 421–434.

Bach, G. R. (1954) *Intensive Group Psychotherapy.* New York: Ronald.

Bales, R. D. (1950) *Interaction Process Analysis.* Cambridge, Mass.: Addison-Wesley.

Bennis, W. (1957) 'A genetic theory of group development.' Unpublished manuscript, Massachusetts Institute of Technology.

Bennis, W. G. (1961) 'Defences against "depressive anxiety" in groups: the case of the absent leader.' *Merrill-Palmer Quart. Behav. Develpm.*, **7**, 3–30.

Bennis, W. G. and H. A. Shepard (1956) 'A theory of group development.' *Hum. Relat.*, **9**, 415–437.

Bibring, E. (1953) 'The mechanisms of depression.' In P. Greenacre (Ed.), *Affective Disorders.* New York: International Universities Press. Pp. 13–48.

Bion, W. R. (1961) *Experiences in Groups.* New York: Basic Books.

Borgetta, E. F., L. S. Cottrell and J. H. Mann (1958) 'The spectrum of individual interaction characteristics: an inter-dimensional analysis.' *Psychol. Rep.*, **4**, 279–319.

Carter, L. F. (1954) 'Recording and evaluating the performance of individuals as members of small groups.' *Personnel Psychol.*, **7**, 477–484.

Coffey, H. S., M. Freedman, T. Leary and A. Orsorio (1950) 'Community service and social research.' *J. soc. Issues*, **6**, No. 1, 25–64.

Couch, A. S. (1960) 'Psychological determinants of interpersonal behaviour.' Unpublished doctoral dissertation, Harvard University.

Ezriel, H. (1952) 'Notes on psychoanalytical group therapy: II. Interpretation and research.' *Psychiatry*, **15**, 119–126.

Foulkes, S. H. and E. J. Anthony (1957) *Group Psychotherapy.* Harmondsworth, Middx.: Penguin Books.

Frank, J. D., J. Margolis, H. T. Nash, A. R. Stone, E. E. Varon and E. Ascher (1952) 'The behaviour patterns in therapeutic groups and their apparent motivation.' *Hum. Relat.*, **5**, 289–317.

Kaplan, S. and M. Roman (1963) 'Phases of development in an adult therapy group.' *Int. J. Group Psychother.*, **13**, 10–26.

Klein, M. (1957) *Envy and Gratitude*. New York: Basic Books.

Mann, J. (1953) 'Group therapy with adults.' *Amer. J. Orthopsychiat.*, **23**, 332–337.

Mann, R. D. (1961) 'Dimensions of individual performance in small groups under task and social-emotional conditions.' *J. Abnorm. soc. Psychol.*, **62**, 674–682.

Mills, T. M. (1964) *Group Transformation: an Analysis of a Learning Group*. Englewood Cliffs, N.J.: Prentice-Hall.

Psathas, G. (1960) 'Phase movement and equilibrium tendencies in interaction process analysis in psychotherapy groups.' *Sociometry*, **23**, 177–194.

Schutz, W. C. (1958) *FIRO: A Three-dimensional Theory of Interpersonal Behaviour*. New York: Holt, Rinehart and Winston.

Shepard, H. A. and W. G. Bennis (1956) 'A theory of training by group methods.' *Hum. Relat.*, **9**, 403–414.

Slater, P. E. (1961a) 'Displacement in groups.' In W. G. Bennis, K. D. Benne and R. Chin (Eds.), *The Planning of Change*. New York: Holt, Rinehart & Winston.

Slater, P. E. (1961b) 'Toward a dualistic theory of identification.' *Merrill-Palmer Quart. Behav. Developm.*, **7**, 113–126.

Stock, D., R. M. Whitman and M. A. Lieberman (1958) 'The deviant member in therapy groups.' *Hum. Relat.*, **11**, 341–372.

Stock, D. and H. A. Thelen (1958) *Emotional Dynamics and Group Culture*. New York: New York University.

Talland, G. A. (1955) 'Task and interaction process: some characteristics of the therapeutic group discussion.' *J. abnorm. soc. Psychol.*, **50**, 105–109.

Thelen, H. (1950) 'Emotional dynamics: theory and research.' *J. soc. Issues*, **6**, No. 2.

Thelen, H. and W. Dickerman (1949) 'Stereotypes and the growth of groups.' *Educ. Leadership*, **6**, 309–316.

Wechsler, I. R. and J. Reisel (1959) *Inside a Sensitivity Training Group*. Los Angeles: University of California.

Recent Publications

Cooper, C. L. (1970) 'T-group training and self-actualisation.' Unpublished manuscript, University of Southampton.

Crawshaw, R. (1969) 'How sensitive is Sensitivity Training.' *American Journal of Psychiatry*, **126** (6), 870–873.

Fiebert, M. S. (1968) 'Sensitivity training: an analysis of trainer intervention and group process.' *Psychological Reports*, **22**, 829–838.

Gertz, B. (1969) 'Peer Group Evaluation in Sensitivity Training Program in Graduate Education.' Paper presented to the American Psychological Association Annual Convention, September 1969.

Gottschalk, L. A. and E. M. Pattison (1969) 'Psychiatric perspectives on T-groups and the laboratory movement: an overview.' *American Journal of Psychiatry*, **126** (6), 823–839.

Keutzer, C., F. R. Fosmire, R. Diller and M. D. Smith (1969) 'Laboratory training in the new social system: evaluation of a two-week program for high school personnel.' Unpublished manuscript, University of Oregon.

Kohn, V. (1969) 'A selected bibliography of evaluation of management training and development programs.' Unpublished manuscript, American Foundation for Management Research.

Koile, E. A. and C. Draeger (1969) 'T-group member ratings of leader and self in a human relations laboratory.' *Journal of Psychology*, **72**, 11–20.

Kuehn, J. L. and F. M. Crinella (1969) 'Sensitivity training: interpersonal "overkill" and other problems.' *American Journal of Psychiatry*, **126** (6), 840–845.

Mangham, I. L. (1970) 'Interpersonal Styles and Group Development.' Ph.D. Thesis, University of Leeds.

Myers, G. E., M. T. Myers, A. Goldberg and C. E. Welch (1969) 'Effects of feedback on interpersonal sensitivity in laboratory training groups.' *Journal of Applied Behavioral Science*, **5** (2), 175–185.

Pollack, D. (1969) 'A sensitivity training approach to group therapy with children.' Unpublished manuscript, San Diego State College.

Powers, J. R. and S. L. Fink (1969) 'The effects of trainer orientation and group composition on the perception of the trainer.' Unpublished manuscript, Case Institute of Technology.

Rawls, J. R., D. J. Rawls and R. L. Frye (1969) 'Membership satisfaction as it is related to certain dimensions of interaction in a T-group.' *Journal of Social Psychology*, **78**, 243–248.

Index

Page numbers followed by the letter 'n' refer to footnotes. Numbers in parenthesis are reference numbers to the author's work quoted in full at the end of the chapter.